Expert F# 4.0

Fourth Edition

Don Syme
Adam Granicz
Antonio Cisternino

Apress®

Expert F# 4.0

ISBN-13 (pbk): 978-1-4842-0741-3

ISBN-13 (electronic): 978-1-4842-0740-6

Managing Director: Welmoed Spahr
Lead Editor: James DeWolf
Development Editor: Douglas Pundick
Technical Reviewer: Phil De Joux and Kit Eason
Editorial Board: Steve Anglin, Pramila Balen, Louise Corrigan, James DeWolf, Jonathan Gennick, Robert Hutchinson, Celestin Suresh John, Michelle Lowman, James Markham, Susan McDermott, Matthew Moodie, Jeffrey Pepper, Douglas Pundick, Ben Renow-Clarke, Gwenan Spearing
Coordinating Editor: Melissa Maldonado
Copy Editor: April Rondeau
Compositor: SPi Global
Indexer: SPi Global
Artist: SPi Global

Distributed to the book trade worldwide by Springer Science+Business Media New York, 233 Spring Street, 6th Floor, New York, NY 10013. Phone 1-800-SPRINGER, fax (201) 348-4505, e-mail orders-ny@springer-sbm.com, or visit www.springer.com. Apress Media, LLC is a California LLC and the sole member (owner) is Springer Science + Business Media Finance Inc (SSBM Finance Inc). SSBM Finance Inc is a Delaware corporation.

For information on translations, please e-mail rights@apress.com, or visit www.apress.com.

Apress and friends of ED books may be purchased in bulk for academic, corporate, or promotional use. eBook versions and licenses are also available for most titles. For more information, reference our Special Bulk Sales–eBook Licensing web page at www.apress.com/bulk-sales.

Any source code or other supplementary material referenced by the author in this text is available to readers at www.apress.com. For detailed information about how to locate your book's source code, go to www.apress.com/source-code/.

Contents at a Glance

Contents

About the Authors

Don Syme is a principal researcher at Microsoft Research and is the main designer of F#. He has been a seminal contributor to a number of leading-edge projects, including generics in C# and the .NET Common Language Runtime, F# itself, F# asynchronous programming, units of measure in F#, and F# type providers. He received a Ph.D. from the University of Cambridge Computer Laboratory in 1999 and the Royal Engineering Academy Silver Medal in 2015.

Adam Granicz is the founder of IntelliFactory, an F# consultancy specialized in building next-generation web and business intelligence applications that serves happy customers from over 20 countries. He has 10 years of experience using F# in commercial projects and works on WebSharper, the main F# web ecosystem, which offers the fastest way to develop robust, client-based web and mobile web applications in F#. Adam is an active F# evangelist, a regular author and speaker at development conferences and workshops, and has a M.Sc. in Computer Science from the California Institute of Technology.

Antonio Cisternino is researcher, faculty member, and professor in the Computer Science Department of University of Pisa, Italy. He is vice director of the IT Center of the University of Pisa. His research focuses on meta-programming and domain-specific languages applied to system architectures. He has been active in the .NET community since 2000. Recent F# projects include evReact, a novel library for reactive programming, and IoX, a runtime for routing messages generated by IoT devices. He uses F# to teach a fundamental course on programming GUIs as part of the computer science degree. He received a Ph.D. from the University of Pisa Computer Science Department in 2003.

About the Technical Reviewers

Phil De Joux: When asked by his teacher at primary school what he would like to do for a job when he grew up, Phil replied, "Stay at home and make things." While not sure exactly what he would make, it would be a cottage industry of sorts. While studying math on a rural campus, he wove flax backpacks to give away to friends. He's worked in the Square Mile of London and the Latin Quarter of Paris, but it was in a small stone cottage in the village of Le Vaudoué on the fringe of the Fontainebleau forest that he lived up to the earlier aspiration. As a long-time remote developer for Block Scope, he weaves functions in code with F#, and possibly with next week's compile-to-JavaScript language.

Kit Eason is a senior software developer for an energy trading systems provider. He has also developed software for automotive engineering companies, universities, energy suppliers, banks, and financial services companies. Kit has run many educational and training courses, including evening classes, women's electronics classes, and CNC training for engineers. Kit is a regular speaker at Skills Matter in London and at various conferences and meet ups. He works mainly in F# and C# and normally speaks on F# and related matters.

Acknowledgments

We would like to thank James DeWolf and Melissa Maldonado from Apress, who have worked with us and kept us on track for publication. Likewise, we thank Phil de Joux and Kit Eason, who acted as technical reviewers and whose comments were invaluable in ensuring that the book is a comprehensive and reliable source of information.

The drafts and first three editions of this book were read and commented on by many people. *Expert F# 4.0* has benefited greatly from their input. In particular, we'd like to thank Ashley Feniello, whose meticulous reviews proved invaluable, as well as John Bates, Nikolaj Bjorner, Luca Bolognese, Ralf Herbrich, and Laurent le Brun, to name but a few people who were helpful.

We also thank the amazing people in the F# community who have contributed so much to the language over the years. Without them neither F# nor this book would have been possible, and we are very grateful for the interactions, help, and support given by others, including Byron Cook, Xavier Leroy, Malcolm Newey, Martin Odersky, Simon Peyton Jones, Mads Torgersen, and Phil Wadler. Finally, we thank our families and loved ones for their long-suffering patience. It would have been impossible to complete this book without their unceasing support.

CHAPTER 1

■ ■ ■

Introduction

F# is an open-source, cross-platform, functional-first programming language that empowers all levels of programmers to write simple, robust code for a huge range of practical purposes. F# combines the succinctness, expressivity, efficiency, and robustness of functional programming–programming based on transformations of data–with the runtime support, libraries, interoperability, tools, and object models of modern programming frameworks. F# is the safe choice for modern programming, embracing both enterprise quality through tools for a wide range of editors and operating systems, and openness, allowing you to contribute to the language and its ecosystem.

This book will help you become an expert in using F# for a broad range of practical problems. F# is a "functional-first" language, where functional programming is the first option used for solving most programming problems. However, F# differs from many functional languages in that it is both highly interoperable and embraces imperative and object-oriented (OO) programming where necessary. It also provides the benefits of both compiled and dynamic languages, allowing both the rapid iteration typical of dynamic languages and the performance and robustness of a strongly-typed compiled language.

Functional programming has long inspired students and programmers alike with its simplicity and expressive power. Applied functional programming is booming. A new generation of functional languages is reaching maturity; some functional language constructs have been integrated into languages such as C#, Java, and Python, and there is now widespread expertise available in the pragmatic application of functional programming techniques. There is also strong evidence that functional programming offers significant productivity gains in important application areas such as data access, ETL (Extract, Transform, Load) pipelines, enterprise architecture, financial modeling, machine learning, and analysis tools. More recently, functional programming is part of the rise of declarative programming models, especially for data queries, concurrent programming, parallel programming, and reactive programming.

The F# designers have adopted a design philosophy that allows you to take the best and most productive aspects of these paradigms and combine them while still placing primary emphasis on simplicity. This book will help you understand the power that F# offers through this combination. The designer of the F# language, Don Syme, is one of the authors of this book. This book benefits from his authority on F# and from all the authors' years of experience with F# and other programming languages.

F# benefits from a supportive and energetic worldwide community that is happy and willing to help you in your journey. You can find them everywhere: on StackOverflow (tag fsharp), Twitter (#fsharp), LinkedIn, GitHub, Slack, Facebook, and more. Most of all, you can find them via fsharp.org–the home of the F# Software Foundation, the non-profit foundation whose mission is to promote and protect the F# language and that acts as a strong voice for the language worldwide. The F# community contributes to an ecosystem of free open-source components and tools, including important core tools such as FSharp.Data, that bridge to a host of other programming libraries and services. F# also combines the best of openness and enterprise support: it is an open-source, cross-platform language under an OSS-approved license, and companies including Microsoft and Xamarin provide supported tooling for F# through tools such as Visual Studio and Xamarin Studio. Combined with its technical features, this makes F# an exciting and safe choice for mainstream professional programming activities.

F# offers an approach to computing that will continue to surprise and delight, and mastering F# programming techniques will help you become a better and happier programmer regardless of the language you use. There has been no better time to dive into the beautiful and productive world of F# programming, and F# offers the best route to learn and apply modern programming techniques so as to solve real-world problems.

The Genesis of F#

F# began in 2002, when Don Syme and others decided to ensure that the "ML" approach to pragmatic functional language design found a high-quality expression for the .NET platform. The project was closely associated with the design and implementation of Generics for the .NET Common Language Runtime. The first stabilized, supported version of F# was F# 2.0 in 2010. F# has always been open source and cross platform, and now adopts open engineering for all its components. In 2015, F# 4.0 was finalized, including commits from both enterprise and community contributors. This is the version of the language described in this book and is also the version included with Visual Studio 2015 and Xamarin Studio 5.0.

F# draws its core language from the programming language OCaml, which in turn comes from the ML family of programming languages, which dates back to 1974. F# also draws from C# for its object model; from Haskell, with regard to two language features–sequence expressions and computation expressions; and from Python, with regard to its indentation-aware syntax.

Despite the similarities to OCaml and Haskell, programming with F# is quite different in practice. In particular, the F# approach to object programming and dynamic language techniques is substantially different from other mainstream functional languages. Programming in F# tends to be more object oriented than in other functional languages. Programming also tends to be more flexible, as F# embraces techniques such as dynamic loading, dynamic typing, and reflection, and it adds techniques such as expression quotation, units-of-measure, type providers, and active patterns. We will cover these topics in this book and use them in many application areas.

F# began as a .NET language interoperating with C# and .NET libraries, and is quickly and easily able to leverage the thousands of libraries and techniques developed by the broader .NET community. However, F# is beginning to escape the .NET box; for example, it may also be compiled to Android, Apple iOS, Linux, JavaScript, and GPUs. F# 4.0 can be compiled to JavaScript through the open-source toolkits FunScript and WebSharper (websharper.com). Also, .NET is beginning to loosen its association with Windows, as the NET Core Framework is open source and cross platform, and you can contribute to it. F# code can also be edited and executed directly in most web browsers through sites such as tryfsharp.org and cloudsharper.com.

About This Book

This book is structured in three parts. Chapters 2 through 11 deal with the F# language and basic techniques such as functional, imperative, and object programming, followed by techniques to program with textual, structured, and numeric data, and then techniques for parallel, reactive, concurrent, and distributed programming. Chapters 12 through 15 deal with a series of applied programming samples and topics. Chapters 16 through 19 deal with more advanced F# programming techniques.

Throughout this book, we address both *programming constructs* and *programming techniques*. Our approach is driven by examples: we show code, and then we explain it. Frequently, we give reference material describing the constructs used in the code and related constructs you may use in similar programming tasks. We've found that an example-driven approach helps bring out the essence of a language and the way the language constructs work together. You can find a complete syntax guide in the appendix, and we encourage you to reference it while reading the book.

The book's chapters are as follows, starting with basic F# techniques:

Chapter 2, "Your First F# Program: Getting Started With F#," begins by introducing F# Interactive, a tool you can use to interactively evaluate F# expressions and declarations and that we encourage you to use while reading this book. In this chapter, you will use F# Interactive to explore some basic F# and .NET constructs, and we introduce many concepts that are described in more detail in later chapters.

Chapter 3, "Introducing Functional Programming," focuses on the basic constructs of typed functional programming, including arithmetic and string primitives, type inference, tuples, lists, options, function values, aggregate operators, recursive functions, function pipelines, function compositions, and pattern matching.

Chapter 4, "Introducing Imperative Programming," introduces the basic constructs used for imperative programming in F#. Although the use of imperative programming is often minimized with F#, it's used heavily in some programming tasks such as scripting. You will learn about loops, arrays, mutability mutable records, locals and reference cells, the imperative .NET collections, exceptions, and the basics of .NET I/O.

Chapter 5, "Understanding Types in Functional Programming," covers types in more depth, especially topics of generics and subtyping. You will learn techniques that you can use to make your code generic as well as how to understand and clarify type error messages reported by the F# compiler.

Chapter 6, "Programming with Objects," introduces object-oriented programming in F#. You will learn how to define concrete object types so as to implement data structures, how to use the notational devices of object-programming such as method overloading with your F# types, and how to create objects with mutable state. You will then learn how to define object interface types and a range of techniques to implement objects, including object expressions, constructor functions, delegation, and implementation inheritance.

Chapter 7, "Encapsulating and Organizing Your Code," shows the techniques you can use to hide implementation details through encapsulation and to organize your code with namespaces and modules. You'll understand the benefits of F# requiring a file-ordering for code in your project and how it helps you avoid the spaghetti-dependencies of unrestricted programming.

Chapter 8, "Working with Textual Data," looks at techniques for formatting data, working with strings, tokenizing text, parsing text, and marshaling binary values. You'll learn how to use the powerful FSharp.Data library to access CSV, JSON, and XML data in type-safe and scalable ways.

Chapter 9, "Working with Sequences and Structured Data," looks at two important sets of functional programming techniques. In this chapter, you will learn succinct and compositional techniques for building, transforming, and querying in-memory data structures and sequences. In addition, you will learn techniques for working with tree-structured data, especially abstract syntax representations; how to use F# active patterns to hide representations; and how to traverse large structured data without causing stack overflows through the use of tail calls.

Chapter 10, "Numeric Programming and Charting," looks at constructs and libraries for programming with numerical data in F#. In this chapter, you will learn about basic numeric types; how to use library routines for summing, aggregating, maximizing and minimizing sequences; how to implement numeric algorithms; how to use the FSharpCharting library for charting; how to use units of measure in F# to give strong typing to numeric data; and how to use the powerful open-source Math.NET library for advanced vector, matrix, statistical, and linear algebra programming.

Chapter 11, "Reactive, Asynchronous, and Parallel Programming," shows how you can use F# for programs that have multiple logical threads of execution and that react to inputs and messages. You will first learn how to construct basic background tasks that support progress reporting and cancellation. You will then learn how to use F# asynchronous workflows to build scalable, massively concurrent reactive programs that make good use of the .NET thread pool and other .NET concurrency-related resources. This chapter concentrates on message-passing techniques that avoid or minimize the use of shared memory. However, you will also learn the fundamentals of concurrent programming with shared memory using .NET.

Chapters 12 to 15 deal with applied topics in F# programming.

Chapter 12, "Symbolic Programming with Structured Data," applies some of the techniques from Chapters 9 and 11 in two case studies. The first is symbolic expression differentiation and rendering, an extended version of a commonly used case study in symbolic programming. The second is verifying circuits with propositional logic; you will learn how to use symbolic techniques to represent digital circuits, specify properties of these circuits, and verify these properties using binary decision diagrams (BDDs).

Chapter 13, "Integrating External Data and Services," looks at several dimensions of querying and accessing data from F#. You will first learn how to use the type-provider feature of F# to give fluent data scripting against databases and web services. You will then learn how to use queries with F#, in particular the LINQ paradigm supported by .NET. You will then look at how to use F# in conjunction with relational databases and how to use FSharp.Data to access REST services.

Chapter 14, "Build Smart Web Applications," shows how to use F# to write server-side scripts that respond to web requests, followed by how to serve webpage content using the Suave.io microservice framework. We also describe how WebSharper lets you write cross-tier HTML5 web applications in F#.

Chapter 15, "Visualization and Graphical User Interfaces," shows how to design and build graphical user-interface applications using F# and the .NET Windows Forms and WPF libraries. We also show how to design new controls using standard OO design patterns and how to script applications using the controls offered directly by the .NET libraries.

Chapters 16 to 19 deal with more advanced techniques in F# programming.

Chapter 16, "Language-Oriented Programming," looks at what is effectively a fourth programming paradigm supported by F#: the manipulation and representation of languages using a variety of concrete and abstract representations. In this chapter, you will learn three advanced features of F# programming: computation expressions (also called workflows), reflection, and quotations. These are also used in other chapters, particularly Chapters 11 and 12.

Chapter 17, "Libraries and Interoperability," shows how to use F# with other software libraries. In particular, you will learn some of the many libraries available, look at how memory management works, and learn how to use the .NET Platform Invoke mechanisms from F#.

Chapter 18, "Developing and Testing F# Code," shows the primary tools and techniques you can use to eliminate bugs from your F# programs. You will learn how to package your code into assemblies, how to share F# packages, how to use debugging tools with F#, how to use F# Interactive for exploratory development and testing, and how to use the NUnit and XUnit testing frameworks with F# code.

Chapter 19, "Designing F# Libraries," gives our advice on methodology and design issues for writing libraries in F#. You will learn how to write interoperable F# libraries that make relatively little use of F# constructs at their boundaries in order to appear as natural as possible to other programmers. We then cover functional programming design methodology and how to combine it with the OO design techniques.

The appendix, "F# Brief Language Guide," gives a compact guide to all key F# language constructs and the key operators used in F# programming.

Because of space limitations, we only partially address some important aspects of programming with F#. There are also hundreds of additional tools and libraries that can be readily used from F#, many explicitly designed for use with F#. Quotation meta-programming and F# type providers are described only briefly in Chapter 16. Also, some software-engineering issues such as performance tuning are largely omitted.

Who This Book Is For

We assume you have some programming knowledge and experience. If you don't have experience with F#, you'll still be familiar with many of the ideas it uses. However, you may also encounter some new and challenging ideas. For example, if you've been taught that OO design and programming are the only ways to think about software, then programming in F# may be a re-education. F# fully supports OO development, but F# programming combines elements of both functional and OO design. OO patterns such as implementation inheritance play a less prominent role than you may have previously experienced. Chapter 6 covers many of these topics in depth.

The following notes will help you set a path through this book, depending on your background:

C++, C#, and Java: If you've programmed in a typed OO language, you may find that functional programming, type inference, and F# type parameters take a while to get used to. However, you'll soon see how to use these to be a more productive programmer. Be sure to read Chapters 2, 3, 5, and 6 carefully.

Python, Scheme, Ruby, and dynamically typed languages: F# is statically typed and type-safe. As a result, F# development environments can discover many errors while you program, and the F# compiler can more aggressively optimize your code. If you've primarily programmed in an untyped language such as Python, Scheme, or Ruby, you may think that static types are inflexible and wordy. However, F# static types are relatively nonintrusive, and you'll find the language strikes a balance between expressivity and type safety. You'll also see how type inference lets you recover succinctness despite working in a statically typed language. Be sure to read Chapters 2 through 6 carefully, paying particular attention to the ways in which types are used and defined.

Typed functional languages: If you're familiar with Swift, Scala, Haskell, or OCaml, you'll find the core of F# readily familiar, with some syntactic differences. However, F# embraces .NET, including the .NET object model, and it may take you a while to learn how to use objects effectively and how to use the .NET libraries themselves. This is best done by learning how F# approaches object programming in Chapter 6, and then exploring applied programming in Chapters 8 through 16, referring to earlier chapters as necessary. Haskell programmers also need to learn the F# approach to imperative programming, described in Chapter 4, because many .NET libraries require a degree of imperative coding to create, configure, connect, and dispose of objects.

We strongly encourage you to use this book in conjunction with a development environment that supports F# 4.0 directly, such as Atom, Vim, Emacs, CloudSharper, Visual Studio 2015. or Xamarin Studio 5.0. In particular, the interactive type inference in these environments is exceptionally helpful for understanding F# code; with a simple mouse movement, you can examine the inferred types of the sample programs. These types play a key role in understanding the behavior of the code.

■ **Note**   You can download and install F# from `fsharp.org`. You can download all the code samples used in this book from A press; they were prepared and checked with F# 4.0. As with all books, it's inevitable that minor errors may exist in the text. An active errata and list of updates is maintained by the publishers.

CHAPTER 2

■ ■ ■

Your First F# Program: Getting Started with F#

This chapter will cover simple interactive programming with F#. To begin, download and install F# from fsharp.org, if you don't have it installed already. The sections that follow use F# Interactive (fsi.exe or fsharpi), a tool you can use to execute fragments of F# code interactively, and that is convenient for exploring the language. Along the way, you will see examples of the most important F# language constructs and many important libraries.

Creating Your First F# Program

Listing 2-1 shows your first complete F# program. You may not understand it all at first glance, but we will explain it piece by piece after the listing.

Listing 2-1. Analyzing a string for duplicate words

```
/// Split a string into words at spaces.
let splitAtSpaces (text: string) =
    text.Split ' '
    |> Array.toList

/// Analyze a string for duplicate words.
let wordCount text =
    let words = splitAtSpaces text
    let numWords = words.Length
    let distinctWords = List.distinct words
    let numDups = numWords - distinctWords.Length
    (numWords, numDups)

/// Analyze a string for duplicate words and display the results.
let showWordCount text =
    let numWords, numDups = wordCount text
    printfn "--> %d words in the text" numWords
    printfn "--> %d duplicate words" numDups
```

Paste this program into F# Interactive, which you can start as follows:

- If using a Linux or Mac OS X command prompt or terminal, run fsharpi from there and paste the code.

- If using Windows, run fsi.exe from a developer command prompt and paste the code

- If using Emacs, install the MELPA package for fsharp-mode, use key combination C-c C-s to start F# Interactive, and send the code from a buffer to F# Interactive using C-c C-r.

- If using Visual Studio, open an F# script and choose F# Interactive from the View menu; send the code to F# Interactive by selecting it and using Alt+Enter.

- If using Xamarin Studio, create an F# script and choose F# Interactive from the Pads menu; send the code to F# Interactive by selecting it and using Ctrl+Enter.

F# editing tools are also available for other editors such as Atom and Sublime Text 3. If you're running from the command line, remember to enter ;; to terminate the Interactive entry—you don't need to do this in Visual Studio or Xamarin Studio or other interactive environments, where you can send text by using a key combination as described above.

■ **Tip**   When using an Interactive Development Environment (IDE) you can usually start F# Interactive via a shortcut—for example, in Visual Studio by selecting F# Interactive in the View menu or by pressing Ctrl+Alt+F in an F# file or script. A tool window appears, and you can send text to F# Interactive by selecting the text and pressing Alt+Enter.

```
> <start F# Interactive as described above>
F# Interactive version xx.x.xxxxx.x
(a banner is printed here, it will depend on your version)
For help type #help;;

> <use the send-to-interactive command or paste the earlier program > ;;

val splitAtSpaces : text:string -> string list
val wordCount : text:string -> int * int
val showWordCount : text:string -> unit
```

Here, F# Interactive reports the types of the functions splitAtSpaces, wordCount, and showWordCount (you will learn more about types in a moment). The keyword val stands for *value*; in F# programming, functions are just values, a topic we will return to in Chapter 3. Also, sometimes F# Interactive shows a little more information than we show in this book (such as some internal details of the generated values); if you're trying out these code snippets, you can ignore that additional information. For now, let's use the wordCount function interactively:

```
> let (numWords,numDups) = wordCount "All the king's horses and all the king's men";;

val numWords : int = 9
val numDups : int = 2
```

This code shows the results of executing the function wordCount and binding its two results to the names numWords and numDups, respectively. Examining the values shows that the given text contains nine words: two duplicates and seven words that occur only once. showWordCount prints the results as a side effect instead of returning them as a value:

```
> showWordCount "Couldn't put Humpty together again";;

--> 5 words in the text
--> 0 duplicate words
```

From the output, you can more or less see what the code does. Now that you've done that, let's go through the program in detail.

Documenting Code

Let's start with the definition of the wordCount function in Listing 2-1. The first line of the definition isn't code; rather, it's a comment:

```
/// Analyze a string for duplicate words.
```

Comments are either lines starting with // or blocks enclosed by (* and *). Comment lines beginning with three slashes (///) are XMLDoc comments and can, if necessary, include extra XML tags and markup. The comments from a program can be collected into a single .xml file and processed with additional tools.

Using let

Now, look at the first two lines of the function wordCount in Listing 2-1. These lines define the function wordCount and the local value words, both using the keyword let:

```
let wordCount text=
    let words = ...
```

let is the single most important keyword you will use in F# programming: it's used to define data, computed values, and functions. The left of a let binding is often a simple identifier, but it can also be a pattern. (See "Using Tuples" later in this chapter for examples.) It can also be a function name followed by a list of argument names, as in the case of wordCount, which takes one argument: text. The right of a let binding (after the =) is an expression.

VALUES AND IMMUTABILITY

In other languages, a local *value* is called a local *variable*. In F#, however, you can't change the immediate value of locals after they've been initialized unless the local is explicitly marked as `mutable`, a topic we will return to in Chapter 4. For this reason, F# programmers and the language specification tend to prefer the term *value* to *variable*.

As you'll see in Chapter 4, data indirectly referenced by a local value can still be mutable even if the local value isn't. For example, a local value that is a handle to a hash table can't be changed to refer to a different table, but the contents of the table itself can be changed by invoking operations that add and remove elements from the table. Many values and data structures in F# programming are completely *immutable*, however; in other words, neither the local value nor its contents can be changed through external mutation. These are usually just called *immutable values*. For example, all basic .NET types— such as integers, strings, and `System.DateTime` values—are immutable. In addition, the F# library defines a range of immutable data structures, such as `Set` and `Map`, based on binary trees, and the NuGET package `System.Collections.Immutable` defines a large number more.

Immutable values offer many advantages. At first it may seem strange to define values you can't change. Knowing a value is immutable, however, means you rarely need to think about the value's *object identity*—you can pass such values to functions and know that they won't be mutated. You can also pass them among multiple threads without worrying about unsafe concurrent access to the values, which will be discussed in Chapter 11.

Understanding Types

F# is a typed language, so it's reasonable to ask what the *type* of wordCount is. F# Interactive has shown it already:

```
val wordCount : text:string -> int * int
```

This indicates that wordCount takes one argument of type string and returns int * int, which is F#'s way of saying "a pair of integers." The symbol -> indicates that wordCount is a *function*. No explicit type is given in the program for the type of the argument text, because the full type for wordCount is *inferred* from its definition. We discuss type inference further in "What Is Type Inference?" and in more detail in later chapters.

Types are significant in F# for reasons that range from performance to coding productivity and interoperability. Types are used to help structure libraries, to guide you through the complexity of an API, and to place constraints on code to ensure that it is correct and can be implemented efficiently. Unlike many other typed languages, F#'s type system is both simple and powerful—and indeed in many ways beautiful—because it uses orthogonal, compositional constructs, such as tuples and functions, to form succinct and descriptive types. Furthermore, type inference means you almost never have to write types in your program, although doing so can be useful.

Table 2-1 shows some of the most important ways of forming types. These are ways F# offers for defining new types. Chapters 3 and 4 will discuss all these ways of forming types in more detail.

Table 2-1. *Some Important Types and Type Constructors and Their Corresponding Values (int is the type representing integer numbers)*

Family of Types	Examples	Description
type option	int option, option<int>	A value of the given type or the special value None. For example: Some 3, Some "3", None.
type list	int list, list<int>	An immutable linked list of values of the given type. All elements of the list must have the same type. For example: [], [3;2;1].
type1 -> *type2*	int -> string	A function type, representing a value that accepts values of the first type and computes results of the second type. For example: (fun x -> x+1).
type1 * ... * *typeN*	int * string	A tuple type, such as a pair, triple, or larger combination of types. For example: (1,"3"), (3,2,1).
type[]	int[]	An array type for a flat, fixed-size, mutable collection.
unit	unit	A type containing a single value (), akin to void in many imperative languages.
'T	'T, 'a, 'Key, 'Value	A variable type, used in generic code.

Some type constructors, such as list and option, are *generic*, which means they can be used to form a range of types by instantiating the generic variables, such as int list, string list, int list list, and so on. You can write instantiations of generic types using either prefix notation (such as int list) or postfix notation (such as list<int>), though by convention prefix notation (int list) is only used for list and option types. Variable types such as 'a and 'T are placeholders for any type. Chapters 3 and 5 will discuss generics and variable types in more detail.

WHAT IS TYPE INFERENCE?

Type inference works by analyzing your code to collect constraints from the way you use names. These are collected over each file (for the F# command-line compiler) and each chunk entered (in F# Interactive). These constraints must be consistent, thus ensuring that your program is well typed; you get a type error if they are not. Constraints are collected from top to bottom, left to right, and outside in. This is important, because in some situations it may affect the inference process.

Type inference also *automatically generalizes* your code, which means that when your code is reusable and generic in certain obvious ways, it's given a suitable generic type without your needing to write down the generic type explicitly. Automatic generalization is the key to succinct but reusable typed programming. Chapter 5 will further discusses automatic generalization.

Calling Functions

Functions are at the heart of most F# programming. It's not surprising that the first thing the wordCount function does is call a function—in this case, the splitAtSpaces function, which is the first function defined in the program:

```
let wordCount text=
    let words = splitAtSpaces text
```

Let's first investigate the splitAtSpaces function by running F# Interactive:

```
> splitAtSpaces "hello world";;

val it : string list = ["hello"; "world"]
```

You can see that splitAtSpaces breaks the given text into words, splitting at spaces. In the sample code, you can also see examples of:

- Literal characters, such as ' ' and 'a'
- Literal strings, such as "hello world"
- Literal lists of strings, such as the returned value ["hello"; "world"]

Chapter 3 will cover literals and lists in detail. Lists are an important data structure in F#, and you will see many examples of their use in this book.

Lightweight Syntax

The F# compiler and F# Interactive use the indentation of F# code to determine where constructs start and finish. The indentation rules are very intuitive; we will discuss them in the appendix, which is a guide to the F# syntax. Listing 2-2 shows a version of the wordCount function that makes explicit all the scopes of names using the in keyword.

Listing 2-2. A version of the wordCount function using explicit "in" tokens

```
/// Analyze a string for duplicate words.
let wordCount text =
    let words = splitAtSpaces text in
    let distinctWords = List.distinct words in
    let numWords = words.Length in
    let numDups = numWords - distinctWords.Length in
    (numWords, numDups)
```

Double semicolons (;;)are still required in order to terminate entries to F# Interactive. If you're using an interactive development environment such as Visual Studio, however, the environment typically adds them automatically when code is selected and executed. We show the double semicolons in the interactive code snippets used in this book, although not in the larger samples.

Sometimes it's convenient to write let definitions on a single line. Do this by separating the expression that follows a definition from the definition itself, using in. For example:

```
let powerOfFour n =
    let nSquared = n * n in nSquared * nSquared
```

Here's an example use of the function:

```
> powerOfFour 3;;
val it : int = 81
```

Indeed, let *pat* = *expr1* in *expr2* is the true primitive construct in the language, with *pat* standing for *pattern,* and *expr1* and *expr2* standing for *expressions.* The F# compiler inserts the in if *expr2* is column-aligned with the let keyword on a subsequent line.

■ **Tip**   We recommend that you use four-space indentation for F# code. Tab characters can't be used, and the F# tools give an error if they're encountered. Most F# editors convert uses of the Tab key to spaces automatically.

Understanding Scope

Local values, such as words and distinctWords, can't be accessed outside their *scope.* In the case of variables defined using let, the scope of the value is the entire expression that follows the definition, although not the definition itself. Here are two examples of invalid definitions that try to access variables outside their scope. As you see, let definitions follow a sequential, top-down order, which helps ensure that programs are well-formed and free from many bugs related to uninitialized values:

```
let badDefinition1 =
    let words = splitAtSpaces text
    let text = "We three kings"
    words.Length
```

gives

```
error FS0039: The value or constructor 'text' is not defined
```

and

```
let badDefinition2 = badDefinition2 + 1
```

gives

```
error FS0039: The value or constructor 'badDefinition2' is not defined
```

Within function definitions, you can *outscope* values by declaring another value of the same name. For example, the following function computes (n*n*n*n)+ 2:

```
let powerOfFourPlusTwo n =
    let n = n * n
    let n = n * n
    let n = n + 2
    n
```

13

This code is equivalent to:

```
let powerOfFourPlusTwo n =
    let n1 = n * n
    let n2 = n1 * n1
    let n3 = n2 + 2
    n3
```

Outscoping a value doesn't change the original value; it just means that the name of the value is no longer accessible from the current scope. Outscoping should be used with care.

Because `let` bindings are simply a kind of expression, you can use them in a nested fashion. For example:

```
let powerOfFourPlusTwoTimesSix n =
    let n3 =
        let n1 = n * n
        let n2 = n1 * n1
        n2 + 2
    let n4 = n3 * 6
    n4
```

Here, n1 and n2 are values defined locally by `let` bindings within the expression that defines n3. These local values aren't available for use outside their scope. For example, this code gives an error:

```
let invalidFunction n =
    let n3 =
        let n1Inner = n + n
        let n2Inner = n1Inner * n1Inner
        n1Inner * n2Inner
    let n4 = n1Inner + n2Inner + n3  // Error! n3 is in scope, but the others are not!
    n4
```

Local scoping is used for many purposes in F# programming, especially to hide implementation details that you don't want revealed outside your functions or other objects. Chapter 7 will cover this topic in more detail.

Using Data Structures

The next portion of the code is:

```
let wordCount text =
    let words = splitAtSpaces text
    let distinctWords = List.distinct words
    ...
```

This gives you your first taste of using data structures from F# code. The last of these lines lies at the heart of the computation performed by wordCount. It uses the function List.distinct from the F# library to convert the given words to a list where all the words are distinct. You can see the results of this function using F# Interactive:

```
> List.distinct ["b"; "a"; "b"; "b"; "c" ];;

val it : string list = [ "b"; "a"; "c" ]

> List.distinct (List.distinct ["abc"; "ABC"]);;

val it : string list = [ "abc"; "ABC" ]
```

Here you can see several things:

- F# Interactive prints the contents of structured values, such as lists.

- Duplicate elements are removed by the conversion.

- The elements in the list remain ordered, as List.distinct does not reorder the distinct elements.

- The default ordering and equality for strings is case sensitive.

The name List references the F# module FSharp.Collections.List in the F# core library. This contains operations associated with values of the list type. It's common for types to have a separate module that contains associated operations. All modules under the FSharp namespaces Core, Collections, Text, and Control can be referenced by simple one-word prefixes, such as List.distinct. Other modules under these namespaces include Set, Option, Map, and Array. The function List.distinct was added in F# 4.0; in prior versions alternatives such as Set.ofList would be used instead.

Using Properties and the Dot-Notation

The next two lines of the wordCount function compute the result you're after—the number of duplicate words. This is done by using the Length property of the values you've computed:

```
let numWords = words.Length
let numDups = numWords - distinctWords.Length
```

F# performs resolution on property names at compile time (or interactively when you're using F# Interactive, in which there is no distinction between compile time and runtime). This is done using compile-time knowledge of the type of the expression on the left of the dot—in this case, words and distinctWords. Sometimes, a type annotation is required in your code in order to resolve the potential ambiguity among possible property names. For example, the following code uses a type annotation to note that inp refers to a list. This allows the F# type system to infer that Length refers to a property associated with values of the list type:

```
let length (inp:'T list) = inp.Length
```

Here, the 'T indicates that the length function is generic; that is, it can be used with any type of list. Chapters 3 and 5 will cover generic code in more detail.

As you can see from the use of the dot-notation, F# is both a functional language and an object-oriented one. In particular, properties are a kind of *member*, a general term used for any functionality associated with a type or value. Members referenced by prefixing a type name are called *static members*, and members associated with a particular value of a type are called *instance members*; in other words, instance members are accessed through an object on the left of the dot. We will discuss the distinction between values, properties, and methods later in this chapter, and Chapter 6 will discuss members in full.

■ **Note**   Type annotations can be useful documentation; when you use them, they should generally be added at the point where a variable is declared.

Sometimes, explicitly named functions play the role of members. For example, you could write the earlier code as:

```
let numWords = List.length words
let numDups = numWords - List.length wordSet
```

You see both styles in F# code. Some F# libraries don't use members at all or use them only sparingly. Judiciously using members and properties, however, can greatly reduce the need for trivial get/set functions in libraries, can make client code much more readable, and can allow programmers who use environments such as Visual Studio to easily and intuitively explore the primary features of the libraries they write.

If your code doesn't contain enough type annotations to resolve the dot-notation, you will see an error such as:

```
> let length inp = inp.Length;;
```

error FS0072: Lookup on object of indeterminate type based on information prior to this program point. A type annotation may be needed prior to this program point to constrain the type of the object. This may allow the lookup to be resolved. You can resolve this by adding a type annotation as shown earlier.

Using Tuples

The final part of the wordCount function returns a *tuple* made up of the number of words and the number of duplicate words:.

```
...
(numWords, numDups)
```

Tuples are the simplest, but perhaps the most useful, of all F# data structures. A tuple expression is a number of expressions grouped together to form a new expression:

```
let site1 = ("www.cnn.com", 10)
let site2 = ("news.bbc.com", 5)
let site3 = ("www.msnbc.com", 4)
let sites = (site1, site2, site3)
```

Here, the inferred types and computed values are:

```
val site1 : string * int = ("www.cnn.com", 10)
val site2 : string * int = ("news.bbc.com", 5)
val site3 : string * int = ("www.msnbc.com", 4)
val sites : (string * int) * (string * int) * (string * int) =
  (("www.cnn.com", 10), ("news.bbc.com", 5), ("www.msnbc.com", 4))
```

Tuples can be decomposed into their constituent components in two ways. For pairs—that is, tuples with two elements—you can explicitly call the functions fst and snd, which, as their abbreviated names imply, extract the first and second parts of the pair:

```
> fst site1;;

val it : string = "www.cnn.com"

> let relevance = snd site1;;

val relevance : int = 10
```

The functions fst and snd are defined in the F# library and are always available for use by F# programs. Here are their simple definitions:

```
let fst (a, _) = a
let snd (_, b) = b
```

More commonly, tuples are decomposed using *patterns*, as in the following code:

```
let url, relevance = site1
let siteA, siteB, siteC = sites
```

In this case, the names in the tuples on the left of the definitions are bound to the respective elements of the tuple value on the right; so, again, url gets the value "www.cnn.com" and relevance gets the value 10.

Tuple values are typed, and, strictly speaking, there are an arbitrary number of families of tuple types: one for pairs holding two values, one for triples holding three values, and so on. This means that if you try to use a triple where a pair is expected, you get a type-checking error before your code is run:

```
> let a, b = (1, 2, 3);;

error FS0001: Type mismatch. Expecting a
    'a * 'b
but given a
    'a * 'b * 'c
The tuples have differing lengths of 2 and 3
```

Tuples are often used to return multiple values from functions, as in the wordCount example earlier. They're also often used for multiple arguments to functions, and frequently the tupled output of one function becomes the tupled input of another function. This example shows a different way of writing the showWordCount function defined and used earlier:

```
let showResults (numWords, numDups) =
    printfn "--> %d words in the text" numWords
    printfn "--> %d duplicate words" numDups

let showWordCount text = showResults (wordCount text)
```

The function showResults accepts a pair as input, decomposed into numWords and numDups. The pair of outputs of wordCount becomes the input pair of showResults.

VALUES AND OBJECTS

In F#, everything is a *value*. In some other languages, everything is an *object*. In practice, you can use the words largely interchangeably, although F# programmers tend to reserve *object* for special kinds of values, as follows:

- Values whose observable properties change as the program executes, usually through the explicit mutation of underlying in-memory data or through external state changes

- Values that refer to data or to a state that reveals an identity, such as a unique integer stamp or the overall object identity, where that identity is used to distinguish the object from otherwise identical values

- Values that can be queried to reveal additional functionality, through the use of casts, conversions, and interfaces

F# thus supports objects, but not all values are referred to as objects. F# programming is not "object-*oriented*"; rather, it supports object programming and uses objects where they are most useful. Chapter 4 will discuss identity and mutation in more detail.

Using Imperative Code

The showWordCount and showResults functions defined in the previous section output results using a library function called printfn:

```
printfn "--> %d words in the text" numWords
printfn "--> %d duplicate words" numDups
```

If you're familiar with OCaml, C, or C++, printfn will look familiar as a variant of printf. printfn also adds a newline character at the end of printing. Here, the pattern %d is a placeholder for an integer, and the rest of the text is output verbatim to the console.

F# also supports related functions, such as printf, sprintf, and fprintf, which will be discussed further in Chapter 4. Unlike C/C++, the printf family of functions are type-safe text formatters in which the F# compiler checks that the subsequent arguments match the requirements of the placeholders.

The "n" suffix in printfn indicates that a new line is started at the end of the ouput. There are also other ways to format text with F#. For example, you can use the .NET libraries directly:

```
System.Console.WriteLine("--> {0} words in the text", numWords)
System.Console.WriteLine("--> {0} duplicate words", numDups)
```

Here, {0} acts as the placeholder, although no checks are made that the arguments match the placeholder before the code is run. The use of printfn also shows how you can use sequential expressions to cause effects in the outside world.

As with let ... in ... expressions, it's sometimes convenient to write sequential code on a single line. Do this by separating two expressions with a semicolon (;). The first expression is evaluated (usually for its side effects), its result is discarded, and the overall expression evaluates to the result of the second. Here is a simpler example of this construct:

```
let two = (printfn "Hello World"; 1 + 1)
let four = two + two
```

When executed, this code prints Hello World precisely once, when the right side of the definition of two is executed. F# doesn't have statements as such—the fragment (printfn "Hello World"; 1 + 1) is an expression, but when evaluated, the first part of the expression causes a side effect, and its result is discarded. It's also often convenient to use parentheses to delimit sequential code. The code from the script could, in theory, be parenthesized, with a semicolon added to make the primitive constructs involved more apparent:

```
(printfn "--> %d words in the text" numWords;
 printfn "--> %d duplicate words" numDups)
```

■ **Note** The token ; is used to write sequential code within expressions, and ;; is used to terminate interactions with the F# Interactive session. Semicolons are optional when the individual fragments of your sequential code are placed on separate lines beginning at the same column position.

Using Object-Oriented Libraries from F#

The value of F# lies not just in what you can do inside the language, but also in what you can connect to outside the language. For example, F# doesn't come with a GUI library. Instead, F# is connected to .NET and via .NET to most of the significant programming technologies available on major computing platforms. You've already seen one use of the .NET libraries, in the first function defined earlier:

```
/// Split a string into words at spaces
let splitAtSpaces (text: string) =
    text.Split ' '
    |> Array.toList
```

Here, text.Split is a call to a .NET library instance method called Split that is defined on all string objects.

To emphasize this, the second sample uses two of the powerful libraries that come with the .NET Framework: System.IO and System.Net. The full sample, seen in Listing 2-3, is a script for use with F# Interactive.

Listing 2-3. Using the .NET networking libraries from F#

```
open System.IO
open System.Net

/// Get the contents of the URL via a web request
let http (url: string) =
    let req = WebRequest.Create(url)
    let resp = req.GetResponse()
    let stream = resp.GetResponseStream()
    let reader = new StreamReader(stream)
    let html = reader.ReadToEnd()
    resp.Close()
    html

http "http://news.bbc.co.uk"
```

The above example uses several important .NET libraries and helps you explore some interesting F# language constructs. The following sections walk you through this listing.

Using open to Access Namespaces and Modules

The first thing you see in the sample is the use of open to access functionality from the namespaces System.IO and System.Net:

```
open System.IO
open System.Net
```

Chapter 7 will discuss namespaces in more detail. The earlier declaration means you can access any content under this path without quoting the long path. If it didn't use open, you'd have to write the following, which is obviously a little verbose:

```
let req = System.Net.WebRequest.Create(url)
```

You can also use open to access the contents of an F# module without using long paths. Chapter 7 will look at modules in more detail.

MORE ABOUT OPEN

Using open is an easy way to access the contents of namespaces and modules. There are some subtleties, however. For example, open doesn't actually load or reference a library—instead, it reveals functionality from already-loaded libraries. You load libraries by referring to a particular DLL, using #r in a script or -r as a command-line option.

Libraries and namespaces are orthogonal concepts: multiple libraries can contribute functionality to the same namespace, and each library can contribute functionality to multiple namespaces. Often, one particular library contributes most of the functionality in a particular namespace. For example, most of the functionality in the System.Net namespace comes from a library called System.Net.dll, but some of the functionality for this namespace can also be found in other system libraries. You can place your code in a namespace by using a namespace declaration at the top of your file, as discussed later on in Chapter 7.

If two namespaces have types, subnamespaces, and/or modules with identical names, when you open these, you can access the contents of both using the same shortened paths. For example, the namespace System contains a type String, and the namespace FSharp.Core contains a module String. In this case, long identifier lookups such as String.map search the values and members under both of these, preferring the most recently opened if there is any ambiguity.

Finally, if you ever have name collisions, you can define your own short aliases for modules and types, such as by using module MyString = My.Modules.String and type SysString = System.String. You cannot alias namespaces.

Fetching a Web Page

The second half of Listing 2-3 uses the System.Net library to define a function http so as to read HTML web pages. You can investigate the operation of the implementation of the function by entering the following lines into F# Interactive:

```
> open System.IO;;

> open System.Net;;

> let req = WebRequest.Create("http://news.bbc.co.uk");;

val req : WebRequest

> let resp = req.GetResponse();;

val resp : WebResponse

> let stream = resp.GetResponseStream();;

val stream : Stream

> let reader = new StreamReader(stream);;

val reader : StreamReader

> let html = reader.ReadToEnd();;

val html : string =
  "<html><head><title>BBC News and Sport</title><meta http-eq"+[959 chars]
```

The first line of the code creates a WebRequest object using the static method Create, a member of the type System.Net.WebRequest. The result of this operation is an object that acts as a handle to a running request to fetch a web page—you could, for example, abandon the request or check to see whether the request has completed. The second line calls the instance method GetResponse. The remaining lines of the sample get a stream of data from the response to the request using resp.GetResponseStream(), make an object with which to read this stream using new StreamReader(stream), and read the full text from this stream. Chapter 4 will cover .NET I/O in more detail; for now, you can test by experimentation in F# Interactive that these actions do indeed fetch the HTML contents of a web page.

VALUES, METHODS, AND PROPERTIES

Here are the differences among values, methods, and properties:

- *Values*: Parameters and top-level items defined using `let` or pattern matching. Examples: `form`, `text`, `wordCount`.

- *Methods*: Named operations associated with types or values. Both simple values and objects may have methods. Methods can be overloaded (see Chapter 6), which means the exact method that gets used can depend on the type and number of arguments. Examples: `System.Net.WebRequest.Create(url)` and `resp.GetResponseStream()`.

- *Properties*: Named "get" or "set" operations associated with types or values. A property is just shorthand for invoking method members that get or set underlying data. Examples: `System.DateTime.Now` and `form.TopMost`.

- *Indexer properties*: A property that accepts index arguments. Indexer properties named `Item` can be accessed using the `.[_]` syntax (note that the dot is required). Examples: `vector.[3]` and `matrix.[3,4]`.

The inferred type for `http` that wraps up this sequence as a function is:

```
val http : url:string -> string
```

XML HELP IN YOUR IDE

In a rich interactive editor such as Visual Studio or Xamarin Studio, you can easily find out more about the functionality of libraries by hovering your mouse over the identifiers in your source code. For example, if you hover over `Create` in `WebRequest.Create`, you see the XML help shown here:

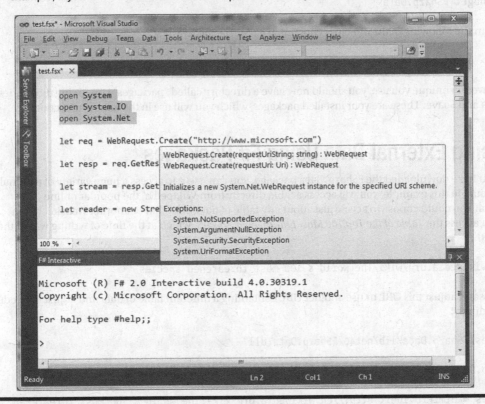

Getting and Using Packages

In the previous section you saw how to use one of the rich set of libraries available as part of your minimal F# installation. However, F# allows you to connect and use much more than these libraries. For example, a vast repository of *packages* is available at http://nuget.org. In the following sample, you will use the F# packages Suave and FSharp.Data.

The two most common ways to download packages with F# are by using nuget.exe and paket.exe. You can use either.

- If using nuget.exe , first download and install nuget.exe from http://nuget.org, then run the following from a command line:

```
> nuget install Suave -ExcludeVersion -OutputDirectory packages
> nuget install FSharp.Data -ExcludeVersion -OutputDirectory packages
```

- If using paket.exe, first download and install Paket from http://fsprojects.
github.io/paket. Then place the following text in a file called paket.dependencies
in an empty directory (create and edit the file using your favorite text editor):

```
source https://nuget.org/api/v2
nuget Suave
nuget FSharp.Data
```

Then run the following in the directory containing paket.dependencies:

```
> paket.exe install
```

Whichever technique you use, you should now have a directory called "packages" containing directories
FSharp.Data and Suave. These are your installed packages, which you will use in the following sections.

Accessing External Data Using F# Packages

Now that you have downloaded the FSharp.Data package, you can use it to access a huge variety of external
sources of data. In this example, you will access a table directly from Wikipedia, the popular online
encyclopedia. You could choose to access just about any table of data from that or another website, but in
this case you access the *Table of the Top 100 Most Endangered Species*, which at the time of writing was at the
following URL:

```
http://en.wikipedia.org/wiki/The_world's_100_most_threatened_species
```

If necessary, adjust this URL or use another URL containing a different table of data and adjust the code
below accordingly:

```
#r "packages/FSharp.Data/lib/net40/FSharp.Data.dll"

open FSharp.Data

type Species = HtmlProvider<"http://en.wikipedia.org/wiki/The_world's_100_most_threatened_
species">

let species =
    [ for x in Species.GetSample().Tables.``Species list``.Rows ->
        x.Type, x.``Common name`` ]
```

These are perhaps the most magical three lines in this chapter. When run, they produce:

```
val species : (string * string) list =
  [("Plant (tree)", "Baishan Fir");
   ("Reptile", "Leaf scaled sea-snake");
   ...
   ("Mammal", "Attenborough's echidna")]
```

In just three lines you have "screen-scraped" and downloaded a significant data set. You can now process this data using functional programming techniques—you will learn more about these techniques in Chapters 3 and 8.

```
let speciesSorted =
    species
      |> List.countBy fst
      |> List.sortByDescending snd
```

Producing:

```
val speciesSorted : (string * int) list =
  [("Plant", 13); ("Bird", 11); ("Fish", 10); ("Plant (tree)", 8);
   ("Amphibian (frog)", 7); ("Mammal (primate)", 6); ("Mammal", 5);
...
   ("Fish (shark)", 1)]
```

This list shows the world's top 100 endangered species, listed by category.

Starting a Web Server and Serving Data using F# Packages

One of the packages you downloaded in the previous section was called Suave. Suave is a lightweight framework for implementing web servers in F#. You can find out more about Suave at http://suave.io. Suave web servers are very efficient and are able to scale so as to handle many simultaneous web requests—they are written in the "non-blocking" style and use F# features you'll learn about in Chapter 11.

In the sample below, you will start a local web server that serves some HTML text generated from the data you downloaded in the previous sample. You will learn more about web programming and programming web sites in Chapter 14. See the following:

```
#r "packages/Suave/lib/net40/Suave.dll"

open Suave
open Suave.Http.Successful
open Suave.Web

let html =
    [ yield "<html><body><ul>"
      for (category,count) in speciesSorted do
          yield sprintf "<li>Category <b>%s</b>: <b>%d</b></li>" category count
      yield "</ul></body></html>" ]
    |> String.concat "\n"

startWebServer defaultConfig (OK html)
```

This web server runs locally and is only accessible to your local machine (you will learn more about making it accessible to other machines in Chapter 14). After running this code, you should see something like this:

```
[I] 2015-02-12T20:15:40.6980929Z: listener started in 14.001 ms with binding
localhost:8083
```

If you now go to a web browser on the same machine, you can enter the URL http://localhost:8083 into the browser address bar. If your web server is running successfully you should now see the content displayed as in Figure 2-1.

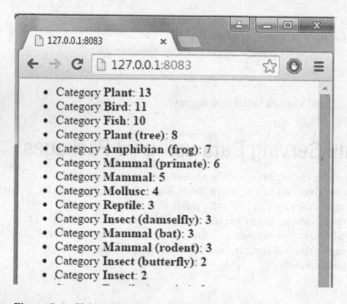

Figure 2-1. *Using a Browser to View a Website Created with Suave*

You'll learn more about web programming in Chapter 14, and in particular how to use the F# WebSharper framework to write HTML, JavaScript, and server-side code—all in F#. With a little more work, you can improve the display using a popular web programming framework called Angular. If you have a working knowledge of HTML, you will recognize many of the display elements here:

```
let angularHeader = """<head>
<link rel="stylesheet" href="http://maxcdn.bootstrapcdn.com/bootstrap/3.2.0/css/bootstrap.
min.css">
<script src="http://ajax.googleapis.com/ajax/libs/angularjs/1.2.26/angular.min.js"></script>
</head>"""

let fancyText =
    [ yield """<html>"""
      yield angularHeader
      yield """ <body>"""
      yield """   <table class="table table-striped">"""
```

```
    yield """   <thead><tr><th>Category</th><th>Count</th></tr></thead>"""
    yield """   <tbody>"""
    for (category,count) in speciesSorted do
        yield sprintf "<tr><td>%s</td><td>%d</td></tr>" category count
    yield """   </tbody>"""
    yield """   </table>"""
    yield """ </body>"""
    yield """</html>""" ]
|> String.concat "\n"

startWebServer defaultConfig (OK fancyText)
```

You may need to restart F# Interactive at this point. The new web content is shown in Figure 2-2.

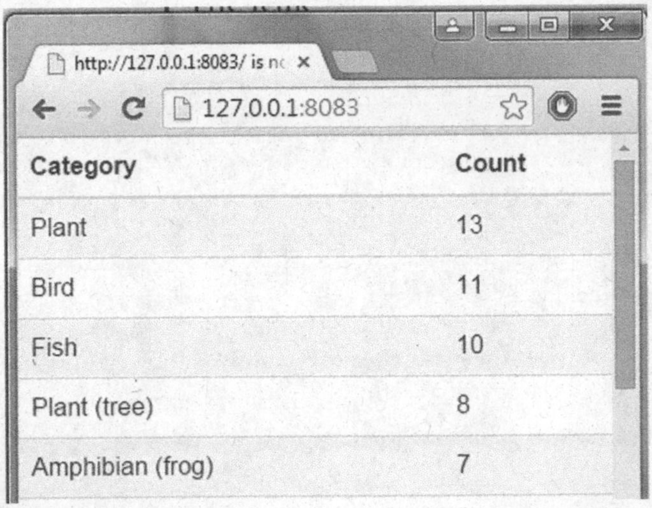

Figure 2-2. *A Website with Better Formatting Created with Suave*

You can use F# for many things besides serving web content, as you will discover throughout this book.

Summary

This chapter looked at some simple interactive programming with F# and .NET. Along the way, you met many of the constructs you would use in day-to-day F# programming. You then learned how to download packages to use with F# and got a taste of using a powerful F# library called FSharp.Data. Finally, you created and started a web server, which serves information extracted from Wikipedia, using HTML as the rendering language.

The next chapter will take a closer look at these and other constructs that are used to perform compositional and succinct functional programming in F#.

■ **Note**   In Chapter 3, you will use some of the functions defined in this chapter. If you're using F# Interactive, you may want to leave your session open as you proceed.

CHAPTER 3

■■■

Introducing Functional Programming

F#'s effectiveness rests on the tried and tested foundation of functional programming. This chapter will cover the core building blocks of functional programming with F#, including simple types and function values, pattern matching, lists, and options. Chapters 4 through 6 will cover imperative programming, generics, and object-oriented programming, and Chapters 8, 9, and 10 will cover more advanced topics in functional programming with text, sequences, and structured and numeric data.

Starting with Numbers and Strings

We will first cover the most common base types of data manipulated in F# code, beginning with numbers and strings.

Some Simple Types and Literals

Table 3-1 lists the basic numeric types used in F# code and their corresponding literal forms. The table also lists the nonnumeric types bool and unit.

Table 3-1. *Some Simple Types and Literals*

Type	Description	Sample Literals	Long Name
bool	True/false values	true, false	System.Boolean
Int/int32	32-bit signed integers	0, 19, 0x0800, 0b0001	System.Int32
float/double	64-bit IEEE floating-point	0.0, 19.7, 1.3e4	System.Double
string	Unicode strings	"abc", @"\a\b"	System.String
unit	The type with only one value	()	Core.Unit

Table 3-2 lists the most commonly used arithmetic operators. These are overloaded to work with all basic numeric types, including int and float/double.

Table 3-2. Arithmetic Operators and Examples

Operator	Description	Sample Use on *int*	Sample Use on *float*
+	Unchecked addition	1 + 2	1.0 + 2.0
-	Unchecked subtraction	12 - 5	12.3 - 5.4
*	Unchecked multiplication	2 * 3	2.4 * 3.9
/	Division	5 / 2	5.0 / 2.0
%	Modulus	5 % 2	5.4 % 2.0
-	Unary negation	-(5+2)	-(5.4 + 2.4)

The behavior of these and other operators can be extended for user-defined types, a topic that will be covered in Chapter 6. In F#, addition, subtraction, and multiplication over integers are unchecked; that is, if overflow or underflow occurs beyond the representable range, wraparound occurs. Checked arithmetic will be discussed in Chapter 10.

Operator overloading interacts with type inference and defaults to operate on 32-bit integers unless constrained to work on a different type via type inference. To constrain a use of an operator to a particular type, you must sometimes give a type annotation that tells the compiler the type on the left of the two arguments to the binary operator. For example, in the absence of additional type information, the following function is assumed to work with integers:

```
> let squareAndAdd a b = a * a + b;;
val squareAndAdd : a:int -> b:int -> int
```

A single type annotation on a is sufficient to indicate that a * a is an operation on float values and thus returns a float value, and that a * a + b is also an operation on float. You can use either float or double for 64-bit IEEE floating-point numbers, as the words abbreviate the same type.

```
> let squareAndAdd (a:float) b = a * a + b;;
val squareAndAdd : a:float -> b:float -> float
```

In general, you can place such annotations on any of the function arguments or directly when you use them in the body of the function. If you want, you can also give full type annotations for the arguments and return type of a function:

```
> let squareAndAdd (a:float) (b:float) : float = a * a + b;;
val squareAndAdd : a:float -> b:float -> float
```

Arithmetic Conversions

Numeric types aren't implicitly converted—conversions between different numeric types must be made explicitly. You do this by using overloaded conversion operators. Table 3-3 shows the simplest and most common conversion operators. More conversion operators will be described in Chapter 10.

Table 3-3. *The Simplest Overloaded Arithmetic Conversions and Examples*

Operator	Description	Sample Use	Result
int/int32	Convert/truncate to int32	int 17.8	17
		int -17.8	-17
string	Convert to string	string 65	"65"
float/double	Convert to float/double	float 65	65.0
		double 65	

Arithmetic Comparisons

When used with numeric values, the binary comparison operators =, <>, <, <=, >, >=, min, and max perform comparisons according to the natural ordering for each particular numeric type. You can also use these operators on other structural data types whose elements are comparable, such as to compare lists of integers. Finally, you can customize the behavior of these operators for new types that you define. Chapter 5 will discuss generic comparison in detail, and Chapter 9 will look at customizing generic comparison.

Simple Strings

The F# type string is an abbreviation for the type System.String and represents a sequence of Unicode UTF-16 characters. The index operator str.[index] is used to access the elements of a string, the property Length retrieves its length, and the slicing operator str.[index..index] can be used to take substrings:

```
> let s = "Couldn't put Humpty";;
val s : string = "Couldn't put Humpty"
> s.Length;;
val it : int = 19
> s.[13];;
val it : char = 'H'
> s.[13..16];;
val it : string = "Hump"
```

Both indexing and slicing can also be used with other data types, as will be discussed in Chapter 9.

Strings are immutable; that is, a string value can't be modified after it's built. For example, the Substring method on the string type doesn't modify the original string but instead returns a new string representing the result. As mentioned in Chapter 2, immutability is a key concept for many F# values, and you will encounter it many places in this book. If you do attempt to mutate a string, you will get an error like the one shown here:

```
> let s = "Couldn't put Humpty";;
val s : string = "Couldn't put Humpty"
> s.[13] <- 'h';;
error FS0810: Property 'Chars' cannot be set
```

The simplest way to build strings is via concatenation using the + operator:

```
> "Couldn't put Humpty" + " " + "together again";;
val it : string = "Couldn't put Humpty together again"
```

Chapter 8 will discuss other techniques for working with strings.

Working with Conditionals: && and ||

A basic control construct in F# programming is if/then/elif/else. Here's an example:

```
let round x =
    if x >= 100 then 100
    elif x < 0 then 0
    else x
```

Conditionals are really shorthand for pattern matching; for example, the previous code could be written like this:

```
let round x =
    match x with
    | _ when x >= 100 -> 100
    | _ when x < 0 -> 0
    | _ -> x
```

Conditionals are always guarded by a Boolean-valued expression. You can build them using && and || (the "and" and "or" operators) as well as any library functions that return Boolean values:

```
let round2 (x, y) =
    if x >= 100 || y >= 100 then 100, 100
    elif x < 0 || y < 0 then 0, 0
    else x, y
```

The operators && and || have the usual short-circuit behavior in that the second argument of && is evaluated only if the first evaluates to true and, likewise, the second argument of || is evaluated only if the first evaluates to false.

Defining Recursive Functions

A fundamental building block of computation in F# is recursion. The following code shows a simple, well-known recursive function:

```
> let rec factorial n = if n <= 1 then 1 else n * factorial (n - 1);;
val factorial : n:int -> int
> factorial 5;;
val it : int = 120
```

This example shows that a recursive function is simply one that can call itself as part of its own definition. Recursive functions are introduced by let rec. Functions aren't recursive by default, because it's wise to isolate recursive functions so as to help you control the complexity of your algorithms and to keep your code maintainable. It may help to visualize the execution of factorial 5 in the following way (note that, in reality, F# executes the function using efficient native code):

```
factorial 5
= 5 * factorial 4
= 5 * (4 * factorial 3)
= 5 * (4 * (3 * factorial 2))
= 5 * (4 * (3 * (2 * factorial 1 )))
= 5 * (4 * (3 * (2 * 1)))
= 5 * (4 * (3 * 2))
= 5 * (4 * 6)
= 5 * 24
= 120
```

As with all calls, the execution of the currently executing instance of the function is suspended while a recursive call is made.

Many of the operators you've encountered so far can be coded as recursive functions. For example, the following is one possible implementation of List.length:

```
let rec length l =
    match l with
    | [] -> 0
    | h :: t -> 1 + length t
```

Likewise, many other list-processing functions, such as List.iter, are often implemented using recursive functions.

Recursion is sometimes used as a means of programming particular patterns of control. For example, the following code repeatedly fetches the HTML for a particular web page, printing each time it's fetched (this code reuses the http function from the previous chapter):

```
let rec repeatFetch url n =
    if n > 0 then
        let html = http url
        printfn "fetched <<< %s >>> on iteration %d" html n
        repeatFetch url (n - 1)
```

Recursion is powerful, but it is not always the ideal way to encode either data manipulations or control constructs, at least if other techniques are readily available. For example, the previous program could be implemented using a for loop (as will be explained in Chapter 4), which would be clearer. Likewise, you should typically avoid explicit recursion if an existing function captures the pattern of recursion being used. For example, explicit uses of loops and recursive functions can be replaced by calls to functions such as List.map and Array.map when working with lists and arrays.

A typical error with recursion is to forget to decrement a variable at the recursive call. For example, the following badFactorial function doesn't terminate:

```
let rec badFactorial n = if n <= 1 then 1 else n * badFactorial n
```

You should always check your recursive calls to ensure that the function is tending toward termination—that is, that the arguments are approaching the base case. This is called *well-founded recursion*.

You can define multiple recursive functions simultaneously by separating the definitions with and. These are called *mutually recursive functions*. For example:

```
let rec even n = (n = 0u) || odd(n - 1u)
and odd n = (n <> 0u) && even(n - 1u)
```

This gives the following types:

```
val even : n:uint32 -> bool
val odd : n:uint32 -> bool
```

Of course, a more efficient, nonrecursive implementation of these is available:

```
let even n = (n % 2u) = 0u
let odd n = (n % 2u) = 1u
```

You must sometimes take care with recursive functions to ensure that they're *tail recursive*, or else the computation stack of your program may be exhausted by large inputs. This is particularly important for library functions or functions that operate over large data structures with very large numbers of recursive calls. Indeed, the implementation of length shown previously isn't tail recursive. Chapter 9 will discuss tail recursion in depth.

Lists

Some of the foundational data structures of F# coding are lists and options. The following sections will discuss these and some related topics by example.

F# lists are a common data structure used in functional programming. You saw some examples of concrete lists in Chapter 2. Table 3-4 shows the primitive constructs for building lists.

Table 3-4. *Some List-Related Language Constructs and Operators*

Operator/Expression	Description	Examples
[]	The empty list	[]
expr :: expr	"Cons" an element with a list	1 :: [2; 3]
[expr; ...; expr]	A list value	[1; 2; 3]
[expr .. expr]	A range	[1 .. 99] and ['A' .. 'Z']
[for x in list ...]	A generated list (see end of chapter)	[for x in 1..99 -> x * x]
expr @ expr	Concatenates two lists	[1; 2] @ [3]

Here are some basic list values:

```
let oddPrimes = [3; 5; 7; 11]
let morePrimes = [13; 17]
let primes = 2 :: (oddPrimes @ morePrimes)
```

The type and value of primes are as follows:

```
val primes : int list = [2; 3; 5; 7; 11; 13; 17]
```

Lists are immutable: The cons :: and append @ operations don't modify the original lists; instead, they create new lists. You can see this in the following interactive session:

```
> let people = [ "Adam"; "Dominic"; "James" ];;

val people : string list = ["Adam"; "Dominic"; "James"]

> "Chris" :: people;;

val it : string list = ["Chris"; "Adam"; "Dominic"; "James"]

> people;;

val it : string list = ["Adam"; "Dominic"; "James"]
```

Note that people has not been changed by the construction of a new list using the cons operator. F# lists are immutable, and they are represented in memory as linked lists; each F# list value is a cons cell containing a value plus a pointer to the next chain in the list, or else it's a special nil object. When you create a new list using the :: operator, then the tail of the new list points to the old list, which ensures that the inner memory associated with lists is often reused as part of multiple list values.

The F# library also includes a module called List that contains functions for programming with lists. You will see many of these functions in the next section and throughout this book. Table 3-5 shows some of them.

Table 3-5. *Some Sample Functions in the List Module*

Function	Type	Description
List.length	'T list -> int	Returns the length of the list
List.head	'T list -> 'T	Returns the first element of a nonempty list
List.tail	'T list -> 'T list	Returns all the elements of a nonempty list except the first
List.init	int -> (int -> 'T) -> 'T list	Returns a new list. The length of the new list is specified by the first parameter. The second parameter must be a generating function that maps list indexes to values.
List.append	'T list -> 'T list -> 'T list	Returns a new list containing the elements of the first list followed by the elements of the second list.
List.filter	('T -> bool) -> 'T list -> 'T list	Returns a new list containing only those elements of the original list where the function returns true
List.map	('T -> 'U) -> 'T list -> 'U list	Creates a new list by applying a function to each element of the original list
List.iter	('T -> unit) -> 'T list -> unit	Executes the given function for each element of the list
List.unzip	('T * 'U) list -> 'T list * 'U list	Returns two new lists containing the first and second elements of the pairs in the input list
List.zip	'T list -> 'U list -> ('T * 'U) list	Returns a new list containing the elements of the two input lists combined pairwise as tuples. The input lists must be the same length; otherwise, an exception is raised.
List.toArray	'T list -> 'T []	Creates an array from the given list
List.ofArray	'T [] -> 'T list	Creates a list from the given array

F# lists aren't appropriate for all circumstances. For example, very large data structures should probably be represented using arrays or other data structures, or even managed by an external tool, such as a relational database. We discuss a number of immutable data structures in the "Some Common Immutable Data Structures" sidebar.

Here are examples of how to use some of the functions from Table 3-5. The last two use *function values,* which we will cover in more detail in "Introducing Function Values" later in this chapter.

```
> List.head [5; 4; 3];;
val it : int = 5
> List.tail [5; 4; 3];;
val it : int list = [4; 3]
> List.map (fun x -> x * x) [1; 2; 3];;
val it : int list = [1; 4; 9]
> List.filter (fun x -> x % 3 = 0) [2; 3; 5; 7; 9];;
val it : int list = [3; 9]
```

SOME COMMON IMMUTABLE DATA STRUCTURES

Data structures are generally divided between *mutable* and *immutable*, a distinction that was touched on in Chapter 2 and will be covered in more detail in Chapter 4. Immutable data structures are sometimes called *persistent,* or simply *functional*. Here are some of the immutable data structures commonly used with F#:

- *Tuple values and option values*: These are immutable and are basic workhorses of F# programming.

- *Immutable linked lists of type* 'T list: These are cheap to access from the left end. They're inefficient for random-access lookup because the list must be traversed from the left for each lookup—that is, random-access lookup is O(*n*), where *n* is the number of elements in the collection. The full name of this type is FSharp.Collections.List<'T>.

- *Immutable sets based on balanced trees*: Chapter 2 showed some examples of uses of immutable sets, and an implementation is provided via the type Set<'T> in the F# library namespace FSharp.Collections. These are cheap to add, access, and union, with O(log(*n*)) access times, where *n* is the number of elements in the collection. Because the type is immutable, internal nodes can be shared among different sets.

- *Immutable maps based on balanced trees*: These are similar to immutable sets but associate keys with values (that is, they're immutable dictionaries). One implementation of these is provided via the F# library type Map<'Key, 'Value> in FSharp.Collections. As with sets, these have O(log(*n*)) access times.

- *More immutable collections*: The System.Collections.Immutable package contains many more immutable collections and is readily usable from F#.

Chapter 4 will cover imperative programming and mutable data structures.

Options

Like lists and tuples, option values are simple constructs frequently used as workhorses in F# coding. An option is simply either a value "Some v" or the absence of a value "None". For example, options are useful for returning the value of a search where you may or may not have a result. You will see in the section "Defining Discriminated Unions" in Chapter 4 that the option type is defined in the F# library essentially as follows:

```
type 'T option =
    | None
    | Some of 'T
```

The following is a data structure (an association list) that uses options to represent the (optional) parents of some well-known mythical characters:

```
let people =
    [("Adam", None);
     ("Eve" , None);
     ("Cain", Some("Adam","Eve"));
     ("Abel", Some("Adam","Eve"))]
```

Giving:

```
val people : (string * (string * string) option) list =
  [("Adam", None); ("Eve", None); ("Cain", Some ("Adam", "Eve"));
   ("Abel", Some ("Adam", "Eve"))]
```

One use of option values is to represent the success or failure of a computation. This can be useful when you're catching an exception, as shown in the following example (which uses the function http from Chapter 2):

```
let fetch url =
    try Some (http url)
    with :? System.Net.WebException -> None
```

Chapter 4 will describe exceptions in more detail. What matters here is that if a network error occurs during the HTTP request, the exception is caught and the result of the fetch function is the value None. Successful web-page requests return a Some value. Option values can then be discriminated and decomposed using pattern matching, as shown here:

```
match (fetch "http://www.nature.com") with
  | Some text -> printfn "text = %s" text
  | None -> printfn "**** no web page found"
```

Giving:

```
text = <!DOCTYPE html PUB (note: the HTML is shown here if connected to the web)
```

Getting Started with Pattern Matching

One important construct in F# programming is *pattern matching*, a general construct that combines decomposition and control. In the previous sections, you got a taste of how you can use pattern matching with some simple values, such as tuples and options. You can use pattern matching in many other situations, however. You will see many other examples of pattern matching in this book, but let's start with some simple pattern matching over strings and integers. As you've already seen, pattern matches on explicit values are introduced using the match ... with ... construct, as follows:

```
let isLikelySecretAgent url agent =
    match (url, agent) with
    | "http://www.control.org", 99 -> true
    | "http://www.control.org", 86 -> true
    | "http://www.kaos.org", _ -> true
    | _ -> false
```

The inferred type of the function is as follows:

```
val isLikelySecretAgent : url:string -> agent:int -> bool
```

The expression (url, agent) after the keyword match is a tuple of type (string*int). You can omit the parentheses here (as in the subsequent | patterns) and use them only when you need to group inner tuples together, but it's a good practice to keep them around the values you are matching against. Each rule of the match is introduced with a | followed by a pattern, then ->, and then a result expression. When executed, the patterns of the rules are checked one by one, and the first successful pattern match determines which result expression is used. In the previous example, the first rule matches if url and agent are "http://www.control.org" and 99. Likewise, the second rule matches "http://www.control.org" and 86. The third rule matches if url is "http://www.kaos.org", regardless of agent number. The last two rules use "wildcard" patterns (represented by the underscore character); these match all inputs.

The overall conditions under which isLikelySecretAgent returns true can be determined by reading through the pattern match: agents 86 and 99 are known agents of http://www.control.org, all agent numbers at http://www.kaos.org are assumed to be agents, and no other inputs are categorized as agents.

Patterns are a rich and powerful technique for simultaneous data analysis and decomposition. For example, pattern matching can be used to decompose list values from the head downward:

```
let printFirst xs =
    match xs with
    | h :: t -> printfn "The first item  in the list is %A" h
    | [] -> printfn "No items in the list"
> printFirst oddPrimes;;
```

The first item in the list is 3

The first line after the match is a pattern-matching rule that matches the input xs against the pattern h :: t. If xs is a nonempty list, then the match is successful, and the first printfn is executed with h bound to the head of the list and t to its tail. The second line considers the case in which xs is an empty list. Note that the :: and [] symbols can be used both to build up lists in expressions and to decompose them in pattern matching. In this example, the order of the pattern matching clauses can be reversed without changing the result.

Likewise, pattern matching can be used to examine option values, as follows:

```
let showParents (name, parents) =
    match parents with
    | Some (dad, mum) -> printfn "%s has father %s and mother %s" name dad mum
    | None -> printfn "%s has no parents!" name
```

Giving type:

```
val showParents : name:string * parents:(string * string) option -> unit
```

And used as follows:

```
> for person in people do showParents person;;

Adam has no parents!
Eve has no parents!
Cain has father Adam and mother Eve
Abel has father Adam and mother Eve
```

Matching on Structured Values

Pattern matching can be used to decompose structured values. Here is an example in which nested tuple values are matched:

```
let highLow a b =
    match (a, b) with
    | ("lo", lo), ("hi", hi) -> (lo, hi)
    | ("hi", hi), ("lo", lo) -> (lo, hi)
    | _ -> failwith "expected a both a high and low value"
```

The match examines two pairs and looks at the strings in the first element of each, returning the associated values:

```
> highLow ("hi", 300) ("lo", 100);;

val it : int * int = (100, 300)
```

The first rule matches if the first parts of the input pairs are the strings "lo" and "hi". The second rule is the mirror of this in case the values appeared in reverse order.

The final cases of both of the previous examples use wildcard patterns to cover remaining cases. This makes the patterns *exhaustive*. Frequently, no wildcard is needed to ensure this, because for many input types, F# is able to determine whether the given set of rules is sufficient to cover all possibilities for the given shape of data. In the following example, the match isn't exhaustive:

```
let urlFilter3 url agent =
    match url,agent with
    | "http://www.control.org", 86 -> true
    | "http://www.kaos.org", _ -> false
```

As a result, a warning is given:

```
warning FS0025: Incomplete pattern matches on this expression. For example, the value
'(_,0)' may indicate a case not covered by the pattern(s).

val urlFilter3 : url:string -> agent:int -> bool
```

In these cases, it may be necessary to add an extra exception-throwing clause to indicate to the F#
compiler that the given inputs aren't expected:

```
let urlFilter4 url agent =
    match url,agent with
    | "http://www.control.org", 86 -> true
    | "http://www.kaos.org", _ -> false
    | _ -> failwith "unexpected input"
```

Nonexhaustive matches are automatically augmented by the compiler with a default case in which a
MatchFailureException is thrown. Chapter 4 will discuss exceptions.

F# is frequently able to determine whether pattern-matching rules are redundant, such as if a rule can
never be selected because previous rules subsume all such cases. In this case, a warning is given. For example:

```
> let urlFilter2 url agent =
    match url,agent with
    | "http://www.control.org", _ -> true
    | "http://www.control.org", 86 -> true
    | _ -> false;;

warning FS0026: This rule will never be matched

val urlFilter2 : url:string -> agent:int -> bool
```

■ **Tip**   Use wildcard patterns with care. F# can often determine whether a match is exhaustive, and the use
of wildcard patterns effectively disables this analysis for any particular pattern match. Sometimes it's better
to write out the extra cases of a match as explicit patterns, because you can then adjust your code when new
kinds of input data are introduced.

Guarding Rules and Combining Patterns

Individual rules of a match can be guarded by a condition that is tested if the pattern itself succeeds. Here is
a simple use of this mechanism to record the three clauses of computing the sign of an integer:

```
let sign x =
    match x with
    | _ when x < 0 -> -1
    | _ when x > 0 -> 1
    | _ -> 0
```

You can combine two patterns to represent two possible paths for matching:

```
let getValue a =
    match a with
    | (("lo" | "low"), v) -> v
    | ("hi", v) | ("high", v) -> v
    | _ -> failwith "expected a both a high and low value"
```

Here, the pattern ("lo" | "low") matches either string. The pattern ("hi", v) | ("high", v) plays essentially the same role by matching pairs values where the left of the pair is "hi" or "high" and by binding the value v on either side of the pattern.

Further Ways of Forming Patterns

Table 3-6 summarizes all the ways to form patterns in F#; many of these involve building up patterns from other patterns. Chapter 8 will cover active patterns and look at further techniques for working with structured data.

***Table 3-6.** Different Ways to Form Patterns*

General Form	Kind	Example
(pat, ... , pat)	Tuple pattern	(1, 2, ("3", x))
[pat; ... ; pat]	List pattern	[x; y; z]
[| pat; ...; pat |]	Array pattern	[|"cmd"; arg1; arg2|]
{id=pat; ...; id=pat}	Record pattern	{ X = 1; Y = 2 }
Tag(pat, ... , pat)	Tagged union or active pattern	Point(x, y)
pat | pat	"Or" pattern	[x] | ["X"; x]
pat & pat	"And" pattern	[p] & [Point(x, y)]
pat as id	Named pattern	[x] as inp
id	Variable pattern	X
_	Wildcard pattern	_
Any literal	Constant pattern	36, "36", 27L, System.DayOfWeek.Monday
:? *type*	Type test pattern	:? String
null	Null test pattern	Null

■ **Note** Individual patterns can't bind the same variables twice. For example, a pattern (x, x) isn't permitted, although (x, y) when x = y is permitted. Furthermore, each side of an "or" pattern must bind the same set of variables, and these variables must be of the same types.

Introducing Function Values

This section will cover the foundational building block of F# functional programming: function values. We will begin with a simple and well-known example: using function values to transform one list into another.

One of the primary uses of F# lists is as a general-purpose, concrete data structure for storing ordered input lists and ordered results. Input lists are often transformed into output lists using collection functions that transform, select, filter, and categorize elements of the list according to a range of criteria. These collection functions provide an excellent introduction to how to use function values. Let's take a closer look at this in the following code sample, which continues from the definition of http from Listing 2-2 in Chapter 2:

```
> let sites = ["http://www.bing.com"; "http://www.google.com"];;

val sites : string list = ["http://www.bing.com"; "http://www.google.com"]

> let fetch url = (url, http url);;

val fetch : url:string -> string * string

> List.map fetch sites;;

val it : (string * string) list =
  [("http://www.bing.com",
    "<!DOCTYPE html PUBLIC ...
</body></html>");
   ("http://www.google.com",
    "<!doctype html>...
</script>")]
```

The first interaction defines sites as a literal list of URLs, and the second defines the function fetch. The third calls the collection function List.map. This accepts the function value fetch as the first argument and the list sites as the second argument. The function applies fetch to each element of the list and collects the results in a new list.

Types are one useful way to help learn what a function does. Here's the type of List.map:

```
val map : mapping: ('T -> 'U) -> list: 'T list -> 'U list
```

This says List.map accepts a function value as the first argument and a list as the second argument, and it returns a list as the result. The function argument can have any type 'T -> 'U, and the elements of the input list must have a corresponding type 'T. The symbols 'T and 'U are called *type parameters,* and functions that accept type parameters are called *generic.* Chapter 5 will discuss type parameters in detail.

■ **Tip** You can often deduce the behavior of a function from its type, especially if its type involves type parameters. For example, look at the type of List.map. Using type parameters, you can observe that the type 'T list of the input list is related to the type 'T accepted by the function passed as the first parameter. Similarly, the type 'U returned by this function is related to the type 'U list of the value returned by List.map. From this, it's reasonable to conclude that List.map calls the function parameter for items in the list and constructs its result using the values returned.

Using Function Values

Function values are so common in F# programming that it's convenient to define them without giving them names. Here is a simple example:

```
> let primes = [2; 3; 5; 7];;

val primes : int list = [2; 3; 5; 7]

> let primeCubes = List.map (fun n -> n * n * n) primes;;

val primeCubes: int list = [8; 27; 125; 343]
```

The definition of primeCubes uses the *lambda function* or *anonymous function value* (fun n -> n * n * n). Such values are similar to function definitions but are unnamed and appear as an expression rather than as a let declaration. fun is a keyword meaning function, n represents the argument to the function, and n * n * n is the result of the function. The overall type of the anonymous function expression is int -> int. You could use an anonymous function instead of the intermediary function fetch in the earlier sample:

```
let resultsOfFetch = List.map (fun url -> (url, http url)) sites
```

You will see anonymous functions throughout this book. Here is another example:

```
> List.map (fun (_,p) -> String.length p) resultsOfFetch;;

val it : int list = [56601; 52321]
```

Here you see two things:

- The argument of the anonymous function is a tuple pattern. Using a tuple pattern automatically extracts the second element from each tuple and gives it the name p within the body of the anonymous function.

- Part of the tuple pattern is a wildcard pattern, indicated by an underscore. This indicates that you don't care what the first part of the tuple is; you're interested only in extracting the length from the second part of the pair.

Computing with Collection Functions

Functions such as List.map are called *combinators* or *collection functions*, and they're powerful constructs, especially when combined with the other features of F#. Here is a longer example that uses the collection functions Array.filter and List.map to count the number of URL links in an HTML page and then collects stats on a group of pages (this sample uses the function http defined in Chapter 2):

```
let delimiters = [| ' '; '\n'; '\t'; '<'; '>'; '=' |]

let getWords (s: string) = s.Split delimiters

let getStats site =
    let url = "http://" + site
    let html = http url
```

```
let hwords = html |> getWords
let hrefs = html |> getWords |> Array.filter (fun s -> s = "href")
(site, html.Length, hwords.Length, hrefs.Length)
```

Here, you use the function getStats with three web pages:

```
> let sites = ["www.bing.com"; "www.google.com"; "search.yahoo.com"];;

val sites : string list

> sites |> List.map getStats;;

val it : (string * int * int * int) list =
    [("www.bing.com", 56601, 3230, 30);
     ("www.google.com", 52314, 2975, 31);
     ("search.yahoo.com", 17691, 1568, 40)]
```

The function getStats computes the length of the HTML for the given website, the number of words in the text of that HTML, and the approximate number of links on that page.

The previous code sample extensively uses the |> operator to *pipeline* operations, discussed in "Pipelining with |>" (see sidebar). The F# library design ensures that a common, consistent set of collection functions is defined for each structured type. Table 3-7 shows how the same convention is used for the map abstraction.

Table 3-7. A Recurring Collection Function Design Pattern from the F# Library

Operator	Type
List.map	('T -> 'U) -> 'T list -> 'U list
Array.map	('T -> 'U) -> 'T [] -> 'U []
Option.map	('T -> 'U) -> 'T option -> 'U option
Seq.map	('T -> 'U) -> seq<'T> -> seq<'U>

Using Fluent Notation on Collections

Some programmers prefer to use "fluent" notation for collection functions, using notation such as

```
sites.map(fun x -> ...).sort()
```

rather than

```
xs |> List.map(fun x -> ...)  |> List.sort
```

For example, you may use

```
sites.map(getStats)
```

to replace

```
sites |> List.map getStats
```

This option is available through the nuget package FSharp.Core.Fluent which you can add to your script and/or project through the techniques described in Chapter 2. This provides a slightly more succinct way of transforming data through a set of (lowercase named) instance extension members on List, Array, and seq types. Chapter 6 will discuss extension members in detail. This style may require the use of a type annotation. In general, both the "pipelining" and the "fluent" styles are used in F# programming, depending on the methods and properties available for a particular data type. For largely historical reasons the fluent style is not used particularly often with the collection types List, Array, and Seq. However, the package FSharp.Core.Fluent does enable it for those who wish to adopt it for consistency reasons.

PIPELINING WITH |>

The |> forward pipe operator is perhaps the most important operator in F# programming. Its definition is deceptively simple:

```
let (|>) x f = f x
```

Here is how to use the operator to compute the cubes of three numbers:

```
[1;2;3] |> List.map (fun x -> x * x * x)
```

This produces [1; 8; 27], just as if you had written:

```
List.map (fun x -> x * x * x) [1; 2; 3]
```

In a sense, |> is function application in reverse. However, using |> has distinct advantages:

- *Clarity:* When used in conjunction with functions such as List.map, the |> operator allows you to perform the data transformations and iterations in a forward-chaining, pipelined style.

- *Type inference:* Using the |> operator lets type information flow from input objects to the functions manipulating those objects. F# uses information collected from type inference to resolve some language constructs, such as property accesses and method overloading. This relies on information being propagated left to right through the text of a program. In particular, typing information to the right of a position isn't taken into account when resolving property access and overloads.

For completeness, here is the type of the operator:

```
val (|>) : 'T -> ('T -> 'U) -> 'U
```

Composing Functions with >>

You saw earlier how to use the |> forward pipe operator to pipe values through a number of functions. This was a small example of the process of *computing with functions*, an essential and powerful programming technique in F#. This section will cover ways to compute new function values from existing ones using compositional techniques. First, let's look at function composition. For example, consider the following code:

```
let google = http "http://www.google.com"

google |> getWords |> Array.filter (fun s -> s = "href") |> Array.length
```

You can rewrite this code using function composition, as follows:

```
let countLinks = getWords >> Array.filter (fun s -> s = "href") >> Array.length

google |> countLinks
```

You define countLinks as the composition of three function values using the >> forward composition operator. This operator is defined in the F# library, as follows:

```
let (>>) f g x = g(f(x))
```

You can see from the definition that f >> g gives a function value that first applies f to the x and then applies g. Here is the type of >>:

```
val (>>) : ('T -> 'U) -> ('U -> 'V) -> ('T -> 'V)
```

Note that >> has only two arguments, here named f and g. The operator takes two functions and returns a function.

F# is good at optimizing basic constructions of pipelines and composition sequences from functions—for example, the function countLinks shown earlier becomes a single function that directly calls the three functions in the pipeline in sequence. This means sequences of compositions can be used with relatively low overhead.

Building Functions with Partial Application

Composing functions is just one way to compute interesting new functions. Another useful way is to use *partial application*. Here's an example, with x and y in Cartesian coordinates:

```
let shift (dx, dy) (px, py) = (px + dx, py + dy)
let shiftRight = shift (1, 0)
let shiftUp = shift (0, 1)
let shiftLeft = shift (-1, 0)
let shiftDown = shift (0, -1)
```

The last four functions are defined by calling shift with only one argument, in each case leaving a residue function that expects an additional argument. F# Interactive reports the types as follows:

```
val shiftRight : (int * int -> int * int)
val shiftUp : (int * int -> int * int)
val shiftLeft : (int * int -> int * int)
val shiftDown : (int * int -> int * int)
```

Here is an example of how to use shiftRight and how to partially apply shift to new arguments (2, 2):

```
> shiftRight (10, 10);;
val it : int * int = (11, 10)

> List.map (shift (2,2)) [(0,0); (1,0); (1,1); (0,1)];;
val it : (int * int) list = [(2, 2); (3, 2); (3, 3); (2, 3)]
```

In the second example, the function shift takes two pairs as arguments. You bind the first parameter to (2, 2). The result of this partial application is a function that takes one remaining tuple parameter and returns the value shifted by two units in each direction. This resulting function can now be used in conjunction with List.map.

Using Local Functions

Partial application is one way in which functions can be computed rather than simply defined. This technique becomes very powerful when combined with additional local definitions. Here's a simple and practical example, representing an idea common in graphics programming:

```
open System.Drawing

open System.Drawing

let remap (r1:RectangleF) (r2:RectangleF) =
    let scalex = r2.Width / r1.Width
    let scaley = r2.Height / r1.Height
    let mapx x = r2.Left + (x - r1.Left) * scalex
    let mapy y = r2.Top + (y - r1.Top) * scaley
    let mapp (p:PointF) = PointF(mapx p.X, mapy p.Y)
    mapp

let rect1 = RectangleF(100.0f, 100.0f, 100.0f, 100.0f)
let rect2 = RectangleF(50.0f, 50.0f, 200.0f, 200.0f)

let mapp = remap rect1 rect2
```

The function remap computes a new function value mapp that maps points in one rectangle to points in another. F# Interactive reports the type as follows:

```
val remap : r1:RectangleF -> r2:RectangleF -> (PointF -> PointF)
val mapp : (PointF -> PointF)
```

The type Rectangle is defined in the library System.Drawing.dll and represents rectangles specified by integer coordinates. The computations on the interior of the transformation are performed in floating point to improve precision. You can use this as follows:

```
> mapp (PointF(100.0f, 100.0f));;

val it : PointF = {X=50, Y=50}

> mapp (Point(150.0f, 150.0f));;

val it : PointF = {X=150, Y=150}

> mapp (Point(200.0f, 200.0f));;

val it : PointF = {X=200, Y=200}
```

The intermediate values scalex and scaley are computed only once, despite the fact that you've called the resulting function mapp three times.

In the previous example, mapx, mapy, and mapp are *local functions*—functions defined locally as part of the implementation of remap. Local functions can be context dependent; in other words, they can be defined in terms of any values and parameters that happen to be in scope. Local functions are said to *capture* the values they depend on. Here, mapx is defined in terms of scalex, scaley, r1, and r2 and captures all of these values.

■ **Note** Local and partially applied functions are, if necessary, implemented by taking the *closure* of the variables they depend on and storing them away until needed. In optimized F# code, the F# compiler often avoids this and instead passes extra arguments to the function implementations. Closure is a powerful technique that is used frequently in this book. It's often used in conjunction with functions, as in this chapter, but it is also used with object expressions, sequence expressions, and class definitions.

Iterating with Functions

It's common to use data to drive control. In functional programming, the distinction between data and control is often blurred: function values can be used as data, and data can influence control flow. One example is using a function such as List.iter to iterate over a list:

```
let sites = ["http://www.bing.com";
             "http://www.google.com";
             "http://search.yahoo.com"]

sites |> List.iter (fun site -> printfn "%s, length = %d" site (http site).Length)
```

The function List.iter simply calls the given function (here an anonymous function) for each element in the input list. Some additional iteration techniques are available in F#, particularly by using values of type seq<type>, which will be discussed in "Getting Started with Sequences" later in this chapter.

Abstracting Control with Functions

As a second example of how you can abstract control using functions, let's consider the common pattern of timing the execution of an operation (measured in wall-clock time). First, let's explore how to use System.DateTime.Now to get the wall-clock time:

```
> open System;;

> let start = DateTime.Now;;

val start : DateTime = 13/06/2015 9:54:36 p.m.

> http "http://www.newscientist.com";;

val it : string = "<!DOCTYPE html...</html>"

> let finish = DateTime.Now;;

val finish : DateTime = 13/06/2015 9:54:39 p.m.
> let elapsed = finish - start;;

val elapsed : TimeSpan = 00:00:01.1550660
```

Note that the type TimeSpan has been inferred from the use of the overloaded operator in the expression finish - start. Chapter 6 will discuss overloaded operators in depth. You can now wrap up this technique as a function time that acts as a new control operator:

```
open System

let time f =
    let start = DateTime.Now
    let res = f()
    let finish = DateTime.Now
    (res, finish - start)
```

This function runs the input function f but takes the time on either side of the call. It then returns both the result of the function and the elapsed time. The inferred type is as follows:

```
val time : f:(unit -> 'a) -> 'a * TimeSpan
```

Here 'a is a *type variable* that stands for any type, and thus the function can be used to time functions that return any kind of result. Note that F# automatically infers a generic type for the function, a technique called *automatic generalization* that lies at the heart of F# type inference. Chapter 5 will discuss automatic generalization in detail. Here is an example of using the time function, which again reuses the http function defined in Chapter 2:

```
> time (fun () -> http "http://www.newscientist.com");;

val it : string * TimeSpan = ...    (The HTML text and time will be shown here)
```

Using Object Methods as First-Class Functions

You can use existing .NET methods as first-class functions. You will learn more about methods in Chapter 6. You can use both static and instance methods as first-class values. The following uses the .NET method System.IO.Path.GetExtension as a first-class method:

```
open System.IO

[ "file1.txt"; "file2.txt"; "file3.sh" ]
    |> List.map Path.GetExtension
```

This gives the result:

```
val it : string list = [".txt"; ".txt"; ".sh"]
```

Sometimes you need to add extra type information to indicate which overload of the method is required. Chapter 6 will discuss method overloading in more detail. For example, the following causes an error:

```
> open System;;

> let f = Console.WriteLine;;

error FS0041: A unique overload for method 'WriteLine' could not be determined based on
type information prior to this program point. A type annotation may be needed.
```

However, the following succeeds:

```
> let f = (Console.WriteLine : string -> unit);;

val f : (string -> unit)
```

Some Common Uses of Function Values

The function remap from the previous section generates values of type PointF -> PointF, representing "transformations for points." You haven't needed to define a new type for "transformations"—you just use functions as a way of modeling transformations. Many useful concepts can be modeled using function types and values. For example:

- Actions. The type unit -> unit can be used to model actions—operations that run and perform some unspecified side effect. For example, consider the expression (fun () -> printfn "Hello World").

- Predicates. Types of the form *type* -> bool can be used to model *predicates*, which return true for a subset of values.

- Counting Functions. Types of the form *type* -> int can be used to model *counting functions*, which give a number for each input; the numbers may then be accumulated.

- Statistical Functions. Types of the form *type* -> `float` can be used to model *statistical functions*, which give a floating point number for each input. These may be used as an input into a statistical routine such `Seq.averageBy`.

- Key Functions. Types of the form *type* -> *keytype* can be used to model *key functions*, which give a key value for each input. For example, a key function may be an integer associated with each input. Operations such as `Seq.groupBy` and `Seq.sortBy` accept key functions.

- Orderings. Types of the form *type* -> *type* -> `int` can be used to model comparison functions over the type type. You also see `type` * `type` -> `int` used for this purpose, where a tuple is accepted as the first argument. In both cases, a negative result indicates less than, zero indicates equals, and a positive result indicates greater than. Operations such as `Seq.sortWith` accept ordering functions.

- Callbacks. Types of the form *type* -> `unit` can be used to model *callbacks*. Callbacks are often run in response to a system event, such as when a user clicks a user interface element. In this case, the parameter sent to the handler has some specific type, such as `System.EventArgs`.

- Delayed Computations. Types of the form `unit` -> *type* can be used to model *delayed computations*, which are values that, when required, produce a value of type *type*. For example, a threading library can accept such a function value and execute it on a different thread, eventually producing a value of type type. Delayed computations are related to lazy computations and sequence expressions; these are discussed in "Using Sequence Expressions" in Chapter 9.

- Sinks. Types of the form *type* -> `unit` can be used to model *sinks*, which are function values that, when required, consume a value of type *type*. For example, a logging API may use a sink to consume values and write them to a log file.

- Generators. Types of the form `int` -> *type* can be used to model *generators*, which are used to initialize a collection. The parameter may be an integer index into the collection. For example, `Array.init` accepts a generator function. More complex generators may propagate state and optionally indicate the end of the generation process. For an example, see `Seq.unfold`.

- Binary Operators. Types of the form *type* -> *type* -> *type* can be used to model binary operations, which take two input values and combine them into one. Operations such as `List.reduce` accept binary operators.

- Transformations. Types of the form *type1* -> *type2* can be used to model *transformers*, which are functions that transform each element of a collection. You see this pattern in the `map` operator for many common collection types.

- Accumulators. Types of the form *type1* -> *type2* -> *type2* can be used to model visitor *accumulating functions*, which are functions that visit each element of a collection (type *type1*) and accumulate a result (type *type2*). For example, a visitor function that accumulates integers into a set of integers has type `int` -> `Set<int>` -> `Set<int>`.

■ **Note**   The power of function types to model many different concepts is part of the enduring appeal of functional programming. This is one of the refreshing features F# brings to programming: many simple abstractions are modeled in very simple ways and often have simple implementations through orthogonal, unified constructs, such as anonymous function values and function compositions.

Summary

F# is a multiparadigm language, and this chapter has looked at the core language constructs used for functional programming. The next chapter will explore how to use F# for imperative programming: how to use a mutable state, raise and handle exceptions, and perform I/O.

CHAPTER 4

■ ■ ■

Introducing Imperative Programming

In Chapter 3, you saw some of the constructs that make up F# functional programming. At the core of the functional programming paradigm is "programming without side effects," also called pure functional programming. In this chapter you will learn about programming *with* side effects, called imperative programming.

About Functional and Imperative Programming

In the functional programming paradigm, programs compute the result of a mathematical expression and don't cause any side effects, simply returning the result of the computation. The formulas used in spreadsheets are often pure, as is the core of functional programming languages such as Haskell.

However, F# is not a pure functional language—functions and expressions *can* have side effects. It is very common to write pure functions and expressions in F#, but you can also write functions and expression that mutate data, perform I/O (input/output), communicate over the network, start new parallel threads, and raise exceptions. These side effects are collectively called *imperative programming*. The F#-type system doesn't distinguish between functions that perform these actions and those that don't. The type of a function doesn't reveal what side effects a function may perform.

If your primary programming experience has been with an imperative language such as C, C#, or Java, you may initially find yourself using imperative constructs fairly frequently in F#. Over time, however, F# programmers learn to perform a surprisingly large proportion of routine programming tasks within the side effect–free subset of the language; functional programming can express an astounding range of computations succinctly and accurately. However, when you reach the limits of what functional programming can do, you will need to turn to imperative programming. In particular, F# programmers tend to use imperative programming in the following situations:

- When scripting and prototyping using F# Interactive

- When working with .NET library components that use side effects heavily, such as GUI libraries and I/O libraries

- When initializing complex data structures

- When using inherently imperative, efficient data structures, such as hash tables, hash sets, and matrices

- When locally optimizing functions in a way that improves performance

- When working with very large data structures or in scenarios in which the allocation of data structures must be minimized for performance reasons

Some F# programs don't use any imperative techniques except as part of the outermost layer of their program architecture. Adopting this form of pure functional programming is good practice and an excellent way to hone your functional programming techniques.

Programming with fewer side effects is attractive for many reasons. For example, eliminating unnecessary side effects nearly always reduces the complexity of your code, so it leads to fewer bugs and more rapid delivery of high-quality components. Another thing experienced functional programmers appreciate is that the programmer or compiler can easily adjust the order in which expressions are computed. If your programs don't have side effects, then it's easier to think clearly about your code; you can visually check when two programs are equivalent, and it's easier to make radical adjustments to your code without introducing new, subtle bugs. Programs that are free from side effects can often be computed on demand or in parallel by your making very small, local changes to the code to introduce the use of delayed data structures or parallelism. Finally, mutation and other side effects introduce complex, time-dependent interactions into your code, making it difficult to test and debug, especially when data is accessed concurrently from multiple threads, which will be discussed further in Chapter 11.

Imperative Looping and Iterating

The first imperative constructs we will look at are those associated with looping and iteration. Three available looping constructs help simplify writing iterative code with side effects:

- Simple for loops: for *val* = *start-expr* to *end-expr* do *work-expr*

- Simple while loops: while *condition-expr* do *work-expr*

- Sequence loops: for *pattern* in *collection-expr* do *work-expr*

All three constructs are for writing imperative programs, indicated partly by the fact that in all cases the body of the loop must have a return type of unit. Note that unit is the F# type that corresponds to void in imperative languages, such as C, and it has the single value (). This means the loops don't produce a useful value, so the only use a loop can have is to perform some kind of side effect. The following sections will cover these three constructs in more detail.

Simple for Loops

Simple for loops are used to iterate over integer ranges. This is illustrated here by a replacement implementation of the repeatFetch function from Chapter 2:

The first looping construct is simple for loops, which iterate over a range of integers. For example, the following construct fetches the same web page n times, printing the result each time:

```
let repeatFetch url n =
    for i = 1 to n do
        let html = http url
        printfn "fetched <<< %s >>>" html
    printfn "Done!"
```

This loop is executed for successive values of i over the given range, including both start and end indexes.

Simple While Loops

The second looping construct is a while loop, which repeats until a given guard is false. For example, here is a way to keep your computer busy until the weekend:

```
open System

let loopUntilSaturday() =
    while (DateTime.Now.DayOfWeek <> DayOfWeek.Saturday) do
        printfn "Still working!"

    printfn "Saturday at last!"
```

When executing this code in F# Interactive, you can interrupt its execution by choosing the "Cancel Interactive Evaluation" command in Visual Studio or by using Ctrl+C when running fsi.exe from the command line.

More Iteration Loops over Sequences

As you will learn in depth in Chapter 9, any values compatible with the type seq<type> can be iterated using the for *pattern* in *seq* do ... construct. The input seq may be an F# list value, any seq<type>, or a value of any type supporting a GetEnumerator method. Here are some simple examples:

```
> for (b, pj) in [("Banana 1", false); ("Banana 2", true)] do
      if pj then
          printfn "%s is in pyjamas today!" b;;

Banana 2 is in pyjamas today!
```

The following example iterates the results of a regular expression match. The type returned by the .NET method Regex.Matches is a MatchCollection, which, for reasons known best to the .NET designers, doesn't directly support the seq<Match> interface. It does, however, support a GetEnumerator method that permits iteration over the individual results of the operation, each of which is of type Match. The F# compiler inserts the conversions necessary to view the collection as a seq<Match> and perform the iteration. You will learn more about using the .NET Regular Expression library in Chapter 8. See the following:

```
> open System.Text.RegularExpressions;;

> for m in Regex.Matches("All the Pretty Horses","[a-zA-Z]+") do
      printfn "res = %s" m.Value;;

res = All
res = the
res = Pretty
res = Horses
```

Using Mutable Records

One of the most common kinds of imperative programming is to use mutation to adjust the contents of values. Values whose contents can be adjusted are called *mutable* values. The simplest mutable values in F# are mutable records. Record types and their use in functional programming will be discussed in more detail in Chapter 5. A record is mutable if one or more of its fields is labeled `mutable`. This means that record fields can be updated using the `<-` operator; that is, the same syntax used to set a property. Mutable fields are generally used for records that implement the internal state of objects, which will be discussed in Chapters 6 and 7.

For example, the following code defines a record that is used to count the number of times an event occurs and the number of times the event satisfies a particular criterion:

```
type DiscreteEventCounter =
    { mutable Total : int;
      mutable Positive : int;
      Name : string }

let recordEvent (s : DiscreteEventCounter) isPositive =
    s.Total <- s.Total + 1
    if isPositive then s.Positive <- s.Positive + 1

let reportStatus (s : DiscreteEventCounter) =
    printfn "We have %d %s out of %d" s.Positive s.Name s.Total

let newCounter nm =
    { Total = 0;
      Positive = 0;
      Name = nm }
```

You can use this type as follows (this example uses the `http` function from Chapter 2):

```
let longPageCounter = newCounter "long page(s)"

let fetch url =
    let page = http url
    recordEvent longPageCounter (page.Length > 10000)
    page
```

Every call to the function `fetch` mutates the mutable-record fields in the global variable `longPageCounter`. For example:

```
> fetch "http://www.smh.com.au" |> ignore;;

> fetch "http://www.theage.com.au" |> ignore;;

> reportStatus longPageCounter;;

We have 2 long page(s) out of 2
```

Record types can also support members (for example, properties and methods) and give explicit implementations of interfaces, which will be discussed in Chapter 6. When compiled, records become .NET classes and can be used in C# and other .NET languages. Practically speaking, this means you can use them as one way to implement objects.

WHICH DATA STRUCTURES ARE MUTABLE?

It's useful to know which data structures are mutable and which aren't. If a data structure can be mutated, this is typically evident in the types of operations you can perform on that structure. For example, if a data structure `Table<'Key,'Value>` has an operation such as the following, in practice you can be sure that updates to the data structure modify the data structure itself:

```
val add : Table<'Key,'Value> -> 'Key -> 'Value -> unit
```

That is, any update to this data structure is destructive and no value is returned. Likewise, the following member indicates that the data structure is almost certainly mutable:

```
member Add : 'Key * 'Value -> unit
```

In both cases, the presence of `unit` as a return type is a sure sign that an operation performs some side effects. In contrast, operations on immutable data structures typically return a new instance of the data structure when an operation such as `add` is performed. For example:

```
val add : 'Key -> 'Value -> Table<'Key,'Value> -> Table<'Key,'Value>
```

Or for example:

```
member Add : 'Key * 'Value -> Table<'Key,'Value>
```

As discussed in Chapter 3, immutable data structures are also called *functional* or *persistent*. The latter name is used because the original table isn't modified when adding an element. Well-crafted persistent data structures don't duplicate the actual memory used to store the data structure every time an addition is made; instead, internal nodes can be shared between the old and new data structures. Example persistent data structures in the F# library are F# lists, options, tuples, and the types `FSharp.Collections.Map<'Key,'Value>`, and `FSharp.Collections.Set<'Key>`. Most data structures in the .NET libraries aren't persistent, although if you're careful, you can use them as persistent data structures by accessing them in read-only mode and copying them if necessary.

Avoiding Aliasing

Like all mutable objects, two names referring to mutable record values may refer to the *same* storage location—this is called *aliasing*. Aliasing of mutable data can lead to problems in understanding code, however. In general, it's good practice to ensure that no two values currently in scope directly alias the same mutable data structures.

The following example shows how an update to `cell1` can affect both `cell1` and `cell2`, as they are aliased.

```
> type Cell = { mutable data : int };;

> let cell1 = { data = 3 };;

val cell1 : Cell = { data = 3;}

> let cell2 = cell1;;

val cell2 : Cell = { data = 3;}

> cell1.data <- 7;;

val it : unit = ()

> cell1;;

val cell1 : Cell = { data = 7;}

> cell2;;

val cell2 : Cell = { data = 7;}
```

Using Mutable let Bindings

F# supports named mutable storage locations defined using let. These may be either top-level definitions or local variables in a function, local values in an object type (see Chapter 5), or local values in a computation expression (see Chapter 16).

```
> let mutable cell1 = 1;;

val mutable cell1 : int = 1

> cell1 <- 3;;

> cell1;;

val it : int = 3
```

The following shows how to use a mutable location:

```
let sum n m =
    let mutable res = 0
    for i = n to m do
        res <- res + i
    res
```

```
> sum 3 6;;

val it : int = 18
```

Hiding Mutable Data

Mutable data is often hidden behind an encapsulation boundary. Chapter 7 will look at encapsulation in more detail, but one easy way to do this is to make data private to a function. For example, the following shows how to hide a mutable reference within the inner closure of values referenced by a function value:

```
let generateStamp =
    let mutable count = 0
    (fun () -> count <- count + 1; count)

val generateStamp: unit -> int
```

The line let mutable count = 0 is executed once, when the generateStamp function is defined. Here is an example of the use of this function:

```
> generateStamp();;

val it : int = 1

> generateStamp();;

val it : int = 2
```

This is a powerful technique for hiding and encapsulating a mutable state without resorting to writing new type and class definitions. It's good programming practice in polished code to ensure that all related items of mutable state are collected under some named data structure or other entity, such as a function.

UNDERSTANDING MUTATION AND IDENTITY

F# encourages the use of objects whose logical identity (if any) is based purely on the characteristics (for example, fields and properties) of the object. For example, the identity of a pair of integers (1,2) is determined by the two integers themselves; two tuple values that each contain these two integers are, for practical purposes, identical. This is because tuples are immutable and support structural equality, hashing, and comparison, which will be discussed further in Chapters 5 and 9.

Mutable reference cells are different; they can reveal their identities through aliasing and mutation. Not all mutable values necessarily reveal their identity through mutation, however. For example, sometimes mutation is used just to bootstrap a value into its initial configuration, such as when connecting the nodes of a graph. These are relatively benign uses of mutation.

Ultimately, you can detect whether two mutable values are the same object by using the function System.Object.ReferenceEquals.

Working with Arrays

Mutable arrays are a key data structure used as a building block in many high-performance computing scenarios. This example illustrates how to use a one-dimensional array of float values:

```
> let arr = [|1.0; 1.0; 1.0|];;

val arr : float [] = [|1.0; 1.0; 1.0|]

> arr.[1];;

val it : float = 1.0

> arr.[1] <- 3.0;;

> arr;;

val it : float [] = [|1.0; 3.0; 1.0|]
```

F# array values are usually manipulated using functions from the Array module; its full path is FSharp.Collections.Array, but you can access it with the short name Array. Arrays are created either by using the creation functions in that module (such as Array.init, Array.create, and Array.zeroCreate) or by using sequence expressions, as will be discussed in Chapter 9. Some useful methods are also contained in the System.Array class. Table 4-1 shows some common functions from the Array module.

Table 4-1. *Some Important Expressions and Functions from the* Array *Module*

Operator	Type	Explanation
Array.append	'T[] -> 'T[] -> 'T[]	Returns a new array containing elements of the first array followed by elements of the second array
Array.sub	'T[] -> int -> int -> 'T[]	Returns a new array containing a portion of elements of the input array
Array.copy	'T[] -> 'T[]	Returns a copy of the input array
Array.iter	('T -> unit) -> 'T[] -> unit	Applies a side-effecting function to all elements of the input array
Array.filter	('T -> bool) -> 'T[] -> 'T[]	Returns a new array containing a selection of elements of the input array
Array.length	'T[] -> int	Returns the length of the input array
Array.map	('T -> 'U) -> 'T[] -> 'U[]	Returns a new array containing the results of applying the function to each element of the input array
Array.fold	('T -> 'U -> 'T) -> 'T -> 'U[] -> 'T	Accumulates left to right over the input array
Array.foldBack	('T -> 'U -> 'U) -> 'T[] -> 'U -> 'U	Accumulates right to left over the input array

F# arrays can be very large, up to the memory limitations of the machine (a 3 GB limit applies on 32-bit systems). For example, the following creates an array of 100 million elements (with a total size of approximately 400 MB for a 32-bit machine):

```
> let bigArray = Array.zeroCreate<int> 100000000;;

val bigArray : int [] = ...
```

The following attempt to create an array more than 4 GB in size causes an OutOfMemoryException on one of our machines:

```
> let tooBig = Array.zeroCreate<int> 1000000000;;

System.OutOfMemoryException: Exception of type 'System.OutOfMemoryException'
was thrown.
```

■ **Note**   Arrays of value types (such as int, float32, float, int64) are stored flat, so only one object is allocated for the entire array. Arrays of other types are stored as an array of object references. Primitive types, such as integers and floating-point numbers, are all value types; many other .NET types are also value types. The .NET documentation indicates whether each type is a value type. Often, the word *struct* is used for value types. You can also define new struct types directly in F# code, as will be discussed in Chapter 6. All other types in F# are reference types, such as all record, tuple, discriminated union, class, and interface values.

Generating and Slicing Arrays

As you will explore in more depth in Chapter 9, you can use "sequence expressions" as a way to generate interesting array values. For example:

```
> let arr = [|for i in 0 .. 5 -> (i, i * i)|];;

val arr : (int * int) [] = [|(0, 0); (1, 1); (2, 4); (3, 9); (4, 16); (5, 25)|]
```

You can also use a convenient syntax for extracting subarrays from existing arrays, called *slice notation*. A slice expression for a single-dimensional array has the form arr.[start..finish], where either one of start and finish may optionally be omitted, and index zero or the index of the last element of the array is assumed instead. For example:

```
> let arr = [|for i in 0 .. 5 -> (i, i * i)|];;

val arr : (int * int) [] = [|(0, 0); (1, 1); (2, 4); (3, 9); (4, 16); (5, 25)|]

> arr.[1..3];;

val it : (int * int) [] = [|(1, 1); (2, 4); (3, 9);|]

> arr.[..2];;

val it : (int * int) [] = [|(0, 0); (1, 1); (2, 4);|]

> arr.[3..];;

val it : (int * int) [] = [|(3, 9); (4, 16); (5, 25)|]
```

Slicing syntax will be used extensively in the example "Verifying Circuits with Propositional Logic" in Chapter 12. You can also use slicing syntax with strings and several other F# types, such as vectors and matrices, and the operator can be overloaded to work with your own type definitions. The F# library definitions of vectors and matrices can be used as a guide.

■ **Note**   Slices on arrays generate fresh arrays. Sometimes it's more efficient to use other techniques, such as accessing the array via an accessor function or object that performs one or more internal index adjustments before looking up the underlying array. If you add support for the slicing operators to your own types, you can choose whether they return copies of data structures or an accessor object.

Two-Dimensional Arrays

Like other .NET languages, F# directly supports two-dimensional array values that are stored flat—that is, where an array of dimensions (N, M) is stored using a contiguous array of N * M elements. The types for these values are written using [,], such as in int[,] and float[,], and these types also support slicing syntax. Values of these types are created and manipulated using the values in the Array2D module. Likewise, there is a module for manipulating three-dimensional array values, whose types are written int[, ,]. You can also use the code in those modules as a template for defining code to manipulate arrays of a higher dimension.

Introducing the Imperative .NET Collections

The .NET framework comes equipped with an excellent set of imperative collections under the namespace System.Collections.Generic. You've seen some of these already. The following sections will look at some simple uses of these collections.

Using Resizable Arrays

As mentioned in Chapter 3, the .NET framework comes with a type System.Collections.Generic. List<'T>, which, although named List, is better described as a resizable array, and is similar to std::vector<T> in C++. The F# library includes the following type abbreviation for this purpose:

```
type ResizeArray<'T> = System.Collections.Generic.List<'T>
```

Here is a simple example of using this data structure:

```
> let names = new ResizeArray<string>();;

val names : ResizeArray<string>

> for name in ["Claire"; "Sophie"; "Jane"] do
      names.Add(name);;

> names.Count;;

val it : int = 3

> names.[0];;
```

```
val it : string = "Claire"

> names.[1];;

val it : string = "Sophie"

> names.[2];;

val it : string = "Jane"
```

Resizable arrays use an underlying array for storage, and they support constant-time random-access lookup. In many situations, this makes a resizable array more efficient than an F# list, which supports efficient access only from the head (left) of the list. You can find the full set of members supported by this type in the .NET documentation. Commonly used properties and members include Add, Count, ConvertAll, Insert, BinarySearch, and ToArray. A module ResizeArray is included in the F# library; it provides operations over this type in the style of the other F# collections.

Like other .NET collections, values of type ResizeArray<'T> support the seq<'T> interface. There is also an overload of the new constructor for this collection type that lets you specify initial values via a seq<'T>. This means you can create and consume instances of this collection type using sequence expressions, as follows:

```
> let squares = new ResizeArray<int>(seq {for i in 0 .. 100 -> i * i});;

val squares : ResizeArray<int>

> for x in squares do
      printfn "square: %d" x;;

square: 0
square: 1
square: 4
square: 9
 ...
square: 9801
square: 10000
```

Using Dictionaries

The type System.Collections.Generic.Dictionary<'Key,'Value> is an efficient hash-table structure that is excellent for storing associations between keys and values. Using this collection from F# code requires a little care, because it must be able to correctly hash the key type. For simple key types such as integers, strings, and tuples, the default hashing behavior is adequate. Here is a simple example:

```
> open System.Collections.Generic;;

> let capitals = new Dictionary<string, string>(HashIdentity.Structural);;

val capitals : Dictionary<string,string> = dict []
```

```
> capitals.["USA"] <- "Washington";;

> capitals.["Bangladesh"] <- "Dhaka";;

> capitals.ContainsKey("USA");;
```

val it : bool = true

```
> capitals.ContainsKey("Australia");;
```

val it : bool = false

```
> capitals.Keys;;
```

val it : Dictionary'2.KeyCollection<string,string> = seq ["USA"; "Bangladesh"]

```
> capitals.["USA"];;
```

val it : string = "Washington"

Dictionaries are compatible with the type seq<KeyValuePair<'key,'value>>, where KeyValuePair is a type from the System.Collections.Generic namespace and simply supports the properties Key and Value. Armed with this knowledge, you can use iteration to perform an operation for each element of the collection, as follows:

```
> for kvp in capitals do
      printfn "%s has capital %s" kvp.Key kvp.Value;;

USA has capital Washington
Bangladesh has capital Dhaka
```

Using Dictionary's TryGetValue

The Dictionary method TryGetValue is of special interest, because its use in F# is a little nonstandard. This method takes an input value of type 'Key and looks it up in the table. It returns a bool indicating whether the lookup succeeded: true if the given key is in the dictionary and false otherwise. The value itself is returned via a .NET idiom called an *out parameter*. In F# code, three ways of using .NET methods rely on out parameters:

- You may use a local mutable in combination with the address-of operator &.
- You may use a reference cell.
- You may simply not give a parameter, and the result is returned as part of a tuple.

Here's how you do it using a mutable local:

```
open System.Collections.Generic

let lookupName nm (dict : Dictionary<string, string>) =
    let mutable res = ""
    let foundIt = dict.TryGetValue(nm, &res)
    if foundIt then res
    else failwithf "Didn't find %s" nm
```

The use of a reference cell can be cleaner. For example:

```
> let mutable res = "";;

val mutable res : string = ""

> capitals.TryGetValue("Australia", &res);;

val it : bool = false

> capitals.TryGetValue("USA", &res);;

val it : bool = true

> res;;

val it : string = "Washington"
```

Finally, with this last technique you don't pass the final parameter, and instead the result is returned as part of a tuple:

```
> capitals.TryGetValue("Australia");;

val it : bool * string = (false, null)

> capitals.TryGetValue("USA");;

val it : bool * string = (true, "Washington")
```

Note that the value returned in the second element of the tuple may be null if the lookup fails when this technique is used; null values will be discussed in the section "Working with null Values" in Chapter 6.

Using Dictionaries with Compound Keys

You can use dictionaries with compound keys, such as tuple keys of type (int * int). If necessary, you can specify the hash function to be used for these values when creating the instance of the dictionary. The default is to use generic hashing, also called *structural hashing*, a topic that will be covered in more detail in Chapter 9. To indicate this explicitly, specify FSharp.Collections.HashIdentity.Structural when creating the collection instance. In some cases, this can also lead to performance improvements, because the F# compiler often generates a hashing function appropriate for the compound type.

This example uses a dictionary with a compound key type to represent sparse maps:

```
> open System.Collections.Generic;;

> open FSharp.Collections;;

> let sparseMap = new Dictionary<(int * int), float>();;

val sparseMap : Dictionary<(int * int),float> = dict []

> sparseMap.[(0,2)] <- 4.0;;

> sparseMap.[(1021,1847)] <- 9.0;;

> sparseMap.Keys;;

val it : Dictionary'2.KeyCollection<(int * int),float> =
  seq [(0, 2); (1021, 1847)]
```

Some Other Mutable Data Structures

Some other important mutable data structures in the F# and .NET libraries are:

- System.Collections.Generic.SortedList<'Key,'Value>: A collection of sorted values. Searches are done by a binary search. The underlying data structure is a single array.

- System.Collections.Generic.SortedDictionary<'Key,'Value>: A collection of key/value pairs sorted by the key, rather than hashed. Searches are done by a binary search. The underlying data structure is a single array.

- System.Collections.Generic.Stack<'T>: A variable-sized last-in/first-out (LIFO) collection.

- System.Collections.Generic.Queue<'T>: A variable-sized first-in/first-out (FIFO) collection.

- System.Text.StringBuilder: A mutable structure for building string values.

- FSharp.Collections.HashSet<'Key>: A hash table structure holding only keys and no values. Since .NET 3.5, a HashSet<'T> type is available in the System. Collections.Generic namespace.

Exceptions and Controlling Them

When an expression encounters a problem, it can respond in several ways: by recovering internally, emitting a warning, returning a marker value or incomplete result, or throwing an exception. The following code indicates how an exception can be thrown by some of the code you've been using:

```
> let req = System.Net.WebRequest.Create("not a URL");;
```

```
System.UriFormatException: Invalid URI: The format of the URI could not be determined.
```

Similarly, the GetResponse method also used in the http function may raise a System.Net.WebException exception. The exceptions that may be raised by functions are typically recorded in the documentation for those routines. Exception values may also be raised explicitly by F# code:

```
> (raise (System.InvalidOperationException("not today thank you")) : unit);;
```

```
System.InvalidOperationException: not today thank you
```

In F#, exceptions are commonly raised using the F# failwith function:

```
> if false then 3 else failwith "hit the wall";;
```

```
System.Exception: hit the wall
```

Types of some common functions used to raise exceptions are:

```
val failwith : string -> 'T
val raise : System.Exception -> 'T
val failwithf : Printf.StringFormat<'T,'U> -> 'T
val invalidArg : string -> string -> 'T
```

Note that the return types of all these are generic type variables: the functions never return normally and instead return by raising an exception. This means they can be used to form an expression of any particular type and can be handy when you're drafting your code. For example, in the following example, we've left part of the program incomplete:

```
if (System.DateTime.Now > failwith "not yet decided") then
    printfn "you've run out of time!"
```

Table 4-2 shows some common exceptions raised by failwith and other operations.

Table 4-2. *Common Categories of Exceptions and F# Functions that Raise Them*

Exception Type	Description	Example
Exception	General failure	`failwith "fail"`
ArgumentException	Bad input	`invalidArg "x" "y"`
DivideByZeroException	Integer divide by 0	`1 / 0`
NullReferenceException	Unexpected null	`(null : string).Length`

Catching Exceptions

You can catch exceptions using the try ... with ... language construct and : ? type-test patterns that filter any exception value caught by the with clause. For example:

```
try
    raise (System.InvalidOperationException ("it's just not my day"))
with
    :? System.InvalidOperationException -> printfn "caught!"
```

Giving:

---

caught!

Chapter 5 will cover these patterns more closely. The following code sample shows how to use try ... with ... to catch two kinds of exceptions that may arise from the operations that make up the http method, in both cases returning the empty string "" as the incomplete result. Note that try ... with ... is just an expression, and it may return a result in both branches:

```
open System.IO

let http (url : string) =
    try
        let req = System.Net.WebRequest.Create(url)
        let resp = req.GetResponse()
        let stream = resp.GetResponseStream()
        let reader = new StreamReader(stream)
        let html = reader.ReadToEnd()
        html
    with
        | :? System.UriFormatException -> ""
        | :? System.Net.WebException -> ""
```

When an exception is thrown, a value is created that records information about the exception. This value is matched against the earlier type-test patterns. It may also be bound directly and manipulated in the with clause of the try ... with constructs. For example, all exception values support the Message property:

```
try
    raise (new System.InvalidOperationException ("invalid operation"))
with err -> printfn "oops, msg = '%s'" err.Message
```

Giving:

---

oops, msg = 'invalid operation'

Using try . . . finally

Exceptions may also be processed using the try ... finally ... construct. This guarantees to run the finally clause both when an exception is thrown and when the expression evaluates normally. This allows you to ensure that resources are disposed of after the completion of an operation. For example, you can ensure that the web response from the previous example is closed as follows:

```
let httpViaTryFinally (url: string) =
    let req = System.Net.WebRequest.Create(url)
    let resp = req.GetResponse()
    try
        let stream = resp.GetResponseStream()
        let reader = new StreamReader(stream)
        let html = reader.ReadToEnd()
        html
    finally
        resp.Close()
```

In practice, you can use a shorter form to close and dispose of resources simply by using a use binding instead of a let binding if the resource implements IDisposable, a technique that will be covered in Chapter 6. This closes the response at the end of the scope of the resp variable. Here is how the previous function looks when using this form:

```
let httpViaUseBinding (url: string) =
    let req = System.Net.WebRequest.Create(url)
    use resp = req.GetResponse()
    let stream = resp.GetResponseStream()
    let reader = new StreamReader(stream)
    let html = reader.ReadToEnd()
    html
```

Defining New Exception Types

F# lets you define new kinds of exception objects that carry data in a conveniently accessible form. For example, here is a declaration of a new class of exceptions and a function that wraps http with a filter that catches particular cases:

```
exception BlockedURL of string

let http2 url =
    if url = "http://www.kaos.org"
    then raise (BlockedURL(url))
    else http url
```

You can extract the information from F# exception values, again using pattern matching:

```
  try
      raise (BlockedURL ("http://www.kaos.org"))
  with
      BlockedURL url -> printfn "blocked! url = '%s'" url
```

Giving:

```
blocked! url = 'http://www.kaos.org'
```

Exception values are always subtypes of the F# type exn, an abbreviation for the .NET type System.Exception. The declaration exception BlockedURL of string is shorthand for defining a new F# class type BlockedURLException, which is a subtype of System.Exception. Exception types can also be defined explicitly by defining new object types. Chapters 5 and 6 will look more closely at object types and subtyping.

Table 4-3 summarizes the exception-related language and library constructs.

Table 4-3. Exception-Related Language and Library Constructs

Example Code	Kind	Notes
raise *expr*	F# library function	Raises the given exception
failwith *expr*	F# library function	Raises an Exception exception
try *expr* with *rules*	F# expression	Catches expressions matching the pattern rules
try *expr* finally *expr*	F# expression	Executes the finally expression both when the computation is successful and when an exception is raised
| :? ArgumentException ->	F# pattern rule	A rule matching the given .NET exception type
| :? ArgumentException as *e* ->	F# pattern rule	A rule matching the given .NET exception type and naming it as its stronger type
| Failure(*msg*) -> *expr*	F# pattern rule	A rule matching the given data-carrying F# exception
| *exn* -> *expr*	F# pattern rule	A rule matching any exception, binding the name exn to the exception object value
| *exn* when *expr* -> *expr*	F# pattern rule	A rule matching the exception under the given condition, binding the name exn to the exception object value

Having an Effect: Basic I/O

Imperative programming and input/output are closely related topics. The following sections will demonstrate some very simple I/O techniques using F# and .NET libraries.

The .NET types System.IO.File and System.IO.Directory contain a number of simple functions to make working with files easier. For example, let's look at a way to output lines of text to a file. You will find the created file in the same directory as the script you are editing (or the current directory of F# Interactive if entering text directly):

```
> open System.IO;;

> let tmpFile = Path.Combine(__SOURCE_DIRECTORY__, "temp.txt");;

> File.WriteAllLines(tmpFile, [|"This is a test file."; "It is easy to read."|]);;
```

Many simple file-processing tasks require reading all the lines of a file. You can do this by reading all the lines in one action as an array using System.IO.File.ReadAllLines:

```
> open System.IO;;

> File.ReadAllLines tmpFile;;
val it : string [] = [|"This is a test file."; "It is easy to read."|]
```

If necessary, the entire file can be read as a single string using System.IO.File.ReadAllText:

```
> File.ReadAllText tmpFile;;

val it : string = "This is a test file.
It is easy to read."
```

You can also use the method System.IO.File.ReadLines, which reads lines on-demand, as a sequence. This is often used as the input to a sequence expression or to a pipeline on sequence operators. For example, this;

```
seq { for line in File.ReadLines tmpFile do
        let words = line.Split [|' '|]
        if words.Length > 3 && words.[2] = "easy" then
            yield line}
```

gives these results:

```
val it : seq<string> = seq ["It is easy to read."]
```

.NET I/O via Streams

The .NET namespace System.IO contains the primary .NET types for reading and writing bytes and text from and to data streams. The primary output constructs in this namespace are:

- System.IO.BinaryWriter: Writes primitive data types as binary values. Create by using new BinaryWriter(stream). You can create output streams using File.Create(filename).

- System.IO.StreamWriter: Writes textual strings and characters to a stream. The text is encoded according to a particular Unicode encoding. Create by using new StreamWriter(stream) and its variants, or by using File.CreateText(filename).

- System.IO.StringWriter: Writes textual strings to a StringBuilder, which eventually can be used to generate a string.

Here is a simple example of using System.IO.File.CreateText to create a StreamWriter and write two strings:

```
> let outp = File.CreateText "playlist.txt";;

val outp : StreamWriter

> outp.WriteLine "Enchanted";;

> outp.WriteLine "Put your records on";;

> outp.Close();;
```

The primary input constructs in the System.IO namespace are:

- System.IO.BinaryReader: Reads primitive data types as binary values. Create by using new BinaryReader(stream).

- System.IO.StreamReader: Reads a stream as textual strings and characters. The bytes are decoded to strings from a particular Unicode encoding. Create by using new StreamReader(stream) and its variants, or by using File.OpenText(filename).

- System.IO.StringReader: Reads a string as textual strings and characters.

Here is a simple example of using System.IO.File.OpenText to create a StreamReader and read two strings:

```
> let inp = File.OpenText("playlist.txt");;

val inp : StreamReader

> inp.ReadLine();;

val it : string = "Enchanted"

> inp.ReadLine();;

val it : string = "Put your records on"

> inp.Close();;
```

■ **Tip** In non-scripting production code, whenever you create objects such as a StreamReader that have a Close or Dispose operation or that implement the IDisposable interface, consider how to eventually close or otherwise dispose of the resource. We will discuss this in Chapter 6.

Some Other I/O-Related Types

The System.IO namespace contains other types for advanced I/O that are useful for corner cases but not day-to-day use. For example, these abstractions appear in the .NET documentation:

- System.IO.TextReader: Reads textual strings and characters from an unspecified source. This is the common functionality implemented by the StreamReader and StringReader types and the System.Console.In object. The latter is used to access the stdin input.

- System.IO.TextWriter: Writes textual strings and characters to an unspecified output. This is the common functionality implemented by the StreamWriter and StringWriter types and the System.Console.Out and System.Console.Error objects. The latter are used to access the stdout and stderr output streams.

- System.IO.Stream: Provides a generic view of a sequence of bytes.

Some functions that are generic over different kinds of output streams make use of these; for example, the formatting function twprintf discussed in "Using printf and Friends" writes to any System. IO.TextWriter.

Using System.Console

Some simple input/output routines are provided in the System.Console class. For example:

```
> System.Console.WriteLine "Hello World";;

Hello World

> System.Console.ReadLine();;

<enter "I'm still here" here>

val it : string = "I'm still here"
```

The System.Console.Out object can also be used as a TextWriter.

Combining Functional and Imperative Efficient Precomputation and Caching

All experienced programmers are familiar with the concept of *precomputation*, in which computations are performed as soon as some of the inputs to a function are known. The following sections cover a number of manifestations of precomputation in F# programming, as well as the related topics of memoization and caching. These represent one common pattern in which imperative programming is used safely and non-intrusively within a broader setting of functional programming.

Precomputation and Partial Application

Let's say you're given a large input list of words, and you want to compute a function that checks whether a word is in this list. You would do this:

```
let isWord (words : string list) =
    let wordTable = Set.ofList words
    fun w -> wordTable.Contains(w)
```

Here, isWord has the following type:

```
val isWord : words:string list -> (string -> bool)
```

The efficient use of this function depends crucially on the fact that useful intermediary results are computed after only one argument is applied and a function value is returned. For example:

```
> let isCapital = isWord ["London"; "Paris"; "Warsaw"; "Tokyo"];;

val isCapital : (string -> bool)

> isCapital "Paris";;

val it : bool = true

> isCapital "Manchester";;

val it : bool = false
```

Here, the internal table wordTable is computed as soon as isCapital is applied to one argument. It would be wasteful to write isCapital as:

```
let isCapitalSlow word = isWord ["London"; "Paris"; "Warsaw"; "Tokyo"] word
```

This function computes the same results as isCapital. It does so inefficiently, however, because isWord is applied to both its first argument and its second argument every time you use the function isCapitalSlow. This means the internal table is rebuilt every time the function isCapitalSlow is applied, somewhat defeating the point of having an internal table in the first place. In a similar vein, the definition of isCapital shown previously is more efficient than either isCapitalSlow2 or isCapitalSlow3 in the following:

```
let isWordSlow2 (words : string list) (word : string) =
    List.exists (fun word2 -> word = word2) words

let isCapitalSlow2 word = isWordSlow2 ["London"; "Paris"; "Warsaw"; "Tokyo"] word

let isWordSlow3 (words : string list) (word : string) =
    let wordTable = Set<string>(words)
    wordTable.Contains(word)

let isCapitalSlow3 word = isWordSlow3 ["London"; "Paris"; "Warsaw"; "Tokyo"] word
```

The first uses an inappropriate data structure for the lookup (an F# list, which has O(n) lookup time), and the second attempts to build a better intermediate data structure (an F# set, which has O(log n) lookup time), but does so on every invocation.

There are often trade-offs among different intermediate data structures, or when deciding whether to use them at all. For example, in the previous example you could just as well use a HashSet as the internal data structure. This approach, in general, gives better lookup times (constant time), but it requires slightly more care to use, because a HashSet is a mutable data structure. In this case, you don't mutate the data structure after you create it, and you don't reveal it to the outside world, so it's entirely safe:

```
let isWord (words : string list) =
    let wordTable = HashSet<string>(words)
    fun word -> wordTable.Contains word
```

Precomputation and Objects

The examples of precomputation given thus far are variations on the theme of computing functions, introduced in Chapter 3. The functions, when computed, capture the precomputed intermediate data structures. It's clear, however, that precomputing via partial applications and functions can be subtle, because it matters when you apply the first argument of a function (triggering the construction of intermediate data structures) and when you apply the subsequent arguments (triggering the real computation that uses the intermediate data structures).

Luckily, functions don't just have to compute functions; they can also return more sophisticated values, such as objects. This can help make it clear when precomputation is being performed. It also allows you to build richer services based on precomputed results. For example, Listing 4-1 shows how to use precomputation as part of building a name-lookup service. The returned object includes both a Contains method and a ClosestPrefixMatch method.

Listing 4-1. Precomputing a eord table before creating an object

```
open System

type NameLookupService =
    abstract Contains : string -> bool

let buildSimpleNameLookup (words : string list) =
    let wordTable = HashSet<_>(words)
    {new NameLookupService with
        member t.Contains w = wordTable.Contains w}
```

The internal data structure used in Listing 4-1 is the same as before: an F# set of type FSharp. Collections.Set<string>. The service can now be instantiated and used as follows:

```
> let capitalLookup = buildSimpleNameLookup ["London"; "Paris"; "Warsaw"; "Tokyo"];;

val capitalLookup : NameLookupService

> capitalLookup.Contains "Paris";;

val it : bool = true
```

In passing, note the following about this implementation:

- You can extend the returned service to support a richer set of queries of the underlying information by adding further methods to the object returned.

Precomputation of the kind used previously is an essential technique for implementing many services and abstractions, from simple functions to sophisticated computation engines. You will see further examples of these techniques in Chapter 9.

Memoizing Computations

Precomputation is one important way to amortize the costs of computation in F#. Another is called *memoization*. A memoizing function avoids recomputing its results by keeping an internal table, often called a *lookaside table*. For example, consider the well-known Fibonacci function, whose naive, unmemoized version is:

```
let rec fib n = if n <= 2 then 1 else fib (n - 1) + fib (n - 2)
```

Not surprisingly, a version keeping a lookaside table is much faster:

```
let fibFast =
    let t = new System.Collections.Generic.Dictionary<int, int>()
    let rec fibCached n =
        if t.ContainsKey n then t.[n]
        elif n <= 2 then 1
        else let res = fibCached (n - 1) + fibCached (n - 2)
             t.Add (n, res)
             res
    fun n -> fibCached n

// From Chapter 2, but modified to use stop watch.
let time f =
    let sw = System.Diagnostics.Stopwatch.StartNew()
    let res = f()
    let finish = sw.Stop()
    (res, sw.Elapsed.TotalMilliseconds |> sprintf "%f ms")

time(fun () -> fibFast 30)
time(fun () -> fibFast 30)
time(fun () -> fibFast 30)
```

```
val fibFast : (int -> int)
val time : f:(unit -> 'a) -> 'a * string
val it : int * string = (832040, "0.727200 ms")
val it : int * string = (832040, "0.066100 ms")
val it : int * string = (832040, "0.077400 ms")
```

On one of our laptops, with n = 30, there's an order of magnitude speed up from the first to second run. Listing 4-2 shows how to write a generic function that encapsulates the memoization technique.

Listing 4-2. A generic memoization function

```
open System.Collections.Generic

let memoize (f : 'T -> 'U) =
    let t = new Dictionary<'T, 'U>(HashIdentity.Structural)
    fun n ->
        if t.ContainsKey n then t.[n]
        else let res = f n
             t.Add (n, res)
             res

let rec fibFast =
    memoize (fun n -> if n <= 2 then 1 else fibFast (n - 1) + fibFast (n - 2))
```

Here, the functions have the types:

```
val memoize : f:('T -> 'U) -> ('T -> 'U) when 'T : equality
val fibFast : (int -> int)
```

In the definition of fibFast, you use let rec because fibFast is self-referential—that is, used as part of its own definition. You can think of fibFast as a *computed, recursive* function. Such a function generates an informational warning when used in F# code, because it's important to understand when this feature of F# is being used; you then suppress the warning with #nowarn "40". As with the examples of computed functions from the previous section, omit the extra argument from the application of memoize, because including it would lead to a fresh memoization table being allocated each time the function fibNotFast was called:

```
let rec fibNotFast n =
    memoize (fun n -> if n <= 2 then 1 else fibNotFast (n - 1) + fibNotFast (n - 2)) n
```

Due to this subtlety, it's often a good idea to define your memoization strategies to generate objects other than functions (think of functions as very simple kinds of objects). For example, Listing 4-3 shows how to define a new variation on memoize that returns a Table object that supports both a lookup and a Discard method.

Listing 4-3. A generic memoization service

```
open System.Collections.Generic

type Table<'T, 'U> =
    abstract Item : 'T -> 'U with get
    abstract Discard : unit -> unit

let memoizeAndPermitDiscard f =
    let lookasideTable = new Dictionary<_, _>(HashIdentity.Structural)
    {new Table<'T, 'U> with
        member t.Item
            with get(n) =
                if lookasideTable.ContainsKey(n) then
                    lookasideTable.[n]
                else
                    let res = f n
```

```
                    lookasideTable.Add(n, res)
                    res

        member t.Discard() =
            lookasideTable.Clear()}
```

```
#nowarn "40" // do not warn on recursive computed objects and functions

let rec fibFast =
    memoizeAndPermitDiscard (fun n ->
        printfn "computing fibFast %d" n
        if n <= 2 then 1 else fibFast.[n - 1] + fibFast.[n - 2])
```

In Listing 4-3, lookup uses the a.[b] associative Item lookup property syntax, and the Discard method discards any internal partial results. The functions have these types:

```
val memoizeAndPermitDiscard : ('T -> 'U) -> Table<'T, 'U> when 'T : equality
val fibFast : Table<int,int>
```

This example shows how fibFast caches results but recomputes them after a Discard:

```
> fibFast.[3];;

computing fibFast 3
computing fibFast 2
computing fibFast 1

val it : int = 2

> fibFast.[5];;

computing fibFast 5
computing fibFast 4

val it : int = 5

> fibFast.Discard();;

> fibFast.[5];;

computing fibFast 5
computing fibFast 4
computing fibFast 3
computing fibFast 2
computing fibFast 1

val it : int = 5
```

■ **Note** Memoization relies on the memoized function being stable and idempotent. In other words, it always returns the same results, and no additional interesting side effects are caused by further invocations of the function. In addition, memoization strategies rely on mutable internal tables. The implementation of `memoize` shown in this chapter isn't thread safe, because it doesn't lock this table during reading or writing. This is fine if the computed function is used only from at most one thread at a time, but in a multithreaded application, use memoization strategies that utilize internal tables protected by locks, such as a .NET `ReaderWriterLock`. Chapter 11 will further discuss thread synchronization and mutable state.

Lazy Values

Memoization is a form of *caching*. Another important variation on caching is a simple *lazy* value, a delayed computation of type `FSharp.Control.Lazy<'T>` for some type `'T`. Lazy values are usually formed by using the special keyword `lazy` (you can also make them explicitly by using the functions in the `FSharp.Core.Lazy` module). For example:

```
> let sixty = lazy (30 + 30);;

val sixty : Lazy<int> = Value is not created.

> sixty.Force();;

val it : int = 60
```

Lazy values of this kind are implemented as thunks holding either a function value that computes the result or the actual computed result. The lazy value is computed only once, and thus its effects are executed only once. For example, in the following code fragment, "Hello world" is printed only once:

```
> let sixtyWithSideEffect = lazy (printfn "Hello world"; 30 + 30);;

val sixtyWithSideEffect: Lazy<int> = Value is not created.

> sixtyWithSideEffect.Force();;

Hello world

val it : int = 60

> sixtyWithSideEffect.Force();;

val it : int = 60
```

Lazy values are implemented by a simple data structure containing a mutable reference cell. The definition of this data structure is in the F# library source code.

Other Variations on Caching and Memoization

You can apply many different caching and memoization techniques in advanced programming, and this chapter can't cover them all. Some common variations are:

- Using an internal data structure that records only the last invocation of a function and basing the lookup on a very cheap test on the input.

- Using an internal data structure that contains both a fixed-size queue of input keys and a dictionary of results. Entries are added to both the table and the queue as they're computed. When the queue is full, the input keys for the oldest computed results are dequeued, and the computed results are discarded from the dictionary.

- Some of these techniques are encapsulated in the .NET type System.Runtime.Caching. MemoryCache that is found in the system library System.Runtime.Caching.dll.

Mutable Reference Cells

One mutable record type that you will see occasionally (especially in F# code before F# 4.0) is the general-purpose type of mutable reference cells, or "ref cells" for short. These play much the same role as pointers in other imperative programming languages. You can see how to use mutable reference cells in this example:

```
> let cell1 = ref 1;;

val cell1 : int ref = {contents = 1;}

> cell1.Value;;

val it : int = 1

> cell1 := 3;;

val it : unit = ()

> cell1;;

val it : int ref = {contents = 3;}

> cell1.Value;;

val it : int = 3
```

The type is 'T ref, and three associated functions are ref, !, and :=. The types of these are:

```
val ref : 'T -> 'T ref
val (:=) : 'T ref -> 'T -> unit
val (!) : 'T ref -> 'T
```

These allocate a reference cell, mutate the cell, and read the cell, respectively. The operation `cell1 := 3` is the key one; after this operation, the value returned by evaluating the expression `!cell1` is changed. You can also use either the `contents` field or the `Value` property to access the value of a reference cell.

Both the `'T ref` type and its operations are defined in the F# library as simple record-data structures with a single mutable field. The type `'T ref` is a synonym for a type `FSharp.Core.Ref<'T>` that is defined in this way:

```
type 'T ref =
    {mutable contents : 'T}
    member cell.Value = cell.contents

let (!) r = r.contents

let (:=) r v = r.contents <- v

let ref v = {contents = v}
```

When using F# 4.0 you don't need to use ref cells as much as with previous versions of F#, as a single "let mutable" can usually be used as an alternative.

Combining Functional and Imperative: Functional Programming with Side Effects

F# stems from a tradition in programming languages in which state is made explicit, largely by passing extra parameters. Many F# programmers use functional programming techniques first before turning to their imperative alternatives, and we encourage you to do the same, for all the reasons listed at the start of this chapter.

F# also integrates imperative and functional programming together in a powerful way. F# is actually an extremely succinct imperative programming language! Furthermore, in some cases no good functional techniques exist to solve a problem, or those that do are too experimental for production use. This means that in practice, using imperative constructs and libraries is common in F#. For example, many examples you saw in Chapters 2 and 3 used side effects to report their results or to create GUI components.

Regardless, we still encourage you to think functionally, even about your imperative programming. In particular, it's always helpful to be aware of the potential side effects of your overall program and the characteristics of those side effects. The following sections describe five ways to help tame and reduce the use of side effects in your programs.

Consider Replacing Mutable Locals and Loops with Recursion

When imperative programmers begin to use F#, they frequently use mutable local variables or reference cells heavily as they translate code fragments from their favorite imperative language into F#. The resulting code often looks very bad. Over time, programmers learn to avoid many uses of mutable locals. For example, consider this naive implementation of factorization, transliterated from C code:

```
let factorizeImperative n =
    let mutable factor1 = 1
    let mutable factor2 = n
    let mutable i = 2
    let mutable fin = false
```

```
    while (i < n && not fin) do
        if (n % i = 0) then
            factor1 <- i
            factor2 <- n / i
            fin <- true
        i <- i + 1

    if (factor1 = 1) then None
    else Some (factor1, factor2)
```

This code can be replaced by use of an inner recursive function:

```
let factorizeRecursive n =
    let rec find i =
        if i >= n then None
        elif (n % i = 0) then Some(i, n / i)
        else find (i + 1)
    find 2
```

The second code is not only shorter, but also uses no mutation, which makes it easier to reuse and maintain. You can also see that the loop terminates (i is increasing toward n) and see the two exit conditions for the function (i >= n and n % i = 0). Note that the state i has become an explicit parameter.

Separating Pure Computation from Side-Effecting Computations

Where possible, separate out as much of your computation as possible using side effect–free functional programming. For example, sprinkling printf expressions throughout your code may make for a good debugging technique, but if not used wisely it can lead to code that is difficult to understand and inherently imperative.

Separating Mutable Data Structures

A common technique of object-oriented programming is to ensure that mutable data structures are private and, where possible, fully separated, which means there is no way that distinct pieces of code can access one another's internal state in undesirable ways. Fully separated state can even be used inside the implementation of what to the outside world appears to be a purely functional piece of code.

For example, where necessary, you can use side effects on private data structures allocated at the start of an algorithm and then discard these data structures before returning a result; the overall result is then effectively a side effect–free function. One example of separation from the F# library is the library's implementation of List.map, which uses mutation internally; the writes occur on an internal, separated data structure that no other code can access. Thus, as far as callers are concerned, List.map is pure and functional.

This second example divides a sequence of inputs into equivalence classes (the F# library function Seq. groupBy does a similar thing):

```
open System.Collections.Generic

let divideIntoEquivalenceClasses keyf seq =
    // The dictionary to hold the equivalence classes
    let dict = new Dictionary<'key, ResizeArray<'T>>()
```

```
// Build the groupings
seq |> Seq.iter (fun v ->
    let key = keyf v
    let ok, prev = dict.TryGetValue(key)
    if ok then prev.Add(v)
    else let prev = new ResizeArray<'T>()
         dict.[key] <- prev
         prev.Add(v))

// Return the sequence-of-sequences. Don't reveal the
// internal collections: just reveal them as sequences
dict |> Seq.map (fun group -> group.Key, Seq.readonly group.Value)
```

This uses `Dictionary` and `ResizeArray` internally, but these mutable data structures aren't revealed externally. The inferred type of the overall function is:

```
val divideIntoEquivalenceClasses :
  keyf:('T -> 'key) -> seq:seq<'T> -> seq<'key * seq<'T>> when 'key : equality
```

Here is an example use:

```
> divideIntoEquivalenceClasses (fun n -> n % 3) [0 .. 10];;

val it : seq<int * seq<int>>
= seq [(0, seq [0; 3; 6; 9]); (1, seq [1; 4; 7; 10]); (2, seq [2; 5; 8])]
```

Not All Side Effects Are Equal

It's often helpful to use the weakest set of side effects necessary to achieve your programming task, and to at least be aware when you're using strong side effects:

- Weak side effects are effectively benign, given the assumptions you're making about your application. For example, writing to a log file is very useful and essentially benign (if the log file can't grow arbitrarily large and crash your machine!). Similarly, reading data from a stable, unchanging file store on a local disk is effectively treating the disk as an extension of read-only memory, so reading these files is a weak form of side effect that isn't difficult to incorporate into your programs.

- Strong side effects have a much more corrosive effect on the correctness and operational properties of your program. For example, blocking network I/O is a relatively strong side effect by any measure. Performing blocking network I/O in the middle of a library routine can destroy the responsiveness of a GUI application, at least if the routine is invoked by the GUI thread of an application. Any constructs that perform synchronization between threads are also a major source of strong side effects.

Whether a particular side effect is stronger or weaker depends on your application and on whether the consequences of the side effect are sufficiently isolated and separated from other entities. Strong side effects can and should be used freely in the outer shell of an application or when you're scripting with F# Interactive; otherwise, not much can be achieved.

When you're writing larger pieces of code, write your application and libraries in such a way that most of your code either doesn't use strong side effects or at least makes it obvious when these side effects are being used. Threads and concurrency are commonly used to mediate problems associated with strong side effects. Chapter 11 will cover these issues in more depth.

Avoid Combining Imperative Programming and Laziness

It's generally thought to be bad style to combine delayed computations (that is, laziness) and side effects. This isn't entirely true; for example, it's reasonable to set up a read from a file system as a lazy computation using sequences. It's relatively easy to make mistakes in this sort of programming, however. For example, consider the following:

```
open System.IO
let reader1, reader2 =
    let reader = new StreamReader(File.OpenRead("test.txt"))
    let firstReader() = reader.ReadLine()
    let secondReader() = reader.ReadLine()

    // Note: we close the stream reader here!
    // But we are returning function values that use the reader
    // This is very bad!
    reader.Close()
    firstReader, secondReader

// Note: stream reader is now closed! The next line will fail!
let firstLine = reader1()
let secondLine = reader2()
firstLine, secondLine
```

This code is wrong, because the StreamReader object reader is used after the point indicated by the comment. The returned function values are then called, and they try to read from the captured variable reader. Function values are just one example of delayed computations; others are lazy values, sequences, and any objects that perform computations on demand. Avoid building delayed objects such as reader that represent handles to transient, disposable resources, unless those objects are used in a way that respects the lifetime of that resource.

The previous code can be corrected to avoid using laziness in combination with a transient resource as follows:

```
open System.IO

let line1, line2 =
    let reader = new StreamReader(File.OpenRead("test.txt"))
    let firstLine = reader.ReadLine()
    let secondLine = reader.ReadLine()
    reader.Close()
    firstLine, secondLine
```

Another technique uses language and/or library constructs that tie the lifetime of an object to some larger object. For example, you can use a use binding within a sequence expression, which augments the sequence object with the code needed to clean up the resource when iteration is finished or terminates. This technique, which will be discussed further in Chapter 9, is shown by example here (see also the System.IO.File.ReadLines, which serves a similar role):

```
let linesOfFile =
    seq { use reader = new StreamReader(File.OpenRead("test.txt"))
          while not reader.EndOfStream do
              yield reader.ReadLine() }
```

The general lesson is to minimize the side effects you use, and to use separated, isolated state where possible.

Summary

In this chapter, you learned how to do imperative programming in F#, from basic mutable data structures like arrays to working with side effects, such as exceptions and I/O. You also looked at general principles for avoiding imperative programming and for isolating your uses of side effects. The next chapter will continue to explore building blocks of typed functional programming in F#, with a deeper look at types, type inference, and generics.

■ ■ ■

CHAPTER 5

Understanding Types in Functional Programming

F# is a typed language, and F# programmers often use types in sophisticated ways. In this chapter, you will learn about the foundations of types, focusing on how they are defined and used in F# functional programming. You also will look closely at *generics*, and closely related to generics is the notion of *subtyping*. Generics and subtyping combine to allow you to write code that is generic over families of types. You will see how F# uses *automatic generalization* to automatically infer generic types for your code, and the chapter will cover some of the basic generic functions in the F# libraries, such as generic comparison, hashing, and binary serialization.

Exploring Some Simple Type Definitions

Given that F# is a typed language, you will often need to declare new shapes of types via type definitions and type abbreviations. This chapter will cover only some of the simpler type definitions that are useful and succinct workhorses for functional programming. F# also lets you define a range of type definitions related to object-oriented programming, which will be discussed in Chapter 6. Often, however, these aren't required in basic functional programming.

Defining Type Abbreviations

Type abbreviations are the simplest type definitions:

```
type index = int
type flags = int64
type results = string * System.TimeSpan * int * int
```

It's common to use lowercase names for type abbreviations, but it's certainly not compulsory. Type abbreviations aren't concrete, because they simply alias an existing type. For example, when doing .NET programming with F#, they're expanded during the process of compiling F# code to the format shared among multiple .NET languages. Because of this, a number of restrictions apply to type abbreviations. For example, you can't augment them with additional members, as can be done for concrete types such as records, discriminated unions, and classes. In addition, you can't truly hide a type abbreviation using a signature (see Chapter 7).

Defining Record Types

The simplest concrete type definitions are records. Here's an example:

```
open System

type Person =
    { Name : string
      DateOfBirth : DateTime }
```

You can construct record values by using the record labels:

```
{ Name = "Bill"; DateOfBirth = DateTime(1962, 09, 02) };;
```

Giving you:

```
val it : Person = {Name="Bill"; DateOfBirth = 02/09/1962 ...}
```

Here, semicolons are used to separate each field; semicolon are optional in the longer, one-field-per-line form above.

Record values are often used to return results from functions:

```
type PageStats =
    { Site : string
      Time : System.TimeSpan
      Length : int
      NumWords : int
      NumHRefs : int }
```

This technique works well when returning a large number of heterogeneous results:

```
//Using the time, http and getWords functions from Chapter 3.
let stats site =
    let url = "http://" + site
    let html, t = time (fun () -> http url)
    let words = html |> getWords
    let hrefs = words |> Array.filter (fun s -> s = "href")
    { Site = site
      Time = t
      Length = html.Length
      NumWords = words.Length
      NumHRefs = hrefs.Length}
```

Here is the type of stats:

```
val stats : site:string -> PageStats
```

Here is how F# Interactive shows the results of applying the function:

```
> stats "www.google.com";;

val it : PageStats = {Site = "www.google.com";
                      Time = 00:00:03.0941770 {Days = 0; ...};
                      Length = 12139;
                      NumWords = 892;
                      NumHRefs = 11;}
```

Handling Non-Unique Record Field Names

Record labels need not be unique among multiple record types. Here is an example:

```
type Person =
    { Name : string
      DateOfBirth : System.DateTime }

type Company =
    { Name: string
      Address : string }
```

When record names are non-unique, constructions of record values may need to use object expressions in order to indicate the name of the record type, thus disambiguating the construction. For example, consider the following type definitions:

```
type Dot = { X : int; Y : int }
type Point = { X : float; Y : float }
```

On lookup, record labels are accessed using the dot (.) notation in the same way as with properties. One slight difference is that in the absence of further qualifying information, the type of the object being accessed is inferred from the record label. This is based on the latest set of record labels in scope from record definitions and uses of open. For example, given the previous definitions, you have the following:

```
> let coords1 (p:Point) = (p.X, p.Y);;

val coords1 : p:Point -> float * float

> let coords2 (d:Dot) = (d.X, d.Y);;

val coords2 : d:Dot -> int * int

> let dist p = sqrt (p.X * p.X + p.Y * p.Y);; // use of X and Y implies type "Point"

val dist : p:Point -> float
```

The accesses to the labels X and Y in the first two definitions have been resolved using the type information provided by the type annotations. The accesses in the third definition have been resolved using the default interpretation (taking the last definition that fits) of record field labels in the absence of any other qualifying information.

Should there be a conflict between labels among multiple records, you can also construct record values by using an explicit type annotation for the whole record:

```
let anna = ({Name = "Anna"; DateOfBirth = new System.DateTime(1968, 07, 23)} : Person)
```

Giving you:

```
val anna : Person = {Name="Anna"; DateOfBirth = 23/07/1968 ... }
```

Cloning Records

Records support a convenient syntax with which to clone all the values in the record, but with some values replaced. Here is a simple example:

```
type Point3D = {X : float; Y : float; Z : float}

let p1 = {X = 3.0; Y = 4.0; Z = 5.0}
let p2 = {p1 with Y = 0.0; Z = 0.0}
```

Giving you:

```
val p1 : Point3D = {X = 3.0; Y = 4.0; Z = 5.0;}
val p2 : Point3D = {X = 3.0; Y = 0.0; Z = 0.0;}
```

The definition of p2 is identical to this:

```
let p2 = {X = 3.0; Y = 0.0; Z = 0.0}
```

This expression form doesn't mutate the values of a record, even if the fields of the original record are mutable.

Defining Discriminated Unions

The second kind of concrete type definition discussed in this section is a discriminated union. Here is a very simple example:

```
type Route = int
type Make = string
type Model = string
type Transport =
    | Car of Make * Model
    | Bicycle
    | Bus of Route
```

Each alternative of a discriminated union is called a *discriminator*. You can build values by using the discriminator much as if it were a function:

```
> let ian = Car("BMW","360");;

val ian : Transport = Car ("BMW","360")

> let don = [Bicycle; Bus 8];;

val don : Transport list = [Bicycle; Bus 8]

> let peter = [Car ("Ford","Fiesta"); Bicycle];;

val peter : Transport list = [Car ("Ford","Fiesta"); Bicycle];;
```

You can also use discriminators in pattern matching:

```
let averageSpeed (tr : Transport) =
    match tr with
    | Car _ -> 35
    | Bicycle -> 16
    | Bus _ -> 24
```

Discriminated unions can include recursive references (the same is true of records and other type definitions). These are frequently used when representing structured languages via discriminated unions, a topic that will be covered in depth in Chapter 9:

```
type Proposition =
    | True
    | And of Proposition * Proposition
    | Or of Proposition * Proposition
    | Not of Proposition
```

Recursive functions can be used to traverse such a type. For example:

```
let rec eval (p : Proposition) =
    match p with
    | True -> true
    | And(p1,p2) -> eval p1 && eval p2
    | Or (p1,p2) -> eval p1 || eval p2
    | Not(p1) -> not (eval p1)
```

Several of the types you've already seen are defined as discriminated unions. For example, the 'T option type and the F# type of immutable lists are effectively defined as:

```
type 'T option =
    | None
    | Some of 'T

type 'T list =
    | ([])
    | (::) of 'T * 'T list
```

A broad range of tree-like data structures are conveniently represented as discriminated unions. For example:

```
type Tree<'T> =
    | Tree of 'T * Tree<'T> * Tree<'T>
    | Tip of 'T
```

You can use recursive functions to compute properties of trees:

```
let rec sizeOfTree tree =
    match tree with
    | Tree(_, l, r) -> 1 + sizeOfTree l + sizeOfTree r
    | Tip _ -> 1
```

Here is the inferred type of sizeOfTree:

```
val sizeOfTree : tree:Tree<'a> -> int
```

Here is an example of a constructed tree term and the use of the size function:

```
> let smallTree = Tree ("1", Tree ("2", Tip "a", Tip "b"), Tip "c");;

val smallTree : Tree<string> = Tree ("1",Tree ("2",Tip "a",Tip "b"),Tip "c")

> sizeOfTree smallTree;;

val it : int = 5
```

Chapters 9 and 12 will discuss symbolic manipulation based on trees.

■ **Note**   Discriminated unions are a powerful and important construct and are useful when modeling a finite, sealed set of choices. This makes them a perfect fit for many constructs that arise in applications and symbolic-analysis libraries. They are, by design, nonextensible–subsequent modules can't add new cases to a discriminated union. This is deliberate, as you get strong and useful guarantees by placing a limit on the range of possible values for a type.

Using Discriminated Unions as Records

Discriminated union types with only one data tag are an effective way to implement record-like types:

```
type Point3D = Vector3D of float * float * float

let origin = Vector3D(0., 0., 0.)
let unitX = Vector3D(1., 0., 0.)
let unitY = Vector3D(0., 1., 0.)
let unitZ = Vector3D(0., 0., 1.)
```

These are particularly effective because they can be decomposed using succinct patterns in the same way as tuple arguments can:

```
let length (Vector3D(dx, dy, dz)) = sqrt(dx * dx + dy * dy + dz * dz)
```

This technique is most useful for record-like values where there is some natural order on the constituent elements of the value (as shown earlier) or where the elements have different types.

It might also be helpful to be aware that when pattern matching against single-case discriminated-union values in a match construct, the use of the pipe | operator is optional. This is also the case above, in the type definition.

Defining Multiple Types Simultaneously

Multiple types can be declared together to give a mutually recursive collection of types, including record types, discriminated unions, and abbreviations. The type definitions must be separated by the keyword and:

```
type Node =
    { Name : string
      Links : Link list }
and Link =
    | Dangling
    | Link of Node
```

Understanding Generics

F# constructs such as lists, tuples, and function values are all *generic*, which means they can be instantiated with multiple different types. For example, int list, string list, and (int * int) list are all instantiations of the generic family of F# list types. Likewise, int -> int and string -> int are both instantiations of the generic family of F# function types. The F# library and the .NET framework have many other generic types and operations in addition to these.

Generic constructs are always represented through the use of *type variables*, which in F# syntax are written 'T, 'U, 'a, 'Key, and so on. For example, the definition of the Set type in the F# library begins like this:

```
type Set<'T> = ...
```

Type abbreviations can also be generic; for example:

```
type StringMap<'T> = Map<string, 'T>
```

```
type Projections<'T, 'U> = ('T -> 'U) * ('U -> 'T)
```

Values can also be generic. A typical generic value is List.map, whose type is as follows:

```
val map : ('T -> 'U) -> 'T list -> 'U list
```

Each time you name a generic type or value, the F# type system must infer instantiations for the type variables involved. For example, in Chapter 3 you used List.map fetch over an input list, where fetch had the following type:

```
val fetch : url:string -> string * string
```

In this case, the type variable 'T in the signature of List.map is instantiated to string, and the type variable 'U is instantiated to string * string, giving a return type of (string * string) list.

Generic values and functions such as List.map are common in F# programming; they're so common that you usually don't even write the declarations of the type variables in the types of these values. Sometimes, however, the declaration point of these variables is made explicit in output from tools and the F# compiler. For example, you may see this:

```
val map<'T, 'U> : ('T -> 'U) -> 'T list -> 'U list
```

Frequently, type variables have an implicit scope, governed by the rules of automatic generalization discussed in the section "Writing Generic Functions." This means you can introduce type variables simply by writing them as part of the type annotations of a function:

```
let rec map (f : 'T -> 'U) (l : 'T list) =
    match l with
    | h :: t -> f h :: map f t
    | [] -> []
```

If you want, you can also write the type parameters explicitly on a declaration. You typically have to use each type variable at least once in a type annotation in order to relate the type parameters to the actual code:

```
let rec map<'T, 'U> (f : 'T -> 'U) (l : 'T list) =
    match l with
    | h :: t -> f h :: map f t
    | [] -> []
```

■ **Note**   By convention, uppercase type-variable names are used for user-declared type parameters, and lowercase names are used for inferred type parameters. In general, the style *TypeName*<'T> is preferred for F# types, although for historical reasons, the style 'T *TypeName* is used for list, option, reference, and array types.

Writing Generic Functions

A key feature of F# is the automatic generalization of code. The combination of automatic generalization and type inference makes many programs simpler, more succinct, and more general. It also greatly enhances code reuse. Languages without automatic generalization force programmers to compute and explicitly write down the most general type of their functions, and often this is so tedious that programmers don't take the time to abstract common patterns of data manipulation and control.

For example, type parameters are automatically introduced when you write simple functions that are independent of some of their arguments:

```
let getFirst (a,b,c) = a
```

The inferred type of getFirst is reported as follows:

```
val getFirst : a:'a * b:'b * c:'c -> 'a
```

Here, getFirst has been *automatically inferred to be generic*. The function is generic in three type variables, where the result type is the first element of the input tuple type. Automatic generalization is applied when a let or member definition doesn't fully constrain the types of inputs or outputs. You can tell automatic generalization has been applied by the presence of type variables in an inferred type and ultimately by the fact that you can reuse a construct with multiple types.

Automatic generalization is particularly useful when taking functions as inputs. For example, the following takes two functions as inputs and applies them to each side of a tuple:

```
let mapPair f g (x, y) = (f x, g y)
```

The generalized, inferred type is as follows:

```
val mapPair : f:('a -> 'b) -> g:('c -> 'd) -> x:'a * y:'c -> 'b * 'd
```

Some Important Generic Functions

The F# and .NET libraries include definitions for some important generic functions. You saw a number of these in action in earlier chapters. It's important to have a working knowledge of these building blocks, because often your code will automatically become generic when you use these primitives.

Generic Comparison

The first primitives are all related to *generic comparison*, which is often also called *structural comparison*. Every time you use operators such as <, >, <=, >=, =, <>, compare, min, and max in F# code, you're using generic comparison. All of these operators are located in the FSharp.Core.Operators module, which is opened by default in all F# code. Some important data structures also use generic comparison internally; for example, you may also be using generic comparison when you use F# collection types such as FSharp.Collections.Set and FSharp.Collections.Map. This is discussed in the documentation for these types. The type signatures of the basic generic comparison operators are shown here:

```
val compare : 'T -> 'T -> int when 'T : comparison
val (=) : 'T -> 'T -> bool when 'T : equality
val (<) : 'T -> 'T -> bool when 'T : comparison
val (<=) : 'T -> 'T -> bool when 'T : comparison
val (>) : 'T -> 'T -> bool when 'T : comparison
val (>=) : 'T -> 'T -> bool when 'T : comparison
val (min) : 'T -> 'T -> 'T when 'T : comparison
val (max) : 'T -> 'T -> 'T when 'T : comparison
```

All of these routines are constrained, which means they may be used only on a subset of types that are known to support either equality (for =) or ordered comparison (for the others). It may help to think of those that implement ordered comparison as being implemented in terms of compare, which returns 0 if the arguments are equal and returns –1 and 1 for less than and greater than, respectively.

On ordinary simple types, such as integers, generic comparison works by invoking the default .NET behavior for these types, giving the natural ordering for these types. For strings, culture-neutral ordinal comparison is used, which means the local culture settings on your machine don't affect string comparison (see System.Globalization, System.Threading.Thread.CurrentThread.CurrentCulture, and String. Compare for more information about local culture settings and culture-specific string ordering). Most other .NET base types, such as System.DateTime values, implement the System.IComparable interface, and generic comparison uses these implementations where necessary.

You can also use the comparison operators on most structured types. For example, you can use them on F# tuple values, where a lexicographic left-to-right comparison is used:

```
> ("abc", "def") < ("abc", "xyz");;

val it : bool = true

> compare (10, 30) (10, 20);;

val it : int = 1
```

Likewise, you can use generic comparison with list and array values:

```
> compare [10; 30] [10; 20];;

val it : int = 1

> compare [|10; 30|] [|10; 20|];;

val it : int = 1

> compare [|10; 20|] [|10; 30|];;

val it : int = -1
```

Generic Hashing

Generic hashing is an important partner of generic comparison. The primary primitive function used to invoke generic hashing is hash, which is also located in the FSharp.Core.Operators module. The type signature is:

```
val hash : 'T -> int when 'T : equality
```

Again, this is a constrained operation, requiring that the type supports equality. Most types support some form of equality, even if it's the default reference equality of .NET.

When used with simple structural types, the function returns an integer that gives a stable hash of the input value:

```
> hash 100;;

val it : int = 100

> hash "abc";;

val it : int = 536991770

> hash (100, "abc");;

val it : int = 536990974
```

Generic hashing is implemented similarly to generic comparison. Like generic comparison, generic hashing should generally be used only with base types, such as integers, and with structural types built using records and discriminated unions.

For the most part, generic hashing and comparison are implemented efficiently—code is autogenerated for each type definition where possible fast-path comparison techniques are used. For example, the generated code uses primitive Common IL/native instructions for integer comparisons. This means that in practice, structural comparison is typically fast when used with appropriately sized keys. However, you should consider the following before using generic comparison over complex new data types:

- When using .NET collections, consider passing the HashIdentity.Structural or ComparisonIdentity.Structural parameters to the object constructor of the collection. This helps the F# compiler optimize the performance of the hashing, equality, and comparison functions for the collection instance.

- Hashing, comparison, and equality on tuples can be slower than expected in those circumstances where the F# compiler can't optimize the hashing, equality, and comparison functions for these types. Consider replacing uses of tuples as keys by the use of a new, named key type, often using a union type with a single case; for example, type Key = Key of string * int. This allows the compiler to optimize the hashing.

- Consider customizing the behavior of generic hashing, comparison, and equality for new types you define, at least when those types will be used as keys in a data structure. You can do this for comparison and equality by implementing the System.IComparable interface and overriding the System.Object.Equals method, which will be covered in Chapter 8. You can customize generic hashing for new types by either overriding the GetHashCode method or implementing the FSharp.Core.IStructuralHash interface, also covered in Chapter 8.

- Both ordered comparison and equality (in combination with hashing) can be used to build interesting indexed data structures. Collections built using these techniques are more efficient than small keys. Performance issues may arise, however, if they're used repeatedly over large structured keys. In this case, using custom comparison may be appropriate.

Disabling Structural Generic Hashing and Comparison

In normal usage, F# tuple, record, union, and struct types support "structural" equality, comparison, and hashing. This is a good default for a data-centric functional language. However, in some circumstances you may wish to "turn off" structural comparison. In F# 4.0, this is possible by opening the module `FSharp.Core.Operators.NonStructuralComparison`—you can just use open `NonStructuralComparison`.

When this is done, the operators =, <, >, <=, >=, <> and functions compare, hash, min, and max are altered and structural comparison is no longer supported. Comparison and equality is then only supported on types supporting the direct comparison and equality operators, which will be discussed in Chapter 9. These are defined on most .NET library types.

```
> open NonStructuralComparison;;

> compare 4 1;; // allowed, gives 1

val it : int = 1

> compare DateTime.Now (DateTime.Now.AddDays(1.0));; // allowed, gives -1

val it : int = -11

> compare (1,3) (5,4);;

ch02.fsx: error FS0001: Expecting a type supporting the operator '<' but given a tuple type
```

Generic Pretty-Printing

Some useful generic functions are available for generic formatting of values. The simplest way to access this functionality is to use the %A specifiers in `printf` format strings. Here is an example:

```
> sprintf "result = %A" ([1], [true]);;

val it : string = "result = ([1], [true])"
```

This code uses .NET and F# reflection to walk the structure of values so as to build a formatted representation of the value. You format structural types such as lists and tuples using the syntax of F# source code. Unrecognized values are formatted by calling the .NET `ToString()` method for these values. F# and .NET reflection are discussed in more depth toward the end of Chapter 17.

Generic Boxing and Unboxing

Two useful generic functions convert any F# data to and from the universal type `System.Object` (the F# type obj):

```
val box : 'T -> obj
val unbox : obj -> 'T
```

Here are some simple examples of these functions in action:

```
> box 1;;

val it : obj = 1

> box "abc";;

val it : obj = "abc"

> let stringObj = box "abc";;

val stringObj : obj = "abc"

> (unbox<string> stringObj);;

val it : string = "abc"

> (unbox stringObj : string);;

val it : string = "abc"
```

Note that using unbox generally requires you to specify the target type, given either as an explicit type parameter such as unbox<string> or as a type constraint such as (unbox stringObj: string)—these forms are equivalent. A runtime check is performed on unboxing to ensure that the object can be safely converted to the target type. Values of type obj carry dynamic type information, and attempting to unbox a value to an incompatible type raises an error, as follows:

```
> (unbox stringObj : int);;

System.InvalidCastException: Specified cast is not valid.
    at <StartupCode$FSI_0046>.$FSI_0046.main@()
Stopped due to error
```

Boxing is important partly because many early .NET libraries provide operations through functions that accept arguments of type obj. You will see an example of this in the next section. Furthermore, some .NET APIs are dynamically typed, and almost all parameters are of type obj. This was common before generics were added in v2.0 of the .NET framework.

Generic Binary Serialization via the .NET Libraries

The .NET libraries provide an implementation of generic binary serialization that is useful as a quick and easy way to save computed values to disk and to send values over the network. Let's use this as an example to see how you can define building-block generic operations using functionality in the .NET libraries combined with box and unbox. You must first define functions with the following signatures:

```
val writeValue : Stream -> 'T -> unit
val readValue : Stream -> 'a
```

The function writeValue takes an arbitrary value and writes a binary representation of its underlying object graph to the given I/O stream. The function readValue reverses this process, in much the same way that unbox reverses the process performed by box. Here are the implementations of the functions in terms of the .NET binary serializer located in the namespace System.Runtime.Serialization.Formatters.Binary:

```
open System.IO
open System.Runtime.Serialization.Formatters.Binary

let writeValue outputStream x =
    let formatter = new BinaryFormatter()
    formatter.Serialize(outputStream, box x)

let readValue inputStream =
    let formatter = new BinaryFormatter()
    let res = formatter.Deserialize(inputStream)
    unbox res
```

Note that box and unbox are used in the implementation, because the Serialize and Deserialize functions accept and return a value of type obj. Here is an example of how to use the functions to write a value of type FSharp.Collections.Map<string,string> to a FileStream and read it back in again:

```
open System.IO
let addresses =
    Map.ofList ["Jeff", "123 Main Street, Redmond, WA 98052"
                "Fred", "987 Pine Road, Phila., PA 19116"
                "Mary", "PO Box 112233, Palo Alto, CA 94301"]

let fsOut = new FileStream("Data.dat", FileMode.Create)
writeValue fsOut addresses
fsOut.Close()

let fsIn = new FileStream("Data.dat", FileMode.Open)
let res : Map<string, string> = readValue fsIn
fsIn.Close()
```

The final result of this code when executed interactively is as follows:

```
> res;;

val it : Map<string,string> =
  map
    [("Fred", "987 Pine Road, Phila., PA 19116");
     ("Jeff", "123 Main Street, Redmond, WA 98052");
     ("Mary", "PO Box 112233, Palo Alto, CA 94301")]
```

Note that values of type Map<string,string> are printed interactively as sequences of key/value pairs. Also, a type annotation is required when reading the data back using readValue, and a runtime type error results if the types of the objects reconstructed from the binary data don't match this type annotation.

The .NET framework provides several other generic serializers that differ in output format and operational characteristics. The most important of these are based around the notion of DataContract serialization:

- System.Runtime.Serialization.Json.DataContractJsonSerializer: Used for serializing public data objects into the popular JavaScript Object Notation (JSON) form using formats that aren't specifically tied to particular .NET types but that are, rather, compatible with a range of types.

- System.Runtime.Serialization.DataContractSerializer: Used for serializing public data objects into XML with its built-in simple types and extensible complex types.

- System.Runtime.Serialization.NetDataContractSerializer: Used for serializing arbitrary object graphs, including private data and closures, into XML using the same idioms as the other DataContract serializers.

In addition, you can use some older serializers with F#. For example, System.Runtime.Serialization. XmlSerializer is used for serializing public data into XML. This serializer is now used less frequently; you should generally use NetDataContractSerializer instead. You can also write your own generic serializer– for example, by using the techniques you will see in Chapter 8. Finally, some excellent serializers are available as F# community libraries, including Nessos.FsPickler.

Making Things Generic

The following sections discuss how to make existing code more generic (that is, reusable) and how to systematically represent the abstract parameters of generic algorithms.

Generic Algorithms through Explicit Arguments

A common pattern in F# programming is to accept function parameters in order to make an algorithm abstract and reusable. A simple sample is the following generic implementation of Euclid's algorithm for finding the highest common factor (HCF) of two numbers:

```
let rec hcf a b =
    if a = 0 then b
    elif a < b then hcf a (b - a)
    else hcf (a - b) b
```

The type of this function is:

```
val hcf : a:int -> b:int -> int
```

For example:

```
> hcf 18 12;;
val it : int = 6

> hcf 33 24;;
val it : int = 3
```

This algorithm isn't generic, however, because as written it works only over integers. In particular, although the operator (-) is by default overloaded in F#, each use of the operator must be associated with at most one type that is decided at compile time. This restriction is discussed in more detail in the section "Understanding Generic Overloaded Operators." In addition, the constant 0 is an integer and isn't overloaded.

Despite this, this algorithm can be easily generalized to work over any type. To achieve this, you must provide an explicit zero, a subtraction function, and an ordering. Here's one way:

```
let hcfGeneric (zero, sub, lessThan) =
    let rec hcf a b =
        if a = zero then b
        elif lessThan a b then hcf a (sub b a)
        else hcf (sub a b) b
    hcf
```

The inferred, generic type of this function is as follows:

```
val hcfGeneric :
  zero:'a * sub:('a -> 'a -> 'a) * lessThan:('a -> 'a -> bool) ->
    ('a -> 'a -> 'a) when 'a : equality
```

The numeric type being manipulated has type 'a in the inferred type, and the result is a function. This approach uses techniques for computing functions similar to those discussed in Chapter 3. Here are some examples of using this generic function:

```
let hcfInt = hcfGeneric (0, (-), (<))
let hcfInt64 = hcfGeneric (0L, (-), (<))
let hcfBigInt = hcfGeneric (0I, (-), (<))
```

Note that when you instantiate the generic function for these cases, you're drawing on particular instances of the default overloaded operator (-). You can check that the code is executing correctly as follows:

```
> hcfInt 18 12;;

val it : int = 6

> hcfBigInt 1810287116162232383039576I 1239028178293092830480239032I;;

val it : System.Numerics.BigInteger = 33224
```

Generic Algorithms through Function Parameters

The generic implementation from the previous section took three related parameters for zero, comparison, and subtraction. It's common practice to package related operations together. One way to do this is to use a concrete record type containing function values, as seen here:

```
type Numeric<'T> =
    {Zero : 'T
     Subtract : ('T -> 'T -> 'T)
     LessThan : ('T -> 'T -> bool) }
```

```
let intOps = {Zero = 0; Subtract = (-); LessThan = (<)}
let bigintOps = {Zero = 0I; Subtract = (-); LessThan = (<)}
let int64Ops = {Zero = 0L; Subtract = (-); LessThan = (<)}

let hcfGeneric (ops : Numeric<'T>) =
    let rec hcf a b =
        if a = ops.Zero then b
        elif ops.LessThan a b then hcf a (ops.Subtract b a)
        else hcf (ops.Subtract a b) b
    hcf

let hcfInt = hcfGeneric intOps
let hcfBigInt = hcfGeneric bigintOps
```

The inferred types are as follows, and the hcfGeneric type is now simpler:

```
val hcfGeneric : ops:Numeric<'T> -> ('T -> 'T -> 'T) when 'T : equality
val hcfInt : (int -> int -> int)
val hcfBigInt :  (bigint -> bigint -> bigint)
```

To double-check that everything works as before:

```
> hcfInt 18 12;;

val it : int = 6

> hcfBigInt 18102871161622323830395761 123902817829309283048023903211;;

val it : bigint = 33224
```

Record types such as Numeric<'T>, often called *dictionaries of operations,* are similar to vtables from object-oriented programming and the compiled form of type classes from Haskell. As you've seen, dictionaries such as these can be represented in different ways according to your tastes, using either tuples or records. For larger frameworks, a carefully constructed classification of *object interface types* is often used in place of records. Here is an interface-type definition that plays the same role as the record in the previous example:

```
type INumeric<'T> =
    abstract Zero : 'T
    abstract Subtract : 'T * 'T -> 'T
    abstract LessThan : 'T * 'T -> bool
```

You can implement interface types with object expressions similarly to record values:

```
let intOps =
    {new INumeric<int> with
        member ops.Zero = 0
        member ops.Subtract(x, y) = x - y
        member ops.LessThan(x, y) = x < y}
```

```
val intOps : INumeric<int>
```

The code for Euclid's algorithm using interface types is essentially the same as for the code based on record types:

```
let hcfGeneric (ops : INumeric<'T>) =
    let rec hcf a b =
        if a = ops.Zero then b
        elif ops.LessThan(a, b) then hcf a (ops.Subtract(b, a))
        else hcf (ops.Subtract(a, b)) b
    hcf
```

GENERIC ALGORITHMS AND FUNCTION PARAMETERS

One of the remarkable features of functional programming with F# is that generic programming is practical even when the types involved aren't explicitly related. For example, the previous generic algorithm shows how you can write reusable code without resorting to relating the types involved through an inheritance hierarchy: the generic algorithm works over any type if an appropriate set of operations is provided to manipulate values of that type. This is a form of *explicit factoring by functions*. Object-oriented programming typically uses *implicit factoring by hierarchy*, because the library designer decides the relationships that exist among various types, and these are fixed in stone.

Type inference in F# makes explicit factoring by functions convenient. Given the simplicity and flexibility of this approach, it's a useful way to write applications and to prototype frameworks. Factoring by hierarchy still plays a role in F# programming, however. For example, all F# values can be implicitly converted to and from the type System.Object, something that is extremely useful when you're interoperating with many libraries. It would obviously be inconvenient to have to pass around functions to marshal (box/unbox) types to System.Object and back. Similarly, many F# values can be implicitly converted to the IDisposable interface. Hierarchical factoring requires careful design choices; in general, we recommend that you use explicit factoring first, moving toward implicit factoring only when an algorithmic pattern is truly universal and repeats itself many times, as is the case with the IDisposable idiom. The .NET and F# libraries contain definitions of many of the implicit factors you should use in practice, such as IDisposable and IEnumerable.

Some functional languages, such as Haskell, allow you to implicitly pass dictionaries of operations through an extension to type inference known as type classes. At the time of writing, this isn't supported by F#, but the designers of F# have stated that they expect a future version of the language to support this. Either way, explicitly passing dictionaries of operations is common in all functional programming and is an important technique to master.

Generic Algorithms through Inlining

An additional way to make code generic is to mark a function as inline. You can use this technique for code that uses F# operators, such as float, int, +, -, *, /, and other arithmetic operations. As we'll discuss in the section "Understanding Generic Overloaded Operators," each use of these operators is normally statically resolved. For example, consider this code:

```
let convertToFloat x = float x
```

In the F# type system, the type of the float function is 'T -> float (requires member op_Explicit). This means the type 'T must support an explicit conversion from 'T to float. Thus, you can use it with integers, singles, doubles, decimals, and so on, but you can't use it with any old type. The 'T is constrained.

As mentioned earlier, F# operators such as float are statically resolved. This means each use of float is associated with one statically inferred type. The same applies to other operators such as +, *, and so on. These operators also generally default to working over integers. For example, this shows float being used with three different statically resolved types:

```
float 3.0 + float 1 + float 3L
```

To make code such as this generic, you can use inline. For example, consider:

```
let inline convertToFloatAndAdd x y = float x + float y
```

The function convertToFloatAndAdd can be used with an integer and a float, or a decimal and an integer, or two decimals. You can use inline to write code and algorithms that are implicitly generic over arithmetic type while still maintaining type safety. This gives you generic, type-safe code while ensuring the static resolution of basic numeric operations, making it easy to reason about the efficiency of your code.

You can also apply this technique to the earlier HCF algorithm, whose code is shown again here:

```
let hcfGeneric (ops : INumeric<'T>) =
    let rec hcf a b =
        if a = ops.Zero then b
        elif ops.LessThan(a, b) then hcf a (ops.Subtract(b, a))
        else hcf (ops.Subtract(a, b)) b
    hcf
```

You can avoid passing the INumeric "dictionary" of operations explicitly by providing a simple wrapper that delegates to a non-inlined generic routine. For example, the following code delegates to the non-inlined routine hcfGeneric, defined earlier in this section:

```
let inline hcf a b =
    hcfGeneric
        {new INumeric<'T> with
            member ops.Zero = LanguagePrimitives.GenericZero<'T>
            member ops.Subtract(x, y) = x - y
            member ops.LessThan(x, y) = x < y}
        a b
```

The type of this function is:

```
val inline hcf :
  a: ^T -> b: ^T -> ^T
    when  ^T : (static member get_Zero : ->  ^T) and  ^T : comparison and
          ^T : (static member ( - ) :  ^T *  ^T ->  ^T)
```

This gives you the best of two worlds: a generic function hcfGeneric that can be used with any explicit set of arithmetic operations, and an inlined generic routine hcf that can be used with any type that supports an implicit set of arithmetic operations. For example:

```
> hcf 18 12;;

val it : int = 6

> hcf 18I 12I;;

val it : bigint = 6
```

The algorithm is now generic. You should use this technique sparingly, but it can be extremely powerful. Note the use of the F# library primitive GenericZero to get a zero value for an arbitrary type supporting a Zero static property.

More on Different Kinds of Types

For the most part, programming in F# involves using types in a simple way: each type has some values, and types are related by using explicit functions to map from one type to another. In reality, however, types in F# are more sophisticated than this statement implies. First, F# types are really .NET types, and .NET makes some distinctions between different kinds of types that are occasionally important, such as between value types and reference types.

Furthermore, .NET and F# support hierarchical relationships between types through *subtyping*. The following sections first cover .NET types from the F# perspective and then cover subtyping.

Reference Types and Value Types

The .NET documentation and other .NET languages often describe types as either *reference types* or *value types*. You can use System.String and System.DateTime as typical examples of each. First note that both of these types are immutable. That is, given a value of type System.String, you can't modify the contents of the string; the same is true for System.DateTime. This is by far the most important fact you need to know about these types; for immutable types the reference/value type distinction is relatively unimportant. It's still useful, however, to know the following:

- *Representation:* Values of type System.String are single pointers into the garbage-collected heap where the actual data for the string reside. Two System.String values may point to the same data. In contrast, values of type System.DateTime are somewhat larger blobs of integer data (64-bits of data, in this case), and no data live on the garbage-collected heap. The full data for the value are copied as needed.

- *Boxing:* All .NET types can be marshaled to and from the .NET type System.Object (the F# type obj) by using F# functions such as box and unbox. All reference types are trivially marshaled to this type without any change of representation or identity, so for reference types, box is a no-op. Boxing a value type involves a heap allocation, resulting in a new object. Often this object is immediately discarded after the operation on the obj type has been performed.

If a value can be mutated, then the distinction between value types and reference types is more serious. Fortunately, essentially all mutable values in the .NET libraries are reference types, which means any mutation actually mutates the heap-allocated data referred to by the reference.

Other Flavors of .NET Types

The .NET type system makes some additional distinctions among types that are occasionally significant for F# programming:

- *Delegate types*: Delegate types, such as `System.EventHandler<'T>`, are a form of named function type supported by all .NET languages. They tend not to be as convenient to use as F# function types are, as they don't support compositional operations such as pipelining and forward composition, but .NET APIs use delegates extensively. To create a delegate value, you name the delegate type and pass it a function value that accepts the same arguments expected by the delegate type, such as `EventHandler(fun sender args -> printfn "click!")`.

- *Attribute types*: Types derived from the `System.Attribute` class are used to add metadata to source-code declarations and typically end in the suffix `Attribute`. You can access these attributes via .NET and F# reflection. You can add attributes to F# declarations using the `[<...>]` syntax. For example, `System.ObsoleteAttribute` marks a function as obsolete, and the F# compiler produces a warning if the function is used. Attribute names such as this one, when used inside the `[<...>]` syntax, can omit the `Attribute` suffix, which is then automatically inserted by the F# compiler.

- *Exception types*: Types derived from the `System.Exception` class are used to represent raised exceptions. Chapter 4 discussed exceptions in detail.

- *Enum types*: .NET enum types are simple integer-like value types associated with a particular name. They're typically used for specifying flags to APIs; for example, `FileMode` in the `System.IO` namespace is an enum type with values such as `FileMode.Open` and `FileMode.Create`. .NET enum types are easy to use from F# and can be combined using bitwise AND, OR, and XOR operations using the `&&&`, `|||`, and `^^^` operators. Most commonly, the `|||` operator is used to combine multiple flags. On occasion, you may have to mask an attribute value using `&&&` and compare the result to enum `0`. You will see how to define .NET-compatible enum types in F# at the end of Chapter 6.

Understanding Subtyping

Simple types are related in simple ways. For example, values of the type `int` are distinct from values of the type `float`, and values of one record type are distinct from values of another. This approach to types is powerful and often sufficient, partly because type inference and function values make it easy to write generic code, although .NET and F# also support hierarchical relationships between types through *subtyping*. Subtyping is a key concept of object-oriented programming and will be discussed in more detail in Chapter 6. In addition, you can use subtyping in conjunction with pure functional programming, because it offers one technique to make algorithms generic over a restricted family of types.

The following sections explain how these constructs appear to the F# programmer and the role they play in F# programming. Subtyping in F# is the same as that used by the .NET framework, so if you're familiar with another .NET language, you already know how things work.

Casting Up Statically

You can explore how subtyping works by using F# Interactive. First, let's look at how some of the F# types you've already seen relate to the type obj:

```
> let xobj = (1 :> obj);;

val xobj : obj = 1

> let sobj = ("abc" :> obj);;

val sobj : obj = "abc"
```

This example shows the subtyping relationship through the use of the built-in coercion (or *upcast*) operator, which is :>. This operator converts a value to any of its supertypes in precisely the same way as the box function does.

The previous code indicates the subtyping between ordinary types and the type obj. Subtyping occurs between other kinds of types as well (Chapters 3 and 6 discuss the various kinds of type definitions, such as records, discriminated unions, classes, and interfaces):

- All types are subtypes of System.Object (called obj in F#).

- Record and discriminated-union types are subtypes of the interface types they implement.

- Interface types are subtypes of the other interfaces they extend.

- Class types are subtypes of both the interfaces they implement and the classes they extend.

- Array types are subtypes of the .NET type System.Array.

- Value types (types such as int32 that are abbreviations of .NET value types) are subtypes of the .NET type System.ValueType. Likewise, .NET enumeration types are subtypes of System.Enum.

Casting Down Dynamically

Values that may have subtypes carry a *runtime type,* and you can use runtime-type tests to query the type of an object and convert it to one of the subtypes. You can do this in three main ways: the unbox operation, downcasts, and pattern-type tests. We've already explained the unbox function. As with most object-oriented languages, the upcasts performed through subtyping are reversible through the use of downcasts—in other words, by using the :?> operator. Consider these examples:

```
> let boxedObject = box "abc";;

val boxedObject : obj = "abc"

> let downcastString = (boxedObject :?> string);;

val downcastString : string = "abc"
```

Downcasts are checked at runtime, and all values of the obj type are implicitly annotated with the runtime type of the value. The operator : ?> raises an exception if the object isn't of a suitable type:

```
> let xobj = box 1;;

val xobj : obj = 1

> let x = (xobj :?> string);;

System.InvalidCastException: Unable to cast object of type 'System.Int32' to type
'System.String'.
  at <StartupCode$FSI_0037>.$FSI_0037.main@()
```

Performing Type Tests via Pattern Matching

A more convenient way of performing dynamic type tests uses *type-test patterns*—in particular the : ? pattern construct, which you encountered in Chapter 4 in the context of catching various .NET exception types. This example uses a pattern-type test to query the dynamic type of a value of type obj:

```
let checkObject (x : obj) =
    match x with
    | :? string -> printfn "The object is a string"
    | :? int -> printfn "The object is an integer"
    | _ -> printfn "The input is something else"
```

```
> checkObject (box "abc");;

The object is a string
```

Such a pattern may also bind the matched value at its more specific type:

```
let reportObject (x : obj) =
    match x with
    | :? string as s -> printfn "The input is the string '%s'" s
    | :? int as d -> printfn "The input is the integer '%d'" d
    | _ -> printfn "the input is something else"
```

```
> reportObject (box 17);;

The input is the integer '17'
```

Knowing When Upcasts Are Applied Automatically

Like most object-oriented languages, F# automatically applies upcasts whenever a function or method is called or wherever a value is used. If a parameter to an F# function has a named type, then the function implicitly accepts parameters that are of any subtype, assuming that type supports subtyping. This is particularly common when working with .NET libraries that use subtyping heavily. For example, consider the following sample:

```
open System
open System.Net
let dispose (c : IDisposable) = c.Dispose()

let obj1 = new WebClient()
let obj2 = new HttpListener()

dispose obj1
dispose obj2
```

Here, the function `dispose` is used on two different subtypes of `IDisposable`. When functions have parameters that accept named types such as `IDisposable`, you don't need to supply an upcast explicitly.

F# doesn't apply upcasts in all the situations where other object-oriented languages do, however. In practice, this means you sometimes have to add explicit upcasts to your code to throw away information. For example, if each branch of an `if ... then ... else ...` construct returns different types, then you need to upcast the results of one or both of the branches. This is shown by the type error given for the following code, which returns `Console.In` (a `TextReader`) from one branch and the results of `File.OpenText` (a `StreamReader`) from the other branch:

```
open System
open System.IO

let textReader =
    if DateTime.Today.DayOfWeek = DayOfWeek.Monday
    then Console.In
    else File.OpenText("input.txt")
```

The error reported is as follows:

```
error FS0001: This expression was expected to have type
    TextReader
but here has type
    StreamReader
```

`StreamReader` is a subtype of `TextReader`, so the code can be corrected by throwing away the information that the returned type is a `StreamReader`:

```
open System
open System.IO

let textReader =
    if DateTime.Today.DayOfWeek = DayOfWeek.Monday
    then Console.In
    else (File.OpenText("input.txt") :> TextReader)
```

Upcasts are applied automatically in the following situations:

- When passing arguments to functions and all members associated with .NET and F# objects and types. This applies when parameters have named types, such as TextReader, rather than generic types.

- When calling functions with flexible parameter types (see in the following section), such as #TextReader.

- When assigning into fields and properties.

- When accessing members using dot notation. For example, given a value of type StreamReader, all the members associated with TextReader can also be accessed without needing to apply an upcast.

Note particularly that upcasts aren't applied automatically for the result of a function. For example, an upcast is needed here, to coerce a StreamReader to a TextReader, despite the presence of an explicit type annotation for the return type:

```
let getTextReader () : TextReader = (File.OpenText("input.txt") :> TextReader)
```

Flexible Types

F# also has the notion of a *flexible type constraint*, which is shorthand for a generic function and a constraint on the type variable. For example, consider this:

```
let disposeMany (cs : seq<#IDisposable>) =
    for c in cs do c.Dispose()
```

giving type:

```
val disposeMany: c: seq<#IDisposable> -> s:string -> unit
```

This function can be used with arguments of type seq<FileStream>, seq<Stream>, or indeed any sequence whose elements are some subtype of IDisposable. You could equally write this:

```
let disposeMany (cs : seq<'T :> IDisposable>) =
    for c in cs do c.Dispose()
```

Flexible type constraints don't occur much in F#, but they sometimes occur when you're working with collections or sequences. For example, consider this function from the F# library:

```
module Seq =
    ...
    val concat : seq<#seq<'T>> -> seq<'T>
    ...
```

When implicit flexibility of arguments is taken into account, the signature of concat means that Seq.concat accepts a list of lists, or a list of arrays, or an array of lists, and so forth. For example:

```
Seq.concat [[1;2;3]; [4;5;6]]
Seq.concat [[|1; 2; 3|]; [|4; 5; 6|]] ]
```

113

Troubleshooting Type-Inference Problems

The following sections cover some of the techniques you can use to understand the type-inference process and to debug problems when inferred types aren't as expected.

Using a Visual Editing Environment

The best and most important technique for debugging and understanding type inference is to use a visual editing environment for F#. For example, Visual Studio performs interactive type-checking as you're writing code. Such tools display errors interactively and show inferred types as you move the mouse pointer over identifiers.

Using Type Annotations

Type inference in F# works through a process of type-constraint *propagation*. As a programmer, you can add further type constraints to your code in several ways. For example, you can do the following:

- Add a rigid type constraint using the : notation, such as let t : float = 5.0.

- Add a type constraint to an argument, such as let setTextOfControl (c : Control) (s : string) = c.Text <- s.

- Apply a function that accepts only a particular type of argument, such as let f x = String.length x. Here, the use of String.length generates a constraint on the type of x.

Adding type annotations to and removing them from your code is the standard technique for troubleshooting type-inference problems. For example, the following code doesn't type-check:

```
> let getLengths inp = inp |> Seq.map (fun y -> y.Length) ;;
```

```
error FS0072: Lookup on object of indeterminate type based on information prior to this
program point. A type annotation may be needed prior to this program point to constrain
the type of the object. This may allow the lookup to be resolved.
```

You can easily solve this problem by adding a type annotation, such as to y:

```
let getLengths inp =
    inp |> Seq.map (fun (y : string) -> y.Length)
```

You can also use type annotations to discover why code isn't as generic as you think it should be. For example, the following code has a mistake, and the F# type checker says the code is less generic than expected:

```
let printSecondElements (inp : seq<'T * int>) =
    inp
    |> Seq.iter (fun (x, y) -> printfn "y = %d" x)
```

```
> ... enter the code above ...
```

```
warning FS0064: This construct causes code to be less generic than indicated by the type
annotations. The type variable 'T has been constrained to be type 'int'.
```

The mistake here is that you're printing the variable x instead of y, but it's not always so easy to spot what has caused this kind of problem. One way to track down this problem is to temporarily change the generic type parameter to some arbitrary, unrelated type. After all, if code is generic, then you should be able to use *any* type; and by changing the type variable to an unrelated type, you can track down where the inconsistency first arises. For example, let's change 'T to the type PingPong:

```
type PingPong = Ping | Pong

let printSecondElements (inp : seq<PingPong * int>) =
    inp
    |> Seq.iter (fun (x,y) -> printfn "y = %d" x)
```

You now get a different and in many ways more informative error message, localized to the first place that the value x marked with type PingPong is used in an unexpected way:

```
> ... enter the code above ...

error FS0001: The type 'PingPong' is not compatible with any of the types byte,int16,
int32,int64,sbyte,uint16,uint32,uint64,nativeint,unativeint, arising from the use of a
printf-style format string
```

Understanding the Value Restriction

F# sometimes requires a little help before a definition is automatically generalized. In particular, only function definitions and simple immutable data expressions are automatically generalized; this is called the *value restriction*. For example, the following definition doesn't result in a generic type and gives an error:

```
> let empties = Array.create 100 [];;

error FS0030: Value restriction. The value 'empties' has been inferred to have generic type
    val empties : '_a list []
Either define 'empties' as a simple data term, make it a function with explicit arguments
or, if you do not intend for it to be generic, add a type annotation.
```

The code attempts to create an array of empty lists. The error message indicates that type inference has given empties the type '_a list []. The underscore (_) indicates that the type variable 'a is *ungeneralized*, meaning this code isn't fully generic. It would make no sense to give empties the truly generic type 'a list [], because this would imply that you've created an array of lists somehow suitable for use with any type 'a. In reality, any particular array should have one specific type, such as int list [] or string list [], but not both. (If it were usable with both types, then you could store an integer list in the array and fetch it out as a string list!)

The value restriction ensures that declarations don't result in this kind of confusion; automatic generalization isn't applied to declarations unless they're functions or simple, immutable data constructs. One way to think of this is that you can create concrete objects only after the type-inference problem is sufficiently constrained so that every concrete object created at the top level of your program has a ground type—a type that doesn't contain any ungeneralized type variables.

The value restriction doesn't apply to simple immutable data constants or function definitions. For example, the following declarations are all automatically generalized, giving the generic types shown:

```
let emptyList = []
let initialLists = ([], [2])
let listOfEmptyLists = [[]; []]
let makeArray () = Array.create 100 []
```

```
val emptyList : 'a list
val initialLists : 'a list * int list
val listOfEmptyLists : 'a list list
val makeArray : unit -> 'a list []
```

Working Around the Value Restriction

The value restriction crops up with mild regularity in F# coding—particularly when you're using F# Interactive, where the scope of type inference is at the granularity of each entry sent to the tool rather than an entire file, and hence, fewer constraints are placed on these code fragments. You can work around the value restriction in several ways, depending on what you're trying to do.

Technique 1: Constrain Values to Be Nongeneric

The first technique applies when you make a definition such as empties, shown earlier, but you meant to create one value. Recall that this definition was problematic because it's not clear what type of array is being created:

```
let empties = Array.create 100 []
```

If you meant to create one value with a specific type, then use an explicit type annotation:

```
let empties : int list [] = Array.create 100 []
```

The value is then not generic, and the value restriction doesn't apply.

Technique 2: Ensure Generic Functions Have Explicit Arguments

The next technique applies when you're defining generic functions. In this case, make sure you define them with explicit arguments. For example, look at the following definition of a function value:

```
let mapFirst = List.map fst
```

You may expect this to be a generic function with type ('a * 'b) list -> 'a list. This isn't what happens. Type variables are automatically generalized at true syntactic function definitions—that is, function definitions with *explicit* arguments. The function mapFirst has *implicit* arguments. Fortunately, it's easy to work around this by making the arguments explicit (or in academic terms, performing η [eta] abstraction):

```
let mapFirst inp = List.map fst inp
```

This function now has the following type:

```
val mapFirst : inp:('a * 'b) list -> 'a list
```

When there is only one argument, our favorite way of writing the extra arguments is as follows:

```
let mapFirst inp = inp |> List.map (fun (x, y) -> x)
```

The same problem arises when you try to define functions by composition. For example:

```
let printFstElements = List.map fst >> List.iter (printf "res = %d")
```

The arguments here are implicit, which causes problems. This definition isn't automatically generalized because this isn't a syntactic function. Again, make the arguments explicit:

```
let printFstElements inp = inp |> List.map fst |> List.iter (printf "res = %d")
```

Technique 3: Add a Unit Argument to Create a Generic Function

Look at this definition again:

```
let empties = Array.create 100 []
```

Given this definition, empties is not a function. It's possible that you really did intend to define a function that generates arrays of different types on demand. In this case, add a unit argument:

```
let empties () = Array.create 100 []
let intEmpties : int list [] = empties ()
let stringEmpties : string list [] = empties ()
```

The dummy argument ensures that empties is a function with generic arguments and that it can be automatically generalized.

Technique 4: Add Explicit Type Arguments

You can use one final technique to make a value generic. This one is rarely used, but it is very handy when it's required. It's normally used when you're defining values that are generic but that are neither functions nor simple data expressions. For example, let's define a sequence of 100 empty lists:

```
let emptyLists = Seq.init 100 (fun _ -> [])
```

The expression on the right isn't a function or simple data expression (it's a function application), so the value restriction applies. One solution is to add an extra dummy argument, as in the previous section. If you're designing a library, however, this can seem very artificial. Instead, you can use the following declaration form to make emptyLists generic:

```
let emptyLists<'T> : seq<'T list> = Seq.init 100 (fun _ -> [])
```

You can now use emptyLists as a *type function* to generate values of different types. For example:

```
> Seq.length emptyLists;;

val it : int = 100

> emptyLists<int>;;

val it : seq<int list> = seq [[]; []; []; []; ...]

> emptyLists<string>;;

val it : seq<string list> = seq [[]; []; []; []; ...]
```

Some values and functions in the F# library are defined in this way, including typeof<_>, Seq.empty, and Set.empty. Chapter 17 will cover typeof.

Understanding Generic Overloaded Operators

There is one further important way in which code doesn't automatically become generic in F#: when you use overloaded operators such as +, -, *, and /, or overloaded conversion functions such as float and int64. For example, the following is *not* a generic function:

```
let twice x = (x + x)
```

In the absence of further information, the type of this function is as follows:

```
val twice : x:int -> int
```

This is because the overloaded operator + defaults to operating on integers. If you add type annotations or further type constraints, you can force the function to operate on any type supporting the overloaded + operator:

```
let twiceFloat (x : float) = x + x
```

```
val twiceFloat : x:float -> float
```

The information that resolves a use of an overloaded operator can come after the use of the operator:

```
let threeTimes x = (x + x + x)
let sixTimesInt64 (x:int64) = threeTimes x + threeTimes x
```

```
val threeTimes : x:int64 -> int64
val sixTimesInt64 : x:int64 -> int64
```

Note how the constraint in the definition of sixTimesInt64 is the only mention of int64 and affects the type of threeTimes. The technical explanation is that overloaded operators such as + give rise to *floating* constraints, which can be resolved later in the type-inference scope.

Summary

F# is a typed language, and F# programmers often use types in sophisticated ways. In this chapter, you learned about the foundations of types, focusing on how types are used in functional programming and with generics and subtyping in particular. The next chapter will cover the related topics of object-oriented and modular programming in F#.

CHAPTER 6

Programming with Objects

Chapters 2 through 5 dealt with the basic constructs of F# functional and imperative programming, and by now we trust you're familiar with the foundational concepts and techniques of practical, small-scale F# programming. This chapter covers language constructs related to *object programming*.

Programming in F# tends to be less "object-*oriented*" than in other languages, since functional programming with values, functions, lists, tuples, and other shaped data is enough to solve many programming problems. Objects are used as a means to an end rather than as the dominant paradigm.

The first part of this chapter will focus on object programming with concrete types. We will assume some familiarity with the basic concepts of object-oriented programming, although you may notice that our discussion of objects deliberately deemphasizes techniques such as implementation inheritance. You will then be introduced to the notion of object interface types and some simple techniques to implement them. The chapter will cover more advanced techniques to implement objects using function parameters, delegation, and implementation inheritance. Finally, it will cover the related topics of modules (which are simple containers of functions and values) and extensions (in other words, how to add ad hoc dot-notation to existing modules and types). Chapter 7 will cover the topic of encapsulation.

This chapter deemphasizes the use of .NET terminology for object types. However, all F# types are ultimately compiled as .NET types.

Getting Started with Objects and Members

One of the most important activities of object programming is defining concrete types equipped with dot-notation. A concrete type has *fixed* behavior; that is, it uses the same member implementations for each concrete value of the type.

You've already met many important concrete types, such as integers, lists, strings, and records (introduced in Chapter 3). It's easy to add object members to concrete types. Listing 6-1 shows an example.

Listing 6-1. A Vector2D record type with object members

```
/// Two-dimensional vectors
type Vector2D =
    { DX : float; DY : float }

    /// Get the length of the vector
    member v.Length = sqrt(v.DX * v.DX + v.DY * v.DY)

    /// Return a vector scaled by the given factor
    member v.Scale k = { DX = k * v.DX; DY = k * v.DY }
```

```
/// Return a vector shifted by the given delta in the X coordinate
member v.ShiftX x = { v with DX = v.DX + x }

/// Return a vector shifted by the given delta in the Y coordinate
member v.ShiftY y = { v with DY = v.DY + y }

/// Return a vector shifted by the given distance in both coordinates
member v.ShiftXY (x,y) = { DX = v.DX + x; DY = v.DY + y }

/// Get the zero vector
static member Zero = { DX = 0.0; DY = 0.0 }

/// Return a constant vector along the X axis
static member ConstX dx = { DX = dx; DY = 0.0 }

/// Return a constant vector along the Y axis
static member ConstY dy = { DX = 0.0; DY = dy }
```

You can use the properties and methods of this type as follows:

```
> let v = { DX = 3.0; DY=4.0 };;

val v : Vector2D = {DX = 3.0; DY = 4.0;}

> v.Length;;

val it : float = 5.0

> v.Scale(2.0).Length;;

val it : float = 10.0

> Vector2D.ConstX(3.0);;

val it : Vector2D = {DX = 3.0; DY = 0.0}
```

As usual, it's useful to look at inferred types to understand a type definition. Here are the inferred types for the Vector2D type definition of Listing 6-1:

```
type Vector2D =
  {DX: float;
   DY: float;}
  member Scale : k:float -> Vector2D
  member ShiftX : x:float -> Vector2D
  member ShiftXY : x:float * y:float -> Vector2D
  member ShiftY : y:float -> Vector2D
  member Length : float
  static member ConstX : dx:float -> Vector2D
  static member ConstY : dy:float -> Vector2D
  static member Zero : Vector2D
```

You can see that the Vector2D type contains the following:

- A collection of record fields
- One instance property (Length)
- Four instance methods (Scale, ShiftX, ShiftY, ShiftXY)
- One static property (Zero)
- Two static methods (ConstX, ConstY)

Let's look at the implementation of the Length property:

```
member v.Length = sqrt(v.DX * v.DX + v.DY * v.DY)
```

Here, the identifier v stands for the Vector2D value on which the property is being defined. In many other languages, this is called this or self, but in F# you can name this parameter as you see fit. The implementation of a property such as Length is executed each time the property is invoked; in other words, properties are syntactic sugar for method calls. For example, let's repeat the earlier type definition with an additional property that adds a side effect:

```
member v.LengthWithSideEffect =
    printfn "Computing!"
    sqrt(v.DX * v.DX + v.DY * v.DY)
```

Each time you use this property, you see the side effect:

```
> let x = {DX = 3.0; DY = 4.0};;

val x : Vector2D = {DX = 3.0; DY = 4.0;}

> x.LengthWithSideEffect;;

Computing!
val it : float = 5.0

> x.LengthWithSideEffect;;

Computing!

val it : float = 5.0
```

The method members for a type look similar to the properties but also take arguments. For example, let's look at the implementation of the ShiftX method member:

```
member v.ShiftX(x) = { v with DX = v.DX + x }
```

Here the object is v, and the argument is dx. The return result clones the input record value and adjusts the DX field to be v.DX+dx. Cloning records is described in Chapter 3. The ShiftXY method member takes two arguments:

```
member v.ShiftXY(x, y) = { DX = v.DX + x; DY = v.DY + y }
```

Like functions, method members can take arguments in either tupled or iterated "curried" form. For example, you could define ShiftXY as follows:

```
member v.ShiftXY x y = { DX = v.DX + x; DY = v.DY + y }
```

However, it's conventional for methods to take their arguments in tupled form. This is partly because OO programming is strongly associated with the design patterns and guidelines of the .NET framework, and arguments for methods defined in other .NET languages always appear as tupled when using them from F#.

Discriminated unions are also a form of concrete type. In this case, the shape of the data associated with a value is drawn from a finite, fixed set of choices. Discriminated unions can also be given members. For example:

```
/// A type of binary tree, generic in the type of values carried at nodes
type Tree<'T> =
    | Node of 'T * Tree<'T> * Tree<'T>
    | Tip

    /// Compute the number of values in the tree
    member t.Size =
        match t with
        | Node(_, l, r) -> 1 + l.Size + r.Size
        | Tip -> 0
```

SHOULD YOU USE MEMBERS OR FUNCTIONS?

F# lets you define both members associated with types and objects via the dot-notation and static functions that can perform essentially the same operations. For example, the length of a string s can be computed by both the s.Length property and the String.length function. Given the choice, which should you use in your code? Although there is no fixed answer to this, here are some general rules:

- Use members (methods and properties) where they already exist, unless you have other good reasons not to do so. It's better to use s.Length than String.length, simply because it's shorter, even if it occasionally requires using an additional type annotation. That is, embrace dot-notation, even though it may require type annotations, but use it tastefully.

- When designing a framework or library, define members for the intrinsic, essential properties and operations associated with a type.

- When designing a framework or library, define additional functionality in new modules or by using extension members. The section "Extending Existing Types and Modules" later in this chapter covers extension members.

Sometimes there is duplication in functionality between dot-notation members and values in associated modules. This is intended and should be accepted as part of the mixed OO/functional nature of F#.

Using Classes

Record and union types are symmetric; the values used to *construct* an object are the same as those *stored* in the object, which are a subset of those *published* by the object. This symmetry makes record and union types succinct and clear, and it helps give them other properties; for example, the F# compiler automatically derives generic equality, comparison, and hashing routines for these types.

However, more advanced object programming often needs to break these symmetries. For example, let's say you want to precompute and store the length of a vector in each vector value. It's clear you don't want everyone who creates a vector to have to perform this computation for you. Instead, you precompute the length as part of the construction sequence for the type. You can't do this using a record, except by using a helper function, so it's convenient to switch to a more general notation for *class types*. Listing 6-2 shows the Vector2D example using a class type.

Listing 6-2. A Vector2D type with length precomputation via a class type

```
type Vector2D(dx : float, dy : float) =

    let len = sqrt(dx * dx + dy * dy)

    /// Get the X component of the vector
    member v.DX = dx

    /// Get the Y component of the vector
    member v.DY = dy

    /// Get the length of the vector
    member v.Length = len

    /// Return a vector scaled by the given factor
    member v.Scale(k) = Vector2D(k * dx, k * dy)

    /// Return a vector shifted by the given delta in the Y coordinate
    member v.ShiftX(x) = Vector2D(dx = dx + x, dy = dy)

    /// Return a vector shifted by the given delta in the Y coordinate
    member v.ShiftY(y) = Vector2D(dx = dx, dy = dy + y)

    /// Return a vector that is shifted by the given deltas in each coordinate
    member v.ShiftXY(x, y) = Vector2D(dx = dx + x, dy = dy + y)

    /// Get the zero vector
    static member Zero = Vector2D(dx = 0.0, dy = 0.0)

    /// Get a constant vector along the X axis of length one
    static member OneX = Vector2D(dx = 1.0, dy = 0.0)

    /// Get a constant vector along the Y axis of length one
    static member OneY = Vector2D(dx = 0.0, dy = 1.0)
```

You can now use this type as follows:

```
> let v = Vector2D(3.0, 4.0);;

val v : Vector2D

> v.Length;;

val it : float = 5.0

> v.Scale(2.0).Length;;

val it : float = 10.0
```

Once again, it's helpful to look at the inferred type signature for the Vector2D type definition of Listing 6-2:

```
type Vector2D =
    new : dx:float * dy:float -> Vector2D
    member Scale : k:float -> Vector2D
    member ShiftX : x:float -> Vector2D
    member ShiftXY : x:float * y:float -> Vector2D
    member ShiftY : y:float -> Vector2D
    member DX : float
    member DY : float
    member Length : float
    static member OneX : Vector2D
    static member OneY : Vector2D
    static member Zero : Vector2D
```

The signature of the type is almost the same as that for Listing 6-1. The primary difference is in the construction syntax. Let's look at what's going on here. The first line says you're defining a type Vector2D with a *primary constructor*. This is sometimes called an *implicit constructor*. The constructor takes two arguments, dx and dy. The variables dx and dy are in scope throughout the (nonstatic) members of the type definition.

The second line is part of the computation performed each time an object of this type is constructed:

```
let len = sqrt(dx * dx + dy * dy)
```

Like the input values, the len value is in scope throughout the rest of the (nonstatic) members of the type. The next three lines publish both the input values and the computed length as properties:

```
member v.DX = dx
member v.DY = dy
member v.Length = len
```

The remaining lines implement the same methods and static properties as the original record type. The Scale method creates its result by calling the constructor for the type using the expression Vector2D(k * dx, k * dy). In this expression, arguments are specified by position.

Class types with primary constructors always have the following form:

```
type TypeName <type-arguments>optional arguments [ as ident ] optional =
    [ inherit type [ as base ] optional ] optional
    [ let-binding | let-rec bindings ] zero-or-more
    [ do-statement ] zero-or-more
    [ abstract-binding | member-binding | interface-implementation ] zero-or-more
```

Later sections will cover inheritance, abstract bindings, and interface implementations.

The Vector2D in Listing 6-2 uses a construction sequence. Construction sequences can enforce object invariants. For example, the following defines a vector type that checks that its length is close to 1.0 and refuses to construct an instance of the value if not:

```
/// Vectors whose length is checked to be close to length one.
type UnitVector2D(dx,dy) =
    let tolerance = 0.000001

    let length = sqrt (dx * dx + dy * dy)
    do if abs (length - 1.0) >= tolerance then failwith "not a unit vector";

    member v.DX = dx

    member v.DY = dy

    new() = UnitVector2D (1.0,0.0)
```

This example shows something else: sometimes it's convenient for a class to have multiple constructors. You do this by adding extra *explicit constructors* using a member named new. These must ultimately construct an instance of the object via the primary constructor. The inferred signature for this type contains two constructors:

```
type UnitVector2D =
    new : unit -> UnitVector2D
    new : dx:float * dy:float -> UnitVector2D
    member DX : float
    member DY : float
```

This represents a form of method overloading, which will be covered in more detail in the "Adding Method Overloading" section later in this chapter.

Class types can also include static bindings. For example, this can be used to ensure only one vector object is allocated for the Zero and One properties of the vector type:

```
/// A class including some static bindings
type Vector2D(dx : float, dy : float) =

    static let zero = Vector2D(0.0, 0.0)
    static let onex = Vector2D(1.0, 0.0)
    static let oney = Vector2D(0.0, 1.0)

    /// Get the zero vector
    static member Zero = zero
```

```
/// Get a constant vector along the X axis of length one
static member OneX = onex

/// Get a constant vector along the Y axis of length one
static member OneY = oney
```

Static bindings in classes are initialized once, along with other module and static bindings in the file. If the class type is generic, it's initialized once per concrete type generic instantiation.

Adding Further Object Notation to Your Types

As we mentioned, one of the most useful aspects of object programming is the notational convenience of dot-notation. This extends to other kinds of notation, in particular expr.[expr] *indexer* notation, named arguments, optional arguments, operator overloading, and method overloading. The following sections cover how to define and use these notational conveniences.

Working with Indexer Properties

Like methods, properties can take arguments; these are called *indexer* properties. The most commonly defined indexer property is called Item, and the Item property on a value v is accessed via the special notation v.[i]. As the notation suggests, these properties are normally used to implement the lookup operation on collection types. The following example implements a sparse vector in terms of an underlying sorted dictionary:

```
open System.Collections.Generic

type SparseVector(items : seq<int * float>)=
    let elems = new SortedDictionary<_, _>()
    do items |> Seq.iter (fun (k, v) -> elems.Add(k, v))

    /// This defines an indexer property
    member t.Item
        with get(idx) =
            if elems.ContainsKey(idx) then elems.[idx]
            else 0.0
```

You can define and use the indexer property as follows:

```
> let v = SparseVector [(3, 547.0)];;

val v : SparseVector

> v.[4];;

val it : float = 0.0

> v.[3];;

val it : float = 547.0
```

You can also use indexer properties as mutable setter properties with the syntax expr.[expr] <- expr. This will be covered in the section "Defining Object Types with Mutable State." Indexer properties can also take multiple arguments; for example, the indexer property for the F# Power Pack type FSharp.Math.Matrix<'T> takes two arguments. Chapter 10 will describe this type.

Adding Overloaded Operators

Types can also include the definition of overloaded operators. Typically, you do this by defining static members with the same names as the relevant operators. Here is an example:

```
type Vector2DWithOperators(dx : float,dy : float) =
    member x.DX = dx
    member x.DY = dy

    static member (+) (v1 : Vector2DWithOperators, v2 : Vector2DWithOperators) =
        Vector2DWithOperators(v1.DX + v2.DX, v1.DY + v2.DY)

    static member (-) (v1 : Vector2DWithOperators, v2 : Vector2DWithOperators) =
        Vector2DWithOperators (v1.DX - v2.DX, v1.DY - v2.DY)
```

```
> let v1 = new Vector2DWithOperators (3.0, 4.0);;

val v1 : Vector2DWithOperators

> v1 + v1;;

val it : Vector2DWithOperators = {DX = 6.0; DY = 8.0;}

> v1 - v1;;

val it : Vector2DWithOperators = {DX = 6.0; DY = 8.0;}
```

If you add overloaded operators to your type, you may also have to customize how generic equality, hashing, and comparison are performed. In particular, the behavior of generic operators such as hash, <, >, <=, >=, compare, min, and max isn't specified by defining new static members with these names, but rather by the techniques that will be described in Chapter 9.

HOW DOES OPERATOR OVERLOADING WORK?

Operator overloading in F# works by having fixed functions that map uses of operators through to particular static members on the static types involved in the operation. These functions are usually defined in the F# library. For example, the F# library includes the following definition for the (+) operator:

```
let inline (+) x y = ((^a or ^b): (static member (+) : ^a * ^b -> ^c) (x, y))
```

This defines the infix function (+) and is implemented using a special kind of expression that says "implement x + y by calling a static member (+) on the type of the left or right operand." The function is marked inline to ensure that F# can always check for the existence of this member and call it efficiently. When you name a static member (+), then that is really shorthand for the name op_Addition, which is the .NET standard encoded name for addition operators.

You can define your own operators if you want, but they aren't automatically overloaded in the same way as F# library definitions like the one shown previously are. For example, the following defines a new infix operator that appends a single element to the end of a list:

```
let (++) x y = List.append x [y]
```

This operator isn't overloaded; it's a single fixed function. Defining non-overloaded operators can help make some implementation code more succinct, and you will use this technique in the symbolic programming examples in Chapter 12.

In principle, you can define new operators that are truly overloaded in the same way as the definition of (+) in the F# library, mapping the operator across to particular static members. However, code is generally much clearer if you stick to the standard overloaded operators.

Using Named and Optional Arguments

F# object programming constructs are designed largely for use in APIs for software components. Two useful mechanisms in APIs permit callers to name arguments and let API designers make certain arguments optional.

Named arguments are simple. For example, in Listing 6-2, the implementations of some methods specify arguments by name, as in the expression Vector2D(dx=dx+x, dy=dy). You can use named arguments with all dot-notation method calls. Code written using named arguments is often much more readable and maintainable than code relying on argument position. The rest of this book frequently uses named arguments.

You declare a member argument optional by prefixing the argument name with ?. Within a function implementation, an optional argument always has an option<_> type; for example, an optional argument of type int appears as a value of type option<int> within the function body. The value is None if no argument is supplied by the caller and Some(arg) if the argument arg is given by the caller. For example:

```
open System.Drawing

type LabelInfo(?text : string, ?font : Font) =
    let text = defaultArg text ""
    let font = match font with
                | None -> new Font(FontFamily.GenericSansSerif, 12.0f)
                | Some v -> v
    member x.Text = text
    member x.Font = font

    /// Define a static method that creates an instance
    static member Create(?text, ?font) = new LabelInfo(?text=text, ?font=font)
```

The inferred signature for this type shows the optional arguments:

```
type LabelInfo =
    new : ?text:string * ?font:System.Drawing.Font -> LabelInfo
    static member Create : ?text:string * ?font:System.Drawing.Font -> LabelInfo
    member Font : System.Drawing.Font
    member Text : string
```

You can now create `LabelInfo` values using several different techniques:

```
> LabelInfo (text="Hello World");;

val it : LabelInfo = LabelInfo  {Font = [Font: Name=Sans Serif, Size=12, ...];

> LabelInfo("Goodbye Lenin");;

val it : LabelInfo = LabelInfo {Font = [Font: Name= Sans Serif, Size=12 ...];

> LabelInfo(font = new Font(FontFamily.GenericMonospace, 36.0f),
            text = "Imagine");;

val it : LabelInfo =  LabelInfo  {Font = [Font: Name=Courier New, Size=36, ...];
```

Optional arguments must always appear last in the set of arguments accepted by a method. They're usually used as named arguments by callers. At the call site, this is done using the syntax *argument-name = argument-value*. If the argument has type *T option*, then *argument-value* must have type *T*.

In the example, you see the static member `Create`, which also takes optional arguments, the code for which is repeated here:

```
type LabelInfo ...  =
    ...

    /// Define a static method that creates an instance
    static member Create(?text, ?font) = new LabelInfo(?text = text, ?font = font)
```

This represents a common pattern when using optional arguments heavily within a framework implementation: one method taking optional arguments is defined in terms of another. The implementation of the `Create` method simply passes the optional arguments through to be optional arguments of the constructor. At the call site, this is done using the syntax *?argument-name = argument-value*. Note the extra question mark at the call site! If the argument has type *T option*, then *argument-value* must have type *T option* as well.

The implementation of `LabelInfo` uses the F# library function `defaultArg`, which is a useful way to specify simple default values for optional arguments. Its type is as follows:

```
val defaultArg : 'T option -> 'T-> 'T
```

■ **Note** The second argument given to the `defaultArg` function is evaluated *before* the function is called. This means you should take care that this argument isn't expensive to compute and doesn't need to be disposed of. The previous example uses a match expression to specify the default for the `font` argument for this reason.

Adding Method Overloading

.NET APIs and other object frameworks frequently use a notational device called *method overloading*. This means a type can support multiple methods with the same name, and various uses of methods are distinguished by name, number of arguments, and argument types. For example, the System.Console. WriteLine method of .NET has 19 overloads!

Method overloading is used relatively rarely in F#-authored classes, partly because optional arguments and mutable property setters tend to make it less necessary. However, method overloading is permitted in F#. First, methods can easily be overloaded by the number of arguments. For example, Listing 6-3 shows a concrete type representing an interval of numbers on the number line. It includes two methods called Span, one taking a pair of intervals and the other taking an arbitrary collection of intervals. The overloading is resolved according to argument count.

Listing 6-3. An Interval type with overloaded methods

```
/// Interval(lo,hi) represents the range of numbers from lo to hi,
/// but not including either lo or hi.
type Interval(lo, hi) =
    member r.Lo = lo
    member r.Hi = hi
    member r.IsEmpty = hi <= lo
    member r.Contains v = lo < v && v < hi

    static member Empty = Interval(0.0, 0.0)

    /// Return the smallest interval that covers both the intervals
    static member Span (r1 : Interval, r2 : Interval) =
        if r1.IsEmpty then r2 else
        if r2.IsEmpty then r1 else
        Interval(min r1.Lo r2.Lo, max r1.Hi r2.Hi)

    /// Return the smallest interval that covers all the intervals
    static member Span(ranges : seq<Interval>) =
        Seq.fold (fun r1 r2 -> Interval.Span(r1, r2)) Interval.Empty ranges
```

Second, multiple methods can also have the same number of arguments and be overloaded by type. One of the most common examples is providing multiple implementations of overloaded operators on the same type. The following example shows a Point type that supports two subtraction operations, one subtracting a Point from a Point to give a Vector and one subtracting a Vector from a Point to give a Point:

```
type Vector =
    { DX : float; DY : float }
    member v.Length = sqrt( v.DX * v.DX + v.DY * v.DY)

type Point =
    { X : float; Y : float }

    static member (-) (p1 : Point, p2 : Point) =
        { DX = p1.X - p2.X; DY = p1.Y - p2.Y }

    static member (-) (p : Point, v : Vector) =
        { X = p.X - v.DX; Y = p.Y - v.DY }
```

Overloads must be unique by signature, and you should take care to make sure your overload set isn't too ambiguous—the more overloads you use, the more type annotations users of your types will need to add.

Defining Object Types with Mutable State

All the types you've seen so far in this chapter have been immutable. For example, the values of the Vector2D types shown in Listing 6-1 and Listing 6-2 can't be modified after they're created. Sometimes you may need to define mutable objects, particularly because object programming is a generally useful technique for encapsulating a mutable and evolving state. Listing 6-4 shows the definition of a mutable representation of a 2D vector.

Listing 6-4. An Object Type with State

```
type MutableVector2D(dx : float, dy : float) =
    let mutable currDX = dx
    let mutable currDY = dy

    member vec.DX with get() = currDX and set v = currDX <- v
    member vec.DY with get() = currDY and set v = currDY <- v

    member vec.Length
        with get () = sqrt (currDX * currDX + currDY * currDY)
        and  set len =
            let theta = vec.Angle
            currDX <- cos theta * len
            currDY <- sin theta * len

    member vec.Angle
        with get () = atan2 currDY currDX
        and  set theta =
            let len = vec.Length
            currDX <- cos theta * len
            currDY <- sin theta * len
```

The mutable state is held in two mutable local let bindings for currDX and currDY. It also exposes additional settable properties, Length and Angle, which interpret and adjust the underlying currDX/currDY values. Here is the inferred signature for the type:

```
type MutableVector2D =
    new : dx:float * dy:float -> MutableVector2D
    member Angle : float with get, set
    member DX : float with get, set
    member DY : float with get, set
    member Length : float with get, set
```

You can use this type as follows:

```
> let v = MutableVector2D(3.0, 4.0);;

val v : MutableVector2D

> (v.DX, v.DY);;

val it : float * float = (3.0, 4.0)

> (v.Length, v.Angle);;

val it : float * float = (5.0, 0.927295218)

> v.Angle <- System.Math.PI / 6.0;;

> (v.DX, v.DY);;

val it : float * float = (4.330127019, 2.5)

> (v.Length, v.Angle);;

val it : float * float = (5.0, 0.523598775)
```

Adjusting the Angle property rotates the vector while maintaining its overall length. This example uses the long syntax for properties, where you specify both set and get operations for the property.

If the type has an indexer (Item) property, then you write an indexed setter as follows:

```
open System.Collections.Generic

type IntegerMatrix(rows : int, cols : int)=
    let elems = Array2D.zeroCreate<int> rows cols

    /// This defines an indexer property with getter and setter
    member t.Item
        with get (idx1, idx2) = elems.[idx1, idx2]
        and set (idx1, idx2) v = elems.[idx1, idx2] <- v
```

■ **Note**   Class types with a primary constructor are useful partly because they implicitly *encapsulate* internal functions and mutable state. This is because all the construction arguments and let bindings are private to the object instance being constructed. This is just one of the ways of encapsulating information in F# programming. Chapter 7 will cover encapsulation more closely.

OBJECTS AND MUTATION

Object programming was originally developed as a technique for controlling the complexity of mutable state. However, many of the concerns of object programming are orthogonal to this. For example, programming constructs such as object interface types, inheritance, and higher-level design patterns such as publish/subscribe stem from the OO tradition, whereas techniques such as functions, type abstraction, and aggregate operations such as map and fold stem from the functional programming tradition. Many object programming techniques have no fundamental relationship to object mutation and identity; for example, interfaces and inheritance can be used very effectively with immutable objects. Much of the expressivity of F# lies in the way it brings the techniques of object programming and functional programming comfortably together.

Using Optional Property Settings

Throughout this book, you've used a second technique to specify configuration parameters when creating objects: *initial property settings* for objects. For example, in Chapter 2, you used the following code:

```
open System.Windows.Forms

let form = new Form(Visible = true, TopMost = true, Text = "Welcome to F#")
```

The constructor for the System.Windows.Forms.Form class takes no arguments, so in this case the named arguments indicate set operations for the given properties. The code is shorthand for this:

```
open System.Windows.Forms

let form -
    let tmp = new Form()
    tmp.Visible <- true
    tmp.TopMost <- true
    tmp.Text <- "Welcome to F#"
    tmp
```

The F# compiler interprets unused named arguments as calls that set properties of the returned object. This technique is widely used for mutable objects that evolve over time, such as graphical components, because it greatly reduces the number of optional arguments that need to be plumbed around.

Here's how to define a version of the LabelInfo type used earlier that is configurable by optional property settings:

```
open System.Drawing

type LabelInfoWithPropertySetting() =
    let mutable text = "" // the default
    let mutable font = new Font(FontFamily.GenericSansSerif, 12.0f)
    member x.Text with get() = text and set v = text <- v
    member x.Font with get() = font and set v = font <- v
```

```
let labelInfo = LabelInfoWithPropertySetting(Text="Hello World")

let form = new Form(Visible = true, TopMost = true, Text = "Welcome to F#")
```

The "Defining Object Types with Mutable State" section later in this chapter will cover mutable objects in more detail.

Declaring Auto-Properties

When declaring properties, especially settable ones, a common pattern occurs where the property storage is defined, the initial value for the property is specified, and the member to allow external access to the property is defined. This has a more convenient syntactic declaration form called an auto-property. An auto-property declaration has the form member val id = expr followed by an optional with get, set if the property storage is mutable and a property setter should be exported. An example is shown here, defining the same type as previously:

```
type LabelInfoWithPropertySetting() =
    member val Name = "label"
    member val Text = "" with get, set
    member val Font = new Font(FontFamily.GenericSansSerif, 12.0f) with get, set
```

Note that the initializer for an auto-property is executed once per object, when the object is initialized. Auto-properties can also be static.

Getting Started with Object Interface Types

So far in this chapter, you've seen only how to define *concrete* object types. One of the key advances in both functional and object-oriented programming has been the move toward using *abstract* types for large portions of modern software. These values are typically accessed via *interfaces*, and we will now look at defining new *object interface types*.

The notion of an object interface type can sound a little daunting at first, but the concept is actually simple; object interface types are ones whose member implementations can vary from value to value. As it happens, you've already met one important family of types whose implementations also vary from value to value: F# function types!

- In Chapter 3, you saw how functions can be used to model a range of concepts such as comparison functions, aggregation functions, and transformation functions.

- In Chapter 5, you saw how records of function values can be used for the parameters needed to make an algorithm generic.

You've also already met some other important object interface types, such as System.Collections.Generic.IEnumerable<'T> and System.IDisposable. .NET object interface types always begin with the letter I by convention.

Definitions of object interface types do not specify the implementation of objects. Listing 6-5 shows an object interface type IShape and a number of implementations of it. This section walks through the definitions in this code piece by piece, because they illustrate the key concepts behind object interface types and how they can be implemented.

Listing 6-5. An object interface type IShape and some implementations

```
open System.Drawing

type IShape =
    abstract Contains : Point -> bool
    abstract BoundingBox : Rectangle

let circle (center : Point, radius : int) =
    { new IShape with

        member x.Contains(p : Point) =
            let dx = float32 (p.X - center.X)
            let dy = float32 (p.Y - center.Y)
            sqrt(dx * dx + dy * dy) <= float32 radius

        member x.BoundingBox =
            Rectangle(
                center.X - radius, center.Y - radius,
                2 * radius + 1, 2 * radius + 1)}

let square (center : Point, side : int) =
    { new IShape with

        member x.Contains(p : Point) =
            let dx = p.X - center.X
            let dy = p.Y - center.Y
            abs(dx) < side / 2 && abs(dy) < side / 2

        member x.BoundingBox =
            Rectangle(center.X - side, center.Y - side, side * 2, side * 2)}

type MutableCircle() =

    member val Center = Point(x = 0, y = 0) with get, set
    member val Radius = 10 with get, set

    member c.Perimeter = 2.0 * System.Math.PI * float c.Radius

    interface IShape with

        member c.Contains(p : Point) =
            let dx = float32 (p.X - c.Center.X)
            let dy = float32 (p.Y - c.Center.Y)
            sqrt(dx * dx + dy * dy) <= float32 c.Radius

        member c.BoundingBox =
            Rectangle(
                c.Center.X - c.Radius, c.Center.Y - c.Radius,
                2 * c.Radius + 1, 2 * c.Radius + 1)
```

Defining New Object Interface Types

The key definition in Listing 6-5 is the following (it also uses `Rectangle` and `Point`, two types from the `System.Drawing` namespace):

```
open System.Drawing

type IShape =
    abstract Contains : Point -> bool
    abstract BoundingBox : Rectangle
```

Here you use the keyword `abstract` to define the member signatures for this type, indicating that the implementation of the member may vary from value to value. Also note that IShape isn't concrete; it's neither a record nor a discriminated union or class type. It doesn't have any constructors and doesn't accept any arguments. This is how F# infers that it's an object interface type.

Implementing Object Interface Types Using Object Expressions

The following code from Listing 6-5 implements the object interface type IShape using an *object expression*:

```
let circle(center : Point, radius : int) =
    { new IShape with

        member x.Contains(p : Point) =
            let dx = float32 (p.X - center.X)
            let dy = float32 (p.Y - center.Y)
            sqrt(dx * dx + dy * dy) <= float32 radius

        member x.BoundingBox =
            Rectangle(
                center.X - radius, center.Y - radius,
                2 * radius + 1, 2 * radius + 1)}
```

The type of the function `circle` is as follows:

```
val circle : center:Point * radius:int -> IShape
```

The construct in the braces, `{ new IShape with ... }`, is the object expression. This is a new expression form that you haven't encountered previously in this book, because it's generally used only when implementing object interface types. An object expression must give implementations for all the members of an object interface type. The general form of this kind of expression is simple:

```
{ new Type optional-arguments with
      member-definitions
  optional-extra-interface-definitions }
```

The member definitions take the same form as members for type definitions described earlier in this chapter. The optional arguments are given only when object expressions inherit from a class type, and the optional interface definitions are used when implementing additional interfaces that are part of a hierarchy of object interface types.

You can use the function `circle` as follows:

```
> let bigCircle = circle(Point(0, 0), 100);;
val bigCircle : IShape

> bigCircle.BoundingBox;;
val it : Rectangle = {X=-100,Y=-100,Width=201,Height=201}

> bigCircle.Contains(Point(70, 70));;
val it : bool = true

> bigCircle.Contains(Point(71, 71));;
val it : bool = false
```

Listing 6-5 also contains another function `square` that gives a different implementation for `IShape`, also using an object expression:

```
> let smallSquare = square(Point(1, 1), 1);;
val smallSquare : IShape

> smallSquare.BoundingBox;;
val it : Rectangle = {X=0,Y=0,Width=2,Height=2}

> smallSquare.Contains(Point(0,0));;
val it : bool = false
```

■ **Note** In object-oriented languages, implementing types in multiple ways is commonly called *polymorphism*, which you may call *polymorphism of implementation*. Polymorphism of this kind is present throughout F#, and not just with respect to the object constructs. In functional programming, the word *polymorphism* is used to mean generic type parameters. These are an orthogonal concept discussed in Chapters 2 and 5.

Implementing Object Interface Types Using Concrete Types

It's common to have concrete types that both implement one or more object interface types and provide additional services of their own. Collections are a primary example, because they always implement IEnumerable<'T>. To give another example, in Listing 6-5 the type MutableCircle is defined as follows:

```
type MutableCircle() =
    let radius = 0
    member val Center = Point(x = 0, y = 0) with get, set
    member val Radius = radius with get, set
    member c.Perimeter = 2.0 * System.Math.PI * float radius

    interface IShape with
        member c.Contains(p : Point) =
            let dx = float32 (p.X - c.Center.X)
            let dy = float32 (p.Y - c.Center.Y)
            sqrt(dx * dx + dy * dy) <= float32 c.Radius

        member c.BoundingBox =
            Rectangle(
                c.Center.X - c.Radius, c.Center.Y - c.Radius,
                2 * c.Radius + 1, 2 * c.Radius + 1)
```

This type implements the IShape interface, which means MutableCircle is a subtype of IShape, but it also provides three properties—Center, Radius, and Perimeter—that are specific to the MutableCircle type, two of which are settable. The type has the following signature:

```
type MutableCircle =
    interface IShape
    new : unit -> MutableCircle
    member Perimeter : float
    member Center : Point with get,set
    member Radius : int with get,set
```

You can now reveal the interface (through a type cast) and use its members. For example:

```
> let circle2 = MutableCircle();;

val circle2 : MutableCircle

> circle2.Radius;;

val it : int = 10

> (circle2 :> IShape).BoundingBox;;

val it : Rectangle = {X=-10,Y=-10,Width=21,Height=21}
```

Using Common Object Interface Types from the .NET Libraries

Like other constructs discussed in this chapter, object interface types are often encountered when using .NET libraries. Some object interface types such as IEnumerable<'T> (called seq<'T> in F# coding) are also used throughout F# programming. It's a .NET convention to prefix the name of all object interface types with I. However, using object interface types is very common in F# object programming, and this convention doesn't have to be followed.

Here's the essence of the definition of the System.Collections.Generic.IEnumerable<'T> type and the related type IEnumerator using F# notation:

```
type IEnumerator<'T> =
    abstract Current : 'T
    abstract MoveNext : unit -> bool

type IEnumerable<'T> =
    abstract GetEnumerator : unit -> IEnumerator<'T>
```

The IEnumerable<'T> type is implemented by most concrete collection types. It can also be implemented by a sequence expression or by calling a library function such as Seq.unfold, which in turn uses an object expression as part of its implementation.

■ **Note** The IEnumerator<'T> and IEnumerable<'T> interfaces are defined in a library component that is implemented using another .NET language. This section uses the corresponding F# syntax. In reality, IEnumerator<'T> also inherits from the nongeneric interfaces System.Collections.IEnumerator and System.IDisposable, and IEnumerable<'T> also inherits from the nongeneric interface System. Collections.IEnumerable. For clarity, we've ignored this. See the F# library documentation for full example implementations of these types.

Some other useful predefined F# and .NET object interface types are as follows:

- System.IDisposable: Represents values that may own explicitly reclaimable resources.

- System.IComparable and System.IComparable<'T>: Represent values that can be compared to other values. F# generic comparison is implemented via these types, as you will see in Chapter 9.

- FSharp.Control.IEvent: Represents mutable ports into which you can plug event listeners, or *callbacks*. This technique will be described in Chapter 11. Some other entity is typically responsible for raising the event and thus calling all the listener callbacks. In F#, .NET events become values of this type or the related type FSharp.Control.IDelegateEvent, and the module FSharp.Control.Event contains many useful functions for manipulating these values. You can open this module by using open Event.

Understanding Hierarchies of Object Interface Types

Object interface types can be arranged in hierarchies using *interface inheritance*. This provides a way to classify types. To create a hierarchy, you use the inherit keyword in an object interface type definition along with each parent object interface type. For example, the .NET framework includes a hierarchical classification of collection types: ICollection<'T> extends IEnumerable<'T>. Here are the essential definitions of these types in F# syntax, with some minor details omitted:

```
type IEnumerable<'T> =
    abstract GetEnumerator : unit -> IEnumerator<'T>

type ICollection<'T> =
    inherit IEnumerable<'T>
    abstract Count : int
    abstract IsReadOnly : bool
    abstract Add : 'T -> unit
    abstract Clear : unit -> unit
    abstract Contains : 'T -> bool
    abstract CopyTo : 'T [] * int -> unit
    abstract Remove : 'T -> unit
```

When you implement an interface that inherits from another interface, you must effectively implement both interfaces.

■ **Caution**   Although hierarchical modeling is useful, you must use it with care: poorly designed hierarchies often have to be abandoned late in the software development life cycle, leading to major disruptions. For many applications, it's adequate to use existing classification hierarchies in conjunction with some new nonhierarchical interface types.

More Techniques for Implementing Objects

Objects can be difficult to implement from scratch; for example, a graphical user interface (GUI) component must respond to many different events, often in regular and predictable ways, and it would be tedious to have to recode all this behavior for each component. This makes it essential to support the process of creating partial implementations of objects, where the *partial implementations* can then be completed or customized. The following sections cover techniques for building partial implementations of objects.

Combining Object Expressions and Function Parameters

One of the easiest ways to build a partial implementation of an object is to qualify the implementation of the object by a number of function parameters that complete the implementation. For example, the following code defines an object interface type called ITextOutputSink, a partial implementation of that type called simpleOutputSink, and a function called simpleOutputSink that acts as a partial implementation of that type. The remainder of the implementation is provided by a function parameter called writeCharFunction:

```
/// An object interface type that consumes characters and strings
type ITextOutputSink =
```

```
/// When implemented, writes one Unicode character to the sink
abstract WriteChar : char -> unit

/// When implemented, writes one Unicode string to the sink
abstract WriteString : string -> unit
```

```
/// Returns an object that implements ITextOutputSink by using writeCharFunction
let simpleOutputSink writeCharFunction =
    { new ITextOutputSink with
        member x.WriteChar(c) = writeCharFunction c
        member x.WriteString(s) = s |> String.iter x.WriteChar }
```

This construction function uses function values to build an object of a given shape. Here the inferred type is as follows:

```
val simpleOutputSink : writeCharFunction:(char -> unit) -> ITextOutputSink
```

The following code instantiates the function parameter to output the characters to a particular System. Text.StringBuilder object, an imperative type for accumulating characters in a buffer before converting these to an immutable System.String value:

```
let stringBuilderOuputSink (buf : System.Text.StringBuilder ) =
    simpleOutputSink (fun c -> buf.Append(c) |> ignore)
```

Here is an example that uses this function interactively:

```
> open System.Text;;

> let buf = new SringBuilder();;

val buf : StringBuilder =

> let c = stringBuilderOuputSink(buf);;

val c : ITextOutputSink

> ["Incy"; " "; "Wincy"; " "; "Spider"] |> List.iter c.WriteString;;

> buf.ToString();;

val it : string = "Incy Wincy Spider"
```

Object expressions must give definitions for all unimplemented abstract members and can't add other members.

One powerful technique implements some or all abstract members in terms of function parameters. As you saw in Chapter 3, function parameters can represent a wide range of concepts. For example, here is type CountingOutputSink that performs the same role as the earlier function simpleOutputSink, except that the number of characters written to the sink is recorded and published as a property:

```
/// A type that fully implements the ITextOutputSink object interface
type CountingOutputSink(writeCharFunction : char -> unit) =

    let mutable count = 0

    interface ITextOutputSink with
        member x.WriteChar(c) = count <- count + 1; writeCharFunction(c)
        member x.WriteString(s) = s |> String.iter (x :> ITextOutputSink).WriteChar

    member x.Count = count
```

■ **Note**   Qualifying object implementations by function parameters can be seen as a simple form of the OO design pattern known as *delegation*, because parts of the implementation are delegated to the function values. Delegation is a powerful and compositional technique for reusing fragments of implementations and is commonly used in F# as a replacement for OO implementation inheritance.

Defining Partially Implemented Class Types

In this chapter, you've seen how to define concrete types, such as Vector2D in Listings 6-2 and 6-3, and you've seen how to define object interface types, such as IShape in Listing 6-5. Sometimes it's useful to define types that are halfway between these types: *partially concrete types*. Partially implemented types are class types that also have abstract members, some of which may be unimplemented and some of which may have default implementations. For example, consider the following class:

```
/// A type whose members are partially implemented
[<AbstractClass>]
type TextOutputSink() =
    abstract WriteChar : char -> unit
    abstract WriteString : string -> unit
    default x.WriteString s = s |> String.iter x.WriteChar
```

This class defines two abstract members, WriteChar and WriteString, but gives a default implementation for WriteString in terms of WriteChar. (In C# terminology, WriteString is virtual and WriteChar is abstract). Because WriteChar isn't yet implemented, you can't create an instance of this type directly; unlike other concrete types, partially implemented types still need to be implemented. One way to do this is to complete the implementation via an object expression. For example:

```
{ new TextOutputSink() with
    member x.WriteChar c = System.Console.Write(c)}
```

Using Partially Implemented Types via Delegation

This section covers how you can use partially implemented types to build complete objects. One approach is to instantiate one or more partially implemented types in order to put together a complete concrete type. This is often done via delegation to an instantiation of the partially concrete type; for example, the following example creates a private, internal TextOutputSink object whose implementation of WriteChar counts the number of characters written through that object. You use this object to build the HtmlWriter object, which publishes three methods specific to the process of writing a particular format:

```
/// A type which uses a TextOutputSink internally
type HtmlWriter() =
    let mutable count = 0
    let sink =
        { new TextOutputSink() with
            member x.WriteChar c =
                count <- count + 1;
                System.Console.Write c }

    member x.CharCount = count
    member x.OpenTag(tagName) = sink.WriteString(sprintf "<%s>" tagName)
    member x.CloseTag(tagName) = sink.WriteString(sprintf "</%s>" tagName)
    member x.WriteString(s) = sink.WriteString(s)
```

Using Partially Implemented Types via Implementation Inheritance

Another technique that uses partially implemented types is called *implementation inheritance*, which is widely used in OO languages despite being a somewhat awkward technique. Implementation inheritance tends to be much less significant in F# because it comes with major drawbacks:

- Implementation inheritance takes base objects and makes a new type that is more complex by adding new members. This is against the spirit of functional programming, where the aim is to build simple, composable abstractions. Functional programming, object expressions, and delegation tend to provide good alternative techniques for defining, sharing, and combining implementation fragments.

- Implementation hierarchies tend to leak across API boundaries, revealing how objects are implemented rather than how they can be used and composed.

- Implementation hierarchies are often fragile in response to minor changes in program specification. There is pressure on developers to put too much functionality in base classes, anticipating the needs of all derivations. There's also pressure to go back and change the base class as new needs arise. This gives rise to the "fragile base class" problem, a major curse of object-oriented programming.

If implementation inheritance is used, you should in many cases consider making all implementing classes private or hiding all implementing classes behind a signature. For example, the FSharp.Collections.Seq module provides many implementations of the seq<'T> interface but exposes no implementation inheritance.

Nevertheless, hierarchies of classes are important in domains such as GUI programming, and the technique is used heavily by .NET libraries written in other .NET languages. For example, System.Windows.Forms.Control, System.Windows.Forms.UserControl and System.Windows.Forms.RichTextBox are part of a hierarchy of visual GUI elements. Should you want to write new controls, you must understand this implementation hierarchy and how to extend it. However, even in this domain, implementation inheritance is often less important than you may think, because these controls can often be configured in powerful and interesting ways by adding function callbacks to events associated with the controls.

Here is a simple example of applying the technique to instantiate and extend the partially implemented type TextOutputSink:

```
/// An implementation of TextOutputSink, counting the number of bytes written
type CountingOutputSinkByInheritance() =
    inherit TextOutputSink()

    let mutable count = 0

    member sink.Count = count

    default sink.WriteChar c =
        count <- count + 1
        System.Console.Write c
```

The keywords override and default can be used interchangeably; both indicate that an implementation is being given for an abstract member. By convention, override is used when giving implementations for abstract members in inherited types that already have implementations, and default is used for implementations of abstract members that didn't previously have implementations.

Implementations are also free to override and modify default implementations such as the implementation of WriteString provided by TextOutputSink. Here is an example:

```
{ new TextOutputSink() with
    member sink.WriteChar c = System.Console.Write c
    member sink.WriteString s = System.Console.Write s }
```

You can also build new partially implemented types by extending existing partially implemented types. The following example takes the TextOutputSink type from the previous section and adds two abstract members called WriteByte and WriteBytes, adds a default implementation for WriteBytes, adds an initial implementation for WriteChar, and overrides the implementation of WriteString to use WriteBytes. The implementations of WriteChar and WriteString use .NET functionality to convert the Unicode characters and strings to bytes under System.Text.UTF8Encoding, documented in the .NET framework class libraries:

```
open System.Text

/// A component to write bytes to an output sink
[<AbstractClass>]
type ByteOutputSink() =
    inherit TextOutputSink()

    /// When implemented, writes one byte to the sink
    abstract WriteByte : byte -> unit
```

```
/// When implemented, writes multiple bytes to the sink
abstract WriteBytes : byte[] -> unit

default sink.WriteChar c = sink.WriteBytes(Encoding.UTF8.GetBytes [|c|])

override sink.WriteString s = sink.WriteBytes(Encoding.UTF8.GetBytes s)

default sink.WriteBytes b = b |> Array.iter sink.WriteByte
```

Combining Functional and Objects: Cleaning Up Resources

Many constructs in the System.IO namespace need to be closed after use, partly because they hold on to operating system resources such as file handles. This is an example of how objects are used to encapsulate and manage resource lifetime. In polished code, you use language constructs such as use *val* = *expr* to ensure that the resource is closed at the end of the lexical scope where a stream object is active. For example:

```
let myWriteStringToFile() =
    use outp = File.CreateText("playlist.txt")
    outp.WriteLine("Enchanted")
    outp.WriteLine("Put your records on")
```

This is equivalent to the following:

```
let myWriteStringToFile () =
    let outp = File.CreateText("playlist.txt")
    try
        outp.WriteLine("Enchanted")
        outp.WriteLine("Put your records on")
    finally
        (outp :> System.IDisposable).Dispose()
```

Both forms ensure that the underlying stream is closed deterministically and the operating system resources are reclaimed when the lexical scope is exited. The longer form uses the :> operator to call Dispose, which was explained further in Chapter 5. This happens regardless of whether the scope is exited because of normal termination or because of an exception.

■ **Note** If you don't use a use binding, or otherwise explicitly close the stream, the stream is closed when the stream object is finalized by the .NET garbage collector. It's generally bad practice to rely on finalization to clean up resources this way, because finalization isn't guaranteed to happen in a deterministic, timely fashion.

Resources and IDisposable

All programming involves the use of real resources on the host machine(s) and operating system. For example:

- *Stack:* Implicitly allocated and deallocated as functions are called

- *Heap allocated memory:* Used by all reference-typed objects

- *File handles:* Such as operating system file handles represented by System.IO.FileStream objects and its subtypes

- *Network connections:* Such as operating system I/O completion ports represented by System.Net.WebResponse and its subtypes

- *Threads:* Such as operating system threads represented by System.Threading.Thread objects and also worker threads in the .NET thread pool

- *Graphics objects:* Such as drawing objects represented by various constructs under the System.Drawing namespace

- *Concurrency objects:* Such as operating system synchronization objects represented by System.Threading.WaitHandle objects and its subtypes

All resources are necessarily finite. In .NET programming, some resources such as memory are fully *managed*, in the sense that you almost never need to consider when to clean up memory. This is done automatically through a process called *garbage collection*. Chapter 18 will look at garbage collection in more detail. Other resources must be *reclaimed* and/or *recycled*.

When prototyping, you can generally assume that resources are unbounded, although it's good practice when you're using a resource to be aware of how much of the resource you're using and roughly what your budget for the resource is. For example:

- On a modern 32-bit desktop machine, 10,000 tuple values occupy only a small fragment of a machine's memory, roughly 160 KB, but 10,000 open file handles is an extreme number and will stress the operating system. Ten thousand simultaneous web requests may stress your network administrator.

- In some cases, even memory should be explicitly and carefully reclaimed. For example, on a modern 64-bit machine, the largest single array you can allocate in a .NET 2.0 program is 2 GB. If your machine has, say, 4 GB of real memory, you may be able to have only a handful of these objects and should strongly consider moving to a regime in which you explicitly recycle these objects and think carefully before allocating them.

With the exception of stack and memory, all objects that own resources should be subtypes of the .NET type System.IDisposable. This is the primary way you can recognize primitive resources and objects that wrap resources. The System.IDisposable interface has a single method; in F# syntax, it can be defined as:

```
namespace System
    type IDisposable =
        abstract Dispose : unit -> unit
```

A simple approach to managing IDisposable objects is to give each resource a *lifetime*; that is, some well-defined portion of the program execution for which the object is active. This is even easier when the lifetime of a resource is lexically scoped, such as when a resource is allocated on entry to a function and deallocated on exit. In this case, the resource can be tied to the scope of a particular variable, and you can protect and dispose of a value that implements IDisposable by using a use binding instead of a let binding. For example, in the following code, three values implement IDisposable, all of which are bound using use:

```
/// Fetch a web page
let http (url : string) =
    let req = System.Net.WebRequest.Create url
    use resp = req.GetResponse()
    use stream = resp.GetResponseStream()
    use reader = new System.IO.StreamReader(stream)
    let html = reader.ReadToEnd()
    html
```

This is an improved version of the similar function you defined in Chapter 2, because it deterministically closes the network connections. In all three cases, the objects (a WebResponse, a Stream, and a StreamReader) are automatically closed and disposed of at the end of an execution of the function.

A number of important types implement IDisposable; Table 6-1 shows some of them. You can use tables such as this to chart the portions of the .NET framework that reveal operating system functionality to .NET applications.

Table 6-1. A Selection of the Types that Implement IDisposable

Namespace	Some Types Implementing IDisposable
System.IO	BinaryReader, BinaryWriter, FileSystemWatcher, IsolatedFileStorage, Stream, TextReader, TextWriter, ...
System.Net	WebResponse, ...
System.Net.Sockets	Socket, TcpClient, ...
System.Data.SqlClient	SqlBulkCopy, SqlCommand, SqlConnection, SqlTransaction, ...
System.Threading	Timer, WaitHandle, AutoResetEvent, ManualResetEvent, Mutex, Semaphore, ...

■ **Tip** IDEs can help you determine when a type has implemented IDisposable. When you rest your mouse pointer over a value, you usually see this noted on the information displayed for a value.

WHEN WILL THE RUNTIME CLEAN UP FOR YOU?

People often ask if the .NET Common Language Runtime automatically cleans up resources such as file handles the same way it cleans up memory. While when an object gets garbage collected, it may be *finalized*, if the object is well implemented, this results in it deallocating any unmanaged resources, closing any outstanding file connections, and releasing any operating system resources. Although it's appropriate to rely on finalization when prototyping, never rely on finalization in code where you're hitting resource limits.

For example, let's say you have a loop where you open files using System.IO.File.OpenRead. If you forget to close the file handles, you may quickly allocate thousands of them. If you're lucky, the garbage collector may finalize these before you run out of OS resources, but if not, one of your File.OpenRead calls will fail with an exception, even if the file exists on disk.

Also, be aware of the potential for memory stickiness. This occurs when the .NET Common Language Runtime is unable to garbage-collect memory even though objects have become unreachable. This happens especially when long-running computations and inactive callbacks hold on to object handles related to the earlier phases of execution of a program. Memory stickiness can also lead to objects never being finalized, reinforcing that you shouldn't rely on finalization to release nonmemory resources. Memory profiling tools such as CLRProfiler are indispensable when you're tracking down memory leaks in production code or long-running applications.

Managing Resources with More-Complex Lifetimes

Sometimes, the lifetime of a resource isn't simple in the sense that it doesn't follow a stack discipline. In these cases, you should almost always adopt one of two techniques:

- Design objects that can own one or more resources and that are responsible for cleaning them up. Make sure that these objects implement System.IDisposable.

- Use control constructs that help you capture the kind of computation you're performing. For example, when generating sequences of data (such as from a database connection), you should strongly consider using sequence expressions, as discussed in Chapter 3. These may have internal use bindings, and the resources are disposed of when each sequence iteration finishes. Likewise, when using asynchronous I/O, it may be helpful to write your computation as an asynchronous workflow. Chapter 11 and the following sections will provide examples.

Consider implementing the IDisposable interface on objects and types in situations such as:

- When you build an object that uses one or more IDisposable objects internally.

- When you're writing a wrapper for an operating system resource or some resource allocated and managed in a native (C or C++) DLL. In this case, implement a finalizer by overriding the Object.Finalize method.

- When you implement the System.Collections.Generic.IEnumerable<'T> (that is, sequence) interface on a collection. The IEnumerable interface isn't IDisposable, but it must generate System.Collection.Generic.IEnumerator<'T> values, and this interface inherits from IDisposable. For nearly all collection types, the disposal action returns without doing anything.

The following sections give some examples of these.

Cleaning Up Internal Objects

Listing 6-6 shows an example that implements an object that reads lines from a pair of text files, choosing the file at random at each line pull. You must implement the type IDisposable, because the object owns two internal System.IO.StreamReader objects, which are IDisposable. You also must explicitly check to see whether the object has already been disposed of.

Listing 6-6. Implementing IDisposable to clean up internal objects

```
open System.IO

type LineChooser(fileName1, fileName2) =
    let file1 = File.OpenText(fileName1)
    let file2 = File.OpenText(fileName2)
    let rnd = new System.Random()

    let mutable disposed = false

    let cleanup() =
        if not disposed then
            disposed <- true;
            file1.Dispose();
            file2.Dispose();
```

```
interface System.IDisposable with
    member x.Dispose() = cleanup()

member obj.CloseAll() = cleanup()

member obj.GetLine() =
    if not file1.EndOfStream &&
        (file2.EndOfStream  || rnd.Next() % 2 = 0) then file1.ReadLine()
    elif not file2.EndOfStream then file2.ReadLine()
    else raise (new EndOfStreamException())
```

You can now instantiate, use, and dispose of this object as follows:

```
> open System;;

> open System.IO;;

> File.WriteAllLines("test1.txt", [|"Daisy, Daisy"; "Give me your hand oh do"|]);;

> File.WriteAllLines("test2.txt", [|"I'm a little teapot"; "Short and stout"|]);;

> let chooser = new LineChooser ("test1.txt", "test2.txt");;

val chooser : LineChooser

> chooser.GetLine();;

val it : string = "Daisy, Daisy"

> chooser.GetLine();;

val it : string = "I'm a little teapot"

> (chooser :> IDisposable).Dispose();;

> chooser.GetLine();;

Error: System.ObjectDisposedException: Cannot read from a closed TextReader.
```

Disposal should leave an object in an unusable state, as shown in the last line of the previous example. It's also common for objects to implement a member with a more intuitive name that does precisely the same thing as its implementation of IDisposable.Dispose, which is CloseAll in Listing 6-6.

Cleaning Up Unmanaged Objects

If you're writing a component that explicitly wraps some kind of unmanaged resource, then implementing IDisposable is a little trickier. Listing 6-7 shows the pattern that is used for this type of cleanup. Here, you mimic an external resource via a data structure that generates fresh, reclaimable integer tickets. The idea is that each customer is given an integer ticket, but this is kept internal to the customer, and customers return their tickets to the pool when they leave (that is, are disposed of).

Listing 6-7. Reclaiming unmanaged tickets with IDisposable

```
open System

type TicketGenerator() =
    let mutable free = []
    let mutable max = 0

    member h.Alloc() =
        match free with
        | [] -> max <- max + 1; max
        | h :: t -> free <- t; h

    member h.Dealloc(n:int) =
        printfn "returning ticket %d" n
        free <- n :: free

let ticketGenerator = new TicketGenerator()

type Customer() =
    let myTicket = ticketGenerator.Alloc()
    let mutable disposed = false
    let cleanup() =
        if not disposed then
            disposed <- true
            ticketGenerator.Dealloc(myTicket)

    member x.Ticket = myTicket

    override x.Finalize() = cleanup()

    interface IDisposable with
        member x.Dispose() = cleanup(); GC.SuppressFinalize(x)
```

Note that you override the Object.Finalize method. This makes sure cleanup occurs if the object isn't disposed of but is still garbage-collected. If the object is explicitly disposed of, you call GC.SuppressFinalize() to ensure that the object isn't later finalized. The finalizer shouldn't call the Dispose() of other managed objects, because they have their own finalizers if needed. The following example session generates some customers, and tickets used by some of the customers are automatically reclaimed as they exit their scopes:

```
> let bill = new Customer();;

val bill : Customer

> bill.Ticket;;

val it : int = 1

> (use joe = new Customer() in printfn "joe.Ticket = %d" joe.Ticket);;
```

```
joe.Ticket = 2
returning ticket 2

> (use jane = new Customer() in printfn "jane.Ticket = %d" jane.Ticket);;

jane.Ticket = 2

returning ticket 2
```

In the example, Joe and Jane get the same ticket. Joe's ticket is returned at the end of the scope where the joe variable is declared as a result of the IDisposable cleanup implicit in the use binding.

Extending Existing Types and Modules

The final topic covered in this chapter is how you can define ad hoc dot-notation extensions to existing library types and modules. This technique is used less commonly than the others in this chapter but can be invaluable in certain circumstances. For example, the following definition adds the member IsPrime to Int32.

```
module NumberTheoryExtensions =

    let factorize i =
        let lim = int (sqrt (float i))
        let rec check j =
            if j > lim  then None
            elif (i % j) = 0 then Some (i / j, j)
            else check (j + 1)
        check 2

    type System.Int32 with
        member i.IsPrime = (factorize i).IsNone
        member i.TryFactorize() = factorize i
```

The IsPrime extension property and the TryFactorize extension method are then available for use in conjunction with int32 values whenever the NumberTheoryExtensions module has been opened. For example:

```
> open NumberTheoryExtensions;;

> (2 + 1).IsPrime;;

val it : bool = true

> (6093704 + 11).TryFactorize();;

val it : (int * int) option = Some (1218743, 5)
```

These type extensions are called *F#-style extension members*. Since F# 3.1, an additional kind of extension member is supported called a *C#-style extension member*. These can be declared in other .NET languages and then accessed by opening a namespace. They can also be declared in F# code. C#-style extension members can only be instance methods; i.e., they can't be static and can't be properties.

```
module CSharpStyleExtensions =

    open System.Runtime.CompilerServices

    let factorize i =
        let lim = int (sqrt (float i))
        let rec check j =
            if j > lim  then None
            elif (i %  j) = 0 then Some (i / j, j)
            else check (j + 1)
        check 2

    [<Extension>]
    type Int32Extensions() =
        [<Extension>]
        static member IsPrime2(i:int) = (factorize i).IsNone

        [<Extension>]
        static member TryFactorize2(i:int) = factorize i

    [<Extension>]
    type ResizeArrayExtensions() =
        [<Extension>]
        static member Product(values:ResizeArray<int>) =
            let mutable total = 1
            for v in values do
                total <- total * v
            total

        [<Extension>]
        static member inline GenericProduct(values:ResizeArray<'T>) =
            let mutable total = LanguagePrimitives.GenericOne<'T>
            for v in values do
                total <- total * v
            total
```

C# -style extension members are *declared* as an (attributed) static method in an (attributed) class. The method takes an extra "this" argument. C# -style extension members are *used* as an instance method taking one fewer parameters. At the usage site they must minimally take at least "zero" arguments through a () parameter. For example:

```
> open CSharpStyleExtensions ;;

> (2 + 1).IsPrime2();;

val it : bool = true

> (6093704 + 11).TryFactorize2();;

val it : (int * int) option = Some (1218743, 5)
```

Despite the limitations of C#-style extension members, they have an important advantage that is useful for some F# API designs: *for generic types, C#-style extension methods can constrain the generic type parameters to either a particular instantiation or some other generic constraint.* For example, in the code just reviewed, the Product method constrains the type of the input ResizeArray to be int. Likewise, GenericProduct constrains the ResizeArray to be a type 'T, which support zero and multiplication (see Chapter 5 for more discussion on generic constraints). Normal F# extensions can't operate on constrained types like this, which sometimes makes a mix of F# and C# extensions useful when designing "Fluent" APIs. For example, see the F# community library **FSharp.Core.Fluent** on GitHub, which uses exactly such a mix.

```
> open System.Collections.Generic;;

> let arr = ResizeArray([ 1 .. 10 ]);;

val arr = ResizeArray<int>

> let arr2 = ResizeArray([ 1L .. 10L ]);;

val arr2 = ResizeArray<int64>

> arr.Product();;
val it : int = 3628800

> arr.GenericProduct();;

val it : int = 3628800

> arr2.GenericProduct();;

val it : int64 = 3628800L
```

Type extensions can be given in any assembly, but priority is always given to the intrinsic members of a type when resolving dot-notation.

Modules can also be extended, in a fashion. For example, say you think the List module is missing an obvious function such as List.pairwise to return a new list of adjacent pairs. You can extend the set of values accessed by the path List by defining a new module List:

```
module List =
    let rec pairwise l =
        match l with
        | [] | [_] -> []
        | h1 :: ((h2 :: _) as t) -> (h1, h2) :: pairwise t
```

```
> List.pairwise [1; 2; 3; 4];;

val it : (int * int) list = [(1,2); (2,3); (3,4)]
```

■ **Note** Type extensions are a good technique for equipping simple type definitions with extra functionality. However, don't fall into the trap of adding too much functionality to an existing type via this route. Instead, it's often simpler to use additional modules and types. For example, the module `FSharp.Collections.List` contains extra functionality associated with the F# `list` type.

USING MODULES AND TYPES TO ORGANIZE CODE

You often have to choose whether to use modules or object types to organize your code. Here are some of the rules for using these to organize your code effectively and to lay the groundwork for applying good .NET library and framework design principles to your code:

- Use modules when prototyping and to organize scripts, ad hoc algorithms, initialization code, and active patterns.

- Use concrete types (records, discriminated unions, and class types) to implement concrete data structures. In the long term, plan on completely hiding the implementation of these types. You will see how to do this in Chapter 7. You can provide dot-notation operations to help users to access parts of the data structure. Avoid revealing other representation details.

- Use object interface types for types that have several possible implementations.

- Implement object interface types by private concrete types or by object expressions.

- In polished libraries, most concrete types exposed in an implementation should also implement one or more object interface types. For example, collections should implement `IEnumerable<'T>`, and many types should implement `IDisposable`.

- Avoid relying on or revealing complex type hierarchies. In particular, avoid relying on implementation inheritance, except as an internal implementation technique or when doing GUI programming or authoring very large objects.

- Avoid nesting modules or types inside other modules or types, especially in public APIs. Nested modules and types are useful implementation details, but they're rarely made public in APIs. Deep hierarchical organization can be confusing; when you're designing a library, you should place nearly all public modules and types immediately inside a well-named namespace.

Working with F# Objects and .NET Types

This chapter has deemphasized the use of .NET terminology for object types, such as class and interface. However, all F# types are ultimately compiled as .NET types. Here is how they relate:

- Concrete types such as record types, discriminated unions, and class types are compiled as .NET classes.

- Object interface types are by default compiled as .NET interface types.

If you want, you can delimit class types using class/end:

```
type Vector2D(dx : float, dy : float) =
    class
        let len = sqrt(dx * dx + dy * dy)
        member v.DX = dx
        member v.DY = dy
        member v.Length = len
    end
```

Or you can use a Class attribute:

```
[<Class>]
type Vector2D(dx : float, dy : float) =
    let len = sqrt(dx * dx + dy * dy)
    member v.DX = dx
    member v.DY = dy
    member v.Length = len
```

You see this in F# code samples on the Internet and in other books. However, we have found that this tends to make types harder to understand, so we've omitted class/end and Class attributes throughout this book. You can also delimit object interface types by interface/end:

```
type IShape =
    interface
        abstract Contains : Point -> bool
        abstract BoundingBox : Rectangle
    end
```

Or you can use an attribute:

```
[<Interface>]
type IShape =
    abstract Contains : Point -> bool
    abstract BoundingBox : Rectangle
```

Again, we omit these attributes in this book.

Structs

It's occasionally useful to direct the F# compiler to use a .NET struct (value type) representation for small, generally immutable objects. You can do this by adding a Struct attribute to a class type and adding type annotations to all arguments of the primary constructor:

```
[<Struct>]
type Vector2DStruct(dx : float, dy : float) =
    member v.DX = dx
    member v.DY = dy
    member v.Length = sqrt (dx * dx + dy * dy)
```

Finally, you can also use a form that makes the values held in a struct explicit:

```
[<Struct>]
type Vector2DStructUsingExplicitVals =
    val dx : float
    val dy : float
    member v.DX = v.dx
    member v.DY = v.dy
    member v.Length = sqrt (v.dx * v.dx + v.dy * v.dy)
```

Structs are often more efficient, but you should use them with care because the full contents of struct values are frequently copied. The performance characteristics of structs can also change depending on whether you're running on a 32-bit or 64-bit machine.

Delegates

Occasionally, you need to define a new .NET delegate type in F#:

```
type ControlEventHandler = delegate of int -> bool
```

This is usually required only when using C code from F#, because some magic performed by the .NET Common Language Runtime lets you marshal a delegate value as a C function pointer. Chapter 18 will look at interoperating with C and COM. For example, here's how you add a new handler to the Win32 Ctrl+C–handling API:

```
open System.Runtime.InteropServices

let ctrlSignal = ref false

[<DllImport("kernel32.dll")>]
extern void SetConsoleCtrlHandler(ControlEventHandler callback, bool add)

let ctrlEventHandler = new ControlEventHandler(fun i ->  ctrlSignal := true; true)

SetConsoleCtrlHandler(ctrlEventHandler,true)
```

Enums

Occasionally, you need to define a new .NET enum type in F#. You do this using a notation similar to that for discriminated unions:

```
type Vowels =
    | A = 1
    | E = 5
    | I = 9
    | O = 15
    | U = 21
```

This type is compiled as a .NET enum whose underlying bit representation is a simple integer. Likewise, you can define enums for other .NET primitive types, such as byte, int64, and uint64.

Working with null Values

The keyword null is used in programming languages as a special, distinguished value of a type that represents an uninitialized value or some other kind of special condition. In general, null isn't used in conjunction with types defined in F# code, although it's common to simulate null with a value of the option type. For example:

```
> let parents = [("Adam", None); ("Cain", Some("Adam", "Eve"))];;

val parents : (string * (string * string) option) list = ...
```

Reference types defined in other .NET languages do support null, however; when using .NET APIs, you may have to explicitly pass null values to the API and also, where appropriate, test return values for null. The .NET framework documentation specifies when null may be returned from an API. It's recommended that you test for this condition using null value tests. For example:

```
match System.Environment.GetEnvironmentVariable("PATH") with
| null -> printf "the environment variable PATH is not defined\n"
| res -> printf "the environment variable PATH is set to %s\n" res
```

The following is a function that incorporates a pattern match with type tests and a null-value test:

```
let switchOnType (a : obj) =
    match a with
    | null -> printf "null!"
    | :? System.Exception as e -> printf "An exception: %s!" e.Message
    | :? System.Int32 as I -> printf "An integer: %d!" i
    | :? System.DateTime as d -> printf "A date/time: %O!" d
    | _ -> printf "Some other kind of object\n"
```

There are other important sources of null values. For example, the semi-safe function Array.zeroCreate creates an array whose values are initially null or, in the case of value types, an array in which each entry is the zero-bit pattern. This function is included with F# primarily because there is no other technique for initializing and creating the array values used as building blocks of larger, more sophisticated data structures, such as queues and hash tables. Of course, you must use this function with care, and in general you should hide the array behind an encapsulation boundary and be sure the values of the array aren't referenced before they're initialized.

■ **Note** Although F# generally enables you to code in a null-free style, F# isn't totally immune to the potential existence of null values: they can come from the .NET APIs, and it's also possible to use Array. zeroCreate and other back-door techniques to generate null values for F# types. If necessary, APIs can check for this condition by first converting F# values to the obj type by calling box and then testing for null (see the F# Informal Language Specification for full details). In practice, this isn't required by the vast majority of F# programs; for most purposes, the existence of null values can be ignored.

Summary

This chapter looked at the basic constructs of object-oriented programming in F#, including concrete object types, object notation, and object interface types and their implementations, as well as more advanced techniques to implement object interface types. You also saw how implementation inheritance is less important as an object implementation technique in F# than in other object-oriented languages, and then learned how the F# object model relates to the .NET object model. The next chapter will cover language constructs and practical techniques related to encapsulating, packaging, and deploying your code.

CHAPTER 7

Encapsulating and Organizing Your Code

Organizing code and making it available for people and programs to use is a key part of best using F#. In this book, you've already seen many of the constructs to help you do this: functions, objects, type definitions, modules, namespaces, and assemblies. In some cases, however, you've encountered these only peripherally when using the libraries that come with F#. This chapter will cover these constructs from the perspective of code organization and encapsulation.

Organizing code can involve four distinct activities:

- *Organizing* code into sensible entities using namespaces, types, and modules.

- *Encapsulating* internal data structures and implementation details by making them private.

- *Assembling* code and data as one component, which for F# is called an *assembly*. An assembly is code that is packaged together with supporting resources as a single, logical unit of deployment.

- *Deploying* one or more assemblies—for example, as a Web application or using a Web-based community packaging mechanism, such as NuGET.

The first two of these topics are associated with the F# language, and the last is more associated with the pragmatics of deploying, installing, configuring, and maintaining software. The third lies in between, because a .NET assembly can act as both a unit of encapsulation and a unit of deployment. In Chapter 19, we will also consider some of the different kinds of software you can write with F# and how you can organize and package your code for these different cases.

Hiding Things

In all kinds of software, it's common to hide implementation details of data structures and algorithms behind *encapsulation boundaries*. Encapsulation is a fundamental technique when writing software and is possibly the most important idea associated with object-oriented programming.

For this book's purposes, *encapsulation* means hiding implementation details behind well-defined boundaries. This lets you enforce consistency properties and makes the structure of a program easier to manage. It also lets an implementation evolve over time. A good rule of thumb is to hide anything you don't want used directly by client code.

Later, this chapter will explain how encapsulation applies when you're building assemblies, frameworks, and applications. In the extreme, you may even be ensuring that your code is *secure* when used in partial-trust mode—in other words, that it can't be inadvertently or deliberately used to achieve malicious results when used as a library by code that doesn't have full permissions. The most important kind of encapsulation, however, is the day-to-day business of hiding the internal implementation details of functions, objects, types, and modules. The primary techniques used to do this are

- local definitions,

- accessibility annotations, and

- explicit signatures.

We will cover the first two of these techniques next, and we will cover explicit signatures in "Hiding Things with Signatures" later in this chapter.

Hiding Things with Local Definitions

The easiest way to hide definitions is to make them local to expressions or constructed class definitions using inner let bindings. These aren't directly accessible from outside their scope. This technique is frequently used to hide state and other computed values inside the implementations of functions and objects. Let's begin with a simple example. Here is the definition of a function that incorporates a single item of encapsulated state:

```
let generateTicket =
    let mutable count = 0
    (fun () -> count <- count + 1; count)
```

If you examine this definition, you will see that the generateTicket function isn't defined immediately as a function; instead, it first declares a local element of state called *count* and then returns a function value that refers to this state. This function value has type unit -> int, and each time it is called, count is incremented, but the ability to mutate the value directly is never published outside the function implementation, and it is thus encapsulated.

Encapsulation through local definitions is a particularly powerful technique in F# when used in conjunction with object expressions. For example, Listing 7-1 shows the definition of an object interface type called IPeekPoke and a function that implements objects of this type using an object expression.

Listing 7-1. Implementing objects with encapsulated state

```
type IPeekPoke =
    abstract member Peek : unit -> int
    abstract member Poke : int -> unit

let makeCounter initialState =
    let mutable state = initialState
    {new IPeekPoke with
        member x.Poke n = state <- state + n
        member x.Peek() = state}
```

The type of the function Counter is:

```
val makeCounter : initialState:int -> IPeekPoke
```

As with the earlier generateTicket function, the internal state for each object generated by the makeCounter function is hidden and is accessible only via the published Peek and Poke methods.

The previous examples showed how to combine let bindings with anonymous functions and object expressions. You saw in Chapter 6 how let bindings can also be used in object types. For example, Listing 7-2 shows a constructed class type with private mutable state count that publishes two methods: Next and Reset.

Listing 7-2. A type for objects with encapsulated state

```
type TicketGenerator() =
    // Note: let bindings in a type definition are implicitly private to the object
    // being constructed. Members are implicitly public.
    let mutable count = 0

    member x.Next() =
        count <- count + 1;
        count

    member x.Reset () =
        count <- 0
```

The variable count is implicitly private to the object being constructed and is hence hidden from outside consumers. By default, member definitions are public, which means they're accessible throughout their scope.

Frequently, more than one item of state is hidden behind an encapsulation boundary. For example, the following code shows a function makeAverager that uses an object expression and two local elements of state, count and total, to implement an instance of the object interface type IStatistic, as shown in Listing 7-3.

Listing 7-3. Implementing an object interface type with encapsulated state

```
type IStatistic<'T,'U> =
    abstract Record : 'T -> unit
    abstract Value : 'U

let makeAverager(toFloat : 'T -> float) =

    let mutable count = 0
    let mutable total = 0.0

    { new IStatistic<'T, float> with

        member __.Record(x) =
            count <- count + 1
            total <- total + toFloat x

        member __.Value =
            total / float count }
```

The code in Listing 7-3 uses the convention that the "self" (or "this") parameter is given the name "__" if it is not used in the code. The inferred types here are:

```
type IStatistic<'T,'U> =
    abstract member Record : 'T -> unit
    abstract member Value : 'U

val makeAverager  : toFloat:('T -> float) -> IStatistic<'T,float>
```

The internal state is held in values count and total and is, once again, encapsulated.

■ **Note**   Most of the examples of encapsulation in this chapter show ways to hide *mutable state* behind encapsulation boundaries. Encapsulation can be just as important for immutable constructs, however, especially in larger software components. For example, the implementation of the immutable System.DateTime type in the .NET BCL hides the way the date and time are stored internally but reveals the information via properties.

Hiding Things with Accessibility Annotations

Local definitions are good for hiding most implementation details. Sometimes, however, you may need definitions that are local to a type, a module, or an assembly. You can change the default accessibility of an item by using an *accessibility annotation* to restrict the code locations that can use a construct. These indicate what is private or partially private to a module, file, or assembly. The primary accessibility annotations are private, internal, and public:

- *private* makes a construct private to the enclosing type definition/module.
- *internal* makes a construct private to the enclosing assembly (DLL or EXE).
- *public* makes a construct available globally, which is the default for most constructs.

As of F# 4.0, F# does not support declaring methods with the *protected* accessibility annotation found in many object-oriented programming languages. This is because this modifier encourages overuse of implementation inheritance and inhibits common refectorings of code. Some of the reasons to avoid overuse of implementation inheritance were explained in Chapter 6.

Accessibility annotations are placed immediately prior to the name of the construct. Listing 7-4 shows how to protect an internal table of data in a module using accessibility annotations.

Listing 7-4. Protecting a table using accessibility annotations

```
open System

module public VisitorCredentials =

    /// The internal table of permitted visitors and the
    /// days they are allowed to visit.
    let private  visitorTable =
        dict [("Anna", set [DayOfWeek.Tuesday; DayOfWeek.Wednesday]);
              ("Carolyn", set [DayOfWeek.Friday])]
```

```
/// This is the function to check if a person is a permitted visitor.
/// Note: this is public and can be used by external code.
let public checkVisitor(person) =
    visitorTable.ContainsKey(person) &&
    visitorTable.[person].Contains(DateTime.Today.DayOfWeek)

/// This is the function to return all known permitted visitors.
/// Note: this is internal and can be used only by code in this assembly.
let internal allKnownVisitors() =
    visitorTable.Keys
```

The private table is visitorTable. Attempting to access this value from another module gives a type-checking error. The function checkVisitor is marked public and is thus available globally. The function allKnownVisitors is available only within the same assembly (or the same F# Interactive session) as the definition of the VisitorCredentials module. Note that you could drop the public annotations from function checkVisitor and module VisitorCredentials, because these declarations are public by default.

Accessibility annotations are often used to hide state or handles to resources such as files. In Listing 7-5, you protect a single reference cell containing a value that alternates between Tick and Tock. This example uses an internal *event*, a technique that will be covered in more detail in Chapter 11.

Listing 7-5. Protecting internal state using accessibility annotations

```
module public GlobalClock =

    type TickTock = Tick | Tock

    let mutable private clock = Tick

    let private tick = new Event<TickTock>()

    let internal oneTick() =
        (clock <- match clock with Tick -> Tock | Tock -> Tick)
        tick.Trigger (clock)

    let tickEvent = tick.Publish

module internal TickTockDriver =

    open System.Threading

    let timer = new Timer(callback = (fun _ -> GlobalClock.oneTick()),
                          state = null, dueTime = 0, period = 100)
```

In Listing 7-5, the private state is clock. The assembly-internal module TickTockDriver uses the System.Threading.Timer class to drive the alternation of the state via the internal function oneTick. The GlobalClock module publishes one IEvent value, tickEvent, which any client can use to add handlers to listen for the event. The sample uses the Event type, which will be covered in more detail in Chapter 11.

Another assembly can now contain the following code, which adds a handler to TickEvent:

```
module TickTockListener =
   GlobalClock.tickEvent.Add(function
      | GlobalClock.Tick -> printfn "tick!"
      | GlobalClock.Tock -> printfn "tock!")
```

This prints a sequence of tick/tock lines—you can stop these by resetting the F# Interactive session. You can add accessibility annotations in a number of places in F# code:

- On let and extern definitions in modules, and in individual identifiers in patterns
- On new(...) object-constructor definitions
- On member definitions associated with types
- On module definitions
- On type definitions associated with types
- On primary constructors, such as type C private (...) = ...

■ **Note** You can add accessibility annotations to type abbreviations. The abbreviation, however, is still just an abbreviation—only the name, and not the actual equivalence, is hidden. That is, if you define a type abbreviation such as type private label = int, then all users of the type label know that it's really just an abbreviation for int and not a distinct type definition of its own. This is because .NET provides no way to hide type abbreviations; the F# compiler expands type abbreviations in the underlying generated .NET IL code.

Listing 7-6 shows a type in which some methods and properties are labeled public, but the methods that mutate the underlying collection (Add and the set method associated with the Item property) are labeled internal.

Listing 7-6. Making property setters internal to a type definition

```
open System.Collections.Generic

type public SparseVector () =

    let elems = new SortedDictionary<int, float>()

    member internal vec.Add (k, v) = elems.Add(k ,v)

    member public vec.Count = elems.Keys.Count

    member vec.Item
        with public get i =
            if elems.ContainsKey(i) then elems.[i]
            else 0.0
        and internal set i v =
            elems.[i] <- v
```

■ **Note**   In class types, `let` bindings in types are always private to the object being constructed, and all `member` bindings default to public—they have the same accessibility as the type definition. This is a useful default, because it corresponds to the common situation in which internal implementation details are fully private and published constructs are available widely, and because omitting accessibility annotations makes code more readable in the common case.

Organizing Code with Namespaces and Modules

The most important organizational technique for large-scale software is giving sensible qualified names to your types and values. A qualified name is, for example, `FSharp.Collections.List` (for the F# list type) or `System.IO.StreamReader` (for one of the types in the .NET framework BCL). Qualified names are particularly important when you're writing frameworks to be used by other people, and they are also a useful way to organize your own code.

You give types and functions qualified names by placing them in namespaces, modules, and type definitions. Table 7-1 shows these three kinds of containers and what they can contain. For completeness, the table also includes type abbreviations, which are slightly different because you can't use them as a container for other constructs.

Table 7-1. *Namespaces, Modules, Types, and What They Can Contain*

Entity	Description	Examples
Namespace	A namespace can contain further namespaces, modules, and types. Multiple DLLs can contribute to the same namespace.	`System, FSharp`
Module	A module can contain nested modules, types, and values.	`FSharp.Collections.Map, FSharp.Collections.List`
Concrete type definition	A type definition can contain members and nested type definitions.	`System.String, System.Int32`
Type abbreviation	A type abbreviation such as `string`, for `System.String`, can't act as a container for additional members, values, or types.	`int, string`

Putting Your Code in a Module

One way to group items together with a common qualified name is to use a *module*. A module is a simple container for values, type definitions, and submodules. For example, here is the `Vector2D` example rewritten to use a module to hold the operations associated with the type:

```
type Vector2D =
    {DX : float; DY : float}

module Vector2DOps =
    let length v = sqrt (v.DX * v.DX + v.DY * v.DY)
    let scale k v = {DX = k * v.DX; DY = k * v.DY}
    let shiftX x v = {v with DX = v.DX + x}
```

```
let shiftY y v = {v with DY = v.DY + y}
let shiftXY (x, y) v = {DX = v.DX + x; DY = v.DY + y}
let zero = {DX = 0.0; DY = 0.0}
let constX dx = {DX = dx; DY = 0.0}
let constY dy = {DX = 0.0; DY = dy}
```

Some people prefer to use classes with static members for this purpose, although modules tend to be more convenient for rapid prototyping. Modules may also contain type and submodule definitions.

Putting Your Modules and Types in Namespaces

When designing a library, it is usually better to place your code in a *namespace*, which can contain only types and modules. Think of this as a restricted form of module, because it is forbidden to use let bindings outside of module or type definitions. Using namespaces forces you to adopt design- and code-organization patterns that are familiar to other F#, C#, and .NET programmers.

For example, Listing 7-7 shows a file that contains two type definitions, both located in the namespace Acme.Widgets.

Listing 7-7. A file containing two type definitions in a namespace

```
namespace Acme.Widgets

type Wheel = Square | Round | Triangle

type Widget = {id : int; wheels : Wheel list; size : string}
```

Most significantly, namespaces are *open*, which means multiple source files and assemblies can contribute to the same namespace. For example, another implementation file or assembly can contain the definitions shown in Listing 7-8.

Listing 7-8. A file containing two type definitions in two mamespaces

```
namespace Acme.Widgets

type Lever = PlasticLever | WoodenLever

namespace Acme.Suppliers

type LeverSupplier = {name : string; leverKind : Acme.Widgets.Lever}
```

The file in Listing 7-8 contributes to two namespaces: Acme.Widgets and Acme.Suppliers. The two files can occur in the same assembly or in different assemblies. Either way, when you reference the assembly (or assemblies), the namespace Acme.Widgets appears to have at least three type definitions (perhaps more, if other assemblies contribute further type definitions), and the namespace Acme.Suppliers has at least one.

You can nest namespaces simply by declaring one namespace with a path that is a suffix of another, e.g., namespace Acme and namespace Acme.Suppliers.

Defining a Module with the Same Name as a Type

Sometimes it is useful to have a module with the same name as one of your types. You can do this by adding a special attribute to your code:

```
type Vector2D =
    { DX : float; DY : float }

[<CompilationRepresentation(CompilationRepresentationFlags.ModuleSuffix)>]
module Vector2D =
    let length v = sqrt(v.DX * v.DX + v.DY * v.DY)
```

This has the effect of adding a Module suffix to the name of the module in the compiled version of your code. If you inspect the compiled version of the Vector2D module, you will see that the name Vector2DModule is used.

Preventing Client Code from Opening a Module

Values in a module can be used via a long path, such as Vector2D.length. Alternatively, you can open the module, which makes all the contents accessible without qualification. For example, open Vector2D makes the identifier length available without qualification.

Modules, however, are often designed in such a way that client code should not normally "open" the module, because doing so will create too many ambiguities among various function and value names. Allowing clients to open your modules may make client code more brittle as you add new functions to your modules. For this reason, you can add an attribute RequireQualifiedAccess, indicating that qualified access to the module or type is required:

```
[<RequireQualifiedAccess>]
module Vector2D =
    let length v = sqrt(v.DX * v.DX + v.DY * v.DY)
    let zero = {DX=0.0; DY=0.0}
```

The following code then gives an error:

```
> open Vector2D;;
```

error FS0892: This declaration opens the module 'FSI_0003.Vector2D', which is marked as 'RequireQualifiedAccess'. Adjust your code to use qualified references to the elements of the module instead, e.g. 'List.map' instead of 'map'. This change will ensure that your code is robust as new constructs are added to libraries.

Using Files as Modules

In F#, a module is a simple container for values and type definitions. Modules also are often used to provide outer structure for fragments of F# code; many of the simple F# programs you've seen so far in this book have been in modules without your knowing about them. In particular:

- Code fragments typed into F# Interactive and delimited by ;; (or sent from an IDE using a keystroke like Alt-Enter) are each implicitly placed in a module of their own. These modules are implicitly opened.

- Files compiled with the command-line compiler using Visual Studio or loaded into F# Interactive with #load have their values and types placed in a namespace or module according to the leading module or namespace declaration in the file. Declarations in files without a leading module or namespace declaration are placed in a module whose name is derived from the name of the implementation file.

Let's look at the second case in more detail. You can explicitly declare the name of the namespace/module for a file by using a leading module declaration. For example, Listing 7-9 defines the module Acme.Widgets.WidgetWheels, regardless of the name of the file containing the constructs.

Listing 7-9. An implementation module with an explicit initial module declaration

```
module Acme.Widgets.WidgetWheels

type Wheel = Square | Triangle | Round

let wheelCornerCount =
    dict [(Wheel.Square, 4)
          (Wheel.Triangle, 3)
          (Wheel.Round, 0)]
```

Here, the first line gives the name for the module defined by the file. The namespace is Acme.Widgets, the module name is WidgetWheels, and the full path to the value is Acme.Widgets.WidgetWheels.wheelCornerCount. An explicit initial module declaration does require "=" at the end of the declaration.

Automatically Opening Modules

Modules can be labeled AutoOpen, meaning they're treated as opened whenever the enclosing namespace or module is opened. This can be useful when you're defining ad hoc top-level operators and functions:

```
namespace Acme.Compenents

[<AutoOpen>]
module private Utilities =
    let swap (x,y) = (y,x)

// Note, the module is not explicitly opened, but 'swap' is accessible throughout the file
swap (3,4)
```

This mechanism can also be useful when designing libraries and frameworks, especially for modules holding extension members and utility functions. For example:

```
namespace Acme.NumberTheory

[<AutoOpen>]
module NumberTheoryExtensions =
    let private isPrime i =
        let lim = int (sqrt (float i))
        let rec check j =
            j > lim || (i % j <> 0 && check (j+1))
        check 2

    type System.Int32 with
        member i.IsPrime = isPrime i
```

In this example, the IsPrime extension property is automatically available as soon as the path Acme. NumberTheory is opened. There is then no need to open the specific extension module directly—you can simply open the enclosing namespace.

You can also attach an AutoOpen attribute to a compiled assembly with a string path. This means the path is opened as soon as the assembly is referenced, in the order in which the assemblies are given to the F# command- line compiler or F# Interactive:

```
[<assembly:AutoOpen("Acme.NumberTheory")>]
do()
```

The path can be to a namespace or to a module. This last mechanism should be used rarely and diligently. It is most useful when writing a framework that configures F# as a scripting environment for a specific programming domain, because referencing an assembly can then automatically add various modules, types, functions, and extension members into the environment of the consuming code, without requiring "open" declarations in client code.

Projects, Assemblies, and Compilation Order

Once your software starts to become larger, it will start to contain multiple files. These are normally organized into a *project*, which, when compiled, produces an *assembly*.

Creating Assemblies, DLLs, and EXEs

F# Interactive is excellent when you're exploring a set of libraries and writing scripts or small applications that use them. But to understand how to write libraries and organize other kinds of applications, you need to learn how to use the F# command-line compiler, fsc.exe, to compile your code into DLLs and EXEs. A dynamic link library (DLL) is a name for library components. They have a .dll extension, and .exe is the extension used for executable programs.

As you saw at the start of this chapter, all .NET code compiled to IL exists in an *assembly*, which is, roughly speaking, either a DLL or an EXE. Assemblies can also contain supporting code and data files. Every time you compile a set of files using fsc.exe, you create one assembly, either a DLL or an EXE. Even when you use F# Interactive (fsi.exe), you're dynamically adding code to a dynamically generated assembly. You will now learn how to use the command-line compiler to create assemblies.

To compile code to an EXE, you call `fsc.exe` with the names of your source-code files in dependency order. For example, if the file `dolphin.fs` contains the code in Listing 7-10, then you can compile the code using `fsc dolphin.fs`. You can also use the -o flag to name the generated EXE.

Listing 7-10. File `dolphins.fs`

```
let longBeaked = "Delphinus capensis"
let shortBeaked = "Delphinus delphis"
let dolphins = [longBeaked; shortBeaked]
printfn "Known Dolphins: %A" dolphins
```

You can now compile this code to an EXE:

```
C:\fsharp> fsc dolphins.fs

C:\fsharp> dir dolphins.exe

...

18/06/2012  02:30 p.m.              4,608 dolphin.exe

C:\fsharp> dolphins.exe

Known Dolphins: ["Delphinus capensis"; "Delphinus delphis"]
```

To compile F# code into a DLL, take one or more source files and invoke `fsc.exe` with the -a option. For example, let's assume the file `whales.fs` contains the code shown in Listing 7-11. (This sample also includes some documentation comments, referred to in the "Generating Documentation" section later in this chapter.)

Listing 7-11. File `whales.fs`

```
module Whales.Fictional

/// The three kinds of whales we cover in this release
type WhaleKind =
    | Blue
    | Killer
    | GreatWhale

/// The main whale
let moby = "Moby Dick, Pacific", GreatWhale

/// The backup whale
let bluey = "Blue, Southern Ocean", Blue

/// This whale is for experimental use only
let orca = "Orca, Pacific", Killer

/// The collected whales
let whales = [|moby; bluey; orca|]
```

172

You can now compile the code as follows:

```
C:\test> fsc -g -a whales.fs
C:\test> dir whales.dll

...

18/06/2012  02:37 p.m.                9,216 whales.dll
```

Here you've added one command-line flag: -g to generate debug output. When compiling other assemblies, you need to reference your DLLs. For example, consider the code in Listing 7-12, which needs to reference whales.dll.

Listing 7-12. File whalewatcher.fs

```
open Whales
open System

let idx = Int32.Parse(Environment.GetCommandLineArgs().[1])
let spotted = Fictional.whales.[idx]

printfn "You spotted %A!" spotted
```

You can compile this file by adding an -r flag to reference the DLLs on which the code depends. You can also use the -o flag to name the generated EXE or DLL and the -I flag to list search paths:

```
C:\fsharp> fsc -g -r whales.dll -o watcher.exe whaleWatcher.fs

C:\fsharp> dir watcher.exe

...

18/06/2012  02:48 p.m.                5,120 watcher.exe

C:\fsharp> watcher.exe 1

You spotted ("Blue, Southern Ocean", Blue)!
```

■ **Note** F# projects and assemblies often contain a large amount of code. For example, a single assembly may contain the compiled output from as many as 30 to 50 F# source-code files in a single project. Having many small projects may seem tempting, but it can lead to difficulties when you're managing updates, and it can be confusing to end users. Large assemblies are easier to version: you have to update only one component, and you can package multiple updates into a single new version of the DLL.

Project Files and Compilation Order

The files in an F# project must be placed in a *compilation order*. Normally this order is dictated by a *project file* (using the .fsproj project file format used by the MSBuild/XBuild tools). Some important fragments of an example of a project file are shown in Listing 7-13.

Listing 7-13. Fragments of an example project file in the .fsproj format

```xml
<?xml version="1.0" encoding="utf-8"?>
<Project ToolsVersion="12.0" ... >
  <PropertyGroup>
    ...
    <OutputType>Library</OutputType>
    <AssemblyName>MyLibrary</AssemblyName>
    <TargetFrameworkVersion>v4.5</TargetFrameworkVersion>
    <TargetFSharpCoreVersion>4.3.1.0</TargetFSharpCoreVersion>
    ...
  </PropertyGroup>
  <PropertyGroup Condition=" '$(Configuration)|$(Platform)' == 'Debug|AnyCPU' ">
    <Optimize>false</Optimize>
    <Tailcalls>false</Tailcalls>
    <DocumentationFile>bin\Debug\MyLibrary.xml</DocumentationFile>
    ...
  </PropertyGroup>
  <PropertyGroup Condition=" '$(Configuration)|$(Platform)' == 'Release|AnyCPU' ">
    <Optimize>true</Optimize>
    <Tailcalls>true</Tailcalls>
    <DocumentationFile>bin\Release\MyLibrary.xml</DocumentationFile>
    ...
  </PropertyGroup>
  <ItemGroup>
    <Reference Include="mscorlib" />
    <Reference Include="FSharp.Core, Version=$(TargetFSharpCoreVersion)..." />
    <Reference Include="System" />
    <Reference Include="System.Core" />
  </ItemGroup>
  <ItemGroup>
    <Compile Include="file1.fsi" />
    <Compile Include="file2.fs" />
    <Compile Include="file3.fs" />
    <Compile Include="file4.fs" />
    <None Include="Script.fsx" />
  </ItemGroup>
  ...
</Project>
```

When that project file is used as input to the MSBuild/XBuild tool, the F# compiler is eventually invoked using

- a set of command-line options implied by the first PropertyGroup;

- an additional set of command-line options implied by either the second or third PropertyGroup depending on whether compilation is being done in Debug or Release mode;

- a set of assembly references implied by the first ItemGroup; and

- a file compilation ordering implied by the second ItemGroup.

The set of command-line options used for this project file is quite large, but instructive (some parts of the command-line arguments have been elided with ... for clarity):

```
...\fsc.exe
    -o:obj\Debug\MyLibrary.dll
    -g
    --debug:full
    --define:DEBUG --define:TRACE
    --doc:bin\Debug\MyLibrary.xml
    --optimize-
    --tailcalls-
    --noframework
    -r:"...\FSharp.Core.dll"
    -r:"...\mscorlib.dll"
    -r:"...\System.Core.dll"
    -r:"...\System.dll"
    --target:library
    file1.fsi file2.fs file3.fs file4.fs
```

On the last line, you can see that the input files have been passed to the compiler in the same order as specified in the project file.

WHY DOES F# USE A COMPILATION ORDERING?

Managing dependencies and circularity is one of the most difficult and fundamental problems in good software design. F# has a number of features designed to help you write code that is reusable and organized into components that are, where possible, independent and not combined into a "tangle" of "spaghetti code".

In order to help achieve this, the files in an F# project are presented to the F# compiler in a *compilation order*. This ordering is relevant to compilation: constructs in the earlier files can't refer to declarations in the later files. This is a mechanism to enforce *layered design*, where software is carefully organized into layers, and where one layer doesn't refer to other layers in a cyclic way.

This has a major effect on how you organize your code. A newcomer might be tempted to organize code in the same way as in object-oriented programming, where each class gets its own file. Instead, it is more normal in F# for a file to contain an entire *layer* of your design—this might be an entire layer of *infrastructure types*, or *domain types*, or *validation logic*, or *logging functionality*, or *user interface types* and so on. Scott Wlaschin of the F# community has written extensively on how to design your application in beautifully layered ways at http://fsharpforfunandprofit.com/.

Scott and others in the F# community have also done extensive statistical analyses of the dependency and circularity properties of F# and C# code in a series of Internet articles called "Circularities and Modularity in the Wild." They demonstrate that, based on the code samples they look at, F# code tends to have fewer dependencies and be much less circular in its dependency structure.

The use of a file ordering in F# can be a significant annoyance to newcomers to the language, and many object-oriented programmers do not like it. When discussing this issue with other programmers it is important to be aware of the differences in design methodology for F# code and the benefits that are gained through this approach.

Using Signature Files

Every piece of F# code you write has a *signature type*. The inferred signature type for a piece of code is shown for every code fragment you enter into F# Interactive, and it can also be reported by using the F# command-line compiler, fsc.exe, with the -i option. For example, consider the following code, placed in an implementation file clock.fs:

```
module Clock

type TickTock = Tick | Tock

let ticker x =
    match x with
    | Tick -> Tock
    | Tock -> Tick
```

You can now invoke the command-line compiler from a command prompt:

```
C:\Users\dsyme\Desktop> fsc –sig:clock.fsi -a clock.fs

module Clock

type TickTock =
  | Tick
  | Tock

val ticker : x:TickTock -> TickTock
```

The inferred signature shows the results of type inference and takes into account other information, such as accessibility annotations.

If you want, you can make the inferred types explicit by using an *explicit signature type* for each implementation file. The syntax used for explicit signature types is identical to the inferred types reported by F# Interactive or fsc.exe, like those shown previously. If you use explicit signatures, they're placed in a *signature file*, and they list the names and types of all values and members that are accessible in some way to the outside world. Signature files should use the same root name as the matching implementation file with the extension `.fsi`. For example, Listing 7-14 shows the explicit signature file `vector.fsi` and the implementation file `vector.fs`.

Listing 7-14. *A signature file* `vector.fsi` *with implementation file* `vector.fs`

```
// The contents of vector.fsi
namespace Acme.Collections
    type SparseVector =
        new: unit -> SparseVector
        member Add : int * float -> unit
        member Item : int -> float with get
```

```
// The contents of vector.fs
namespace Acme.Collections
    open System.Collections.Generic
    type SparseVector() =
        let elems = new SortedDictionary<int, float>()
        member vec.Add(k, v) = elems.Add(k, v)
        member vec.Item
            with get i =
                if elems.ContainsKey(i) then elems.[i]
                else 0.0
            and set i v =
                elems.[i] <- v
```

You can now invoke the command-line compiler from a command-line shell:

```
C:\Users\dsyme\Desktop> fsc -a vector.fsi vector.fs
```

■ **Note** You can use signature types to hide constructs, which can be used as an alternative to giving accessibility annotations on types, values, and members. Neither accessibility annotations nor signatures can hide type abbreviations, for the reasons discussed earlier in "Hiding Things with Accessibility Annotations." Some additional restrictions apply to both hiding techniques. For example, if a type is revealed to be a constructed class type or an interface type, all of its abstract members must be included in the signature. Similarly, a record type must reveal all of its fields, and a discriminated union type must reveal all of its cases. Also, in some languages, such as OCaml, a signature may restrict the type of an implementation construct. For example, if a function is inferred to have a generic type `'a -> 'a`, then in OCaml, the signature may specify a more restricted type, such as `int -> int`. This isn't permitted in F#.

Designing with Signatures

Although explicit signature types are optional, many programmers like to use them, especially when writing a library framework, because the signature file gives a place to document and maintain a component's public interface. For example, a signature file can be used to contain the "public-facing" API and documentation for a library, while the implementation contains the implementation.

Using explicit signature types comes with a cost: the signature files duplicate names, documentation, attributes, and some other information found in the implementation.

When Are Signature Types Checked?

A signature file appears *before* the implementation file in the compilation order for the files in an F# program. The conformance between the signature type and the corresponding implementation is checked *after* an implementation has been fully processed, however. This is unlike type annotations that occur directly in an implementation file, which are applied *before* an implementation fragment is processed. This means that the type information in a signature file isn't used as part of the type-inference process when processing the implementation.

■ **Note**   Each signature file must appear before its corresponding implementation file in the compilation order in an F# project. In Visual Studio, this means that the signature file must come before the implementation file in the project listing.

Reusing Your Code

This book has used F# Interactive for most of the samples. F# Interactive is excellent when you're exploring a set of libraries and writing scripts or small applications that use them. As your F# programming progresses, however, you will need to venture beyond these small scripts and start to write libraries and components that are reused across multiple projects and scripts.

Using Files as Small Reusable Components

One of the simplest kinds of reusable components in F# is the "single standalone F# file with optional signature," which we'll call a *single file component*. We've seen examples of these earlier in this chapter—for example, in Listing 7-14, showing implementation-file vector.fs and signature-file vector.fsi.

A single file component can be included in multiple assemblies simply by referencing the common file in multiple compilations. In Visual Studio, you can link to a single file from multiple projects—for example, using "Add Existing File" ➤ "Add as Link" and using Alt-Up and Alt-Down to move the file(s) to the right place in the compilation order for the project.

A single file component can be referenced from an F# Interactive script using #load; e.g.,

```
#load "vector.fs"
```

In F#, a single file may sometimes contain a very large amount of functionality, especially if accompanied by a signature file. If a single file component has a signature file, you can also refer to that in the #load directive; e.g.,

```
#load "vector.fsi" "vector.fs"
```

A single file component may not list its dependencies in terms of other components or assemblies. This means the project that hosts the single file must list the dependencies in its references. For use from F# Interactive, however, you can place the dependencies in an accompanying script file that contains the necessary #r directives. For example, if you are using an F# wrapper for a charting library, and the wrapper is in charting.fs and charting.fsi, then it can be useful to also create a charting.fsx containing any necessary #r directives.

```
#load "charting.fsi" "charting.fs" "charting.fsx"
```

The #load directive for F# Interactive is not limited to a single file—you can include multiple signature files and implementation files in a single directive. For example:

```
#load "matrix.fsi" "matrix.fs" "vector.fsi" "vector.fs"
```

Again, the #load is only used in F# Interactive and is not valid in .fs or .fsi files.

Creating and Sharing Packages

Sharing is at the heart of modern communities! Once you have organized your code into files and assemblies, you can make these available to a wider audience using some of these mechanisms:

- *NuGET.* The most widely used package-sharing mechanisms for F# and .NET code; see www.nuget.org.

- *Paket.* A popular package-dependency management tool that supports both NuGET and individual file references; see fsprojects.github.com/Paket.

- *Open Source Snippet Sites.* Place your code on a snippet site, such as www.fssnip.net.

- *Open Source Forges.* Make your code a project on a forge site, such as www.github.com.

- *Blogs and Web Sites.* Make a ZIP of your code available on the Web.

- *Installers.* Package your code as an installer that installs local copies of components on a target machine in known locations.

Summary

In this chapter, you learned about a number of techniques related to encapsulating and organizing your code, from the language mechanisms used for accessibility, encapsulation, modules, namespaces, and signatures to building assemblies and the related topics of building applications and DLLs.

The next three chapters will look at some of the techniques you need to master in order to work with different kinds of data as you progress with learning to program in F#.

CHAPTER 8

■ ■ ■

Working with Textual Data

Chapters 2 and 3 introduced the F# type for strings. While F#'s specialty is in programming with structured data, unstructured textual data is exceptionally common in programming, both as a data format and as an internal representation in algorithms that work over documents and text. In this chapter, you will learn some of the techniques available for working with textual data in F# programs, including working with the XML and JSON semi-structured data formats, which are initially represented as text.

Building Strings and Formatting Data

In Chapter 3, you saw the different forms of string literals (strings with escape characters and verbatim strings) and the most typical operations, such as concatenation using string builders. You may also remember that string values are *immutable* and that string operations that seem to change their input actually return a new string that represents the result. The following sections will cover further ways to work with strings.

Building Strings

In Chapter 3, you saw how the + operator is one simple tool for building strings, and you saw a number of simple string literals. You can also build strings using objects of the type System.Text.StringBuilder. These objects are mutable buffers that you can use to accumulate and modify text, and they're more efficient than repeated uses of the + operator. Here's an example:

```
> let buf = System.Text.StringBuilder();;

val buf : System.Text.StringBuilder

> buf.Append("Humpty Dumpty");;

> buf.Append(" sat on the wall");;

> buf.ToString();;

val it : string = "Humpty Dumpty sat on the wall"
```

More about String Literals

The F# type string is an abbreviation for the type System.String and represents a sequence of Unicode UTF-16 characters. The following sections will briefly introduce strings and the most useful functions for formatting them. Table 8-1 shows the different forms for writing string literals.

Table 8-1. *String and Character Literals*

Example	Kind	Type
"Humpty Dumpty"	String	String
"c:\\Program Files"	String	String
@"c:\Program Files"	Verbatim string	String
"""I "like" you"""	Triple quote string	String
"xyZy3d2"B	Literal byte array	byte []
'c'	Character	Char

As shown in Table 8-1, a literal form is also available for arrays of bytes: the characters are interpreted as ASCII characters, and non-ASCII characters can be embedded using escape codes. This can be useful when you're working with binary protocols. Verbatim string literals are particularly useful for file and path names that contain the backslash character (\):

```
> "MAGIC"B;;

val it : byte [] = [|77uy; 65uy; 71uy; 73uy; 67uy|]

> let dir = @"c:\Program Files";;
val dir : string = "c:\Program Files"

> let text = """I "like" you""";;
val text : string = "I "like" you"
```

Triple-quote string literals can contain both embedded quotation marks (") and backslashes (\) without escape, and include all the text until the terminating triple quote. You can also use multi-line string literals:

```
> let s = "All the kings horses
- and all the kings men";;

val s : string = "All the kings horses
and all the kings men"

> let s2 = """All the kings' "horses"
- and all the kings men""";;

val s2 : string = "All the kings' "horses"
- and all the kings men"
```

Table 8-2 shows the escape characters you can use in strings and characters.

Table 8-2. *Escape Characters in Nonverbatim Strings*

Escape	Character	ASCII/Unicode Value	Examples
\n	New line	10	"\n"
\r	Carriage return	13	"\r"
\t	Tab	9	"\t"
\b	Backspace	8	"a\b" ("a")
\NNN	Trigraph	NNN	"\032" (space)
\uNNNN	Unicode character	NNNN	"\u00a9" (©)
\UNNNNNNNN	Long Unicode character	NNNN NNNN	"\U00002260" (≠)

Using printf and Friends

Throughout this book, you've used the `printfn` function, which is one way to print strings from F# values. This is a powerful, extensible technique for type-safe formatting. A related function called `sprintf` builds strings:

```
> sprintf "Name: %s, Age: %d" "Anna" 3;;

val it : string = "Name: Anna, Age: 3"
```

The format strings accepted by `printf` and `sprintf` are recognized and parsed by the F# compiler, and their use is statically type-checked to ensure that the arguments given for the formatting holes are consistent with the formatting directives. For example, if you were to use an integer where a string is expected, you would see a type error:

```
> sprintf "Name: %s, Age: %d" 3 10;;

error FS0001: This expression was expected to have type
    string
but here has type
    int
```

Several `printf`-style formatting functions are provided in the `FSharp.Text.Printf` module. Table 8-3 shows the most important of these.

Table 8-3. *Formatting Functions in the* `printf` *Module*

Function(s)	Outputs via Type	Outputs via Object	Example
`printf(n)`[a]	`TextWriter`	`Console.Out`	`printf "Result: %d" res`
`eprintf(n)`	`TextWriter`	`Console.Error`	`eprintf "Result: %d" res`
`fprintf(n)`	`TextWriter`	Any `TextWriter`	`fprintf stderr "Error: %d" res`
`Sprintf`	`String`	Generates strings	`sprintf "Error: %d" res`
`bprintf(n)`	`StringBuilder`	Any `StringBuilder`	`bprintf buf "Error: %d" res`

[a] *The functions with a suffix n add a new line to the generated text.*

Table 8-4 shows the basic formatting codes for `printf`-style formatting.

Table 8-4. *Formatting Codes for* `printf`-*style String and Output Formatting*

Code	Type Accepted	Notes
`%b`	`Bool`	Prints `true` or `false`
`%s`	`String`	Prints the string
`%d, %u, %x, %X, %o`	`int/int32`	Signed and unsigned decimal whole numbers, hex in lower- and uppercase, and octal formats for any integer types
`%e, %E, %f, %g`	`Float`	Floating-point formats
`%M`	`Decimal`	See the .NET documentation.
`%A`	Any type	Uses structured formatting, discussed in the section "Generic Structural Formatting" in this chapter and in Chapter 5
`%+A`	Any type	Uses structured formatting, but accesses to private internals of data structures if they are accessible via reflection
`%O`	Any type	Uses `Object.ToString()`
`%a`	Any type	Takes two arguments: one is a formatting function, and one is the value to format
`%t`	Function	Runs the function given as an argument

Any value can be formatted using a `%O` or `%A` pattern; these patterns are extremely useful when you're prototyping or examining data. `%O` converts the object to a string using the `Object.ToString()` function, which is supported by all values. For example:

```
// Note, the formatting of dates and times will vary in some regions.
> System.DateTime.Now.ToString();;

val it : string = "28/06/20.. 17:14:07 PM"

> sprintf "It is now %O" System.DateTime.Now;;

val it : string = "It is now 28/06/20... 17:14:09"
```

■ **Note** The format strings used with `printf` are scanned by the F# compiler during type checking, which means the use of the formats are type safe; if you forget arguments, a warning is given, and if your arguments are of the wrong type, an error is given. The format strings may also include the usual range of specifiers for padding and alignment used by languages such as C, as well as some other interesting specifiers for computed widths and precisions. You can find the full details in the F# library documentation for the `Printf` module.

Generic Structural Formatting

`Object.ToString()` is a somewhat undirected way of formatting data. Structural types—such as tuples, lists, records, discriminated unions, collections, arrays, and matrices—are often poorly formatted by this technique. The `%A` pattern uses .NET reflection to format any F# value as a string based on the structure of the value. For example:

```
> printf "The result is %A\n" [1; 2; 3];;

The result is [1; 2; 3]
```

Generic structural formatting can be extended to work with any user-defined data types, a topic covered on the F# website. It is covered in detail in the F# library documentation for the `printf` function.

Formatting Strings Using .NET Formatting

Throughout this book, you've used F# `printf` format strings to format text and output; Chapter 4 and the previous section introduced the basic format specifiers for this kind of text formatting. Functions such as `printf` and `printfn` are located in the `FSharp.Text.Printf` module.

Another way to format strings is to use the `System.String.Format` static method or the other .NET composite formatting functions, such as `System.Console.WriteLine` and `TextWriter.WriteLine`. This is a distinct set of formatting functions and directives redesigned and implemented from the ground up for the .NET platform. Like `printf`, these methods take a format specifier as well as the objects to be formatted. The format specifier is a string with any number of format items acting as placeholders and designating which object is to be formatted and how. Consider this simple example:

```
> System.String.Format("{0} {1} {2}", 12, "a", 1.23);;

val it : string = "12 a 1.23"
```

Each format item is enclosed in braces, giving the index of the object to be formatted, and each can include an optional alignment specification (always preceded by a comma after the index, giving the width of the region in which the object is to be inserted, as in {0, 10}), and a format type that guides how the given object is formatted (as in {0:C}, where C formats as a system currency). The general syntax of the format item is:

{index[,alignment][:formatType]}

You can use the alignment value to pad the formatted object with spaces; text alignment is left if its value is negative and right if positive. Table 8-5 summarizes the format types used most often.

Table 8-5. *The .NET Format Specifiers*

Specifier	Type
C	Currency
D	Decimal/lVong date
E	Scientific
F	Fixed-point
G	General
N	Number
P	Percent
X	Hexadecimal
d/D	Short/long date
t/T	Short/long time
M	Month
Y	Year

Parsing Strings and Textual Data

In this section you will learn some basic techniques to work with strings and textual data.

Parsing Basic Values

The following session shows some sample uses of the parsing capabilities of the DateTime type:

```
> open System;;

> DateTime.Parse("23 July 1968");;

val it : DateTime = 23/07/1968 00:00:00

> let date x = DateTime.Parse(x);;

val date : x:string -> DateTime

> printfn "date = %A" (date "23 July 1968");;

date = 23/07/1968 00:00:00

> printfn "birth = %A" (date "18 March 2003, 6:21:01pm");;

birth = 18/03/2003 18:21:01
```

Note that formatting dates depends on the user's localization settings; you can achieve more explicit formatting by using the System.DateTime.ToString overload, which accepts explicit format information.

Next, use the System.Uri type to parse a URL:

```
> open System;;

> Uri.TryCreate("http://www.thebritishmuseum.ac.uk/", UriKind.Absolute);;

val it : bool * Uri =
  (true,
   http://www.thebritishmuseum.ac.uk/)

> Uri.TryCreate("e3£%//ww.gibberish.com", UriKind.Absolute);;

val it : bool * Uri = (false, null)
```

Processing Line-Based Input

A common, simple case of parsing and lexing occurs when you're working with an existing line-based, text-file format. In this case, parsing is often as easy as splitting each line of input at a particular separator character and trimming whitespace off the resulting partial strings:

```
> let line = "Smith, John, 20 January 1992, Software Developer";;

val line : string = "Smith, John, 20 January 1992, Software Developer"

> line.Split ',';;

val it : string [] = [|"Smith"; " John"; " 20 January 1992"; " Software Developer"|]

> line.Split ',' |> Array.map (fun s -> s.Trim());;

val it : string [] = [|"Smith"; "John"; "20 January 1992"; "Software Developer"|]
```

You can then process each column in the data format:

```
let splitLine (line : string) =
    line.Split [|','|] |> Array.map (fun s -> s.Trim())

let parseEmployee (line : string) =
    match splitLine line with
    | [|last; first; startDate; title|] ->
        last, first, System.DateTime.Parse(startDate), title
    | _ ->
        failwithf "invalid employee format: '%s'" line
```

The type of this function is:

```
val parseEmployee : line:string -> string * string * DateTime * string
```

Here is an example use:

```
> parseEmployee line;;

val it : string * string * DateTime * string
    = ("Smith", "John", 20/01/1992 00:00:00 { ... }, "Software Developer")
```

You can now use on-demand reading of files to turn a file into an on-demand sequence of results. The following example takes the first three entries from an artificially generated file containing 10,000 copies of the same employee, sets up a processing pipeline for the lines of the file, and then truncates that to the first three elements.

```
open System.IO

File.WriteAllLines("employees.txt", Array.create 10000 line)

let readEmployees (fileName : string) =
    fileName |> File.ReadLines |> Seq.map parseEmployee

let firstThree = readEmployees "employees.txt" |> Seq.truncate 3 |> Seq.toList
```

```
> firstThree |> Seq.iter (fun (last, first, startDate, title)  ->
      printfn "%s %s started on %A" first last startDate);;

John Smith started on 20/01/1992 00:00:00
John Smith started on 20/01/1992 00:00:00
John Smith started on 20/01/1992 00:00:00
```

This technique often is used to do an exploratory analysis of large data files. After the algorithm is refined using a prefix of the data, the analysis can then be run directly over the full data file by removing the Seq.truncate 3 step.

Using Regular Expressions

Another technique that's frequently used to extract information from strings is the use of regular expressions. The System.Text.RegularExpressions namespace provides convenient string-matching and -replacement functions. For example, let's say you have a log file containing a record of HTML GET requests. Here is a sample request:

```
GET /favicon.ico HTTP/1.1
```

The following code captures the name of the requested resource (`favicon.ico`) and the lower version number of the HTML protocol (1) used:

```
open System.Text.RegularExpressions

let parseHttpRequest line =
    let result = Regex.Match(line, @"GET (.*?) HTTP/1\.([01])$")
    let file = result.Groups.[1].Value
    let version = result.Groups.[2].Value
    file, version
```

The relevant fields are extracted by using the `Groups` attribute of the regular expression match to access the matched strings for each parenthesized group in the regular expression.

More on Matching with System.Text.RegularExpressions

Matching with regular expressions can be made more fluent using some auxiliary definitions:

```
open System.Text.RegularExpressions
let regex s = new Regex(s)
let (=~) s (re:Regex) = re.IsMatch(s)
let (<>~) s (re:Regex) = not (s =~ re)
```

Here, the inferred types are:

```
val regex : s:string -> Regex
val ( =~ ) : s:string -> re:Regex -> bool
val ( <>~ ) : s:string -> re:Regex -> bool
```

The infix operators allow you to test for matches:

```
> let samplestring = "This is a string";;

val samplestring : string = "This is a string"

> if samplestring =~ regex "his" then printfn "A Match! ";;

A Match!
```

Regular expressions can include *, +, and ? symbols for zero or more occurrences, one or more occurrences, and zero or one occurrences of the immediately preceding regular expression, respectively, and they can include parentheses to group regular expressions. For example:

```
> "This is a string" =~ regex "(is )+";;

val it : bool = true
```

Regular expressions also can be used to split strings:

```
> regex(" ").Split("This is a string");;

val it : string [] = [|"This"; "is"; "a"; "string"|]
```

Here, you use the regular expression " " for whitespace. In reality, you probably want to use the regular expression " +" to match multiple spaces. Better still, you can match any Unicode whitespace character using \s, including end-of-line markers. When using escape characters, however, you should use verbatim strings to specify the regular expression, such as @"\s+". Let's try:

```
> regex(@"\s+").Split("I'm a little       teapot");;

val it : string [] = [|"I'm"; "a"; "little"; "teapot"|]

> regex(@"\s+").Split("I'm a little  \t\t\n\t\n\t teapot");;

val it : string [] = [|"I'm"; "a"; "little"; "teapot"|]
```

Let's look at how to match using the method Match instead of using =~ and IsMatch. This lets you examine the positions of a match:

```
> let m = regex("joe").Match("maryjoewashere");;

val m : Match = joe

> if m.Success then printfn "Matched at position %d" m.Index;;

Matched at position 4
```

Replacing text is also easy:

```
> let text = "was a dark and stormy night";;

val text : string = "was a dark and stormy night"

> let t2 = regex(@"\w+").Replace(text, "WORD");;

val t2: string  = "WORD WORD WORD WORD WORD WORD"
```

Here, you use the regular expression "\w+" for a sequence of word characters. Table 8-6 shows the broad range of specifiers you can use with .NET regular expressions.

Table 8-6. *Regular Expression Escape Characters*

Characters	Description
Ordinary characters	Characters other than . $ ^ { [(	) * + ? \ match themselves.
.	Matches any character except \n. If RegexOptions.SingleLine is specified, it matches every character.
[aeiou0-9]	Matches any of the given characters or character ranges
[^aeiou0-9]	Matches any character other than the given characters or character ranges
\p{name}	Matches any character in the named character class specified by {name}. See the .NET documentation for full details.
\P{name}	Matches text not included in groups and block ranges specified in {name}
\w	Matches any word character
\W	Matches any nonword character
\s	Matches any whitespace character
\S	Matches any nonwhitespace character
\d	Matches any decimal digit
\D	Matches any nondigit
\a	Matches a bell (alarm) \u0007
\b	Matches a backspace \u0008 if in a [ ] character class; otherwise, in a regular expression, \b denotes a word boundary (between \w and \W characters). In a replacement pattern, \b always denotes a backspace.
\t	Matches a tab \u0009
\r	Matches a carriage return \u000D
\v	Matches a vertical tab \u000B
\f	Matches a form feed \u000C
\n	Matches a new line \u000A
\e	Matches an escape \u001B
\digit	Matches a back reference
\040	Matches an ASCII character as octal
\x20	Matches an ASCII character using hexadecimal representation (exactly two digits)
\cC	Matches an ASCII control character; for example, \cC is Ctrl+C
\u0020	Matches a Unicode character using hexadecimal representation (exactly four digits)
\	When followed by a character that isn't recognized as an escaped character, matches that character. For example, * is the same as \x2A.

You can specify case-insensitive matches by using (?i) at the start of a regular expression:

```
> samplestring =~ regex "(?i)HIS";;

val it : bool = true

> samplestring =~ regex "HIS";;

val it : bool = false
```

This final example shows the use of named groups:

```
let entry = @"
Jolly Jethro
13 Kings Parade
Cambridge, Cambs CB2 1TJ
"

let re =
  regex @"(?<=\n)\s*(?<city>[^\n]+)\s*,\s*(?<county>\w+)\s+(?<pcode>.{3}\s*.{3}).*$"
```

You can now use this regular expression to match the text and examine the named elements of the match:

```
> let r = re.Match(entry);;

val r : Match = Cambridge, Cambs CB2 1TJ

> r.Groups.["city"].Value;;

val it : string = "Cambridge"

> r.Groups.["county"].Value;;

val it : string = "Cambs"

> r.Groups.["pcode"].Value;;

val it : string = "CB2 1TJ"
```

You can also combine regular-expression matching with active patterns, which are described in Chapter 9. For example:

```
let (|IsMatch|_|) (re : string) (inp : string) =
    if Regex(re).IsMatch(inp)  then Some() else None
```

This active pattern can now be used as:

```
> match "This is a string" with
| IsMatch "(?i)HIS" -> "yes, it matched"
| IsMatch "ABC" -> "this would not match"
| _ -> "nothing matched"

val it : string = "yes, it matched "
```

Likewise, you can define functions or active patterns that extract and return named results from the match:

```
let firstAndSecondWord (inp : string) =
    let re = regex "(?<word1>\w+)\s+(?<word2>\w+)"
    let results = re.Match(inp)
    if results.Success then
        Some (results.Groups.["word1"].Value, results.Groups.["word2"].Value)
    else
        None
```

```
> firstAndSecondWord "This is a super string"

val it : (string * string) option = Some ("This", "is")
```

The string-based lookup of group names "word1" and "word2" in the result set is a little dissatisfying in a strongly typed language, and there are a couple of things you can do to improve this. First, you can use the dynamic operator, described in Chapter 17, to make the lookups slightly more natural. This code requires

```
let (?) (results : Match) (name : string) =
    results.Groups.[name].Value

let firstAndSecondWord (inp : string) =
    let re = regex "(?<word1>\w+)\s+(?<word2>\w+)"
    let results = re.Match(inp)
    if results.Success then
        Some (results ? word1, results ? word2)
    else
        None
```

More Robust Code with the Regular Expression Type Provider

Regular expressions are an embedded language, written in strings, and it is relatively easy to make mistakes with them. In the recent versions of F#, it is possible to statically check regular expressions at compile time using the F# type provider FSharp.Text.RegexProvider. You will learn more about type providers in Chapter 18. To use this provider, first install the FSharp.Text.RegexProvider package, using either NuGET or Paket, as described in Chapter 2:

```
paket add nuget FSharp.Text.RegexProvider
```

Then, reference the type provider component:

```
#r @"packages/FSharp.Text.RegexProvider/lib/net40/FSharp.Text.RegexProvider.dll"
```

You can now define and use a strongly checked regular expression as follows:

```
open FSharp.Text.RegexProvider

type PhoneRegex = Regex< @"(?<AreaCode>^\d{3})-(?<PhoneNumber>\d{3}-\d{4}$)">

let results = PhoneRegex().Match("425-123-2345")

let areaCode = results.AreaCode.Value
```

This gives you:

```
val results : Regex<...>.MatchType2 = 425-123-2345
val areaCode : string = "425"
```

Somewhat magically, if the regular expression has an error, you will get an error message at compile time—which helps you catch bugs much earlier than otherwise. This example

```
type FaultyAreaCodeRegex = Regex< @"(?<AreaCode>^\d{3}">
```

gives a static error:

```
The type provider 'FSharp.Text.RegexProvider.RegexProvider' reported an error: parsing
"(?<AreaCode>^\d{3}" - Not enough )'s.
```

■ **Note** .NET regular expressions have many more features than those described here. For example, you can compile regular expressions to make them match very efficiently. You can also use regular expressions to define sophisticated text substitutions. The `FSharp.Text.RegexProvider` has further useful features in addition to those shown here. The `FSharp.Text.RegexProvider` is open source, and you can contribute to it at `http://fsprojects.github.io/FSharp.Text.RegexProvider/`.

Using XML as a Concrete Language Format

Two common sources of structured data in a textual format are data formatted in the Extensible Markup Language (XML) and in JavaScript Object Notation (JSON). F# comes with well-engineered libraries for reading and generating both XML and JSON, and in both cases you can manipulate a typed abstract representation of an XML or JSON document in memory, without having to worry about parsing or generating strings corresponding to the concrete format. Let's first look at using XML data.

Using the System.Xml Namespace

XML is a general-purpose markup language; it is extensible, because it allows its users to define their own tags. Its primary purpose is to facilitate the sharing of data across different information systems, particularly via the Internet. Here is a sample fragment of XML, defined as a string directly in F#:

```
let inp = """<?xml version="1.0" encoding="utf-8" ?>
            <Scene>
             . <Composite>
               <Circle radius='2' x='1' y='0'/>
               <Composite>
                 <Circle radius='2' x='4' y='0'/>
                 <Square side='2' left='-3' top='0'/>
               </Composite>
               <Ellipse top='2' left='-2' width='3' height='4'/>
             </Composite>
            </Scene>"""
```

The backbone of an XML document is a hierarchical structure, and each node is decorated with attributes keyed by name. You can parse XML using the types and methods in the System.Xml namespace provided by the .NET libraries and then examine the structure of the XML interactively:

```
> open System.Xml;;

> let doc = new XmlDocument();;
val doc : XmlDocument

> doc.LoadXml(inp);;
val it : unit = ()

> doc.ChildNodes;;
val it : XmlNodeList =
  seq [seq []; seq [seq [seq []; seq [seq []; seq []]; seq []]]]
```

The default F# Interactive display for the XmlNode type isn't particularly useful. Luckily, you can add an interactive printer to the fsi.exe session using the AddPrinter method on the fsi object:

```
> fsi.AddPrinter(fun (x:XmlNode) -> x.OuterXml);;

> doc.ChildNodes;;
val it : XmlNodeList =
  seq
    [<?xml version="1.0" encoding="utf-8"?>;
     <Scene><Composite><Circle radius="2" x="1" y="0" /><Composite>...</Scene>]

> doc.ChildNodes.Item(1);;
val it : XmlNode =
```

```
  <Scene><Composite><Circle radius="2" x="1" y="0" /><Composite>...</Scene>

> doc.ChildNodes.Item(1).ChildNodes.Item(0);;

val it : XmlNode =
  <Composite><Circle radius="2" x="1" y="0" />...</Composite>

> doc.ChildNodes.Item(1).ChildNodes.Item(0).ChildNodes.Item(0);;

val it : XmlNode = <Circle radius="2" x="1" y="0" />

> doc.ChildNodes.Item(1).ChildNodes.Item(0).ChildNodes.Item(0).Attributes;;

val it : XmlAttributeCollection = seq [radius="2"; x="1"; y="0"]
```

Table 8-7 shows the most commonly used types and members from the System.Xml namespace.

Table 8-7. *Commonly Used Types and Members from the System.Xml Namespace*

Type/Member	Description
type XmlNode	Represents a single node in an XML document
member ChildNodes	Gets all the child nodes of an XmlNode
member Attributes	Gets all the attributes of an XmlNode
member OuterXml	Gets the XML text representing the node and all its children
member InnerText	Gets the concatenated values of the node and all its children
member SelectNodes	Selects child nodes using an XPath query
type XmlElement	Represents an element in an XML document; also an XmlNode
type XmlAttribute	Represents one attribute for an XmlNode; also an XmlNode
member Value	Gets the string value for the attribute
type XmlDocument	Represents an entire XML document; also an XmlNode
member Load	Populates the document from the given XmlReader, stream, or file name
member LoadXml	Populates the document object from the given XML string
type XmlReader	Represents a reader for an XML document or source
type XmlWriter	Represents a writer for an XML document

From Concrete XML to Abstract Syntax

Often, your first task in processing a concrete language is to bring the language fragments under the type discipline of F#. This section shows how to transform the data contained in the XML from the previous section into an instance of the recursive type shown here. This kind of type is usually called an *abstract syntax tree* (AST):

```
open System.Drawing
type Scene =
    | Ellipse of RectangleF
    | Rect of RectangleF
    | Composite of Scene list
```

This example uses the types PointF and RectangleF from the System.Drawing namespace, although you can also define your own types to capture the information carried by the leaves of the tree. Listing 8-1 shows a recursive transformation that converts XML documents like the one used in the previous section into the type Scene.

Listing 8-1. Converting XML into a typed format using the System.Xml namespace

```
open System.Xml
open System.Drawing
type Scene =
    | Ellipse of RectangleF
    | Rect of RectangleF
    | Composite of Scene list

    /// A derived constructor
    static member Circle(center : PointF, radius) =
        Ellipse(RectangleF(center.X - radius, center.Y - radius,
                           radius * 2.0f, radius * 2.0f))

    /// A derived constructor
    static member Square(left, top, side) =
        Rect(RectangleF(left, top, side, side))

/// Extract a number from an XML attribute collection
let extractFloat32 attrName (attribs : XmlAttributeCollection) =
    float32 (attribs.GetNamedItem(attrName).Value)

/// Extract a Point from an XML attribute collection
let extractPointF (attribs : XmlAttributeCollection) =
    PointF(extractFloat32 "x" attribs, extractFloat32 "y" attribs)

/// Extract a Rectangle from an XML attribute collection
let extractRectangleF (attribs : XmlAttributeCollection) =
    RectangleF(extractFloat32 "left" attribs, extractFloat32 "top" attribs,
               extractFloat32 "width" attribs, extractFloat32 "height" attribs)
```

```
/// Extract a Scene from an XML node
let rec extractScene (node : XmlNode) =
    let attribs = node.Attributes
    let childNodes = node.ChildNodes
    match node.Name with
    | "Circle" ->
        Scene.Circle(extractPointF(attribs), extractFloat32 "radius" attribs)
    | "Ellipse" ->
        Scene.Ellipse(extractRectangleF(attribs))
    | "Rectangle" ->
        Scene.Rect(extractRectangleF(attribs))
    | "Square" ->
        Scene.Square(extractFloat32 "left" attribs, extractFloat32 "top" attribs,
                     extractFloat32 "side" attribs)
    | "Composite"  ->
        Scene.Composite [for child in childNodes -> extractScene(child)]
    | _ -> failwithf "unable to convert XML '%s'" node.OuterXml
/// Extract a list of Scenes from an XML document
let extractScenes (doc : XmlDocument) =
    [for node in doc.ChildNodes do
        if node.Name = "Scene" then
            yield (Composite
                    [for child in node.ChildNodes -> extractScene(child)])]
```

The inferred types of these functions are:

```
type Scene =
  | Ellipse of RectangleF
  | Rect of RectangleF
  | Composite of Scene list
  static member Circle : center:PointF * radius:float32 -> Scene
  static member Square : left:float32 * top:float32 * side:float32 -> Scene

val extractFloat32 : attrName:string -> attribs:XmlAttributeCollection -> float32
val extractPointF : attribs:XmlAttributeCollection -> PointF
val extractRectangleF : attribs:XmlAttributeCollection -> RectangleF
val extractScene : node:XmlNode -> Scene
val extractScenes : doc:XmlDocument -> Scene list
```

The definition of extractScenes in Listing 8-1 generates lists using sequence expressions, which are covered in Chapter 3. You can now apply the extractScenes function to the original XML. (You must first add a pretty-printer to the F# Interactive session for the RectangleF type using the AddPrinter function on the fsi object.)

```
> fsi.AddPrinter(fun (r:RectangleF) ->
    sprintf "[%A,%A,%A,%A]" r.Left r.Top r.Width r.Height);;
> extractScenes doc;;

val it : Scene list
= [Composite
    [Composite
      [Ellipse [-1.0f,-2.0f,4.0f,4.0f];
       Composite [Ellipse [2.0f,-2.0f,4.0f,4.0f]; Rect [-3.0f,0.0f,2.0f,2.0f]];
       Ellipse [-2.0f,2.0f,3.0f,4.0f]]]]
```

The following sections more closely explain some of the choices we've made in the abstract syntax design for the type Scene.

Using the FSharp.Data XmlTypeProvider

In the last section, we saw how F# includes components for working with embedded languages such as regular expressions in a strongly typed and strongly-checked way. For XML, the F# package System.Data includes FSharp.Data.XmlProvider as type provider for doing some limited work with XML in a similarly strongly-typed and strongly checked way. You will learn more about type providers in Chapter 18. To reference the type provider, first get the NuGET package and then add the necessary references:

```
> #r @"packages\FSharp.Data\lib\net40\FSharp.Data.dll";;

//--> Referenced '...FSharp.Data.dll'

> #r "System.Xml.Linq";;

//--> Referenced '...System.Xml.Linq.dll'
```

The XmlTypeProvider is sample-driven; the "schema" is specified using a sample of XML data, drawn from a literal string, a file, or a URL:

```
[<Literal>]
let customersXmlSample = """
  <Customers>
    <Customer name="ACME">
      <Order Number="A012345">
        <OrderLine Item="widget" Quantity="1"/>
      </Order>
      <Order Number="A012346">
        <OrderLine Item="trinket" Quantity="2"/>
      </Order>
    </Customer>
```

```
    <Customer name="Southwind">
      <Order Number="A012347">
        <OrderLine Item="skyhook" Quantity="3"/>
        <OrderLine Item="gizmo" Quantity="4"/>
      </Order>
    </Customer>
  </Customers>"""
```

```
type InputXml = XmlProvider<customersXmlSample>
```

The shape of the schema dictates the shape of the data that is accepted to match the schema; for example, multiple elements indicate the element corresponds to a sequence. The type provider can then be used as follows:

```
let inputs = InputXml.GetSample().Customers
```

In this case, the type provider is being used to process the sample input itself. You can also use it to load or parse other data by using InputXml.Parse or InputXml.Load. The results are:

```
val inputs : XmlProvider<...>.Customer [] =
  [|<Customer name="ACME">
  <Order Number="A012345">
    <OrderLine Item="widget" Quantity="1" />
  </Order>
  <Order Number="A012346">
    <OrderLine Item="trinket" Quantity="2" />
  </Order>
</Customer>;
    <Customer name="Southwind">
  <Order Number="A012347">
    <OrderLine Item="skyhook" Quantity="3" />
    <OrderLine Item="gizmo" Quantity="4" />
  </Order>
</Customer>|]
```

This is a strongly typed representation of the contents of the file and can be processed using strongly typed code, as follows:

```
let orders =
  [ for customer in inputs do
      for order in customer.Orders do
        for line in order.OrderLines do
          yield (customer.Name,order.Number,line.Item,line.Quantity) ]
```

Giving

```
val orders : (string * string * string * int) list =
  [("ACME", "A012345", "widget", 1);
   ("ACME", "A012346", "trinket", 2);
   ("Southwind", "A012347", "skyhook", 3);
   ("Southwind", "A012347", "gizmo", 4)]
```

But what happens if you want to produce new XML rather than just consume it? The type provider also helps you to do that. First, give a schema indicating the shape of the output XML you would like to use and instantiate the type provider with this schema:

```
[<Literal>]
let orderLinesXmlSample = """
  <OrderLines>
      <OrderLine Customer="ACME" Order="A012345" Item="widget" Quantity="1"/>
      <OrderLine Customer="ACME" Order="A012346" Item="trinket" Quantity="2"/>
      <OrderLine Customer="Southwind" Order="A012347" Item="skyhook" Quantity="3"/>
      <OrderLine Customer="Southwind" Order="A012347" Item="gizmo" Quantity="4"/>
  </OrderLines>"""

type OutputXml = XmlProvider<orderLinesXmlSample>
```

You can then create the objects in the strongly typed XML representation derived from the schema:

```
let orderLines =
    OutputXml.OrderLines
        [| for (name, number, item, quantity) in orders do
               yield OutputXml.OrderLine(name, number, item, quantity) |]
```

and convert these to textual XML:

```
> orderLines.XElement.ToString();;

val it : string =
  "<OrderLines>
  <OrderLine Customer="ACME" Order="A012345" Item="widget" Quantity="1" />
  <OrderLine Customer="ACME" Order="A012346" Item="trinket" Quantity="2" />
  <OrderLine Customer="Southwind" Order="A012347" Item="skyhook" Quantity="3" />
  <OrderLine Customer="Southwind" Order="A012347" Item="gizmo" Quantity="4" />
</OrderLines>"
```

■ **Tip** Translating to a typed representation isn't always necessary. Some manipulations and analyses are better performed directly on heterogeneous, general-purpose formats, such as XML or even strings. For example, XML libraries support XPath, accessed via the SelectNodes method on the XmlNode type. If you need to query a large, semi-structured document whose schema is frequently changing in minor ways, using XPath is the right way to do it. Likewise, if you need to write a significant amount of code that interprets or analyzes a tree structure, converting to a typed abstract syntax tree is usually better.

Using JSON as a Concrete Language Format

Next, we will look briefly at doing similar tasks, but with the JSON data format replacing the XML format. There are several good NuGet packages available with which to work with JSON data. In this chapter you use the JSON data support in the `FSharp.Data` library. Another widely used library is `Json.NET` by Newtonsoft.

Parsing JSON Data

First, consider the simple task of parsing JSON data to an untyped format. Reference the `FSharp.Data` library and open the namespace:

```
> #r @"packages\FSharp.Data\lib\net40\FSharp.Data.dll";;

> open FSharp.Data;;
> open FSharp.Data.JsonExtensions;;
```

Next, use the `JsonValue.Parse` method to get a weakly typed `JsonValue` for some JSON data:

```
let animals =
    JsonValue.Parse """
        { "dogs":
            [ { "category": "Companion dogs",
                "name": "Chihuahua" },
              { "category": "Hounds",
                "name": "Foxhound" } ] }
        """
```

Giving:

```
val animals : JsonValue =
  { "dogs": [
      { "category": "Companion dogs",
        "name": "Chihuahua" },
      { "category": "Hounds",
        "name": "Foxhound" } ] }
```

You can also load JSON data directly from a file or a URL (using an HTTP GET); for instance, these examples (the output is not shown):

```
let data2 =
  JsonValue.Load (__SOURCE_DIRECTORY__ + "data/file.json")

let data3 =
  JsonValue.Load
      "http://api.worldbank.org/country/cz/indicator/GC.DOD.TOTL.GD.ZS?format=json"
```

Properties of `JsonValue` objects can be accessed using the `?` dynamic lookup operator defined in the `FSharp.Data.JsonExtensions`, and arrays of `JsonValue` can be iterated using for loops. For example:

```
let dogs = [ for dog in animals?dogs  -> dog?name ]
```

gives the result:

```
val dogs : JsonValue list = ["Chihuahua"; "Foxhound"]
```

A full guide to the `FSharp.Data JsonExtensions` is available at the `FSharp.Data` project website documentation.

Using the FSharp.Data JsonProvider

In the last example, the JSON data was parsed to the `JsonValue` type, which is a weakly typed representation. We will now look at how to use the `JsonProvider` from `FSharp.Data` to access JSON data directly in a strongly typed way.

Like the `XmlTypeProvider`, the `JsonProvider` is sample driven: the "schema" is specified by using a sample of JSON data, drawn from a literal string, a file, or a URL:

```
type Customers = JsonProvider<"""
  { "customers" :
    [ { "name" : "ACME",
        "orders" :
          [ { "number" : "A012345",
              "item" : "widget",
              "quantity" : 1 } ] } ] }
""">
```

Once again, the shape of the sample data used as a schema dictates the shape of the data that is accepted when parsing. The type provider can then be used to parse as follows:

```
Customers.Parse """
  { "customers" :
    [ { "name" : "Apple Store",
        "orders" :
          [ { "number" : "B73284",
              "item" : "iphone5",
              "quantity" : 18373 },
            { "number" : "B73238",
              "item" : "iphone6",
              "quantity" : 3736 } ] },
      { "name" : "Samsung Shop",
        "orders" :
          [ { "number" : "N36214",
              "item" : "nexus7",
              "quantity" : 18373 } ] } ] }
"""
```

The results are:

```
val customers : JsonProvider<...>.Root =
  { "customers": [
    { "name": "Apple Store",
      "orders": [
        { "number": "B73284",
          "item": "iphone5",
          "quantity": 18373 },
        { "number": "B73238",
          "item": "iphone6",
          "quantity": 3736 } ] },
    { "name": "Samsung Shop",
      "orders": [
        { "number": "N36214",
          "item": "nexus7",
          "quantity": 18373 } ] } ] }
```

This is a strongly typed representation of the contents of the file and can be processed using strongly typed code, as follows:

```
let customerNames = [ for c in customers.Customers -> c.Name ]
```

giving

```
val customerNames : string list = ["Apple Store"; "Samsung Shop"]
```

As with the XML type provider, you can create new JSON data using the strong types:

```
let newOrder = Customers.Order(number = "N36214", item = "nexus7", quantity = 1636)

let newCustomer = Customers.Customer(name = "FabPhone", orders = [| newOrder|])

let jsonText = newCustomer.JsonValue.ToString()
```

Giving the following for the final generated textual JSON data:

```
val jsonText : string =
  """{"name": "FabPhone",
      "orders": [
        { "number": "N36214",
          "item": "nexus7",
          "quantity": 1636 } ] }"""
```

Some Recursive Descent Parsing

Sometimes, you want to tokenize and parse a nonstandard language format, such as XML or JSON. The typical task is to parse the user input into your internal representation by breaking down the input string into a sequence of tokens ("lexing") and then constructing an instance of your internal representation based on a grammar ("parsing"). Lexing and parsing don't have to be separated, and there are often convenient .NET methods for extracting information from text in particular formats, as shown in this chapter. Nevertheless, it's often best to treat the two processes separately.

In this section, you will implement a simple tokenizer and parser for a language of polynomial expressions for inputted text fragments, such as

```
x^5 - 2x^3 + 20
```

or

```
x + 3
```

The aim is simply to produce a structured value that represents the polynomial to permit subsequent processing. For example, this may be necessary when writing an application that performs simple symbolic differentiation—say, on polynomials only. You want to read polynomials, such as x^5 - 2x^3 + 20, as input from your users, which in turn is converted to your internal polynomial representation so that you can perform symbolic differentiation and pretty-print the result to the screen. One way to represent polynomials is as a list of terms that are added or subtracted to form the polynomial:

```
type Term =
    | Term  of int * string * int
    | Const of int

type Polynomial = Term list
```

For instance, the polynomial x^5 - 2x^3 + 20 is represented as:

```
[Term (1,"x",5); Term (-2,"x",3); Const 20]
```

A Simple Tokenizer

First, you implement a tokenizer for the input, using regular expressions. See Listing 8-2.

Listing 8-2. Tokenizer for polynomials using regular expressions

```
type Token =
    | ID of string
    | INT of int
    | HAT
    | PLUS
    | MINUS

let regex s = new System.Text.RegularExpressions.Regex(s)

let tokenR = regex @"((?<token>(\d+|\w+|\^|\+|-))\s*)*"
```

```
let tokenize (s : string) =
    [for x in tokenR.Match(s).Groups.["token"].Captures do
        let token =
            match x.Value with
            | "^" -> HAT
            | "-" -> MINUS
            | "+" -> PLUS
            | s when System.Char.IsDigit s.[0] -> INT (int s)
            | s -> ID s
        yield token]
```

The inferred type of the function is:

```
val tokenize : s:string -> Token list
```

We can now test the tokenizer on some sample inputs:

```
> tokenize "x^5 - 2x^3 + 20";;
val it : Token list =
    [ID "x"; HAT; INT 5; MINUS; INT 2; ID "x"; HAT; INT 3; PLUS; INT 20]
```

The tokenizer works by simply matching the entire input string, and for each text captured by the labeled "token" pattern, we yield an appropriate token depending on the captured text.

Recursive-Descent Parsing

You can now turn your attention to parsing. In Listing 8-2, you built a lexer and a token type suitable for generating a token stream for the inputted text (shown as a list of tokens here):

```
[ID "x"; HAT; INT 5; MINUS; INT 2; ID "x"; HAT; INT 3; PLUS; INT 20]
```

Listing 8-3 shows a *recursive-descent parser* that consumes this token stream and converts it into the internal representation of polynomials. The parser works by generating a list for the token stream.

Listing 8-3. Recursive-descent parser for polynomials

```
type Term =
    | Term of int * string * int
    | Const of int

type Polynomial = Term list
type TokenStream = Token list

let tryToken (src : TokenStream) =
    match src with
    | tok :: rest -> Some(tok, rest)
    | _ -> None
```

```
let parseIndex src =
    match tryToken src with
    | Some (HAT, src) ->
        match tryToken src with
        | Some (INT num2, src) ->
            num2, src
        | _ -> failwith "expected an integer after '^'"
    | _ -> 1, src

let parseTerm src =
    match tryToken src with
    | Some (INT num, src) ->
        match tryToken src with
        | Some (ID id, src) ->
            let idx, src = parseIndex src
            Term (num, id, idx), src
        | _ -> Const num, src
    | Some (ID id, src) ->
        let idx, src = parseIndex src
        Term(1, id, idx), src
    | _ -> failwith "end of token stream in term"

let rec parsePolynomial src =
    let t1, src = parseTerm src
    match tryToken src with
    | Some (PLUS, src) ->
        let p2, src = parsePolynomial src
        (t1 :: p2), src
    | _ -> [t1], src

let parse input =
    let src = tokenize input
    let result, src = parsePolynomial src
    match tryToken src with
    | Some _ -> failwith "unexpected input at end of token stream!"
    | None -> result
```

The functions here have these types (using the type aliases you defined):

```
val tryToken : src:TokenStream -> (Token * Token list) option
val parseIndex : src:TokenStream -> int * Token list
val parseTerm : src:TokenStream -> Term * Token list
val parsePolynomial : src:TokenStream -> Term list * Token list
val parse : input:string -> Term list
```

Note in the previous examples that you can successfully parse either constants or complete terms, but after you locate a HAT symbol, a number must follow. This sort of parsing, in which you look only at the next token to guide the parsing process, is referred to as *LL(1)*, which stands for left-to-right, leftmost derivation parsing; 1 means that only one look-ahead symbol is used. To conclude, you can look at the parse function in action:

```
> parse "1+3";;

val it : Term list = [Const 1; Const 3]

> parse "2x^2+3x+5";;

val it : Term list = [Term (2,"x",2); Term (3,"x",1); Const 5]
```

Binary Parsing and Formatting

One final case of parsing is common when working with binary data. That is, say you want to work with a format that is conceptually relatively easy to parse and generate (such as a binary format) but in which the process of actually writing the code to crack and encode the format is somewhat tedious. This section covers a useful set of techniques to write readers and writers for binary data quickly and reliably.

The running example shows a set of *pickling* (also called *marshalling*) and *unpickling* combinators to generate and read a binary format of our design. You can easily adapt the combinators to work with existing binary formats, such as those used for network packets. Picklers and unpicklers for different data types are function values that have signatures, as follows:

```
type OutState = System.IO.BinaryWriter
type InState = System.IO.BinaryReader

type Pickler<'T> = 'T -> OutState -> unit
type Unpickler<'T> = InState -> 'T
```

Here, OutState and InState are types that record information during the pickling or unpickling processes. In this section, these are just binary readers and writers; more generally, they can be any type that can collect information and help compact the data during the writing process, such as by ensuring that repeated strings are given unique identifiers during the pickling process.

At the heart of every such library lies a set of primitive leaf functions for the base cases of aggregate data structures. For example, when you're working with binary streams, this is the usual set of primitive read/write functions:

```
// P is the suffix for pickling and U is the suffix for unpickling
let byteP (b : byte) (st : OutState) = st.Write(b)
let byteU (st : InState) = st.ReadByte()
```

You can now begin to define additional pickler/unpickler pairs:

```
let boolP b st = byteP (if b then 1uy else 0uy) st
let boolU st = let b = byteU st in (b = 1uy)

let int32P i st =
    byteP (byte (i &&& 0xFF)) st
    byteP (byte ((i >>> 8) &&& 0xFF)) st
    byteP (byte ((i >>> 16) &&& 0xFF)) st
    byteP (byte ((i >>> 24) &&& 0xFF)) st

let int32U st =
    let b0 = int (byteU st)
    let b1 = int (byteU st)
    let b2 = int (byteU st)
    let b3 = int (byteU st)
    b0 ||| (b1 <<< 8) ||| (b2 <<< 16) ||| (b3 <<< 24)
```

These functions have the following types (to keep output readable, Pickler and Unpickler types are used in the output instead of their expanded versions that are reported by F# Interactive):

```
val byteP  : Pickler<byte>
val byteU  : Unpickler<byte>
val boolP  : Pickler<bool>
val boolU  : Unpickler<bool>
val int32P : Pickler<int>
val int32U : Unpickler<int>
```

So far, so simple. One advantage of this approach comes as you write combinators that put these together in useful ways. For example, for tuples:

```
let tup2P p1 p2 (a, b) (st : OutState) =
    (p1 a st : unit)
    (p2 b st : unit)

let tup3P p1 p2 p3 (a, b, c) (st : OutState) =
    (p1 a st : unit)
    (p2 b st : unit)
    (p3 c st : unit)

let tup2U p1 p2 (st : InState) =
    let a = p1 st
    let b = p2 st
    (a, b)

let tup3U p1 p2 p3 (st : InState) =
    let a = p1 st
    let b = p2 st
    let c = p3 st
    (a, b, c)
```

and for lists:

```
/// Outputs a list into the given output stream by pickling each element via f.
/// A zero indicates the end of a list, a 1 indicates another element of a list.
let rec listP f lst st =
    match lst with
    | [] -> byteP 0uy st
    | h :: t -> byteP 1uy st; f h st; listP f t st

// Reads a list from a given input stream by unpickling each element via f.
let listU f st =
    let rec loop acc =
        let tag = byteU st
        match tag with
        | 0uy -> List.rev acc
        | 1uy -> let a = f st in loop (a :: acc)
        | n -> failwithf "listU: found number %d" n
    loop []
```

These functions conform to the types:

```
val tup2P : Pickler<'a> -> Pickler<'b> -> Pickler<'a * 'b>
val tup3P : Pickler<'a> -> Pickler<'b> -> Pickler<'c> -> Pickler<'a * 'b * 'c>
val tup2U : Unpickler<'a> -> Unpickler<'b> -> Unpickler<'a * 'b>
val tup3U : Unpickler<'a> -> Unpickler<'b> -> Unpickler<'c> -> Unpickler<'a* 'b* 'c>
val listP : Pickler<'a> -> Pickler<'a list>
val listU : Unpickler<'a> -> Unpickler<'a list>
```

It's now beginning to be easy to pickle and unpickle aggregate data structures using a consistent format. For example, imagine that the internal data structure is a list of integers and Booleans:

```
type format = list<int32 * bool>

let formatP = listP (tup2P int32P boolP)
let formatU = listU (tup2U int32U boolU)

open System.IO

let writeData file data =
    use outStream = new BinaryWriter(File.OpenWrite(file))
    formatP data outStream

let readData file =
    use inStream = new BinaryReader(File.OpenRead(file))
    formatU inStream
```

You can now invoke the pickle/unpickle process:

```
> writeData "out.bin" [(102, true); (108, false)] ;;

> readData "out.bin";;

val it : (int * bool) list = [(102, true); (108, false)]
```

Combinator-based pickling is a powerful technique that can be taken well beyond what has been shown here. For example, it's possible to do the following:

- Ensure data are compressed and shared during the pickling process by keeping tables in the input and output states. Sometimes this requires two or more phases in the pickling and unpickling process.

- Build in extra-efficient primitives that compress leaf nodes, such as writing out all integers using BinaryWriter.Write7BitEncodedInt and BinaryReader.Read7BitEncodedInt.

- Build extra combinators for arrays, sequences, and lazy values and for lists stored in binary formats other than the 0/1 tag scheme used here.

- Build combinators that allow dangling references to be written to the pickled data, usually written as a symbolic identifier. When the data are read, the identifiers must be resolved and relinked, usually by providing a function parameter that performs the resolution. This can be a useful technique when processing independent compilation units.

Combinator-based pickling is used mainly because it allows data formats to be created and read in a relatively bug-free manner. It isn't always possible to build a single pickling library suitable for all purposes, and you should be willing to customize and extend code samples, such as those listed previously, in order to build a set of pickling functions suitable for your needs.

■ **Note**   Combinator-based parsing borders on a set of techniques called *parser combinators* that we don't cover in this book. The idea is very much the same as the combinators presented here; parsing is described using a compositional set of functions. You also can write parser combinators using the workflow notation described in Chapter 17.

Encoding and Decoding Unicode Strings

It's often necessary to convert string data between different formats. For example, files read using the ReadLine method on the System.IO.StreamReader type are read with respect to a Unicode encoding. You can specify this when creating the StreamReader. If left unspecified, the .NET libraries attempt to determine the encoding for you.

One common requirement is to convert strings to and from ASCII representations, assuming that all the characters in the strings are in the ASCII range 0 to 127. You can do this using System.Text.Encoding.ASCII.GetString and System.Text.Encoding.ASCII.GetBytes. Table 8-8 shows the predefined encodings and commonly used members in the System.Text.Encoding type.

Table 8-8. *Types and Members Related to Unicode Encodings*

Type/Member	Description
`System.Text.Encoding`	Represents a character encoding
`UTF8 : Encoding`	The encoding for the UTF-8 Unicode format
`ASCII : Encoding`	The encoding for the ASCII 7-bit character set
`Unicode : Encoding`	The encoding for the UTF-16 Unicode format
`UTF32 : Encoding`	The encoding for the UTF-32 Unicode format
`GetEncoding : string -> Encoding`	Fetches an encoding by name
`member GetBytes : string -> byte[]`	Encodes a string to bytes
`member GetChars: byte[] -> char[]`	Decodes a sequence of bytes
`member GetString : byte[] -> string`	Decodes a sequence of bytes

Encoding and Decoding Binary Data

Another common requirement is to convert binary data to and from the standard 64-character, string-encoded representation of binary data used in XML, email, and other formats. You can do this using `System.Convert.FromBase64String` and `System.Convert.ToBase64String`.

Summary

In this chapter, you explored several topics related to working with textual data. You learned about formatting text using both F# type-safe formatting and .NET formatting, some simple techniques to parse data to primitive types, and the basics of working with regular expressions. You also learned how to work with JSON and XML as concrete text formats for structured data, and you saw three examples of how type providers can make working with data and embedded languages simpler and safer. Finally, you learned how to use recursive descent parsing and some combinator-based approaches for generating and reading binary data to and from structured data types. The next chapter will go deeper into working with structured data itself using the strongly typed functional-programming facilities of .NET.

CHAPTER 9

■ ■ ■

Working with Sequences and Tree-Structured Data

In the previous chapter, you learned to manipulate textual data, including how to convert text to structured data through parsing and back again through formatting. In this chapter, you will focus on F# programming techniques related to structured data.

Structured data and its processing are broad topics that lie at the heart of much applied F# programming. In this chapter, you will learn about a number of applied topics in structured programming, including:

- *producing, transforming, and querying* in-memory data—in particular, using sequence-based programming

- *defining and working with domain models,* including some efficiency-related representation techniques

- *working with tree-structured data,* including recursive processing and rewriting of trees

- *building new data structures,* including implementing *equality* and *comparison* operations for these types

- *defining structured views* of existing data structures using *active patterns*

Closely related to programming with structured data is the use of *recursion* in F# to describe some algorithms. In order to use recursion effectively over structured data, you will also learn about *tail calls* and how they affect the use of the "stack" as a computational resource.

Getting Started with Sequences

Many programming tasks require the iteration, aggregation, and transformation of data streamed from various sources. One important and general way to code these tasks is in terms of values of the type System.Collections.Generic.IEnumerable<type>, which is typically abbreviated to seq<type> in F# code. A seq<type> is a value that can be *iterated*, producing results of type type on demand. Sequences are used to wrap collections, computations, and data streams and are frequently used to represent the results of database queries. The following sections will present some simple examples of working with seq<type> values.

213

Using Range Expressions

You can generate simple sequences using *range expressions*. For integer ranges, these take the form of seq {n .. m} for the integer expressions n and m:

```
> seq {0 .. 2};;

val it : seq<int> = seq [0; 1; 2;]
```

You can also specify range expressions using other numeric types, such as double and single:

```
> seq {-100.0 .. 100.0};;

val it : seq<float> = seq [-100.0; -99.0; -98.0; -97.0; ...]
```

By default, F# Interactive shows the value of a sequence only to a limited depth; seq<'T> values are *lazy* in the sense that they compute and return the successive elements on demand. This means you can create sequences representing very large ranges, and the elements of the sequence are computed only if they're required by a subsequent computation. In the next example, you don't actually create a concrete data structure containing one trillion elements, but rather you create a sequence value that has the *potential* to yield this number of elements on demand. The default printing performed by F# Interactive forces this computation up to depth 4:

```
> seq {1 .. 10000000 };;

val it : seq<int> =  seq [1 ; 2; 3; 4; ...]
```

The default increment for range expressions is always 1. A different increment can be used via range expressions of the form seq {n .. skip .. m}:

```
> seq {1 .. 2 .. 5};;

val it : seq<int> = seq [1; 3; 5]

> seq {1 .. -2 .. -5};;

val it : seq<int> = seq [1; -1; -3; -5]
```

If the skip causes the final element to be overshot, then the final element isn't included in the result:

```
> seq {0 .. 2 .. 5};;

val it : seq<int> = seq [0; 2; 4]
```

The (..) and (.. ..) operators are overloaded operators in the same sense as (+) and (-), which means their behavior can be altered for user-defined types. Chapter 6 discussed this in more detail.

Iterating a Sequence

You can iterate sequences using the for ... in ... do construct, as well as the Seq.iter function discussed in the next section. Here is a simple example of the first:

```
> let range = seq {0 .. 2 .. 6};;

val range : seq<int>

> for i in range do printfn "i = %d" i;;
i = 0
i = 2
i = 4
i = 6
```

This construct forces the iteration of the entire seq. Use it with care when you're working with sequences that may yield a large number of elements.

Transforming Sequences with Functions

Any value of type seq<type> can be iterated and transformed using functions in the FSharp.Collections. Seq module. For example:

```
> let range = seq {0 .. 10};;

val range : seq<int>

> range |> Seq.map (fun i -> (i, i*i));;

val it : seq<int * int> = seq [(0, 0); (1, 1); (2, 4); (3, 9); ...]
```

Table 9-1 shows some important functions in this library module. The following operators necessarily evaluate all the elements of the input seq immediately:

- Seq.iter: This iterates all elements, applying a function to each.

- Seq.toList: This iterates all elements, building a new list.

- Seq.toArray: This iterates all elements, building a new array.

Table 9-1. *Some Important Functions from the Seq Module*

Operator	Type
Seq.append	seq<'T> -> seq<'T> -> seq<'T>
Seq.concat	seq<#seq<'T>> -> seq<'T>
Seq.choose	('T -> 'U option) -> seq<'T> -> seq<'U>
Seq.delay	(unit -> seq<'T>) -> seq<'T>
Seq.empty	seq<'T>
Seq.iter	('T -> unit) -> seq<'T> -> unit
Seq.filter	('T -> bool) -> seq<'T> -> seq<'T>
Seq.map	('T -> 'U) -> seq<'T> -> seq<'U>
Seq.singleton	'T -> seq<'T>
Seq.truncate	int -> seq<'T> -> seq<'T>
Seq.toList	seq<'T> -> 'T list
Seq.ofList	'T list -> seq<'T>
Seq.toArray	seq<'T> -> 'T[]
Seq.ofArray	'T[] -> seq<'T>

Most other operators in the Seq module return one or more seq<type> values and force the computation of elements in any input seq<type> values only on demand.

Which Types Can Be Used as Sequences?

Table 9-1 includes many uses of types such as seq<'T>. When a type appears as the type of an argument, the function accepts any value that's compatible with this type. Chapter 5 explained the notions of subtyping and compatibility in more detail; the concept should be familiar to OO programmers, because it's the same as that used by languages such as C#, which itself is close to that used by Java and C++. In practice, you can easily discover which types are compatible with which others by using F# Interactive and tools such as Visual Studio: when you hover over a type name, the compatible types are shown. You can also refer to the online documentation for the F# libraries and the .NET Framework, which you can easily obtain using the major search engines.

Here are some of the types compatible with seq<'T>:

- *Array types:* For example, int[] is compatible with seq<int>.

- *F# list types:* For example, int list is compatible with seq<int>.

- *All other F# and .NET collection types:* For example, SortedList<string> in the System.Collections.Generic namespace is compatible with seq<string>.

Using Lazy Sequences from External Sources

Sequences are frequently used to represent the process of streaming data from an external source, such as from a database query or from a computer's file system. For example, the following recursive function constructs a seq<string> that represents the process of recursively reading the names of all the files under a given path. The return types of Directory.GetFiles and Directory.GetDirectories are string[]; and, as noted earlier, this type is always compatible with seq<string>:

```
open System
open System.IO

let rec allFiles dir =
    Seq.append
        (dir |> Directory.GetFiles)
        (dir |> Directory.GetDirectories |> Seq.map allFiles |> Seq.concat)
```

This gives the following type:

```
val allFiles : dir:string -> seq<string>
```

Here is an example of the function being used on one of our machines:

```
> allFiles Environment.SystemDirectory;;

val it : seq<string> =
  seq
    ["c:\WINDOWS\system32\12520437.cpx"; "c:\WINDOWS\system32\12520850.cpx";
     "c:\WINDOWS\system32\aaclient.dll";
     "c:\WINDOWS\system32\accessibilitycpl.dll"; ...]
```

The allFiles function is interesting, partly because it shows many aspects of F# working seamlessly together:

- *Functions as values:* The function allFiles is recursive and is used as a first-class function value within its own definition.

- *Pipelining:* The pipelining operator |> provides a natural way to present the transformations applied to each subdirectory name.

- *Type inference:* Type inference computes all types in the obvious way, without any type annotations.

- *NET interoperability:* The System.IO.Directory operations provide intuitive primitives, which can then be incorporated in powerful ways using succinct F# programs.

- *Laziness where needed:* The function Seq.map applies the argument function lazily (on demand), which means subdirectories aren't read until required.

One subtlety with programming with on-demand or lazy values such as sequences is that side effects like reading and writing from an external store shouldn't generally happen until the lazy sequence value is consumed. For example, the previous allFiles function reads the system directory as soon as allFiles is applied to its argument. This may not be appropriate if the contents of the system directory are changing. You can delay the computation of the sequence by using the library function Seq.delay or by using a sequence expression, covered in the next section, in which delays are inserted automatically by the F# compiler.

Using Sequence Expressions

Functions are a powerful way of working with seq<type> values. However, F# also provides a convenient and compact syntax called *sequence expressions* for specifying sequence values that can be built using operations such as choose, map, filter, and concat. You can also use sequence expressions to specify the shapes of lists and arrays. It's valuable to learn how to use sequence expressions for the following reasons:

- They're a compact way of specifying interesting data and generative processes.

- They're used to specify database queries when using data-access layers such as Microsoft's Language Integrated Queries (LINQ). See Chapter 15 for examples of using sequence expressions this way.

- They're one particular use of *computation expressions*, a more general concept that has several uses in F# programming. This chapter discusses computation expressions, and we will show how to use them for asynchronous and parallel programming in Chapter 13.

The simplest form of a sequence expression is seq { for value in expr .. expr -> expr }. Here, -> should be read as "yield." This is a shorthand way of writing Seq.map over a range expression. For example, you can generate an enumeration of numbers and their squares as follows:

```
> let squares = seq { for i in 0 .. 10 -> (i, i * i) };;

val squares : seq<int * int>
```

The more complete form of this construct is seq { for pattern in sequence -> expression }. The pattern allows you to decompose the values yielded by the input enumerable. For example, you can consume the elements of squares using the pattern (i, iSquared):

```
> seq { for (i, iSquared) in squares -> (i, iSquared, i * iSquared) };;

val it : seq<int * int * int> =
  seq [(0, 0, 0); (1, 1, 1); (2, 4, 8); (3, 9, 27); ...]
```

The input sequence can be a seq<type> or any type supporting a GetEnumerator method.

Enriching Sequence Expressions with Additional Logic

A sequence expression often begins with for ... in ..., but you can use additional constructs. For example:

- A *secondary iteration:* for pattern in seq do seq-expr
- A *filter:* if expression then seq-expr
- A *conditional:* if expression then seq-expr else seq-expr
- A let *binding:* let pattern = expression in seq-expr
- Yielding a value: yield expression

Secondary iterations generate additional sequences, all of which are collected and concatenated together. Filters let you skip elements that don't satisfy a given predicate. To show both of these in action, the following computes a checkerboard set of coordinates for a rectangular grid:

```
let checkerboardCoordinates n =
    seq { for row in 1 .. n do
              for col in 1 .. n do
                  let sum = row + col
                  if sum % 2 = 0 then
                      yield (row, col)}
```

```
> checkerboardCoordinates 3;;
```

```
val it : seq<int * int> = seq [(1, 1); (1, 3); (2, 2); (3, 1); ...]
```

Using let clauses in sequence expressions allows you to compute intermediary results. For example, the following code gets the creation time and last access time for each file in a directory:

```
let fileInfo dir =
    seq { for file in Directory.GetFiles dir do
              let creationTime = File.GetCreationTime file
              let lastAccessTime = File.GetLastAccessTime file
              yield (file, creationTime, lastAccessTime)}
```

In the previous examples, each step of the iteration produces zero or one result. The final yield of a sequence expression can also be another sequence, signified through the use of the yield! keyword. The following sample shows how to redefine the allFiles function from the previous section using a sequence expression. Note that multiple generators can be included in one sequence expression; the results are implicitly collated together using Seq.append:

```
let rec allFiles dir =
    seq { for file in Directory.GetFiles dir do
              yield file
          for subdir in Directory.GetDirectories dir do
              yield! allFiles subdir}
```

Generating Lists and Arrays Using Sequence Expressions

You can also use range and sequence expressions to build list and array values. The syntax is identical, except the surrounding braces are replaced by the usual [ ] for lists and [| |] for arrays (Chapter 4 discussed arrays in more detail):

```
> [1 .. 4];;

val it: int list = [1; 2; 3; 4]

> [for i in 0 .. 3 -> (i, i * i)];;

val it : (int * int) list = [(0, 0); (1, 1); (2, 4); (3, 9)]

> [|for i in 0 .. 3 -> (i, i * i)|];;

val it : (int * int) [] = [|(0, 0); (1, 1); (2, 4); (3, 9)|]
```

■ **Caution**   F# lists and arrays are finite data structures built immediately rather than on demand, so you must take care that the length of the sequence is suitable. For example, [1I .. 1000000000I] attempts to build a list that is 1 billion elements long.

More on Working with Sequences

In this section, we will look at more techniques for working with sequences of data. These extend the initial techniques you learned in the previous section. For example, consider the map and filter operations. You can use these operators in a straightforward manner to query and transform in-memory data. For instance, given a table representing some people in your contacts list, you can select those names that start with the letter *A*:

```
/// A table of people in our startup
let people =
    [("Amber", 27, "Design")
     ("Wendy", 35, "Events")
     ("Antonio", 40, "Sales")
     ("Petra", 31, "Design")
     ("Carlos", 34, "Marketing")]

/// Extract information from the table of people
let namesOfPeopleStartingWithA =
    people
        |> Seq.map (fun (name, _age, _dept) -> name)
        |> Seq.filter (fun name -> name.StartsWith "A")
        |> Seq.toList
```

At the end of the set of sequence operations, we use Seq.toList to evaluate the sequence once and convert the results into a concrete list. Similarly, the following finds all those in the design department:

```
/// Extract the names of designers from the table of people
let namesOfDesigners =
    people
        |> Seq.filter  (fun (_, _, dept) -> dept = "Design")
        |> Seq.map (fun (name, _, _) -> name)
        |> Seq.toList
```

The output from evaluating these declarations is:

```
val people : (string * int * string) list =
  [("Amber", 27, "Design"); ("Wendy", 35, "Events"); ("Antonio", 40, "Sales");
   ("Petra", 31, "Design"); ("Carlos", 34, "Marketing")]
val namesOfPeopleStartingWithA : string list = ["Amber"; "Antonio"]
val namesOfDesigners : string list = ["Amber"; "Petra"]
```

The map and filter operations on sequences, arrays, lists, and other structured data types are examples of *queries*. In these cases, the queries are expressed by using pipelined combinators that accept the data structure as input. In database terminology, the map and filter operations are, respectively, called "select" and "where." Sequence-based functional programming gives you the tools to apply in-memory query logic on all types that are compatible with the F# sequence type, such as F# lists, arrays, sequences, and anything else that implements the IEnumerable<'a>/seq<'a> interface.

In the rest of this section, you will learn about additional operations over sequences. Some further statistical and numeric operations, such as summing and averaging over sequences, will be described in Chapter 10.

Using Other Sequence Operators: Truncate and Sort

The Seq module contains many other useful functions in addition to the map and filter operators, some of which were described in Chapter 3. For instance, a useful query-like function is Seq.truncate, which takes the first *n* elements of a sequence and discards the rest. Likewise, you can sort a sequence by using Seq.sort. In the following example, you extract the first 3,000 even numbers from an unbounded stream of random numbers, and for each result you return a pair of the number and its square. The sort operation uses the default comparison semantics for the type of elements in the sequence.

```
/// A random-number generator
let rand = System.Random()

/// An infinite sequence of numbers
let randomNumbers = seq { while true do yield rand.Next(100000) }

/// The first 10 random numbers, sorted
let firstTenRandomNumbers =
    randomNumbers
        |> Seq.truncate 10
        |> Seq.sort                          // sort ascending
        |> Seq.toList

/// The first 3000 even random numbers and sort them
let firstThreeThousandEvenNumbersWithSquares =
    randomNumbers
```

```
|> Seq.filter (fun i -> i % 2 = 0)  // "where"
|> Seq.truncate 3000
|> Seq.sort                         // sort ascending
|> Seq.map (fun i -> i, i*i)        // "select"
|> Seq.toList
```

The output for evaluating this expression is:

```
// random - results will vary!

val rand : Random
val randomNumbers : seq<int>
val firstTenRandomNumbers : int list =
  [9444; 14443; 15015; 20448; 31038; 46145; 69447; 85050; 85509; 92181]
val firstThreeThousandEvenNumbersWithSquares : (int * int) list =
  [(56, 3136); (62, 3844); (66, 4356); (68, 4624); (70, 4900); (86, 7396);
   (144, 20736); (238, 56644); (248, 61504); (250, 62500); ... ]
```

The operations Seq.sortBy and Seq.sortWith take custom key-extraction and key-comparison functions, respectively. For example, the next code sample takes the first ten numbers from our random-number sequence and sorts them by the *last* digit only (so 17510 appears before 16351, because the last digit 0 is lower than 1):

```
/// The first 10 random numbers, sorted by last digit
let firstTenRandomNumbersSortedByLastDigit =
    randomNumbers
        |> Seq.truncate 10
        |> Seq.sortBy (fun x -> x % 10)
        |> Seq.toList
```

The output is:

```
val firstTenRandomNumbersSortedByLastDigit : int list =
  [51220; 56640; 88543; 97424; 90744; 11784; 23316; 1368; 71878; 89719]
```

Selecting Multiple Elements from Sequences

Often, you will find yourself writing sequence transformations that select *multiple* elements or *zero-or-one* elements for each input element in the sequence. This is in contrast to the operation Seq.map, which always selects *one* new element. The types of Seq.collect and Seq.choose are:

```
module Seq =
    val choose : chooser : ('T -> 'U option) -> source : seq<'T> -> seq<'U>
    val collect : mapping : ('T -> #seq<'U>) -> source : seq<'T> -> seq<'U>
    val map : mapping : ('T -> 'U) -> source : seq<'T> -> seq<'U>
```

For example, given a list of numbers 1 to 10, the following sample shows how to select the "triangle" of numbers 1, 1, 2, 1, 2, 3, 1, 2, 3, 4, and so on. At the end of the set of sequence operations, we use Seq.toList to evaluate the sequence once and convert the results into a concrete list:

```
// Take the first 10 numbers and build a triangle 1, 1, 2, 1, 2, 3, 1, 2, 3, 4, ...
let triangleNumbers =
    [ 1 .. 10 ]
      |> Seq.collect (fun i -> [ 1 .. i ] )
      |> Seq.toList
```

The output is:

```
val triangleNumbers : int list =
  [1; 1; 2; 1; 2; 3; 1; 2; 3; 4; 1; 2; 3; 4; 5; 1; 2; 3; 4; 5; 6; 1; 2; 3; 4;
   5; 6; 7; 1; 2; 3; 4; 5; 6; 7; 8; 1; 2; 3; 4; 5; 6; 7; 8; 9; 1; 2; 3; 4; 5;
   6; 7; 8; 9; 10]
```

Likewise, you can use Seq.choose for the special case in which returning only zero-or-one elements, returning an option value None to indicate no new elements are produced and Some *value* to indicate the production of one element. The Seq.choose operation is logically the same as combining filter and map operations into a single step. In the example below, you will create an 8 x 8 "game board" full of random numbers, in which each element of the data structure includes the index position and a "game value" at that position. (Note that you will reuse this data structure later to explore several other sequence operations.)

```
let gameBoard =
    [ for i in 0 .. 7 do
          for j in 0 .. 7 do
              yield (i, j, rand.Next(10)) ]
```

We then select the positions containing an even number:

```
let evenPositions =
    gameBoard
      |> Seq.choose (fun (i, j, v) -> if v % 2 = 0 then Some (i, j) else None)
      |> Seq.toList
```

The output is:

```
// random - results will vary!

val gameBoard : (int * int * int) list =  [(0, 0, 9); (0, 1, 2); (0, 2, 8); (0, 3, 2); ...]
val evenPositions : (int * int) list =  [(0, 1); (0, 2); (0, 3); ... ]
```

Finding Elements and Indexes in Sequences

One of the most common operations in sequence programming is searching a sequence for an element that satisfies a specific criteria. The operations you use to do this are Seq.find, Seq.findIndex, and Seq. pick. These will raise an exception if an element or index is not found, and they also have corresponding nonfailing partners Seq.tryFind, Seq.tryFindIndex, and Seq.tryPick. The types of these operations are:

```
module Seq =
    val find : predicate : ('T -> bool) -> source : seq<'T> -> 'T
    val findIndex : predicate : ('T -> bool) -> source : seq<'T> -> int
    val pick : chooser : ('T -> 'U option) -> source : seq<'T> -> 'U
    val tryFind : predicate : ('T -> bool) -> source : seq<'T> -> 'T option
    val tryFindIndex : predicate : ('T -> bool) -> source : seq<'T> -> int option
    val tryPick : chooser : ('T -> 'U option) -> source : seq<'T> -> 'U option
```

For example, given the board you previously defined, you can search the game board for the first location with a zero game value by using Seq.tryFind. This will return None if the search fails and Some *value* if it succeeds. Likewise, you can combine a selection and projection into a single operation using Seq.tryPick.

```
let firstElementScoringZero =
    gameBoard |> Seq.tryFind (fun (i, j, v) -> v = 0)

let firstPositionScoringZero =
    gameBoard |> Seq.tryPick (fun (i, j, v) -> if v = 0 then Some(i, j) else None)
```

The output is:

```
// random - results will vary!

val firstElementScoringZero : (int * int * int) option = Some (1, 5, 0)
val firstPositionScoringZero : (int * int) option = Some (1, 5)
```

Grouping and Indexing Sequences

Search operations such as Seq.find search the input sequence linearly, from left to right. Frequently, it will be critical to the performance of your code to *index* your operations over your data structures. There are numerous ways to do this, usually by building an indexed data structure, such as a Dictionary (see Chapter 4) or an indexed functional map (see Chapter 3).

In the process of building an indexed collection, you will often start with sequences of data and then *group* the data into buckets. Grouping is useful for many other reasons when categorizing data for structural and statistical purposes. In the following example, you will group the elements of the game board defined previously into buckets according to the game value at each position:

```
open System.Collections.Generic
let positionsGroupedByGameValue =
    gameBoard
        |> Seq.groupBy (fun (i, j, v) -> v)
        |> Seq.sortBy (fun (k, v) -> k)
        |> Seq.toList
```

The output is:

```
val positionsGroupedByGameValue : (int * seq<int * int * int>) list =
  [(0, <seq>); (1, <seq>); (2, <seq>); (3, <seq>); (4, <seq>); (5, <seq>);
   (6, <seq>); (7, <seq>); (8, <seq>); (9, <seq>)]
```

Note that each element in the grouping is a key and a sequence of values for that key. It is very common to immediately post-process the results of grouping into a dictionary or map. The built-in functions dict and Map.ofSeq are useful for this purpose, as they build dictionaries and immutable tree-maps, respectively. For example:

```
let positionsIndexedByGameValue =
    gameBoard
        |> Seq.groupBy (fun (i, j, v) -> v)
        |> Seq.sortBy (fun (k, v) -> k)
        |> Seq.map (fun (k, v) -> (k, Seq.toList v))
        |> dict
let worstPositions = positionsIndexedByGameValue.[0]
let bestPositions = positionsIndexedByGameValue.[9]
```

The output is:

```
// random - results will vary!

val positionsIndexedByGameValue :
   IDictionary<int,(int * int * int) list>
val worstPositions : (int * int * int) list =
  [|(0, 6, 0); (2, 1, 0); (2, 3, 0); (6, 0, 0); (7, 0, 0)|]
val bestPositions : (int * int * int) list =
  [|(0, 3, 9); (0, 7, 9); (5, 3, 9); (6, 4, 9); (6, 7, 9)|]
```

Note that for highly-optimized grouping and indexing, it can be useful to rewrite your core indexed tables into direct uses of highly optimized data structures, such as System.Collections.Generic. Dictionary, as described in Chapter 4.

Folding Sequences

Some of the most general functions supported by most F# data structures are fold and foldBack. These apply a function to each element of a collection and accumulate a result. For fold and foldBack, the function is applied in left-to-right or right-to-left order, respectively. If you use the name fold, the ordering typically is left to right. Both functions also take an initial value for the accumulator. For example:

```
> List.fold (fun acc x -> acc + x) 0 [4; 5; 6];;

val it : int = 15
```

These can be used with the ||> pipelining operator, which takes two arguments in a tuple and pipes them into a function expecting two (curried) arguments:

```
> (0, [4;5;6]) ||> List.fold (fun acc x -> acc + x);;
val it : int = 15

> (0.0, [4.0; 5.0; 6.0]) ||> Seq.fold (fun acc x -> acc + x);;
val it : float = 15.0

> ([4; 5; 6; 3; 5], System.Int32.MaxValue) ||> List.foldBack (fun x acc -> min x acc);;
val it : int = 3
```

The following are equivalent, but no explicit anonymous function values are used:

```
> (0, [4; 5; 6]) ||> List.fold (+);;
val it : int = 15

> (0.0, [4.0; 5.0; 6.0]) ||> Seq.fold (+);;
val it : float = 15.0

> ([4; 5; 6; 3; 5], System.Int32.MaxValue ) ||> List.foldBack min;;
val it : int = 3
```

If used carefully, the various foldBack operators are pleasantly compositional, because they let you apply a selection function as part of the accumulating function:

```
> ([(3, "three"); (5, "five")], System.Int32.MaxValue) ||> List.foldBack (fst >> min);;
val it : int = 3
```

The F# library also includes more direct accumulation functions, such as Seq.sum and Seq.sumBy. These use a fixed accumulation function (addition) with a fixed initial value (zero), and are described in Chapter 10.

■ **Caution** Folding operators are very powerful and can help you avoid many explicit uses of recursion or loops in your code. They're sometimes overused in functional programming, however, and they can be hard for novice users to read and understand. Take the time to document uses of these operators, or consider using them to build simpler operators that apply a particular accumulation function.

Cleaning Up in Sequence Expressions

It's common to implement sequence computations that access external resources such as databases but that return their results on demand. This raises a difficulty: How do you manage the lifetime of the resources for the underlying operating-system connections? One elegant solution is via use bindings in sequence expressions:

- When a use binding occurs in a sequence expression, the resource is initialized each time a client enumerates the sequence.

- The connection is closed when the client disposes of the enumerator.

For example, consider the following function that creates a sequence expression that reads the first two lines of a file on demand:

```
open System.IO

let firstTwoLines file =
    seq { use s = File.OpenText(file)
          yield s.ReadLine()
          yield s.ReadLine() }
```

Let's now create a file and a sequence that reads the first two lines of the file on demand:

```
> File.WriteAllLines("test1.txt", [|"Es kommt ein Schiff";
                                    "A ship is coming"|]);;

> let twolines () = firstTwoLines "test1.txt";;

val twolines : unit -> seq<string>
```

At this point, the file hasn't yet been opened, and no lines have been read from the file. If you now iterate the sequence expression, the file is opened, the first two lines are read, and the results are consumed from the sequence and printed. Most important, the file has now also been closed, because the Seq.iter function is careful to dispose of the underlying enumerator it uses for the sequence, which in turn disposes of the file handle generated by File.OpenText:

```
> twolines() |> Seq.iter (printfn "line = '%s'")

line = 'Es kommt ein Schiff'
line = 'A ship is coming'
```

Expressing Operations Using Sequence Expressions

Sequences written using map, filter, choose, and collect can often be rewritten to use a sequence expression. For example, the triangleNumbers and evenPositions examples can also be written as:

```
let triangleNumbers =
    [ for i in 1 .. 10 do
          for j in 1 .. i do
              yield (i, j) ]
```

```
let evenPositions =
    [ for (i, j, v) in gameBoard do
        if v % 2 = 0 then
            yield (i, j) ]
```

The output in each case is the same. In many cases, rewriting to use generative sequence expressions results in considerably clearer code. There are pros and cons to using sequence-expression syntax for some parts of queries:

- Sequence expressions are very good for the subset of queries expressed using iteration (for), filtering (if/then), and mapping (yield). They're particularly good for queries containing multiple nested for statements.

- Other query constructs, such as ordering, truncating, grouping, and aggregating, must be expressed directly using aggregate operators, such as Seq.sortBy and Seq. groupBy, or by using the more general notion of "query expressions" (see Chapter 14).

- Some queries depend on the index position of an item within a stream. These are best expressed directly using aggregate operators such as Seq.map.

- Many queries are part of a longer series of transformations chained by |> operators. Often, the type of the data being transformed at each step varies substantially through the chain of operators. These queries are best expressed using operator chains.

■ **Note**   F# also has a more general "query-expression" syntax that includes support for specifying grouping, aggregation, and joining operations. This is mostly used for querying external data sources and will be discussed in Chapter 13.

Structure beyond Sequences: Domain Modeling

In Chapters 5 and 6, you learned about some simple techniques to represent record and tree-structured data in F# using *record types*, *union types*, and *object types*. Together this constitutes *domain modeling* using types. Further, in Chapter 8, you learned how to move from an unstructured, textual representation such as XML to a domain model in the form of a structured representation. In the following sections, you will learn techniques for working with domain models.

Let's look at the design of the type Scene from the previous chapter, in Listing 8-1, repeated below. The type Scene uses fewer kinds of nodes than the concrete XML representation from Chapter 8; the concrete XML has node kinds Circle, Square, Composite, and Ellipse, whereas Scene has just three (Rect, Ellipse, and Composite), with two derived constructors, Circle and Square, defined as static members of the Scene:

```
open System.Xml
open System.Drawing

type Scene =
    | Ellipse of RectangleF
    | Rect of RectangleF
    | Composite of Scene list

    static member Circle(center:PointF,radius) =
        Ellipse(RectangleF(center.X-radius,center.Y-radius,
                           radius*2.0f,radius*2.0f))
```

```
/// A derived constructor
static member Square(left,top,side) =
    Rect(RectangleF(left,top,side,side))
```

This is a common step when building a domain model; details are dropped and unified to make the domain model simpler and more general. Extra functions are then added that compute specific instances of the domain model. This approach has pros and cons:

- Manipulations are easier to program if you have fewer constructs in your domain model.

- You must be careful not to eliminate truly valuable information from a domain model. For some applications, it may really matter if the user specified a Square or a Rectangle in the original input; for example, an editor for this data may provide different options for editing these objects.

The domain model uses the types PointF and RectangleF from the System.Drawing namespace. This simplification is a design decision that should be assessed: PointF and RectangleF use 32-bit, low-precision, floating-point numbers, which may not be appropriate if you're eventually rendering on high-precision display devices. You should be wary of deciding on domain models on the basis of convenience alone, although of course this is useful during prototyping.

The lesson here is that you should look carefully at your domain models, trimming out unnecessary nodes and unifying constructs where possible, but only so long as doing so helps you achieve your ultimate goals.

Common operations on domain models include traversals that collect information and transformations that generate new models from old ones. For example, the domain model from Listing 8-1 has the property that, for nearly all purposes, the Composite nodes are irrelevant (this wouldn't be the case if you added an extra construct, such as an Intersect node). This means you can flatten to a sequence of Ellipse and Rectangle nodes:

```
let rec flatten scene =
    seq { match scene with
          | Composite scenes -> for x in scenes do yield! flatten x
          | Ellipse _ | Rect _ -> yield scene }
```

Here, flatten is defined using sequence expressions that were introduced in Chapter 3. Its type is:

```
val flatten : scene:Scene -> seq<Scene>
```

Let's look at this more closely. Recall that sequences are on-demand (lazy) computations. Using functions that recursively generate seq<'T> objects can lead to inefficiencies in your code if your domain model is deep. It's often better to traverse the entire tree in an *eager* way (eager traversals run to completion immediately). For example, it's typically faster to use an accumulating parameter to collect a list of results. Here's an example:

```
let rec flattenAux scene acc =
    match scene with
    | Composite(scenes) -> List.foldBack flattenAux scenes acc
    | Ellipse _
    | Rect _ -> scene :: acc

let flatten2 scene = flattenAux scene [] |> Seq.ofList
```

The following does an eager traversal using a local mutable instance of a `ResizeArray` as the accumulator and then returns the result as a sequence. This example uses a local function and ensures that the mutable state is locally encapsulated:

```
let flatten3 scene =
    let acc = new ResizeArray<_>()
    let rec flattenAux s =
        match s with
        | Composite(scenes) -> scenes |> List.iter flattenAux
        | Ellipse _ | Rect _ -> acc.Add s
    flattenAux scene
    Seq.readonly acc
```

The types of these are:

```
val flatten : scene: Scene -> seq<Scene>
val flattenAux : scene: Scene -> acc: Scene list -> Scene list
val flatten2 : scene: Scene -> seq<Scene>
val flatten3 : scene: Scene -> seq<Scene>
```

There is no hard and fast rule about which of these is best. For prototyping, the second option—doing an efficient, eager traversal with an accumulating parameter—is often the most effective. Even if you implement an accumulation using an eager traversal, however, returning the result as an on-demand sequence still can give you added flexibility later in the design process.

■ **Note** Domain modeling with F# types is a rich topic. The F# expert Scott Wlaschin and others in the domain-driven-design community have written extensively on domain modeling techniques for real-world business problems. You can read about this at `http://fsharpforfunandprofit.com`. Domain modeling with types is not restricted to business problems, but rather occurs under different names in almost every field of programming.

Transforming Domain Models

In the previous section, you saw examples of accumulating traversals over a domain model. It's common to traverse domain models in other ways:

- *Leaf rewriting (mapping)*: Translating some leaf nodes of the representation but leaving the overall shape of the model unchanged

- *Bottom-up rewriting*: Traversing a model but making local transformations on the way up

- *Top-down rewriting*: Traversing a model, but before traversing each subtree, attempting to locally rewrite the tree according to some particular set of rules

- *Accumulating and rewriting transformations*: For example, transforming the model left to right but accumulating a parameter along the way

For example, this mapping transformation rewrites all leaf ellipses to rectangles:

```
let rec rectanglesOnly scene =
    match scene with
    | Composite scenes -> Composite (scenes |> List.map rectanglesOnly)
    | Ellipse rect | Rect rect -> Rect rect
```

Often, whole classes of transformations are abstracted into aggregate transformation operations, taking functions as parameters. For example, here is a function that applies one function to each leaf rectangle:

```
let rec mapRects f scene =
    match scene with
    | Composite scenes -> Composite (scenes |> List.map (mapRects f))
    | Ellipse rect -> Ellipse (f rect)
    | Rect rect -> Rect (f rect)
```

The types of these functions are:

```
val rectanglesOnly : scene:Scene -> Scene
val mapRects : f:(RectangleF -> RectangleF) -> scene:Scene -> Scene
```

Here is a use of the mapRects function that adjusts the aspect ratio of all the RectangleF values in the scene (RectangleF values support an Inflate method):

```
let adjustAspectRatio scene =
    scene |> mapRects (fun r -> RectangleF.Inflate(r, 1.1f, 1.0f / 1.1f))
```

Using On-Demand Computation with Domain Models

Sometimes it's feasible to delay loading or processing some portions of a domain model. For example, imagine that the XML for the small geometric language from the previous section included a construct such as the following, in which the File nodes represent entire subtrees defined in external files:

```
<Composite>
    <File file='spots.xml'/>
    <File file='dots.xml'/>
</Composite>
```

It may be useful to delay loading these files. One general way to do this is to add a Delay node to the Scene type:

```
type Scene =
    | Ellipse of RectangleF
    | Rect of RectangleF
    | Composite of Scene list
    | Delay of Lazy<Scene>
```

You can then extend the extractScene function of Listing 9-1 with the following code to handle this node:

```
let rec extractScene (node : XmlNode) =
    let attribs = node.Attributes
    let childNodes = node.ChildNodes
    match node.Name with
    | "Circle" ->
        ...
    | "File" ->
        let file = attribs.GetNamedItem("file").Value
        let scene = lazy (let d = XmlDocument()
                          d.Load(file)
                          extractScene(d :> XmlNode))
        Scene.Delay scene
```

Code that analyzes domain models (for example, via pattern matching) must typically be adjusted to force the computation of delayed values. One way to handle this is to first call a function to eliminate immediately delayed values:

```
let rec getScene scene =
    match scene with
    | Delay d -> getScene (d.Force())
    | _ -> scene
```

Here is the function flatten2 from the "Processing Domain Models" section, but redefined to first eliminate delayed nodes:

```
let rec flattenAux scene acc =
    match getScene(scene) with
    | Composite scenes -> List.foldBack flattenAux scenes acc
    | Ellipse _ | Rect _ -> scene :: acc
    | Delay _ -> failwith "this lazy value should have been eliminated by getScene"

let flatten2 scene = flattenAux scene []
```

It's generally advisable to have a single representation of laziness within a single domain model design. For example, the following abstract syntax design uses laziness in too many ways:

```
type SceneVeryLazy =
    | Ellipse of Lazy<RectangleF>
    | Rect of Lazy<RectangleF>
    | Composite of seq<SceneVeryLazy>
    | LoadFile of string
```

The shapes of ellipses and rectangles are lazy computations; each Composite node carries a seq<SceneVeryLazy> value to compute subnodes on demand, and a LoadFile node is used for delayed file loading. This is a bit of a mess, because a single Delay node would, in practice, cover all these cases.

■ **Note** The Lazy<'T>type is defined in System and represents delayed computations. You access a lazy value via the Value property. F# includes the special keyword lazy for constructing values of this type. Chapter 8 also covered lazy computations.

Caching Properties in Domain Models

For high-performance applications of domain models, it can occasionally be useful to cache computations of some derived attributes within the model itself. For example, let's say you want to compute bounding boxes for the geometric language described in Listing 9-1. It's potentially valuable to cache this computation at Composite nodes. You can use a type such as the following to hold a cache:

```
type SceneWithCachedBoundingBox =
    | EllipseInfo of RectangleF
    | RectInfo of RectangleF
    | CompositeInfo of CompositeScene
and CompositeScene =
    { Scenes: SceneWithCachedBoundingBox list
      mutable BoundingBoxCache : RectangleF option  }
```

This is useful for prototyping, although you should be careful to encapsulate the code that is responsible for maintaining this information. Listing 9-1 shows the full code for doing this.

Listing 9-1. Adding the cached computation of a local attribute to a domain model

```
type SceneWithCachedBoundingBox =
    | EllipseInfo of RectangleF
    | RectInfo of RectangleF
    | CompositeInfo of CompositeInfo
and CompositeInfo =
    { Scenes: SceneWithCachedBoundingBox list
      mutable BoundingBoxCache : RectangleF option  }

    member x.BoundingBox =
        match x with
        | EllipseInfo rect | RectInfo rect -> rect
        | CompositeInfo info ->
            match info.cache with
            | Some v -> v
            | None ->
                let bbox =
                    info.Scenes
                    |> List.map (fun s -> s.BoundingBox)
                    |> List.reduce (fun r1 r2 -> RectangleF.Union(r1, r2))
                info.cache <- Some bbox
                bbox
    /// Create a Composite node with an initially empty cache
    static member Composite scenes = CompositeInfo { Scenes=scenes; BoundingBoxCache=None }
    static member Ellipse rect = EllipseInfo rect
    static member Rect rect = CompositeInfo rect
```

Other attributes that are sometimes cached include the hash values of tree-structured terms and the computation of all the identifiers in a subexpression. The use of caches makes it more awkward to pattern-match on terms. This issue can be largely solved by using active patterns, covered later in this chapter.

Memoizing Construction of Domain Model Nodes

In some cases, domain model nodes can end up consuming significant portions of the application's memory budget. In this situation, it can be worth memoizing some or all of the nodes constructed in the model. You can even go as far as memoizing *all* equivalent nodes, ensuring that equivalence between nodes can be implemented by pointer equality, a technique often called *hash-consing*. Listing 9-2 shows a domain model for propositional logic terms that ensures that any two nodes that are syntactically identical are shared via a memoizing table. Propositional logic terms are terms constructed using *P* AND *Q*, *P* OR *Q*, NOT *P*, and variables *a*, *b*, and so on. A noncached version of the expressions is:

```
type Prop =
    | And of Prop * Prop
    | Or of Prop * Prop
    | Not of Prop
    | Var of string
    | True
```

Listing 9-2. Memoizing the construction of domain model nodes

```
type Prop =
    | Prop of int

and PropRepr =
    | AndRepr of Prop * Prop
    | OrRepr of Prop * Prop
    | NotRepr of Prop
    | VarRepr of string
    | TrueRepr

open System.Collections.Generic

module PropOps =
    let uniqStamp = ref 0
    type internal PropTable() =
        let fwdTable = new Dictionary<PropRepr, Prop>(HashIdentity.Structural)
        let bwdTable = new Dictionary<int, PropRepr>(HashIdentity.Structural)
        member t.ToUnique repr =
            if fwdTable.ContainsKey repr then fwdTable.[repr]
            else let stamp = incr uniqStamp; !uniqStamp
                 let prop = Prop stamp
                 fwdTable.Add (repr, prop)
                 bwdTable.Add (stamp, repr)
                 prop
        member t.FromUnique (Prop stamp) =
            bwdTable.[stamp]
```

```
let internal table = PropTable ()

// Public construction functions
let And (p1, p2) = table.ToUnique (AndRepr (p1, p2))
let Not p = table.ToUnique (NotRepr p)
let Or (p1, p2)  = table.ToUnique (OrRepr (p1, p2))
let Var p = table.ToUnique (VarRepr p)
let True = table.ToUnique TrueRepr
let False = Not True

// Deconstruction function
let getRepr p = table.FromUnique p
```

You construct terms using the operations in PropOps much as you would construct terms using the nonmemoized representation:

```
> open PropOps;;

> True;;

val it : Prop = Prop 1

> let prop = And (Var "x",Var "y");;

val prop  : Prop = Prop 5

> let repr = getRepr prop;;

val repr : PropRepr = AndRepr (Prop 3, Prop 4)

> let prop2 = And (Var "x",Var "y");;

val prop2 : Prop = Prop 5
```

In this example, when you create two trees using the same specification, And (Var "x",Var "y"), you get back the same Prop object with the same stamp 5. You can also use memoization techniques to implement interesting algorithms; in Chapter 12, you will see an important representation of propositional logic called a *binary decision diagram* (BDD) that is based on a memoization table similar to that in the previous example.

The use of unique integer stamps and a lookaside table in the previous representation also has some drawbacks; it's harder to pattern match on abstract syntax representations, and you may need to reclaim and recycle stamps and remove entries from the lookaside table if a large number of terms is created or if the overall set of stamps must remain compact. You can solve the first problem by using active patterns, which will be covered next. If necessary, you can solve the second problem by scoping stamps in an object that encloses the uniqStamp state, the lookaside table, and the construction functions. Alternatively, you can explicitly reclaim the stamps by using the IDisposable idiom described in Chapter 6, although this approach can be intrusive to your application.

Active Patterns: Views for Structured Data

Pattern matching is a key technique provided in F# for decomposing domain models and other representations. So far in this book, all the examples of pattern matching have been directly over the core representations of data structures; for example, directly matching on the structure of lists, options, records, and discriminated unions. But pattern matching in F# is also *extensible*—that is, you can define new ways of matching over existing types. You do this through a mechanism called *active patterns*.

This book covers only the basics of active patterns. They can be indispensable, because they can let you continue to use pattern matching with your types even after you hide their representations. Active patterns also let you use pattern matching with .NET object types. The following section covers active patterns and how they work.

Converting the Same Data to Many Views

In high-school math courses, you were probably taught that you can view complex numbers in two ways: as rectangular coordinates $x + yi$ or as polar coordinates of a phase r and magnitude ϕ. In most computer systems, complex numbers are stored in the first format, although often the second format is more useful.

Wouldn't it be nice if you could look at complex numbers through either lens? You could do this by explicitly converting from one form to another when needed, but it would be better to have your programming language look after the transformations needed to do this for you. Active patterns let you do exactly that. First, here is a standard definition of complex numbers:

```
[<Struct>]
type Complex(r : float, i : float) =
    static member Polar(mag, phase) = Complex(mag * cos phase, mag * sin phase)
    member x.Magnitude = sqrt(r * r + i * i)
    member x.Phase = atan2 i r
    member x.RealPart = r
    member x.ImaginaryPart = i
```

Here are active patterns that let you view complex numbers as rectangular coordinates and polar coordinates, respectively:

```
let (|Rect|) (x : Complex) = (x.RealPart, x.ImaginaryPart)
let (|Polar|) (x : Complex) = (x.Magnitude, x.Phase)
```

The key thing to note is that these definitions let you use Rect and Polar as tags in pattern matching. For example, you can now write the following to define addition and multiplication over complex numbers:

```
let addViaRect a b =
    match a, b with
    | Rect (ar, ai), Rect (br, bi) -> Complex (ar + br, ai + bi)

let mulViaRect a b =
    match a, b with
    | Rect (ar, ai), Rect (br, bi) -> Complex (ar * br - ai * bi, ai * br + bi * ar)
```

As it happens, multiplication on complex numbers is easier to express using polar coordinates, implemented as:

```
let mulViaPolar a b =
    match a, b with
    | Polar (m, p), Polar (n, q) -> Complex.Polar (m * n, p + q)
```

Here is an example of using the (|Rect|) and (|Polar|) active patterns directly on some complex numbers via the pattern tags Rect and Polar. You first make the complex number 3+4i:

```
> fsi.AddPrinter (fun (c : Complex) -> sprintf "%gr + %gi" c.RealPart c.ImaginaryPart)

> let c = Complex (3.0, 4.0);;

val c : Complex = 3r + 4i

> c;;

val it : Complex = 3r + 4i

>   match c with
    | Rect (x, y) -> printfn "x = %g, y = %g" x y;;

x = 3, y = 4

>   match c with
    | Polar (x, y) -> printfn "x = %g, y = %g" x y;;

x = 5, y = 0.927295

> addViaRect c c;;

val it : Complex = 6r + 8i

> mulViaRect c c;;

val it : Complex = -7r + 24i

> mulViaPolar c c;;

val it : Complex = -7r + 24i
```

As you may expect, you get the same results if you multiply via either rectangular or polar coordinates. The execution paths are quite different, however. Let's look closely at the definition of mulViaRect:

```
let mulViaRect a b =
    match a, b with
    | Rect (ar, ai), Rect (br, bi) ->
        Complex (ar * br - ai * bi, ai * br + bi * ar)
```

When F# needs to match the values a and b against the patterns Rect (ar, ai) and Rect (br, bi), it doesn't look at the contents of a and b directly. Instead, it runs a function as part of pattern matching (which is why they're called *active* patterns). In this case, the function executed is (|Rect|), which produces a pair as its result. The elements of the pair are then bound to the variables ar and ai. Likewise, in the definition of mulViaPolar, the matching is performed partly by running the function (|Polar|).

The functions (|Rect|) and (|Polar|) are allowed to do anything, as long as each ultimately produces a pair of results. You should think of the names of these functions as including the (| and |). Here are the types of (|Rect|) and (|Polar|):

```
val (|Rect|) : x:Complex -> float * float
val (|Polar|) : x:Complex -> float * float
```

These types are identical, but they implement completely different views of the same data. The definitions of addViaRect and mulViaPolar can also be written using pattern matching in argument position:

```
let add2 (Rect (ar, ai)) (Rect (br, bi)) = Complex (ar + br, ai + bi)
let mul2 (Polar (r1, th1)) (Polar (r2, th2)) = Complex (r1 * r2, th1 + th2)
```

Matching on .NET Object Types

One useful thing about active patterns is that they let you use pattern matching with existing .NET object types. For example, the .NET object type System.Type is a runtime representation of types in .NET and F#. Here are the members found on this type:

```
type System.Type with
    member IsGenericType : bool
    member GetGenericTypeDefinition : unit -> Type
    member GetGenericArguments : unit -> Type[]
    member HasElementType : bool
    member GetElementType : unit -> Type
    member IsByRef : bool
    member IsPointer : bool
    member IsGenericParameter : bool
    member GenericParameterPosition : int
```

This type looks very much like one you'd like to pattern match against. There are clearly three or four distinct cases here, and pattern matching helps you isolate them. You can define an active pattern to achieve this, as shown in Listing 9-3.

Listing 9-3. Defining an active pattern for matching on System.Type values

```
let (|Named|Array|Ptr|Param|) (typ : System.Type) =
    if typ.IsGenericType
    then Named(typ.GetGenericTypeDefinition(), typ.GetGenericArguments())
    elif typ.IsGenericParameter then Param(typ.GenericParameterPosition)
    elif not typ.HasElementType then Named(typ, [|||])
    elif typ.IsArray then Array(typ.GetElementType(), typ.GetArrayRank())
```

```
elif typ.IsByRef then Ptr(true, typ.GetElementType())
elif typ.IsPointer then Ptr(false, typ.GetElementType())
else failwith "MSDN says this can't happen"
```

This then lets you use pattern matching against a value of this type:

```
open System
let rec formatType typ =
    match typ with
    | Named (con, [||]) -> sprintf "%s" con.Name
    | Named (con, args) -> sprintf "%s<%s>" con.Name (formatTypes args)
    | Array (arg, rank) -> sprintf "Array(%d,%s)" rank (formatType arg)
    | Ptr(true, arg) -> sprintf "%s&" (formatType arg)
    | Ptr(false, arg) -> sprintf "%s*" (formatType arg)
    | Param(pos) -> sprintf "!%d" pos

and formatTypes typs =
    String.Join(",", Array.map formatType typs)
```

or collect the free generic type variables:

```
let rec freeVarsAcc typ acc =
    match typ with
    | Array (arg, rank) -> freeVarsAcc arg acc
    | Ptr (_, arg) -> freeVarsAcc arg acc
    | Param _ -> (typ :: acc)
    | Named (con, args) -> Array.foldBack freeVarsAcc args acc

let freeVars typ = freeVarsAcc typ []
```

Defining Partial and Parameterized Active Patterns

Active patterns can also be *partial*. You can recognize a partial pattern by a name such as (|MulThree|_|) and by the fact that it returns a value of type 'T option for some 'T. For example:

```
let (|MulThree|_|) inp = if inp % 3 = 0 then Some(inp / 3) else None
let (|MulSeven|_|) inp = if inp % 7 = 0 then Some(inp / 7) else None
```

Finally, active patterns can also be *parameterized*. You can recognize a parameterized active pattern by the fact that it takes several arguments. For example:

```
let (|MulN|_|) n inp = if inp % n = 0 then Some(inp / n) else None
```

The F# quotation API FSharp.Quotations uses both parameterized and partial patterns extensively.

Hiding Representations with Active Patterns

Earlier in this chapter, you saw the following type that defines an optimized representation of propositional logic terms using a unique stamp for each syntactically unique term:

```
type Prop = Prop of int
and internal PropRepr =
    | AndRepr of Prop * Prop
    | OrRepr of Prop * Prop
    | NotRepr of Prop
    | VarRepr of string
    | TrueRepr
```

What happens, however, if you want to pattern match against values of type Prop? Even if you exposed the representation, all you would get is an integer, which you would have to look up in an internal table. You can define an active pattern for restoring matching on that data structure, as shown in Listing 9-4.

Listing 9-4. Extending Listing 9-2 with an active pattern for the optimized representation

```
module PropOps =
    ...
    let (|And|Or|Not|Var|True|) prop =
        match table.FromUnique prop with
        | AndRepr (x, y) -> And (x, y)
        | OrRepr (x, y) -> Or (x, y)
        | NotRepr x -> Not x
        | VarRepr v -> Var v
        | TrueRepr -> True
```

This code defines an active pattern in the auxiliary module PropOps that lets you pattern match against Prop values, despite the fact that they're using optimized unique-integer references under the hood. For example, you can define a pretty-printer for Prop terms as follows, even though they're using optimized representations:

```
open PropOps

let rec showProp precedence prop =
    let parenIfPrec lim s = if precedence < lim then "(" + s + ")" else s
    match prop with
    | Or (p1, p2) -> parenIfPrec 4 (showProp 4 p1 + " || " + showProp 4 p2)
    | And (p1, p2) -> parenIfPrec 3 (showProp 3 p1 + " && " + showProp 3 p2)
    | Not p -> parenIfPrec 2 ("not " + showProp 1 p)
    | Var v -> v
    | True -> "T"
```

Likewise, you can define functions to place the representation in various normal forms. For example, the following function computes *negation normal form* (NNF), where all instances of NOT nodes have been pushed to the leaves of the representation:

```
let rec nnf sign prop =
    match prop with
    | And (p1, p2) ->
```

```
            if sign then And (nnf sign p1, nnf sign p2)
            else Or (nnf sign p1, nnf sign p2)
    | Or (p1, p2) ->
            if sign then Or (nnf sign p1, nnf sign p2)
            else And (nnf sign p1, nnf sign p2)
    | Not p ->
            nnf (not sign) p
    | Var _ | True ->
            if sign then prop else Not prop

let NNF prop = nnf true prop
```

The following demonstrates that two terms have equivalent NNF normal forms:

```
> let t1 = Not (And (Not (Var "x"), Not (Var "y")));;

val t1 : Prop = Prop 8

> fsi.AddPrinter(showProp 5);;

> t1;;

val it : Prop = not (not x && not y)

> let t2 = Or(Not(Not(Var("x"))),Var("y"));;

val t2 : Prop = not (not x) || y

> (t1 = t2);;

val it : bool = false

> NNF t1;;

val it : Prop = x || y

> NNF t2;;

val it : Prop = x || y

> NNF t1 = NNF t2;;

val it : bool = true
```

241

Equality, Hashing, and Comparison

Many efficient algorithms over structured data are built on primitives that efficiently compare and hash representations of information. In Chapter 5, you saw a number of predefined generic operations, including generic comparison, equality, and hashing, accessed via functions such as:

```
val compare : 'T -> 'T -> int when 'T : comparison
val (=) : 'T -> 'T -> bool when 'T : equality
val (<) : 'T -> 'T -> bool when 'T : comparison
val (<=) : 'T -> 'T -> bool when 'T : comparison
val (>) : 'T -> 'T -> bool when 'T : comparison
val (>=) : 'T -> 'T -> bool when 'T : comparison
val min : 'T -> 'T -> 'T when 'T : comparison
val max : 'T -> 'T -> 'T when 'T : comparison
val hash : 'T -> int when 'T : equality
```

First, note that these are *generic* operations—they can be used on objects of many different types. This can be seen by the use of 'T in the signatures of these operations. The operations take one or two parameters of the same type. For example, you can apply the = operator to two Form objects, or two System.DateTime objects, or two System.Type objects, and something reasonable happens. Some other important derived generic types, such as the immutable (persistent) Set<_> and Map<_,_> types in the F# library, also use generic comparison on their key type:

```
type Set<'T when 'T : comparison> = ...
type Map<'Key, 'Value when 'Key : comparison> = ...
```

These operations and types are all *constrained*, in this case by the equality and/or comparison constraints. The purpose of constraints on type parameters is to make sure the operations are used only on a particular set of types. For example, consider equality and ordered comparison on a System.Net.WebClient object. Equality is permitted, because the default for nearly all .NET object types is reference equality:

```
let client1 = new System.Net.WebClient()
let client2 = new System.Net.WebClient()
client1 = client1 // true
client1 = client2 // false
```

Ordered comparison isn't permitted, however:

```
> client1 <= client2;;
```

```
error FS0001: The type 'System.Net.WebClient does not support the 'comparison' constraint.
For example, it does not support the 'System.IComparable' interface
```

That's good! There is no natural ordering for WebClient objects, or at least no ordering is provided by the .NET libraries.

Equality and comparison can work over the structure of types. For example, you can use the equality operators on a tuple only if the constituent parts of the tuple also support equality. This means that using equality on a tuple of WebClient objects is permitted:

```
> (client1, client2) = (client1, client2);;

val it : bool = true

> (client1, client2) = (client2, client1);;

val it : bool = false
```

But using ordered comparison of a tuple isn't:

```
> (client1, "Data for client 1") <= (client2, " Data for client 2");;

error FS0001: The type 'System.Net.WebClient' does not support the 'comparison'
constraint. For example, it does not support the 'System.IComparable' interface
```

Again, that's good—this ordering would be a bug in your code. Now, let's take a closer look at when equality and comparison constraints are satisfied in F#.

- The equality constraint is satisfied if the type definition doesn't have the NoEquality attribute, and any dependencies also satisfy the equality constraint.

- The comparison constraint is satisfied if the type definition doesn't have the NoComparison attribute, the type definition implements System.IComparable, and any dependencies also satisfy the comparison constraint.

An equality constraint is relatively weak, because nearly all CLI types satisfy it. A comparison constraint is a stronger constraint, because it usually implies that a type must implement System. IComparable.

Asserting Equality, Hashing, and Comparison Using Attributes

These attributes control the comparison and equality semantics of type definitions:

- StructuralEquality and StructuralComparison: Indicate that a structural type must support equality and comparison

- NoComparison and NoEquality: Indicate that a type doesn't support equality or comparison

- CustomEquality and CustomComparison: Indicate that a structural type supports custom equality and comparison

Let's look at examples of these. Sometimes you may want to assert that a structural type must support structural equality, and you want an error at the definition of the type if it doesn't. Do this by adding the StructuralEquality or StructuralComparison attributes to the type:

```
[<StructuralEquality; StructuralComparison>]
type MiniIntegerContainer = MiniIntegerContainer of int
```

This adds extra checking. In the following example, the code gives an error at compile time—the type can't logically support automatic structural comparison, because one of the element types doesn't support ordered comparison:

```
[<StructuralEquality; StructuralComparison>]
type MyData = MyData of int * string * string * System.Net.WebClient
```

```
error FS1177: The struct, record or union type 'MyData' has the
'StructuralComparison' attribute but the component type
'System.Net.WebClient' does not satisfy the 'comparison' constraint
```

Fully Customizing Equality, Hashing, and Comparison on a Type

Many types in the .NET libraries come with custom equality, hashing, and comparison implementations. For example, System.DateTime has custom implementations of these.

F# also allows you to define custom equality, hashing, and comparison for new type definitions. For example, values of a type may carry a unique integer tag that can be used for this purpose. In such cases, we recommend that you take full control of your destiny and define custom comparison and equality operations on your type. For example, Listing 9-5 shows how to customize equality, hashing (using the predefined hash function), and comparison based on a unique stamp integer value. The type definition includes an implementation of System.IComparable and overrides of Object.Equals and Object.GetHashCode.

Listing 9-5. Customizing equality, hashing, and comparison for a record type definition

```
/// A type abbreviation indicating we're using integers for unique stamps
/// on objects
type stamp = int

/// A structural type containing a function that can't be compared for equality
[<CustomEquality; CustomComparison>]
type MyThing =
    {Stamp : stamp;
     Behavior : (int -> int)}

    override x.Equals(yobj) =
        match yobj with
        | :? MyThing as y -> (x.Stamp = y.Stamp)
        | _ -> false

    override x.GetHashCode() = hash x.Stamp
    interface System.IComparable with
      member x.CompareTo yobj =
          match yobj with
          | :? MyThing as y -> compare x.Stamp y.Stamp
          | _ -> invalidArg "yobj" "cannot compare values of different types"
```

The System.IComparable interface is defined in the .NET libraries:

```
namespace System

    type IComparable =
        abstract CompareTo : obj -> int
```

Recursive calls to compare subexpressions are processed using the functions:

```
val hash : 'T -> int when 'T : equality
val (=) : 'T -> 'T -> bool when 'T : equality
val compare : 'T -> 'T -> int when 'T : comparison
```

Listing 9-6 shows the same for a union type, this time using some helper functions.

Listing 9-6. Customizing generic hashing and comparison on a union type

```
let inline equalsOn f x (yobj : obj) =
    match yobj with
    | :? 'T as y -> (f x = f y)
    | _ -> false

let inline hashOn f x = hash (f x)

let inline compareOn f x (yobj : obj) =
    match yobj with
    | :? 'T as y -> compare (f x) (f y)
    | _ -> invalidArg "yobj" "cannot compare values of different types"

type stamp = int

[<CustomEquality; CustomComparison>]
type MyUnionType =
    | MyUnionType of stamp * (int -> int)

    static member Stamp (MyUnionType (s, _)) = s

    override x.Equals y = equalsOn MyUnionType.Stamp x y
    override x.GetHashCode() = hashOn MyUnionType.Stamp x
    interface System.IComparable with
        member x.CompareTo y = compareOn MyUnionType.Stamp x y
```

Listing 9-6 also shows how to implement the System.Object method GetHashCode. This follows the same pattern as generic equality. Finally, you can declare that a structural type should use reference equality:

```
[<ReferenceEquality>]
type MyFormWrapper = MyFormWrapper of System.Windows.Forms.Form * (int -> int)
```

There is no such thing as reference comparison (the object pointers used by .NET move around, so the ordering would change). You can implement that by using a unique tag and custom comparison.

Suppressing Equality, Hashing, and Comparison on a Type

You can suppress equality on an F# defined type by using the NoEquality attribute on the definition of the type. This means the type isn't considered to satisfy the equality constraint. Likewise, you can suppress comparison on an F# defined type by using the NoComparison attribute on the definition of the type:

```
[<NoEquality; NoComparison>]
type MyProjections =
    | MyProjections of (int * string) * (string -> int)
```

Adding these attributes to your library types makes client code safer, because it's less likely to inadvertently rely on equality and comparison over types for which these operations make no sense.

Customizing Generic Collection Types

Programmers love defining new generic collection types. This is done less often in .NET and F# programming than in other languages, because the F# and .NET built-in collections are so good, but it's still important.

Equality and comparison play a role here. For example, it's common to have collections in which some of the values can be indexed using hashing, compared for equality when searching, or compared using an ordering. For example, seeing a constraint on this signature on a library type would come as no surprise:

```
type Graph<'Node when 'Node : equality>() = ...
```

The presence of the constraint is somewhat reassuring, because the requirement on node types is made clearer. Sometimes it's also desirable to be able to compare entire containers; for example, to compare one set with another, one map with another, or one graph with another. Consider the simplest generic collection type of all, which holds only one element. You can define it easily in F#:

```
type MiniContainer<'T> = MiniContainer of 'T
```

In this case, this is a structural type definition, and F# infers that there is an equality and comparison dependency on 'T. All done! You can use MiniContainer<_> with values of any type, and you can do equality and comparison on MiniContainer values only if the element type also supports equality and comparison. Perfect.

If MiniContainer is a class type or has customized comparison and equality logic, however, then you need to be more explicit about dependencies. You can declare dependencies using the EqualityConditionalOn and ComparisonConditionalOn attributes on the type parameter. You should also use the operators Unchecked.equals, Unchecked.hash, and Unchecked.compare to process elements recursively. With these attributes, MiniContainer<A> satisfies the equality and comparison constraints if A itself satisfies these constraints. Here's a full example:

```
type MiniContainer<[<EqualityConditionalOn; ComparisonConditionalOn >]'T>(x : 'T) =
    member x.Value = x
    override x.Equals(yobj) =
        match yobj with
        | :? MiniContainer<'T> as y -> Unchecked.equals x.Value y.Value
        | _ -> false

    override x.GetHashCode() = Unchecked.hash x.Value
```

```
interface System.IComparable with
    member x.CompareTo yobj =
        match yobj with
        | :? MiniContainer<'T> as y -> Unchecked.compare x.Value y.Value
        | _ -> invalidArg "yobj" "cannot compare values of different types"
```

■ **Note** Be careful about using generic equality, hashing, and comparison on mutable data. Changing the value of a field may change the value of the hash or the results of the operation. It's normally better to use the operations on immutable data or on data with custom implementations.

Tail Calls and Recursive Programming

In the previous section, you saw how to process nested, tree-structured domain models using recursive functions. In this section, you will learn about important topics associated with programming with recursive functions: stack usage and tail calls.

When F# programs execute, two resources are managed automatically, *stack-* and *heap*-allocated memory. Stack space is needed every time you call an F# function and is reclaimed when the function returns or when it performs a *tail call*. It's perhaps surprising that stack space is more limited than space in the garbage-collected heap. For example, on a 32-bit Windows machine, the default settings are such that each thread of a program can use up to 1 MB of stack space. Because stack is allocated every time a function call is made, a very deep series of nested function calls causes a StackOverflowException to be raised. For example, on a 32-bit Windows machine, the following program causes a stack overflow when n reaches about 79000:

```
let rec deepRecursion n =
    if n = 1000000 then () else
    if n % 100 = 0 then
        printfn "--> deepRecursion, n = %d" n
    deepRecursion (n+1)
    printfn "<-- deepRecursion, n = %d" n
```

You can see this in F# Interactive:

```
> deepRecursion 0;;

--> deepRecursion, n = 0
...
--> deepRecursion, n = 79100
--> deepRecursion, n = 79200
--> deepRecursion, n = 79300
Process is terminated due to StackOverflowException
Session termination detected. Press Enter to restart.
```

Stack overflows are extreme exceptions, because it's often difficult to recover correctly from them. For this reason, it's important to ensure that the amount of stack used by your program doesn't grow in an unbounded fashion as your program proceeds, especially as you process large inputs. Furthermore, deep stacks can hurt in other ways; for example, the .NET garbage collector traverses the entire stack on every garbage collection. This can be expensive if your stacks are very deep.

Because recursive functions are common in F# functional programming, this may seem to be a major problem. There is, however, one important case in which a function call recycles stack space eagerly: a *tail call*. A tail call is any call that is the last piece of work done by a function. For example, Listing 9-7 shows the same program with the last line deleted.

Listing 9-7. A simple tail-recursive function

```
let rec tailCallRecursion n : unit =
    if n = 1000000 then () else
    if n % 100 = 0 then
        printfn "--> tailCallRecursion, n = %d" n
    tailCallRecursion (n+1)
```

The code now runs to completion without a problem:

```
> tailCallRecursion 0;;
...
--> tailCallRecursion, n = 999600
--> tailCallRecursion, n = 999700
--> tailCallRecursion, n = 999800
--> tailCallRecursion, n = 999900
```

When a tail call is made, the F# execution machinery can drop the current stack frame before executing the target function, rather than waiting for the call to complete. Sometimes this optimization is performed by the F# compiler. If the n = 1000000 check were removed in the previous program, the program would run indefinitely. (As an aside, note that n would cycle around to the negative numbers, because arithmetic is unchecked for overflow unless you open the module FSharp.Core.Operators.Checked.)

Functions such as tailCallRecursion are known as *tail-recursive* functions. When you write recursive functions, you should check either that they're tail recursive or that they won't be used with inputs that cause them to recurse to an excessive depth. The following sections will give some examples of techniques you can use to make your functions tail recursive.

Tail Recursion and List Processing

Tail recursion is particularly important when you're processing F# lists, because lists can be long, and recursion is the natural way to implement many list-processing functions. For example, here is a function to find the last element of a list (this must traverse the entire list, because F# lists are pointers to the head of the list):

```
let rec last l =
    match l with
    | [] -> invalidArg "l" "the input list should not be empty"
    | [h] -> h
    | h::t -> last t
```

This function is tail recursive, because no work happens after the recursive call `last t`. Many list functions are written most naturally in non-tail-recursive ways, however. Although it can be a little annoying to write these functions using tail recursion, it's often better to use tail recursion than to leave the potential for stack overflow lying around your code. For example, the following function creates a list of length n in which every entry in the list is the value x:

```
let rec replicateNotTailRecursiveA n x =
    if n <= 0 then []
    else x :: replicateNotTailRecursiveA (n - 1) x
```

The problem with this function is that work is done after the recursive call. This becomes obvious when you write the function in this fashion:

```
let rec replicateNotTailRecursiveB n x =
    if n <= 0 then []
    else
        let recursiveResult = replicateNotTailRecursiveB (n - 1) x
        x :: recursiveResult
```

Clearly, a value is being constructed by the expression `x :: recursiveResult` after the recursive call `replicateNotTailRecursiveB (n - 1) x`. This means that the function isn't tail recursive. The solution is to write the function using an *accumulating parameter*. This is often done by using an auxiliary function that accepts the accumulating parameter:

```
let rec replicateAux n x acc =
    if n <= 0 then acc
    else replicateAux (n - 1) x (x :: acc)

let replicate n x = replicateAux n x []
```

Here, the recursive call to `replicateAux` is tail recursive. Sometimes the auxiliary functions are written as inner recursive functions:

```
let replicate n x =
    let rec loop i acc =
        if i >= n then acc
        else loop (i + 1) (x :: acc)
    loop 0 []
```

The F# compiler optimizes inner recursive functions such as these to produce an efficient pair of functions that pass extra arguments as necessary.

When you're processing lists, accumulating parameters often accumulate a list in reverse order. This means a call to `List.rev` may be required at the end of the recursion. For example, consider this implementation of `List.map`, which isn't tail recursive:

```
let rec mapNotTailRecursive f inputList =
    match inputList with
    | [] -> []
    | h :: t -> (f h) :: mapNotTailRecursive f t
```

Here is an implementation that neglects to reverse the accumulating parameter:

```
let rec mapIncorrectAcc f inputList acc =

    match inputList with
    | [] -> acc              // whoops! Forgot to reverse the accumulator here!
    | h :: t -> mapIncorrectAcc f t (f h :: acc)

let mapIncorrect f inputList = mapIncorrectAcc f inputList []
```

This function executes as follows:

```
> mapIncorrect (fun x -> x * x) [1; 2; 3; 4];;

val it : int list = [16; 9; 4; 1]
```

Here is a correct implementation:

```
let rec mapAcc f inputList acc =
    match inputList with
    | [] -> List.rev acc
    | h::t -> mapAcc f t (f h :: acc)

let mapCorrect f inputList = mapAcc f inputList []
```

```
> mapCorrect (fun x -> x * x) [1; 2; 3; 4];;

val it : int list = [1; 4; 9; 16]
```

Tail Recursion and Object-Oriented Programming

You may need to implement object members with a tail-recursive implementation. For example, consider this list-like data structure:

```
type Chain =
    | ChainNode of int * string * Chain
    | ChainEnd of string

    member chain.LengthNotTailRecursive =
        match chain with
        | ChainNode(_, _, subChain) -> 1 + subChain.LengthNotTailRecursive
        | ChainEnd _ -> 0
```

The implementation of LengthNotTailRecursive is *not* tail recursive, because the addition 1 + applies to the result of the recursive property invocation. One obvious tail-recursive implementation uses a local recursive function with an accumulating parameter, as shown in Listing 9-8.

Listing 9-8. Making an object member tail recursive

```
type Chain =
    | ChainNode of int * string * Chain
    | ChainEnd of string

    // The implementation of this property is tail recursive.
    member chain.Length =
        let rec loop c acc =
            match c with
            | ChainNode(_, _, subChain) -> loop subChain (acc + 1)
            | ChainEnd _ -> acc
        loop chain 0
```

■ **Note**   The list-processing functions in the F# library module `FSharp.Collections.List` are tail recursive,
except where noted in the documentation. Some of them have implementations that are specially optimized to
take advantage of the implementation of the `list` data structure.

Tail Recursion and Processing Unbalanced Trees

This section will consider tail-recursion problems that are much less common in practice but for which
it's important to know the techniques to apply if required. The techniques also illustrate some important
aspects of functional programming—in particular, an advanced technique called *continuation passing*.

Tree-structured data are generally more difficult to process in a tail-recursive way than list-structured
data are. For example, consider this tree structure:

```
type Tree =
    | Node of string * Tree * Tree
    | Tip of string

let rec sizeNotTailRecursive tree =
    match tree with
    | Tip _ -> 1
    | Node(_, treeLeft, treeRight) ->
        sizeNotTailRecursive treeLeft + sizeNotTailRecursive treeRight
```

The implementation of this function isn't tail recursive. Luckily, this is rarely a problem, especially if
you can assume that the trees are *balanced*. A tree is balanced when the depth of each subtree is roughly the
same. In that case, a tree of depth 1,000 will have about 21,000 entries. Even for a balanced tree of this size,
the recursive calls to compute the overall size of the tree won't recurse to a depth greater than 1,000—not
deep enough to cause stack overflow, except when the routine is being called by some other function already
consuming inordinate amounts of stack. Many data structures based on trees are balanced by design; for
example, the Set and Map data structures implemented in the F# library are based on balanced binary trees.

Some trees can be unbalanced, however. For example, you can explicitly make a highly unbalanced tree:

```
let rec mkBigUnbalancedTree n tree =
    if n = 0 then tree
    else Node("node", Tip("tip"), mkBigUnbalancedTree (n - 1) tree)
```

```
let tree1 = Tip("tip")
let tree2 = mkBigUnbalancedTree 15000 tree1
let tree3 = mkBigUnbalancedTree 15000 tree2
let tree4 = mkBigUnbalancedTree 15000 tree3
let tree5 = mkBigUnbalancedTree 15000 tree4
let tree6 = mkBigUnbalancedTree 15000 tree5
```

Calling sizeNotTailRecursive(tree6) now risks a stack overflow (note that this may depend on the amount of memory available on a system; change the size of the tree to force the stack overflow). You can solve this in part by trying to predict whether the tree will be unbalanced to the left or the right and by using an accumulating parameter:

```
let rec sizeAcc acc tree =
    match tree with
    | Tip _ -> 1 + acc
    | Node(_, treeLeft, treeRight) ->
        let acc = sizeAcc acc treeLeft
        sizeAcc acc treeRight

let size tree = sizeAcc 0 tree
```

This algorithm works for tree6, because it's biased toward accepting trees that are skewed to the right. The recursive call that processes the right branch is a tail call, while the call that processes the left branch isn't. This may be okay if you have prior knowledge of the shape of your trees. This algorithm still risks a stack overflow, however, and you may have to change techniques. One way to do this is to use a much more general and important technique known as *continuation passing*.

Using Continuations to Avoid Stack Overflows

A continuation is a function that receives the result of an expression after it's been computed. Listing 9-9 shows an example implementation of the previous algorithm that handles trees of arbitrary size.

Listing 9-9. Making a function tail recursive via an explicit continuation

```
let rec sizeCont tree cont =
    match tree with
    | Tip _ -> cont 1
    | Node(_, treeLeft, treeRight) ->
        sizeCont treeLeft (fun leftSize ->
        sizeCont treeRight (fun rightSize ->
          cont (leftSize + rightSize)))

let size tree = sizeCont tree (fun x -> x)
```

What's going on here? Let's look at the type of sizeCont and size:

```
val sizeCont : tree:Tree -> cont:(int -> 'a) -> 'a
val size : tree:Tree -> int
```

The type of sizeCont tree cont can be read as "compute the size of the tree and call cont with that size." If you look at the type of sizeCont, you can see that it will call the second parameter of type int -> 'T at some point—how else could the function produce the final result of type 'T? When you look at the implementation of sizeCont, you can see that it does call cont on both branches of the match.

Now, if you look at recursive calls in sizeCont, you can see that they're both tail calls:

```
sizeCont treeLeft (fun leftSize ->
  sizeCont treeRight (fun rightSize ->
    cont (leftSize + rightSize)))
```

That is, the first call to sizeCont is a tail call with a new continuation, as is the second. The first continuation is called with the size of the left tree, and the second is called with the size of the right tree. Finally, you add the results and call the original continuation cont. Calling size on an unbalanced tree such as tree6 now succeeds:

```
> size tree6;;
val it : int = 50001
```

How did you turn a tree walk into a tail-recursive algorithm? The answer lies in the fact that continuations are function objects, which are allocated on the garbage-collected heap. Effectively, you've generated a work list represented by objects, rather than keeping a work list via a stack of function invocations.

As it happens, using a continuation for both the right and left trees is overkill, and you can use an accumulating parameter for one side. This leads to a more efficient implementation, because each continuation-function object is likely to involve one allocation (short-lived allocations such as continuation objects are very cheap but not as cheap as not allocating at all). For example, Listing 9-10 shows a more efficient implementation.

Listing 9-10. Combining an accumulator with an explicit continuation

```
let rec sizeContAcc acc tree cont =
    match tree with
    | Tip _ -> cont (1 + acc)
    | Node (_, treeLeft, treeRight) ->
        sizeContAcc acc treeLeft (fun accLeftSize ->
        sizeContAcc accLeftSize treeRight cont)

let size tree = sizeContAcc 0 tree (fun x -> x)
```

The behavior of this version of the algorithm is:

1. You start with an accumulator acc of 0.

2. You traverse the left spine of the tree until a Tip is found, building up a continuation for each node along the way.

3. When a Tip is encountered, the continuation from the previous node is called, with accLeftSize increased by 1. The continuation makes a recursive call to sizeContAcc for its right tree, passing the continuation for the second-to-last node along the way.

4. When all is done, all the left and right trees have been explored, and the final result is delivered to the (fun x -> x) continuation.

As you can see from this example, continuation passing is a powerful control construct, although it's used only occasionally in F# programming.

Another Example: Processing Syntax Trees

One real-world example where trees may become unbalanced is syntax trees for parsed languages when the inputs are very large and machine generated. In this case, some language constructs may be repeated many times in an unbalanced way. For example, consider this data structure:

```
type Expr =
    | Add of Expr * Expr
    | Bind of string * Expr * Expr
    | Var of string
    | Num of int
```

This data structure would be suitable for representing arithmetic expressions of the forms *var*, *expr + expr*, and *bind var = expr in expr*. This chapter and Chapter 11 are dedicated to techniques for representing and processing languages of this kind. As with all tree structures, most traversal algorithms over this type of abstract syntax tree aren't naturally tail recursive. For example, here is a simple evaluator:

```
type Env = Map<string, int>

let rec eval (env : Env) expr =
    match expr with
    | Add (e1, e2) -> eval env e1 + eval env e2
    | Bind (var, rhs, body) -> eval (env.Add(var, eval env rhs)) body
    | Var var -> env.[var]
    | Num n -> n
```

The recursive call eval env rhs isn't tail recursive. For the vast majority of applications, you never need to worry about making this algorithm tail recursive. Stack overflow may be a problem; however, if bindings are nested to great depth, such as in bind v1 = (bind v2 = . . . (bind v1000000 = 1. . .)) in v1+v1. If the syntax trees come from human-written programs, you can safely assume this won't be the case. If you need to make the implementation tail recursive, however, you can use continuations, as shown in Listing 9-11.

Listing 9-11. A tail-recursive expression evaluator using continuations

```
let rec evalCont (env : Env) expr cont =
    match expr with
    | Add (e1, e2) ->
        evalCont env e1 (fun v1 ->
        evalCont env e2 (fun v2 ->
        cont (v1 + v2)))
    | Bind (var, rhs, body) ->
        evalCont env rhs (fun v1 ->
        evalCont (env.Add(var, v1)) body cont)
```

```
  | Num n ->
      cont n
  | Var var ->
      cont (env.[var])

let eval env expr = evalCont env expr (fun x -> x)
```

■ **Note**   Programming with continuations can be tricky, and you should use them only when necessary, or use the F# async type as a way of managing continuation-based code. Where possible, abstract the kind of transformation you're doing on your tree structure (for example, a map, fold, or bottom-up reduction) so you can concentrate on getting the traversal right. In the previous examples, the continuations all effectively played the role of a work list. You can also reprogram your algorithms to use work lists explicitly and to use accumulating parameters for special cases. Sometimes this is necessary to gain maximum efficiency, because an array or a queue can be an optimal representation of a work list. When you make a work list explicit, the implementation of an algorithm becomes more verbose, but in some cases debugging can become simpler.

Summary

This chapter covered some of the techniques you're likely to use in your day-to-day F# programming when working with *sequences, domain models,* and *tree-structured data.* Nearly all the remaining chapters use some of the techniques described in this chapter, and Chapter 12 goes deeper into symbolic programming based on structured-data programming techniques.

In the next chapter, you'll learn about programming with numeric data using structural and statistical methods.

CHAPTER 10

■■■

Numeric Programming and Charting

In Chapters 8 and 9, you learned constructs and techniques for programming with three important kinds of data in F#: *textual data*, *sequences of data*, and *structured data*. In this chapter, we will return to constructs and techniques for one of the most important kinds of data in programming systems: *numeric data*.

Programming with numbers is a huge topic, ultimately overlapping with many fields of mathematics, statistics, and computer science, and used industrially in applied science, engineering, economics, and finance. In this chapter, you will learn about the following:

- getting FsLab, which includes all the packages used in this chapter

- some *charting* with F#, using the FSharp.Charting library

- programming with additional basic numeric types and literals beyond simple integers and floating-point numbers already covered in Chapter 3

- using library and hand-coded routines for *summing, aggregating, maximizing,* and *minimizing* sequences

- some simple algorithmic programming with F#, implementing the KMeans clustering algorithm and applying it to some input data

- using the Math.NET library for *statistics, distributions,* and *linear algebra*

- using the Deedle library for *time series data* and *data frames*

- Using the unique F# feature *units of measure* for giving strong types to numeric data

Getting Started with FsLab

All of the FSharp.Data, Math.NET, Deedle, and FSharp.Charting packages are part of FsLab. FsLab is an integrated set of open-source packages and tools for data-science programming with F#. You can find out more about FsLab at http://www.fslab.org. You can access all the packages by downloading the single FsLab package from NuGET. Use either paket.exe or nuget.exe, as described in Chapter 2. After you download it, you can reference FsLab as follows:

```
#load "packages/FsLab/FsLab.fsx"
```

Alternatively, you can reference the load scripts and components for individual packages; for example, as follows:

```
#load "packages/FSharp.Charting/FSharp.Charting.fsx"
```

Basic Charting with FSharp.Charting

Your primary focus in this chapter will be on numeric programming itself. A very common activity associated with working with numbers is *charting*. You will now explore some basic uses of the FSharp. Charting library (use FSharp.Charting.Gtk on Linux and OSX). For example, consider creating 1,000 random points and plotting them:

```
open FSharp.Charting

let rnd = System.Random()
let rand() = rnd.NextDouble()

let randomPoints = [for i in 0 .. 1000 -> 10.0 * rand(), 10.0 * rand()]

randomPoints |> Chart.Point
```

This gives the chart shown in Figure 10-1.

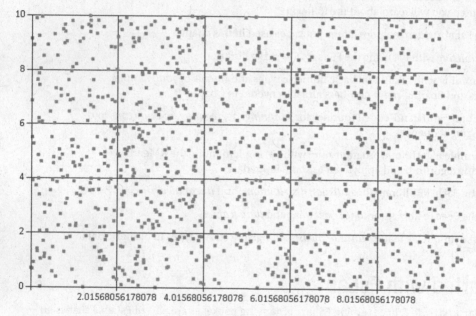

Figure 10-1. *A point chart showing a cloud of random points*

Likewise, consider two sinusoidal datasets with some random noise added:

```
let randomTrend1 = [for i in 0.0 .. 0.1 .. 10.0 -> i, sin i + rand()]
let randomTrend2 = [for i in 0.0 .. 0.1 .. 10.0 -> i, sin i + rand()]
```

You can combine two charts—the first dataset as a line, and the second as a set of points—as follows:

```
Chart.Combine [Chart.Line randomTrend1; Chart.Line randomTrend2]
```

Giving the result shown in Figure 10-2:

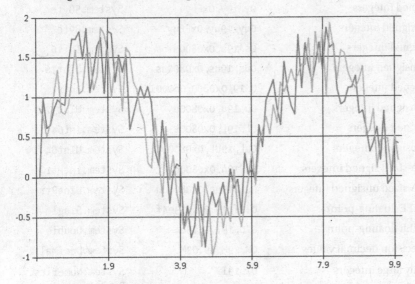

Figure 10-2. *Two line charts composed together*

Many other chart types and options are available for use with `FSharpCharting`. For example, you can add a title to your chart:

```
Chart.Line (randomTrend1,Title = "Random Trend")
```

Charting is often used with pipelining, so attributes like this are often specified using `|> fun c ->` as follows:

```
randomPoints
    |> fun c -> Chart.Line (c,Title = "Expected Trend")
```

Basic Numeric Types and Literals

We will first cover the most common base types of data manipulated in F# code, beginning with the basics of F# arithmetic. Table 10-1 lists the basic numeric types used in F# code and their corresponding literal forms. The table also lists the non-numeric types `bool` and `unit`.

Table 10-1. *Basic Types and Literals*

Type	Description	Sample Literals	Long Name
bool	True/false values	true, false	System.Boolean
sbyte	8-bit signed integers	0y, 19y, 0xFFy	System.SByte
byte	8-bit unsigned integers	0uy, 19uy, 0xFFuy	System.Byte
int16	16-bit signed integers	0s, 19s, 0x0800s	System.Int16
uint16	16-bit unsigned integers	0us, 19us, 0x0800us	System.UInt16
int, int32	32-bit signed integers	0, 19, 0x0800, 0b0001	System.Int32
uint32	32-bit unsigned integers	0u, 19u, 0x0800u	System.UInt32
int64	64-bit signed integers	0L, 19L, 0x0800L	System.Int64
uint64	64-bit unsigned integers	0UL, 19UL, 0x0800UL	System.UInt64
nativeint	Machine-sized signed integers	0n, 19n, 0x0800n	System.IntPtr
unativeint	Machine-sized unsigned integers	0un, 19un, 0x0800un	System.UIntPtr
single, float32	32-bit IEEE floating-point	0.0f, 19.7f, 1.3e4f	System.Single
double, float	64-bit IEEE floating-point	0.0, 19.7, 1.3e4	System.Double
decimal	High-precision decimal values	0M, 19M, 19.03M	System.Decimal
bigint	Arbitrarily large integers	0I, 19I	System.Numerics.BigInteger

Arithmetic Operators

Table 10-2 lists the most commonly used arithmetic operators. These are overloaded so as to work with all the numeric types listed in Table 10-1.

Table 10-2. *Arithmetic Operators and Examples*

Operator	Description	Sample Use on int	Sample Use on float
+	Unchecked addition	1 + 2	1.0 + 2.0
-	Unchecked subtraction	12 - 5	12.3 - 5.4
*	Unchecked multiplication	2 * 3	2.4 * 3.9
/	Division	5 / 2	5.0 / 2.0
%	Modulus	5 % 2	5.4 % 2.0
-	Unary negation	-(5+2)	-(5.4+2.4)

Checked Arithmetic

The behavior of these and other operators can be extended for user-defined types, a topic covered in Chapter 6. In F#, addition, subtraction, and multiplication over integers are unchecked; that is, if overflow or underflow occur beyond the representable range, wraparound occurs. For example, 2147483647 is the largest representable 32-bit integer of the int type:

```
> 2147483647 + 1;;

val it : int = -2147483648
```

You can access checked versions of arithmetic operators that raise System.OverflowException exceptions by opening the FSharp.Core.Operators.Checked module. If avoiding overflow is a priority, using the decimal, bigint, and bignum types is recommended. Division by zero raises a System.DivideByZeroException exception, except in the case of floating-point numbers, in which case it returns one of the special floating-point numbers: Infinity, -Infinity, and NaN. Operator overloading interacts with type inference—if a use of an overloaded operator isn't otherwise constrained to work on a particular type, F# assumes it works on 32-bit integers.

Arithmetic Conversions

Numeric types aren't implicitly converted—conversions among different numeric types must be made explicitly. You do this by using overloaded conversion operators. These work the same way as overloaded infix operators such as + and *. Table 10-3 shows the primary conversion operators.

Table 10-3. *Overloaded Arithmetic Conversions and Examples*

Operator	Description	Sample Use	Result
sbyte	Convert/truncate to sbyte	sbyte (-17)	-17y
byte	Convert/truncate to byte	byte 255	255uy
int16	Convert/truncate to int16	int16 0	0s
uint16	Convert/truncate to uint16	uint16 65535	65535us
int/int32	Convert/truncate to int32	int 17.8	17
uint32	Convert/truncate to uint32	uint32 12	12u
int64	Convert/truncate to int64	int64 (-100.4)	-100L
uint64	Convert/truncate to uint64	uint64 1	1UL
decimal	Convert to decimal	decimal 65.3	65.3M
float32	Convert to float32/single	float32 65	65.0f
float	Convert to float/double	float 65	65.0

These conversions are all unchecked in the sense that they won't raise exceptions. Again, the FSharp.Core.Operators.Checked module has corresponding definitions of these operators. An alternative is to use the library static methods contained in the type System.Convert, such as System.Convert.ToDouble( ). These do perform checking, which means they raise an exception if the source number can't be represented within the numeric range of the target type. As with many object-oriented library constructs, uses of System.Convert methods may require type annotations to resolve overloading, which is discussed in Chapters 5 and 6.

Arithmetic Comparisons

When used with numeric values, the binary comparison operators =, <>, <, <=, >, and >= as well as the functions min and max perform comparisons according to the natural ordering for each particular numeric type. You can also use these operators on other data types, such as to compare lists of integers, and you can customize their behavior for new types that you define. Chapter 5 discusses generic comparison in detail, and Chapter 8 discusses customizing generic comparison.

When used with floating-point values, these operators implement the IEEE semantics for NaN (Not a Number) values. For example, (NaN = NaN) is false, as are (NaN <= NaN) and (NaN < NaN).

Overloaded Math Functions

The module FSharp.Core.Operators includes the definition of a number of useful overloaded math operators. These are shown in Table 10-4 and are overloaded either on a suitable range of integer types or on the basic floating-point types.

Table 10-4. *Overloaded Math Functions and Examples*

Function	Description	Sample Use	Result
abs	Absolute value of signed numeric types	abs -10.0	10.0
cos, sin, tan	Trigonometric functions	cos 0.0	1.0
cosh, sinh, tanh	Hyperbolic trigonometric functions	cosh 1.0	1.543080635
acos, asin, atan, atan2	Inverse trigonometric functions	acos 1.0	0.0
ceil, floor	Round up, round down	ceil 1.001	2.0
truncate	Round toward zero	truncate 8.9	8.0
exp, log, log10	Exponent, logarithm, base-10 logarithm	exp 1.0	2.718281828
(**)	Power	2.0 ** 4.0	16.0

Bitwise Operations

All the integer types listed in Table 10-1 support bitwise manipulations on their underlying representations. Table 10-5 shows the bitwise manipulation operators.

Table 10-5. *Bitwise Arithmetic Operators and Examples*

Operator	Description	Sample Use	Result
&&&	Bitwise "and"	0x65 &&& 0x0F	0x05
|||	Bitwise "or"	0x65 ||| 0x18	0x7D
^^^	Bitwise "exclusive or"	0x65 ^^^ 0x0F	0x6A
~~	Bitwise negation	~~~0x65	0xFFFFFF9a
<<<	Left shift	0x01 <<< 3	0x08
>>>	Right shift (arithmetic if signed)	0x65 >>> 3	0x0C

The following sample shows how to use these operators to encode 32-bit integers into 1, 2, or 5 bytes, represented by returning a list of integers. Integers in the range from 0 to 127 return a list of length 1:

```
/// Encode an integer into 1, 2, or 5 bytes
let encode (n : int32) =
    if (n >= 0 && n <= 0x7F) then [n]
    elif (n >= 0x80 && n <= 0x3FFF) then
        [(0x80 ||| (n >>> 8)) &&& 0xFF;
         (n &&& 0xFF)]
    else [0xC0;
          ((n >>> 24) &&& 0xFF);
          ((n >>> 16) &&& 0xFF);
          ((n >>> 8) &&& 0xFF);
          (n &&& 0xFF)]
```

Here's an example of the function in action:

```
> encode 32;;

val it : int32 list = [32]

> encode 320;;

val it : int32 list = [129; 64]

> encode 32000;;

val it : int32 list = [192; 0; 0; 125; 0]
```

Sequences, Statistics, and Numeric Code

Some of the most common and simplest numeric-programming techniques with F# involve taking aggregate statistics over sequences of objects. In this section, you will learn how to use the built-in aggregation operators, such as Seq.sum and Seq.averageBy. Further, you will look at how to define additional functions with similar characteristics. In later sections, you will learn how to use functionality from the Math.NET library to perform more-advanced statistical analyses of sequences of numbers.

Summing, Averaging, Maximizing, and Minimizing Sequences

The table that follows shows how to compute the average, sum, maximum, and minimum over input sequences using operations from the Seq module to process the data.

```
data |> Seq.average
data |> Seq.sum
data |> Seq.max
data |> Seq.min
data |> Seq.averageBy (fun x -> proj)
data |> Seq.sumBy (fun x -> proj)
data |> Seq.maxBy (fun x -> proj)
data |> Seq.minBy (fun x -> proj)
```

If you are using the `FSharp.Core.Fluent` package (see Chapter 2), you can use:

```
open FSharp.Core.Fluent

data.average()
data.sum()
data.max()
data.min()
data.averageBy(fun x -> proj)
data.sumBy(fun x -> proj)
data.maxBy(fun x -> proj)
data.minBy(fun x -> proj)
```

For example, consider taking the average, sum, maximum, and minimum of a set of 1,000 numbers between 0 and 1, each generated by multiplying two random numbers drawn from a random-number generator:

```
let rnd = new System.Random()
let rand() = rnd.NextDouble()
let data = [for i in 1 .. 1000 -> rand() * rand()]

let averageOfData = data |> Seq.average
let sumOfData = data |> Seq.sum
let maxOfData = data |> Seq.max
let minOfData = data |> Seq.min
```

The results are:

```
// Random numbers, results may differ!
val averageOfData : float = 0.2365092084
val sumOfData : float = 236.5092084
val maxOfData : float = 0.9457838635
val minOfData : float = 6.153537535e-05
```

As expected, the average of the sequence lies near 0.25.

Normally, however, statistics are generated by projecting information from particular objects using operators such as `Seq.sumBy`. For example, consider taking the average X, Y, and Z positions of a random set of 1,000 points drawn in three dimensions:

```
type RandomPoint = {X : float; Y : float; Z : float}

let random3Dpoints =
    [for i in 1 .. 1000 -> {X = rand(); Y = rand(); Z = rand()}]

let averageX = random3Dpoints |> Seq.averageBy (fun p -> p.X)
let averageY = random3Dpoints |> Seq.averageBy (fun p -> p.Y)
let averageZ = random3Dpoints |> Seq.averageBy (fun p -> p.Z)
```

As expected, the results center on 0.5:

```
// Random numbers, results may differ!
val averageX : float = 0.4910144491
val averageY : float = 0.5001688922
val averageZ : float = 0.5170302648
```

Likewise, you can use Seq.maxBy to determine the element where a maximum occurs for a particular measure:

```
let maxY = random3Dpoints |> Seq.maxBy (fun p -> p.Y)
```

This operator returns the object that corresponds to the maximum:

```
// Random numbers, results may differ!
val maxY : RandomPoint = {X = 0.9829979292;
                          Y = 0.9997189497;
                          Z = 0.4552816481;}
```

Likewise, you can use minimize and maximize by other measures. For example, consider finding the point that minimizes the distance from the origin to the point:

```
let distanceFromOrigin (p : RandomPoint) = sqrt (p.X * p.X + p.Y * p.Y + p.Z * p.Z)
let closest = random3Dpoints |> Seq.minBy distanceFromOrigin
```

As expected, the point has relatively low values for all of X, Y, and Z:

```
// Random numbers, results may differ!
val distanceFromOrigin: p:RandomPoint -> float
val closest : RandomPoint = {X = 0.05287901873;
                             Y = 0.0570056001;
                             Z = 0.1018355787;}
```

Note that Seq.maxBy and Seq.minBy return the input object that maximizes or minimizes the function respectively—that is, they return the *input object* and not the *maximum/minimum* value. Some other similar operations in the F# libraries and .NET Framework return the value itself; the type signature of the operation allows you to tell the difference.

■ **Note** Sums, averages, maximums, and minimums can also be computed by using F# 3.0 *query expressions*, which will be discussed in Chapter 13. For example, you can compute an average by using an expression such as query { for x in *data* do averageBy p.X }. The advantage of this approach is that, for some external data sources such as databases, the queries and aggregation can be executed on the remote server. As we shall see in Chapter 13, this depends on how *data* has been defined. While queries can be used over sequences and other in-memory data, for most in-memory processing, you should just use operations such as Seq.averageBy to process the data.

Counting and Categorizing

A common statistical operation is categorizing elements according to some *key* (a grouping, as discussed in Chapter 9) and counting the number of elements in each group. This corresponds to building a histogram for the data based on a selection function.

The simplest way to generate a histogram for in-memory data is to use Seq.countBy, which returns a sequence of key/count pairs. For example, consider the random3Dpoints you generated in the previous section. These can be categorized into 10 quantiles depending on how far they are from the origin. The maximum distance a point can be away from the origin is $\sqrt{3}$, so we multiply by 10, divide by $\sqrt{3}$, and round down to the nearest integer to compute the bucket a point belongs to:

```
let histogram =
    random3Dpoints
    |> Seq.countBy (fun p -> int (norm p * 10.0 / sqrt 3.0) )
    |> Seq.sortBy fst
    |> Seq.toList
```

As an aside, when using FSharp.Core.Fluent these can be written as follows:

```
let histogram2 =
    random3Dpoints
      .countBy(fun p -> int (norm p * 10.0 / sqrt 3.0) )
      .sortBy(fst)
      .toList()
```

The results reveal a concentration of points at distance 0.6 * $\sqrt{3}$ = 1.03.

```
// Random numbers, results may differ!
val closest : (int * int) list =
  [(0, 1); (1, 15); (2, 52); (3, 97); (4, 173); (5, 233); (6, 256); (7, 116);
   (8, 52); (9, 5)]
```

Note that you usually have to sort the counted results by the key and convert the overall results to a concrete data structure, such as a list, array, map, or dictionary.

■ **Note**   The Math.NET library includes the type Statistics.Histogram for incrementally computing histograms from numerical input sets. You will use this type later in this chapter.

Writing Fresh Numeric Code

If you are writing a lot of numeric code, you will almost certainly want to use one of the standard math and statistical packages that can be used with F# programming, such as Math.NET, described later in this chapter. It is often necessary, however, to define new statistical computations in F# to extend the basic set of operations that are available for routine use.

As an example of this, consider defining the *variance* and *standard deviation* of a sequence of numbers. These are simple computations based on taking the average of a sequence and then the average of the sum-of-squares of variations from the average.

First, the simplest form of the operation simply computes the variance over an input array of floating-point numbers:

```
/// Compute the variance of an array of inputs
let variance (values : float[]) =
    let sqr x = x * x
    let avg = values |> Array.average
    let sigma2 = values |> Array.averageBy (fun x -> sqr (x - avg))
    sigma2

let standardDeviation values =
    sqrt (variance values)
```

These operations have types:

```
val variance : values:float [] -> float
val standardDeviation : values:float [] -> float
```

You can apply the functions to sequences of data. For example:

```
let sampleTimes = [|for x in 0 .. 1000 -> 50.0 + 10.0 * rand()|]

let exampleDeviation = standardDeviation  sampleTimes
let exampleVariance = variance sampleTimes
```

Giving results:

```
val exampleDeviation : float = 2.865331753
val exampleVariance : float = 8.210126054
```

In some circumstances, it may make sense to define projection "By" versions of these operations, and, further, it may make sense to place the operations in a utility module called "Seq", "Array", or "List", depending on the kind of input data accepted by the routine:

```
module Seq =
    /// Compute the variance of the given statistic from from the input data
    let varianceBy (f : 'T -> float) values =
        let sqr x = x * x
        let xs = values |> Seq.map f |> Seq.toArray
        let avg = xs |> Array.average
        let res = xs |> Array.averageBy (fun x -> sqr (x - avg))
        res

    /// Compute the standard deviation of the given statistic drawn from the input data
    let standardDeviationBy f values =
        sqrt (varianceBy f values)
```

■ **Note** The Math.NET library includes the functions Statistics.StandardDeviation, Statistics.Variance, Statistics.Mean, Statistics.Maximum, Statistics.Minimum, and Statistics.DescriptiveStatistics for computing basic statistics from sequences.

Making Numeric Code Generic

It is often sufficient to define statistical functions over base types, such as floating-point numbers. If necessary, this code can be made *generic*. You have already seen generic numeric algorithms in Chapter 5. You can make the code for variance and standardDeviation generic, as the underlying operations Array.average and Array.averageBy are themselves generic. For example:

```
let inline variance values =
    let sqr x = x * x
    let avg = values |> Array.average
    let sigma2 = values |> Array.averageBy (fun x -> sqr (x - avg))
    sigma2

let inline standardDeviation values =
    sqrt (variance values)
```

This code can now be used with any numeric type. The downside is that a complex relationship is asserted between the input and output types:

```
val inline variance :
  values: ^a [] ->  ^c
    when  ^a : (static member ( + ) :  ^a *  ^a ->  ^a) and
          ^a : (static member DivideByInt :  ^a * int ->  ^a) and
          ^a : (static member get_Zero : ->  ^a) and
          ^a : (static member ( - ) :  ^a *  ^a ->  ^b) and
          ^b : (static member ( * ) :  ^b *  ^b ->  ^c) and
          ^c : (static member ( + ) :  ^c *  ^c ->  ^c) and
          ^c : (static member DivideByInt :  ^c * int ->  ^c) and
          ^c : (static member get_Zero : ->  ^c)
val inline standardDeviation :
  values: ^a [] ->  ^d
    when  ^a : (static member ( + ) :  ^a *  ^a ->  ^a) and
          ^a : (static member DivideByInt :  ^a * int ->  ^a) and
          ^a : (static member get_Zero : ->  ^a) and
          ^a : (static member ( - ) :  ^a *  ^a ->  ^b) and
          ^b : (static member ( * ) :  ^b *  ^b ->  ^c) and
          ^c : (static member ( + ) :  ^c *  ^c ->  ^c) and
          ^c : (static member DivideByInt :  ^c * int ->  ^c) and
          ^c : (static member get_Zero : ->  ^c) and
          ^c : (static member Sqrt :  ^c ->  ^d)
```

This cost can sometimes be worth it, as the operation is very general—it can be used on decimals, floating-point numbers, and unitized versions of these. Further, the code produced is also usually as efficient as can be without writing a highly case-specific optimized routine.

Example: KMeans

As an example, in Listing 10-1, we will use one simple machine-learning algorithm, called *KMeans clustering*. This algorithm accepts a set of inputs, each with a vector of numbers representing *features*. For example, each input may represent an observed object, such as a flower or animal in a biology field experiment, and the features may represent a set of observed measurements of that object.

The algorithm proceeds by clustering the data around a fixed number of centroids in the feature space. Each object is assigned to the "nearest" centroid according to a distance function. Once the groups are determined, new centers are then computed, and the process is repeated.

In this implementation of the algorithm, we keep a reference to the original data, of some type T, and assume a function is given that extracts the actual feature vectors from the parameters.

Listing 10-1. KMeans clustering algorithm

```
type Input<'T> = {Data : 'T; Features : float[]}
type Centroid = float[]

module Array =
    /// Like Seq.groupBy, but returns arrays
    let classifyBy f (xs : _ []) =
        xs |> Seq.groupBy f |> Seq.map (fun (k, v) -> (k, Seq.toArray v)) |> Seq.toArray

module Seq =
    /// Return x, f(x), f(f(x)), f(f(f(x))), ...
    let iterate f x = x |> Seq.unfold (fun x -> Some (x, f x))

/// Compute the norm distance between an input and a centroid
/// using the double-pipe operator
let distance (xs : Input<_>) (ys : Centroid) =
    (xs.Features,ys)
        ||> Array.map2 (fun x y -> (x - y) * (x - y))
        |> Array.sum

/// Find the average of set of inputs. First compute xs1 + ... + xsN, pointwise,
/// then divide each element of the sum by the number of inputs.
let computeCentroidOfGroup (_, group : Input<_>[]) =
    let e0 = group.[0].Features
    [|for i in 0 .. e0.Length - 1 -> group |> Array.averageBy (fun e -> e.Features.[i])|]

/// Group all the inputs by the nearest centroid
let classifyIntoGroups inputs centroids =
    inputs |> Array.classifyBy (fun v -> centroids |> Array.minBy (distance v))

/// Repeatedly classify the inputs, starting with the initial centroids
let rec computeCentroids inputs centroids = seq {
    let classification = classifyIntoGroups inputs centroids
    yield classification
    let newCentroids = Array.map computeCentroidOfGroup classification
    yield! computeCentroids inputs newCentroids}
```

```fsharp
/// Extract the features and repeatedly classify the inputs, starting with the
/// initial centroids
let kmeans inputs featureExtractor initialCentroids =
    let inputsWithFeatures =
        inputs
        |> Seq.map (fun i -> {Data = i; Features = featureExtractor i})
        |> Seq.toArray
    let initialCentroids = initialCentroids |> Seq.toArray
    computeCentroids inputsWithFeatures initialCentroids
```

We now generate a synthetic input dataset that features four clusters of data:

```fsharp
open FSharp.Data.UnitSystems.SI.UnitSymbols

type Observation = {Time : float<s>; Location : float<m>}

let rnd = System.Random()
let rand() = rnd.NextDouble()
let randZ() = rnd.NextDouble() - 0.5

/// Create a point near the given point
let near p = {Time= p.Time + randZ() * 20.0<s>;
              Location = p.Location + randZ() * 5.0<m>}

let data =
    [for i in 1 .. 1000 -> near {Time= 100.0<s>; Location = 60.0<m>}
     for i in 1 .. 1000 -> near {Time= 120.0<s>; Location = 80.0<m>}
     for i in 1 .. 1000 -> near {Time= 180.0<s>; Location = 30.0<m>}
     for i in 1 .. 1000 -> near {Time= 70.0<s>; Location = 40.0<m>}]
```

The algorithm is run by extracting two features from the data into a normalized (0,1) range and choosing ten initial centroids at random in this two-dimensional feature space.

We discard the classifications of the points to the centroids and simply report the centroids that have been found, renormalized into the original input space:

```fsharp
let maxTime = data |> Seq.maxBy (fun p -> p.Time) |> fun p -> p.Time
let maxLoc = data |> Seq.maxBy (fun p -> p.Location) |> fun p -> p.Location

let initialCentroids = [for i in 0 .. 9 -> [|rand(); rand()|]]
let featureExtractor (p : Observation) = [|p.Time / maxTime; p.Location / maxLoc|]

kmeans data featureExtractor initialCentroids
```

This gives an infinite sequence of centroid/classification groups representing repeated iterations of the algorithm. We discard the classifications and simply report the centroids that have been found, taking only the one-hundredth iteration of the algorithm, and then we renormalize the centroids into the original input space:

```fsharp
kmeans data featureExtractor initialCentroids
    |> Seq.map (Array.map (fun (c, _) -> c.[0] * maxTime, c.[1] * maxLoc))
    |> Seq.item 100
```

This gives the resulting centroids. For example, on one sample execution, the discovered centroids for the one-hundredth iteration are:

```
> val it : (float<s> * float<m>) [] =
  [|(95.21297664, 59.92134092); (105.128182, 60.03017317);
    (120.0522592, 79.99954457); (179.7447501, 29.96446713);
    (65.97080136, 38.75120135); (75.63604991, 40.05351476);
    (64.8228706, 41.26265782)|]
```

The algorithm has determined seven centroids—those that don't classify any points are discarded—and each of these corresponds to one of the four original centroids—(100,60), (120,80), (180,30), (70,40)—used in the random generation of the data. (Several discovered centroids correspond to one original centroid; thus, the data are "over-fitted." The over-fitting of the centroid model to the data is characteristic of naïve clustering algorithms. The use of more-advanced statistical methods can avoid this.)

Statistics, Linear Algebra, and Distributions with Math.NET

In this chapter so far, you have seen how to use F# language and library constructs to implement a variety of numeric-programming tasks "from scratch." This is commonly done when using F# for writing simulators or doing basic data scripting, charting, and reporting.

For even moderately advanced math and numeric programming, however, you will want to make use of an existing F# or .NET math library. Several high-quality .NET libraries are available, and more are appearing all the time. Also, math and statistics libraries tend to have different characteristics:

- Some libraries use C/C++ code "under the hood." For example, many managed .NET libraries use the Intel MKL library or an equivalent.

- Some libraries also have an "all managed" mode, meaning that most or all of the functionality in the library is authored in C# and F#. This means, for example, that math libraries can be highly portable and used across a number of situations in which .NET code is accepted.

- Some libraries implement optimizations such as "GPU" execution, allowing some or all of the routines to execute on a graphics processor.

- The libraries differ by license and availability. Some are open source, and some are commercial.

- Some libraries are designed for use from C# or F# but also have an F#-specific wrapper.

A detailed overview of math library choices for F# can also be found at http://fsharp.org. People often ask us which libraries we recommend. Table 10-6 shows some of the frameworks and libraries available at the time of writing that may interest you.

Table 10-6. *Some Math Frameworks and Libraries Not Covered in This Chapter*

Library Name	Description	URL
Extreme Optimization	A commercial math, vector, statistics, and matrix library for .NET	www.extremeoptimization.com
FCore	A commercial F#-specific math and statistics library, particularly suitable for quantitative development	www.statfactory.co.uk
Math.NET	The standard open-source math library for the .NET Framework. Includes special functions, linear algebra, probability models, statistics, random numbers, interpolation, and integral transforms (FFT)	www.mathdotnet.com www.fslab.org
NMath	A commercial object-oriented .NET math library that supports linear algebra and function optimization. NMath Stats is a .NET statistics library that can be used for data manipulation and statistical computation, as well as for biostatistics.	www.centerspace.net

Basic Statistical Functions in Math.NET Numerics

Throughout the rest of this book, we will use the open-source library Math.NET Numerics. This is the preferred open-source math library for use with F#. It is part of a larger project called Math.NET, an umbrella project for open-source math libraries on the .NET and Mono Frameworks, and included in the FsLab suite of packages. Math.NET Numerics includes:

- types representing dense as well as sparse vectors and matrices
- a library containing a full set of standard linear-algebra routines
- a range of random-number generators with different strengths
- additional features that include support for certain numerical integration and statistical functions.

Math.NET Numerics is available for use as a pure-managed library, but it also includes wrappers for highly optimized native math libraries, such as Intel MKL and AMD ACML. This library is available under a broad open-source license, and it is available as a NuGET package. To install the library, either use the FsLab package directly (as described at the start of this chapter) or reference the NuGET package for MathNet.Numerics.FSharp and add explicit DLL references.

Some basic statistical functions in Math.NET are shown in Table 10-7. We can use the functions in the expected way:

```
open MathNet.Numerics.Statistics

let data = [for i in 0.0 .. 0.01 .. 10.0 -> sin i]

let exampleVariance = data |> Statistics.Variance
let exampleMean = data |> Statistics.Mean
let exampleMin = data |> Statistics.Minimum
let exampleMax = data |> Statistics.Maximum
```

Giving us:

```
val exampleVariance : float = 0.443637494
val exampleMean : float = 0.1834501596
val exampleMin : float = -0.9999971464
val exampleMax : float = 0.9999996829
```

Table 10-7. *Some Statistical Functions in Math.NET, in Namespace* `MathNet.Numerics.Statistics`

Notation	Description	URL
σ	Standard Deviation	`Statistics.StandardDeviation`
σ2	Variance	`Statistics.Variance`
μ	Mean	`Statistics.Mean`
max	Maximum	`Statistics.Maximum`
min	Minimum	`Statistics.Minimum`
	Computes an object giving a range of descriptive statistics for a set of numbers	`Statistics.DescriptiveStatistics`
$\binom{n}{k}$	Binomial function, number of ways of choosing k elements from n choices, "n choose k"	`Combinatorics.Combinations` `SpecialFunctions.Binomial`
$\binom{n}{k_1,k_2,\ldots,k_r}$	Multinomial function	`SpecialFunctions.Multinomial`
erf(x)	Error function	`SpecialFunctions.Erf`
erfc(x)	Complementary error function	`SpecialFunctions.Erfc`
Γ(x)	Gamma function	`SpecialFunctions.Gamma`
B(x,y)	Beta function	`SpecialFunctions.Beta`
n!	Factorial function	`SpecialFunctions.Factorial`

Using Histograms and Distributions from Math.NET Numerics

The `Math.NET Numerics` library includes implementations of all the most important statistical distributions in the namespace `MathNet.Numerics.Distributions`. For example, consider a normal (bell-curve) distribution centered on 100.0 with standard deviation 10.0:

```
open MathNet.Numerics.Distributions
open System.Collections.Generic

let exampleBellCurve = Normal(100.0, 10.0)
let samples = exampleBellCurve.Samples()
```

```
val exampleBellCurve : Normal = Normal(μ = 100, σ = 10)
val samples : seq<float> = seq [93.15201095; 107.1097763; 106.0871014; 94.16559639; ...]
```

Math.NET Numerics also includes type MathNet.Numerics.Distributions.Histogram for categorizing numeric data into a histogram. For example, we can define a function that categorizes data into a given number of buckets and generates a label for each bucket as:

```
let histogram n data =
    let h = Histogram(data, n)
    [|for i in 0 .. h.BucketCount - 1 ->
        (sprintf "%.0f-%.0f" h.[i].LowerBound h.[i].UpperBound, h.[i].Count)|]
```

Using this function, we can now chart the sample data drawn from the normal distribution as:

```
exampleBellCurve.Samples()
    |> Seq.truncate 1000
    |> histogram 10
    |> Chart.Column
```

Giving us the chart shown in Figure 10-3:

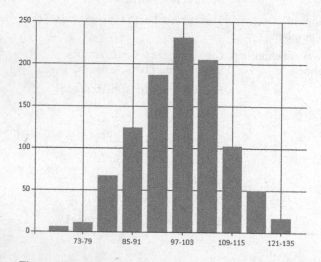

Figure 10-3. *Results from sampling a histogram distribution*

The Math.NET library supports many more-sophisticated distribution types, including multivariate Gaussian distributions (MatrixNormal), coin flips (Bernoulli), decaying-exponential distributions (Exponential), and distributions that can be used to simulate the time delays between occurrences of events (Poisson).

Using Matrices and Vectors from Math.NET

The Math.NET Numerics library includes extensive support for matrices, vectors, and linear algebra. For example, you can create and add two vectors:

```
open MathNet.Numerics
open MathNet.Numerics.LinearAlgebra
```

```
let vector1 = vector [1.0; 2.4; 3.0]
let vector2 = vector [7.0; 2.1; 5.4]

vector1 + vector2
```

Giving us:

```
val it : Vector<float> = seq [8.0; 4.5; 8.4]
```

Likewise, you can define and multiply two matrices:

```
let matrix1 = matrix [[1.0; 2.0]; [1.0; 3.0]]
let matrix2 = matrix [[1.0; -2.0]; [0.5; 3.0]]
let matrix12 = matrix1 * matrix2
```

Giving us:

```
val matrix1 : Matrix<float> = DenseMatrix 2x2-Double
1  2
1  3

val matrix2 : Matrix<float> = DenseMatrix 2x2-Double
  1  -2
0.5   3

val matrix12 : Matrix<float> = DenseMatrix 2x2-Double
  2  4
2.5  7
```

Matrix Inverses, Decomposition, and Eigenvalues

The linear-algebra support in the Math.NET Numerics library is extensive and can be configured to use highly optimized native linear-algebra packages under the hood. The default method is to use fully managed linear algebra. For example, to compute the inverse of a matrix, simply call the .Inverse() method on the matrix.

First, define a large 100x100 matrix with random numbers and compute its inverse:

```
let largeMatrix = matrix [for i in 1 .. 100 -> [for j in 1 .. 100 -> rand()]]

let inverse = largeMatrix.Inverse()
```

Next, multiply the two to check that the inverse is correct:

```
let check = largeMatrix * largeMatrix.Inverse()
```

Giving us:

```
val check : Matrix<float> =
  [[1.0; 2.775557562e-16; 4.371503159e-15; 1.887379142e-15; 1.887379142e-15;
   -1.054711873e-15; -2.664535259e-15; 6.689093723e-15; 4.440892099e-16;
   -5.551115123e-16; -2.664535259e-15; -5.551115123e-16; 2.664535259e-15;
   -2.220446049e-15; 1.110223025e-16; -1.776356839e-15; -2.886579864e-15;
   ...
```

As expected, this is numerically very close to the identity matrix. Likewise, common decompositions of matrices can be computed using the Svd(), Evd(), LU(), and QR() methods on the matrix itself. For example, to compute the eigenvalues and eigenvectors of a matrix:

```
let evd = largeMatrix.Evd()
let eigenValues = evd.EigenValues
```

Giving us:

```
val evd : Factorization.Evd
val eigenValues : Vector<Numerics.Complex>

> eigenValues;;
val it : Vector<Numerics.Complex> =
  seq
    [(49.9915503772098, 0);
     (-0.406120558380603, 2.92962073514449);
     ...
```

Adding a printer for complex numbers as follows:

```
fsi.AddPrinter (fun (c : System.Numerics.Complex) -> sprintf "%fr + %fi" c.Real c.Imaginary)
```

Gives us:

```
val eigenValues : Vector<Numerics.Complex> =
  seq
    [49.991550r + 0.000000i; -0.406121r + 2.929621i; -0.406121r + -2.929621i;
     3.095556r + 0.000000i; ...]
    ...
```

Time Series and Data Frames with Deedle

An increasingly common technique in numeric programming is the use of time-series data and data frames, popularized by R and the Pandas library of Python. You can use time-series and data-frame programming in F# via the Deedle library, which is part of the FsLab suite of numeric packages. Deedle also lets you interoperate with R and Python. Time-series and data-frame programming is a big topic, and in this book you will use just a small sample of the functionality available in Deedle.

First, you open the necessary namespaces and generate data:

```
open System
open Deedle
open MathNet.Numerics.Distributions

let start = DateTimeOffset(DateTime.Today)

let randomPrice drift volatility initial (span:TimeSpan) count =    let dist = Normal(0.0,
1.0, RandomSource=Random())
  let dt = span.TotalDays / 250.0
  let driftExp = (drift - 0.5 * pown volatility 2) * dt
  let randExp = volatility * (sqrt dt)
  (start, initial) |> Seq.unfold (fun (dt, price) ->
    let price = price * exp (driftExp + randExp * dist.Sample())
    Some((dt, price), (dt + span, price))) |> Seq.take count

let stock1 = randomPrice 0.1 3.0 20.0 (TimeSpan.FromMinutes(1.0)) 500
let stock2 = randomPrice 0.2 1.5 20.0 (TimeSpan.FromSeconds(30.0)) 1000
```

Giving us:

```
val start : DateTimeOffset = 26/10/2015 00:00:00 +00:00
val randomPrice :
  drift:float ->
    volatility:float ->
      initial:float ->
        span:TimeSpan -> count:int -> seq<DateTimeOffset * float>
val stock1 : seq<DateTimeOffset * float>
val stock2 : seq<DateTimeOffset * float>
```

The raw data can now be turned into a time series of the Deedle library:

```
let stockSeries1 = series stock1
let stockSeries2 = series stock2
```

```
val stockSeries1 : Series<DateTimeOffset,float> =

26/10/2015 00:00:00 +00:00 -> 19.9621208550249
26/10/2015 00:01:00 +00:00 -> 20.0473700064037
...                        -> ...
26/10/2015 08:18:00 +00:00 -> 22.4659473574845
26/10/2015 08:19:00 +00:00 -> 22.4642226226483

val stockSeries2 : Series<DateTimeOffset,float> =

26/10/2015 00:00:00 +00:00 -> 20.0128595701374
26/10/2015 00:00:30 +00:00 -> 19.9783872009122
...                        -> ...
26/10/2015 08:19:00 +00:00 -> 21.8583967272075
26/10/2015 08:19:30 +00:00 -> 21.8421959339634
```

Note that a time series differs from a regular sequence in that the Deedle library "knows" that the time acts as a special sort of ordered key for the data. This is used to support many time-series and data-frame operations. For example, you can zip series together:

```
let zippedSeriesWhereBothHaveData = stockSeries1.Zip(stockSeries2, JoinKind.Left)
let zippedSeriesWhereOneHasData = stockSeries1.Zip(stockSeries2, JoinKind.Right)
```

Giving us:

```
val zippedSeriesWhereBothHaveData : Series<DateTimeOffset,(float opt * float opt)> =

26/10/2015 00:00:00 +00:00 -> (20.0362216597634, 20.0128595701374)
26/10/2015 00:01:00 +00:00 -> (19.9385876603037, 19.9347932573347)
...                        -> ...
26/10/2015 08:18:00 +00:00 -> (22.4659473574845, 21.8507518100555)
26/10/2015 08:19:00 +00:00 -> (22.4642226226483, 21.8583967272075)


val zippedSeriesWhereOneHasData :Series<DateTimeOffset,(float opt * float opt)> =

26/10/2015 00:00:00 +00:00 -> (20.0362216597634, 20.0128595701374)
26/10/2015 00:00:30 +00:00 -> (<missing>, 19.9783872009122)
...                        -> ...
26/10/2015 08:19:00 +00:00 -> (22.4642226226483, 21.8583967272075)
26/10/2015 08:19:30 +00:00 -> (<missing>, 21.8421959339634)
```

The key sets are aligned and matched using rules similar to those used for database tables. For left joins, both datasets must have values. For outer joins, if any data is missing from one set the results will still contain a row. It is this kind of database thinking applied to time-series data that makes Deedle very powerful.

This kind of idea can also be applied to whole collections of related time series called data frames. For example:

```
// Contains value every minute
let f1 = Frame.ofColumns ["S1" => stockSeries1]
// Contains value every 30 seconds
let f2 = Frame.ofColumns ["S2" => stockSeries2]
let alignedData = f1.Join(f2, JoinKind.Outer)
```

Giving us:

```
val alignedData : Frame<DateTimeOffset,string> =

                              S1                S2
26/10/2015 00:00:00 +00:00 -> 20.0362216597634  20.0128595701374
26/10/2015 00:00:30 +00:00 -> <missing>         19.9783872009122
:                          -> ...               ...
26/10/2015 08:19:00 +00:00 -> 22.4642226226483  21.8583967272075
26/10/2015 08:19:30 +00:00 -> <missing>         21.8421959339634
```

■ **Note**   Time-series and data-frame programming is a powerful data-analysis programming paradigm that you have only touched on in passing in this book. See `bluemountaincapital.github.io/Deedle/` for a fully detailed guide on this topic.

Units of Measure

F# includes a beautiful feature in its type system called *units of measure*. This feature lets you annotate numeric types with annotations such as kg, m, and sec that indicate the kind of quantity the number represents—that is, its unit of measure. You can also use the feature to annotate other, user-defined types that are ultimately based on numeric quantities. This feature is best explained using code for physical simulations and is rooted in scalable quantities. It also has a wide range of surprising applications outside physical simulation, including annotating code with units for integer quantities, such as pixels, currencies, or click-counts.

The F# 3.0 library comes with predefined unit definitions matching the Système International (SI) standard in the namespace `FSharp.Data.UnitSystems.SI.UnitNames` (for base unit names such as `kilogram` and derived units such as `hertz`) and namespace `FSharp.Data.UnitSystems.SI.UnitSymbols` (for standard abbreviations of these names, such as `kg` and `hz`, respectively). To define a new kind of measure annotation, use a type definition with a `Measure` attribute. (Note, while it is uncommon to use lowercase for types–see Chapter 19–for unit types the casing matches the expected case of the name and the abbreviation of the unit)

```
[<Measure>]
type click

[<Measure>]
type pixel

[<Measure>]
type money
```

Once a set of measures is defined or chosen from the library, the basic numeric types and literals can include these qualifications. For example, consider the computation "we are receiving 200 clicks every second, and the website has been running 3.5 seconds." This computation can be performed as:

```
open FSharp.Data.UnitSystems.SI.UnitNames
open FSharp.Data.UnitSystems.SI.UnitSymbols

let rateOfClicks = 200.0<click/s>
let durationOfExecution = 3.5<s>
```

A calculation involving these quantities is:

```
let numberOfClicks = rateOfClicks * durationOfExecution
```

The inferred type of `numberOfClicks` is `float<click>`.

```
val numberOfClicks: float<click> = 700.0
```

If a mismatched unit type is used in such a calculation, a type error is reported.

Adding Units to a Numeric Algorithms

Code that uses units of measure may also be generic over the units involved. This is particularly important for generic algorithms. To demonstrate this, consider three simple algorithms for integrating a function, as learned in elementary calculus. We will take the first three numerical-integration techniques for integrating a function $f(x)$ of one variable over the range from a to b, taken from http://en.wikipedia.org/wiki/Numerical_integration. These are

- integrating by evaluating f at a midpoint

$$\int_a^b f(x)\ dx \approx (b-a)\ f\left(\frac{a+b}{2}\right).$$

- integrating by evaluating f at the endpoints

$$\int_a^b f(x)\ dx \approx (b-a)\ \frac{f(a)+f(b)}{2}.$$

- integrating by evaluating f at a mesh of n sub-intervals evenly spaced between a and b

$$\int_a^b f(x)\ dx \approx \frac{b-a}{n}\left(\frac{f(a)+f(b)}{2} + \sum_{k=1}^{n-1} f\left(a+k\frac{b-a}{n}\right)\right)$$

Translating these into code, the non-unitized implementations are:

```
let integrateByMidpointRule f (a, b) = (b - a) * f ((a + b) / 2.0)

let integrateByTrapezoidalRule f (a, b) = (b - a) * ((f a + f b) / 2.0)

let integrateByIterativeRule f (a, b) n =
    (b - a) / float n *
    ((f a + f b) / 2.0 +
      List.sum [for k in 1 .. n - 1 -> f (a + float k * (b - a) / float n)])
```

Giving us types:

```
val integrateByMidpointRule : f:(float -> float) -> a:float * b:float -> float
val integrateByTrapezoidalRule :  f:(float -> float) -> a:float * b:float -> float
val integrateByIterativeRule :  f:(float -> float) -> a:float * b:float -> n:int -> float
```

Take a look at the unitized implementations. Note that you author the unitized numbers by introducing type annotations:

```
let integrateByMidpointRule (f : float<'u> -> float<'v>) (a : float<'u>, b : float<'u>) =
    (b - a) * f ( (a+b) / 2.0)

let integrateByTrapezoidalRule (f : float<'u> -> float<'v>) (a : float<'u>, b : float<'u>) =
    (b - a) * ((f a + f b) / 2.0)
```

```
let integrateByIterativeRule (f : float<'u> -> float<'v>) (a : float<'u>, b : float<'u>) n =
    (b - a) / float n *
    ((f a + f b) / 2.0 +
      List.sum [for k in 1 .. n - 1 -> f (a + float k * (b - a) / float n)])
```

In all three cases, the inferred, generic unitized type for the functions gives a return type of float<'u 'v>:

```
val integrateByMidpointRule :
  f:(float<'u> -> float<'v>) -> a:float<'u> * b:float<'u> -> float<'u 'v>

val integrateByTrapezoidalRule :
  f:(float<'u> -> float<'v>) -> a:float<'u> * b:float<'u> -> float<'u 'v>

val integrateByIterativeRule :
  f:(float<'u> -> float<'v>) -> a:float<'u> * b:float<'u> -> n:int -> float<'u 'v>
```

For example, if the x dimension is "time" (for example, float<s>) and the y dimension is "velocity" (for example, float<m/s>), the result type is float<s m/s>, which simplifies to float<m> (for example, a distance). This is as expected; integrating a velocity over a period of time gives the distance traveled.

When we run these implementations of integration using a linear function as input, they all give the same answer. For example, consider a velocity function for a ball thrown upward at an initial velocity of 100.0<m/s> and falling back to earth at 9.81<m/s>. Using the numeric-integration techniques, we can evaluate the distance the ball is above the earth at time 10 seconds as:

```
let velocityFunction (t : float<s>) = 100.0<m/s> + t * -9.81<m/s^2>

let distance1 = integrateByMidpointRule velocityFunction (0.0<s>, 10.0<s>)
let distance2 = integrateByTrapezoidalRule velocityFunction (0.0<s>, 10.0<s>)
let distance3 = integrateByIterativeRule velocityFunction (0.0<s>, 10.0<s>) 10
```

As expected, the results of these approximate integration techniques are precise for a linear function, and in all three cases, the distance computed is 509.5 meters:

```
val distance1 : float<m> = 509.5
val distance2 : float<m> = 509.5
val distance3 : float<m> = 509.5
```

As our second example, consider adding units to the variance function you defined earlier in this chapter. In this case, we also change the input to be a sequence, to make the operation more general still:

```
let variance (values : seq<float<_>>) =
    let sqr x = x * x
    let xs = values |> Seq.toArray
    let avg = xs |> Array.average
    let variance = xs |> Array.averageBy (fun x -> sqr (x - avg))
    variance

let standardDeviation values =
    sqrt (variance values)
```

The types of the operations are now unitized:

```
val variance : values:seq<float<'u>> -> float<'u ^ 2>
val standardDeviation : values:seq<float<'u>> -> float<'u>
```

You can now apply the functions to unitized sequences of data. For example:

```
let sampleTimes = [for x in 0 .. 1000 -> 50.0<s> + 10.0<s> * rand()]

let exampleDeviation = standardDeviation sampleTimes

let exampleVariance = variance sampleTimes
```

Giving us:

```
val exampleDeviation : float<s> = 2.865331753
val exampleVariance : float<s ^ 2> = 8.210126054
```

Adding Units to a Type Definition

When you define a new type, you may include measure parameters as part of the definition of the type. These parameters must be marked with the Measure attribute. For example:

```
type Vector2D<[<Measure>] 'u> = {DX : float<'u>; DY : float<'u>}
```

You can use units of measure in conjunction with object-oriented programming, discussed in Chapter 6. For example, here is a vector-type generic over units of measure:

```
/// Two-dimensional vectors
type Vector2D<[<Measure>] 'u>(dx : float<'u>, dy : float<'u>) =

    /// Get the X component of the vector
    member v.DX = dx

    /// Get the Y component of the vector
    member v.DY = dy

    /// Get the length of the vector
    member v.Length = sqrt(dx * dx + dy * dy)

    /// Get a vector scaled by the given factor
    member v.Scale k = Vector2D(k * dx, k * dy)

    /// Return a vector shifted by the given delta in the X coordinate
    member v.ShiftX x = Vector2D(dx + x, dy)

    /// Return a vector shifted by the given delta in the Y coordinate
    member v.ShiftY y = Vector2D(dx, dy + y)
```

```
/// Get the zero vector
static member Zero = Vector2D<'u>(0.0<_>, 0.0<_>)

/// Return a constant vector along the X axis
static member ConstX dx = Vector2D<'u>(dx, 0.0<_>)

/// Return a constant vector along the Y axis
static member ConstY dy = Vector2D<'u>(0.0<_>, dy)

/// Return the sum of two vectors
static member (+) (v1 : Vector2D<'u>, v2 : Vector2D<'u>) =
    Vector2D(v1.DX + v2.DX, v1.DY + v2.DY)

/// Return the difference of two vectors
static member (-) (v1 : Vector2D<'u>, v2 : Vector2D<'u>) =
    Vector2D(v1.DX - v2.DX, v1.DY - v2.DY)

/// Return the pointwise-product of two vectors
static member (.*) (v1 : Vector2D<'u>, v2 : Vector2D<'u>) =
    Vector2D(v1.DX * v2.DX, v1.DY * v2.DY)
```

Note that some measure annotations are needed on zero values in this sample. In addition, a vector type such as this should normally implement the IComparable interface as well as the Equals and GetHashCode methods, as described in Chapter 8.

Applying and Removing Units

When you have a unitized value, you can remove the units by simply applying the float function. When you have a nonunitized value, you can apply units to it by using LanguagePrimitives.FloatWithMeasure. For example:

```
let three = float 3.0<kg>

let sixKg = LanguagePrimitives.FloatWithMeasure<kg> (three + three)
```

Giving us:

```
val three : float. = 3.0
val sixKg : float<kg> = 6.0
```

Some Limitations of Units of Measure

Units of measure can help tame the sea of floating-point numbers that tends to characterize numerical programming. It is important, however, to be aware of the limitations of this feature so as to avoid its overzealous application to the detriment of productivity, code stability, and readability. In particular:

- Units of measure work best for algorithms that deal with summing, multiplying, dividing, and taking integral roots of inputs, such as square roots. Units of measure do not work well for algorithms or computations that deal with other functions, such as exponentials. Algorithms that use these functions can still often be "coarsely" unitized, first by removing units from the inputs and then by reapplying them to the outputs.

- Units of measure must be applied to a particular type, such as float<_>, decimal<_>, or a user-defined type, such as Vector2D<_> earlier. In particular, you can't easily be generic over both this type *and* the unit of measure, except by writing an inlined generic algorithm, as explained in Chapter 5.

- Units of measure are an F#-only feature, and they are "erased" at runtime. This means that the unit information isn't available to "reflective" metaprogramming. Unit information *can* be provided by F# type providers, something we will look at in Chapter 17.

■ **Note** F# units of measure are covered only briefly in this book. For more information, see the MSDN documentation or Andrew Kennedy's four-part introduction to the topic; search for "Andrew Kennedy Units of Measure Part One" or visit http://blogs.msdn.com/andrewkennedy.

EXERCISE: UNITIZING KMEANS

The KMeans algorithm uses distances between feature vectors based on sums of squares. This means that the feature vectors should, ideally, be "normalized" to prevent one dimension from dominating another.

This indicates that units of measure can be used with the algorithm, in the sense that the algorithm should be generic with respect to the "dimension" of the normalized numbers used in the feature space. As an exercise, try to apply units of measure to the earlier code. Start by making the type definitions unitized in this way:

```
type Input<'T, [<Measure>] 'u> =
  { Data : 'T
    Features: float<'u>[] }

type Centroid<[<Measure>] 'u> = float<'u>[]
```

You then simply need to adjust the code in a couple of places, and type inference will look after the rest. The adjustments needed are:

```
let distance (xs : Input<_, _>) (ys : Centroid<_>) = ...

let computeCentroidOfGroup (_, group : Input<_>[]) = ...
```

Summary

In this chapter, you've seen how to use F# to perform a range of numeric-programming tasks, including the use of the powerful open-source Math.NET library. In the next chapter, we will turn to an increasingly important part of programming––building parallel, reactive, and event-driven systems.

CHAPTER 11

■■■

Reactive, Asynchronous, and Parallel Programming

So far in this book, you've seen functions and objects that process their inputs immediately using a single thread of execution in which the code runs to completion and produces useful results or state changes. In this chapter, you will turn your attention to *concurrent, parallel, asynchronous,* and *reactive* programs. These represent substantially different approaches to programming from those you've seen so far. Some reasons for turning to these techniques are the following:

- To achieve better scalability in a web server

- To achieve better responsiveness in a graphical user interface (GUI)

- To report progress results during a long-running computation and to support the cancellation of these computations

- To achieve greater throughput in a reactive application

- To achieve faster processing rates on a multiprocessor machine or cluster

- To take advantage of the I/O parallelism available in modern disk drives or network connections

- To sustain processing while network and disk I/O operations are in process

This chapter will cover techniques that can help achieve these outcomes, including:

- Using events to report results back from a component

- Using F# async computations to handle network requests and other asynchronous I/O operations

- Using F# agents and pattern matching to process message queues

- Interoperating with .NET tasks

- Using low-level shared-memory primitives to implement new concurrency techniques and control access to mutable data structures

   In Chapter 15, you will see one of the most common type of reactive programs: GUI programs that respond to events raised on the GUI thread. The inner loop of such an application (contained in the GUI library) spends most of its time blocked and waiting for the underlying operating system to notify it of a relevant event, such as a click from the user or a timer event from the operating system. This notification is received as an event in a message queue. Many GUI programs have only a single thread of execution, so all computation happens on the GUI thread. This can lead to problems, such as nonresponsive user interfaces. This is one of many reasons why it's important to master some techniques of concurrent and asynchronous programming.

Introducing Terminology

Let's begin by looking more closely at some terminology:

- *Processes* are, in the context of this chapter, standard operating-system (OS) processes. Each F# program runs in its own process, and multiple instances of different F# programs are often running on the same machine.

- *Threads* are, in the context of this chapter, standard operating-system threads. Each process has many threads running within the one process.

- *Concurrent programs* are ones with multiple threads of execution, each typically executing different code, or running at different execution points within the same code. Simultaneous execution may be simulated by scheduling and descheduling the threads, which is done by the OS. For example, most OS services and GUI applications are concurrent.

- *Parallel programs* are one or more processes or threads executing simultaneously. For example, many modern microprocessors have two or more physical CPUs capable of executing processes and threads in parallel. Parallel programs can also be *data parallel*. For example, a massively parallel device, such as a graphics processor unit (GPU), can process arrays and images in parallel. Parallel programs can also be a cluster of computers on a network, communicating via message passing. Historically, some parallel scientific programs have even used email for communication.

- *Asynchronous programs* perform requests that don't complete immediately but rather are fulfilled at a later time; the program issuing the request does meaningful work in the meantime. For example, most network I/O is inherently asynchronous. A web crawler is also a highly asynchronous program, managing hundreds or thousands of simultaneous network requests.

- *Reactive programs* are ones whose normal mode of operation is to be in a state of waiting for some kind of input, such as waiting for user input or for input from a message queue via a network socket. For example, GUI applications and web servers are reactive programs.

Parallel, asynchronous, concurrent, and reactive programs bring many challenges. For example, these programs are nearly always *nondeterministic*. This makes debugging more challenging, because it's difficult to step through a program; even pausing a running program with outstanding asynchronous requests may cause timeouts. Most dramatically, incorrect concurrent programs may *deadlock*, which means that all threads are waiting for results from some other thread, and no thread can make progress. Programs may also *livelock*, in which processing is occurring and messages are being sent between threads, but no useful work is being performed.

Events

One recurring idiom in .NET programming is that of *events*. An event is something you can listen to by registering a callback with it. For example, here's how you can create a file watcher that raises events when changes occur to files in a local directory:

```
> open System.IO;;

> let watcher = new FileSystemWatcher(__SOURCE_DIRECTORY__, EnableRaisingEvents=true);;

val watcher: FileSystemWatcher = FileSystemWatcher

> watcher.Changed.Add(fun args -> printfn "File %s was changed!" args.Name);;
```

If you run this code in F# Interactive and then edit files in the current directory of your script (__SOURCE_DIRECTORY__), messages will appear showing that the program is reacting to events being raised corresponding to your edits.

```
File script.fsx was changed!
```

In F# terminology, watcher.Changed is an event, and watcher.Changed.Add registers an event handler, also known as a callback, with the event. You can register multiple callbacks with the same event, and some objects make multiple events available to register with.

If necessary, you can remove event handlers by first adding them using the AddHandler method and then removing them using RemoveHandler. In this case, you can also stop events from being raised by disposing of the watcher object:

```
> watcher.Dispose();;
```

The process of saving the file *triggers* (or fires) the event, which means that the callbacks are called in the order they were registered. Events can't be triggered "from the outside." In other words, you can't trigger the Changed event on a file watcher from your program (except by actually changing a file); you can only handle it. Events also have *event arguments*. In the first example shown, the event arguments are called args, and they are ignored. Many events from libraries often pass arguments of type System.EventArgs or some related type, such as FileSystemEventArgs. These arguments usually carry pieces of information. For example, a value of type FileSystemEventArgs has the properties FullName, Name, and ChangeType.

■ **Note** .NET event handlers also have an argument meant to bring information about the object source of the event. F# hides this argument in the process of making events first class and allowing their composition, as will be explained later.

Events occur throughout the design of the .NET libraries. Table 11-1 shows some of these.

Table 11-1. *A Selection of Events from the .NET Libraries*

Type	Some Sample Events
System.AppDomain	AssemblyLoad, AssemblyResolve, DomainUnload, ProcessExit, UnhandledException (and others)
System.Diagnostics.Process	ErrorDataReceived, Exited, OutputDataReceived (and others)
System.IO.FileSystemWatcher	Changed, Created, Deleted, Error, Renamed (and others)
System.Timers.Timer	Elapsed

Creating and Publishing Events

As you write code in F#, particularly object-oriented code, you will sometimes need to implement, publish, and trigger events. The normal method for doing this is to call new Event<_>(). Listing 11-1 shows how to define an event object that is triggered at random intervals.

Listing 11-1. Creating a RandomTicker that defines, publishes, and triggers an event

```
open System
open System.Windows.Forms

type RandomTicker(approxInterval) =
    let timer = new Timer()
    let rnd = new System.Random(99)
    let tickEvent = new Event<int> ()

    let chooseInterval() : int =
        approxInterval + approxInterval / 4 - rnd.Next(approxInterval / 2)

    do timer.Interval <- chooseInterval()

    do timer.Tick.Add(fun args ->
        let interval = chooseInterval()
        tickEvent.Trigger interval;
        timer.Interval <- interval)

    member x.RandomTick = tickEvent.Publish
    member x.Start() = timer.Start()
    member x.Stop() = timer.Stop()
    interface IDisposable with
        member x.Dispose() = timer.Dispose()
```

Here's how you can instantiate and use this type:

```
> let rt = new RandomTicker(1000);;

val rt : RandomTicker

> rt.RandomTick.Add(fun nextInterval -> printfn "Tick, next = %A" nextInterval);;

> rt.Start();;

Tick, next = 1072
Tick, next = 927
Tick, next = 765
...

> rt.Stop();;
```

Events are understood by all .NET languages, but F# event values are not. This is because F# allows you to go one step further and use events as first-class values. If you need to ensure that your events can be used by other .NET languages, do both of the following:

- Create the events using new Event<*DelegateType*, *Args*> instead of new Event<*Args*>.

- Publish the event as a property of a type with the [<CLIEvent>] attribute.

Events as First-Class Values

In F#, an event such as watcher.Changed is a *first-class value*, which means you can pass it around like any other value. The main advantage this brings is that you can use the combinators in the F# library module FSharp.Control.Event to map, filter, and otherwise transform the event stream in compositional ways. For example, the following code filters the event stream from form.MouseMove so that only events with X > 100 result in output to the console:

```
form.MouseMove
    |> Event.filter (fun args -> args.X > 100)
    |> Event.listen (fun args -> printfn "Mouse, (X, Y) = (%A, %A)" args.X args.Y)
```

If you work with events a lot, you will find yourself factoring out useful portions of code into functions that preprocess event streams. Table 11-2 shows some functions from the F# Event module. One interesting combinator is Event.partition, which splits an event into two events based on a predicate.

Table 11-2. Some Functions from the Event Module, with Simplified Types

Function	Type
Event.choose	: ('T -> 'U option) -> IEvent<'T> -> IEvent<'U>
Event.filter	: ('T -> bool) -> IEvent<'T> -> IEvent<'T>
Event.scan	: ('U -> 'T -> 'U) -> 'U -> IEvent<'T> -> IEvent<'U>
Event.map	: ('T -> 'U) -> IEvent<'T> -> IEvent<'U>
Event.partition	: ('T -> bool) -> IEvent<'T> -> IEvent<'T> * IEvent<'T>

From Events to Observables

Events are a common F# way to express configurable callback structures. F# also supports a more advanced mechanism for configurable callbacks that is more compositional than events. These are called *observables*, and, in particular, they are characterized by the System.IObservable and System.IObserver types in the core libraries.

F# makes working with observables very easy, because all event objects also implement these interfaces and so can be used as observables. The FSharp.Core library contains a small library of combinators for working with observables. For example, here's how you can use observables to work with click events raised by a form:

```
> rt.RandomTick |> Observable.add (fun evArgs -> printfn "Tick!");;
```

When you run this code in F# Interactive, you will see the expected printing each time the form is clicked. Likewise, you can filter and map using Observable.filter and Observable.map combinators

Programming with observables is powerful and compositional, and many further combinators are supported by the Rx programming library, available through the Rx library website on www.github.com. While we don't cover Rx in detail in this book, it is commonly used with F#.

■ **Note** Because events and observables allow you to register callbacks, it's sometimes important to be careful about the thread on which an event is being raised. This is particularly true when you're programming with parallel or background threads.

Asynchronous Computations

Most of the code you've seen so far in this book has run in a "blocking" fashion using active loops and recursion with limited support for cancellation. Event-driven code is the first exception, but structuring all your code with events can lead to "callback spaghetti." In practice, a lot of modern code has to be "non-blocking" or asynchronous, responding to completed web requests or waiting to acquire shared resources. Fortunately, F# comes with a powerful set of techniques for structuring non-blocking programs in a natural way without using explicit callbacks. These are called *asynchronous computations*, or just *async*. The next three sections will cover how to use async to structure asynchronous and message-processing tasks in ways that preserve the essential logical structure of your code.

Fetching Multiple Web Pages in Parallel, Asynchronously

One of the most intuitive asynchronous tasks is fetching a web page; we all use web browsers that can fetch multiple pages simultaneously. The samples in Chapter 2 show how to fetch pages synchronously. This is useful for many purposes, but browsers and high-performance web crawlers have tens of thousands of connections in flight at once. Listing 11-2 shows how to use async computations to fetch several web pages simultaneously using F# async programing.

Listing 11-2. Fetching three web pages simultaneously

```
open System.Net
open System.IO

let museums =
    [ "MOMA", "http://moma.org/";
        "British Museum", "http://www.thebritishmuseum.ac.uk/";
        "Prado", "http://www.museodelprado.es/" ]

let fetchAsync(nm, url : string) =
    async {
        printfn "Creating request for %s..." nm
        let req = WebRequest.Create(url)

        let! resp = req.AsyncGetResponse()

        printfn "Getting response stream for %s..." nm
        let stream = resp.GetResponseStream()

        printfn "Reading response for %s..." nm
        let reader = new StreamReader(stream)
        let html = reader.ReadToEnd()

        printfn "Read %d characters for %s..." html.Length nm
    }

Async.Parallel [for nm, url in museums -> fetchAsync(nm, url)]
    |> Async.Ignore
    |> Async.RunSynchronously
```

The types of these functions and values are:

```
val museums : (string * string) list
val fetchAsync : nm:string * url:string -> Async<unit>
```

When run on one of our machines via F# Interactive, the output of the code from Listing 11-2 is:

```
Creating request for MOMA...
Creating request for British Museum...
Creating request for Prado...
Getting response for MOMA...
Reading response for MOMA...
Getting response for Prado...
Reading response for Prado...
Read 188 characters for Prado...
Read 41635 characters for MOMA...
Getting response for British Museum...
Reading response for British Museum...
Read 24341 characters for British Museum...
```

F# async computations are characterized by async { ... } blocks of type Async<'T>. A value of type Async<'T> represents a program fragment that will generate a value of type 'T at some point in the future. In Listing 11-2, the key operation is the let! operation within the async { ... } expression. Let's take a closer look:

```
async { ...
        let! resp  = req.AsyncGetResponse()
        ... }
```

Within async expressions, the construct let! var = expr in body means "perform the operation expr asynchronously and bind the result to var when the operation completes. Then, continue by executing the rest of the computation body." With this in mind, you can now see what fetchAsync does:

- It synchronously requests a web page.

- It asynchronously awaits a response to the request.

- It gets the response Stream.

- It reads to the end of the stream synchronously with a StreamReader.

- It prints the total number of characters read synchronously.

Finally, you would use the method Async.RunSynchronously to initiate the execution of the overall asynchronous computation, blocking until it completes.

Understanding Asynchronous Computations

Asynchronous computations are different from normal computations for one primary reason: an *asynchronous operation* (e.g., let!) is different from a *synchronous operation* (e.g., let). When an asynchronous wait is performed, the remainder of the computation is "captured" (or "suspended") and placed aside, registered for execution when the operation completes. In the meantime, the program can get on with other work. This means slightly different things in different contexts, but it may mean, for example, that a request handler in a web server can get on with processing other requests while the operation completes.

One side effect of this is that async { ... } computations tend to "hop" between different operating-system threads. To see this, let's augment the asynchronous computation from Listing 11-2 with diagnostics that show the ID of the underlying .NET thread at each point of active execution. You can do this by replacing uses of printfn in the function fetchAsync with uses of the following function:

```
let tprintfn fmt =
    printf "[Thread %d]" System.Threading.Thread.CurrentThread.ManagedThreadId;
    printfn fmt
```

After doing this, the output changes to:

```
[Thread 12]Creating request for MOMA...
[Thread 13]Creating request for British Museum...
[Thread 12]Creating request for Prado...
[Thread 8]Getting response for MOMA...
[Thread 8]Reading response for MOMA...
[Thread 9]Getting response for Prado...
[Thread 9]Reading response for Prado...
[Thread 9]Read 188 characters for Prado...
```

```
[Thread 8]Read 41635 characters for MOMA...
[Thread 8]Getting response for British Museum...
[Thread 8]Reading response for British Museum...
[Thread 8]Read 24341 characters for British Museum...
```

Note how each individual async { ... } computation hops between threads; the MOMA request started on thread 12 and finished life on thread 8. Each async computation in Listing 11-2 executes in the same way:

- It starts life running in the "thread pool." For .NET programs, the thread pool is a pool of operating-system threads processing a queue containing user work items. The number of threads in the thread pool is automatically tuned.

- When the async computation reaches the AsyncGetResponse call, the rest of the computation is registered as an I/O completion action in the .NET thread pool. No thread is blocked while the request is in progress.

- When the requests complete, they trigger a callback executed as a new task in the thread pool. This callback may be serviced by a different thread than the one that initiated the call.

Another way to look at this is that async { ... } values provide a form of *managed asynchronous computation*, which means that several aspects of asynchronous programming are handled automatically:

- *Exception propagation is added for free*: If an exception is raised during an asynchronous step, the exception terminates the entire asynchronous computation and cleans up any resources declared using use, and the exception value is then handed to a continuation. Exceptions may also be caught and managed within the asynchronous computation by using try/with/finally.

- *Cancellation checking is added for free*: The execution of an Async<'T> workflow automatically checks a cancellation flag at each asynchronous operation. Cancellation can be controlled through the use of cancellation tokens.

- *Resource lifetime management* is fairly simple: You can protect resources across parts of an asynchronous computation by using use inside the workflow syntax.

Table 11-3 shows the common constructs used in asynchronous computation expressions. For example, the asynchronous computation

```
async {
    let req = WebRequest.Create("http://moma.org/")
    let! resp = req.AsyncGetResponse()
    let stream = resp.GetResponseStream()
    let reader = new StreamReader(stream)
    let html = reader.ReadToEnd()
    return html
}
```

is shorthand for the code

```
async.Delay(fun () ->
    let req = WebRequest.Create("http://moma.org/")
    async.Bind(req.AsyncGetResponse(), (fun resp ->
```

```
let stream = resp.GetResponseStream()
let reader = new StreamReader(stream)
let html = reader.ReadToEnd()
async.Return html)))
```

The key to understanding the F# async expressions is to understand the meaning of let!. In the case of async workflows, let! executes one asynchronous computation and schedules the next computation for execution after the first asynchronous computation completes. This is syntactic sugar for the async.Bind operation.

Table 11-3. Common Constructs Used in async { ... } Workflow Expressions

Construct	Description
let! pat = expr	Executes the async computation expr and binds its result to pat when it completes. If expr has type Async<'T>, then pat has type 'T. Equivalent to async.Bind(expr,(fun pat -> ...))
let pat = expr	Executes an expression synchronously and binds its result to pat immediately. If expr has type 'T, pat has type 'T.
do! expr	Equivalent to let! () = expr
do expr	Equivalent to let () = expr
return expr	Evaluates the expression and returns its value as the result of the containing asynchronous computation. Equivalent to async.Return(expr)
return! expr	Executes the expression as an asynchronous computation and returns its result as the overall result of the containing asynchronous computation. Equivalent to expr
use pat = expr	Executes the expression immediately and binds its result immediately. Calls the Dispose method on each variable bound in the pattern when the subsequent asynchronous computation terminates, regardless of whether it terminates normally or by an exception. Equivalent to async.Using(expr,(fun pat -> ...))

ASYNC COMPUTATIONS AND CONTINUATIONS

async { ... } values have type Async<'T> and are essentially a way of writing continuation-passing or structured-callback programs implicitly. Continuations themselves were described in Chapter 9 along with techniques to pass them explicitly. Under the hood, async computations call a *success continuation* when the asynchronous computation completes and an *exception continuation* if it fails. If you put aside the question of cancellation, values of type Async<'T> are effectively identical to the following type:

```
type Async<'T> = Async of ('T -> unit) * (exn -> unit) -> unit
```

Here, the functions are the success continuation and exception continuations, respectively. Each value of type Async<'T> should eventually call one of these two continuations.

Example: Parallel File Processing Using Async Computations

This section will show a slightly longer example of asynchronous I/O processing. The running sample is an application that must read a large number of image files and perform some processing on them. This kind of application may be *compute bound* (if the processing takes a long time and the file system is fast) or *I/O bound* (if the processing is quick and the file system is slow). Using asynchronous techniques tends to give good overall performance gains when an application is I/O bound, and it can also give performance improvements for compute-bound applications if asynchronous operations are executed in parallel on multicore machines.

Listing 11-3 shows a synchronous implementation of the image-transformation program.

Listing 11-3. A synchronous image processor

```
open System.IO
let numImages = 200
let size = 512
let numPixels = size * size

let makeImageFiles () =
    printfn "making %d %dx%d images... " numImages size size
    let pixels = Array.init numPixels (fun i -> byte i)
    for i = 1 to numImages  do
        System.IO.File.WriteAllBytes(sprintf "Image%d.tmp" i, pixels)
    printfn "done."

let processImageRepeats = 20

let transformImage (pixels, imageNum) =
    printfn "transformImage %d" imageNum;
    // Perform a CPU-intensive operation on the image.
    for i in 1 .. processImageRepeats do
        pixels |> Array.map (fun b -> b + 1uy) |> ignore
    pixels |> Array.map (fun b -> b + 1uy)

let processImageSync i =
    use inStream =  File.OpenRead(sprintf "Image%d.tmp" i)
    let pixels = Array.zeroCreate numPixels
    let nPixels = inStream.Read(pixels,0,numPixels);
    let pixels' = transformImage(pixels,i)
    use outStream =  File.OpenWrite(sprintf "Image%d.done" i)
    outStream.Write(pixels',0,numPixels)

let processImagesSync () =
    printfn "processImagesSync...";
    for i in 1 .. numImages do
        processImageSync(i)
```

You assume the image files already are created using the code:

```
> System.Environment.CurrentDirectory <- __SOURCE_DIRECTORY__;;

> makeImageFiles();;
```

You leave the transformation on the image largely unspecified, such as the function `transformImage`. By changing the value of `processImageRepeats`, you can adjust the computation from compute bound to I/O bound.

The problem with this implementation is that each image is read and processed sequentially when in practice multiple images can be read and transformed simultaneously, giving much greater throughput. Listing 11-4 shows the implementation of the image processor using an async computation.

Listing 11-4. The async image processor

```
let processImageAsync i =
    async {
        use inStream = File.OpenRead(sprintf "Image%d.tmp" i)
        let! pixels = inStream.AsyncRead(numPixels)
        let  pixels2 = transformImage(pixels, i)
        use outStream = File.OpenWrite(sprintf "Image%d.done" i)
        do! outStream.AsyncWrite(pixels2)
    }

let processImagesAsync() =
    printfn "processImagesAsync...";
    let tasks = [for i in 1 .. numImages -> processImageAsync(i)]
    Async.RunSynchronously (Async.Parallel tasks) |> ignore
    printfn "processImagesAsync finished!"
```

On one of our machines, the async version of the code ran up to three times as fast as the synchronous version (in total elapsed time) when `processImageRepeats` is 20 and `numImages` is 200. A factor of 2 was achieved consistently for any number of `processImageRepeats`, because this machine had two CPUs.

Let's take a closer look at this code. The call `Async.RunSynchronously (Async.Parallel ...)` executes a set of asynchronous operations, collects their results (or their exceptions), and returns the overall array of results to the original code. The core async computation is introduced by the `async { ... }` construct. Let's look at the inner workflow line by line:

```
async { use inStream = File.OpenRead(sprintf "Image%d.tmp" i)
        ... }
```

This line opens the input stream synchronously using `File.OpenRead`. Although this is a synchronous operation, the use of `use` indicates that the lifetime of the stream is managed over the remainder of the workflow. The stream is closed when the variable is no longer in scope—that is, at the end of the workflow—even if async activations occur in between. If any step in the workflow raises an uncaught exception, the stream is also closed while handling the exception.

The next line reads the input stream asynchronously using `inStream.AsyncRead`:

```
async { use inStream =  File.OpenRead(sprintf "Image%d.tmp" i)
        let! pixels = inStream.AsyncRead(numPixels)
        ... }
```

`Stream.AsyncRead` is an extension method added to the .NET `System.IO.Stream` class that is defined in the F# library, and it generates a value of type `Async<byte[]>`. The use of `let!` executes this operation asynchronously and registers a callback. When the callback is invoked, the value `pixels` is bound to the result of the operation, and the remainder of the async computation is executed. The next line transforms the image synchronously using transformImage:

```
async { use inStream = File.OpenRead(sprintf "Image%d.tmp" i)
        let! pixels = inStream.AsyncRead(numPixels)
        let  pixels' = transformImage(pixels, i)
        ... }
```

Like the first line, the next line opens the output stream. Using use guarantees that the stream is closed by the end of the workflow regardless of whether exceptions are thrown in the remainder of the workflow:

```
async { use inStream = File.OpenRead(sprintf "Image%d.tmp" i)
        let! pixels = inStream.AsyncRead(numPixels)
        let  pixels' = transformImage(pixels, i)
        use outStream = File.OpenWrite(sprintf "Image%d.done" i)
        ... }
```

The final line of the workflow performs an asynchronous write of the image. Once again, AsyncWrite is an extension method added to the .NET System.IO.Stream class that is defined in the F# library:

```
async { use inStream = File.OpenRead(sprintf "Image%d.tmp" i)
        let! pixels = inStream.AsyncRead(numPixels)
        let  pixels' = transformImage(pixels,i)
        use outStream = File.OpenWrite(sprintf "Image%d.done" i)
        do! outStream.AsyncWrite(pixels')  }
```

If you now return to the first part of the function, you can see that the overall operation of the function is to create numImages individual async operations, using a sequence expression that generates a list:

```
let tasks = [ for i in 1 .. numImages -> processImageAsync(i) ]
```

You can compose these tasks in parallel using Async.Parallel and then run the resulting process using Async.RunSynchronously. This waits for the overall operation to complete and returns the result:

```
Async.RunSynchronously (Async.Parallel tasks)
```

Table 11-4 shows some of the primitives and combinators commonly used to build async computations. Take the time to compare Listings 11-3 and 11-4. Notice:

- The overall structure and flow of the core of Listing 11-4 is similar to that of Listing 11-3 (that is, the synchronous algorithm), even though it includes steps executed asynchronously.

- The performance characteristics of Listing 11-4 are the same as those of Listing 11-3. Any overhead involved in executing the asynchronous computation is easily dominated by the overall cost of I/O and image processing. It's also much easier to experiment with modifications, such as making the write operation synchronous.

Table 11-4. *Some Common Primitives Used to Build* `Async<'T>` *Values*

Member/Type	Description
`Async.FromContinuations(callback)`	Builds a single primitive step of an async computation. The function that implements the step is passed continuations to call after the step is complete or if the step fails.
`Async.FromBeginEnd(beginAction, endAction)`	Builds a single async computation from a pair of `BeginOperation`/`EndOperation` methods.
`Async.AwaitTask(task)`	Builds a single async computation from a .NET 4.0 task. .NET tasks are returned by many .NET 4.0 APIs.
`Async.Parallel(computations)`	Builds a composite async computation that runs the given async computations in parallel and waits for results from all to be returned. Each may either terminate with a value or return an exception. If any raises an exception, then the others are canceled, and the overall async computation also raises the same exception.

Running Async Computations

Values of type `Async<'T>` are usually run using the functions listed in Table 11-5. You have already seen samples of `Async.RunSynchronously` earlier in this chapter.

Table 11-5. *Common Methods in the* `Async` *Type Used to Run* `Async<'T>` *Values*

Member/Type	Description
`Async.RunSynchronously(async)`	Runs an operation in the thread pool and waits for its result.
`Async.Start(async)`	Queues the async computation as an operation in the thread pool.
`Async.StartImmediate(async)`	Starts the async computation on the current thread. It will run on the current thread until the first point where a continuation in scheduled for the thread; for example, at a primitive asynchronous I/O operation.
`Async.StartChild(async)`	Queues the async computation, initially as a work item in the thread pool, but inherits the cancellation handle from the current async computation.

The most important function in this list is `Async.StartImmediate`. This starts an async computation using the current thread to run the prefix of the computation. For example, if you start an async computation from a GUI thread, the prefix of the computation will run on the GUI thread. This should be your primary way of starting async computations when doing GUI programming or when implementing server-side asynchronous processes using systems such as ASP.NET that have a dedicated "page handling" thread.

Common I/O Operations in Asynchronous Computations

Async programming is becoming more widespread because of the increased use of multicore machines and networks in applications. Many .NET APIs now come with both synchronous and asynchronous versions of their functionality. For example, all web-service APIs generated by .NET tools have async versions of their requests. A quick scan of the .NET API documentation on the Microsoft website reveals the asynchronous operations listed in Table 11-6. These all have equivalent `Async<'T>` operations that are defined in the F# libraries as extensions of the corresponding .NET types.

Table 11-6. *Some Async Operations in the .NET Libraries and Corresponding Expected F# Naming Scheme*

.NET Asynchronous Operations	F# Naming Scheme	Description
`Stream.Begin/EndRead` (pair) `Stream.ReadAsync` (task)	`AsyncRead`	Reads a stream of bytes asynchronously. See also `FileStream`, `NetworkStream`, `DeflateStream`, `IsolatedStorageFileStream`, and `SslStream`.
`Stream.Begin/EndWrite` (pair) `Stream.WriteAsync` (task)	`AsyncWrite`	Writes a stream of bytes asynchronously. See also `FileStream`.
`Socket.Begin/EndAccept` (pair) `Socket.AcceptAsync` (task)	`AsyncAccept`	Accepts an incoming network socket request asynchronously.
`Socket.Begin/EndReceive` (pair) `Socket.ReceiveAsync` (task)	`AsyncReceive`	Receives data on a network socket asynchronously.
`Socket.Begin/EndSend` (pair) `Socket.SendAsync` (task)	`AsyncSend`	Sends data on a network socket asynchronously.
`WebRequest.Begin/ EndGetResponse` `WebRequest.GetResponseAsync`	`AsyncGetResponse`	Makes an asynchronous web request. See also `FtpWebRequest` and `HttpWebRequest`.

Sometimes, you may need to write a few primitives to map .NET asynchronous operations into the F# asynchronous framework. You will see some examples later in this section.

Understanding Exceptions and Cancellations

Two recurring topics in asynchronous programming are exceptions and cancellations. Let's first explore some of the behavior of asynchronous programs with regard to exceptions:

```
> let failingAsync = async { do failwith "fail" };;

val failingAsync: Async<unit>

> Async.RunSynchronously failingAsync;;

System.Exception
Stopped due to error

> let failingAsyncs = [async {do failwith "fail A"};
                       async {do failwith "fail B"}];;

val failingAsyncs : Async<unit> list
```

```
> Async.RunSynchronously (Async.Parallel failingAsyncs);;

System.Exception: fail A
stopped due to error

> Async.RunSynchronously (Async.Parallel failingAsyncs);;

System.Exception: fail B
stopped due to error
```

From these examples, you can see the following:

- Async computations fail only when they're actually executed. The construction of an async using the async { ... } syntax never fails directly.

- Async computations that are run using Async.RunSynchronously report any failure back to the controlling thread as an exception.

- It's nondeterministic which async computation will fail first.

- Async computations composed using Async.Parallel report the first failure from among the various computations. An attempt is made to cancel other tasks by setting the cancellation flag for the group of tasks, and any further failures are ignored.

You can wrap a task using the Async.Catch combinator. This has the type:

```
static member Catch : computation:Async<'T> -> Async<Choice<'T,exn>>
```

For example:

```
> Async.RunSynchronously (Async.Catch failingAsync);;

val it : Choice<unit,exn> =
  Choice2Of2
    System.Exception: fail
```

You can also handle errors by using try/finally in an async { ... } workflow.

Interoperating with .NET Tasks

In C# 5.0 and .NET 4.0, the .NET Framework was updated with *tasks*. Tasks represent already-started computations with a mutable register to hold the result, and many tasks are returned by many .NET 4.0 APIs. Some of the operations producing tasks are shown in Table 11-6. In F#, the best way to deal with tasks is normally to immediately consume them in an asynchronous computation by using Async.AwaitTask, and you publish F# async computations as tasks using Async.StartAsTask.

Table 11-7. *Some Methods with Which to Consume and Produce Tasks*

Member/Usage	Description
`Async.AwaitTask(task)`	Builds a single asynchronous computation that awaits the completion of an already-running .NET 4.0 task
`Async.StartAsTask(computation)`	Starts an asynchronous computation as a .NET 4.0 task

It can also sometimes be useful to program with tasks directly using the library primitives available in the .NET libraries. In particular, tasks support a rich (and somewhat bewildering) number of primitives for controlling the timing and scheduling of computations. Examples of doing this can be found in C# programming guides on the web, and they can readily be translated to F#.

Agents

A distinction is often made between *shared-memory* concurrency and *message-passing* concurrency. The former is often more efficient on local machines and is covered in the section "Using Shared-Memory Concurrency" later in this chapter. The latter scales to systems in which there is no shared memory—for example, distributed systems—and also can be used to avoid performance problems associated with shared memory. Asynchronous message passing and processing is a common foundation for concurrent programming, and this section will look at some simple examples of message-passing programs.

Introducing Agents

This section will cover a simple kind of message processing called *mailbox processing* that's popular in languages such as Erlang. A *mailbox* is a message queue that you can scan for a message that is particularly relevant to the message-processing agent you're defining. Listing 11-5 shows a concurrent agent that implements a simple counter by processing a mailbox as messages arrive. The type `MailboxProcessor` is defined in the F# library—in this book, we use the name `Agent` for this type through the use of a type alias.

Listing 11-5. Implementing a counter using an agent

```
type Agent<'T> = MailboxProcessor<'T>

let counter =
    new Agent<_>(fun inbox ->
        let rec loop n =
            async {printfn "n = %d, waiting..." n
                   let! msg = inbox.Receive()
                   return! loop (n + msg)}
        loop 0)
```

The type of the counter is `Agent<int>`, in which the type argument indicates that this object expects to be sent messages of type `int`:

```
type Agent<'T> = MailboxProcessor<'T>
val counter : Agent<int>
```

The "Message Processing and State Machines" sidebar describes the general pattern of Listing 11-5 and the other MailboxProcessor examples in this chapter, all of which can be thought of as *state machines*. With this in mind, let's take a closer look at Listing 11-5. First, let's use counter on some simple inputs:

```
> counter.Start();;

n = 0, waiting...

> counter.Post(1);;

n = 1, waiting...

> counter.Post(2);;

n = 3, waiting...

> counter.Post(1);;

n = 4, waiting...
```

Looking at Listing 11-5, note that calling the Start method causes the processing agent to enter loop with n = 0. The agent then performs an asynchronous Receive request on the inbox for the MailboxProcessor; that is, the agent waits asynchronously until a message has been received. When the message msg is received, the program calls loop (n+msg). As additional messages are received, the internal counter (actually an argument) is incremented further.

You post messages to the agent using counter.Post. The type of inbox.Receive is as follows:

```
member Receive: ?timeout:int -> Async<'Message>
```

Using an asynchronous Receive ensures that no real threads are blocked for the duration of the wait. This means the previous techniques scale to many thousands of concurrent agents.

MESSAGE PROCESSING AND STATE MACHINES

Listing 11-5 shares a common structure with many of the other message-processing components you see in this chapter, all of which are *state machines*. This general structure is:

```
let agent =
    MailboxProcessor.Start(fun inbox ->

        // The states of the state machine
        let rec state1(args) = async { ... }
        and state2(args) = async { ... }
        ...
        and stateN(args) = async { ... }

        // Enter the initial state
        state1(initialArgs))
```

That is, message-processing components typically use sets of recursive functions, each defining an asynchronous computation. Each of these functions can be thought of as a state, and one of these states is identified as the initial state. You can pass arguments between these states just as you can pass them between any other set of recursive functions.

Creating Objects That React to Messages

Often, it's wise to hide the internals of an asynchronous computation behind an object, because the use of message passing can be seen as an implementation detail. Listing 11-5 doesn't show you how to retrieve information from the counter, except by printing it to the standard output. Furthermore, it doesn't show how to ask the processing agent to exit. Listing 11-6 shows how to implement an object wrapping an agent that supports Increment, Stop, and Fetch messages.

Listing 11-6. Hiding a mailbox and supporting a fetch method

```
/// The internal type of messages for the agent
type internal msg = Increment of int | Fetch of AsyncReplyChannel<int> | Stop

type CountingAgent() =
    let counter = MailboxProcessor.Start(fun inbox ->
        // The states of the message-processing state machine...
        let rec loop n =
            async {let! msg = inbox.Receive()
                   match msg with
                   | Increment m ->
                       // increment and continue...
                       return! loop(n + m)
                   | Stop ->
                       // exit
                       return ()
                   | Fetch replyChannel  ->
                       // post response to reply channel and continue
                       do replyChannel.Reply n
                       return! loop n}

        // The initial state of the message-processing state machine...
        loop(0))

    member a.Increment(n) = counter.Post(Increment n)
    member a.Stop() = counter.Post Stop
    member a.Fetch() = counter.PostAndReply(fun replyChannel -> Fetch replyChannel)
```

The inferred public types indicate how the presence of a concurrent agent is successfully hidden by the use of an object:

```
type CountingAgent =
    new : unit -> CountingAgent
    member Fetch : unit -> int
    member Increment : n:int -> unit
    member Stop : unit -> unit
```

Here, you can see an instance of this object in action:

```
> let counter = new CountingAgent();;

val counter : CountingAgent

> counter.Increment(1);;

> counter.Fetch();;

val it : int = 1
> counter.Increment(2);;

> counter.Fetch();;

val it : int = 3

> counter.Stop();;
```

Listing 11-6 shows several important aspects of message passing and processing using the mailbox-processing model:

- Internal message protocols are often represented using discriminated unions. Here, the type msg has cases Increment, Fetch, and Stop, corresponding to the three methods accepted by the object that wraps the overall agent implementation.

- Pattern matching over discriminated unions gives a succinct way to process messages. A common pattern is a call to inbox.Receive() or inbox.TryReceive() followed by a match on the message contents.

- The PostAndReply on the MailboxProcessor type gives us a way to post a message and wait for a reply. The temporary *reply channel* created should form part of the message. A reply channel is an object of type FSharp.Control. AsyncReplyChannel<'reply>, which in turn supports a Post method. The MailboxProcessor can use this to post a reply to the waiting caller. In Listing 11-6, the channel is sent to the underlying message-processing agent counter as part of the Fetch message.

Table 11-8 summarizes the most important members available on the MailboxProcessor type.

Table 11-8. *Some Members of the* `MailboxProcessor<'Message>` *Type*

Member/Usage	Description
`agent.Post(message)`	Posts a message to a mailbox queue
`agent.Receive(?timeout)`	Returns the next message in the mailbox queue. If no messages are present, it performs an asynchronous wait until the message arrives. If a timeout occurs, then it raises a `TimeoutException`.
`agent.Scan(scanner, ?timeout)`	Scans the mailbox for a message in which the function returns a `Some(_)` value. Returns the chosen result. If no messages are present, performs an asynchronous wait until more messages arrive. If a timeout occurs, then raises a `TimeoutException`.
`agent.TryReceive(?timeout)`	Like `Receive`, but if a timeout occurs, then returns `None`
`agent.TryScan(scanner, ?timeout)`	Like `Scan`, but if a timeout occurs, then returns `None`

Scanning Mailboxes for Relevant Messages

It's common for a message-processing agent to end up in a state in which it's not interested in all messages that may appear in a mailbox, but rather is interested only in a subset of them. For example, you may be awaiting a reply from another agent and aren't interested in serving new requests. In this case, it's essential that you use `MailboxProcessor.Scan` rather than `MailboxProcessor.Receive`. Table 11-8 shows the signatures of both of these. The former lets you choose between available messages by processing them in order, whereas the latter forces you to process every message. Listing 11-7 shows an example of using `MailboxProcessor.Scan`.

Listing 11-7. Scanning a mailbox for relevant messages

```
type Message =
    | Message1
    | Message2 of int
    | Message3 of string

let agent =
    MailboxProcessor.Start(fun inbox ->
        let rec loop() =
            inbox.Scan(function
                | Message1 ->
                    Some (async {do printfn "message 1!"
                                 return! loop()})
                | Message2 n ->
                    Some (async {do printfn "message 2!"
                                 return! loop()})
                | Message3 _ ->
                    None)
        loop())
```

You can now post these agent messages, including messages of the ignored kind Message3:

```
> agent.Post(Message1);;

message 1!

> agent.Post(Message2(100));;

message 2!

> agent.Post(Message3("abc"));;

> agent.Post(Message2(100));;

message 2!

> agent.CurrentQueueLength;;

val it : int = 1
```

When you send Message3 to the message processor, the message is ignored. The last line, however, shows that the unprocessed Message3 is still in the message queue, which you could examine using the backdoor property UnsafeMessageQueueContents.

Example: An Asynchronous Agent for Web Crawling

At the start of this chapter, we mentioned that the rise of the web and other forms of networks is a major reason for the increasing importance of concurrent and asynchronous programming. Listing 11-8 shows an implementation of a web crawler using asynchronous programming and mailbox-processing techniques.

Listing 11-8. A scalable, controlled, asynchronous web crawler

```
open System.Collections.Generic
open System.Net
open System.IO
open System.Threading
open System.Text.RegularExpressions

let limit = 50
let linkPat = "href=\s*\"[^\"h]*(http://[^&\"]*)\""
let getLinks (txt:string) =
    [ for m in Regex.Matches(txt,linkPat)  -> m.Groups.Item(1).Value ]

// A type that helps limit the number of active web requests
type RequestGate(n:int) =
    let semaphore = new Semaphore(initialCount=n,maximumCount=n)
    member x.AsyncAcquire(?timeout) =
        async {
            let! ok = Async.AwaitWaitHandle(semaphore,
                                            ?millisecondsTimeout=timeout)
```

```fsharp
            if ok then
                return
                  { new System.IDisposable with
                        member x.Dispose() =
                            semaphore.Release() |> ignore }
            else
                return! failwith "couldn't acquire a semaphore"
        }

// Gate the number of active web requests
let webRequestGate = RequestGate(5)

// Fetch the URL, and post the results to the urlCollector.
let collectLinks (url:string) =
    async {
        // An Async web request with a global gate
        let! html =
            async {
                // Acquire an entry in the webRequestGate. Release
                // it when 'holder' goes out of scope
                use! holder = webRequestGate.AsyncAcquire()

                let req = WebRequest.Create(url,Timeout=5)

                // Wait for the WebResponse
                use! response = req.AsyncGetResponse()

                // Get the response stream
                use reader = new StreamReader(response.GetResponseStream())

                // Read the response stream (note: a synchronous read)
                return reader.ReadToEnd()
            }

        // Compute the links, synchronously
        let links = getLinks html

        // Report, synchronously
        printfn "finished reading %s, got %d links" url (List.length links)

        // We're done
        return links
    }

/// 'urlCollector' is a single agent that receives URLs as messages. It creates new
/// asynchronous tasks that post messages back to this object.
let urlCollector =
    MailboxProcessor.Start(fun self ->

        // This is the main state of the urlCollector
        let rec waitForUrl (visited : Set<string>) =
```

```
async {
    // Check the limit
    if visited.Count < limit then

        // Wait for a URL...
        let! url = self.Receive()
        if not (visited.Contains(url)) then
            // Start off a new task for the new url. Each collects
            // links and posts them back to the urlCollector.
            do! Async.StartChild
                    (async { let! links = collectLinks url
                             for link in links do
                                self.Post link }) |> Async.Ignore


        return! waitForUrl(visited.Add(url))
}

// This is the initial state.
waitForUrl(Set.empty))
```

You can initiate a web crawl from a particular URL as follows:

```
> urlCollector.Post "http://news.google.com";;

finished reading http://news.google.com, got 191 links
finished reading http://news.google.com/?output=rss, got 0 links
finished reading http://www.ktvu.com/politics/13732578/detail.html, got 14 links
finished reading http://www.washingtonpost.com/wp-dyn/content/art..., got 218 links
finished reading http://www.newsobserver.com/politics/story/646..., got 56 links
finished reading http://www.foxnews.com/story/0,2933,290307,0...1, got 22 links
...
```

The key techniques shown in Listing 11-8 are as follows:

- The type RequestGate encapsulates the logic needed to ensure that you place a global limit on the number of active web requests occurring at any point. This is instantiated to the particular instance webRequestGate with limit 5. This uses a System.Threading.Semaphore object to coordinate access to this shared resource. Semaphores are discussed in more detail in "Using Shared-Memory Concurrency."

- The RequestGate type ensures that web requests sitting in the request queue don't block threads but rather wait asynchronously as callback items in the thread pool until a slot in the webRequestGate becomes available.

- The collectLinks function is a regular asynchronous computation. It first enters the RequestGate (that is, acquires one of the available entries in the Semaphore). After a response has been received, it reads off the HTML from the resulting reader, scrapes the HTML for links using regular expressions, and returns the generated set of links.

- The urlCollector is the only message-processing program. It's written using a MailboxProcessor. In its main state, it waits for a fresh URL and spawns a new asynchronous computation to call collectLinks once one is received. For each collected link, a new message is sent back to the urlCollector's mailbox. Finally, it recurses to the waiting state, having added the fresh URL to the overall set of URLs you've traversed so far.

- The AsyncAcquire method of the RequestGate type uses a design pattern called a *holder*. The object returned by this method is an IDisposable object that represents the acquisition of a resource. This holder object is bound using use, and this ensures that the resource is released when the computation completes or when the computation ends with an exception.

Listing 11-8 shows that it's relatively easy to create sophisticated, scalable asynchronous programs using a mix of message-passing and asynchronous-I/O techniques. Modern web crawlers have thousands of outstanding open connections, indicating the importance of using asynchronous techniques in modern, scalable, web-based programming.

Example: Using async for CPU Parallelism

One of the great advantages of F# async programming is that it can be used for both CPU and I/O parallel-programming tasks. For example, you can use it for many CPU parallelism tasks that don't perform any I/O but rather carry out straight CPU-bound computations.

Optimized, partitioned CPU parallelism is often done by using Async.Parallel with a number of tasks that exactly matches the number of physical processors on a machine. For example, the following code shows parallel initialization of an array in which each cell is filled by running the input function. The implementation of this function makes careful use of shared-memory primitives (a topic discussed later in this book) and is highly efficient:

```
open System.Threading
open System

// Initialize an array by a parallel init using all available processors
// Note, this primitive doesn't support cancellation.
let parallelArrayInit n f =
    let currentLine = ref -1
    let res = Array.zeroCreate n
    let rec loop () =
        let y = Interlocked.Increment(currentLine)
        if y < n then res.[y] <- f y; loop()

    // Start just the right number of tasks, one for each physical CPU
    Async.Parallel [for i in 1 .. Environment.ProcessorCount -> async {do loop()}]
        |> Async.Ignore
        |> Async.RunSynchronously

    res
```

```
> let rec fib x = if x < 2 then 1 else fib (x - 1) + fib (x - 2)

> parallelArrayInit 25 (fun x -> fib x);;

val it : int [] =
  [|1; 1; 2; 3; 5; 8; 13; 21; 34; 55; 89; 144; 233; 377; 610; 987; 1597; 2584;
    4181; 6765; 10946; 17711; 28657; 46368; 75025 |]
```

Under the Hood: Implementing Async.Parallel

Async.Parallel can appear magical. Computation tasks are created, executed, and resynchronized almost without effort. Listing 11-9 shows that a basic implementation of this operator is simple and again helps you see how Async<'T> values work under the hood.

Listing 11-9. A basic implementation of a fork-join parallel operator

```
let forkJoinParallel(taskSeq) =
    Async.FromContinuations (fun (cont, econt, ccont) ->
        let tasks = Seq.toArray taskSeq
        let count = ref tasks.Length
        let results = Array.zeroCreate tasks.Length
        tasks |> Array.iteri (fun i p ->
            Async.Start
                (async {let! res = p
                        results.[i] <- res;
                        let n = System.Threading.Interlocked.Decrement(count)
                        if n = 0 then cont results}))) 
```

This basic implementation first converts the input task sequence to an array and then creates mutable state count and results to record the progress of the parallel computations. It then iterates through the tasks and queues each for execution in the .NET thread pool. Upon completion, each writes its result and decrements the counter using an atomic Interlocked.Decrement operator, discussed further in the section "Using Shared-Memory Concurrency" at the end of this chapter. The last process to finish calls the continuation with the collected results.

In practice, Async.Parallel is implemented more efficiently than shown above and takes into account exceptions and cancellations; again, see the F# library code for full details.

Using Shared-Memory Concurrency

The final topics covered in this chapter are the various primitive mechanisms used for threads, shared-memory concurrency, and signaling. In many ways, these are the assembly language of concurrency.

This chapter has concentrated mostly on techniques that work well with immutable data structures. That isn't to say you should *always* use immutable data structures. It is, for example, perfectly valid to use mutable data structures as long as they're accessed from only one particular thread. Furthermore, private mutable data structures can often be safely passed through an asynchronous computation, because at each point the mutable data structure is accessed by only one thread, even if different parts of the asynchronous computation are executed by different threads. This doesn't apply to workflows that use operators such as Async.Parallel and Async.StartChild that start additional threads of computation.

This means we've largely avoided covering shared-memory primitives so far, because F# provides powerful declarative constructs, such as async computations and message passing, that often subsume the need to resort to shared-memory concurrency. A working knowledge of thread primitives and shared-memory concurrency is still very useful, however, especially if you want to implement your own basic constructs or highly efficient concurrent algorithms on shared-memory hardware.

Creating Threads Explicitly

This chapter has avoided showing how to work with threads directly, instead relying on abstractions like F# async and the .NET thread pool. If you want to create threads directly, here is a short sample:

```
open System.Threading
let t = new Thread(ThreadStart(fun _ ->
                printfn "Thread %d: Hello" Thread.CurrentThread.ManagedThreadId));
t.Start()
printfn "Thread %d: Waiting!" Thread.CurrentThread.ManagedThreadId

t.Join()
printfn "Done!"
```

When run, this gives us:

```
val t : Thread

Thread 1: Waiting!
Thread 10: Hello
Done!
```

■ **Caution** Always avoid using `Thread.Suspend`, `Thread.Resume`, and `Thread.Abort`. These are guaranteed to put obscure concurrency bugs in your program. One of the only compelling uses for `Thread.Abort` is to implement Ctrl+C in an interactive development environment for a general-purpose language, such as F# Interactive.

Creating Tasks Explicitly

Just as you can create threads explicitly, you can also create .NET tasks explicitly. In general, F# coding prefers async { ... } to direct uses of tasks, because the cancellation tokens and mutable registers used to hold intermediate results are hidden when doing async { ... } programming. If all other things are equal, use async. However, if you need to program more directly with tasks, you can do so. Listing 11-10 shows some of the basic coding patterns for creating and using .NET tasks directly.

Listing 11-10. Shared-memory code with a race condition

```
open System.Threading
open System.Threading.Tasks

// Simulate doing something
let doSomething(ct: CancellationToken) =
    printfn "doing something..."
    System.Threading.Thread.Sleep 100
    printfn "done something..."

// Creating a task
let task = Task.Run (fun () -> doSomething())

// A cancellable operation
let doSomethingCancellable(ct:CancellationToken) =
    printfn "doing something..."
    ct.ThrowIfCancellationRequested()
    System.Threading.Thread.Sleep 100
    ct.ThrowIfCancellationRequested()
    printfn "done something..."

// Create a handle for cancellation
let cts = new CancellationTokenSource()

// Start the task...
let task2 = Task.Run (fun () -> doSomethingCancellable(cts.Token))

// Attempt to cancel the task
cts.Cancel()
```

Shared Memory, Race Conditions, and the .NET Memory Model

Many multithreaded applications use mutable data structures shared among multiple threads. Without synchronization, these data structures will almost certainly become corrupt: threads may read data that have been only partially updated (because not all mutations are *atomic*), or two threads may write to the same data simultaneously (a *race condition*). Mutable data structures are usually protected by *locks*, although lock-free mutable data structures are also possible.

Shared-memory concurrency is a difficult and complicated topic, and a considerable amount of good material on .NET shared-memory concurrency is available on the web. All this material applies to F# when you're programming with mutable data structures such as reference cells, arrays, and hash tables, and the data structures can be accessed from multiple threads simultaneously. F# mutable data structures map to .NET memory in fairly predictable ways; for example, mutable references become mutable fields in a .NET class, and mutable fields of word size can be assigned atomically.

On modern microprocessors, multiple threads can see views of memory that aren't consistent; that is, not all writes are propagated to all threads immediately. The guarantees given are called a *memory model* and are usually expressed in terms of the ordering dependencies among instructions that read/write memory locations. This is, of course, deeply troubling, because you have to think about a huge number of possible reorderings of your code, and it's one of the main reasons why shared mutable data structures are difficult to work with.

Using Locks to Avoid Race Conditions

Locks are the simplest way to enforce mutual exclusion between two threads attempting to read or write the same mutable memory location. Listing 11-11 shows an example of code with a race condition.

Listing 11-11. Shared-memory code with a race condition

```
type MutablePair<'T, 'U>(x : 'T, y : 'U) =
    let mutable currentX = x
    let mutable currentY = y
    member p.Value = (currentX, currentY)
    member p.Update(x, y) =
        // Race condition: This pair of updates is not atomic
        currentX <- x
        currentY <- y

let p = new MutablePair<_, _>(1, 2)
do Async.Start (async {do (while true do p.Update(10, 10))})
do Async.Start (async {do (while true do p.Update(20, 20))})
```

Here is the definition of the F# lock function:

```
open System.Threading
let lock (lockobj : obj) f =
    Monitor.Enter lockobj
    try
        f()
    finally
        Monitor.Exit lockobj
```

The pair of mutations in the Update method isn't atomic; that is, one thread may have written to currentX, another then writes to both currentX and currentY, and the final thread then writes to currentY, leaving the pair holding the value (10,20) or (20,10). Mutable data structures are inherently prone to this kind of problem if shared among multiple threads. Luckily, F# code tends to have fewer mutations than imperative languages, because functions normally take immutable values and return a calculated value. When you do use mutable data structures, they shouldn't be shared among threads, or you should design them carefully and document their properties with respect to multithreaded access.

Here is one way to use the F# lock function to ensure that updates to the data structure are atomic. Locks are also required on uses of the property p.Value:

```
do Async.Start (async { do (while true do lock p (fun () -> p.Update(10,10))) })
do Async.Start (async { do (while true do lock p (fun () -> p.Update(20,20))) })
```

■ **Caution** If you use locks inside data structures, do so only in a simple way that uses them to enforce the concurrency properties you've documented. Don't lock just for the sake of it, and don't hold locks longer than necessary. In particular, beware of making indirect calls to externally supplied function values, interfaces, or abstract members while a lock is held. The code providing the implementation may not be expecting to be called when a lock is held, and it may attempt to acquire further locks in an inconsistent fashion.

Using ReaderWriterLock

It's common for mutable data structures to be read more than they're written. Indeed, mutation often is used only to initialize a mutable data structure. In this case, you can use a .NET ReaderWriterLock to protect access to a resource. For example, consider the functions:

```
open System.Threading

let readLock (rwlock : ReaderWriterLock) f =
  rwlock.AcquireReaderLock(Timeout.Infinite)
  try
      f()
  finally
      rwlock.ReleaseReaderLock()

let writeLock (rwlock : ReaderWriterLock) f =
  rwlock.AcquireWriterLock(Timeout.Infinite)
  try
      f()
      Thread.MemoryBarrier()
  finally
      rwlock.ReleaseWriterLock()
```

Listing 11-12 shows how to use these functions to protect the MutablePair class.

Listing 11-12. Shared-memory code with a race condition

```
type MutablePair<'T, 'U>(x : 'T, y : 'U) =
    let mutable currentX = x
    let mutable currentY = y
    let rwlock = new ReaderWriterLock()
    member p.Value =
        readLock rwlock (fun () ->
            (currentX, currentY))
    member p.Update(x, y) =
        writeLock rwlock (fun () ->
            currentX <- x
            currentY <- y)
```

Some Other Concurrency Primitives

Table 11-9 shows some other shared-memory concurrency primitives available in the .NET Framework.

Table 11-9. *.NET Shared-Memory Concurrency Primitives*

Type	Description
`System.Threading.WaitHandle`	A synchronization object for signaling the control of threads
`System.Threading.AutoResetEvent`	A two-state (on/off) `WaitHandle` that resets itself to "off" automatically after the signal is read. Similar to a two-state traffic light
`System.Threading.ManualResetEvent`	A two-state (on/off) `WaitHandle` that requires a call to `ManualResetEvent.Reset()` to set it "off"
`System.Threading.Mutex`	A lock-like object that can be shared among operating-system processes
`System.Threading.Semaphore`	Used to limit the number of threads simultaneously accessing a resource. Use a mutex or lock if at most one thread can access a resource at a time, however.
`System.Threading.Interlocked`	Atomic operations on memory locations. Especially useful for atomic operations on F# reference cells

Summary

This chapter covered concurrent, reactive, and asynchronous programming, topics of growing importance in modern programming because of the widespread adoption of multicore microprocessors, network-aware applications, and asynchronous I/O channels. It discussed, in depth, background processing and a powerful F# construct called *asynchronous computations*. Finally, you looked at applications of asynchronous computations to message-processing agents and web crawling, and examined some of the shared-memory primitives for concurrent programming on the .NET platform. In the next chapter, you will look at further applied topics in symbolic programming.

CHAPTER 12

◼ ◼ ◼

Symbolic Programming with Structured Data

Symbols are everywhere. Numbers are symbols that stand for quantities, and you can add, multiply, or take square roots of numbers that are so small or large that it's hard to imagine the quantity they represent. You can solve equations, multiply polynomials, approximate functions using series, and differentiate or integrate numerically or symbolically—these are just a few everyday examples of using symbols in mathematics.

It would be a mistake to think symbols are useful only in mathematics and related fields. General problem solving can't do without symbols; they provide the ability to abstract away details to make the larger picture clearer and help you understand relationships that may not appear obvious otherwise. Symbols always stand for something and have an attached meaning; they're created to bind this additional content to an existing object. This gives you an extraordinary tool to solve problems, describe behavior, make strategic decisions, create new words, and write poetry—the list could go on forever.

F# is well suited for symbolic computations. This chapter will cover in depth two symbolic manipulation problems. The first example will show how you can use symbolic programming to model hardware circuits and will present the core of a symbolic hardware-verification engine based on binary decision diagrams. The second example will present an implementation of a symbolic differentiation application. We could have chosen other examples of symbolic programming, but we found these two particularly enjoyable to code in F#.

Chapter 9 already covered many of the foundational techniques for symbolic programming. One technique that will be particularly important in this chapter is the use of discriminated unions to capture the shape of the abstract syntax trees for symbolic languages. Using functions as first-class values and applying recursive problem decomposition also leads to a natural and clean approach to computations on symbolic entities. These and other features of F# combine to make symbolic programming concise and painless, allowing you to focus on the really interesting parts of your application domain.

Verifying Circuits with Propositional Logic

The next example turns to a traditional application area for functional programming: describing digital hardware circuits and symbolically verifying their properties. We assume a passing familiarity with hardware design, but if you haven't looked inside a microprocessor chip for some time, a brief recap is included in the "About Hardware Design" sidebar.

In this example, you will model circuits by *propositional logic*, a simple and familiar symbolic language made up of constructs such as AND, OR, NOT, and TRUE/FALSE values. You will then implement an analysis that converts propositional-logic formulae into a canonical form called *binary decision diagrams* (BDDs). Converting to a canonical form allows you to check conditions and properties associated with the digital circuits.

317

ABOUT HARDWARE DESIGN

Digital hardware circuits such as microprocessors almost universally manipulate *bits*—that is, signals that are either low or high, represented by 0/1 or false/true values, respectively. The building blocks of interesting hardware circuits are primitives such as *gates* and *registers*. Gates are logical components that relate their inputs to their outputs; for example, an AND gate takes two input signals, and if both are high, it gives a high signal on its output. Registers are stateful components associated with a clock. This chapter doesn't consider registers and stateful circuits, although they can be tackled using techniques similar to those described here.

Hardware design is largely about building interesting behavior out of these primitives. For example, you can build arithmetic circuits that compute the sum or product of integers by using logical gates alone. These combinatorial circuits can be massive, and a key concern is to both verify their correctness and minimize the overall electrical delay through the circuit.

■ **Note** The examples in this section are inspired by the tutorials for the HOL88 system, a symbolic theorem prover implemented using an F#-like language that has been used for many purposes, including hardware verification. The carry/select adder and the BDD implementation follow those given by John Harrison in his HOL Light version of the same system. You can find out more about these and other systems, as well as delve into theorem proving, in *Handbook of Practical Logic and Automated Reasoning* by John Harrison (Cambridge University Press, 2009).

Representing Propositional Logic

You will begin by using language-oriented programming techniques to implement a little logic of Boolean expressions, of the kind that might be used to describe part of a hardware circuit or a constraint. Let's assume these have forms like the following:

```
P1 AND P2
P1 OR P2
P1 IMPLIES P2
NOT(P1)
v                       -- variable, ranging over true/false
TRUE
FALSE
Exists v. P[v]          -- v ranges over true/false, P may use v
Forall v. P[v]          -- v ranges over true/false, P may use v
```

This is known as *quantified Boolean formulae* (QBF) and is an expressive way of modeling many interesting problems and artifacts that work over finite data domains. Listing 12-1 shows how you model this language in F#.

Listing 12-1. A Minimalistic representation of propositional logic

```
type Var = string

type Prop =
    | And of Prop * Prop
    | Var of Var
    | Not of Prop
    | Exists of Var * Prop
    | False

let True            = Not False
let Or(p, q)        = Not(And(Not(p), Not(q)))
let Iff(p, q)       = Or(And(p, q), And(Not(p), Not(q)))
let Implies(p, q)   = Or(Not(p), q)
let Forall(v, p)    = Not(Exists(v, Not(p)))

let (&&&) p q = And(p, q)
let (|||) p q = Or(p, q)
let (~~~) p   = Not p
let (<=>) p q = Iff(p, q)
let (===) p q = (p <=> q)
let (==>) p q = Implies(p, q)
let (^^^) p q = Not (p <=> q)

let var (nm: Var) = Var nm

let fresh =
    let mutable count = 0
    fun nm -> count <- count + 1; (sprintf "_%s%d" nm count : Var)
```

Listing 12-1 uses a *minimalistic* encoding of propositional-logic terms, where True, Or, Iff, Implies, and Forall are *derived* constructs, defined using their standard classical definitions in terms of the primitives Var, And, Not, Exists, and False. This is adequate for your purposes, because you aren't so interested in preserving the original structure of formulae; if you do need to display a symbolic propositional formula, you're happy to display a form different than the original input.

Variables in formulae of type Prop are *primitive propositions*. A primitive proposition is often used to model some real-world possibility. For example, "it is raining," "it is cold," and "it is snowing" can be represented by Var("raining"), Var("cold"), and Var("snowing"). A Prop formula may be a *tautology*—that is, something that is always true regardless of the interpretation of these primitives. A formula is *satisfiable* if there is at least one interpretation for which it's true. A formula can also be an *axiom*; for example, "if it's snowing, then it's cold" can be represented as the assumption Implies(Var("snowing"), Var("cold")). In this example, variables are used to represent a wire in a digital circuit that may be low or high.

When you're dealing directly with the abstract syntax for Prop, it can be convenient to define infix operators to help you build abstract syntax values. Listing 12-1 shows the definition of seven operators (&&&, |||, ~~~, <=>, ===, ==>, and ^^^) that look a little like the notation you expect for propositional logic. You also define the function var for building primitive propositions and fresh for generating fresh variables. The types of these functions are as follows:

```
val var : nm:Var -> Prop
val fresh : (string -> Var)
```

■ **Note**   The operators in Listing 12-1 aren't overloaded and indeed outscope the default overloaded bitwise operations on integers discussed in Chapter 3. However, that doesn't matter for the purposes of this chapter. If necessary, you can use alternative operator names.

Evaluating Propositional Logic Naively

Before tackling the problem of representing hardware using propositional logic, let's look at some naive approaches for working with propositional-logic formulae. Listing 12-2 shows routines that evaluate formulae given an assignment of variables and that generate the rows of a truth table for a *Prop* formula.

Listing 12-2. Evaluating propositional-logic formulae

```
let rec eval (env: Map<Var,bool>) inp =
    match inp with
    | Exists(v, p) -> eval (env.Add(v, false)) p || eval (env.Add(v, true)) p
    | And(p1, p2)  -> eval env p1 && eval env p2
    | Var v        -> if env.ContainsKey(v) then env.[v]
                      else failwithf "env didn't contain a value for %A" v
    | Not p        -> not (eval env p)
    | False        -> false

let rec support f =
    match f with
    | And(x, y)    -> Set.union (support x) (support y)
    | Exists(v, p) -> (support p).Remove(v)
    | Var p        -> Set.singleton p
    | Not x        -> support x
    | False        -> Set.empty

let rec cases supp =
    seq {
        match supp with
        | [] ->  yield Map.empty
        | v :: rest ->
            yield! rest |> cases |> Seq.map (Map.add v false)
            yield! rest |> cases |> Seq.map (Map.add v true)
    }

let truthTable x =
    x |> support |> Set.toList |> cases
    |> Seq.map (fun env -> env, eval env x)

let satisfiable x =
    x
    |> truthTable
    |> Seq.exists (fun (env, res) -> res)
```

```
let satisfiableWithExample x =
    x
    |> truthTable
    |> Seq.tryFind (fun (env, res) -> res)
    |> Option.map fst

let tautology x =
    x
    |> truthTable
    |> Seq.forall (fun (env, res) -> res)

let tautologyWithCounterExample x =
    x
    |> truthTable
    |> Seq.tryFind (fun (env, res) -> not res)
    |> Option.map fst

let printCounterExample x =
    match x with
    | None     -> printfn "tautology verified OK"
    | Some env -> printfn "tautology failed on %A" (Seq.toList env)
```

The types of these functions are as follows:

```
val eval : env:Map<Var,bool> -> inp:Prop -> bool
val support : f:Prop -> Set<Var>
val cases : supp:'a list -> seq<Map<'a,bool>> when 'a : comparison
val truthTable : x:Prop -> seq<Map<Var,bool> * bool>
val satisfiable : x:Prop -> bool
val satisfiableWithExample : x:Prop -> Map<Var,bool> option
val tautology : x:Prop -> bool
val tautologyWithCounterExample : x:Prop -> Map<Var,bool> option
val printCounterExample : x: #seq<'b> option -> unit
```

The function eval computes the value of a formula given assignments for each variable that occurs in the formula. support computes the set of variables that occurs in the formula. You can now use these functions to examine truth tables for some simple formulae, although first you may want to define the following functions so as to display truth tables neatly in F# Interactive:

```
let stringOfBit b = if b then "T" else "F"

let stringOfEnv env =
    Map.fold (fun acc k v -> sprintf "%s=%s;" k (stringOfBit v) + acc) "" env

let stringOfLine (env, res) =
    sprintf "%20s %s" (stringOfEnv env) (stringOfBit res)

let stringOfTruthTable tt =
    "\n" + (tt |> Seq.toList |> List.map stringOfLine |> String.concat "\n")
```

Here are some examples of computing the satisfiability and the truth tables for x, x AND y, and x OR NOT(x):

```
> fsi.AddPrinter(fun tt -> tt |> Seq.truncate 20 |> stringOfTruthTable);;

> satisfiable (var "x");;

val it : bool = true

> satisfiableWithExample (var "x");;

val it : Map<Var,bool> option = Some (map [("x", true)])

> truthTable (var "x" &&& var "y");;

val it : seq<Map<Var,bool> * bool> =

        y=F;x=F;  F
        y=T;x=F;  F
        y=F;x=T;  F
        y=T;x=T;  T

> tautology (var "x" ||| ~~~(var "x"));;

val it : bool = true
```

From this, you can see that x OR NOT(x) is a tautology, because it always evaluates to TRUE regardless of the value of the variable x.

From Circuits to Propositional Logic

Figure 12-1 shows a diagrammatic representation of three hardware circuits: a *half adder*, a *full adder*, and a *2-bit carry ripple adder*. The first of these has two input wires, x and y, and sets the *sum* wire high if exactly one of these is high. If both x and y are high, then the sum is low, and the carry wire is high instead. Thus, the circuit computes the 2-bit sum of the inputs. Likewise, a full adder computes the sum of three Boolean inputs, which, because it's at most three, can still be represented by 2 bits. A 2-bit carry ripple adder is formed by composing a half adder and a full adder together by wiring the carry from the first adder to one of the inputs of the second adder. The overall circuit has four inputs and three outputs.

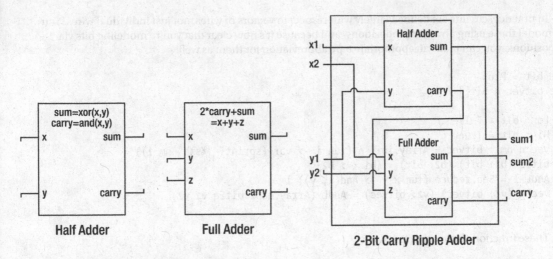

Figure 12-1. *Three simple hardware circuits*

The following code models these circuit components. This uses *relational modeling*, where each circuit is modeled not as a function but rather as a propositional-logic predicate that relates its input wires to its output wires:

```
let sumBit x y = (x ^^^ y)
let carryBit x y = (x &&& y)
let halfAdder x y sum carry =
    (sum === sumBit x y)  &&&
    (carry === carryBit x y)

let fullAdder x y z sum carry =
    let xy = (sumBit x y)
    (sum === sumBit xy z) &&&
    (carry === (carryBit x y ||| carryBit xy z))

let twoBitAdder (x1, x2) (y1, y2) (sum1, sum2) carryInner carry =
    halfAdder x1 y1 sum1 carryInner &&&
    fullAdder x2 y2 carryInner sum2 carry
```

Note the close relationship between the diagram for the 2-bit adder and its representation as code. You can read the implementation as a specification of the diagram, and vice versa. But the types of these functions are a little less informative:

```
val sumBit : x:Prop -> y:Prop -> Prop
val carryBit : x:Prop -> y:Prop -> Prop
val halfAdder : x:Prop -> y:Prop -> sum:Prop -> carry:Prop -> Prop
val fullAdder : x:Prop -> y:Prop -> z:Prop -> sum:Prop -> carry:Prop -> Prop
val twoBitAdder :
  x1:Prop * x2:Prop ->
    y1:Prop * y2:Prop ->
      sum1:Prop * sum2:Prop -> carryInner:Prop -> carry:Prop -> Prop
```

In practice, circuits are defined largely with respect to vectors of wires, not just individual wires. You can model these using arrays of propositions, and because it's now clear that you're modeling bits via propositions, you can make an appropriate type abbreviation for them as well:

```
type bit = Prop
type bitvec = bit[]

let Lo : bit = False
let Hi : bit = True
let vec n nm : bitvec = Array.init n (fun i -> var (sprintf "%s%d" nm i))
let bitEq (b1: bit) (b2: bit) = (b1 <=> b2)
let AndL l = Seq.reduce (fun x y -> And(x, y)) l
let vecEq (v1: bitvec) (v2: bitvec) = AndL (Array.map2 bitEq v1 v2)
```

These functions have types as follows:

```
type bit = Prop
type bitvec = bit []
val Lo : bit = False
val Hi : bit = Not False
val vec : n:int -> nm:string -> bitvec
val bitEq : b1:bit -> b2:bit -> Prop
val AndL : l:seq<Prop> -> Prop
val vecEq : v1:bitvec -> v2:bitvec -> Prop
```

You can now proceed to define larger circuits. For example:

```
let fourBitAdder (x: bitvec) (y: bitvec) (sum: bitvec) (carry: bitvec) =
    halfAdder  x.[0] y.[0]           sum.[0] carry.[0] &&&
    fullAdder  x.[1] y.[1] carry.[0] sum.[1] carry.[1] &&&
    fullAdder  x.[2] y.[2] carry.[1] sum.[2] carry.[2] &&&
    fullAdder  x.[3] y.[3] carry.[2] sum.[3] carry.[3]
```

Or, more generally, you can chain an arbitrary series of adders to form an *N*-bit adder. First, you define an abbreviation for the AndL function to represent the composition of multiple circuit blocks:

```
let Blocks l = AndL l
```

And here is the definition of an *N*-bit adder with a halfAdder at one end:

```
let nBitCarryRippleAdder (n: int) (x: bitvec) (y: bitvec)
                         (sum: bitvec) (carry: bitvec) =
    Blocks [ for i in 0 .. n-1 ->
                if i = 0
                then halfAdder x.[i] y.[i] sum.[i] carry.[i]
                else fullAdder x.[i] y.[i] carry.[i-1] sum.[i] carry.[i]  ]
```

Using a similar approach, you can get the following satisfying specification of a symmetric *N*-bit adder that accepts a carry as input and also gives a carry as output:

```
let rippleAdder (n: int) (x: bitvec) (y: bitvec)
                (sum: bitvec) (carry: bitvec) =
    Blocks [ for i in 0 .. n-1 ->
                fullAdder x.[i] y.[i] carry.[i] sum.[i] carry.[i+1] ]
```

Let's now look at the propositional formula for a halfAdder with variable inputs and outputs:

```
> halfAdder (var "x") (var "y") (var "sum") (var "carry");;
val it : Prop =
  And
   (Not
      (And
         (Not
            (And
               (Var "sum",
                Not
                   (Not
                      (And
                         (Not (And (Var "x",Var "y")),
                          Not (And (Not (Var "x"),Not (Var "y"))))))))),
          Not
             (And
                (Not (Var "sum"),
                 Not
                    (Not
                       (Not
                          (And
                             (Not (And (Var "x",Var "y")),
                              Not (And (Not (Var "x"),Not (Var "y"))))))))))),
     Not
        (And
           (Not (And (Var "carry",And (Var "x",Var "y"))),
            Not (And (Not (Var "carry"),Not (And (Var "x",Var "y")))))))
```

Clearly, you don't want to be doing too much of that! You will see better ways of inspecting circuits and the symbolic values of bit vectors in the section "Representing Propositional Formulae Efficiently Using BDDs."

In passing, note that the twoBitAdder uses an internal wire. You can model this using an existential formula:

```
let twoBitAdderWithHiding (x1, x2) (y1, y2) (sum1, sum2) carry =
    let carryInnerVar = fresh "carry"
    let carryInner = var(carryInnerVar)
    Exists(carryInnerVar, halfAdder x1 y1 sum1 carryInner &&&
                          fullAdder x2 y2 carryInner sum2 carry)
```

However, this brings up issues beyond the scope of this chapter. Instead, you will take an approach to modeling where there are no boundaries to the circuits and where all internal wires are exposed.

Checking Simple Properties of Circuits

Now that you've modeled the initial hardware circuits, you can check simple properties of these circuits. For example, you can check that if you give a fullAdder all low (that is, false) inputs, the output wires may be low as well, and, conversely, that you have a contradiction if one of the output wires is high:

```
> tautology (fullAdder Lo Lo Lo Lo Lo);;

val it : bool = true

> satisfiable (fullAdder Lo Lo Lo Hi Lo);;

val it : bool = false
```

It's of course much better to check these results *symbolically* by giving symbolic inputs. For example, you can check that if the same value is given to the two inputs of a halfAdder, the sum output is low and the carry output is the same as the input:

```
> tautology (halfAdder (var "x") (var "x") Lo (var "x"));;

val it : bool = true
```

Likewise, you can check that a 2-bit adder is commutative—in other words, that it doesn't matter if you swap the *x* and *y* inputs:

```
> tautology
    (nBitCarryRippleAdder 2 (vec 2 "x") (vec 2 "y") (vec 2 "sum") (vec 3 "carry")
 === nBitCarryRippleAdder 2 (vec 2 "y") (vec 2 "x") (vec 2 "sum") (vec 3 "carry"));;

val it : bool = true
```

However, if you repeat the same for sizes of 5 or bigger, things start to slow down, and the naive implementation of checking propositional-logic tautology based on truth tables begins to break down. Hence, you have to turn to more efficient techniques to process propositional formulae.

Representing Propositional Formulae Efficiently Using BDDs

In practice, propositional formulae used to describe hardware can be enormous, involving hundreds of thousands of nodes. As a result, hardware companies have an interest in smart algorithms to process these formulae and check them for correctness. The circuits in the computers you on a daily basis have almost certainly been verified using advanced propositional-logic techniques, often using a functional language as the means to drive and control the analysis of the circuits.

A major advance in the application of symbolic techniques to hardware design occurred in the late 1980s with the discovery of *binary decision diagrams*, a representation for propositional-logic formulae that is compact for many common circuit designs. BDDs represent a propositional formula via the use of if ... then ... else conditionals alone, which you write as (variable => true-branch | false-branch). Special nodes are used for true and false at the leaves; you write these as T and F. Every BDD is constructed with respect to a global variable ordering, so x AND NOT y can be represented as (x => (y => F | T) | F) if x comes before y in this ordering and as (y => F | (x => T | F)) if y comes before x. The variable ordering can be critical for the performance of the representation.

BDDs are efficient because they use some of the language-representation techniques you saw in Chapter 9. In particular, they work by *uniquely memoizing* all BDD nodes that are identical, which works by representing a BDD as an integer index for a lookup table that stores the real information about the node. Furthermore, negative indexes are used to represent the negation of a particular BDD node without creating a separate entry for the negated node. Listing 12-3 shows an implementation of BDDs. Fully polished BDD packages are often implemented in C. It's easy to access those packages from F# using the techniques described in Chapter 19. Here, you have a clear and simple implementation entirely in F# code.

Listing 12-3. Implementing binary decision diagrams

```
open System.Collections.Generic

let memoize f =
    let tab = new Dictionary<_, _>()
    fun x ->
        if tab.ContainsKey(x) then tab.[x]
        else let res = f x in tab.[x] <- res; res

type BddIndex = int
type Bdd = Bdd of BddIndex
type BddNode = Node of Var * BddIndex * BddIndex
type BddBuilder(order: Var -> Var -> int) =

    // The core data structures that preserve uniqueness
    let nodeToIndex = new Dictionary<BddNode, BddIndex>()
    let indexToNode = new Dictionary<BddIndex, BddNode>()

    // Keep track of the next index
    let mutable nextIdx = 2
    let trueIdx = 1
    let falseIdx = -1
    let trueNode = Node("", trueIdx, trueIdx)
    let falseNode = Node("", falseIdx, falseIdx)

    // Map indexes to nodes. Negative indexes go to their negation.
    // The special indexes -1 and 1 go to special true/false nodes.
    let idxToNode(idx) =
        if idx = trueIdx then trueNode
        elif idx = falseIdx then falseNode
        elif idx > 0 then indexToNode.[idx]
        else
            let (Node(v, l, r)) = indexToNode.[-idx]
            Node(v, -l, -r)
```

```
// Map nodes to indexes. Add an entry to the table if needed.
let nodeToUniqueIdx(node) =
    if nodeToIndex.ContainsKey(node) then nodeToIndex.[node]
    else
        let idx = nextIdx
        nodeToIndex.[node] <- idx
        indexToNode.[idx] <- node
        nextIdx <- nextIdx + 1
        idx

// Get the canonical index for a node. Preserve the invariant that the
// left-hand node of a conditional is always a positive node
let mkNode(v: Var, l: BddIndex, r: BddIndex) =
    if l = r then l
    elif l >= 0 then nodeToUniqueIdx(Node(v, l, r) )
    else -nodeToUniqueIdx(Node(v, -l, -r))

// Construct the BDD for a conjunction "m1 AND m2"
let rec mkAnd(m1, m2) =
    if m1 = falseIdx || m2 = falseIdx then falseIdx
    elif m1 = trueIdx then m2
    elif m2 = trueIdx then m1
    else
        let (Node(x, l1, r1)) = idxToNode(m1)
        let (Node(y, l2, r2)) = idxToNode(m2)
        let v, (la, lb), (ra, rb) =
            match order x y with
            | c when c = 0 -> x, (l1, l2), (r1, r2)
            | c when c < 0 -> x, (l1, m2), (r1, m2)
            | c -> y, (m1, l2), (m1, r2)
        mkNode(v, mkAnd(la, lb), mkAnd(ra, rb))

// Memoize this function
let mkAnd = memoize mkAnd

// Publish the construction functions that make BDDs from existing BDDs
member g.False = Bdd falseIdx
member g.And(Bdd m1, Bdd m2) = Bdd(mkAnd(m1, m2))
member g.Not(Bdd m) = Bdd(-m)
member g.Var(nm) = Bdd(mkNode(nm, trueIdx, falseIdx))
member g.NodeCount = nextIdx
```

The types of these functions are as follows:

```
val memoize : f:('a -> 'b) -> ('a -> 'b) when 'a : equality
type BddIndex = int
type Bdd = | Bdd of BddIndex
type BddNode = | Node of Var * BddIndex * BddIndex
type BddBuilder =
    new : order:(Var -> Var -> int) -> BddBuilder
    member And : Bdd * Bdd -> Bdd
```

```
member Not : Bdd -> Bdd
member Var : nm:Var -> Bdd
member False : Bdd
member NodeCount : int
```

In addition to the functions that ensure that nodes are unique, the only substantial function in the implementation is mkAnd. It relies on the following logical rules for constructing BDD nodes formed by taking the conjunction of existing nodes. Note how the second rule is used to interleave variables:

- (x => P | Q) AND (x => R | S) is identical to (x => P AND R | Q AND S).

- (x => P | Q) AND (y => R | S) is identical to (x => P AND T | Q AND T) where T is simply (y => R | S).

One final important optimization in the implementation is to memoize the application of the mkAnd operation.

Given the previous implementation of BDDs, you can now add the members ToString to convert BDDs to strings, Build to convert a Prop representation of a formula into a BDD, and Equiv to check for equivalence between two BDDs:

```
type BddBuilder(order: Var -> Var -> int) =
    ...
    member g.ToString(Bdd idx) =
        let rec fmt dep idx =
            if dep > 3 then "..." else
            let (Node(p, l, r)) = idxToNode(idx)
            if p = "" then if l = trueIdx then "T" else "F"
            else sprintf "(%s => %s | %s)" p (fmt (dep+1) l) (fmt (dep+1) r)
        fmt 1 idx

    member g.Build(f) =
        match f with
        | And(x, y) -> g.And(g.Build x, g.Build y)
        | Var(p) -> g.Var(p)
        | Not(x) -> g.Not(g.Build x)
        | False -> g.False
        | Exists(v, p) -> failwith "Exists node"

    member g.Equiv(p1, p2) = (g.Build(p1) = g.Build(p2))
```

You can now install a pretty-printer and inspect the BDDs for some simple formulae:

```
> let bddBuilder = BddBuilder(compare);;

val bddBuilder: BddBuilder

> fsi.AddPrinter(fun bdd -> bddBuilder.ToString(bdd));;

> bddBuilder.Build(var "x");;

val it : Bdd = (x => T | F)
```

```
> bddBuilder.Build(var "x" &&& var "x");;

val it : Bdd = (x => T | F)

> bddBuilder.Build(var "x") = bddBuilder.Build(var "x" &&& var "x");;

val it : bool = true

> (var "x") = (var "x" &&& var "x");;

val it : bool = false

> bddBuilder.Build(var "x" &&& var "y");;

val it : Bdd = (x => (y => T | F) | F)

> bddBuilder.Equiv(var "x", var "x" &&& var "x");;

val it : bool = true
```

Note that the BDD representations of x and x AND x are identical, whereas the Prop representations aren't. The Prop representation is an *abstract syntax* representation, whereas the BDD representation is more of a *semantic* or *computational* representation. The BDD representation incorporates all the logic necessary to prove propositional formulae to be equivalent; in other words, this logic is built into the representation.

Circuit Verification with BDDs

You can now use BDDs to perform circuit verification. For example, the following verifies that you can swap the *x* and *y* inputs to an 8-bit adder:

```
> bddBuilder.Equiv(
    nBitCarryRippleAdder 8 (vec 8 "x") (vec 8 "y") (vec 8 "sum") (vec 9 "carry"),
    nBitCarryRippleAdder 8 (vec 8 "y") (vec 8 "x") (vec 8 "sum") (vec 9 "carry"));;

val it : bool = true
```

Thirty-three variables are involved in this circuit. A naive exploration of this space would involve searching a truth table of more than eight billion entries. The BDD implementation takes moments on any modern computer. Efficient symbolic representations pay off!

A more substantial verification problem involves checking the equivalence of circuits that have substantial structural differences. To explore this, let's take a different implementation of addition called a *carry select adder*. This avoids a major problem with ripple adders that is caused by the fact that the carry signal must propagate along the entire length of the chain of internal adders. This causes longer delays in the electrical signals and thus reduces the clock rates of a circuit or possibly increases power consumption. A carry select adder gets around this through a common hardware trick–speculative execution. It divides the inputs into blocks and adds each block twice: once assuming the carry is low and once assuming it's high. The result is then selected *after* the circuit, when the carry for the block has been computed. Listing 12-4 shows the specification of the essence of the hardware layout of a carry select adder using the techniques developed so far. The specification uses the slicing syntax for arrays described in Chapter 4.

Listing 12-4. A carry select adder modeled using propositional logic

```
let mux a b c = ((~~~a ==> b) &&& (a ==> c))

let carrySelectAdder
        totalSize maxBlockSize
        (x: bitvec) (y: bitvec)
        (sumLo: bitvec) (sumHi: bitvec)
        (carryLo: bitvec) (carryHi: bitvec)
        (sum: bitvec) (carry: bitvec) =
  Blocks
    [ for i in 0..maxBlockSize..totalSize-1 ->
        let sz = min (totalSize-i) maxBlockSize
        let j = i+sz-1
        let carryLo = Array.append [| False |] carryLo.[i+1..j+1]
        let adderLo = rippleAdder sz x.[i..j] y.[i..j] sumLo.[i..j] carryLo
        let carryHi = Array.append [| True  |] carryHi.[i+1..j+1]
        let adderHi = rippleAdder sz x.[i..j] y.[i..j] sumHi.[i..j] carryHi
        let carrySelect = (carry.[j+1] === mux carry.[i] carryLo.[sz] carryHi.[sz])
        let sumSelect =
            Blocks
                [ for k in i..j ->
                    sum.[k] === mux carry.[i] sumLo.[k] sumHi.[k] ]
        adderLo &&& adderHi &&& carrySelect &&& sumSelect ]
```

You can now check that a `carrySelectAdder` is equivalent to a `rippleAdder`. Here's the overall verification condition:

```
let checkAdders n k =
    let x = vec n "x"
    let y = vec n "y"
    let sumA    = vec n "sumA"
    let sumB    = vec n "sumB"
    let sumLo   = vec n "sumLo"
    let sumHi   = vec n "sumHi"
    let carryA  = vec (n+1) "carryA"
    let carryB  = vec (n+1) "carryB"
    let carryLo = vec (n+1) "carryLo"
    let carryHi = vec (n+1) "carryHi"
    let adder1 = carrySelectAdder n k x y sumLo sumHi carryLo carryHi sumA carryA
    let adder2 = rippleAdder n x y sumB carryB
    (adder1 &&& adder2 &&& (carryA.[0] === carryB.[0]) ==>
        (vecEq sumA sumB &&& bitEq carryA.[n] carryB.[n]))
```

Ignoring the construction of the inputs, the verification condition specifies the following:

- Assume you have the two adder circuits, with the same inputs.

- Assume the input carry bits are the same.

- Then, the output sum vectors are identical, and the final output carry bits are identical.

Here is the verification condition being checked interactively, for 5-bit inputs, in chunks of 2 for the carrySelectAdder:

```
> bddBuilder.Equiv(checkAdders 5 2, True);;

val it : bool = true
```

In practice, BDDs require a good variable ordering, and the default alphabetic ordering is unlikely to be the best. Here is a larger verification using a more random ordering induced by first comparing the hash codes of the names of the variables:

```
let approxCompareOn f x y =
    let c = compare (f x) (f y)
    if c <> 0 then c else compare x y

let bddBuilder2 = BddBuilder(approxCompareOn hash)
```

```
> bddBuilder2.Equiv(checkAdders 7 2, True);;

val it : bool = true
```

Seventy-four Boolean variables are involved in this last verification problem. You would have to generate up to 2^{74} test cases to explore this systematically via testing; that's 22 thousand billion billion test cases. By using symbolic techniques, you've explored this entire space in a matter of seconds and in only a few hundred lines of code.

■ **Note**   Hardware and software verification are highly active areas of research and one of the most important applications of symbolic programming techniques in the industrial arena. The verifications performed here aim to give you a taste of how symbolic techniques can provide nontrivial results about circuits in a matter of seconds. We've omitted some simple techniques that can make these verifications scale to very large circuits; for example, we can expand equivalence nodes in propositional formulae. Preserving them can lead to smaller symbolic descriptions and more-efficient processing with BDDs.

Expression Simplification and Differentiation

A classic application of symbolic programming is working with algebraic expressions like the kind you find in high school mathematics. In this section you will learn how to do this kind of programming in F#.

Let's take it easy at first and assume you're dealing with simple algebraic expressions that can consist only of numbers, a single variable (it doesn't matter what it is, but let's assume it's *x*), sums, and products. Listing 12-5 shows the implementation of symbolic differentiation over this simple expression type.

Listing 12-5. Symbolic differentiation over a simple expression type

```
open System

type Expr =
    | Var
    | Num of int
    | Sum of Expr * Expr
    | Prod of Expr * Expr

let rec deriv expr =
    match expr with
    | Var            -> Num 1
    | Num _          -> Num 0
    | Sum (e1, e2)  -> Sum (deriv e1, deriv e2)
    | Prod (e1, e2) -> Sum (Prod (e1, deriv e2), Prod (e2, deriv e1))
```

The type of the deriv function is as follows:

```
val deriv : expr:Expr -> Expr
```

Now, let's find the derivative of a simple expression, say 1+2x:

```
> let e1 = Sum (Num 1, Prod (Num 2, Var));;

val e1 : Expr = Sum (Num 1, Prod (Num 2, Var))

> deriv e1;;

val it : Expr = Sum (Num 0, Sum (Prod (Num 2, Num 1), Prod (Var, Num 0)))
```

The resulting expression is a symbolic representation of 0+(2*1+x*0), which indeed is 2–so it's right. You should do a couple of things next. First, install a custom printer so that F# Interactive responds using expressions that you're more used to using. Before you apply brute force and put parentheses around the expressions in each sum and product, let's contemplate it a bit. Parentheses are usually needed to give precedence to operations that would otherwise be applied later in the sequence of calculations. For instance, 2+3*4 is calculated as 2+(3*4) because the product has a higher precedence; if you wanted to find (2+3)*4, you would need to use parentheses to designate the new order of calculation. Taking this argument further, you can formulate the rule for using parentheses: they're needed in places where an operator has lower precedence than the one surrounding it. You can apply this reasoning to the expression printer by passing a context-precedence parameter:

```
let precSum = 10
let precProd = 20

let rec stringOfExpr prec expr =
    match expr with
    | Var    -> "x"
    | Num i -> i.ToString()
    | Sum (e1, e2) ->
```

```
        let sum = stringOfExpr precSum e1 + "+" + stringOfExpr precSum e2
        if prec > precSum then
            "(" + sum + ")"
        else
            sum
    | Prod (e1, e2) ->
        stringOfExpr precProd e1 + "*" + stringOfExpr precProd e2
```

You can add this as a custom printer for this expression type:

```
> fsi.AddPrinter (fun expr -> stringOfExpr 0 expr);;

> let e3 = Prod (Var, Prod (Var, Num 2));;

val e3 : Expr = x*x*2

> deriv e3;;

val it : Expr = x*(x*0+2*1)+x*2*1
```

Parentheses are omitted only when a sum is participating in an expression that has a higher precedence, which in this simplified example means products. If you didn't add precedence to the pretty-printer, you'd get x*x*0+2*1+x*2*1 for the last expression, which is incorrect.

Implementing Local Simplifications

The next thing to do is to get your symbolic manipulator to simplify expressions so you don't have to do so. One easy modification is to replace the use of the Sum and Prod constructors in deriv with local functions that perform local simplifications, such as removing identity operations, performing arithmetic, bringing forward constants, and simplifying across two operations. Listing 12-6 shows how to do this.

Listing 12-6. Symbolic differentiation with local simplifications

```
let simpSum (a, b) =
    match a, b with
    | Num n, Num m -> Num (n+m)         // constants!
    | Num 0, e | e, Num 0 -> e          // 0+e = e+0 = e
    | e1, e2 -> Sum(e1, e2)

let simpProd (a, b) =
    match a, b with
    | Num n, Num m -> Num (n*m)         // constants!
    | Num 0, e | e, Num 0 -> Num 0      // 0*e=0
    | Num 1, e | e, Num 1 -> e          // 1*e = e*1 = e
    | e1, e2 -> Prod(e1, e2)

let rec simpDeriv e =
    match e with
    | Var           -> Num 1
    | Num _         -> Num 0
```

```
    | Sum (e1, e2)  -> simpSum (simpDeriv e1, simpDeriv e2)
    | Prod (e1, e2) -> simpSum (simpProd (e1, simpDeriv e2),
                               simpProd (e2, simpDeriv e1))
```

These measures produce a significant improvement over the previous naive approach, but they don't place the result in a normal form, as the following shows:

```
> simpDeriv e3;;

val it : Expr = x*2+x*2
```

However, you can't implement all simplifications using local rules; for example, collecting like terms across a polynomial involves looking at every term of the polynomial.

A Richer Language of Algebraic Expressions

This section goes beyond the approach presented so far and shows a richer language of algebraic expressions with which to simplify and differentiate. This project uses the FsLexYacc package for parsing and lexing. For convenience, you can add the lexer ExprLexer.fsl and the parser ExprParser.fsy to the project so you can quickly edit them if necessary.

The main Expr type that represents algebraic expressions is contained in Expr.fs. Although you can use the expression constructors defined in this type to create expression values on the fly, the most convenient method for embedding complex expressions into this representation is by parsing them. Armed with the ability to encode and parse algebraic expressions, you place the derivation and simplification logic in its own module and file ExprUtil.fs. A parser is added in ExprParser.fsy, and a tokenizer in ExprLexer.fsl. A simple driver added to Main.fs completes the application.

Listing 12-7 shows the definition of the abstract syntax representation of expressions using a single Expr type. Expressions contain numbers, variables, negation, sums, differences, products, fractions, exponents, basic trigonometric functions (sin x, cos x), and e^x.

Let's look at this abstract syntax design more closely. In Chapter 9, you saw that choosing an abstract syntax often involves design choices, and that these choices often relate to the roles the abstract syntax representation should serve. In this case, you use the abstract syntax to compute symbolic derivatives and simplifications (using techniques similar to those seen earlier in this chapter) and also to graphically visualize the resulting expressions in a way that is pleasant for the human user. For this reason, you don't use an entirely minimalistic abstract syntax (for example, by replacing quotients with an inverse node), because it's helpful to maintain some additional structure in the input.

Here, you represent sums and differences not as binary terms (as you do for products and quotients) but instead as a list of expression terms. The Sub term also carries the *minuend*, the term that is to be reduced, separately. As a result, you have to apply different strategies when simplifying them.

Listing 12-7. Expr.fs: the core expression type for the visual symbolic differentiation application

```
namespace Symbolic.Expressions

type Expr =
    | Num  of decimal
    | Var  of string
    | Neg  of Expr
    | Add  of Expr list
    | Sub  of Expr * Expr list
```

```
  | Prod of Expr * Expr
  | Frac of Expr * Expr
  | Pow  of Expr * decimal
  | Sin  of Expr
  | Cos  of Expr
  | Exp  of Expr

  static member StarNeeded e1 e2 =
      match e1, e2 with
      | Num _, Neg _ | _, Num _ -> true
      | _ -> false

  member self.IsNumber =
      match self with
      | Num _ -> true | _ -> false

  member self.NumOf =
      match self with
      | Num num -> num | _ -> failwith "NumOf: Not a Num"

  member self.IsNegative =
      match self with
      | Num num | Prod (Num num, _) -> num < 0M
      | Neg e -> true | _ -> false

  member self.Negate =
      match self with
      | Num num -> Num (-num)
      | Neg e -> e
      | exp -> Neg exp
```

Listing 12-7 also shows the definition of some miscellaneous augmentations on the expression type, mostly related to visual layout and presentation. The StarNeeded member is used internally to determine whether the multiplication operator (the star symbol, or asterisk) is needed in the product of two expressions, e1 and e2. You may want to extend this simple rule: any product whose right side is a number requires the explicit operator, and all other cases don't. Thus, expressions such as $2(x+1)$ and $2x$ are rendered without the asterisk.

The IsNumber member returns true if the expression at hand is numeric and is used in conjunction with NumOf, which returns this numeric component. Similarly, the IsNegative and Negate members determine whether you have an expression that starts with a negative sign, and they negate it on demand.

Parsing Algebraic Expressions

This sample uses a lexer and a parser generated by the F# tools fsyacc.exe and fslex.exe, available as part of the FsLexYacc NuGet package. This chapter skips over the details of how the tools work; instead, it assumes that you have these tools already installed. Listings 12-8 and 12-9 show the code for the lexer and parser respectively. You need to manually build the lexer (generating ExprLexer.fs) and parser (generating ExprParser.fs) from the Windows command line as follows:

```
C:\samples> fsyacc ExprParser.fsy --module Symbolic.Expressions.ExprParser
C:\samples> fslex ExprLexer.fsl --unicode
```

Listing 12-8. `ExprLexer.fsl`: tokenizing the concrete syntax for algebraic expressions

```
{
module Symbolic.Expressions.ExprLexer

open System
open Symbolic.Expressions
open Symbolic.Expressions.ExprParser
open Microsoft.FSharp.Text.Lexing

let lexeme = LexBuffer<_>.LexemeString

let special s =
    match s with
    | "+" -> PLUS     | "-" -> MINUS
    | "*" -> TIMES    | "/" -> DIV
    | "(" -> LPAREN   | ")" -> RPAREN   | "^" -> HAT
    | _   -> failwith "Invalid operator"

let id s =
    match s with
    | "sin" -> SIN   | "cos" -> COS
    | "e"   -> E     | id    -> ID id
}

let digit     = ['0'-'9']
let int       = digit+
let float     = int ('.' int)? (['e' 'E'] int)?
let alpha     = ['a'-'z' 'A'-'Z']
let id        = alpha+ (alpha | digit | ['_' '$'])*
let ws        = ' ' | '\t'
let nl        = '\n' | '\r' '\n'
let special   = '+' | '-' | '*' | '/' | '(' | ')' | '^'

rule main = parse
    | int        { INT (Convert.ToInt32(lexeme lexbuf)) }
    | float      { FLOAT (Convert.ToDouble(lexeme lexbuf)) }
    | id         { id (lexeme lexbuf) }
    | special    { special (lexeme lexbuf) }
    | ws | nl    { main lexbuf }
    | eof        { EOF }
    | _          { failwith (lexeme lexbuf) }
```

The parser has some syntactic sugar for polynomial terms, so it can parse 2x, 2x^3, or x^4 without requiring you to add an explicit multiplication symbol after the coefficient.

Listing 12-9. ExprParser.fsy: parsing the concrete syntax for algebraic expressions

```
%{
open System
open Symbolic.Expressions
%}

%token <int> INT
%token <float> FLOAT
%token <string> ID

%token EOF LPAREN RPAREN PLUS MINUS TIMES DIV HAT SIN COS E

%left ID
%left prec_negate
%left LPAREN
%left PLUS MINUS
%left TIMES DIV
%left HAT

%start expr
%type <Expr> expr
%%

expr:
    | exp EOF { $1 }

number:
    | INT                     { Convert.ToDecimal($1) }
    | FLOAT                   { Convert.ToDecimal($1) }
    | MINUS INT %prec prec_negate  { Convert.ToDecimal(-$2) }
    | MINUS FLOAT %prec prec_negate { Convert.ToDecimal(-$2) }


exp:
    | number              { Num $1 }
    | ID                  { Var $1 }
    | exp PLUS exp        { Add [$1; $3] }
    | exp MINUS exp       { Sub ($1, [$3]) }
    | exp TIMES exp       { Prod ($1, $3) }
    | exp DIV exp         { Frac ($1, $3) }
    | SIN LPAREN exp RPAREN  { Sin $3 }
    | COS LPAREN exp RPAREN  { Cos $3 }
    | E HAT exp           { Exp $3 }
    | term                { $1 }
    | exp HAT number      { Pow ($1, $3) }
    | LPAREN exp RPAREN   { $2 }
    | MINUS LPAREN exp RPAREN { Neg $3 }
```

```
term:
    | number ID                 { Prod (Num $1, Var $2) }
    | number ID HAT number      { Prod (Num $1, Pow (Var $2, $4)) }
    | ID HAT number             { Prod (Num 1M, Pow (Var $1, $3)) }
```

Simplifying Algebraic Expressions

At the start of this chapter, you simplified expressions using local techniques, but you also saw the limitations of this approach. Listing 12-10 shows a more complete implementation of a separate function (Simplify) that performs some nonlocal simplifications as well. Both this function and the one for derivation shown in the subsequent section are placed in a separate file (ExprUtil.fs).

Simplify uses two helper functions (collect and negate). The former collects constants from products using a bottom-up strategy that reduces constant subproducts and factors out constants by bringing them outward (to the left). Recall that product terms are binary.

Listing 12-10. ExprUtils.fs: simplifying algebraic expressions

```
module Symbolic.Expressions.Utils

open Symbolic.Expressions

/// A helper function to map/select across a list while threading state
/// through the computation
let collectFold f l s =
    let l,s2 = (s, l) ||> List.mapFold (fun z x -> f x z)
    List.concat l,s2

/// Collect constants
let rec collect e =
    match e with
    | Prod (e1, e2) ->
        match collect e1, collect e2 with
        | Num n1, Num n2         -> Num (n1 * n2)
        | Num n1, Prod (Num n2, e)
        | Prod (Num n2, e), Num n1 -> Prod (Num (n1 * n2), e)
        | Num n, e | e, Num n      -> Prod (Num n, e)
        | Prod (Num n1, e1), Prod (Num n2, e2) ->
            Prod (Num (n1 * n2), Prod (e1, e2))
        | e1', e2'                 -> Prod (e1', e2')
    | Num _ | Var _ as e    -> e
    | Neg e                 -> Neg (collect e)
    | Add exprs             -> Add (List.map collect exprs)
    | Sub (e1, exprs)       -> Sub (collect e1, List.map collect exprs)
    | Frac (e1, e2)         -> Frac (collect e1, collect e2)
    | Pow (e1, n)           -> Pow (collect e1, n)
    | Sin e                 -> Sin (collect e)
    | Cos e                 -> Cos (collect e)
    | Exp _ as e            -> e
```

```
/// Push negations through an expression
let rec negate e =
    match e with
    | Num n             -> Num (-n)
    | Var v as exp      -> Neg exp
    | Neg e             -> e
    | Add exprs         -> Add (List.map negate exprs)
    | Sub _             -> failwith "unexpected Sub"
    | Prod (e1, e2)     -> Prod (negate e1, e2)
    | Frac (e1, e2)     -> Frac (negate e1, e2)
    | exp               -> Neg exp

let filterNums (e:Expr) n =
    if e.IsNumber
    then [], n + e.NumOf
    else [e], n

let summands e =
    match e with
    | Add es -> es
    | e -> [e]

/// Simplify an expression
let rec simp e =
    match e with
    | Num n -> Num n
    | Var v -> Var v
    | Neg e -> negate (simp e)
    | Add exprs ->
        let exprs2, n =
            (exprs, 0M) ||> collectFold (simp >> summands >> collectFold filterNums)
        match exprs2 with
        | [] -> Num n
        | [e] when n = 0M -> e
        | _   when n = 0M -> Add exprs2
        | _ -> Add (exprs2 @ [Num n])
    | Sub (e1, exprs) -> simp (Add (e1 :: List.map Neg exprs))
    | Prod (e1, e2) ->
        match simp e1, simp e2 with
        | Num 0M, _ | _, Num 0M -> Num 0M
        | Num 1M, e | e, Num 1M -> e
        | Num n1, Num n2 -> Num (n1 * n2)
        | e1, e2 -> Prod (e1, e2)
    | Frac (e1, e2) ->
        match simp e1, simp e2 with
        | Num 0M, _ -> Num 0M
        | e1, Num 1M -> e1
        | Num n, Frac (Num n2, e) -> Prod (Frac (Num n, Num n2), e)
        | Num n, Frac (e, Num n2) -> Frac (Prod (Num n, Num n2), e)
        | e1, e2 -> Frac (e1, e2)
```

```
    | Pow (e, 1M) -> simp e
    | Pow (e, n) -> Pow (simp e, n)
    | Sin e -> Sin (simp e)
    | Cos e -> Cos (simp e)
    | Exp e -> Exp (simp e)

let simplify e = e |> simp |> simp |> collect
```

The main simplification algorithm works as follows:

- Constants and variables are passed through verbatim. You use negate when simplifying a negation, which assumes the expression at hand no longer contains differences and that sums were flattened (see the next item in this list).

- Sums are traversed and nested sums are flattened; at the same time all constants are collected and added up. This reduces the complexity of further simplification considerably.

- Differences are converted to sums: for instance, *A-B-C* is converted to *A+(-B)+(-C)*. Thus, the first element is preserved without negation.

- When simplifying a product, you first simplify its factors, and then you remove identity operations (multiplying by zero or one) and reduce products of constants.

- Fractions are handled similarly. Zero divided by anything is 0, anything divided by 1 is itself, and multiline fractions can be collapsed if you find numeric denominators or numerators.

- The rest of the match cases deal with simplifying subexpressions.

Symbolic Differentiation of Algebraic Expressions

Applying symbolic differentiation is a straightforward translation of the mathematical rules of differentiation into code. You could use local functions that act as constructors and perform local simplifications, but with the simplification function described earlier, this isn't needed. Listing 12-11 shows the implementation of symbolic differentiation for the Expr type. Note how beautifully and succinctly the code follows the math behind it: the essence of the symbolic processing is merely 20 lines of code!

Listing 12-11. ExprUtil.fs (continued): symbolic fifferentiation for algebraic expressions

```
let rec diff v e =
    match e with
    | Num _ -> Num 0M
    | Var v2 when v2=v -> Num 1M
    | Var _ -> Num 0M
    | Neg e -> diff v (Prod ((Num -1M), e))
    | Add exprs -> Add (List.map (diff v) exprs)
    | Sub (e1, exprs)  -> Sub (diff v e1, List.map (diff v) exprs)
    | Prod (e1, e2) -> Add [Prod (diff v e1, e2); Prod (e1, diff v e2)]
    | Frac (e1, e2) -> Frac (Sub (Prod (diff v e1, e2), [Prod (e1, diff v e2)]),Pow (e2, 2M))
    | Pow (e1, n) -> Prod (Prod (Num n, Pow (e1, n - 1M)), diff v e1)
    | Sin e -> Prod (Cos e, diff v e)
    | Cos e -> Neg (Prod (Sin e, diff v e))
```

```
| Exp (Var v2) as e when v2=v  -> e
| Exp (Var v2) -> Num OM
| Exp e -> Prod (Exp e, diff v e)
```

The Driver

Listing 12-12 is the next piece: the command-line driver (main.fsx). It reads lines from the input, tokenizes them, parses them, and applies the symbolic simplification and differentiation functions.

Listing 12-12. Main.fsx: the driver code for the symbolic differentiation application

```fsharp
#r "packages/FsLexYacc.Runtime/lib/net40/FsLexYacc.Runtime.dll"
#load "Expr.fs" "ExprParser.fs" "ExprLexer.fs" "ExprUtils.fs"

open System
open Symbolic.Expressions
open Microsoft.FSharp.Text.Lexing

let ProcessOneLine text =
    let lex = LexBuffer<char>.FromString text
    let e1 = ExprParser.expr ExprLexer.main lex
    printfn "After parsing: %A" e1

    let e2 = Utils.simplify e1
    printfn "After simplifying: %A" e2

    let e3 = Utils.diff "x" e2
    printfn "After differentiating: %A" e3

    let e4 = Utils.simplify e3
    printfn "After simplifying: %A" e4

let main () =
    while true do
        let text = Console.ReadLine()
        try
            ProcessOneLine text
        with e -> printfn "Error: %A" e

main()
```

The Web API

Listing 12-13 is the final piece: the symbolic analysis delivered as a web server using the script server.fsx. It does much the same thing as the command-line interface but uses Suave (see Chapter 2) to process requests:

Listing 12-13. server.fsx: the symbolic differentiation application as a simplistic web API

```
#r "packages/FsLexYacc.Runtime/lib/net40/FsLexYacc.Runtime.dll"
#r "packages/Suave/lib/net40/Suave.dll"
#load "Expr.fs" "ExprParser.fs" "ExprLexer.fs" "ExprUtils.fs"

open Symbolic.Expressions
open Symbolic.Expressions.ExprUtils
open Microsoft.FSharp.Text.Lexing

open Suave
open Suave.Http
open Suave.Http.Applicatives
open Suave.Http.Successful
open Suave.Web

let parse text =
    let lex = LexBuffer<char>.FromString text
    ExprParser.expr ExprLexer.main lex

let toJson x =
    OK (sprintf """{ "result": "%A" }""" x)
    >>= Writers.setMimeType "application/json"

let webServerSpec () =
  choose
    [ path "/" >>= OK "Welcome to the analyzer"
      pathScan "/simp/%s" (parse >> simp >> toJson)
      pathScan "/diff/%s" (parse >> diff "x" >> toJson)
      pathScan "/diffsimp/%s" (parse >> diff "x" >> simp >> toJson)
      pathScan "/parse/%s" (parse >> toJson) ]

startWebServer defaultConfig (webServerSpec())
```

After running this code in F# Interactive, you will see the website running the following:

```
[I] ...listener started ...with binding 127.0.0.1:8083 [Suave.Tcp.tcpIpServer]
```

Once running, you can make requests using URLs such as the following:

```
http://localhost:8083/simp/x+0
http://localhost:8083/diff/x*x
```

343

For each of these, you will get a JSON file served as a result that contains a textual form of the result of the parse. For example

```
http://localhost:8083/diff/x+x+x+x
```

performs differentiation, returning

```
{ "result": "Add [Add [Add [Num 1M; Num 1M]; Num 1M]; Num 1M]" }
```

and

```
http://localhost:8083/diffsimp/x+x+x+x
```

performs both differentiation and simplification, returning

```
{ "result": "Num 4M" }
```

We leave it as an exercise for the reader to format the expression result as more idiomatic JSON content. To recap, in this example you've seen the following:

- Two abstract syntax representations for different classes of algebraic expressions: one simple, and one more realistic

- How to implement simplification and symbolic differentiation routines on these representations of algebraic expressions

- How to implement parsing and lexing for concrete representations of algebraic expressions

- How to put this together into both a final console application and prototype web service

Summary

This chapter looked at two applications of language-oriented symbolic programming. The first was hardware modeling and verification using propositional logic and binary decision diagrams, where you saw how to use symbolic techniques to describe circuits as propositional-logic formulae and then used brute-force and/or binary decision diagram techniques to analyze these for correctness. In the second you learned how to transform and simplify algebraic expressions. These examples are only two of many in the large domain of symbolic computation problems, a domain where both functional programming and F# excel.

CHAPTER 13

■■■

Integrating External Data and Services

One of the major trends in modern computing is the "data deluge," meaning the rapid rise in digital information available for analysis, especially through reliable networked services and large-scale data-storage systems. Some of this data may be collected by an individual or an organization, some may be acquired from data providers, and some may be gathered from free data sources.

In this world, programmed services and applications can be viewed as components that consume, filter, transform, and re-republish information within a larger connected and reactive system. Nearly all modern software components or applications incorporate one or more external information sources. This may include static data in tables, static files copied into your application, data coming from relational databases, data coming from networked services (including the web or the local enterprise network), or data from the ambient context of sensors and devices. When the whole web is included, there are an overwhelming number of data sources that you might use, and hundreds more appearing every month! The digital world is exploding with information, almost beyond imagination.

For example, consider the data provided by the World Bank (http://api.worldbank.org), which includes thousands of data sets for hundreds of countries. From one perspective, this is a lot of data—it would take you a long time to learn and explore all this, and there are a lot of practical things you can do with it. However, from another perspective, the World Bank data is *tiny*—it is just one data source hidden in one remote corner of the Internet that you've probably never heard of until just now.

Because the world of external data is so big, in this chapter we can't hope to describe how to use every data source, or even every kind of data source. We also can't cover the incredible range of things you might want to do with different data sources. Instead, this chapter will introduce a selection of topics in data-rich programming. Along the way you will get to use and learn about some important and innovative F# features related to this space.

- You will first learn some simple and pragmatic techniques to work with external web data using HTTP REST requests, XML, and JSON.

- You will look at how F# allows for the language integration of some schematized data sources through the *type provider* feature. You will learn how to use the F# built-in type providers to query SQL databases directly from F# code.

- You will learn how to author more advanced queries, including sorting, grouping, joins, and statistical aggregates.

- You will learn how to use the lower-level ADO.NET libraries for some data-programming tasks for relational databases.

Some Basic REST Requests

We will begin our adventures in working with external information sources by looking at some simple examples of making HTTP REST requests to web-hosted resources. FSharp.Data comes with function Http. RequestString to download the content of a website. This can also be used to fetch structured data in formats such as XML and JSON from web-hosted services. For example, one such service is the World Bank API mentioned in the introduction to this chapter. This service exposes a data space containing regions, countries, and indicators, where the indicators are a time series of (time, value) pairs. You can fetch the list of countries by using:

```
let worldBankCountriesXmlPage1 = Http.RequestString "http://api.worldbank.org/country"
```

This fetches the first page of the country list as XML, and the results will look like the following:

```
val worldBankCountriesXmlPage1 : string =

  "<?xml version="1.0" encoding="utf-8"?>
<wb:countries page="1"+[25149 chars]

> worldBankCountriesXmlPage1;;

val it : string =
  "<?xml version="1.0" encoding="utf-8"?>
<wb:countries page="1" pages="5" per_page="50" total="246" xmlns:wb="http://www.worldbank.org">
  <wb:country id="ABW">
    <wb:iso2Code>AW</wb:iso2Code>
    <wb:name>Aruba</wb:name>
    <wb:region id="LCN">Latin America &amp; Caribbean (all income levels)</wb:region>
    <wb:adminregion id="" />
    <wb:incomeLevel id="NOC">High income: nonOECD</wb:incomeLevel>
    <wb:lendingType id="LNX">Not classified</wb:lendingType>
    <wb:capitalCity>Oranjestad</wb:capitalCity>
    <wb:longitude>-70.0167</wb:longitude>
    <wb:latitude>12.5167</wb:latitude>
  </wb:country>
  <wb:country id="AFG">
...
  </wb:country>
...
</wb:countries>"
```

This data is a string that you can now parse to a partially typed format using the techniques from Chapter 8, "Programming with Text." Additionally, you can use the URL as a schema specification inputted directly into the XmlProvider type provider in the FSharp.Data library:

```
type CountriesXml = XmlProvider<"http://api.worldbank.org/country">

let sampleCountries = CountriesXml.GetSample()
```

The sample data is now available in a strongly typed form under a schema suitable for all the sample entries the data source is providing:

```
> sampleCountries.Countries.Length;;

val it : int = 50

> sampleCountries.Countries.[0].Name;;

val it : string = "Aruba"
```

Only 50 countries have been returned by our request in the sample. You will see next how to make the multiple requests needed to get all the countries from the data source.

Getting Data in JSON Format

Web-based data sources typically support both XML and JSON result formats. For example, you can fetch the same data in JSON format as follows:

```
let worldBankCountriesJsonPage1 = Http.RequestString "http://api.worldbank.org/
country?format=json"
```

The results will then look like this:

```
val worldBankCountriesJsonPage1 : string =
  "[{"page":1,"pages":5,"per_page":"50","total":246},[{"id":"ABW"+[17322 chars]
```

You learned how to parse and produce JSON data in Chapter 8, "Programming with Text." As with the XML, you can use the sample from the previous URL as a schema specification for the JsonProvider in the FSharp.Data library:

```
type CountriesJson = JsonProvider<"http://api.worldbank.org/country?format=json">

let sampleCountriesFromJson = CountriesJson.GetSample()
```

The sample data is now available in a strongly typed form under a schema suitable for all the sample entries the data source is providing:

```
> sampleCountriesFromJson.Array.Length;;

val it : int = 50

> sampleCountriesFromJson.Array.[0].Name;;

val it : string = "Aruba"
```

There are a couple of minor differences here: the schema inferred from the returned JSON has the countries under a property called `Array` rather than `Countries`. But, apart from that, the results are as before, except this time the underlying request has used JSON data.

Parsing and Handling Multiple Pages

Web-hosted services like the WorldBank API are "stateless"—they will essentially respond to identical requests with identical responses. Accessing services like this uses a technique known as REST, which stands for *REpresentational State Transfer*. This means that any "state" is passed back and forth between the client and the services as data.

One simple example of how this works is the way we collect multiple pages of data from the services. So far, we have only retrieved the first page of countries. If we want to collect all the pages, we need to make multiple requests, where we give a page parameter. For example, we can get the second page as follows:

```
let worldBankCountriesXmlPage2 = http "http://api.worldbank.org/country?page=2"
```

Note that the "state" of the process of iterating through the collection is passed simply by using a different URL, one with "page=2" added. This is very typical of REST requests. The total number of pages can be fetched by parsing the first page, which contains the total page count as an attribute. If using XML, we use the following:

```
let loadPageFromXml n = CountriesXml.Load(sprintf "http://api.worldbank.org/country?page=%d" n)
```

```
let countries =
    let page1 = loadPageFromXml 1
    [ for i in 1 .. page1.Pages do
        let page = loadPageFromXml i
        yield! page.Countries ]
```

This code loads the first page, whose payload also contains a count of the total number of pages available, and then fetches each subsequent page, using the schema inferred from the first page. When executed, this reveals a total of 256 countries (note: the list also includes regions, which are collections of countries):

```
> countries.Length;;

val it : int = 256

> [ for c in countries -> c.Name ];;

val it : string list =
  ["Aruba"; "Afghanistan"; "Africa"; "Angola"; "Albania"; "Andorra";
   "Andean Region"; "Arab World"; "United Arab Emirates"; "Argentina";
   "Armenia"; "American Samoa"; "Antigua and Barbuda"; "Australia"; "Austria";...
```

Almost identical code can be used if loading from JSON; we leave this as an exercise for the reader. The skeleton of the code is shown here:

```
let loadPageFromJson n =
    CountriesJson.Load(sprintf "http://api.worldbank.org/country?format=json&page=%d" n)
```

```
let countriesFromJson =
    let page1 = loadPageFromJson 1
    [ for i in 1 .. page1.Record.Pages do
      ... ]
```

As an alternative, you can often simply increase a REST parameter that indicates how many results to return per page. For example, in the case of the WorldBank API this is the per_page parameter; e.g.:

```
http://api.worldbank.org/country?format=json&per_page=1000
```

This will return all the results in a single page, which can then be parsed. However, not all services allow arbitrarily high numbers of items per page, so parsing multiple pages is still often necessary.

MORE ABOUT TYPE PROVIDERS

The previous examples use two F# type providers from the FSharp.Data library, in this code:

```
type CountriesXml = XmlProvider<" http://api.worldbank.org/country?format=xml">
type CountriesJson = JsonProvider<" http://api.worldbank.org/country?format=json">
```

You've used F# type providers a number of times in this book already, in Chapters 2 and 8. A type provider is an adapter component that reads schematized data and services and transforms them into types in the target programming language. The static parameters <"http://... > identify an external information space, and the type provider supplies the host F# compiler with information describing the namespaces, types, methods, and properties of an F#-friendly version of the information space. This allows you to quickly leverage rich, schematized information sources without an explicit transcription process (such as code generation, a manually created schema, or an ontology). Also, if the data source contains additional descriptive metadata (such as a description of various columns in a database), it can be transformed by the type provider into information that is visible to the programmer within the IDE (such as documentation contained in tooltips).

A type provider is a form of compile-time meta-programming—a compiler plugin that augments the set of types that are known to the type-checker and compiler. Importantly, a type provider can provide types and methods on demand, i.e., lazily, as the information is required by the host tool, such as the F# compiler. This allows the provided type space to be very large, or even infinite.

Getting Started with Queries

In the first section, you performed some basic REST requests in F#. However, you will have noticed that working with external information in this way is somewhat tedious without the help of type providers, because you must manually construct REST API calls and manually parse the XML or JSON returned by the service. This gets progressively harder as services become more complex, as services change, and as additional features like authentication are required. Furthermore, it is very easy to make mistakes in all parts of this process, including parsing the XML or JSON.

In this section, we look at the F# language/tooling feature called *queries*, which, in combination with the F# type providers, are designed to make information sources directly available in the F# language in a simpler, more intuitive, and more directly strongly typed way.

Example: Language-Integrated SQL

For our example of working with queries, we will use data drawn from a relational database and queried using SQL. The following sections will show how to perform relational database queries using F# queries. F# uses quotation metaprogramming to represent SQL queries. These are then translated across to SQL and executed using the LINQ libraries that are part of .NET Framework 4.0 or higher.

We assume you're working with the Northwnd.mdf database, a common database used in many database samples. You can download this sample database from https://northwinddatabase.codeplex.com/, or from many other sources on the Internet. The code used to access the database is very simple:

```
#r "System.Data.Linq.dll"
#r "FSharp.Data.TypeProviders.dll"

open FSharp.Linq
open FSharp.Data.TypeProviders

type NorthwndDb =
    SqlDataConnection<ConnectionString =
                      @"AttachDBFileName  = 'C:\Scripts\northwnd.mdf';
                        Server='.\SQLEXPRESS';User Instance=true;Integrated
Security=SSPI",
                      Pluralize=true>

let db = NorthwndDb.GetDataContext()
```

In this code, you first reference two libraries: the "runtime" library for SQL data access, System.Data.Linq, and the F# library for the F# SQL type providers, which is called FSharp.Data.TypeProviders.dll. You then create an instance of a "data context" to access the database. You can now get data from the service as follows:

```
let customersSortedByCountry =
    query { for c in db.Customers do
            sortBy c.Country
            select (c.Country, c.CompanyName) }
    |> Seq.toList
```

When run, this gives the full list of customers from the database:

```
val customersSortedByCountry : (string * string) list =
  [("Argentina", "Cactus Comidas para llevar");
   ("Argentina", "Océano Atlántico Ltda."); ("Argentina", "Rancho grande");
   ...
   ("Venezuela", "LINO-Delicateses"); ("Venezuela", "HILARION-Abastos");
   ("Venezuela", "GROSELLA-Restaurante")]
```

To understand what's going on, it's helpful to add the following line before executing the code:

```
db.DataContext.Log <- System.Console.Out
```

After you add this, you will see that the output begins:

```
SELECT [t0].[Country] AS [Item1], [t0].[ContactName] AS [Item2]
FROM [dbo].[Customers] AS [t0]
ORDER BY [t0].[Country]
-- Context: SqlProvider(Sql2008) Model: AttributedMetaModel Build: 4.0.30319.17929
```

As you can see, the query has been converted into SQL text and sent to the relational database for execution. A slightly more complex query is shown here:

```
let selectedEmployees =
    query { for emp in db.Employees do
            where (emp.BirthDate.Value.Year > 1960)
            where (emp.LastName.StartsWith "S")
            select (emp.FirstName, emp.LastName)
            take 5 }
    |> Seq.toList
```

The results are as follows (only one employee is ultimately selected):

```
SELECT TOP (5) [t0].[FirstName] AS [Item1], [t0].[LastName] AS [Item2]
FROM [dbo].[Employees] AS [t0]
WHERE ([t0].[LastName] LIKE @p0) AND (DATEPART(Year, [t0].[BirthDate]) > @p1)
-- @p0: Input NVarChar (Size = 4000; Prec = 0; Scale = 0) [S%]
-- @p1: Input Int (Size = -1; Prec = 0; Scale = 0) [1960]
-- Context: SqlProvider(Sql2008) Model: AttributedMetaModel Build: 4.0.30319.17929

val selectedEmployees : (string * string) list = [("Michael", "Suyama")]
```

In this code, this construct is a query:

```
query { for c in db.Customers do
        take 10
        select c }
```

If you know C#, you will recognize this as a way of writing LINQ queries. A LINQ query is simply a manner of specifying a query of a data source using a set of operators such as select, where, take, and so on. In F#, the code inside query { ... } is converted by a LINQ query provider into an actual request that is sent to the service.

In the following sections, you will learn how to perform a number of relational query operations in the F# query syntax.

Sorting

The sorting operations in queries are sortBy, sortByDescending, thenBy, thenByDescending, and their corresponding versions for nullable values, such as sortByNullable. These are added to a query starting with one of the sortBy operations (for the first sorting key) and a sequence of thenBy operations (for secondary and subsequent sorting keys). Sorting is done in ascending order unless the "descending" variations are used. For example:

```
let customersSortedTwoColumns =
    query { for c in db.Customers do
            sortBy c.Country
            thenBy c.Region
            select (c.Country, c.Region, c.CompanyName) }
    |> Seq.toList
```

This gives you:

```
val customersSortedTwoColumns : (string * string * string) list =
  [("Argentina", null, "Cactus Comidas para llevar");
   ("Argentina", null, "Océano Atlántico Ltda.");
   ("Argentina", null, "Rancho grande"); ("Austria", null, "Piccolo und mehr");
   ("Austria", null, "Ernst Handel"); ("Belgium", null, "Maison Dewey");
   ...
   ("Venezuela", "DF", "GROSELLA-Restaurante");
   ("Venezuela", "Lara", "LILA-Supermercado");
   ("Venezuela", "Nueva Esparta", "LINO-Delicateses");
   ("Venezuela", "Táchira", "HILARION-Abastos")]
```

Aggregation

Aggregation operations (sum, average, maximum, minimum) are performed by using the query operators sumBy, sumByNullable, averageBy, averageByNullable, maxBy, maxByNullable, minBy, or minByNullable. For example:

```
let totalOrderQuantity =
    query { for order in db.OrderDetails do
            sumBy (int order.Quantity) }

let customersAverageOrders =
    query { for c in db.Customers do
            averageBy (float c.Orders.Count) }
```

Giving:

```
val totalOrderQuantity : int = 51317
val customersAverageOrders : float = 9.120879121
```

Nullables

Data in XML, JSON, SQL tables, and other data sources may be missing values. When using these data sources via type providers (e.g., `XmlProvider`, `JsonProvider`, `SqlCommandProvider`, `SqlDataProvider`, and `SqlEntityProvider`), the potential for missing primitive values is represented by using either the F# type `option<_>`, discussed in Chapter 2 and used throughout this book, or the .NET type `System.Nullable<_>`. In this section we will discuss the latter.

Full techniques to handle nullable values are discussed in the MSDN documentation for F# queries. Here we show just some examples. For instance, to compute the average price over the range of products on offer, you can use `averageByNullable`:

```
let averagePriceOverProductRange =
    query { for p in db.Products do
            averageByNullable p.UnitPrice }
```

This gives you:

```
val averagePriceOverProductRange : System.Nullable<decimal> = 28.8663M
```

Note that the result of the averaging is itself a nullable value. Working with nullable values can be slightly awkward in F#. Here are some techniques to use:

- Very often, you will need to eliminate nullable values using either the `.Value` property or the `.GetValueOrDefault()` method. You can also call conversion functions such `int` or `float`.

- To create a nullable value, use the constructor for the System.Nullable type, e.g., `System.Nullable(3)`.

- To compare, add, subtract, multiply, or divide nullable values, use the special operators such as `?+?` in `FSharp.Linq.NullableOperators`.

Inner Queries

It is very common to use one or more "inner" queries to collect information about an entity before selecting it. For example, consider the task of writing a query that iterates the customers, sums the number of orders (if any), and finds the average unit price of orders (if any) for that customer. Here is the query:

```
open System

let totalOrderQuantity =
    query { for c in db.Customers do
            let numOrders =
                query { for o in c.Orders do
                        for od in o.OrderDetails do
                        sumByNullable (Nullable(int od.Quantity)) }
            let averagePrice =
                query { for o in c.Orders do
                        for od in o.OrderDetails do
                        averageByNullable (Nullable(od.UnitPrice)) }
            select (c.ContactName, numOrders, averagePrice) }
    |> Seq.toList
```

This gives you:

```
val totalOrderQuantity :
  (string * System.Nullable<int> * System.Nullable<decimal>) list =
  [("Maria Anders", 174, 26.7375M); ("Ana Trujillo", 63, 21.5050M);
   ("Antonio Moreno", 359, 21.7194M); ("Thomas Hardy", 650, 19.1766M);
   ...
   ("Zbyszek Piestrzeniewicz", 205, 20.6312M)]
```

Grouping

The previous example showed how to use inner queries to compute and return a number of statistical properties of an entity using a query. Very often, this is instead done over a group of entities. To group entities, you use the groupBy .. into ... operator:

```
let productsGroupedByNameAndCountedTest1 =
    query { for p in db.Products do
            groupBy p.Category.CategoryName into group
            let sum =
                query { for p in group do
                        sumBy (int p.UnitsInStock.Value) }
            select (group.Key, sum) }
    |> Seq.toList
```

Giving:

```
val productsGroupedByNameAndCountedTest1 : (string * int) list =
  [("Beverages", 559); ("Condiments", 507); ("Confections", 386);
   ("Dairy Products", 393); ("Grains/Cereals", 308); ("Meat/Poultry", 165);
   ("Produce", 100); ("Seafood", 701)]
```

Joins

You can write both normal SQL joins and "group" joins using F# queries. For example, a simple join is written as follows:

```
let innerJoinQuery =
    query { for c in db.Categories do
            join p in db.Products on (c.CategoryID =? p.CategoryID)
            select (p.ProductName, c.CategoryName) }
    |> Seq.toList
```

The operator =? is a nullable comparison operator, mentioned in the previous section, and it is used because p.CategoryID may be missing. This gives you:

```
val innerJoinQuery : (string * string) list =
  [("Chai", "Beverages"); ("Chang", "Beverages");
   ("Aniseed Syrup", "Condiments");
   ...
   ("Lakkalikööri", "Beverages");
   ("Original Frankfurter grüne Soße", "Condiments")]
```

As it happens, many joins are actually implicit in F# queries over types provided by the usual type providers. For example, the query could have been written:

```
let innerJoinQuery =
    query { for p in db.Products do
              select (p.ProductName, p.Category.CategoryName) }
    |> Seq.toList
```

Likewise, you can also write group joins, where the inner iteration results in an overall group of elements that satisfy the joining constraint. For example:

```
let innerGroupJoinQueryWithAggregation =
    query { for c in db.Categories do
              groupJoin p in db.Products on (c.CategoryID =? p.CategoryID) into prodGroup
              let groupMax = query { for p in prodGroup do maxByNullable p.UnitsOnOrder }
              select (c.CategoryName, groupMax) }
    |> Seq.toList
```

This gives you:

```
val innerGroupJoinQueryWithAggregation : (string * Nullable<int16>) list =
  [("Beverages", 40s); ("Condiments", 100s); ("Confections", 70s);
   ("Dairy Products", 70s); ("Grains/Cereals", 80s); ("Meat/Poultry", 0s);
   ("Produce", 20s); ("Seafood", 70s)]
```

More Choices for SQL

So far in this chapter, you have seen how to perform simple "raw" HTTP web requests to an information service, and how to use the type provider and query mechanisms to access SQL data in a more directly strongly typed and clear way. In this section we will examine databases more generally and other ways to access them. Some of the important factors for database choice are:

- *Data security:* When you have centralized control of your data, you can erect a full security system around the data, implementing specific access rules for each type of access or parts of the database.

- *Sharing data*: Any number of applications with the appropriate access rights can connect to your database and read the data stored within—without needing to worry about containing the logic to extract this data. As you will see shortly, applications use various query languages (most notably SQL) to communicate with databases.

- *A logical organization of data*: You can write new applications that work with the same data without having to worry about how the data is physically represented and stored. On the basic level, this logical structure is provided by a set of entities (data tables) and their relationships.

- *Avoiding data redundancy*: Having all requirements from each consuming application up front helps to identify a logical organization for your data that minimizes possible redundancy. For instance, you can use foreign keys instead of duplicating pieces of data. *Data normalization* is the process of systematically eliminating data redundancy, a large but essential topic that we don't consider in this book.

- *Transactions*: Reading from and writing to databases occurs atomically, and, as a result, two concurrent transactions can never leave data in an inconsistent, inaccurate state. *Isolation levels* refer to specific measures taken to ensure transaction isolation by locking various parts of the database (fields, records, tables). Higher isolation levels increase locking overhead and can lead to a loss of parallelism by rendering concurrent transactions sequential; on the other hand, no isolation can lead to inconsistent data.

- *Maintaining data integrity*: Databases make sure data is stored accurately. Having no redundancy is one way to maintain data integrity (if a piece of data is changed, it's changed in the only place it occurs; thus, it remains accurate). On the other hand, data security and transaction isolation are needed to ensure that the data stored is modified in a controlled manner.

Table 13-1 shows some of the most common database engines, all of which can be used from both F# and .NET.

Table 13-1. Common Databases

Name	Type	Description	Available From
PostgreSQL	Open source	Open-source database engine	www.postgresql.org
SQLite	Open source	Small, embeddable, zero-configuration SQL database engine	www.sqlite.org
DB2	Commercial	IBM's database engine	www-01.ibm.com/software/data/db2/ad/dotnet.html
Firebird	Open source	Based on Borland Interbase	www.firebirdsql.org
MySQL	Open source	Reliable and popular database	www.mysql.com
Mimer SQL	Commercial	Reliable database engine	www.mimer.com
Oracle	Commercial	One of the most popular enterprise database engines	www.oracle.com
SQL Server	Commercial	Microsoft's main database engine	www.microsoft.com/sql
SQL Server Express	Commercial	Free and easy-to-use version of SQL Server	www.microsoft.com/express/database
Sybase iAnywhere	Commercial	Mobile database engine	www.ianywhere.com

Applications communicate with relational databases using Structured Query Language (SQL). Each time you create tables, create relationships, insert new records, or update or delete existing ones, you are explicitly or implicitly issuing SQL statements to the database. The examples in this chapter use a dialect of Standard SQL called Transact-SQL (T-SQL), used by SQL Server and SQL Server Express. SQL has syntax to define the structure of a database schema (loosely speaking, a collection of data tables and their relations) and also syntax to manage the data within. These subsets of SQL are called *Data Definition Language* (DDL) and *Data Manipulation Language* (DML), respectively.

Directly Embedding T-SQL Using SqlCommandProvider

In F# 4.0, the F# community has developed a new approach to embedding raw but type-checked T-SQL directly within F#. This is done through the `FSharp.Data.SqlClient` package, which contains the `SqlCommandProvider`, a type provider for F# that accepts SQL commands statically and checks them at compile time against the schema of the database. We don't cover this type provider in detail in this book, though the following code sample shows the style of the integration (it assumes you are accessing the AdventureWorks2014 database, available from `http://msftdbprodsamples.codeplex.com/`):

```
#r "FSharp.Data.SqlClient.dll"

open FSharp.Data

[<Literal>]
let connectionString =
    @"Data Source=.;Initial Catalog=AdventureWorks2014;Integrated Security=True"

let cmd =
    new SqlCommandProvider<
        "SELECT TOP(@topN) FirstName, LastName, SalesYTD
        FROM Sales.vSalesPerson
        WHERE CountryRegionName = @regionName AND SalesYTD > @salesMoreThan
        ORDER BY SalesYTD" , connectionString>()

cmd.Execute(topN = 3L, regionName = "United States", salesMoreThan = 1000000M) |> printfn "%A"
```

Note that the T-SQL text is embedded directly into the F# program: it is a template of a query with some holes in it, such as `@topN`. This is then handed to the database at compile time for pre-checking. If you already know SQL, then `SqlCommandProvider` is a very powerful way to interact with the database while still getting strong checking. The same F# community package also includes two additional type providers (`SqlProgrammabilityProvider` and `SqlEnumProvider`) that allow access to functions, stored procedures, tables, and static lookup data.

Raw Access to Databases Using ADO.NET

Often it is necessary to access databases in a "raw" way rather than through the strongly typed techniques discussed so far in this chapter. To do this, you use the ADO.NET library, which has been part of .NET since its first releases. Like web requests, this is a "lowest common denominator" way of doing information access from F# code. While it is usually nicer to use the type-provider mechanism where possible, this is not always possible for all databases, and is also not really possible for cases where you are creating tables dynamically. Furthermore, some data-access standards (e.g., ODBC, a common data-connectivity standard developed in the late 1990s) will definitely require you to use lower-level libraries that look a lot like ADO.NET. Note that you can also use the newer Entity Framework to work with databases on a higher conceptual level. However, in this current discussion, we are mostly concerned with low-level details such as programmatically creating tables, executing update and insert statements, and querying using plain SQL code.

ADO.NET is the underlying database-access machinery in the .NET Framework, and it provides full XML support, disconnected and typed datasets, scalability, and high performance. This section gives a brief overview of the ADO.NET fundamentals.

With ADO.NET, data is acquired through a *connection* to the database via a provider. This connection serves as a medium against which to execute a *command*; this can be used to fetch, update, insert, or delete data from the data store. Statements and queries are articulated as SQL text (CREATE, SELECT, UPDATE, INSERT, and DELETE statements) and are passed to the command object's constructor. When you execute these statements, you obtain data (in the case of queries) or the number of affected rows (in the case of UPDATE, INSERT, and DELETE statements). The data returned can be processed via two main mechanisms: sequentially in a read-only fashion using a DataReader object or by loading it into an in-memory representation (a DataSet object) for further disconnected processing. DataSet objects store data in a set of table objects along with metadata that describes their relationships and constraints in a fully contained model.

Establishing Connections Using ADO.NET

Before you can do any work with a database, you need to establish a connection to it. For instance, you can connect to a locally running instance of SQL Server Express using the following code:

```
open System.Data
open System.Data.SqlClient

let connString = @"Server='.\SQLEXPRESS';Integrated Security=SSPI"
let conn = new SqlConnection(connString)
```

The value connString is a connection string. Regardless of how you created your connection object, to execute any updates or queries on it, you need to open it first:

```
> conn.Open();;
```

If this command fails, then you may need to do one of the following:

- consult the latest SQL Server Express samples for alternative connection strings.

- add UserInstance='true' to the connection string. This starts the database engine as a user-level process.

- change the connection string if you have a different database engine installed and running (for instance, if you're using SQL Server instead of SQL Server Express).

Connections established using the same connection string are pooled and reused depending on your database engine. Connections are often a limited resource and should generally be closed as soon as possible within your application.

Creating a Database Using ADO.NET

Now that you've established a connection to the database engine, you can explicitly create a database from F# code by executing a SQL statement directly. For example, you can create a database called company as follows:

```
open System.Data
open System.Data.SqlClient

let execNonQuery conn s =
    let comm = new SqlCommand(s, conn, CommandTimeout = 10)
    comm.ExecuteNonQuery() |> ignore

execNonQuery conn "CREATE DATABASE company"
```

You will use execNonQuery in the subsequent sections. This method takes a connection object and a SQL string and executes it as a SQL command, ignoring its result.

■ **Note**   If you try to create the same database twice, you will receive a runtime exception. However, if you intend to drop an existing database, you can do so by issuing a DROP DATABASE company SQL command. The DROP command can also be used for other database artifacts, including tables, views, and stored procedures.

Creating Tables Using ADO.NET

You can execute a simple SQL command to create a table; all you need to do is specify its data fields and their types and whether null values are allowed. The following example creates an Employees table with a primary key EmpID and FirstName, LastName, and Birthday fields:

```
execNonQuery conn "CREATE TABLE Employees (
    EmpID int NOT NULL,
    FirstName varchar(50) NOT NULL,
    LastName varchar(50) NOT NULL,
    Birthday datetime,
    PRIMARY KEY (EmpID))"
```

You can now insert two new records as follows:

```
execNonQuery conn "INSERT INTO Employees (EmpId, FirstName, LastName, Birthday)
    VALUES (1001, 'Joe', 'Smith', '02/14/1965')"

execNonQuery conn "INSERT INTO Employees (EmpId, FirstName, LastName, Birthday)
    VALUES (1002, 'Mary', 'Jones', '09/15/1985')"
```

and retrieve two columns of what was inserted using a fresh connection and a data reader:

```
let query() =
    seq {
        use conn = new SqlConnection(connString)
        conn.Open()
        use comm = new SqlCommand("SELECT FirstName, Birthday FROM Employees", conn)
```

```
        use reader = comm.ExecuteReader()
        while reader.Read() do
            yield (reader.GetString 0, reader.GetDateTime 1)
    }
```

When you evaluate the query expression in F# Interactive, a connection to the database is created and opened, the command is built, and the reader is used to read successive elements:

```
> fsi.AddPrinter(fun (d: DateTime) -> d.ToString());;

> query();;

val it : seq<string * DateTime> =
    seq [("Joe", 14/02/1965 12:00:00AM); ("Mary", 15/09/1985 12:00:00AM)]
```

The definition of query uses sequence expressions that locally define new IDisposable objects such as conn, comm, and reader using declarations of the form use var = expr. These ensure that the locally defined connection, command, and reader objects are disposed of after exhausting the entire sequence. See Chapters 4, 8, and 9 for more details about sequence expressions of this kind.

F# sequences are on demand (that is, lazy), and the definition of query doesn't open a connection to the database. This is done when the sequence is first iterated; a connection is maintained until the sequence is exhausted.

Note that the command object's ExecuteReader method returns a DataReader instance that is used to extract the typed data returned from the query. You can read from the resulting sequence in a straightforward manner using a sequence iterator. For instance, you can use a simple anonymous function to print data on the screen:

```
> query() |> Seq.iter (fun (fn, bday) -> printfn "%s has birthday %O" fn bday);;

Joe has birthday 14/02/1965 00:00:00
Mary has birthday 15/09/1985 00:00:00
```

The query brings the data from the database in memory, although still as a lazy sequence. You can then use standard F# in-memory data transformations on the result:

```
> query()
  |> Seq.filter (fun (_, bday) -> bday < DateTime.Parse("01/01/1985"))
  |> Seq.length;;

val it : int = 1
```

However, be aware that these additional transformations are happening in memory and not in the database.

The command object has different methods for executing different queries. For instance, if you have a statement, you need to use the ExecuteNonQuery method (for UPDATE, INSERT, and DELETE statements, as previously in execNonQuery), which returns the number of rows affected (updated, inserted, or deleted), or the ExecuteScalar method, which returns the first column of the first row of the result, providing a fast and efficient way to extract a single value, such as the number of rows in a table or a result set.

In the previous command, you extracted fields from the result rows using Get*XXX* methods on the reader object. The particular methods have to match the types of the fields selected in the SQL query, as a mismatch results in a runtime `InvalidCastException`. For these and other reasons, `DataReader` tends to be suitable only in situations when the following items are true:

- You need to read data only in a sequential order (as returned from the database). `DataReader` provides forward-only data access.

- The field types of the result are known, and the query isn't configurable.

- You're reading only and not writing data. `DataReader` provides read-only access.

- Your use of `DataReader` is localized. The data connection is open throughout the reader loop.

Database connections are precious resources, and you should always release them as soon as possible. In the previous case, you did this by using a locally defined connection. It's also sufficient to implicitly close the reader by constructing it with the `CloseConnection` option that causes it to release and close the data connection upon closing the reader instance.

Common options include `SchemaOnly`, which you can use to extract field information only (without any data returned); `SingleResult` to extract a single value only (the same as using the `ExecuteScalar` method discussed earlier); `SingleRow` to extract a single row; and `KeyInfo` to extract additional columns (appended to the end of the selected ones) automatically that uniquely identify the rows returned.

Using Stored Procedures via ADO.NET

Stored procedures are defined and stored in your relational database and provide a number of benefits over literal SQL. First, they're external to the application and thus provide a clear division of the data logic from the rest of the application. This enables you to make data-related modifications without having to change application code or having to redeploy the application. Second, they're stored in the database in a prepared or compiled form and thus are executed more efficiently than literal SQL statements (although those can be prepared as well at a one-time cost, they're still contained in application space, which is undesirable). Supplying arguments to stored procedures instantiates the compiled formula.

In Visual Studio, you can add stored procedures just like any other database artifacts using the Server Explorer window: right-click the Stored Procedures item in the appropriate database and select Add New Stored Procedure. Doing so creates a stored procedure template that you can easily customize. Alternatively, you can add stored procedures programmatically using the `CREATE PROCEDURE` SQL command. Consider the following stored procedure that returns the first and last names of all employees whose last name matches the given pattern:

```
execNonQuery conn "
CREATE PROCEDURE dbo.GetEmployeesByLastName ( @Name nvarchar(50) ) AS
    SELECT Employees.FirstName, Employees.LastName
    FROM Employees
    WHERE Employees.LastName LIKE @Name"
```

You can wrap this stored procedure in a function as follows:

```
let GetEmployeesByLastName (name: string) =
    use comm = new SqlCommand("GetEmployeesByLastName", conn,
                              CommandType = CommandType.StoredProcedure)
    comm.Parameters.AddWithValue("@Name", name) |> ignore
    use adapter = new SqlDataAdapter(comm)
    let table = new DataTable()
    adapter.Fill(table) |> ignore
    table
```

You can execute the stored procedure as follows to find employees with the last name Smith:

```
> for row in GetEmployeesByLastName("Smith").Rows do
    printfn "row = %O, %O" (row.Item "FirstName") (row.Item "LastName");;

row = Joe, Smith
```

Summary

In this chapter, you learned about how the growing availability of data is changing programming, forcing programmers to incorporate more data- and network-access code into their applications. You learned both low-level and high-level techniques for accessing a range of web, database, and service technologies. Along the way, you learned the basics of two important F# features that are used for data access: F# queries and F# type providers. Together these give an elegant and direct way of integrating data into your programs. You also learned low-level techniques for REST requests and database access with ADO.NET. These are pragmatic techniques that allow you to do more, but less directly.

The next chapter will continue on the theme of web programming by looking at a range of topics on delivering content via the Internet, from delivering HTML directly to writing full web applications using WebSharper, a web application framework for F#.

CHAPTER 14

∎∎∎

Building Smart Web Applications

Delivering content and applications via web browsers is one of the most important aspects of modern software development. This chapter will examine how you can build web applications using F#. Some of the topics covered are the following:

- Serving static files and dynamic content by directly responding to HTTP requests

- Techniques to build client-based web applications with WebSharper, the main F# web framework

- A walkthrough of the main WebSharper features, including pagelets, sitelets, formlets, flowlets, and piglets

- Working with HTML markup programmatically using `UI.Next` and `WebSharper.Html`

- Using static and dynamic templates and sitelets to build WebSharper applications

- Building sitelets that handle different HTTP requests

- Using dependent formlets and flowlets to model user-interface dependencies and wizard-like sequences of web forms

- Defining resources and attaching them to different code units

- A brief overview of developing WebSharper extensions to third-party JavaScript libraries

- Defining WebSharper proxies to extend the JavaScript translation coverage to additional .NET types

Serving Web Content Directly

When you point your browser at a web page or call a web service from your application, you're effectively issuing one or more requests (commands) to a web (HTTP) server. HTTP commands are simple text-based instructions that are automatically generated by your web browser. For instance, when your browser goes to a particular URL, it does the following:

- Requests the page from the web server and waits for the response

- Analyzes the contents of the page in the response for further content to be fetched (images, for example) and issues the appropriate requests if necessary

- Displays the results and executes any dynamic scripts and content contained in the page

A response can be a verbatim copy of a resource found on the web server (most often a static file such as an image, a style sheet, or a media file) or can be generated on the fly. This section will show how you can use F# to serve content directly.

Listing 14-1 shows a simple web server written directly in F#.

Listing 14-1. A simple web server

```
open System.Net
open System.Net.Sockets
open System.IO
open System.Text.RegularExpressions
open System.Text

/// A table of MIME content types.
let mimeTypes =
    dict [".html", "text/html"
          ".htm",  "text/html"
          ".txt",  "text/plain"
          ".gif",  "image/gif"
          ".jpg",  "image/jpeg"
          ".png",  "image/png"]

/// Compute a MIME type from a file extension.
let getMimeType(ext) =
    if mimeTypes.ContainsKey(ext) then mimeTypes.[ext]
    else "binary/octet"

/// The pattern Regex1 uses a regular expression to match one element.
let (|Regex1|_|) (patt : string) (inp : string) =
    try Some(Regex.Match(inp, patt).Groups.Item(1).Captures.Item(0).Value)
    with _ -> None

/// The root for the data we serve
let root = @"c:\inetpub\wwwroot"

/// Handle a TCP connection for an HTTP GET request.
let handleRequest (client: TcpClient) (port: int) =
    async {
        use stream = client.GetStream()
        use out = new StreamWriter(stream)
        let sendHeaders (lines: seq<string>) =
            let printLine = fprintf out "%s\r\n"
            Seq.iter printLine lines
            // An empty line is required before content, if any.
            printLine ""
            out.Flush()
        let notFound () = sendHeaders ["HTTP/1.0 404 Not Found"]
        let inp = new StreamReader(stream)
        let request = inp.ReadLine()
        match request with
```

```fsharp
        // Requests to root are redirected to the start page.
        | "GET / HTTP/1.0" | "GET / HTTP/1.1" ->
            sendHeaders
                [
                    "HTTP/1.0 302 Found"
                    sprintf "Location: http://localhost:%d/iisstart.htm" port
                ]
        | Regex1 "GET /(.*?) HTTP/1\\.[01]$" fileName ->
            let fname = Path.Combine(root, fileName)
            let mimeType = getMimeType(Path.GetExtension(fname))
            if not (File.Exists(fname)) then notFound()
            else
                let content = File.ReadAllBytes fname
                sendHeaders
                    [
                        "HTTP/1.0 200 OK";
                        sprintf "Content-Length: %d" content.Length;
                        sprintf "Content-Type: %s" mimeType
                    ]
                stream.Write(content, 0, content.Length)
        | _ ->
            notFound()
}

/// The server as an asynchronous process. We handle requests sequentially.
let server =
    let port = 8090
    async {
        let socket = new TcpListener(IPAddress.Parse("127.0.0.1"), port)
        socket.Start()
        while true do
            use client = socket.AcceptTcpClient()
            do! handleRequest client port
    }
```

You can use this code as follows, where http is the function defined in Chapter 2 for requesting web pages and where you assume the directory c:\inetpub\wwwroot contains the file iisstart.htm:

```fsharp
> Async.Start server;;

val it : unit = ()

> http "http://localhost:8090";;

val it : string = "..."    // the text of the iisstart.htm file will be shown here
```

This HTTP request (you can also open the previous URL in a browser) ultimately sends the following text down the TCP socket connection:

```
GET iisstart.htm HTTP/1.1
```

When started, the server in Listing 14-1 attaches itself to a given port (8090) on the local machine (which has IP 127.0.0.1) and listens for incoming requests. These requests are line-based, so when one comes in, you read the full input line and attempt to parse a valid GET request using regular expression matching. Other commands and error recovery aren't dealt with.

The server's actions in response are simple: it locates the requested file relative to a root web directory, determines the MIME type from a fixed table, and sends the necessary response header and content of the file through the client TCP connection. When all this is done, the connection is disposed, and the session ends. The main loop of the server task is a busy-waiting loop, so you busy wait for requests indefinitely and handle them one by one.

Listing 14-1 uses two techniques not directly related to web programming:

- Regex1 is a simple and common *active pattern* for regular expression pattern matching. You learned about active patterns in Chapter 9. This example is particularly interesting because it also shows how to use a parameterized active pattern.

- The value server is an asynchronous task, as is the handleRequest function. You learned about asynchronous tasks in Chapter 11. Many web servers handle multiple requests simultaneously, and high-performance web servers use asynchronous techniques extensively. In this example, the server task serves requests sequentially using a single thread, but you can just as well start a dedicated thread for the server using more explicit threading techniques from System.Threading.

While this example may look simple, many common server-side applications are primarily TCP-based, and you can use the pattern shown here to implement many of these. For example, the following encapsulates an arbitrary TCP server:

```
open System.Net
open System.Net.Sockets

type AsyncTcpServer(addr, port, handleServerRequest) =
    let socket = new TcpListener(addr, port)

    member x.Start() = async { do x.Run() } |> Async.Start

    member x.Run() =
        socket.Start()
        while true do
            let client = socket.AcceptTcpClient()
            async {
                try do! handleServerRequest client with e -> ()
            }
            |> Async.Start
```

This class can now be instantiated and developed in many ways, including more interesting applications than simple HTTP servers. For example, the code that follows is a simulation of a "quote server" that serves "quotes" (represented here as a blob of bytes) to a TCP client every second. Because serving each quote is very simple (simply writing a few bytes to the socket), you can serve many thousands of clients simultaneously using this technique.

```
module Quotes =
    let private quoteSize = 8
    let private quoteHeaderSize = 4
    let private quoteSeriesLength = 3
```

```
module Server =
    let HandleRequest (client: TcpClient) =
        // Dummy header and quote
        let header = Array.init<byte> quoteSize (fun i -> 1uy)
        let quote = Array.init<byte> quoteSize (fun i -> byte(i % 256))
        async {
            use stream = client.GetStream()
            do! stream.AsyncWrite(header, 0, quoteHeaderSize) // Header
            for _ in [0 .. quoteSeriesLength] do
                do! stream.AsyncWrite(quote, 0, quote.Length)
                // Mock an I/O wait for the next quote
                do! Async.Sleep 1000
        }

    let Start () =
        let S = new AsyncTcpServer(IPAddress.Loopback,10003,HandleRequest)
        S.Start()

module Client =
    let RequestQuote =
        async {
            let client = new TcpClient()
            client.Connect(IPAddress.Loopback, 10003)
            use stream = client.GetStream()
            let header = Array.create quoteHeaderSize 0uy
            let! read = stream.AsyncRead(header, 0, quoteHeaderSize)
            if read = 0 then return () else printfn "Header: %A" header
            while true do
                let buffer = Array.create quoteSize 0uy
                let! read = stream.AsyncRead(buffer, 0, quoteSize)
                if read = 0 then return () else printfn "Quote: %A" buffer
        }
        |> Async.Start
```

Additionally, you should consider using secure sockets (HTTPS) for your application. Secure network programming is a vast topic that is beyond the scope of this book, but the code that follows indicates the basic shape of an SSL server, built compositionally using the non-secure AsyncTcpServer detailed previously, and indicates the .NET types you can use to implement authentication-related functionality:

```
open System.Net.Security
open System.Security.Authentication
open System.Security.Cryptography.X509Certificates

type AsyncTcpServerSecure(addr, port, handleServerRequest) =

    // Gets the first certificate with a friendly name of localhost.
    let getCertficate() =
        let store = new X509Store(StoreName.My, StoreLocation.LocalMachine)
        store.Open(OpenFlags.ReadOnly)
        let certs =
            store.Certificates.Find(
```

```
                findType = X509FindType.FindBySubjectName,
                findValue = Dns.GetHostName(),
                validOnly = true)
        certs
        |> Seq.cast<X509Certificate2>
        |> Seq.tryFind (fun c -> c.FriendlyName = "localhost")

    let handleServerRequestSecure (client: TcpClient) =
        async {
            let cert = getCertficate()
            if cert.IsNone then printfn "No cert"; return ()
            let stream = client.GetStream()
            let sslStream = new SslStream(innerStream = stream, leaveInnerStreamOpen = true)
            try
                sslStream.AuthenticateAsServer(
                    serverCertificate = cert.Value,
                    clientCertificateRequired = false,
                    enabledSslProtocols = SslProtocols.Default,
                    checkCertificateRevocation = false)
            with _ -> printfn "Can't authenticate"; return()

            printfn "IsAuthenticated: %A" sslStream.IsAuthenticated
            if sslStream.IsAuthenticated then
                // In this example only the server is authenticated.
                printfn "IsEncrypted: %A" sslStream.IsEncrypted
                printfn "IsSigned: %A" sslStream.IsSigned

                // Indicates whether the current side of the connection
                // is authenticated as a server.
                printfn "IsServer: %A" sslStream.IsServer

            return! handleServerRequest stream
        }

    let server = AsyncTcpServer(addr, port, handleServerRequestSecure)

    member x.Start() = server.Start()
```

TCP-based applications achieve excellent scaling, and cloud-computing solutions such as Azure allow you to host your TCP-based services on a load-balanced set of machines dedicated to serving requests under one common TCP address. The modern web is built with server-side programs following architectures similar to those just laid out.

Rich Client Web Applications with WebSharper

Today, most web pages are *rich client* applications that incorporate a substantial amount of JavaScript code that is executed on the client side of the application in the web browser. You can develop these applications in multiple ways using F#, as follows:

- You can manually write and serve additional JavaScript files as part of your server-side web application using a server-side web framework such as Suave (see Chapter 2) or ASP.NET.

- You can use WebSharper (`http://websharper.com`) to write both client and server code in F#. You can then self-host your WebSharper applications using Suave or WebSharper.Warp, or host them in an ASP.NET container such as IIS.

Developing rich client web applications with the first technique follows a fairly standard path where the client side is mostly independent of F#. The remainder of this section will focus on the second technique and will give a brief overview of some of the core WebSharper features, including *sitelets*, *pagelets*, *formlets*, *flowlets*, and *piglets*, and the foundations of developing reactive WebSharper applications using UI.Next, WebSharper's reactive extension.

WebSharper is an open-source web ecosystem that enables rapid web application development with F#, and it is the recommended way of developing rich client applications with F#, offering unparalleled productivity and ease of use. It provides a wealth of composable primitives for writing robust, efficient, integrated client/server applications in a single, type-checked framework. This ecosystem consists of an F#-to-JavaScript compiler and over 50 libraries that bring powerful web abstractions and extensions to popular JavaScript libraries for client-side development. In particular, WebSharper employs several advanced features of F#, the combination of which offers a unique programming experience for developing web applications; see the following:

- Client-side and server-side code are marked with custom attributes and can be authored in a single F# project. Client-side code, called *pagelets*, is automatically translated to JavaScript using F# quotations and reflection and other metaprogramming techniques, and is served to the client on demand. (See Chapter 16 for details on F# quotations and reflection.)

- Web applications are expressed as *sitelets*, involving an endpoint type that describes their various endpoints and access methods, and a mapping from those endpoints to content served asynchronously. Sitelets play nicely with ASP.NET MVC and can easily be adopted for use in conjunction with Web API as well.

- *HTML markup* in pagelets and sitelets can use any available conforming implementation, including UI.Next, with support for *reactive* DOM and templates via type providers, as well as a dynamic dataflow layer to provide *two-way data binding* between underlying data models and the reactive UI.

- Web forms can be expressed in an extraordinarily compact form as first-class, type-safe values and are represented as *formlets* or *piglets*. They can be composed and enhanced with just a few lines of code, including adding validation and complex user interactions and defining *dependent* formlets. Piglets also enable the tailoring of the presentation layer with custom markup. Both formalisms are available for reactive use as well.

- Sequences of web forms, or *flowlets*, are first-class values that provide an elegant and concise way to express larger-than-page functionality.

- Client-side code can use functionality from many .NET and F# libraries. The calls are mapped to corresponding JavaScript functionality through sophisticated techniques. You can also provide custom proxies to any .NET type, describing how to translate it to JavaScript.

- The client side may make calls to any JavaScript technology via WebSharper stubs implemented for that technology. At the time of writing, WebSharper comes with a number of extensions to various JavaScript libraries, including jQuery, jQuery UI, jQuery Mobile, Google Maps, Google Visualization, Sencha Ext JS, Sencha Touch, Win JS, and Kendo UI, among others.

- The client side may make asynchronous calls to the server using variations of the techniques described in Chapter 11.

- Resulting web applications are dramatically shorter and easier to maintain and extend, and can be readily deployed under IIS on top of ASP.NET, in any other ASP. NET- or OWIN-compatible web container including Suave, or be self-hosted using `WebSharper.Warp`.

■ **Note** While this section serves as a quick and somewhat thorough introduction to WebSharper and some of its features, you may want to consult the main WebSharper documentation for more details. This documentation is largely found in the open-source repository (`http://github.com/IntelliFactory/websharper`) in the `/docs` folder. In addition, you can read more about the core WebSharper features such as sitelets and formlets online at `http://websharper.com/docs`, and you can check out the samples on the home page and the samples page. These samples come with fully annotated descriptions; you can copy and paste the code into your own projects, and you can even try them online.

Getting Started with WebSharper

Perhaps the easiest way to get started with WebSharper is to visit Try WebSharper (`http://try.websharper.com`) or any of the links that point to individual snippets on that site. The Twitter handle for it, `trywebsharper`, has many of these links, and it is a good point of entry for exploring WebSharper samples. Try WebSharper collects WebSharper snippets from the community and makes it easy and fun to create, fork, and edit them. It uses a backend service to provide on-the-fly type checking and code assistance features as you type, and gives you nearly all available WebSharper extensions for experimentation.

Developing with WebSharper involves using various project templates to start new applications and utilizing a set of tools to build and run them. The main compiler as well as the standard libraries and extensions are available as NuGet packages, and in this chapter you will be exploring applications that require the installation of various WebSharper packages. For this, you will use NuGet or Paket (`https://fsprojects.github.io/Paket`) as described in their documentation.

The project templates required for new applications are easiest to obtain by using the installers that are available for various IDEs at `http://websharper.com/downloads`. They are also available within CloudSharper, an online F# IDE developed with WebSharper, at `http://cloudsharper.com`. Next to using the standard installers, you can also install templates via generator-fsharp, a community project (`https://github.com/fsprojects/generator-fsharp`) that is an extension to the popular scaffolding tool Yeoman (`http://yeoman.io`) that only requires command-line access. The examples in this chapter use the UI.Next Single-Page Application (UI.Next SPA) and the UI.Next Client-Server Application (UI.Next Client-Server) templates, which are available in the standard installers and in generator-fsharp as well.

■ **Note**   To install generator-fsharp, assuming you have Node.js installed and `npm.bat` is in your path, you first do:

```
npm install –g yo
```

```
npm install –g generator-fsharp
```

Once installed, you can run Yeoman with the `fsharp` option from your desired root folder:

```
yo fsharp
```

Here, select "Create standalone project" and the desired project template, give your new project a name, and choose whether you would like to use Paket as your package manager option (otherwise, the project will use NuGet). This will create your project files and fetch the necessary packages, and you are ready to run or make changes to your application.

For your very first WebSharper application, shown in Figure 14-1, go ahead and create a UI.Next SPA application. This project contains a single F# file (`Client.fs`) and an HTML master document (`index.html`). You will learn about HTML templates later in this chapter; for now, just trim the `<body>` tag in `index.html` to only contain a DIV node with `id="main"`:

```
<html>
...
<body>
    <div id="main"></div>
    <script type="text/javascript" ...
</body>
```

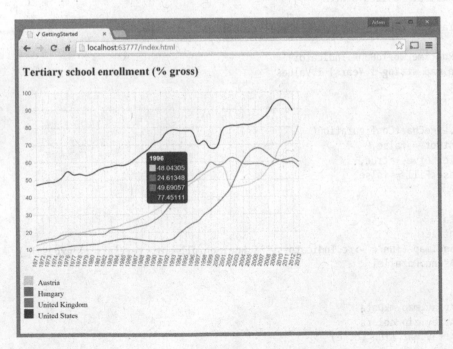

Figure 14-1.   Querying the World Bank database and charting the results

Check that the target framework for your project is set to 4.5. Then add a NuGet reference to
WebSharper.Charting and WebSharper.Data, ensuring that you set the NuGet option "Dependency
behavior" to "Highest." Then change the code in Client.fs to:

```fsharp
namespace GettingStarted

open FSharp.Data
open WebSharper
open WebSharper.UI.Next
open WebSharper.UI.Next.Html
open WebSharper.UI.Next.Client
open WebSharper.Charting

[<JavaScript>]
module Client =
    type WorldBank = WorldBankDataProvider<Asynchronous=true>

    let data = WorldBank.GetDataContext()

    let randomColor =
        let r = System.Random()
        fun () -> Color.Rgba(r.Next 256, r.Next 256, r.Next 256, 1.)

    let countries =
        [| data.Countries.Austria
           data.Countries.Hungary
           data.Countries.``United Kingdom``
           data.Countries.``United States`` |]

    let colors = Array.map (fun _ -> randomColor()) countries

    let mkData (i: Runtime.WorldBank.Indicator) =
        Seq.zip (Seq.map string i.Years) i.Values

    let chart =
        let cfg =
            ChartJs.LineChartConfiguration(
                PointDot = false,
                BezierCurve = true,
                DatasetFill = false)

        async {
            let! data =
                countries
                |> Seq.map (fun c -> c.Indicators.``School enrollment, tertiary (% gross)``)
                |> Async.Parallel
            return
                data
                |> Array.map mkData
                |> Array.zip colors
                |> Array.map (fun (c, e) ->
```

```
                    Chart.Line(e)
                        .WithStrokeColor(c)
                        .WithPointColor(c))
              |> Chart.Combine
              |> fun c ->
                  Renderers.ChartJs.Render(c, Size = Size(600, 400), Config = cfg)
        }

    let legend =
        colors
        |> Array.zip countries
        |> Array.map (fun (c, color) ->
            div [
                spanAttr ["width:20px; height:20px;\
                          margin-right:10px;\
                          display:inline-block;\
                          background-color:" + color.ToString() |> attr.style] []
                span [text c.Name]
            ])
        |> Seq.cast
        |> div

    let Main =
        Doc.Concat [
            h2 [text "Tertiary school enrollment (% gross)"]
            Doc.Async chart
            legend
        ]
        |> Doc.RunById "main"
```

This application runs entirely on the client. It generates JavaScript code (as instructed by the [<JavaScript>] attribute on its single module), which in turn calls the World Bank database to fetch real-time data for a handful of countries, puts those in a combined chart, and adds the resulting markup dynamically into the master template at the selected placeholder (the DIV node with ID "main").

In the remainder of this chapter, you will learn how to create similar SPAs (single-page HTML applications without a sitelet), HTML applications ("offline" sitelets), and client-server applications ("online" sitelets, including REST applications) with WebSharper. As a first step, you will see how to construct HTML programmatically using pagelets and work with HTML design templates, giving you a foundation for taking the next step and embedding those in sitelets.

Pagelets - Working with Reactive HTML and Client-Side Code

Interacting with the user in a typical web application involves employing server-side controls that render to HTML and JavaScript, or writing client-side code by hand using a combination of HTML, JavaScript, and CSS. In various web frameworks, you can further enhance server-side controls, connecting them to other controls in various ways to reach the desired effects. For instance, simple ASP.NET input controls such as a textbox can be paired with event handlers and validators either by following a predefined naming convention or by connecting them via strings in ASPX markup.

This type of loose coupling between the various server-side components can easily lead to problems when you need to code more complex web applications. Furthermore, the server-centric mode of operation requires that all components be rendered to code on the server side, employing post backs and other opaque calls to the server, leaving few opportunities to customize this interaction on the client side.

WebSharper takes a fundamentally different approach and views web applications primarily from a client-based perspective. Client-side functionality in WebSharper applications are made up of *pagelets*: annotated F# code that is automatically translated to JavaScript to run on the client on demand. You can combine pagelets to form larger pagelets and you can develop full web pages and even entire websites as a single pagelet. Pagelets that create DOM nodes can be exposed in a way compatible with traditional server controls and composed into markup seamlessly.

Getting Started with Pagelets

Consider the following simple example, based on the UI.Next SPA template and the trimmed index.html you worked with for the Getting Started example earlier in this chapter, and with Client.fs replaced with:

```
module MyApplication

open WebSharper
open WebSharper.UI.Next.Html
open WebSharper.UI.Next.Client

[<JavaScript>]
let HelloWorld =
    let welcome = p [text "Welcome"]
    div [
        welcome
        inputAttr [
            attr.``type`` "Button"; attr.value "Click me!"
            on.click (fun e args ->
                welcome.Text <- "Hello, world!")
        ] []
    ]
    |> Doc.RunById "main"
```

Here, HelloWorld defines a pagelet that constructs a DOM node: a DIV tag with two child nodes. The first child node is a paragraph containing a welcome text, and the second is an HTML button with "Click me!" as its title. The key thing to note here is the use of the [<JavaScript>] attribute, which defines a particular code element as being available in JavaScript on the client side. The button's click event handler is attached using on.click in attribute position like in normal HTML.

HTML Implementations for Pagelets

WebSharper features a pluggable infrastructure to work with markup. The foundations of this infrastructure are defined in core WebSharper, allowing a uniform treatment for basic templating and ASP.NET backwards compatibility across the available implementations. This chapter and the example above uses UI.Next, WebSharper's next-generation reactive markup language, shipped in the WebSharper.UI.Next NuGet package, which makes it easy to develop reactive web applications. The earlier HTML implementation, now placed in a standalone NuGet package WebSharper.Html, is a simpler implementation that often comes in handy, especially for ordinary, non-reactive applications. Table 14-1 gives a brief summary of these two markup languages.

Table 14-1. *HTML Combinators in UI.Next and WebSharper.Html*

HTML	UI.Next	WebSharper.Html
Plain text	text "Plain text"	Text "Plain text"
class "abc" src "abc"	attr.``class`` "abc" attr.src "abc"	Attr.Class "abc" Attr.Src "abc"
\<h1>ABC\</h1>	h1 [text "ABC"]	H1 [Text "ABC"]
\<div> \<div>..\</div> \</div>	div [div [...]]	Div [Div [...]]
\<div class="abc"> \<div>..\</div> \</div>	divAttr [attr.``class`` "abc"] [div [...]]	Div [Attr.Class "abc"] -< [Div [...]]
\<div onclick="..."> \<div>...\</div> \</div>	divAttr [on.click <@ fun e arg -> ... @>] [div [...]]	Div [Div [...]] |>! OnClick (fun e arg -> ...)

You will learn about the reactive aspects of UI.Next in the next section. One important difference between UI.Next and WebSharper.Html, other than the lack of reactive features in the latter, is that the HTML constructors in UI.Next can be used in both client- and server-side code, unlike in WebSharper.Html, where the same set of HTML constructors are available for client- and server-side use in the WebSharper. Html.Client and WebSharper.Html.Server namespaces, respectively. This bypasses the need in certain situations to have to recreate the same markup in client- and server-side representations, but it also introduces a couple of additional details to pay attention to.

UI.Next markup is represented by the Doc interface, various client-server markup constructors in WebSharper.UI.Next.Html, and a matching module with various operations on Docs in WebSharper. UI.Next. In particular, you can use in both client and server markup:

- Doc.Empty to create an empty markup node. This is often useful in operations on DOM nodes that produce no markup, instead of resorting to the empty parent nodes that would be commonplace with WebSharper.Html.

- Doc.TextNode or simply text to create a text node.

- Doc.Verbatim to create verbatim markup content from a string. For instance, the following are equivalent:

  p [text "Hello World"] and Doc.Verbatim "\<p>Hello World\</p>"

- Doc.Concat to concatenate a sequence of Docs into a single one. This is a useful way to represent multiple DOM nodes as a single Doc, without using a superfluous parent node.

- Doc.Append to append one Doc to another. Typical scenarios include adding content to a given node or populating a placeholder node.

- Doc.ClientSide or simply client to embed client-side code in markup. Note, however, that the range of expressions allowed vary in client-side versus server-side markup. In the latter, only the form <@ FunctionCall(arguments) @> is allowed.

You can use Doc.WebControl to embed server controls in UI.Next server-side markup, and you must open WebSharper.UI.Next.Server for this function to be available.

Other operations, including an array of reactive primitives detailed later in this chapter, are defined on Docs for client-side use only by opening the WebSharper.UI.Next.Client namespace. In particular, Doc.RunById, Doc.RunAfter*, Doc.RunAppend*, and Doc.RunPrepend* are used to attach Docs to the DOM, as you have seen in the SPA examples. Furthermore, in the same client-only namespace, all HTML elements are extended with further functionality, as shown in Table 14-2.

Table 14-2. *Doc Instance Members in WebSharper.UI.Next.Client*

HTML	UI.Next	WebSharper.Html
Prepend	Doc -> unit	Adds the given Doc as first child(ren) of this element
Append	Doc -> unit	Adds the given Doc as the last child(ren) of this element
Clear	unit -> unit	Removes all children nodes of this element
Html	string	Gets the HTML string for this element
Id	string	Gets the ID of this element
Value	string	Gets the value of this element
Text	string	Gets the text content of this element
GetAttribute	string -> string	Gets the given attribute's value of this element
SetAttribute	(string * string) -> unit	Sets the given attribute's value of this element
HasAttribute	string -> bool	Checks whether this element has the given attribute
RemoveAttribute	string -> unit	Removes the given attribute of this element
GetProperty	string -> 'T	Gets the given property of this element
SetProperty	string * 'T -> unit	Sets the given property for this element
AddClass	string -> unit	Adds the given CSS class to this element
RemoveClass	string -> unit	Removes the given CSS class from this element
HasClass	string -> bool	Checks whether this element has the given CSS class
SetStyle	string * string -> unit	Sets the given style element to the given value

EMBEDDING PAGELETS IN ASP.NET MARKUP

You can embed your pagelets into ASP.NET markup by wrapping them into WebSharper web controls, which provide legacy support for ASP.NET. Because these controls are rendered on the server side, you should make sure that you change any direct pagelet binding to a function. For instance, the Hello World pagelet would look like the following:

```
[<JavaScript>]
let HelloWorld () =
    let welcome = p [text "Welcome"]
    div [
        welcome
```

```
        inputAttr [
            attr.``type`` "Button"; attr.value "Click me!"
            on.click (fun e args ->
                welcome.Text <- "Hello, world!")
        ] []
    ]

open WebSharper.Web

type MyHelloWorldControl() =
    inherit Web.Control()

    [<JavaScript>]
    override this.Body = HelloWorld () :> _
```

Here, `WebSharper.Web.Control` is a subclass of `System.Web.UI.Control`, and it includes a `Body` member that bootstraps your pagelet when it is embedded into ASP.NET markup. This control type and an instance of the WebSharper *script manager control* act as a conduit between server- and client-side code, ensuring that client-side dependencies are correctly managed, and computes and injects the DOM placeholder node into the containing page. This then "comes alive" once the associated scripts and tracked dependencies start executing on the client.

To be able to add `MyHelloWorldControl` to your ASPX markup, your `web.config` file has to contain a `controls` declaration for the WebSharper web assembly and the assembly that contains your server-side controls:

```
<configuration>
  <system.web>
    <pages>
      <controls>
        <add tagPrefix="WebSharper"
             namespace="WebSharper.Web"
             assembly="WebSharper.Web" />
        <add tagPrefix="ws"
             namespace="YourApplication"
             assembly=" YourContainingAssembly" />
      </controls>
...
```

With these set up, you can embed the Hello World pagelet into your ASPX markup as follows:

```
<html xmlns="http://www.w3.org/1999/xhtml">
  <head runat="server">
    <title>Your WebSharper Application</title>
    <WebSharper:ScriptManager runat="server" />
  </head>
  <body>
    <ws:MyHelloWorldControl runat="server"/>
  </body>
</html>
```

Incorporating Reactivity with UI.Next

Next to constructing markup, UI.Next also provides *reactive programming* primitives and *two-way data binding* to enable the development of reactive web applications. It includes a dataflow layer for expressing user inputs (visual controls, mouse clicks, and coordinates, etc.) and primarily views values originating from them as functions of time. It also includes a reactive DOM layer for incorporating these time-varying values into the DOM. The result is a powerful combination of a reactive data model and the corresponding UI, where the two are always guaranteed to be in sync. For instance, you can change the value of a reactive variable programmatically, and the parts of the user interface bound to it will update automatically. Similarly, a user-triggered change in the corresponding UI element will update the value of its bound reactive variable.

As a quick glance at reactive DOM, consider the following short snippet:

```
open WebSharper
open WebSharper.UI.Next
open WebSharper.UI.Next.Html
open WebSharper.UI.Next.Client

[<JavaScript>]
let EchoTextBox() =
    let input = Var.Create ""
    let upperInput =
        input.View
        |> View.Map (fun txt -> txt.ToUpper())

    div [
        Doc.Input [] input
        label [textView upperInput]
    ]
```

This implements a reactive label whose value is bound to what the user types in the textbox above it, and it shows the entered text in uppercase. You can see in this example how a reactive variable is bound to an input control, how its "view" (the last value of it) is obtained and mapped to a different view, and how these views can be embedded into markup (using textView).

A number of reactive input controls are implemented in UI.Next, including Doc.Input, Doc.InputArea, Doc.PasswordBox, Doc.IntInput, Doc.Button, Doc.Link, Doc.CheckBox, Doc.CheckBoxGroup, Doc.Select, and Doc.Radio, among others. You can also drive markup in attribute positions based on reactive attributes. These are contained in the Attr module, and include functions such as Attr.Dynamic, Attr.Handler, Attr.DynamicClass, Attr.Style, Attr.DynamicStyle, and Attr.DynamicPred, among others.

Next to reactive variables, you can also create *list models* and bind them to collections of user-interface elements. Most likely you will want to use a design template for this markup and binding. You will find a short example in the subsequent section on UI.Next templates.

Further work is under way to enable the two-way data binding mechanism via reactive variables and list models to survive page refreshes. In its basic form, data models bound to any given UI live on the client, as do all interactions between the reactive model and the bound markup. This means that page refreshes re-initialize the data model, losing all changes since the last page load. One solution is persisting the data model on the client, such as by using HTML5 local storage. This can be accomplished by creating a custom storage for list models via the Storage module and passing that storage implementation to the list model.

This section can only give a brief overview and a small taste of reactivity in UI.Next; for a more comprehensive treatment you should refer to http://websharper.com/docs/ui.next.

HTML Templates

Next to outputting markup programmatically, WebSharper also provides advanced server-side templating facilities (or view engines) that enable you to externalize some or all of your markup into HTML template files. At the time of writing, two separate templating implementations are available, each with different capabilities beyond a set of baseline features. This includes three regular and a handful of managed placeholders:

- Placeholder tags with a data-hole attribute, such as <div data-hole="xyz"></div>. This mode causes HTML content to be added underneath/inside the annotated node.

- Placeholder tags with a data-replace attribute, such as <div data-replace="xyz"></div>. This mode causes HTML content to be added in place of the annotated node, replacing it.

- Placeholders in the form of ${var} can be used to define string placeholders.

- Managed placeholders "scripts", "meta", "styles" are used to instruct WebSharper to embed the tracked resources and dependencies, meta information about embedded controls, and external style sheets of the page, respectively. You can also include these all at once in a single placeholder by adding a single "scripts" placeholder in the <HEAD> section of your template.

A typical base template with a title and body placeholder looks something like the following:

```
<!DOCTYPE html>
<html>
<head>
    <meta charset="utf-8" />
    <meta name="viewport" content="width=device-width,initial-scale=1.0" />
    <title>${title}</title>
    <meta data-replace="meta" />
    <meta data-replace="styles" />
</head>
<body>
    <div data-replace="body"></div>
    <script data-replace="scripts"></script>
</body>
</html>
```

Static HTML Templates with UI.Next

One potential problem with external design templates is that they get out of sync with the code that relies on them. The templating implementation shipped with UI.Next takes a radical approach here: HTML template files are converted at compile time (using a type provider) into F# types that provide a convenient notation to instantiate placeholders with typed content. Assuming you have the above typical base template as `Main.html`, the following implements a `Main` function that constructs HTML responses (that you can plug directly into sitelets, as you will see shortly):

```
module Templating =
    open WebSharper.UI.Next

    type MainTemplate = Templating.Template<"Main.html">

    let Main title body =
        Content.Page(
            MainTemplate.Doc(
                title = title,
                body = body
            )
        )
```

For this code to work, you need a reference to the `WebSharper.UI.Next` NuGet package in your project. Compile-time code generation also means that these templates are static: if you make any change in them you will need to recompile your project for those changes to take effect.

`UI.Next` templates, however, also support reactive programming, and they bring powerful capabilities to your developer tool set. In addition to those placeholders listed in the previous section, `UI.Next` templating also supports the following reactive placeholders:

- Placeholder tags with a `data-var` attribute, such as `<input type="checkbox" data-var="xyz" />`. This enables the binding of a reactive variable to the annotated (input) node.

- Placeholder tags with a `data-attr` attribute, such as `<p data-attr="xyz">...</p>`. This allows you to reactively set attributes on the annotated node.

- Placeholder tags with a `data-event-xxx` attribute, such as `<button data-event-click="HandleClick" />`. This enables you to register event handlers on the annotated node.

- Placeholder tags with `data-template` or `data-children-template`. This enables you to define inner templates, which in turn can be used to generate reactive markup.

- `$!{xxx}` to stand for the value of the given reactive variable.

For instance, you can implement a small people catalog by starting a UI.Next SPA project and adding the following markup to `index.html`, which defines a `Main` template and a nested `ListItem` template, an input field that will supply `Name`, which will be echoed underneath, and an `Add` event handler, which will add the name typed in to our data model.

```
...
<body>
    <h1>My people list</h1>
    <div id="main" data-children-template="Main">
        <ul data-hole="ListContainer">
            <li data-template="ListItem">$!{Name}</li>
        </ul>
```

```
        <div>
            <input data-var="Name" placeholder="Name" />
            <button data-event-click="Add">Add</button>
            <div>You are about to add: $!{Name}</div>
        </div>
    </div>
</div>
<script type="text/javascript" ...
```

Then change Client.fs as follows:

```
namespace ListOfPeople

open WebSharper
open WebSharper.JavaScript
open WebSharper.JQuery
open WebSharper.UI.Next
open WebSharper.UI.Next.Client

[<JavaScript>]
module Client =
    type IndexTemplate = Templating.Template<"index.html">

    let People = ListModel.FromSeq ["John"; "Paul"]

    let Main =
        JQuery.Of("#main").Empty().Ignore

        let newName = Var.Create ""

        IndexTemplate.Main.Doc(
            ListContainer = [
                People.View.DocSeqCached(fun name ->
                    IndexTemplate.ListItem.Doc(Name = View.Const name)
                )
            ],
            Name = newName,
            Add = (fun el ev ->
                People.Add(newName.Value)
                newName.Value <- ""
            )
        )
        |> Doc.RunById "main"
```

There are several key observations to be made here:

- We use a list model, containing strings and initialized with two names.

- We use an internal reactive variable (newName) to transfer the value of the input box (via Name), which we then use when new names are submitted.

- The ListContainer placeholder is instantiated with markup we get by plugging in every name in our data model to the inner markup template (ListItem).

- People.View.DocSeqCached takes care of updating the corresponding DOM for only those names that change, or are added or removed from our list model.

A more complete example can be found at `http://try.websharper.com/example/todo-list`, implementing a reactive TODO application in 40 lines of F# with the help of a reactive HTML template, and is shown in Figure 14-2.

Figure 14-2. *A reactive TODO application in 40 LOC F#*

Dynamic HTML Templates with WebSharper.Html

Dynamic templates in `WebSharper.Html` enable the instantiation of placeholders with HTML and string content dynamically at runtime, without static guarantees about their structure and content. This has the obvious disadvantage that templates may be incompatible when instantiated with the content that your application intends to serve, but they have the flexibility to change markup dynamically, without requiring recompilation, greatly reducing the time it takes to go through various design iterations.

To use dynamic templates, you must first define a record type that holds the content your template will be instantiated with. For instance, the following defines a `Placeholders` type for two placeholders, as well as a `MainTemplate` template (of type `Content.Template<Placeholders>`) that is defined over this placeholder type and that serves a local `Main.html` file with two matching placeholders, "title" and "body." As in the previous example, the function `Main` constructs the actual HTML content response by putting the pieces together:

```
open WebSharper.Sitelets

module Templating =
    open WebSharper.Html.Server

    type Placeholders =
        {
            Title: string
            Body: Element list
        }
```

```
let MainTemplate =
    Content.Template<Placeholders>("~/Main.html")
        .With("title", fun x -> x.Title)
        .With("body", fun x -> x.Body)

let Main title body =
    Content.WithTemplate MainTemplate
        {
            Title = title
            Body = body
        }
```

The key point here is the combined use of calling Content.Template and a number of With calls chained together to define string-to-value instantiations over the given placeholder type. Actual checking that the inserted content is of the right type is done here, along with various other checks such as checking for uninstantiated placeholders, resulting in a runtime error if things don't match up.

Sitelets

The application in Figure 14-1 generated JavaScript code from your F# code, magically referenced in your master template file. This meant that loading this HTML file would execute your application, which in turn would assemble a dynamic chart with real-time data from the World Bank database and inject it into a given DOM node to yield your HTML application.

While applications like this, with full control over how the generated JavaScript code interacts with the HTML document hosting it, are very typical, especially for HTML and client-based applications, WebSharper also has a more robust model for developing applications: representing them in the type system as F# values called *sitelets*. These have a set of endpoints (accessed via GET, POST, etc.) to which they respond by serving web content asynchronously. Sitelets are especially useful for client-server applications, but you can use them to develop single-page and HTML applications as well. Sitelets have a number of advantages over traditional web development practices:

- They can represent *seamless client-server communication* by enabling you to embed client-side functionality into server-side markup and enabling client-side code to call the server using a plain F# function call. You saw a glimpse of the former in the section on "Working with HMTL," and you will learn more about it and client-server calls in the section on *pagelets*.

- They represent the *endpoints* of your web application as an F# type (we refer to it as the EndPoint type in this chapter), thereby enumerating all possible entry points within the type system.

- They provide *safe links* to server-side resources so your hyperlinks never go stale. This is done by giving you a serving context (see section "Serving Contexts" later in this chapter) via which URLs can be computed to any endpoint.

- They provide an abstraction via annotations on the endpoint type and the runtime machinery for mapping incoming requests to endpoints (this is called a *router*) and endpoints to content to be served (this is called a *controller*). You can also define routers and controllers manually.

- They enable dealing with *addressing endpoints and parsing various forms of incoming requests using F# types*. This makes them super useful for REST applications and others that work via serving and taking JSON, form data, or GET parameters. With minimal syntax noise, this feature is a lifesaver for WebSharper developers.

- They integrate nicely with *HTML templates*, which enable you to externalize some or all of the markup from your applications. You saw some of this already in the previous section.

Your First Sitelet

One of the easiest ways to get started with sitelets is by using the UI.Next Client-Server template. This creates a client-server application that consists of a server-side component (in Remoting.fs), a client-side component (in Client.fs), a main component that implements basic templating and your main *sitelet* (in Main.fs), and an optional start-up module (in Startup.fs) that can self-host your sitelet. You will also learn how to host your WebSharper applications in Suave and Microsoft's Katana project shortly, and you can easily change the code in Startup.fs accordingly; otherwise, you can run your application in IIS or the built-in web server in Visual Studio.

To start with your first sitelet, you can trim your project a bit by deleting Remoting.fs, Client.fs, and Startup.fs from your project, and then simply change Main.fs as follows:

```
module MyApplication1

open WebSharper
open WebSharper.Sitelets

[<Website>]
let Main =
    Application.Text (fun ctx -> "Hello World!")
```

This implements a single "page" sitelet, shown in Figure 14-3, which listens on web root and returns a simple plain-text response. Application.Text is a shorthand for creating a single-endpoint application that computes a plain-text response using the serving context. You will learn more about serving contexts later this chapter, and also about the other application shorthands: Application.SinglePage and Application. MultiPage for creating single-page and multi-page applications, respectively.

Figure 14-3. A simple Hello World application

Running Sitelets in an ASP.NET-Compatible Container (IIS, etc.)

Marking your sitelet with the [<Website>] attribute enables an ASP.NET container (IIS, etc.) to easily recognize and run your application. This needs the WebSharper sitelet and RPC modules set up in web.config, as provided in the UI.Next Client-Server template:

```
<configuration>
  <system.webServer>
    <modules>
      <add name="WebSharper.RemotingModule" type="WebSharper.Web.RpcModule, WebSharper.Web" />
      <add name="WebSharper.Sitelets" type="WebSharper.Sitelets.HttpModule,
      WebSharper.Sitelets" />
    </modules>
    ...
```

You may also need to provide assembly redirects for FSharp.Core, especially if you are using F# 4.0:

```
<runtime>
  <assemblyBinding xmlns="urn:schemas-microsoft-com:asm.v1">
    <dependentAssembly>
      <assemblyIdentity name="FSharp.Core" publicKeyToken="b03f5f7f11d50a3a"
      culture="neutral" />
      <bindingRedirect oldVersion="0.0.0.0-4.3.1.0" newVersion="4.4.0.0" />
    </dependentAssembly>
  </assemblyBinding>
</runtime>
```

Self-Hosting Sitelets Using OWIN

If you prefer to self-host your applications, you can use WebSharper.Owin to generate an OWIN-based host executable. The following code assumes you have a console application project, you added WebSharper. Owin to it as a NuGet reference, and your sitelet is available as MySite:

```
module SelfHostedServer =

    open global.Owin
    open Microsoft.Owin.Hosting
    open Microsoft.Owin.StaticFiles
    open Microsoft.Owin.FileSystems
    open WebSharper.Owin

    [<EntryPoint>]
    let Main args =
        let rootDirectory, url =
            match args with
            | [| rootDirectory; url |] -> rootDirectory, url
            | [| url |] -> "..", url
            | [| |] -> "..", "http://localhost:9000/"
            | _ -> eprintfn "Usage: SelfHostedApplication ROOT_DIRECTORY URL"; exit 1
        use server = WebApp.Start(url, fun appB ->
        appB.UseStaticFiles(
```

```
            StaticFileOptions(
                FileSystem = PhysicalFileSystem(rootDirectory)))
          .UseSitelet(rootDirectory, MySite)
      |> ignore)
    stdout.WriteLine("Serving {0}", url)
    stdin.ReadLine() |> ignore
    0
```

Here, Main starts an OWIN container and uses the default http://localhost:9000 URL or the one passed as a command-line argument to serve your sitelet (which it assumes is located in your project root folder, unless otherwise specified). Some of the benefits of self-hosting applications include easy deployment, no existing or installed web server as a prerequisite, and simple configuration. However, not having a full-blown web server also means fewer features are available to your web application, such as logging, resource management, HTTPS, and web socket support, among others.

Self-Hosting Sitelets with WebSharper.Warp

There is also a simpler way to run your sitelets without a web server—by using WebSharper.Warp, a WebSharper library for building scripted/interactive and self-hosted applications. For instance, you can add the following tiny snippet to your WebSharper project (a console one, similar to the OWIN case above) to enable self-hosting:

```
[<EntryPoint>]
do Warp.RunAndWaitForInput(MySite) |> ignore
```

This unceremonial method will start an OWIN container just like the one you saw earlier. In fact, WebSharper.Warp as a project got started so as to provide similar shorthands around WebSharper constructs, which proved so useful that these in turn moved to the main WebSharper repository shortly thereafter. What remains in WebSharper.Warp now is the self-hosting and dynamic code-generation machinery. This latter piece is useful for on-the-fly code-generation scenarios and interactively developing and running sitelets.

Hosting Sitelets in Suave

You can hit a sweet spot between running a full-blown web server such as IIS and self-hosting by using Suave, a feature-rich yet light web server implemented in F#. The adapter required to run sitelets is in the WebSharper.Suave NuGet package. Once you have added this reference to your project, you can run your sitelets on Suave with a couple lines:

```
open global.Suave
open Suave.Web
open WebSharper.Suave

startWebServer defaultConfig
    (WebSharperAdapter.ToWebPart(MySite, RootDirectory="../.."))
```

Online Versus Offline Sitelets: Client-Server Versus HTML+JavaScript Applications

You may often see in the WebSharper documentation references to *offline* sitelets; for instance, in HTML Application projects and mobile web projects for Android or Windows Phone. An offline sitelet is a sitelet without a server side, and it is made up by all the HTML and JavaScript code used and generated by that sitelet.

HTML Applications are offline sitelets, and as opposed to the Getting Started and the Hello World SPAs you saw already in this chapter, are based on sitelets. These applications consist of 100% client-side code without a server component. They can make calls to web services or involve other forms of dynamism, but their content is rendered into pure HMTL and JavaScript when these applications are compiled.

Offline sitelets are useful from a number of perspectives. First, offline sitelet–based applications you develop can be served by any web container, without having to pin yourself to a particular web server and platform, such as IIS. Second, they provide the vehicle to develop self-contained mobile applications, which are essentially HTML applications packaged for various mobile operating systems using standard tools such as Adobe PhoneGap.

Online sitelets, e.g., ordinary client-server applications, in contrast involve a server-side component that responds to client queries via RPC. These sitelets can also be rendered into HTML and JavaScript, and packed into native mobile applications; however, their active server side must also be available in order for these applications to work properly.

At the time of writing, the necessary build logic to compile online and offline sitelets is directed using a setting in the WebSharper project file:

- `<WebSharperProject>Html</WebSharperProject>` for HTML Applications

- `<WebSharperProject>Site</WebSharperProject>` for Client-Server Applications

- `<WebSharperProject>Bundle</WebSharperProject>` for Single-Page Applications

Single-Endpoint Sitelets

The Hello World application you saw earlier has a single endpoint: the root URL accessed via GET. This endpoint is provided as a helper single-case union (`Application.SPA.EndPoint`) and is largely hidden from the user, as the functions operating on it do not take it as an argument (unlike `Application.MultiPage` in the following sections). However, you are free to create any other single-endpoint type that may fit you better.

Consider the following application that has a single-integer endpoint:

```
type EndPoint = int

[<Website>]
let Main =
    Sitelet.Infer (fun ctx (endpoint: EndPoint) ->
        match endpoint with
        | i -> Content.Text (string (i*i))
    )
```

As you may expect, this application will not serve under the root URL, but instead it needs an integer argument such as `http://localhost:16151/25`. It will then return the square of that argument when accessed.

You can construct similar single-endpoint sitelets using types as summarized in Table 14-3. Integers, floats, strings, enumerations, and `DateTimes` are supported as base types. Tuples and records are encoded as consecutive URL path segments, in the order of their definition. Options have a segment identifying the case, followed by segments for the argument(s). Lists and arrays encode their length first, then their elements recursively.

Table 14-3. *Sitelets with Single-Endpoint Types and Their Requests*

Sample Endpoint Type	Sample Request	Parsed Request
Int	/12	12
Float	/12.34	12.34
String	/abc1234	"abc1234"
System.Net.HttpStatusCode	/200	HttpStatusCode.OK
System.DateTime	/2015-08-24-12.55.14	System.DateTime(2015,8,24,12,55,14)
string * int	/abc/1234	("abc", 1234)
{ Name: string; Age: int }	/john/12	{ Name="John"; Age=12 }
string option	/None /Some/abc	None Some "abc"
int list float list string list	/2/1/2 /2/1.1/2.2 /2/abc/1234	[1; 2] [1.1; 2.2] ["abc"; "1234"]
int array float array string array	/2/1/2 /2/1.1/2.2 /2/abc/1234	[|1; 2|] [|1.1; 2.2|] [|"abc"; "1234"|]

The Hello World application can also be written as a Single Page Application (SPA): an application that has a single endpoint, now serving web content instead of plain text via Content.Page:

```
module MyApplication1

open WebSharper
open WebSharper.Sitelets
open WebSharper.UI.Next.Html
open WebSharper.UI.Next.Server

[<Website>]
let Main =
    Application.SinglePage (fun ctx -> Content.Page(h1 [text "Hello World!"]))
```

HTML Responses

Content.Page is WebSharper's way of returning an HTML response asynchronously. It is an abstraction that constructs an empty, well-formed HTML5 document with a handful of managed placeholders: Title, Head, Body, and Doctype. Next to passing a single HTML element as the body of the document, you can set these optional placeholders directly as well:

```
Content.Page(
    Title = "Hello world!",
    Body = [
        h1 [text "Hello World!"]
        p [text "This is a simple paragraph."]
    ]
)
```

You will soon see how you can embed client-side functionality or calls to JavaScript libraries written in F# into HTML responses. When doing so, `Content.Page` will manage and auto-include the minimal subset of JavaScript and CSS dependencies implied by your F# code, in the right order, into the resulting HTML response. This way, you will not have to manually track these artifacts, saving both time and effort.

Other Responses

There are a number of other asynchronous responses you can return from sitelets. These include:

- **Plain text**, using `Content.Text`:

  ```
  Content.Text "Hello World!"
  ```

- **JSON values**, using `Content.Json`:

  ```
  type Person = { First: string; Last: string; Age: int }

  Content.Json { First="John"; Last="Smith"; Age=30 }
  ```

- **Files**, using `Content.File`:

  ```
  Content.File("../../Main.fs", AllowOutsideRootFolder=true,
               ContentType="text/plain")
  ```

  Here, the optional fields `AllowOutsideRootFolder` and `ContentType` determine whether files can be served outside of the web root folder and the content type for the response, respectively.

- **HTTP error codes**:

  - `Content.Unauthorized` (401)

  - `Content.Forbidden` (403)

  - `Content.NotFound` (404)

  - `Content.MethodNotAllowed` (405)

  - `Content.ServerError` (500)

  You can also return your own custom HTTP error code:

  ```
  Content.Custom(Status=Http.Status.Custom 402 (Some "Payment Required"))
  ```

  You can also construct your own custom responses by providing a low-level implementation using `Content.Custom`.

Multi-Endpoint Sitelets

In the previous examples, you saw how to create single-entry sitelets using `Application.Text` and `Application.SinglePage`. These functions took as an argument a function that returned an asynchronous string or content response for a single entry point. You can also easily define sitelets that have multiple endpoints using discriminated unions:

```
type EndPoint =
    | [<EndPoint "/">] Home
    | [<EndPoint "/order">] Order of int
```

```
let Main =
    Application.MultiPage (fun ctx endpoint ->
        match endpoint with
        | EndPoint.Home ->
            // Content here...
        | EndPoint.Order id ->
            // Content here...
    )
```

Here, Application.MultiPage takes a function that computes its response from an additional endpoint argument and returns a sitelet that is parameterized over that same type. This endpoint type represents all endpoints to the sitelet, and as such plays an important role in defining them.

Specifying Endpoints

As you saw in Table 14-1, URLs for endpoints are inferred by a simple heuristic: base types are represented by a single path segment (/12, /abc, /12.34), and more complex types are converted to multiple segments recursively. In the case of discriminated unions, it is often desirable to give more URL-friendly names, hiding implementation details and code artifacts (union case names) from end-users. You can use the following modifiers/attributes to drive URL inference for endpoints:

- [<Method("GET", ...)>] to specify the HTTP verb/method that the endpoint is accessiblé on.

- [<EndPoint "GET /path">] to specify the URL path for the endpoint, with an optional HTTP method (GET is assumed if HTTP method is omitted). This helpful shorthand is your friend for almost all non-trivial sitelets, including REST applications. You can use an empty path "/" to assign an endpoint to the root of the application.

- [<Query("param1", ...)>] to specify that the arguments passed for the given parameters should be parsed from *query parameters* instead of from URL path segments. The endpoint parameters given must be base types (int, float, string) or options of a base type, in which case they indicate optional arguments.

```
type EndPoint =
    | [<EndPoint "/doc"; Query "version">] Document of int * version: int option
```

Sample Request	Parsed Request
/doc/1234?version=1	Document(1234, Some 1)
/doc/1234	Document(1234, None)

- [<Json "param">] to specify that the argument passed for the given parameter should be parsed as JSON. This is always accompanied by a POST method.

```
type EndPoint =
    | [<EndPoint "POST /create"; Json "order">] CreateOrder of data: OrderData

and OrderData =
    { item: string; quantity: int }
```

Sample Request	Parsed Request
/create { item:"Book", quantity:1 }	CreateOrder({ item="Book";quantity=1 })

- [<FormData("param1", ...)>] to specify that the arguments passed for the given parameters should be parsed from form data passed with the request. Similar to Json, this mode is also only available for POST requests.

Calling Server Code from the Client

In your client-server applications you will inevitably need to deal with client-server communication. In its simplest form, you can define server-side functions, such as functions to fetch data from server files or databases, to be callable from the client via RPC. These calls are normal F# function calls between annotated functions, and the communication protocol is automatically inserted and implemented by the WebSharper runtime. The following skeleton code shows the necessary annotations:

```
module MyApplication =
    open WebSharper

    module Server =
        [<Rpc>]
        let YourServerFunction (...) =
            ...

    module Client =

        [<JavaScript>]
        let YourClientFunction (...) =
            ...
            let data = Server.YourServerFunction (...)
            ...
```

It is a good idea to add your client- and server-side code into separate modules for better readability and encapsulation. Mixing the two in a single module is possible, but adds an extra constraint: all your client-side bindings and pagelets must be functions; e.g., you can't have top-level client-side value bindings, which would otherwise be triggered as server-side code while your application initializes.

Constructing and Combining Sitelets

Building sitelets from smaller sitelets is a fundamental operation used in nearly all sitelet-based WebSharper applications. The most basic sitelet serves a response for a GET HTTP command at a given URL:

```
let EntireSite = Sitelet.Content "/" MyEndPoint.Home MyPages.Home
```

This constructs a sitelet over the MyEndPoint type, which serves MyPages.Home when the root path is requested. As you saw in the previous section, you have a number of alternatives for constructing responses, including basic HTML markup, non-HTML content such as JSON or plain text, files, and various error codes.

Next to Sitelet.Content, there are a number of useful sitelet combinators in the WebSharper.Sitelets namespace. These are summarized in Table 14-4.

Table 14-4. *Sitelet Combinators in* WebSharper.Sitelets

Function	Type	Description
Sitelet.Empty	Sitelet<_>	An empty sitelet
Sitelet.Protect	Filter<'A> -> Sitelet<'A> -> Sitelet<'A>	Protects the given sitelet with the given filter
Sitelet.Content	string -> 'A -> Content<'A> -> Sitelet<'A>	Constructs a sitelet that serves the given content for the given URL and endpoint
Sitelet.Map	('A -> 'B) -> ('B -> 'A) -> Sitelet<'A> -> Sitelet<'B>	Maps a sitelet to another endpoint type
<|>	Sitelet<'A> -> Sitelet<'A> -> Sitelet<'A>	Merges two sitelets
Sitelet.Sum	seq<Sitelet<'A>> -> Sitelet<'A>	Combines several sitelets, with the leftmost taking precedence
Sitelet.Shift	string -> Sitelet<'A> -> Sitelet<'A>	Shifts all sitelet URLs by the specified folder prefix
Sitelet.Folder	string -> seq<Sitelets<'A>> -> Sitelet<'A>	Serves the sum of the given sitelets under the specified "folder" prefix
Sitelet.Infer	('A -> Content<'A>) -> Sitelet<'A>	Constructs a sitelet with an inferred router and the given controller function

Authenticated Sitelets

Another important sitelet primitive, Sitelet.Protect, constructs authenticated sitelets—e.g., sitelets whose contents require an authenticated user. Consider the following endpoints for your sitelet, where Authenticated requires authentication before revealing its response and Login takes an optional EndPoint value where the user is redirected after logging in:

```
module MyApplication

open WebSharper
open WebSharper.Sitelets
open WebSharper.UI.Next
open WebSharper.UI.Next.Server

type EndPoint =
    | [<EndPoint "/">] Home
    | [<EndPoint "/authenticated">] Authenticated
    | [<EndPoint "/login">] Login of EndPoint option
    | [<EndPoint "/logout">] Logout
```

The contents you serve for these endpoints are defined next, with a `Links` function that generates a list of menu choices; do note how these are assembled from endpoints and using `ctx.Link`:

```
module Site =
    open WebSharper.UI.Next.Html

    module Pages =
        /// A helper function to create a 'fresh' URL with a random parameter
        /// in order to make sure that browsers don't show a cached version.
        let R url =
            url + "?d=" + System.Uri.EscapeUriString (System.DateTime.Now.ToString())
        let Links (ctx: Context<_>) =
            let ( => ) title ep = aAttr [attr.href (ctx.Link ep)] [text title]
            let user = ctx.UserSession.GetLoggedInUser() |> Async.RunSynchronously
            ul [
                li ["Home" => EndPoint.Home]
                li ["Authenticated" => EndPoint.Authenticated]
                (if user.IsNone then
                    li ["Login" => EndPoint.Login None]
                 else
                    li ["Logout" => EndPoint.Logout])
            ]

        let Home ctx =
            Content.Page(
                Title = "Home",
                Body = [Links ctx; h1 [text "Home page, use links above"]])

        let Authenticated ctx =
            Content.Page(
                Title = "Authenticated",
                Body = [Links ctx; h1 [text "This page requires a login!"]])

        let Logout ctx =
            Content.Page(
                Title = "Logout",
                Body = [Links ctx; h1 [text "You have been logged out."]])

        let Login ctx endpoint =
            let redirectUrl =
                match endpoint with
                | None -> EndPoint.Home
                | Some ep -> ep
                |> ctx.Link
                |> R
            Content.Page(
                Title = "Login",
                Body = [
                    h1 [text "Login"]
                    p [text "and... you are logged in magically..."]
                    aAttr [attr.href redirectUrl] [text "Proceed further"]
                ])
```

Now you can build two sitelets, one for the non-authenticated and one for the authenticated part of your application, and combine them to form the complete web application. The former looks like this:

```
let Authenticated =
    let filter : Sitelet.Filter<EndPoint> =
        { VerifyUser = fun _ -> true
          LoginRedirect = Some >> EndPoint.Login }

    Sitelet.Protect filter
        (Sitelet.Content "/authenticated" EndPoint.Authenticated Pages.Authenticated)
```

This code defines a new response available at /authenticated, servicing the EndPoint.Authenticated endpoint with the content that Pages.Authenticated generates. In addition, this response is protected with a Sitelet.Filter value defined over your global endpoint type. This filter requires that the requesting user is logged in. In addition, you can impose further conditions by giving a user predicate in VerifyUser. In this example, no additional filtering is defined, and we allow any logged-in user to proceed. When the filter determines that the authenticated content can't be served (e.g., there is no logged-in user or the VerifyUser predicate fails), it redirects to the endpoint specified by LoginRedirect, which tells the filter where to redirect for logging in (note the use of the forward composition operator >> to wrap this endpoint into an option first). In this example, EndPoint.Login takes an optional EndPoint parameter, which acts as a return URL.

What's left is to combine these parts by "summing" two sitelets and making sure that Authenticated appears first so that no 500 server error response is raised by the sitelet serving the rest of the application. You can sum several sitelets using the <|> operator, or alternatively the Sitelet.Sum combinator, as follows:

```
[<Website>]
let Main =
    Authenticated
    <|> Application.MultiPage (fun ctx endpoint ->
        match endpoint with
        | EndPoint.Home -> Pages.Home ctx
        | EndPoint.Login endpoint ->
            async {
                // Log in as "visitor" without requiring anything
                do! ctx.UserSession.LoginUser "visitor"
                return! Pages.Login ctx endpoint
            }
        | EndPoint.Logout ->
            async {
                // Log out the "visitor" user and redirect to home
                do! ctx.UserSession.Logout ()
                return! Pages.Logout ctx
            }
        | EndPoint.Authenticated -> Content.ServerError
    )
```

Serving Contexts

As you have seen so far in this section, the serving context provides access to a number of facilities from the serving pipeline, including information on the logged-in user, the current session, the physical folder for the application, and so forth, and you can use the serving context to construct the context-sensitive markup ubiquitous in most applications. These Context<_> fields are summarized in Table 14-5.

Table 14-5. `WebSharper.Sitelets.Context<_>` *Static Members*

Field	Type	Description
ApplicationPath	String	The virtual application root path on the server
Environment	Dictionary<string,obj>	Web (ASP.NET or OWIN) server environment data
Json	Core.Json.Provider	The JSON provider for interacting with the client
Link	'EndPoint -> string	Computes the URL of the given endpoint
Metadata	Core.Metadata.Info	Metadata required for serializing client controls
Request	Http.Request	Provides access to the underlying request object
ResolveUrl	string -> string	Resolves a URL, respecting the application path
ResourceContext	Core.Resources.Context	Metadata required for working with resources
RootFolder	String	The root folder in the file system for the application
UserSession	Web.IUserSession	The UserSession instance for working with logins

Developing REST Applications

In this section, we will walk through creating a small REST application to manage a set of orders. It will feature a simple page with a user form to create a new order and list existing ones, and also to extract JSON for the list of current orders.

To get started, create a new UI.Next Client-Server application and remove `Client.fs` and `Remoting.fs` from your project. You will be updating the `Main.fs` file within this solution for this sample. First, create the `Order` type that represents orders. To keep things simple, your representation will cover an item name and ordered quantity only, although extending these fields to cover a realistic set of order attributes is straightforward. See the following:

```
namespace Website

open WebSharper
open WebSharper.Sitelets
open WebSharper.UI.Next
open WebSharper.UI.Next.Server

type Order =
    { ItemName: string; Quantity: int }
```

Next, implement a basic `Orders` store where orders are stored. This store provides an API to generate IDs (finding the largest ID assigned and increasing that by one) and to save, update, and delete orders, as well as to find them by IDs. In a real-life application, you would want to save these orders into a database or some other form of persistent storage. Another useful approach would be to model the order store as a

UI.Next data-list model and plug in a persistency model that pushes model updates to the server. Storing the orders on the client would also remove page redirects and refreshes, and you could implement the entire application as a single-page application. This is left as an exercise to the reader.

```
type OrderStore(items: Map<int, Order>) =
    let store = ref items

    new () = OrderStore(Map.empty)

    member this.Store = !store
    member this.Orders = !store |> Map.toList |> List.map snd

    member this.Save (id: int) (order: Order) =
        store := this.Store.Add(id, order)

    member this.FindById (id: int) =
        this.Store.TryFind id

    member this.Delete (id: int) =
        if this.Store.ContainsKey id then
            store := this.Store.Remove id

    member this.GetId () =
        if Map.isEmpty !store then 1 else
            !store |> Map.toList |> List.map fst |> List.max |> fun i -> i+1
```

Now, create a type to represent the various endpoints to your application, describing how these endpoints will be accessed:

```
type EndPoint =
    | [<EndPoint "/">] Home
    | [<EndPoint "GET /order">] GetOrder of int
    | [<EndPoint "PUT /order"; Json "order">] UpdateOrder of int * order: Order
    | [<EndPoint "POST /order"; Json "order">] CreateOrder of order: Order
    | [<EndPoint "DELETE /order"; Json "id">] DeleteOrder of id: int
    | [<EndPoint "/edit">] EditOrder of int
    | [<EndPoint "/orders">] ListOrders
```

Here, GetOrder, UpdateOrder, CreateOrder, and DeleteOrder correspond to the REST API you are providing. Note that these actions carry strongly-typed Order values when they need to.

Your application will use static UI.Next templating based on the main.html file in the root of your web project, along with a helper function to compute a relevant menu bar (the project template uses Bootstrap):

```
module Templating =
    open WebSharper.UI.Next.Html

    type MainTemplate = Templating.Template<"Main.html">

    // Compute a menu bar where the menu item for the given endpoint is active
    let MenuBar (ctx: Context<EndPoint>) endpoint : Doc list =
        let (=>) txt act =
```

```
            liAttr [if endpoint = act then yield attr.``class`` "active"] [
                aAttr [attr.href (ctx.Link act)] [text txt]
            ] :> Doc
        [
            "Home" => EndPoint.Home
            "List orders" => EndPoint.ListOrders
        ]

    let Main ctx action title body =
        Content.Page(
            MainTemplate.Doc(
                title = title,
                menubar = MenuBar ctx action,
                body = body
            )
        )
```

The client side will use a few utility functions to build AJAX requests using jQuery, as well as the REST operations and hyperlinks involving them:

```
[<JavaScript>]
module Client =
    open WebSharper.JavaScript
    open WebSharper.UI.Next
    open WebSharper.UI.Next.Html
    open WebSharper.UI.Next.Client
    open WebSharper.Forms
    open WebSharper.JQuery

    /// General function to send an AJAX request with a body.
    let Ajax (met: string) (url: string) (serializedData: string) : Async<string> =
        Async.FromContinuations (fun (ok, ko, _) ->
            JQuery.Ajax(
                JQuery.AjaxSettings(
                    Url = url,
                    Type = As<JQuery.RequestType> met,
                    ContentType = "application/json",
                    DataType = JQuery.DataType.Text,
                    Data = serializedData,
                    Success = (fun (result, _, _) -> ok (result :?> string)),
                    Error = (fun (jqXHR, _, _) -> ko (System.Exception(jqXHR.ResponseText)))
                )
            )
            |> ignore)

    let private OP(met, url, data) =
        async {
            let! response = Ajax met ("/order" + url) data
            JS.Window.Location.Replace "/"
        } |> Async.StartImmediate
```

```
    let private LINK(met, url, data) =
        aAttr [
            on.click (fun e arg -> OP(met, url, data))
        ] [text met]

    let DeleteOrder id = LINK("DELETE", "", string id)
    let CreateOrder data = OP("POST", "", data)
    let UpdateOrder(id, data) = OP("PUT", "/" + string id, data)
```

The form to enter a new order or update an existing one uses a piglet. You will learn about formlets and piglets in the remainder of this chapter, but for now just observe the clarity piglets bring to defining user forms and how they are rendered and run. You will to use NuGet to add a reference to WebSharper.Forms (see later in this chapter), ensuring that "Dependency behavior" is set to "Latest":

```
let OrderForm (orderOpt: (int * Order) option) =
    let title, quantity =
        match orderOpt with
        | None ->
            Var.Create "", Var.Create (CheckedInput.Blank "")
        | Some (id, o) ->
            Var.Create o.ItemName,
            Var.Create (CheckedInput.Valid(o.Quantity, string o.Quantity))
    Form.Return (fun title qty -> { ItemName = title; Quantity = qty })
    <*> (Form.YieldVar title
        |> Validation.IsNotEmpty "Must enter a title")
    <*> (Form.YieldVar quantity
        |> Validation.MapValidCheckedInput "Must enter a valid quantity")
    |> Form.WithSubmit
    |> Form.Run (fun order ->
        match orderOpt with
        | None -> CreateOrder (Json.Serialize order)
        | Some (id, _) -> UpdateOrder(id, Json.Serialize order)
    )
    |> Form.Render (fun title quantity submit ->
        form [
            label [
                text "Title: "
                Doc.Input [] title
            ]
            br []
            label [
                text "Quantity: "
                Doc.IntInput [] quantity
            ]
            br []
            Doc.Button "Submit" [] submit.Trigger
            div [
                submit.View.Doc (function
                    | Success _ -> Doc.Empty
                    | Failure msgs ->
```

```
        Doc.Concat (msgs |> List.map (fun m -> p [text m.Text] :> _))
    )
  ]
]
)
```

Here, OrderForm takes an optional pair of the internal store ID and its corresponding order, and renders a basic web form to edit this data. When the user submits, either a new order is created or the existing one is updated.

Now, you are ready to put together the pages of your application. First up, the Create/Edit page, which displays an order form (possibly initialized if editing an existing order) and the list of orders already saved:

```
module Site =
    open WebSharper.UI.Next.Html

    let MyStore = new OrderStore(Map.ofList [1, { ItemName="Pair of socks"; Quantity=2 }])

    let CreateOrEditOrderPage ctx orderOpt =
        let (=>) txt endpoint = aAttr [attr.href (ctx.Link endpoint)] [text txt]
        Templating.Main ctx EndPoint.Home "Create order" [
            h1 [text "Create/edit order"]
            hr []
            div [client <@ Client.OrderForm orderOpt @>]
            h1 [text "Orders"]
            tableAttr [attr.``class`` "table table-striped table-hover"] [
                thead [
                    td [text "Order #"]
                    td [text "Item"]
                    td [text "Quantity"]
                ]
                tbody
                    (MyStore.Store
                    |> Map.toList
                    |> Seq.map (fun (id, order) ->
                        tr [
                            td [sprintf "#%d" id => EndPoint.GetOrder id]
                            td [text order.ItemName]
                            td [text (string order.Quantity)]
                            td [
                                client <@ Client.DeleteOrder id @>
                                text " | "
                                "EDIT" => EndPoint.EditOrder id                    ]
                        ] :> Doc
                    ))
            ]
        ]
```

Getting a given order is straightforward: either return 404 or the JSON for that order:

```
let GetOrder id =
    match MyStore.FindById id with
    | None -> Content.NotFound
    | Some order -> Content.Json order
```

With these defined, you can now build your sitelet to represent the entire web application:

```
[<Website>]
let Main =
    Application.MultiPage (fun ctx endpoint ->
        match endpoint with
        | EndPoint.Home ->
            CreateOrEditOrderPage ctx None
        | EndPoint.EditOrder i ->
            MyStore.FindById i
            |> Option.bind (fun order -> Some (i, order))
            |> CreateOrEditOrderPage ctx
        | EndPoint.CreateOrder order ->
            MyStore.Save (MyStore.GetId()) order
            Content.Text "Order created successfully."
        | EndPoint.DeleteOrder id ->
            MyStore.Delete id
            Content.Text "Order deleted successfully."
        | EndPoint.GetOrder id ->
            GetOrder id
        | EndPoint.ListOrders ->
            Content.Json MyStore.Orders
        | EndPoint.UpdateOrder (id, order) ->
            MyStore.Save id order
            Content.RedirectTemporary EndPoint.ListOrders
    )
```

Figure 14-4 shows the application in action.

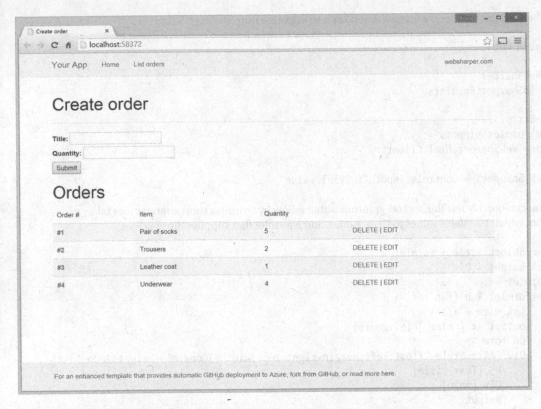

Figure 14-4. *A simple REST client for taking orders*

Formlets and Piglets: Building Functional Web Forms

Nearly all web pages need to take user input in one way or another. For example, users may click buttons or links, or enter values in a web form. In addition, web forms typically impose various limitations for the values entered; for instance, many fields are required and must be supplied a value, certain fields such as date fields require values in a specific format, yet others expect values that contain alpha, numeric, and/or special characters only, and the list goes on.

WebSharper formlets, shipped in the WebSharer.Formlets NuGet package, provide an elegant, type-safe, and robust way to build web forms and encapsulate the structural makeup, the validations involved, and the layout and other presentation details as a single F# value. They are composable building blocks that can be nested, enhanced, and customized to an arbitrary complexity. This section will take a cursory look at formlets. For more details, please refer to http://websharper.com/docs/formlets.

The WebSharper.Formlets namespace contains various formlet controls and enhancements that you can apply to them, along with important formlet combinators such as Formlet.Run, which renders a formlet into a DOM node. The rest of this section will use the SPA project template, with references to the WebSharper.Formlets and WebSharper.Html NuGet packages. You should also add a "main" placeholder to index.html and continue with a fresh Client.fs:

```
...
<body>
    <div id="main"></div>
    <script ...>
```

The simplest formlet is a textbox that takes a string value from the user: Snippet1:

```
namespace Website

open WebSharper
open WebSharper.Formlets

[<JavaScript>]
module FormletSnippets =
    open WebSharper.Html.Client

    let Snippet1 = Controls.Input "initial value"
```

You can quickly test this and other formlets that follow by writing a short wrapper that takes a render function, which translates values to DOM nodes, and a formlet that supplies those values:

```
let RunInBlock title f formlet =
    let output = Div []
    formlet
    |> Formlet.Run (fun res ->
        let elem = f res
        output -< [ elem ] |> ignore)
    |> fun form ->
        Div [Attr.Style "float:left;margin-right:20px;width:300px;min-height:200px"]-<[
            H5 [Text title]
            Div [form]
            output
        ]
```

You can then use this helper function to take a formlet and echo what has been accepted by it:

```
let RunSnippet<'T> title formlet =
    formlet
    |> RunInBlock title (fun (s: 'T) ->
        Div [
            P [Text ("You entered: " + string (box s))]
        ])
```

When testing Snippet1 with RunSnippet, each time you press a key an event is triggered, and the formlet enters an accepting state; subsequently, it displays a new echo message that is appended to the previous ones. Note that this formlet is in an accepting state even without typing anything into it.

To remove the initial empty echo message, e.g., to cause the formlet not to start in an accepting state, and impose further conditions for its acceptance, you can add various validators that "block" until a certain condition holds. For instance, you can use Validator.Is to inspect a formlet's current value and reject or accept based on any criteria you define. For example, here is a basic input formlet, enhanced with a validator that doesn't accept values with fewer than three characters:

```
let Snippet1a =
    Formlet.Yield id
    <*> (Controls.Input ""
        |> Validator.Is (fun s -> s.Length > 3) "Enter a valid name")
```

This is a slightly more elaborate version of the input formlet, enhanced with a general validator and wrapped in a `Formlet.Yield` combinator. This function defines how the values collected in the formlet are combined and returned from the formlet, and it comes in handy when composing larger formlets that contain multiple input fields. The general form of `Formlet.Yield` looks like this:

```
Formlet.Yield (fun v1 ... vn -> <compose into a single return value>)
<*> formlet1
<*> ...
<*> formletn
```

Here, v1, ..., vn correspond to the return values of `formlet1`, ..., `formletn`, respectively. Note how these formlets are combined using the `<*>` formlet operator. Combining two formlets yields another formlet, with the visuals of the combined formlets laid out vertically. You will learn about changing the layout later in this section.

Now that you are familiar with constructing basic formlets with validators and combining them to build larger formlets, let's look at a few more snippets that apply progressive enhancement to your basic input formlet. Table 14-6 contains the most-used enhancements.

Table 14-6. *Formlet Enhancement Functions in* `WebSharper.Formlets.Enhance`

Function	Description
WithCssClass	Enhances the given formlet with a CSS class
WithCustomFormContainer	Enhances the given formlet with a custom form container
WithCustomResetButton	Enhances the given formlet with a custom Reset button
WithCustomSubmitAndResetButtons	Enhances the given formlet with custom Submit and Reset buttons
WithCustomSubmitButton	Enhances the given formlet with a custom Submit button
WithCustomValidationFrame	Enhances the given formlet with a custom validation frame
WithCustomValidationIcon	Enhances the given formlet with a custom validation icon
WithErrorFormlet	Enhances the given formlet with a formlet for displaying error messages
WithErrorSummary	Enhances the given formlet with an error summary that contains a list of error messages when in a failing state
WithFormContainer	Enhances the given formlet with a standard form container
WithLabel	Enhances the given formlet with a label generated by the first argument
WithLabelAbove	Enhances the given formlet by displaying labels above components
WithLabelAndInfo	Enhances the given formlet by including a text label and an info tooltip
WithLabelConfiguration	Enhances the given formlet with a custom label
WithLabelLeft	Enhances the given formlet by displaying labels on the left
WithLegend	Enhances the given formlet with a legend box
WithResetButton	Enhances the given formlet with a basic Reset button
WithResetFormlet	Enhances the first formlet with reset capabilities defined by the second formlet

(continued)

Table 14-6. (*continued*)

Function	Description
WithResetAction	Adds a reset predicate that controls the resetting behavior of the containing formlet
WithRowConfiguration	Enhances the given formlet with a custom row configuration
WithSubmitAndReset	Enhances the given formlet with the given submitting formlet and reset function
WithSubmitAndResetButtons	Enhances the given formlet with basic Submit and Reset buttons
WithSubmitButton	Enhances the given formlet with a basic Submit button
WithSubmitFormlet	Enhances the given formlet by applying a submitting formlet
WithTextLabel	Enhances the given formlet by a text label
WithValidationIcon	Enhances the given formlet with a basic validation icon
WithValidationFrame	Enhances the given formlet with a standard validation frame
CustomMany	Creates a custom formlet for inputting a list of values using the given formlet
Many	Creates a formlet for inputting a list of values using the given formlet
WithJsonPost	Wraps the given formlet in an element and submits the values entered in a POST to a given URL

Many features of the WebSharper formlet library are driven by pure CSS, and the necessary CSS resources are automatically included in your page when you use formlet form containers by applying the Enhance.WithFormContainer function. This applies a clean visual theme to your buttons and input fields and lights up the validation and informational features. For instance, here is a basic input control wrapped in a form container with a validator that accepts any non-empty string (so it blocks on empty input):

```
let Snippet1b =
    Formlet.Yield id
    <*> (Controls.Input ""
        |> Validator.IsNotEmpty "Enter a valid name"
        |> Enhance.WithFormContainer)
```

You can also cause this formlet not to accept until a Submit button is pressed. In addition, you can supply a Reset button that resets the formlet to its original state. This example adds both:

```
let Snippet1c =
    Formlet.Yield id
    <*> (Controls.Input ""
        |> Validator.IsNotEmpty "Enter a valid name"
        |> Enhance.WithFormContainer
        |> Enhance.WithSubmitAndResetButtons)
```

The accepting status of this formlet and any validation error messages can be revealed to the user via a validation icon or an error-summary enhancement. For these to work properly, your formlet needs to be in a form container. You can add a validation icon and/or a validation error summary as follows:

```
let Snippet1d =
    Formlet.Yield id
    <*> (Controls.Input ""
        |> Validator.IsNotEmpty "Enter a valid name"
        |> Enhance.WithValidationIcon
        |> Enhance.WithErrorSummary "Errors"
        |> Enhance.WithSubmitAndResetButtons
        |> Enhance.WithFormContainer)
```

Adding a label for the input control is yet another enhancement:

```
let Snippet1e =
    Formlet.Yield id
    <*> (Controls.Input ""
        |> Validator.IsNotEmpty "Enter a valid name"
        |> Enhance.WithValidationIcon
        |> Enhance.WithTextLabel "Name"
        |> Enhance.WithSubmitAndResetButtons
        |> Enhance.WithFormContainer)
```

And, finally, you can add an information icon before the label:

```
let Snippet1f =
    Formlet.Yield id
    <*> (Controls.Input ""
        |> Validator.IsNotEmpty "Enter a valid name"
        |> Enhance.WithValidationIcon
        |> Enhance.WithLabelAndInfo "Name" "Enter your name"
        |> Enhance.WithSubmitAndResetButtons
        |> Enhance.WithFormContainer)
```

You can test these formlets side by side by wrapping them in a DIV node and adding it to the main placeholder in the master page:

```
let Main =
    Div([
        RunSnippet "Snippet1"  Snippet1
        RunSnippet "Snippet1a" Snippet1a
        RunSnippet "Snippet1b" Snippet1b
        RunSnippet "Snippet1c" Snippet1c
        RunSnippet "Snippet1d" Snippet1d
        RunSnippet "Snippet1e" Snippet1e
        RunSnippet "Snippet1f" Snippet1f
    ]).AppendTo "main"
```

The formlets up to this point are shown in Figure 14-5. Although these examples contain a single input field, you can also create input formlets with multiple fields, as shown in the following example:

```
let input label err =
    Controls.Input ""
    |> Validator.IsNotEmpty err
    |> Enhance.WithValidationIcon
    |> Enhance.WithTextLabel label

let inputInt label err =
    Controls.Input ""
    |> Validator.IsInt err
    |> Formlet.Map int
    |> Enhance.WithValidationIcon
    |> Enhance.WithTextLabel label

let Snippet2 : Formlet<string * int> =
    Formlet.Yield (fun name age -> name, age)
    <*> input "Name" "Please enter your name"
    <*> inputInt "Age" "Please enter a valid age"
    |> Enhance.WithSubmitAndResetButtons
    |> Enhance.WithFormContainer
```

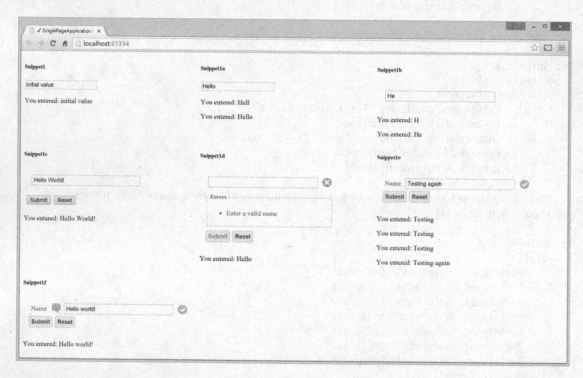

Figure 14-5. *Simple formlets*

Note how this formlet returns a `string-int` pair for the name and age obtained from the user, in essence providing a type-safe and robust way to collect and handle the input values.

Another useful formlet combinator is `Enhance.Many`. It gives you the ability to collect a list of values based on a formlet that collects a single value:

```
let Snippet3 =
    Formlet.Yield (fun name age -> name, age)
    <*> input "Name" "Please enter your name"
    <*> inputInt "Age" "Please enter a valid age"
    |> Enhance.WithLegend "Person"
    |> Enhance.WithTextLabel "Person"
    |> Enhance.Many
    |> Enhance.WithLegend "People"
    |> Enhance.WithSubmitAndResetButtons
    |> Enhance.WithFormContainer
```

These formlets are shown in Figure 14-6.

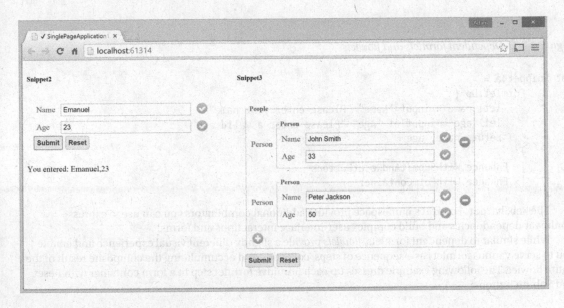

Figure 14-6. *Composite formlets*

Dependent Formlets and Flowlets

Often, web forms need more elaborate considerations. For instance, part of a web form may depend on a value entered in another part. You can express these dependencies using *dependent formlets*, which you can create most conveniently using the `Formlet.Do` computation expression builder. As plain formlets, dependent formlets are also first-class values and further encode linear dependencies between the various form parts. Consider the following simple example in which the name and age are obtained one after the other, requiring that a name is entered before the input field for the age is displayed:

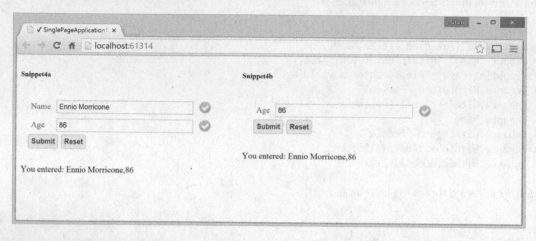

Figure 14-7. Dependent formlets and flowlets

```
let Snippet4a =
        Formlet.Do {
            let! name = input "Name" "Please enter your name"
            let! age = inputInt "Age" "Please enter a valid age"
            return name, age
        }
        |> Enhance.WithSubmitAndResetButtons
        |> Enhance.WithFormContainer
```

The WebSharper.Formlets namespace provides additional combinators you can use to express nonlinear dependencies and build complex user-interface interactions and forms.

While similar to dependent formlets, *flowlets* provide a slightly different visual experience and enable you to serve various formlets as a sequence of steps, collecting and accumulating the composite result of the entire flowlet. The following example dresses up each primitive formlet step in a form container with Reset and Submit buttons:

```
let Snippet4b =
    Formlet.Do {
        let! name = input "Name" "Please enter your name"
                    |> Enhance.WithSubmitAndResetButtons
                    |> Enhance.WithFormContainer
        let! age =  inputInt "Age" "Please enter a valid age"
                    |> Enhance.WithSubmitAndResetButtons
                    |> Enhance.WithFormContainer
        return name, age
    }
    |> Formlet.Flowlet
```

Reactive Formlets with UI.Next

There is an alternative implementation of formlets using UI.Next, at the time of writing available as an alpha release of the WebSharper.UI.Next.Formlets NuGet package, with many missing features compared to the original formlets library presented earlier.

The fundamental enhancement of the UI.Next-based library is that formlet input controls can also be initialized via reactive variables. The following application requires WebSharper.UI.Next.Formlets and implements a Login web form; note how each textbox is bound to a reactive variable:

```
namespace ReactiveFormlets

open WebSharper
open WebSharper.JavaScript
open WebSharper.UI.Next
open WebSharper.UI.Next.Html
open WebSharper.UI.Next.Client
open WebSharper.UI.Next.Formlets

[<JavaScript>]
module LoginForm =

    let Main =
        let username = Var.Create ""
        let password = Var.Create ""
        Formlet.Return (fun user pass -> (user, pass))
        <*> (Controls.InputVar username
            |> Formlet.WithLabel (text "Username: "))
        <*> (Controls.InputVar password
            |> Formlet.WithLabel (text "Password: "))
        |> Formlet.WithSubmit "Log in"
        |> Formlet.WithFormContainer
        |> Formlet.Run (fun (user, pass) ->
            JS.Alert ("Welcome, " + user + "!"))
        |> Doc.RunById "main"
```

This construction has a number of advantages over standard non-reactive formlets. In particular, data binding becomes possible, which you can now do by simply setting the reactive variables—the two-way binding provided by UI.Next will update the input controls automatically.

Piglets

Piglets are closely related to formlets, as they both provide the capability to declaratively describe web forms, including data validation and feedback. The main difference, however, comes from the way they are rendered: formlets automatically generate their corresponding markup based on a backed-in implementation, while piglets let developers compose custom markup for their web forms and connect those with similar declarative syntax to formlets. Therefore, piglets can be seen as a useful extension of formlets, as they provide absolute control over rendering. You can read more about piglets at http://websharper.com/docs/piglets.

One unique ability of piglets is being able to render markup for different presentation channels. For instance, you could define the UI of your application as a piglet and provide rendering implementations for mobile and web users in the same code base.

Piglets are created by a simple `Piglet.Yield` call, taking an initial string value. They can also be enhanced with validation, much like formlets, and `Piglet.Return` can return accumulated values from a piglet. Here is the Login form you saw earlier using piglets and some extra validation:

```
open WebSharper
open WebSharper.JavaScript
open WebSharper.Html.Client
open WebSharper.Piglets

[<JavaScript>]
module LoginForm =

    let Main =
        Piglet.Return (fun user pass -> (user, pass))
        <*> (Piglet.Yield ""
            |> Validation.IsNotEmpty "Must enter a valid username")
        <*> (Piglet.Yield ""
            |> Validation.IsNotEmpty "Must enter a valid password")
        |> Piglet.WithSubmit
        |> Piglet.Run (fun (user, pass) ->
            JS.Alert ("Welcome, " + user + "!"))
        |> Piglet.Render (fun user pass submit ->
            Div [
                Div [Label [Text "Username: "]; Controls.Input user]
                Div [Label [Text "Password: "]; Controls.Password pass]
                Controls.Button submit -< [Text "Log in"]
                Div [] |> Controls.ShowErrors submit (fun errors ->
                    List.map (fun error -> P [Text error]) errors)
            ]
        )
        |> fun s -> s.AppendTo "main"
```

The key here is `Piglet.Render`, which enables you to render markup based on the inner values from the piglet (available as `Stream<'T>` values), various piglet input controls (with `Controls.Input` and friends), and the submitter (which resulted by applying `Piglet.WithSubmit` on the piglet). The submitter can also be used to verify that the values entered into each part of the composed piglet produce an accepting state and are rendered accordingly via `Controls.ShowResult`. If you are only interested in validation errors, you can use `Controls.ShowError` as in the example.

WebSharper.Forms: Reactive Piglets with UI.Next

As with reactive formlets, a matching (at the time of writing, an experimental) version for piglets is shipped in the `WebSharper.Forms` NuGet package, enabling you to use piglets with `UI.Next` and to bind reactive variables to input controls in rendered markup.

Consider the same Login form using `WebSharper.Forms`:

```
namespace ReactivePiglets

open WebSharper
open WebSharper.JavaScript
open WebSharper.UI.Next
```

```
open WebSharper.UI.Next.Html
open WebSharper.UI.Next.Client
open WebSharper.Forms

[<JavaScript>]
module LoginForm =

    let Main =
        Form.Return (fun user pass -> (user, pass))
        <*> (Form.Yield ""
            |> Validation.IsNotEmpty "Must enter a valid username")
        <*> (Form.Yield ""
            |> Validation.IsNotEmpty "Must enter a valid password")
        |> Form.WithSubmit
        |> Form.Run (fun (user, pass) ->
            JS.Alert ("Welcome, " + user + "!"))
        |> Form.Render (fun user pass submit ->
            div [
                div [label [text "Username: "]; Doc.Input [] user]
                div [label [text "Password: "]; Doc.PasswordBox [] pass]
                Doc.Button "Log in" [] submit.Trigger
                div [
                    Doc.ShowErrors submit.View (fun errors ->
                        errors
                        |> List.map (fun error -> p [text error.Text])
                        |> Seq.cast
                        |> Doc.Concat)
                ]
            ]
        )
        |> Doc.RunById "main"
```

The main difference from the regular piglet implementation, apart from using UI.Next, is that the inner piglet values are available as reactive variables inside Piglet.Render, and these can be bound to Doc input controls directly. The submitter and error facilities are also available as Doc members. You can also use Piglet.YieldVar when composing the piglet, using reactive variables for the initial values and enabling direct data binding.

WebSharper.Forms.Bootstrap is a WebSharper.Forms library, available in the similarly named NuGet package. It provides convenient shorthands for various UI controls using Bootstrap, a popular JavaScript library for front-end development. You can easily modify the Form.Render call to use Bootstrap as follows:

```
...
open WebSharper.Forms.Bootstrap

[<JavaScript>]
module LoginForm =
    module C = Controls.Simple

    let Main =
        ...
        |> Form.Render (fun user pass submit ->
```

```
        div [
            C.InputWithError "Username" user submit.View
            C.InputPasswordWithError "Password" pass submit.View
            C.Button "Log in" submit.Trigger
            C.ShowErrors submit.View  // Optional to get a list of errors
        ]
    )
    |> Doc.RunById "main"
```

The WebSharper.Forms.Bootstrap.Controls namespace contains a number of user-interface control variants such as Button, Checkbox, Input, InputPassword, or Radio, each taking a list of UI.Next attributes for configurability. Defaults for each are provided in the Controls.Simple module, as used in the previous snippet. You can see this Bootstrap-based Login form in action in Figure 14-8.

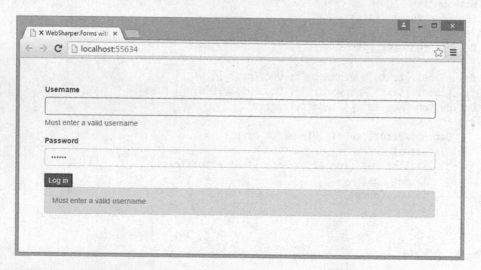

Figure 14-8. *A simple Login form using WebSharper.Forms.Bootstrap*

Automated Resource Tracking and Handling

Pagelets often need to define their own resource dependencies, such as style sheets, JavaScript code, and other artifacts that they might need in order to work properly. These dependencies are automatically referenced and included in sitelets or by the WebSharper script manager when those pagelets are used in an ASPX markup. For instance, the formlet examples in the preceding section came with a dependency on the main formlet style sheet provided by WebSharper.Formlets (along with additional skins), giving the appearance shown in Figures 14-5, 14-6, and 14-7.

Resources can be defined and tagged on various parts of your code, most typically on functions or modules when binding various JavaScript libraries, and when those parts are referenced, the corresponding resources are included in the consuming page. From this automation point of view, resource annotations serve to define anchors to external artifacts using generated HTML markup that is inserted into the <head> section of the containing page or at the location specified in WebSharper.Html or UI.Next templates using various meta placeholders.

The most low-level implementation of a resource thus renders this HTML markup:

```
namespace Website

open WebSharper
open WebSharper.Core

// Put "my.js" in the root of the web project.
type MyResource() =
    interface Resources.IResource with
        member this.Render ctx writer =
            let writer = writer Resources.RenderLocation.Scripts
            writer.WriteLine "<script src='my.js' type='javascript'></script>"
```

You rarely need to use custom-rendered resources. Instead, to define a resource pointing to a CSS or JavaScript file, you can simply use the BaseResource class. This class has two constructors: one that you can use to define a resource embedded into the assembly, and another that can address an external resource relative to an absolute base URL (in the first argument). An example of an embedded resource (be sure to mark my.js as an embedded resource in your solution) is as follows:

```
[<assembly:System.Web.UI.WebResource("my.js", "text/javascript")>]
do ()

type MyEmbeddedResource() =
    inherit Resources.BaseResource("my.js")
```

An example using the multi-argument constructor:

```
type MyExternalResource() =
    inherit Resources.BaseResource(@"http:\\your.net", "lib.js", "style.css")
```

The advantage of using Resources.BaseResource is that you can avoid having to render HTML in your resource declaration. Instead, Resources.BaseResource is smart enough to tell apart JavaScript and CSS artifacts, and outputs the right markup for each.

Once you have defined the resources you need, you can annotate them on any type (or module) or any static member using the Require attribute, specifying the type of the resource that is to be pinned to the given code unit:

```
[<Require(typeof<MyExternalResource>)>]
type Hello = ..
```

From this point, any use of the Hello type will trigger a dependency defined in MyExternalResource.

Using Third-Party JavaScript Libraries

One of WebSharper's great strengths is its ability to use any JavaScript library in client-side F# code, freeing you from having to develop untyped JavaScript code as a separate code base. To talk to these JavaScript libraries in F#, you need a WebSharper *extension* for each library. At the time of writing, WebSharper comes with a number of extensions to various JavaScript libraries, including jQuery, Google Maps and

Visualization, Highcharts, D3, jQuery UI, jQuery Mobile, and many others. Some of these come with the main WebSharper installer (for instance, jQuery and the HTML5 extensions), and some you have to download from the WebSharper site (http://websharper.com) or obtain via NuGet separately.

You can also develop WebSharper extensions to your own or third-party JavaScript libraries. Many JavaScript libraries use loosely typed constructs, such as functions that take a variable number and type of arguments and return objects with different structures. To bind these libraries, you often need to resort to a low-level, weakly typed extension often referred to as a *native extension* and build a derived, more strongly typed and safer F# abstraction around it as second library.

WebSharper extensions are defined in F# using embedded domain-specific language syntax and are processed through the WebSharper Interface Generator (WIG) tool. These definitions are meant to be terse and compact, reiterating the underlying JavaScript API in F# using a set of convenient notations and operators.

You can quickly get started with a new extension by using the Extension project template that comes with the standard WebSharper installers. This creates a new F# project with a single source file Main.fs that contains two important pieces: first, a Definition module that uses the WIG syntax to define various types, interfaces, classes, and members that form an "assembly," which is a code unit that represents a JavaScript library as a single F# value, and second, a Main module that triggers the generation of the extension from this "assembly" value. The generation of the extension involves outputting source code decorated with Inline attributes and compiling it to a .NET assembly that contains the extension. You could also write the code that WIG generates by hand, but you would quickly start to appreciate the amount of effort WIG saves you by automating many of the abstraction chores and common JavaScript usage patterns.

The full WIG language definition is outside the scope of this chapter, and you should consult the WebSharper documentation for more details at http://websharper.com/docs/wig.

Working with .NET Proxies

WebSharper enables you to use F# in your client-side coding and gives you nearly the entire F# language with which to develop client-side code, including powerful language features such as pattern matching, active patterns, discriminated unions and records, classes, interfaces, exceptions, and asynchronous computations, among others. This is coupled with the ability to use a large part of the F# core libraries and standard .NET namespaces in client-side code without having to worry about how to map them to JavaScript. The mechanism to enable this seamless translation experience is *proxying*, a fundamental WebSharper concept that you should be familiar with, as you may need to add proxies yourself to your own or third-party libraries to extend translation coverage.

WebSharper proxies provide a JavaScript interpretation for a .NET type. This proxy type is annotated with the Proxy attribute, giving the type of the underlying target .NET type for which the proxy is provided. Here is a small, partial example to proxy the standard F#/.NET int type:

```fsharp
open WebSharper
open WebSharper.JavaScript

[<Proxy(typeof<System.Int32>)>]
type private Int32 =

    static member MaxValue with [<Inline "2147483647">]  get () = X<int>
    static member MinValue with [<Inline "-2147483648">] get () = X<int>

    [<Inline "parseInt($s)">]
    static member Parse(s: string) = X<int>
```

Note how the three static members use the `Inline` attribute to express their counterparts in JavaScript, and these inline expressions will be evaluated and used in the translation of client-side code instead of invoking the right-hand side of each member. This snippet also demonstrates a subtle point in how proxies (and JavaScript stubs as well) are defined, e.g., what you supply as the .NET implementation for each member. You can apply the following techniques in defining your JavaScript mapping for proxying a .NET type or stubbing JavaScript code:

- You should never call proxies directly. Remember, they are only used in translating .NET types to JavaScript. Hence, you can leave their implementation empty (say, by constructing the default value of the return type) or yield an exception. For this, you can use the `X<'T>` construct, as in the `Parse` member above (requiring opening `WebSharper.JavaScript`). Yielding an exception is a preferred approach, so in case you accidentally call proxy members, you are notified at runtime.

- Since stubbed (that is, inlined) code is designed to be called, you need to take care in how you call these stubbed functions and members. Calling from client code is the intended behavior; here, WebSharper will evaluate and use the attached inline expressions and ignore the .NET implementation. However, if you also want to make your stubbed functions available for server-side use (a rare but useful device when used in a controlled fashion), you should attach a semantically correct .NET implementation.

Summary

In this chapter, you've seen how to use F# to perform a range of web programming tasks. You started by using sockets and TCP/IP to implement a web server and other TCP-based services directly, an example of a system or web-network programming task. In the larger part of the chapter, you looked at using WebSharper, the main F# web framework, to develop client-based applications that incorporate significant client-side scripting, and authored them in pure F# code. You saw in the "Getting Started" example how you can use client-side code to connect to the World Bank database, fetch country statistics in real time, and chart these using `WebSharper.Charting`, a cross-platform web-charting and visualization library built for WebSharper applications. You then looked at pagelets, learned how you can use them to embed client-side functionality into your pages, and learned about the available HTML implementations, including `WebSharper.UI.Next` and `WebSharper.Html`. You also learned about sitelets to represent entire web applications as server-side F# values in a type-safe and composable manner. You saw how to build user interfaces and web forms in a declarative fashion, employ progressive enhancement techniques, and represent these client-side user interfaces as strongly-typed F# values that can be combined and nested to an arbitrary complexity. As well, you saw a number of powerful formlet and piglet combinators that yield a massive productivity factor when it comes to building more complex web forms, such as accepting a list of user inputs, expressing dependencies within form elements, and applying different visual rendering techniques and validation functions.

You also became familiar with WebSharper's extensibility framework and how you can develop WebSharper extensions to any third-party JavaScript library or create proxies to extend the .NET-to-JavaScript translation coverage. With these techniques, you can leverage a massive paradigm shift toward building more client-oriented, reactive applications using less code, while enjoying more robustness and type safety.

CHAPTER 15

Visualization and Graphical User Interfaces

GUI applications revolve around events, and F# provides a natural way to process events with functions. Graphical interfaces are often developed using visual editors, in particular to build GUIs by assembling *controls*. Applications, however, often need drawing capabilities for displaying and manipulating data, which requires custom programming to augment available controls. This chapter will discuss how to develop graphical applications with F# and why the functional traits of the language suit the event-driven programming paradigm typical of GUIs.

In this chapter, you will use the cross-platform and open-source Eto Forms library. This library allows you to use similar widgets on different graphics systems, but also makes it possible to perform drawing operations.

Getting Started with Eto

Eto Forms is an open-source library available on GitHub (https://github.com/picoe/Eto) that is designed for building portable graphical applications. It can also be obtained using NuGet. The library has a modular structure implementing a driver model: the assembly Eto.dll contains the APIs accessed by your application, and a second one named Eto.*XXX*.dll is used as the implementation for the specific platform XXX.

To get started with Eto Forms simply download the platform-specific version of the library. Additional assemblies may be needed for the chosen platform—for instance, on the Windows platform, if WPF is used then the Windows Presentation Foundation libraries must be referenced too.

Eto Forms allows the shipping of binaries targeting multiple graphical environments without the need for recompilation, as Eto.dll implements a dynamic loading mechanism using .NET reflection abilities.

When a graphical application is compiled, everything is linked by the compilation process; however, the dynamic loading technique used may affect the F# Interactive system by failing to properly load the appropriate assemblies. At the time of writing fsharpi, the F# Interactive on Mono (the .NET runtime for running F# on Linux and MacOS), fails to load the platform-specific library, and on Windows fsi.exe must be executed with the --gui- command-line argument in order to use Windows Forms as the target platform, though WPF can be used as an alternative. You can compile the examples on any platform to avoid these issues, and perhaps contribute to fixing and improving specific support for F# in Eto.

```
┌─────────────────────────────────────────────────────────────────────┐
│            ETO FORMS VERSUS OTHER UI FRAMEWORKS                      │
└─────────────────────────────────────────────────────────────────────┘
```

Eto Forms is a framework for programming cross-platform GUI applications by mapping its own abstractions to multiple platforms using widely available .NET-to-native libraries. The design of the library is inspired by Windows Forms, one of the presentation systems available on the Windows platform. The essential elements of GUI programming are similar across different frameworks, since the way systems handle with graphics is similar. If you learn how to program GUI applications using Eto Forms it will be easy to switch to a different framework, since most of the patterns are similar to those learned in this chapter.

The approach taken by Eto Forms is to build a wrapper around similar components on different platforms (i.e., textbox, button, etc.) and offer a unified interface to manipulate them. With Eto it is possible to lay out components that render using the native implementation of the chosen platform. The only exception is the Drawable type, which is a special control designed to allow drawing and not just the composition of preexisting controls.

Writing "Hello, World!" in a Click

It's traditional to start with a "Hello, World!" application, so let's honor that and begin with a simple program that provides a button to display the magic phrase when clicked:

```
open Eto
open Eto.Forms
open Eto.Drawing

let app = new Application()

let form = new Form(Title="Hello world Eto Forms", Topmost=true, Size=Size(640, 480))
let button = new Button(Text="Click me")
button.Click.Add(fun _ -> MessageBox.Show(form, "Hello world!", "Hey!") |> ignore)
form.Content <- button
form.Show()

app.Run(form)
```

Even in its simplicity, the application captures many traits typical of GUI applications. After opening the namespace associated with Eto Forms, you create the application app and the form form that contains the button button, and you set the form and button captions by assigning their Text properties. In Eto Forms controls have a main child element that is accessed through the Content property. It is possible to combine multiple graphics controls with adaptive layouts by using containers, as you will do shortly.

Most GUI programming is devoted to handling events through callbacks from the graphical interface. Events are described in Chapter 11. To display a message box containing the "Hello, World!" string, you have to configure the button so that when its Click event is fired, a function is called. In the example, you pass a function to the Add method for the button's Click event, which adds an event handler to an event source. You then add the button to the form and call the form's Show method to display it.

At the end, you start the event loop of the application using app.Run(form), which is required to handle events such as button clicks.

Understanding the Anatomy of a Graphical Application

Graphical applications are built on the abstractions provided by the graphical environment hosting them. The application must interact with its environment and process input in an unstructured way. User input isn't the only kind of input received from a windowing system. Window management often involves requests to or from the application itself, such as painting or erasing a form.

Windowing systems provide a common and abstract way to interact with a graphical application: the notion of an *event*. When an event occurs, the application receives a message in the *message queue* with information about the event.

The graphical application is responsible for delivering messages from the message queue to the control for which they're meant. A set of functions provided by the API of the windowing system supports this. This activity of reading messages from the message queue and dispatching them is known as the *event loop* of the application. If the loop fails for any reason, the GUI components cease to work, the application hangs, and Windows may eventually inform you that the application isn't responding.

It's rare for an application to program the event loop explicitly. Programming toolkits encapsulate this functionality, because it's basically always the same. The Run method of the Application class is responsible for handling the event loop, and it ensures that messages related to events are delivered to targets within the application.

GUI programs often involve multiple *threads* of execution. Chapter 11 discusses threading and concurrency in more detail; for this chapter, it's important to remember that event dispatching is a single-threaded activity, even if it may seem to be the opposite. The thread executing the event loop calls the functions and methods registered for handling the various events. In the "Hello, World!" example, for instance, you told the button to call back the function to show the message box when clicked.

AN EXPLICIT EVENT LOOP

An Eto Forms event loop can also be explicitly defined by the application using the Application. RunIteration method; in this case, each invocation performs a step in event handling and returns the control to the caller. Some programs can benefit from this control, because they can interleave event processing and computation using a single thread. Computer games, for instance, tend to use this approach, because event-based timers provided by the framework aren't reliable for producing the frames of the game at the required pace. The following is a typical explicit event loop:

```
let form = new Form(Text = "Explicit Event Loop")
form.Show()
while form.Loaded do
    // Perform some task
    Application.RunIterations()
```

When events are handled explicitly, a program must frequently call the RunIterations method: if events aren't processed, the graphical interface may become unresponsive, which provides the wrong feedback to the user.

Software reuse has always been a priority in the world of graphical applications because of the many details involved in realizing even simple behaviors. It's not surprising that programming techniques favoring software reuse have always flourished in this context. You can develop a GUI application without writing a single line of code by combining existing controls into a new interface.

Articulated frameworks provide a significant number of reusable controls so that you can develop entire applications without needing to use the drawing facilities provided by the interface. For this reason, frameworks have started to support two kinds of customers: those composing interfaces with controls and those who need to develop new controls or explicitly use drawing primitives. The following sections explore the Eto Forms framework from both perspectives; the functional nature of F# is very effective for using controls, and the ability to define objects helps you to develop new ones.

Composing Controls and Menus

Graphical controls, also known as widgets, occupy a portion of the visual area of their parent and they need to be positioned and be given a size. In the old days, it was up to programmers to lay out controls by setting location and size; fortunately, nowadays frameworks provide some form of automatic layout management to adjust the location and size of widgets. Eto Forms uses the notion of Layout that is a specialization of the Container class, which in turn inherits from Control.

The available layouts are

- Panel, meant to decorate a single control

- TableLayout, used to lay out controls in a table structure

- PixelLayout, used to lay out controls using explicit location

You will mostly use the TableLayout layout for configuring your layouts. A table is made of rows and cells; with an object-oriented approach the syntax of building a table would require you to create several objects (one for each row and cell), leading to a verbose syntax that is hard to read.

We will implement a module named EtoUtils to define a nice syntax for building table layouts. We first define union types defining cells, rows, and the table itself:

```
type TCell =
| El of Control
| StretchedEl of Control
| EmptyElement
| TableEl of Table

and TRow =
| Row of TCell list
| StretchedRow of TCell list
| Spacing of Size
| Pad of Padding

and Table = Tbl of TRow list
```

Now, we can write a recursive function makeLayout that recursively converts a Table definition into a TableLayout control:

```
let rec makeLayout (Tbl t) =
  let ret = new TableLayout()

  for r in t  do
    let makeTd (tds:TCell list) =
      let row = new TableRow()
      for td in tds do
        match td with
```

```
            | El c -> row.Cells.Add(new TableCell(c, false))
            | StretchedEl c -> row.Cells.Add(new TableCell(c, true))
            | EmptyElement -> row.Cells.Add(new TableCell(null, true))
            | TableEl t -> row.Cells.Add(new TableCell(makeLayout t, true))
        row
    match r with
    | Row tds -> let r = makeTd tds in ret.Rows.Add(r)
    | StretchedRow tds -> let r = makeTd tds in r.ScaleHeight <- true; ret.Rows.Add(r)
    | Spacing sz -> ret.Spacing <- sz
    | Pad pad -> ret.Padding <- pad
  ret
```

The makeLayout function simply visits the Table expression that defines the structure of the table and creates TableRow and TableCell objects accordingly. The union type Table defines the syntax of the table so that you are guaranteed that the argument passed to makeLayout defines a well-formed table.

You can modify the "Hello, World!" example for use in testing the table definition by transforming it into a counter that increases the number displayed in the label when the button is pressed:

```
let form = new Form(Title="Hello world Eto Forms", Topmost=true, Size=Size(640, 480))
let mutable counter = 0
let button = new Button(Text="+1")
let display = new Label(Text=string(counter))
let table = Tbl[ Row[ El(display) ]; Row[ El(button) ]]
let updateCounter c = counter <- c; display.Text <- string(c)
button.Click.Add(fun _ -> updateCounter(counter + 1))
form.Content <- table |> makeLayout

form.Show()
```

The layout is made of two rows. each containing the label used as display and the button for the increment. As you resize the form figure observe the layout policy adopted by the TableLayout. How can you prevent the unwanted resize of the button?

Tables are defined as trees of rows containing cells; UI menus have a similar structure. You can use the same approach used for tables to extend the EtoUtils module with a better syntax for defining menus. As you did for tables, define the syntax with a union type:

```
type Menu =
    | Item of MenuItem
    | ActionMenuItem of string
    | RadioMenuItem of string*string
    | CheckMenuItem of string
    | SubMenu of string*Menu list
    | Action of Menu*(MenuItem -> unit)
    | Check of Menu*bool
    | Shortcut of Menu*Keys
    member m.WithAction cb = Action(m, cb)
    member m.WithCheck () = Check(m, true)
    member m.WithShortcut v = Shortcut(m, v)
```

In this case we used a single type Menu, but defined three members so that we can annotate menu items with a nicer syntax. You can define a menu item and decorate it with actions, checks, or keyboard shortcuts. The result of using the WithXXX methods is the same ActionMenuItem with the related property set.

As you did for the Table, the recursive function makeMenu creates the Eto objects representing the menu described by a Menu instance. Radio buttons are used to allow the user choose a single option from a group. In Eto radio menu items are grouped when a RadioMenuItem of a group is created using another RadioMenuItem of the same group. The Menu union type uses string labels to identify groups, the radioGroup dictionary is used by makeMenu to store the RadioMenuItem objects representing the different groups.

```
let private radioGroup = new System.Collections.Generic.Dictionary<string, RadioMenuItem>()

let rec makeMenu (menu) =
    match menu with
    | Item m -> m
    | ActionMenuItem lbl ->
        let m = new ButtonMenuItem(Text=lbl)
        m :> _
    | RadioMenuItem (group, lbl) ->
        let m = if radioGroup.ContainsKey(group) then
                    new RadioMenuItem(radioGroup.[group], Text=lbl)
                else
                    let g = new RadioMenuItem(Text=lbl)
                    radioGroup.[group] <- g
                    g
        m :> _
    | CheckMenuItem lbl ->
        let m = new CheckMenuItem(Text=lbl)
        m :> _
    | SubMenu (lbl, lst) ->
        let m = new ButtonMenuItem(Text=lbl)
        for el in lst do
            m.Items.Add(makeMenu el)
        m :> _
    | Action (m, cb) ->
        let ret = makeMenu m
        ret.Click.Add(fun _ -> cb(ret))
        ret
    | Check (m, def) ->
        let ret = makeMenu m
        match ret with
        | :? RadioMenuItem as r -> r.Checked <- def
        | :? CheckMenuItem as c -> c.Checked <- def
        | _ -> ()
        ret
    | Shortcut (m, k) ->
        let ret = makeMenu m
        ret.Shortcut <- k
        ret
```

It is worth noting the difference between ActionMenuItem and Item; the former creates a menu item given a string, while the second is meant to insert an Eto menu item created without the help of our library.

If you add the following lines just before the form.Show() line of the counter example you will get a form with a menu allowing for counter reset:

```
let menu = new MenuBar()
let resetMenu = SubMenu("&File",
                        [
                         ActionMenuItem("Reset").WithAction(fun _ -> updateCounter(0));
                         ActionMenuItem("Exit").WithAction(fun _ -> form.Close())
                        ])
menu.Items.Add(resetMenu |> makeMenu)

form.Menu <- menu
```

You created a MenuBar object, then you added one or more menus obtained by invoking the makeMenu function; the WithAction method allowed you to annotate the item with a callback defining what happens when the menu item is selected. You finally set the configured menu bar as the form menu by setting the Menu property of the form.

Composing User Interfaces

A control is represented by an object inheriting, either directly or indirectly, from the Control class in the Eto.Forms namespace. Building interfaces using controls involves two tasks: placing controls into containers (that are themselves a particular type of control) such as panels or forms, and registering controls with event handlers to be notified of relevant events.

As an example, let's develop a simple web browser based on the web view control, which is a control that allows wrapping the HTML renderer (the interior of a Web Browser window) into an application. Start by opening the libraries required for both using Eto Forms and our own EtoUtils module and creating the Application object needed to process UI events:

```
open Eto

open Eto.Forms
open Eto.Drawing
open EtoUtils

let app = new Application()
```

Now, you have to decide what the browser application should look like (see Figure 15-1). The bare minimum is a toolbar featuring the address bar and the classic Go button, a status bar with a progress bar shown during page loading, and the browser control in the middle of the form.

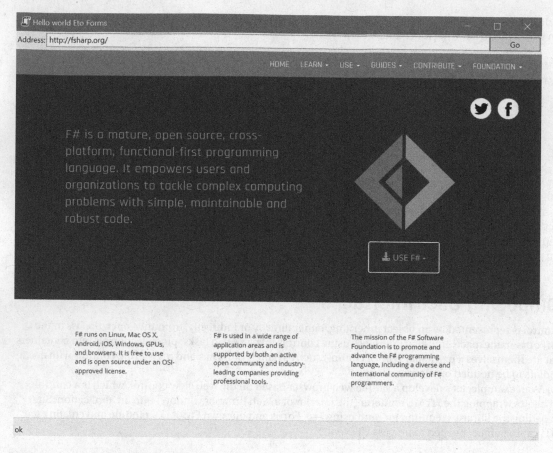

Figure 15-1. *The web browser application*

Next, create and configure the web view, the Go button, the address text box, the status label, and the progress bar, as shown in the following code. The textbox for the address is initially set by the home value to the about:blank URL. The progress bar is resized, and then its Indeterminate property is set to true, meaning that you don't want to show any specific progress but just something moving during download:

```
let home = "about:blank"

let browser = new WebView(Url=System.Uri(home))
let btnGo = new Button(Text="Go")
let txtAddr = new TextBox(Text=home)
let lblStatus = new Label(Text="ok",VerticalAlign=VerticalAlign.Middle)

let progress = new ProgressBar(Indeterminate=true,Visible=false,Width=200)
```

First, associate an event handler for the txtAddr textbox with its KeyUp event. This way, you can catch the Enter key and start browsing the typed URL without having to wait for the Go button. Then, configure the Go button by associating an event handler with the Click event:

```
btnGo.Click.Add(fun _ -> browser.Url <- System.Uri(txtAddr.Text))
txtAddr.KeyUp.Add(fun e -> if e.Key = Keys.Enter then browser.Url <- System.Uri(txtAddr.Text))
```

Both event handlers set the Url property of the browser object, causing the web view control to load the given Uri. Notice how nicely and compactly F# lets you specify event handlers. This is possible because F# lets you use functions directly as arguments to Add.

You can now take care of the browser control and subscribe to two events, DocumentLoading and DocumentLoaded, in order to be notified by the browser when document loading starts and completes. When the browser begins fetching a URL, you show the progress bar in the status bar, setting its Visible property to true. You also update the address bar so that if the user follows a link, the address shown remains consistent with the current document. After the document is loaded, hide the progress bar and update the status label text:

```
browser.DocumentLoading.Add(fun _ ->
  txtAddr.Text <- browser.Url.ToString()
  lblStatus.Text <- "loading..."
  progress.Visible <- true
)

browser.DocumentLoaded.Add(fun _ ->
  lblStatus.Text <- "ok"
  progress.Visible <- false
)
```

You're almost finished with the interface. You have to define the layout of the controls using a TableLayout. Using the layout language created in EtoUtils, you can define the layout in a way that recalls the final output. The main table is 3 x 1 and contains the toolbar, the web view, and the status bar, respectively. The first and the third rows contain a table each to further refine the available space for the remaining controls of the address and status bars:

```
let layout =

    Tbl [
        Spacing(Size(2, 2))
        Row [ TableEl(Tbl [
                         Pad(Padding(2))
                         Row [
                             El(new Label(Text="Address:",VerticalAlign=VerticalAlign.
                             Middle))
                             StretchedEl(txtAddr)
                             El(btnGo)
                         ]
                     ]) ];
        StretchedRow [ StretchedEl(browser) ];
        Row [ TableEl(Tbl [ Pad(Padding(2)); Row [ El(lblStatus); El(progress);
        EmptyElement ]]) ]

    ] |> makeLayout
```

You can now create the form and set its Content to the value of layout, obtained with the help of the makeLayout function. Next, create and start the application:

```
let form = new Form(Title="Hello world Eto Forms", Topmost=true, Size=Size(640, 480))
form.Content <- layout
form.Show()
app.Run(form)
```

WATCH THE APPLICATION GROW

If your `Eto Forms` platform supports F# Interactive, you can see the form growing interactively using `fsi.exe`. Usually, applications first configure forms and controls and then call `Show` to present the user with a form that's ready to use. It's also useful to set the properties `TopMost=true` and `Visible=true`. The properties of a form can also be set after the form is visible, allowing you to see the effects of each operation on it. F# Interactive offers the unique opportunity to watch the form growing interactively; you can, for instance, build the interface of the simple web browser by showing the form immediately and then proceed to add controls and set their properties. Thus, you can experiment with the various properties of controls and see how they affect the interface.

What have you learned by developing this application? It's clear that building interfaces based on controls requires a significant amount of code as you configure controls by setting their properties. The form's layout is also set by defining properties of controls, as you did in the browser. Moreover, an ever-increasing number of controls are available, and each provides a large number of properties. F# syntax supports this process by letting you set initial values for control properties within the call to the control constructor and letting you add functions as event handlers, leading to very compact programs that are easier to understand.

Visual designers are graphical applications that allow you to design interfaces using a visual metaphor. Controls are dragged and dropped onto forms and then configured through a property window; the visual designer generates the code required to obtain the designed layout. However, when you use a cross-platform framework such as `Eto Forms`, you are aware that different platforms render controls differently, and you are looking more for functionality than for appearance. In this case, the logical layouts offered by layout managers are more than enough to build graphical interfaces. If you are looking to create graphical UIs with a specific platform in mind, you can use the framework that usually is accessible through the relevant .NET library.

Leverage on existing designers and .NET interoperability suits many graphical-application scenarios, allowing programmers to exploit the F# data-processing expressivity and power to fuel the UI created using productivity tools. You can easily define simple interfaces with F# code, however, and the rest of this chapter will show you how to do so. You will now focus on the more important part of designing graphical applications: drawing and control development.

Drawing Applications

So far, you've developed graphical applications based on the composition of predeveloped graphical controls, but what do you do if no graphical control suits your needs? You need to learn how to draw using the drawing primitives provided by the graphical system.

To understand how drawing works, you need to review the model behind the rendering process of a graphical application. You know already that the event-driven programming paradigm best suits graphical applications; so far, you've associated event handlers with user actions, but events are used by the graphical system as a general mechanism to communicate with the graphical application.

An application uses resources provided by the graphical system, and these resources are mostly windows. A *window* is a rectangular area on the screen, not necessarily a top-level window with buttons, a title bar, and all the amenities you usually associate with it. Windows can be nested, and they are the unit of traditional windowing systems. Windows can contain other windows, and the windowing system is responsible for ensuring that events are routed to the callbacks registered for handling the events for each window.

Windows are allowed to draw in their own client areas, and the drawing is performed through the *device context*, an object provided by the graphical system and used to perform the *graphic primitives* to draw the content. The graphic primitives issued to the graphics system aren't retained by it; therefore, when the window is covered for some reason, the portion that becomes hidden must be repainted when it's uncovered. Because the information required to redraw the hidden portion is held by the application owning the window, the graphical system sends a *paint* message to the window.

DRAWING WITH ETO FORMS

Since Eto Forms is a library targeting multiple presentation systems, the traditional approach where almost every control of the library can override the Paint message handling is not feasible. For this reason, the library provides a special control designed to allow drawing, as it is custom in the various frameworks. To perform drawing you either make an instance or inherit from the class Drawable.

To better understand the drawing model, consider a simple graphical application that shows how to draw a curved line using the Bézier curve and canonical splines, given four control points. First, open the namespaces of the Eto Forms library, the model you developed, EtoUtils, and create the application object:

```
open Eto
open Eto.Forms
open Eto.Drawing
open EtoUtils

let app = new Application()
```

Next, create the form and the drawable control used for drawing, then define the initial values of the control points. The movingPoint variable keeps track of the point the user is dragging to adjust the curve:

```
let form = new Form(Title="Curves", Topmost=true, Size=Size(640, 480))
let cpt = [|PointF(20.f, 60.f); PointF(40.f, 50.f); PointF(130.f, 60.f); PointF(200.f, 200.f)|]
let mutable movingPoint = -1
let draw = new Drawable()
```

Let's introduce three menus to configure the application. They're used to check features to be drawn:

```
let menuBezier = new CheckMenuItem(Text="Show &Beziér",Checked=true)
let menuCanonical = new CheckMenuItem(Text="Show &Canonical spline")
let menuControlPoints = new CheckMenuItem(Text="Show control &points")
```

Use a scrollbar to define different values for the tension parameter of the canonical spline curve:

```
let tension = new Slider(Orientation=SliderOrientation.Vertical,
                         MinValue=0,MaxValue=10,TickFrequency=1,Visible=false)
```

Control points are drawn if required, and an ellipse is used to mark each of them. The function receives the device context in the form of a Graphics object; draw the ellipse by invoking the DrawEllipse primitive on it. Use a Pen to draw the ellipse—in this case, a red pen:

```
let drawPoint (g : Graphics) (p : PointF) =
    g.DrawEllipse(Pens.Red, p.X - 2.f, p.Y - 2.f, 4.f, 4.f)
```

BRUSHES AND PENS

Eto Forms, like many other libraries, uses two kinds of objects to define colored primitives: brushes and pens. A *brush* is used to fill an area with a given pattern. A number of different patterns are available; solid colors are provided by the SolidBrush class, gradients are provided by LinearGradientBrush, and textured gradients are provided by TextureBrush. The Brushes class provides a number of static brush objects describing solid colors.

Pens represent lines. The line drawn by a pen has a filling (with a given color) and also a width and different styles (dashed or not, with different caps at the beginning and at the end). The Pens class provides a number of static pen objects with the basic solid colors.

Both pen and brush objects utilize resources of the graphical system; it's important to dispose of them as soon as they aren't required anymore. A use binding or the using function discussed in Chapters 4 and 8 help ensure that you don't forget to call the Dispose method, which all these objects provide from the IDisposable interface, method that otherwise should be called explicitly.

You're now ready to define the function responsible for drawing in your window. You can't assume anything about the current state of the window; thus, the paint function always draws the visible primitives[1] depending on the state of menu entries:

```
let paint (g : Graphics) =
    if (menuBezier.Checked) then
        g.DrawLine(Pens.Red, cpt.[0], cpt.[1])
        g.DrawLine(Pens.Red, cpt.[2], cpt.[3])
        let path = new GraphicsPath()
        path.AddBezier(cpt.[0], cpt.[1], cpt.[2], cpt.[3])
        g.DrawPath(Pens.Black, path)
    if (menuCanonical.Checked) then
        let path = new GraphicsPath()
        path.AddCurve(cpt, single tension.Value)
        g.DrawPath(Pens.Blue, path)
    if (menuControlPoints.Checked) then
        for i = 0 to cpt.Length - 1 do

            drawPoint g cpt.[i]
```

Figure 15-2 shows the result of drawing all the elements. The Bézier curve, widely used in image-processing and vector applications, uses the four control points to define the start and end points of the curve and the two segments tangent to the curve at its ends. The cubic parametric curve is calculated from these points and produces the lines shown. The canonical spline, on the other hand, is a curve that traverses all the control points; the tension parameter controls how curvy the curve is.

---

[1]If primitives fall out of the area allowed for drawing, they're clipped in part or entirely.

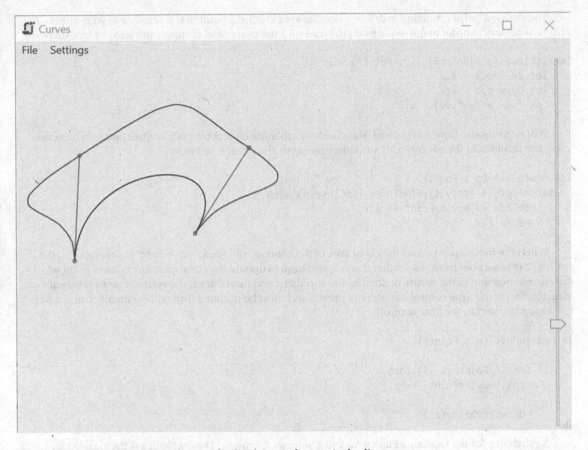

Figure 15-2. *The curve editor showing both Bézier and canonical spline curves*

You now want to allow users to move control points by dragging and dropping. You're interested in mouse events—in particular, when the mouse button is pressed, when it moves, and when the button is released. Thanks to the well-defined model for rendering the application, you can update the state of your variables and ask the graphical system to issue a paint message that causes the window to receive the message and update the current frame.

BACKGROUND PAINTING

In the Curves application, you draw assuming that the window is clean—but who is responsible for clearing the previous drawing in the window? Some frameworks have a special event for background painting where the default implementation clears the area with the color returned by the BackgroundColor property. Eto Forms offers only the ability to handle the paint event, leaving to the platform implementation to decide how to efficiently handle the background filling. However, when the function responsible for painting draws in the area entirely, painting the background could be useless and even problematic: the quick repaint may flicker because the eye can perceive both the background as clear and then the drawing of the current frame. In this case. the only workaround is to use an offscreen bitmap where the drawing is performed, and then only draw the resulting image.

You define a helper function to define a circular area around a point that is sensible to your interaction. This is necessary in order to not require that the user pick the exact pixel corresponding to the control point:

```
let isClose (p : PointF) (l : PointF) =
    let dx = p.X - l.X
    let dy = p.Y - l.Y
    (dx * dx + dy * dy) < 6.f
```

When the mouse button is pressed, you check whether the click is over any control point. In this case, you store its index in the movingPoint variable; otherwise, the event is ignored:

```
let mouseDown (p : PointF) =
  match cpt |> Array.tryFindIndex (isClose p) with
  | Some idx -> movingPoint <- idx
  | None -> ()
```

When the mouse moves over the client area of the window, the mouse move event is generated. If the movingPoint member has a value other than −1, you have to update the corresponding control point with the current position of the mouse defined by the variable p and then inform the system that the current visualization of the draw control has become invalid and must be updated (this will eventually cause a paint message to be sent to the draw control):

```
let mouseMove (p : PointF) =

    if (movingPoint <> -1) then
        cpt.[movingPoint] <- p

    draw.Invalidate()
```

Next, define for the window a File menu and a Settings submenu. The first features the classic Exit option, and the second shows the three checked menu items that control what the paint method should draw. You define menus by composing objects that correspond to the various menu entries. You also define the event handlers associated with each menu item. When Exit is clicked, the form is disposed. In all the other cases, you rely on the menu item's ability to change its checked state, and you invalidate the form content to force the redraw of the window:

```
let updatemenu _ = draw.Invalidate()

let menu = new MenuBar()
let menuFile = SubMenu ("&File", [ ActionMenuItem("E&xit").WithAction(fun _ -> app.Quit()) ])
|> makeMenu
let menuSettings =
  SubMenu
    ("&Settings",
     [
       Item(menuBezier).WithAction(updatemenu)
       Item(menuCanonical).WithAction(fun _ -> draw.Invalidate(); tension.Visible <-
       menuCanonical.Checked)
```

```
        Item(menuControlPoints).WithAction(updatemenu)
    ]) |> makeMenu

[ menuFile; menuSettings ] |> List.iter(fun m -> menu.Items.Add(m))

form.Menu <- menu
```

You're now ready to use the functions you defined to configure the controls. Set up the scrollbar and register the controls in the form, as well as the event handlers for the various events. Finally, start the application's event loop and play with it:

```
tension.ValueChanged.Add(fun _ -> draw.Invalidate())

draw.Paint.Add(fun e -> paint e.Graphics)
draw.MouseDown.Add(fun e -> mouseDown(e.Location))
draw.MouseMove.Add(fun e -> mouseMove(e.Location))
draw.MouseUp.Add(fun e -> movingPoint <- -1)

let l = Tbl [ StretchedRow[ StretchedEl(draw); El(tension) ] ] |> makeLayout

form.Content <- l
form.Show()

app.Run(form)
```

The Paint event on the draw control is responsible for ensuring that whenever the display needs to be updated, the graphics context is extracted from the event's argument and passed to our paint function.

Creating a Mandelbrot Viewer

Fractals are one of the diamonds of mathematics. They show the beauty of mathematical structures visually, which allows nonexperts to see something that is often hidden by formulas that few really appreciate. The Mandelbrot set is one of the most famous fractals. This section will show how to develop an application to browse this set. The result is shown in Figure 15-3.

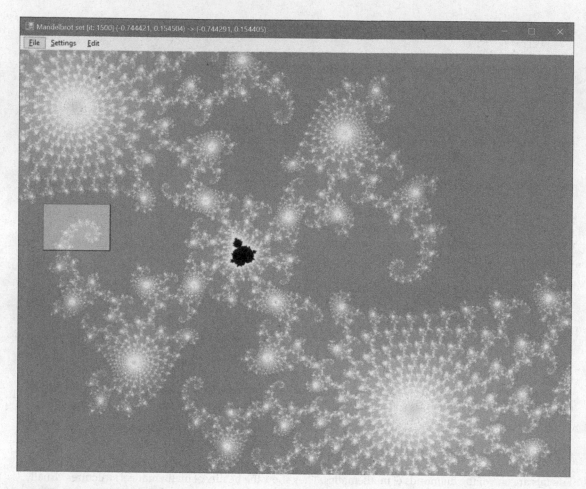

Figure 15-3. The Mandelbrot viewer

This application adopts the *delegation* programming style, subscribing to events rather than using inheritance to override the behavior of a component. This allows you to develop the application interactively using `fsi.exe`. This is a good example of how effectively you can use F# to develop an application interactively while retaining the performance of a compiled language, which is extremely important in such CPU-intensive tasks as computing the points of the Mandelbrot set.

Computing Mandelbrot

First, you need to be familiar with the math required to generate the Mandelbrot set. The set is defined over the set of complex numbers, which is an extension of the real numbers, allowing the computation of square roots over negative numbers. A complex number has the following form, where a and b are real numbers and i is the imaginary unit (by definition, $i^2 = -1$):

```
c = a + bi
```

Using standard algebraic calculations, you can define the sum and product of these numbers:

```
c1 + c2 = (a1 + a2) + (b1 + b2) i
c1 • c2 = (a1 • a2 - b1 • b2) + (a1 • b2 + a2 • b1) i
```

Because you have two components in the definition of the number, you can graphically represent complex numbers using a plane.

This Mandelbrot viewer shows a portion of the complex plane in which each point in the plane is colored according to a relation that defines the Mandelbrot set. The relation is based on the iterative definition seen here:

$$M(c) = \begin{cases} z_0 = c \\ z_{i+1} = z_i^2 + c \end{cases}$$

A complex number belongs to the Mandelbrot set if z^n converges for n. You can test each number c in the complex plane and decide whether the number belongs to the Mandelbrot set. Because it's not practical to perform an infinite computation to test each number of the complex plane, there is an approximation of the test based on a theorem that says if the distance of z^i from the origin passes 2, then the sequence will diverge, and the corresponding z^0 won't belong to the set.

The code to compute membership of the Mandelbrot set is:

```
open System.Numerics

let sqrMod (x : Complex) = x.Real * x.Real + x.Imaginary * x.Imaginary

let rec mandel maxit (z : Complex) (c : Complex) count =
    if (sqrMod(z) < 4.0) && (count < maxit) then
        mandel maxit ((z * z) + c) c (count + 1)

    else count
```

You can create a simple visual representation of the Mandelbrot set by coloring all the points belonging to the set. In this way, you obtain the black portion of Figure 15-3. How can you obtain the richness of color? The trick is to color points depending on how fast the sequence reaches the distance of 2 from the origin. You use 250 colors and map the [0, maxit] interval to the [0, 250] discrete color interval.

Setting Colors

In order for the Mandelbrot viewer application to have appealing coloring, you need to produce some form of continuity in the color variation in the chosen range. You use an array of colors to store these values, but you need a procedure to fill this array so that colors change continuously.

Colors in the Red Green Blue (RGB) space used in graphics libraries are known to define a color space that isn't perceived as continuous by human vision. A color space known to be more effective in this respect is the Hue Saturation Value (HSV), in which a color is defined in terms of hue, color saturation, and the value of luminance (see Figure 15-4). This model was inspired by the method used by painters to create colors in oil painting.

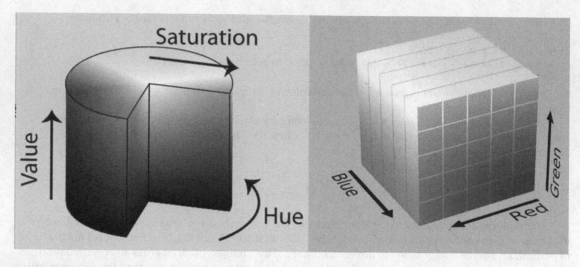

Figure 15-4. *The HSV (left) and RGB (right) color space representations*

Figure 15-4 shows a typical geometric representation of the two color spaces. In the RGB color model, the three axes represent the three base colors varying from black to the full color; in the HSV space, the angle is used to indicate the hue, the distance from the axis of the cylinder represents the saturation, and the value corresponds to the height of the point inside the cylinder.

You can define a conversion from RGB color space to HSV, and vice versa. Listing 15-1 shows the F# functions performing the conversions between the two models. These functions assume the three components R, G, and B are in the interval [0, 1] rather than integers between 0 and 255.

Listing 15-1. Conversion from RGB to HSV, and vice versa

```
let RGBtoHSV (r, g, b) =

    let (m : float) = min r (min g b)
    let (M : float) = max r (max g b)
    let delta = M - m
    let posh (h : float) = if h < 0.0 then h + 360.0 else h
    let deltaf (f : float) (s : float) = (f - s) / delta
    if M = 0.0 then (-1.0, 0.0, M) else
        let s = (M - m) / M
        if r = M then (posh(60.0 * (deltaf g b)), s, M)
        elif g = M then (posh(60.0 * (2.0 + (deltaf b r))), s, M)
        else (posh(60.0 * (4.0 + (deltaf r g))), s, M)

let HSVtoRGB (h, s, v) =
    if s = 0.0 then (v, v, v) else
    let hs = h / 60.0
    let i = floor (hs)
    let f = hs - i
    let p = v * ( 1.0 - s )
    let q = v * ( 1.0 - s * f )
    let t = v * ( 1.0 - s * ( 1.0 - f ))
```

```
match int i with
    | 0 -> (v, t, p)
    | 1 -> (q, v, p)
    | 2 -> (p, v, t)
    | 3 -> (p, q, v)
    | 4 -> (t, p, v)

    | _ -> (v, p, q)
```

To let users choose the coloring of the set, create an array of 10 functions, given an integer between 0 and 250, for a corresponding color. The default color function is based on the HSV color model; it uses the input parameter to set the hue of the color, leaving the saturation and luminance at the maximum values. The other functions use the RGB color space, following directions in the color cube. You use the createPalette function to generate the color palette that is used while drawing fractal points; the palette mutable variable holds this palette. Listing 15-2 shows the code that deals with colors. The pickColor function is responsible for mapping the iteration it, at which the computation of the Mandelbrot set terminates given the maximum number of iterations allowed, maxit.

Listing 15-2. Color-palette definition

```
let makeColor (r, g, b) =
    let f x = int32(x * 255.0)
    Color.FromArgb(f(r), f(g), f(b))

let defaultColor i = makeColor(HSVtoRGB(360.0 * (float i / 250.0), 1.0, 1.0))

let coloring =
    [|
        defaultColor;
        (fun i -> Color.FromArgb(i, i, i));
        (fun i -> Color.FromArgb(i, 0, 0));
        (fun i -> Color.FromArgb(0, i, 0));
        (fun i -> Color.FromArgb(0, 0, i));
        (fun i -> Color.FromArgb(i, i, 0));
        (fun i -> Color.FromArgb(i, 250 - i, 0));
        (fun i -> Color.FromArgb(250 - i, i, i));
        (fun i -> if i % 2 = 0 then Color.White else Color.Black);
        (fun i -> Color.FromArgb(250 - i, 250 - i, 250 - i))
    |]

let createPalette c =
    Array.init 253 (function
        | 250 -> Color.Black
        | 251 -> Color.White
        | 252 -> Color.LightGray
        | i ->   c i)

let mutable palette = createPalette coloring.[0]

let pickColor maxit it =
    palette.[int(250.0 * float it / float maxit)]
```

Creating the Visualization Application

You're now ready to implement the graphical application. The basic idea is to map a rectangle of the complex plane in the client area of your form. Each point of your window corresponds to a complex number and is colored according to the value computed by the mandel function.

A typical value for maxit is 150 for the initial rendering of the Mandelbrot set, although it should be incremented when zooming into the fractal. The total computation required to generate an entire image is significant; therefore, you can't rely on the main thread to perform the computation of the various points. It's important to recall that event handlers are invoked by the graphical interface's thread, and if this thread is used to perform heavy computations, the application windows won't respond to other events.

Introduce a thread responsible for performing the computations required by the Mandelbrot set so that the GUI thread can continue to handle events. (Chapter 11 discusses threads in more detail.) Use shared memory to communicate the results between the threads, using a bitmap image in memory that is referenced by the bitmap variable, which is updated by the thread performing the computation task and read by the GUI thread when the form must be painted. The bitmap is convenient, because you need a matrix of points to be colored, and the device context is designed to avoid pixel coloring being device independent (it doesn't provide a SetColor(x, y) operation). To avoid race conditions, use the lock function to guarantee exclusive access to the bitmap shared between the two threads. Chapter 11 looks at this in more detail. The thread responsible for the set computation executes the following function:

```
// t=top, l=left, r=right, b=bottom, bm=bitmap, p=pixel, w=width, h=height

let run filler (form : #Form) (bitmap : Bitmap) (tlx, tly) (brx, bry) =
    let dx = (brx - tlx) / float bmpw
    let dy = (tly - bry) / float bmph
    let maxit = iterations (tlx, tly) (brx, bry)
    let x = 0
    let y = 0
    let transform x y = new Complex(tlx + (float x)* dx, tly - (float y) * dy)
    app.AsyncInvoke(fun _ ->
      form.Title <- sprintf "Mandelbrot set [it: %d] (%f, %f) -> (%f, %f)"
      maxit tlx tly brx bry
    )
    filler maxit transform

    timer.Stop()
```

Use dx and dy variables to map the x and y coordinates of the bitmap into the complex plane. Then, invoke the filler function responsible for performing the calculation. There are different possible filling strategies with which to compute the colors of the set; the straightforward approach is left to right and top to bottom, implemented by the linearFill function:

```
let linearFill (bw : int) (bh : int) maxit map =

    for y = 0 to bh - 1 do
        for x = 0 to bw - 1 do
            let c = mandel maxit Complex.Zero (map x y) 0

            lock bitmap (fun () -> bitmap.SetPixel(x, y, pickColor maxit c))
```

Another typical filling strategy is to gradually refine the set by computing points in blocks and filling the blocks with the appropriate color; then, the missing points are computed by refining the block size. Using this strategy, you can provide a quick preview of the fractal without having to wait for the entire computation. The blockFill function implements this strategy:

```
let blockFill (bw : int) (bh : int) maxit map =
    let rec fillBlock first sz x y =
        if x < bw then
            let c = mandel maxit Complex.Zero (map x y) 0
            lock bitmap (fun () ->
                use g = new Graphics(bitmap)
                use b = new SolidBrush(pickColor maxit c)
                g.FillRectangle(b, single x, single y, single sz, single sz)
                )
            fillBlock first sz
                      (if first || ((y / sz) % 2 = 1) then x + sz
                                                       else x + 2 * sz) y
        elif y < bh then
            fillBlock first sz
                      (if first || ((y / sz) % 2 = 0) then 0 else sz) (y + sz)
        elif sz > 1 then
            fillBlock false (sz / 2) (sz / 2) 0

    fillBlock true 64 0 0
```

The variable fillFun is used to store the current filling function:

```
let mutable fillFun = blockFill
```

You clear the bitmap by obtaining a device context to the bitmap and clearing it. The global variable bitmap is used to access the image from the code; this is an effective choice to speed up the development of the application. This technique can be a problem from a software-engineering standpoint, however, because the program is less modular, and the mutable state isn't encapsulated:

```
let clearOffScreen (b : Bitmap) =

    use g = new Graphics(b)
    g.Clear(Brushes.White)

let mutable bitmap = new Bitmap(form.Width, form.Height, PixelFormat.Format32bppRgba)
let mutable bmpw = form.Width

let mutable bmph = form.Height
```

To refresh the application form while the fractal computation is ongoing, use a timer that triggers a refresh of the form every tenth of a second (the Interval property of the UITimer type is expressed in seconds). The paint function draws the bitmap that is updated by the worker thread:

```
let paint (g : Graphics) =

    lock bitmap (fun () -> g.DrawImage(bitmap, 0.f, 0.f))
    g.DrawRectangle(Pens.Black, rect)
    use bg = new SolidBrush(Color.FromArgb(0x80FFFFFF))
    g.FillRectangle(bg, rect)

let timer = new UITimer(Interval = 0.1)
timer.Elapsed.Add(fun _ -> draw.Invalidate())
```

```
let stopWorker () =
    if worker <> Thread.CurrentThread then
        worker.Abort()

        worker <- Thread.CurrentThread
```

The drawMandel function is responsible for starting the rendering process:

```
let drawMandel () =

    let bf = fillFun bmpw bmph
    stopWorker()
    timer.Start()
    worker <- new Thread(fun () -> run bf form bitmap tl br)
    worker.IsBackground <- true
    worker.Priority <- ThreadPriority.Lowest
    worker.Start()
```

Creating the Application Plumbing

Now that you've defined the architecture of the application, you can define the graphical aspects, the form, and the menus, as well as how users will interact with the application. The code is similar to the previous applications, as shown in Listing 15-3. Note two aspects: the rect variable contains the current selection, and it's drawn as a rectangle filled with transparent white. The application uses the clipboard to store and retrieve the coordinates of a particular fractal view or to save the current state of the drawn bitmap. When Ctrl+C is pressed, a small XML document similar to the following is saved to the clipboard:

```
<Mandel iter="1000">

  <topleft>
    <re>-7.47421339220139e-001</re>
    <im>1.64667039391667e-001</im>
  </topleft>
  <bottomright>
    <re>-7.47082959511805e-001</re>
    <im>1.64413254610417e-001</im>
  </bottomright>

</Mandel>
```

The saved parameters are the most compact representation of the current view, and they are loaded back if Ctrl+V is pressed; this way, you can save the state of navigation. You save and read text from the clipboard using the Clipboard class's Text property. When the Ctrl+Shift+C key sequence is pressed, the current bitmap is copied to the clipboard using the Image property; the bitmap can be pasted into any program capable of pasting images.

The selection rectangle is updated by the mouse event handlers. You obtain the zoom facility by setting the bounds of the complex plane defined by the variables tl and br.

Listing 15-3. Setup of the application form and event handling

```
let app = new Application()

// Creates the Form
let form = new Form(Title="Mandelbrot set", Size=Size(800, 600))
let draw = new Drawable()
let timer = new UITimer(Interval = 0.1)
timer.Elapsed.Add(fun _ -> draw.Invalidate())

let mutable worker = Thread.CurrentThread
let mutable bitmap = new Bitmap(form.Width, form.Height, PixelFormat.Format32bppRgba)
let mutable bmpw = form.Width
let mutable bmph = form.Height
let mutable rect = RectangleF.Empty
let mutable tl = (-3.0, 2.0)
let mutable br = (2.0, -2.0)
let clipboard = new Clipboard()

let mutable menuIterations = 150

let iterations (tlx, tly) (brx, bry) =
    menuIterations
let RGBtoHSV (r, g, b) = ...
let HSVtoRGB (h, s, v) = ...
let makeColor (r, g, b) = ...
let defaultColor i = ...
let coloring = ...
let createPalette c = ...
let mutable palette = createPalette coloring.[0]
let pickColor maxit it = ...
let sqrMod (x : Complex) = ...
let run filler (form : #Form) (bitmap : Bitmap) (tlx, tly) (brx, bry) = ...
let linearFill (bw : int) (bh : int) maxit map = ...
let blockFill (bw : int) (bh : int) maxit map = ...
let mutable fillFun = blockFill
let clearOffScreen (b : Bitmap) = ...
let paint (g : Graphics) = ...
let stopWorker () = ...
let drawMandel () = ...

let mutable startsel = PointF.Empty

let setCoord (tlx : float, tly : float) (brx : float, bry : float)  =
    let dx = (brx - tlx) / float bmpw
    let dy = (tly - bry) / float bmph
    let mapx x = tlx + float x * dx
    let mapy y = tly - float y * dy
    tl <- (mapx rect.Left, mapy rect.Top)
    br <- (mapx rect.Right, mapy rect.Bottom)
```

```
let ensureAspectRatio (tlx : float, tly : float) (brx : float, bry : float) =
    let ratio = (float bmpw / float bmph)
    let w, h = abs(brx - tlx), abs(tly - bry)
    if ratio * h > w then
        br <- (tlx + h * ratio, bry)
    else
        br <- (brx, tly - w / ratio)

let updateView () =
    if rect <> RectangleF.Empty then setCoord tl br
    ensureAspectRatio tl br
    rect <- RectangleF.Empty
    stopWorker()
    clearOffScreen bitmap
    drawMandel()

let click (arg : MouseEventArgs) =
    if rect.Contains(arg.Location) then
        updateView()
    else
        draw.Invalidate()
        rect <- RectangleF.Empty
        startsel <- arg.Location

let mouseMove (arg : MouseEventArgs) =
    if arg.Buttons = MouseButtons.Primary then
        let tlx = min startsel.X arg.Location.X
        let tly = min startsel.Y arg.Location.Y
        let brx = max startsel.X arg.Location.X
        let bry = max startsel.Y arg.Location.Y
        rect <- new RectangleF(tlx, tly, brx - tlx, bry - tly)
        draw.Invalidate()

let resize () =
    if bmpw <> form.ClientSize.Width ||
       bmph <> form.ClientSize.Height then
         stopWorker()
         rect <- new RectangleF(SizeF(single form.ClientSize.Width, single form.ClientSize.
         Height))
         bitmap <- new Bitmap(form.ClientSize.Width, form.ClientSize.Height, PixelFormat.
         Format32bppRgba)
         bmpw <- form.ClientSize.Width
         bmph <- form.ClientSize.Height

         updateView()

let zoom amount (tlx, tly) (brx, bry) =
    let w, h = abs(brx - tlx), abs(tly - bry)
    let nw, nh = amount * w, amount * h
    tl <- (tlx + (w - nw) / 2., tly - (h - nh) / 2.)
    br <- (brx - (w - nw) / 2., bry + (h - nh) / 2.)
    rect <- RectangleF.Empty
    updateView()
```

```
let selectDropDownItem (l : ToolStripMenuItem) (o : ToolStripMenuItem) =
    for el in l.DropDownItems do
        let item = (el :?> ToolStripMenuItem)
        item.Checked <- (o = item)

let setFillMode (p : ToolStripMenuItem) (m : ToolStripMenuItem) filler _ =
    if (not m.Checked) then
        selectDropDownItem p m
        fillFun <- filler
        drawMandel()

let setupMenu () =
  let m = new MenuBar()
  let setFillMode filler =
    fillFun <- filler
    drawMandel()

  let itchg = fun (m:MenuItem) ->
    menuIterations <- System.Int32.Parse(m.Text)
    stopWorker()
    drawMandel()

  let setPalette idx =
    palette <- createPalette coloring.[idx]
    stopWorker()
    drawMandel()

  let f = SubMenu ("&File", [ MenuItem "E&xit" |> action (fun _ -> app.Quit()) ])

  let c =
    SubMenu
      ("&Settings",
        [
          SubMenu
            ("Color Scheme",
              [
                RadioMenuItem("colscheme", "HSL Color") |> check |> action (fun _ ->
                setPalette 0)
                RadioMenuItem("colscheme", "Gray") |> action (fun _ -> setPalette 1)
                RadioMenuItem("colscheme", "Red")  |> action (fun _ -> setPalette 2)
                RadioMenuItem("colscheme", "Green") |> action(fun _ -> setPalette 3)
              ])
          SubMenu
            ("Iterations",
              [
                RadioMenuItem ("iter", "150")  |> check |> action itchg
                RadioMenuItem ("iter", "250")  |> action itchg
                RadioMenuItem ("iter", "500")  |> action itchg
                RadioMenuItem ("iter", "1000") |> action itchg
              ])
```

```
        SubMenu
          ("Fill mode",
           [
             RadioMenuItem ("fillmode", "Line")  |> action (fun _ -> setFillMode
             linearFill)
             RadioMenuItem ("fillmode", "Block") |> check |> action (fun _ -> setFillMode
             blockFill)
           ])
      ])

  let copyf () =
      let maxit = (iterations tl br)
      let tlx, tly = tl
      let brx, bry = br
      clipboard.Text <- sprintf "<Mandel iter=\"%d\"><topleft><re>%.14e</re><im>%.14e</im>
      </topleft><bottomright><re>%.14e</re><im>%.14e</im></bottomright></Mandel>"
      maxit tlx tly brx bry

  let pastef () =
      if clipboard.Text.StartsWith("<Mandel") then
        let doc = new XmlDocument()
        try
          doc.LoadXml(clipboard.Text)
          menuIterations <-
              int (doc.SelectSingleNode("/Mandel").Attributes.["iter"].Value)
          tl <- (float (doc.SelectSingleNode("//topleft/re").InnerText),
                 float (doc.SelectSingleNode("//topleft/im").InnerText))
          br <- (float (doc.SelectSingleNode("//bottomright/re").InnerText),
                 float (doc.SelectSingleNode("//bottomright/im").InnerText))
          rect <- RectangleF.Empty
          updateView()
        with _ -> ()

  let e =
    SubMenu
      ("&Edit",
       [
         MenuItem "&Copy"  |> action (fun _ -> copyf()) |> shortcut (Keys.Control |||
         Keys.C)
         MenuItem "&Paste" |> action (fun _ -> pastef()) |> shortcut (Keys.Control |||
         Keys.V)
         MenuItem "Copy &bitmap"  |> action (fun _ -> lock bitmap (fun _ -> clipboard.Image
         <- bitmap)) |> shortcut (Keys.Control ||| Keys.Shift ||| Keys.C)
         MenuItem "Zoom &In"  |> action (fun _ -> zoom 0.9 tl br) |> shortcut (Keys.Control
         ||| Keys.T)
         MenuItem "Zoom &Out"  |> action (fun _ -> zoom 1.25 tl br) |> shortcut (Keys.
         Control ||| Keys.W)
       ])
  [f; c; e ] |> List.iter (fun i -> m.Items.Add(i |> mkmenu))
  m
```

```
clearOffScreen bitmap
form.Menu <- setupMenu()
draw.Paint.Add(fun arg -> paint arg.Graphics)
draw.MouseDown.Add(click)
draw.MouseMove.Add(mouseMove)
form.Content <- draw
form.SizeChanged.Add(fun _ -> resize())

app.RunIteration()

drawMandel()

[<System.STAThread>]

do app.Run(form)
```

Decoration on the app.Run invocation with the STAThread attribute is needed only on Windows and is used by the Windows Forms presentation layer. Without this annotation, the clipboard would not work; however, the annotation itself is passive and is ignored on other platforms. As already noted, the plumbing code is dominated by setting up menus and configuring the application form; the rest contains the event handlers that are registered with the various controls.

PERFORMANCE CONSIDERATIONS: IMMEDIATE VERSUS RETENTION GRAPHICS

As you learned in this chapter, Eto Forms is a library that abstracts UI notions across several platforms. Even though the goal is to get the same behavior on all the platforms, the projection of the library on a specific one may introduce subtle differences or even significant differences. You can check for yourself using the Mandelbrot example we just discussed on Windows. Microsoft Windows supports two main frameworks for UI programming: Windows Forms (WinForms) and Windows Presentation Foundation (WPF). The former takes a traditional immediate mode for graphics, meaning that whenever you draw something using the graphics context, it is sent to the frame buffer (the video memory of your system) immediately; the latter retains all the graphics primitives organized in a visual tree, and it's up to the system to decide when changes to this structure must trigger an update of the display.

If you try to switch between WPF and WinForms presentation systems on a Windows computer, you can observe how the memory consumption is very different for the two. Eto Forms tends to implement an immediate mode style of API since it's the most used approach. Thus, on WinForms the application uses far fewer resources, especially in memory usage, than does its WPF counterpart. The reason for this is that retention graphics is memory hungry, and Eto has to map its immediate-mode approach to a retention-based system, leading to additional overheads. However, the application runs smoothly using both presentation systems without changing a line of code.

Writing Your Own Controls

The Curves example from the previous section draws inside an instance of Drawable by handling events. This is a rare way to draw things in graphical applications, because the resulting code is scarcely reusable.

It is possible to create new controls in Eto Forms that specialize in the Drawable class. If delegation is used to handle events generated from controls, inheritance and method overriding are the tools used to handle them in controls.

Developing a Custom Control

To make this discussion concrete, consider a control that implements a simple button.

You start your control by inheriting from the Drawable class:

```
namespace ExpertFSharp4.UserControls

open System
open System.ComponentModel
open Eto
open Eto.Forms
open Eto.Drawing

type OwnerDrawButton() =
  inherit Drawable()
```

You then define the state of the control in terms of the class's fields:

```
    let mutable text = ""
    let mutable pressed = false
    let clickevt = new Event<System.EventArgs>()
```

The text field contains the button's label. As with the movingPoint variable in the Curves example, the pressed field is responsible for remembering whether the button is currently pressed, allowing the paint handler to behave appropriately. To inform the users of the class that a click on the button has occurred, we use the clickevt field, which represents a queue of listeners for the event and a trigger function to perform the notification. You override the OnPaint method to handle the paint event. You allocate the pens and the brush required to draw and then invert the role of the border colors in order to achieve the raised effect when the button isn't pressed and the depressed look otherwise. You also measure the size of the label string, because you're interested in drawing the string in the center of the button. You can then draw the lines on the borders, playing with colors to obtain a 3D effect. You obtain lighter and darker versions of the base color by using Eto Forms support for HSL (a model closer to the HSV you used in the Mandelbrot example) to increase or decrease the luminance. Conversion between RGB and HSL color models is made by the framework. The pens and brushes are disposed of at the end of the function. See here:

```
override x.OnPaint (e : PaintEventArgs) =

  let changeLuminance factor c =
    let mutable hc = ColorHSL(c)
    hc.L <- hc.L * factor
    hc.ToColor()

  let lighter = changeLuminance 1.1f

  let darker = changeLuminance (1.f / 1.1f)
```

```
let g = e.Graphics
let bc = Colors.LightGrey
use pll = new Pen(bc |> lighter |> lighter)
use pl = new Pen(bc |> lighter)
use pd = new Pen(bc |> darker)
use pdd = new Pen(bc |> darker |> darker)
use bfg = new SolidBrush(Colors.Black)
use bbg = new SolidBrush(bc)
let f = new Font(SystemFont.Default)
let szf = g.MeasureString(f, text)
let off = if pressed then 1.0f else 0.0f
let spt = PointF((float32(x.Width) - szf.Width) / 2.0f + off,
                 (float32(x.Height) - szf.Height) / 2.0f + off)
let ptt, pt, pb, pbb =
                    if pressed then pdd, pd, pll, pl
                    else pl, pll, pd, pdd

g.Clear(bbg)
g.DrawLine(ptt, 0.f, 0.f, single(x.Width - 1), 0.f)
g.DrawLine(ptt, 0.f, 0.f, 0.f, single(x.Height - 1))
g.DrawLine(pt, 1.f, 1.f, single(x.Width - 2), 1.f)
g.DrawLine(pt, 1.f, 1.f, 1.f, single(x.Height - 2))
g.DrawLine(pbb, 0.f, single(x.Height - 1), single(x.Width - 1), single(x.Height - 1))
g.DrawLine(pbb, single(x.Width - 1), 0.f, single(x.Width - 1), single(x.Height - 1))
g.DrawLine(pb, 1.f, single(x.Height - 2), single(x.Width - 2), single(x.Height - 2))
g.DrawLine(pb, single(x.Width - 2), 1.f, x.Width - 2 |> single, x.Height - 2 |> single)

g.DrawText(f, bfg, spt, text)
```

Now that you've defined the drawing procedure, you can define the behavior of the control by handling mouse events. You restrict the implementation to mouse events, although a key event handler should be provided in order to react to a press of the Enter key:

```
override x.OnMouseUp (e : MouseEventArgs) =
  pressed <- false
  clickevt.Trigger(new System.EventArgs())
  x.Invalidate()

override x.OnMouseDown (e : MouseEventArgs) =
  pressed <- true

  x.Invalidate()
```

The OnMouseDown event sets the pressed member and asks the control to repaint by invalidating its content. When the mouse is released, the OnMouseUp is called, and you reset the flag, ask for repaint, and then trigger the Click event.

Controls are usually configured through the assignment of properties. Custom attributes allow the passive annotation of the program. This annotation is usable by external tools to properly handle the various elements of a control. The namespace System.ComponentModel includes attributes like the type Category and the type Browsable, which can be used to annotate properties of a control. A visual designer can then browse the control metadata by using reflection and rely on these extra annotations so as to produce the appropriate input properties for configuring it. Visual Studio uses these attributes in the visual designer for

Windows Forms to control the property grid that the user uses for configuring a control that is inserted into the visual designer. As an example, you define the Text property, which exposes the button's label to users of the control:

```
[<Category("Behavior")>]
[<Browsable(true)>]
member x.Text
  with get() = text

  and  set(t : string) = text <- t; x.Invalidate()
```

You also publish the clickevt as the Click event:

```
member x.Click = clickevt.Publish
```

You're now ready to test your new control by writing a few lines of F# code as follows:

```
let app = new Application()
let form = new Form(Title="Hello world Eto Forms", Topmost=true, Size=Size(640, 480))
let c = new OwnerDrawButton(Text="Hello Button")
let p = new Panel()
p.Content <- c
p.Padding <- Padding(10)
form.Content <- p
c.Click.Add(fun _ -> MessageBox.Show("Clicked!") |> ignore)

form.Show()
```

Compile your control as a separate library and reference it from an Eto Forms project. Open the namespace of the control, then simply instantiate it and add it to the appropriate container.

Custom controls are seen as black-box objects by the applications that host them. Several hacks are possible to handle the behavior of controls from outside (subclassing is often used on Windows), but none of them are really satisfactory.

Anatomy of a Control

As illustrated by the OwnerDrawButton control example, the structure of a graphic control tends to assume the form of a finite state automaton. Events received by the control make the automaton change its internal state, usually causing an update of its actual display.

A well-known model that describes this structure is the Model-View-Controller design pattern. As shown in Figure 15-5, the model organizes a graphical element (either an application or a single control) into three parts: the model, the view, and the controller.

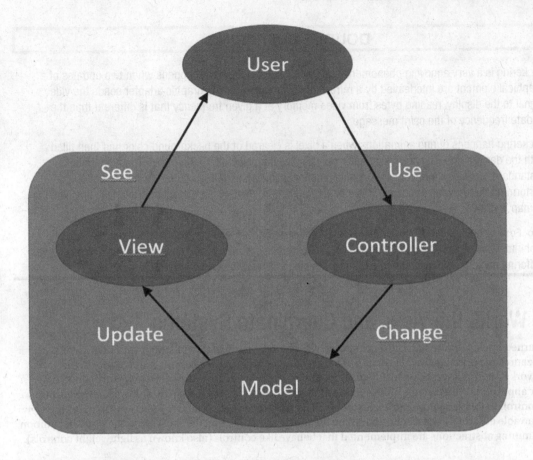

Figure 15-5. *The Model-View-Controller design pattern*

The model constitutes the internal representation of the information displayed by the control. A word processor, for instance, stores a document in memory as part of the model, even though the entire text doesn't fit the current visible area. In your simple button, the model is defined by the pressed and text values.

When the model changes, the view must be updated, and a rendering of the information kept in memory should be performed. Usually, the paint method corresponds to the view portion of the control. Event handlers triggered by the user form the controller of the control. The controller defines how these elements affect the model.

The Model-View-Controller pattern isn't the only model developed to describe graphical interfaces. It captures the intrinsic nature of the problem, however, providing a good framework for classifying the elements of an interface or a control. The rest of this chapter will refer to this pattern to indicate the various elements of the applications you will learn how to develop.

DOUBLE BUFFERING

Flickering is a very annoying phenomenon of graphical applications. It happens when two updates of a graphical element are interleaved by a refresh of its background. The graphic adapter sends the video signal to the display, reading bytes from video memory at a given frequency that is different than the update frequency of the paint message.

Flickering happens during animations when a pixel is cleared of the background color and then filled with the desired one. The graphic adapter may display the pixel before the update, making it blink. A standard technique for avoiding this phenomenon is known as *double buffering*: it consists of performing the drawing primitives into a bitmap offscreen; then, when the entire drawing is finished, the bitmap is drawn.

`Eto Forms` handles double buffering in a platform-specific way, and you should not experience the problem while updating your drawing to create animations. However, you can always implement double buffering on your own by creating a bitmap, drawing in it, and then drawing it to screen.

The World, the View, and Coordinate Systems

You learned how to draw using `Eto Forms`, which is useful if you want to implement your own data visualization in a portable way. The `Drawable` class, used for drawing, represents a singularity in the framework as it disallows the inclusion of additional controls inside it. Therefore, when you need to draw in your application, you can rely only on basic drawing primitives, thus losing the ability to add controls to your control. In this section, some useful tools will be introduced with which to effectively manage the view of a drawable control by consistently handling the process of projecting the model into the view. In addition, programming abstractions are implemented that behave like controls (also known as lightweight controls).

Drawing an Analog Clock

So far you have drawn bitmaps or simple primitives, where basic considerations about the coordinates of the points involved were enough. Now, the interest is in drawing a simple analog clock like the one in Figure 15-6. To simplify the implementation, the quadrant is made by 12 ticks that are segments of lines passing from the center and starting at radius r_1 and ending at r_2. For simplicity, the clock is assumed to be contained in a square 100 pixel wide located in the top-left corner of our control.

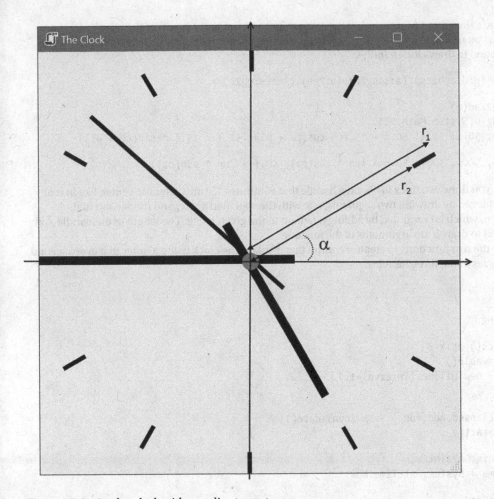

Figure 15-6. *Analog clock with coordinates system*

Using basic trigonometry, you can easily compute the segment endings, as shown by the drawQuadrant function:

```
let deg2rad a =
  single(System.Math.PI) * (a - 90.f) / 180.f

let drawQuadrant (g:Graphics) =
  for i = 1 to 12 do
    let a = single(i - 1) * 30.f |> deg2rad

    g.DrawLine(Pens.Black, 50.f + 40.f * cos(a), 50.f + 40.f * sin(a), 50.f + 50.f * cos(a),
    50.f + 50.f * sin(a))
```

You compute sin and cos functions as if the circle were centered in the origin of the coordinate system, and then you translate it by (50, 50), which is the center of the circle. Similarly, you can define the drawHandle function to draw clock handles:

```
let drawHandle (g:Graphics) (a:single) (p:Pen) (len:single) =

  let ca = deg2rad(a)
  let pi = single(System.Math.PI)
  g.DrawLine(p, 50.f, 50.f, 50.f + 15.f * cos(ca + pi), 50.f + 15.f * sin(ca + pi))

  g.DrawLine(p, 50.f, 50.f, 50.f + len * cos(ca), 50.f + len * sin(ca))
```

In this case, you draw two lines to obtain a handle that continues 15 units after the center, like in real clocks. This is achieved by drawing two segments, one with the specified angle, and the second in the opposite direction, which is computed by adding π radiant to the given angle. The length of the handle and the pen to be used to draw it are arguments of the function.

You can use the two functions to create a control that displays the clock using a timer that every second computes the angles of the three handles:

```
open Eto
open Eto.Forms
open Eto.Drawing

type AnalogClock() as x =
    inherit Drawable()
    let timer = new UITimer(Interval=1.)

    do
        timer.Elapsed.Add(fun _ -> x.Invalidate())
        timer.Start()

    override this.OnPaint e =
        let time = System.DateTime.Now

        let deg2rad = ...
        let drawQuadrant (g:Graphics) = ...
        let drawHandle (g:Graphics) (p:Pen) (len:single) (a:single)= ...

        let g = e.Graphics
        drawQuadrant g
        use p = new Pen(Colors.Black)
        p.Thickness <- 1.f
        drawHandle g p 50.f (single(time.Second) * 6.f)
        p.Thickness <- 2.f
        drawHandle g p 50.f (single(time.Minute) * 6.f)
        drawHandle g p 30.f (single(time.Hour) * 30.f)
        g.FillEllipse(Brushes.Red, 48.f, 48.f, 4.f, 4.f)

let app = new Application()
let form = new Form(Title="The Clock", Topmost=true, Size=Size(640, 480))
let my = new AnalogClock()
form.Content <- my

form.Show()
```

When you need to draw geometrical figures, you may have to resort to trigonometry and other geometrical techniques. There are operations that have been repeated in the drawing, like moving the center of the clock from (0, 0) to (50, 50).

A powerful technique commonly used in vector graphics is to transform the coordinate system used for drawing primitives. The technique used for implementing this transformation, referred to as *homogenous coordinates*, is based on matrix multiplication and can be implemented very efficiently. In modern frameworks it is possible to set a transformation matrix in the current context, and you can do it in Eto Forms on the Graphics context. For instance, if you invoke g.TranslateTransform(50.f, 50.f), every coordinate specified in a graphics primitive gets translated by 50 units on both axes.

Homogenous coordinates allow the expression of affine transformations of the 2D space, which include translation, rotation, and scaling. Transformations can be accumulated, combining their effects; moreover, it is possible to save and then restore the current transformation in order to make local changes that can be easily discarded.

To make the topic more concrete, the AnalogClock class is rewritten using transformations. We assume again that the clock is 100 by 100 units:

```
let sz = SizeF(100.f, 100.f)
let r = sz.Width / 2.f
```

First, let's consider the drawQuadrant function:

```
let drawQuadrant (g:Graphics) =
  g.SaveTransform()
  for i = 1 to 12 do
    g.DrawLine(Pens.Black, 0.9f * r, 0.f, r, 0.f)
    g.RotateTransform(30.f)

  g.RestoreTransform()
```

The function saves the current transformation of the graphics context, then draws 12 times the same horizontal line, which is a tenth of the clock radius r and starts in 0.9f*r on the x axis. The magic happens when you invoke the RotateTransform method and rotate the coordinate system by an additional 30 degrees: it is like rotating a piece of paper before drawing the same line twelve times. Once we are finished with our drawing, we restore the original transformation on the graphics context by invoking RestoreTransform.

The same is done for the drawHand function, for which a single DrawLine suffices because we can use the x axis to go negative instead of having to rotate by π:

```
let drawHand (g:Graphics) (p:Pen) (len:single) (a:single) =
    g.SaveTransform()
    g.RotateTransform(a)
    g.DrawLine(p, -0.2f * r, 0.f, len * r, 0.f)

    g.RestoreTransform()
```

The transformations we perform assumes that the origin of the coordinate system is already in the middle of the clock; therefore, you have to prepare the transformation before the graphics context is passed to your drawing functions. Thus, we translate the coordinate system with TranslateTransform, and we also rotate it with RotateTransform by -90 degrees in order to have the angular coordinate initially used by the rotations aligned with the y axis; angles grow in a clockwise manner.

Using the new functions, the AnalogClock class can be replaced in the previous example:

```
type AnalogClock() as x =
    inherit Drawable()
    let timer = new UITimer(Interval=1.)
```

```
let sz = SizeF(100.f, 100.f)
let r = sz.Width / 2.f

do
    timer.Elapsed.Add(fun _ -> x.Invalidate())
    timer.Start()
override this.OnPaint e =
    let time = System.DateTime.Now

    let drawQuadrant (g:Graphics) = ...

    let drawHand (g:Graphics) (p:Pen) (sz:single) (a:single) = ...
    let g = e.Graphics
    g.TranslateTransform(PointF(sz.Width / 2.f, sz.Height / 2.f))
    g.RotateTransform(-90.f)
    drawQuadrant g
    use p = new Pen(Colors.Black)
    p.Thickness <- 1.f
    drawHand g p 1.f (single(time.Second) * 6.f)
    p.Thickness <- 2.f
    drawHand g p 1.f (single(time.Minute) * 6.f)
    p.Thickness <- 2.f
    drawHand g p 0.7f (single(time.Hour) * 30.f)

    g.FillEllipse(Brushes.Red, -2.f, -2.f, 4.f, 4.f)
```

As a last remark, you have to remember that we used fixed coordinates for drawing a 100-by-100 clock. This may still seem to be a limitation, but in fact you can use ScaleTransform to scale your clock to whatever size you like. Try adding the following line to the OnPaint method just below the binding of g with e.Graphics:

```
g.ScaleTransform(single(this.Width) / sz.Width, single(this.Height) / sz.Height)
```

With this you can scale the coordinate system to fill the whole client area of your control. Try to resize the form to find out whether your clock will fill all the available space. Notice how the scale transformation also affects the thickness of the lines; to avoid this effect you should scale the thickness of the pen appropriately, even though this works only by scaling the two dimensions by the same factor.

HOMOGENOUS COORDINATES

Transforming coordinates is very useful in both 2D and 3D vector graphics. These transformations—namely scale, rotation with regard to the origin, and translation—can be represented respectively as follows (we omit skew for sake of brevity):

$$S\left(\sigma_x, \sigma_y\right) = \begin{cases} x' = \sigma_x x \\ y' = \sigma_y y \end{cases}$$

$$R(a) = \begin{cases} x' = x \cdot cosa + y \cdot sina \\ y' = y \cdot cosa - x \cdot sina \end{cases}$$

$$T\left(t_x, t_y\right) = \begin{cases} x' = x + t_x \\ y' = y + t_y \end{cases}$$

Applying these transformations repeatedly allows us to express affine transformations of the 2D space (remember that affine transformations map parallel lines into parallel lines). The combination of these transformations using these formulas has the defect of requiring a number of operations for transforming a single point. Fortunately, a mathematical trick allows us to represent the three transformations as three 3 x 3 matrices in such a way that the matrix multiplication operation corresponds to applying the three corresponding operations:

$$S(\sigma_x,\sigma_y)=\begin{pmatrix} \sigma_x & 0 & 0 \\ 0 & \sigma_y & 0 \\ 0 & 0 & 1 \end{pmatrix} \quad R(a)=\begin{pmatrix} cosa & sina & 0 \\ -sina & cosa & 0 \\ 0 & 0 & 1 \end{pmatrix} \quad T(t_x,t_y)=\begin{pmatrix} 1 & 0 & t_x \\ 0 & 1 & t_y \\ 0 & 0 & 1 \end{pmatrix}$$

We represent points as three-dimensional column vectors, with the last element set to 1. In this way it is easy to verify that multiplying the rotation matrix by a vector leads to the original formula:

$$R(a)\cdot\vec{P}=\begin{pmatrix} cosa & sina & 0 \\ -sina & cosa & 0 \\ 0 & 0 & 1 \end{pmatrix}\cdot\begin{pmatrix} x \\ y \\ 1 \end{pmatrix}=\begin{pmatrix} x\cdot cosa + y\cdot sina \\ y\cdot cosa - x\cdot sina \\ 1 \end{pmatrix}$$

Composing matrices allows you to obtain a single matrix that represents the combination of the transformations. For example, the matrix of the rotation around a given point can be obtained by composition as follows:

$$R_{\bar{x},\bar{y}}(a)=T(-\bar{x},-\bar{y})\cdot R(a)\cdot T(\bar{x},\bar{y})$$

In essence, we first translate the origin at the point $(\bar{x},\bar{y})$, then we rotate around the origin by α, and finally we translate the coordinate system back by applying the opposite translation.

An important aspect to keep in mind is that matrix multiplication has the associative property but is not commutative, thus the order of application leads to different results. Many frameworks allow you to specify whether to prepend or append a matrix to a matrix multiplication list.

World and View Coordinates

Homogenous coordinates were long used in 3D graphics before finding their way in traditional 2D graphics, and some concepts widely used in the former are not yet so well known or used in the latter. You will now develop an abstraction that will help in implementing flexible handling of the view by offering scroll, rotation, and zoom using coordinate transformation.

As noted when the Model-View-Control pattern was introduced, the view can be seen as the projection of the model. It is normal that the information contained in the model is larger than the available space for the view; for this reason, scrollbars were invented. It is as though the model contains the description of a world, and the view is a camera showing a portion of it. Things lie in the world in a place, but their position may vary with respect to the camera, as exemplified in Figure 15-7.

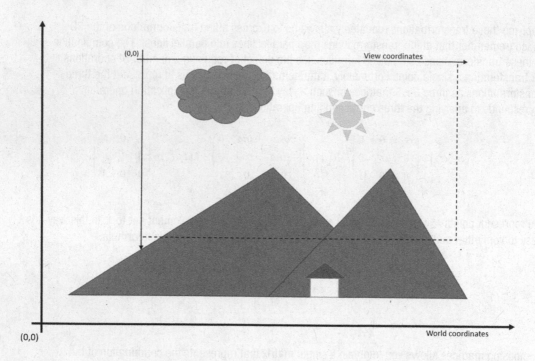

Figure 15-7. *World versus view coordinate systems*

The goal is to refine the drawable control to include the plumbing for transforming the view while keeping the world coordinates of our objects the same. Let's first open the usual namespaces and define two names for the two coordinate systems:

```
open Eto
open Eto.Forms
open Eto.Drawing

type CoordinateSystem =
  | World
  | View
```

View coordinates correspond with the system we have used so far, with (0,0) in the top-left corner of the window. We assume that by default world coordinates coincide with those of the view.

Two transformation matrices will be used, `w2v` and `v2w`, representing the world-to-view and the view-to-world transformations respectively. The `Paint` event is normally expressed in view coordinates because the graphics context draws the primitives in that coordinate system; it is possible to switch the two coordinate systems explicitly during the paint event handling using the matrices. To better support the two coordinate systems, `WorldPaint` and a `ViewPaint` events are introduced. The former will receive a graphics context that is already configured for using world coordinates, while the latter corresponds to the paint-in-view coordinates, but is triggered only after the first is (normally the use of paint-in-view coordinates is done to add annotations to the camera-like HUDs).

You first extend the Drawable class:

```
type TransformableViewControl() as this =
    inherit Drawable()
```

Then the two matrices are created along with the two events for the two new flavors of paint:

```
let w2v = Matrix.Create()
let v2w = Matrix.Create()
let viewpaintEvt = new Event<PaintEventArgs>()

let worldpaintEvt = new Event<PaintEventArgs>()
```

The control of the view is by default performed using the keyboard. For this reason, you declare that the control can get the focus so that it can receive keyboard messages (in Eto Forms this is required in order to get keyboard messages):

```
do this.CanFocus <- true
```

The main reason for having two matrices is that we are interested in converting coordinates from world to view and vice versa. We could have used a single matrix and computed the inverse, but the additional memory occupation is not significant, and this way numerical problems are avoided.

The trick to building two matrices that allow a two-way coordinate conversion between two systems is to perform the same operation in the opposite order. Define a method for each transformation type, allowing the user to indicate in which coordinate space it is expressed:

```
member this.Translate (v:CoordinateSystem) (p:PointF) =
    let am, bm = match v with World -> w2v, v2w | View -> v2w, w2v
    am.Translate(p)
    bm.Append(Matrix.FromTranslation(-p.X, -p.Y))

member this.Rotate (v:CoordinateSystem) (a:single) =
    let am, bm = match v with World -> w2v, v2w | View -> v2w, w2v
    am.Rotate(a)
    bm.Append(Matrix.FromRotation(-a))

member this.Scale (v:CoordinateSystem) (s:SizeF) =
    let am, bm = match v with World -> w2v, v2w | View -> v2w, w2v
    am.Scale(s)
    bm.Append(Matrix.FromScale(1.f/s.Width, 1.f/s.Height))

member this.RotateAt (v:CoordinateSystem) (a:single, p:PointF) =
    let am, bm = match v with World -> w2v, v2w | View -> v2w, w2v
    am.RotateAt(a, p)
    bm.Append(Matrix.FromRotationAt(-a, p))

member this.ScaleAt (v:CoordinateSystem) (s:SizeF, p:PointF) =
    let am, bm = match v with World -> w2v, v2w | View -> v2w, w2v
    am.ScaleAt(s, p)

    bm.Append(Matrix.FromScaleAt(1.f/s.Width, 1.f/s.Height, p.X, p.Y))
```

As you may have noticed, matrices implement the various operations as side effects. It is possible to create matrices for a specific transformation using static methods of the Matrix class. These methods have been used because the side effects methods prepend the transformation, but to build the inverse matrix it is required that you append the needed transformation using the Append method.

Direct access to the matrices may be useful, as they document the current transformation:

```
member this.View2WorldMatrix = v2w
member this.World2ViewMatrix = w2v
```

As already discussed, the Paint event is split into two events, one for the view coordinate system, and the other for the world coordinate system. We publish the events and define two abstract methods that can be overridden by inheriting classes:

```
member this.WorldPaint = worldpaintEvt.Publish
member this.ViewPaint = viewpaintEvt.Publish

abstract OnViewPaint : e:PaintEventArgs -> unit
default this.OnViewPaint _ = ()
abstract OnWorldPaint : e:PaintEventArgs -> unit

default this.OnWorldPaint _ = ()
```

We override the OnPaint event to transform the coordinate system before invoking the OnWorldPaint event and triggering the WorldPaint event. Notice the creation of a new PaintEventArgs object to express the clip rectangle in world coordinates rather than in view coordinates. We save and then restore the transformation of the graphics context to ensure that its state is consistent when OnViewPaint and ViewPaint are raised:

```
override this.OnPaint e =
  let g = e.Graphics
  let wr = e.ClipRectangle |> v2w.TransformRectangle

  g.SaveTransform()
  g.MultiplyTransform(w2v)
  let wpe = PaintEventArgs(g, wr)
  this.OnWorldPaint(wpe)
  worldpaintEvt.Trigger(wpe)
  g.RestoreTransform()

  this.OnViewPaint(e)
  viewpaintEvt.Trigger(e)

  base.OnPaint e
```

We finally override the OnKeyDown event to transform the view when certain keys are pressed. Scale and rotate transformations are performed with respect to the center of the view. Note how you transform the view matrix before invalidating the view:

```
override this.OnKeyDown e =
  let translateV = this.Translate View
  let rotateAtV = this.RotateAt View
  let scaleAtV = this.ScaleAt View
```

```
let mid = PointF(single(this.ClientSize.Width) / 2.f,
single(this.ClientSize.Height) / 2.f)
match e.Key with
| Keys.W -> translateV(PointF(0.f, -10.f)); this.Invalidate()
| Keys.A -> translateV(PointF(-10.f, 0.f)); this.Invalidate()
| Keys.S -> translateV(PointF(0.f, 10.f)); this.Invalidate()
| Keys.D -> translateV(PointF(10.f, 0.f)); this.Invalidate()
| Keys.Q -> rotateAtV(10.f, mid); this.Invalidate()
| Keys.E -> rotateAtV(-10.f, mid); this.Invalidate()
| Keys.Z -> scaleAtV(SizeF(1.1f, 1.1f), mid); this.Invalidate()
| Keys.X -> scaleAtV(SizeF(1.f/1.1f, 1.f/1.1f), mid); this.Invalidate()
| _ -> ()
```

To test TransformableViewControl you can modify the Curves example by creating an instance of this type rather than Drawable:

```
let draw = new TransformableViewControl()
```

You then have to register for the WorldPaint event rather than Paint:

```
draw.PaintWorld.Add(fun e -> paint e.Graphics)
```

If you test this example with these two lines you will be able to scroll, rotate, and scale the view. But if you try to edit the curve by moving the control points after changing the view, you will notice that the point won't move. The reason is that the coordinates that the mouse event handler receives are in the view coordinate space. You can easily transform the location point in world coordinates by using the TransformPoint method of View2WorldMatrix:

```
draw.MouseDown.Add(fun e ->
  let we = draw.View2WorldMatrix.TransformPoint(e.Location)
  mouseDown(we)
)
draw.MouseMove.Add(fun e ->
  let we = draw.View2WorldMatrix.TransformPoint(e.Location)
  mouseMove(we)

)
```

Lightweight Controls

If you need to implement interactive graphics by drawing using Eto Forms, you cannot rely on controls as previously discussed. However, it would be useful to have a control abstraction so that you can encapsulate the view model and control for a portion of the view of your control.

You want to create consistent behavior for subareas of a control, not only because of the limitations of the framework, but also to reduce the overhead of interprocess communication between your application and the graphical system. A common solution to this problem is to implement programming abstractions that mimic the graphical system in creating coherent areas of the view that are autonomous. This kind of abstraction is often referred as *lightweight controls*, and it has been implemented by several graphical frameworks.

In our example you will implement the two types `LightWeightControl` and
`LightWeightContainerControl`. The former defines the abstractions of a graphical control, and the latter is a
graphical control capable of hosting instances of the former. In this small but powerful library, the world and
view coordinate systems introduced in the previous section are used so that a lightweight control can lie in
the world or in the view, and can be subject to either moving or sticking to the view.

Listing 15-4 shows the definition of the `LightWeightControl` type, which is full of members and
properties to resemble as much as possible a normal control. The control has `Location`, `Size`, and `Parent`
properties to define its location size and to which container the control belongs. Invalidating the control
view is performed by delegating the same operation to its parent, if defined. The control also allows
you to manage focus so as to receive keystrokes with the support of the container. The interface of your
`LightWeightControl` base type is given by the long list of abstract methods at the end of the type definition;
the majority of these are similar to those available on real controls and simply define the operation that can
be overridden by derived types. The `HitTest` method is used to test whether a point with certain coordinates
lies inside the control; by default, the method checks if the point is in the bounding rectangle.

Listing 15-4. Definition of the LightWeightControl type

```
type LightWeightControl() =
  let mutable coordinateSystem = World
  let mutable location = PointF()
  let mutable size = SizeF()
  let mutable parent:LightWeightContainerControl option = None

  member this.CoordinateSystem
    with get () = coordinateSystem
    and set (v) = coordinateSystem <- v

  member this.Location
    with get() = location
    and set(v) = location <- v; this.Invalidate()

  member this.Size
    with get() = size
    and set(v) = size <- v; this.OnSizeChanged(new System.EventArgs())

  member this.Bounds = RectangleF(location, size)

  member this.Parent
    with get() = parent
    and set(v) = parent <- v

  member this.Invalidate () =
    match parent with
    | Some v -> v.Invalidate(this.Bounds)
    | None -> ()

  member this.Invalidate (r:Rectangle) =
    match parent with
    | Some v ->
      let tr = RectangleF(r)
      tr.Offset(location)
```

```
      if coordinateSystem = World then
        v.Invalidate(tr |> v.World2ViewMatrix.TransformRectangle |> Rectangle)
      else
        v.Invalidate(tr |> Rectangle)
    | None -> ()

member this.Focus () =
  match parent with
  | Some p -> p.SetFocus(this)
  | None -> ()

member this.Unfocus () =
  match parent with
  | Some p -> p.UnsetFocus()
  | None -> ()

abstract OnPaint : PaintEventArgs -> unit
default this.OnPaint _ = ()
abstract OnMouseDown : MouseEventArgs -> unit
default this.OnMouseDown _ = ()
abstract OnMouseUp : MouseEventArgs -> unit
default this.OnMouseUp _ = ()
abstract OnMouseMove : MouseEventArgs -> unit
default this.OnMouseMove _ = ()
abstract OnMouseEnter : MouseEventArgs -> unit
default this.OnMouseEnter _ = ()
abstract OnMouseLeave : MouseEventArgs -> unit
default this.OnMouseLeave _ = ()
abstract OnKeyDown : KeyEventArgs -> unit
abstract OnMouseDoubleClick : MouseEventArgs -> unit
default this.OnMouseDoubleClick _ = ()
abstract OnMouseWheel : MouseEventArgs -> unit
default this.OnMouseWheel _ = ()
default this.OnKeyDown _ = ()
abstract OnKeyUp : KeyEventArgs -> unit
default this.OnKeyUp _ = ()
abstract OnSizeChanged : System.EventArgs -> unit
default this.OnSizeChanged _ = ()
abstract HitTest : PointF -> bool

default this.HitTest p = RectangleF(PointF(), size).Contains(p)
```

The LightWeightContainerControl type defines where lightweight controls live and is responsible for dispatching them to events if appropriate. A ResizeArray named children is used to store the list of lightweight controls hosted by the container. Some functions acting as helpers are defined to help you look for controls and to transform coordinates before dispatching mouse events. For the class inheriting from LightWeightControl, the illusion of having its own coordinate system should be as close as possible to the coordinate system of regular controls.

459

Listing 15-5 shows the structure of the control that is defined together with the LightWeightControl type, since the two types are mutually recursive. The container paints the contained lightweight children by delegating part of its Paint event handling. Being inherited from the TransformableViewControl type, it defines the two paint methods for view- and world-coordinate paint handling:

```
override this.OnViewPaint e =
  for v in controlsIn View do
    e.Graphics.SaveTransform()
    e.Graphics.TranslateTransform(v.Location)
    v.OnPaint(e)
    e.Graphics.RestoreTransform()

override this.OnWorldPaint e =
  for v in controlsIn World do
    e.Graphics.SaveTransform()
    e.Graphics.TranslateTransform(v.Location)
    v.OnPaint(e)

    e.Graphics.RestoreTransform()
```

In both cases, controls are filtered depending in the coordinate system they declare they belong to, and they invoke their OnPaint method after having translated the coordinate system into the control origin. The transformation is saved and then restored to ensure that the graphics context is consistent across the Paint event handling.

Whenever the container decides whether an event should be dispatched or not to one of its children, it uses the correlate helper function:

```
let correlate (loc:PointF) =
  let cv = controlsIn View |> Seq.tryFindBack (fun v -> v.HitTest(PointF(loc.X -
  v.Location.X, loc.Y - v.Location.Y)))
  match cv with
  | Some c -> Some c
  | None ->
    let l = this.View2WorldMatrix.TransformPoint(loc)
    controlsIn World
      |> Seq.tryFindBack (fun v ->
          v.HitTest(PointF(l.X - v.Location.X, l.Y - v.Location.Y))
  )
```

This function looks for the last control returning true on the HitTest method, checking first the controls in the view space, and then those lying in the world space. As you may guess, the order is not casual; it is the reverse order of paint, where world space controls are painted before those in view space, and where controls are painted in the order returned by the controlsIn function.

Mouse events handling done by the handleMouseEvent rely on the correlating function to decide whether to send the event to the target control or not; in the first case the event argument is updated with the coordinates transformed in the target control's space.

Mouse capturing is implemented; when the mouse-down event occurs inside a lightweight control, the subsequent mouse-move events will be sent to it, even when outside its area, until a mouse-up event is received and dispatched. This behavior is common in GUI frameworks and is meant to ensure that the control produces consistent behavior if the user by will or accident exits the control area while dragging the mouse.

The Z-order of lightweight controls is obtained by moving controls inside the children array; the higher the index the more on top the control is. The methods BringToFront and SendToBack allow type users to change the Z-index of controls.

The container also keeps track of which control has the keyboard focus and when the mouse enters or exits from a control in order to raise the appropriate events.

Listing 15-5. Definition of LightWeightContainerControl type

```
and LightWeightContainerControl() as this =
  inherit TransformableViewControl()

  let children = new ResizeArray<LightWeightControl>()
  let mutable gotFocus : LightWeightControl option = None
  let controlsIn view = children |> Seq.filter (fun v -> v.CoordinateSystem = view)
  let mutable captured : LightWeightControl option = None

  let correlate (loc:PointF) = ...

  let cloneMouseEvent (e:MouseEventArgs) (newloc:PointF) =
    new MouseEventArgs(e.Buttons, e.Modifiers, newloc, new System.Nullable<SizeF>(e.Delta),
    e.Pressure)

  let lightweightCoord (c:LightWeightControl) (loc:PointF) =
    if c.CoordinateSystem = World then
      let l = this.View2WorldMatrix.TransformPoint(loc)
      PointF(l.X - c.Location.X, l.Y - c.Location.Y)
    else
      let l = loc
      PointF(l.X - c.Location.X, l.Y - c.Location.Y)

  let handleMouseEvent (e:MouseEventArgs) (f:LightWeightControl->MouseEventArgs->unit) =
    let cv = correlate e.Location
    match cv with
    | Some c -> f c (cloneMouseEvent e (lightweightCoord c e.Location))
    | None -> ()

  let mutable lastControl:LightWeightControl option = None

  member this.AddControl (c:LightWeightControl) = children.Add(c)

  member this.RemoveControl (c:LightWeightControl) = children.Remove(c)

  member this.BringToFront (c:LightWeightControl) = if children.Remove(c) then children.
  Add(c)

  member this.SendToBack (c:LightWeightControl) = if children.Remove(c) then children.
  Insert(0, c)

  member this.SetFocus(c:LightWeightControl) = gotFocus <- Some c

  member this.UnsetFocus() = gotFocus <- None
```

```
override this.OnMouseDown e =
  handleMouseEvent e (fun c e -> captured <- Some c; c.OnMouseDown e)
  base.OnMouseDown(e)

override this.OnMouseUp e =
  match captured with
  | Some c ->
    c.OnMouseUp (cloneMouseEvent e (lightweightCoord c e.Location))
    captured <- None
  | None -> ()
  handleMouseEvent e (fun c e -> c.OnMouseUp e)
  base.OnMouseUp(e)

override this.OnMouseMove e =
  let lc = lastControl
  let mutable ce = null
  lastControl <- None
  match captured with
  | Some c -> c.OnMouseMove (cloneMouseEvent e (lightweightCoord c e.Location))
  | None -> ()
  handleMouseEvent e (fun c e -> lastControl <- Some(c); ce <- e; c.OnMouseMove e)
  if lastControl <> lc then
    if lastControl = None then lc.Value.OnMouseLeave(ce)
    else lastControl.Value.OnMouseEnter(ce)
  base.OnMouseMove(e)

override this.OnMouseDoubleClick e =
  handleMouseEvent e (fun c e -> c.OnMouseDoubleClick e)
  base.OnMouseDoubleClick(e)

override this.OnMouseWheel e =
  handleMouseEvent e (fun c e -> c.OnMouseWheel e)
  base.OnMouseWheel(e)

override this.OnKeyDown e =
  match gotFocus with
  | Some c -> c.OnKeyDown e
  | None -> ()

override this.OnKeyUp e =
  match gotFocus with
  | Some c -> c.OnKeyUp e
  | None -> ()

override this.OnViewPaint e = ...

override this.OnWorldPaint e = ...
```

To test the lightweight controls framework, let's implement a simple segment editor. We first define the Handle type as a lightweight control that lives in world coordinates and is circle shaped. The handle receives mouse events and changes its location to the new position of the mouse. When the mouse-down event is received, the control saves the offset so that you can preserve the same point under the mouse cursor when dragging. Since the hit test for a circle is a known function, you can define a better test than the bounds check used previously:

```
type Handle() =
  inherit LightWeightControl(CoordinateSystem=World,Size=SizeF(10.f,10.f))

  let mutable off : PointF option = None

  override this.OnMouseDown e =
    off <- Some(e.Location)

  override this.OnMouseMove e =
    match off with
    | Some p ->
      this.Location <- PointF(e.Location.X + this.Location.X - p.X, e.Location.Y + this.
      Location.Y - p.Y)
    | None -> ()

  override this.OnMouseUp _ =
    off <- None

  override this.OnPaint e =
    let g = e.Graphics
    let p = PointF(-(this.Size.Width / 2.f), -(this.Size.Height / 2.f))
    g.DrawEllipse(Colors.Black, RectangleF(p, this.Size))

  override this.HitTest p =
    let xa, yb = p.X / this.Size.Width, p.Y / this.Size.Height

    xa * xa + yb * yb <= 1.f
```

To show the center of the control, a cross would help, and since it lives in view space you can define a straightforward lightweight control of this kind:

```
type Cross() =
  inherit LightWeightControl(CoordinateSystem=View,Size=SizeF(20.f,20.f))

  override this.OnPaint e =
    let g = e.Graphics
    g.DrawLine(Colors.Black, -10.f, 0.f, 10.f, 0.f)

    g.DrawLine(Colors.Black, 0.f, -10.f, 0.f, 10.f)
```

You now can define a Line control that inherits from LightWeightContainerControl; simply add two handles and the cross to the lightweight controls children list using the AddControl method. Whenever the size of the control changes, the cross location should be updated to keep it in the middle. The OnWorldPaint event simply draws a line between the two handles that encapsulate the dragging behavior:

```
type Line() as this =
  inherit LightWeightContainerControl()

  let handles = [|
    Handle(Parent=Some(this :> LightWeightContainerControl), Location=PointF(0.f, 0.f));
    Handle(Parent=Some(this :> LightWeightContainerControl), Location=PointF(100.f, 100.f))
  |]

  let cross = new Cross()

  do
    for h in handles do this.AddControl(h)
    this.AddControl(cross)

  override this.OnSizeChanged _ =
    cross.Location <- PointF(single(this.Width / 2), single(this.Height / 2))

  override this.OnWorldPaint e =
    let g = e.Graphics
    let h1, h2 = handles.[0].Location, handles.[1].Location
    g.DrawLine(Colors.Red, h1, h2)
    base.OnWorldPaint(e)

let app = new Application()

let form = new Form(Title="Hello world Eto Forms", Topmost=true, Size=Size(640, 480))
let my = new Line()
form.Content <- my
form.Show()

app.Run(form)
```

It is interesting to notice how lightweight controls are not clipped to their bounding box, allowing you to draw the cross at a negative location. This is one of the advantages of this abstraction: you can encapsulate behavior while remaining in control of the drawing. With ordinary graphic controls you would be more constrained by system assumptions.

Summary

Event-driven programming is the dominant paradigm of graphical applications. Although object-oriented programming is used to build the infrastructure for graphical frameworks, events are naturally expressed in terms of calling back a given function. F# is effective in GUI programming because it supports both paradigms and provides access to full-featured frameworks, such as Windows Forms.

This chapter covered the basics of GUI programming. It introduced controls and applications, including details typical of real-world applications. The presentation was based on the Eto Forms framework, but many of the ideas discussed can be easily transposed to other graphical frameworks, as the fundamental structure of this class of applications stays mostly unchanged.

CHAPTER 16

███

Language-Oriented Programming

Chapters 3 to 6 covered three well-known programming paradigms in F#: *functional*, *imperative*, and *object* programming. Throughout this book, however, you have in many ways been exploring what is essentially a fourth programming paradigm: *language-oriented programming*. In this chapter, you will focus on advanced aspects of language-oriented programming through language-integrated, domain-specific languages and meta-programming.

The word *language* can have a number of meanings in this context. For example, take the simple language of arithmetic expressions and algebra that you learned in high school mathematics, made up of named variables, such as x and y, and composite expressions, such as $x + y$, xy, $-x$, and x^2. For the purposes of this chapter, this language can have a number of manifestations:

- one or more *concrete representations*: for example, using an ASCII text format or an XML representation of arithmetic expressions

- one or more *abstract representations*: for example, as F# types and values representing the normalized form of an arithmetic expression tree

- one or more *computational representations*, either by functions that compute the values of arithmetic expressions or via other engines that perform analysis, interpretation, compilation, execution, or transformation of language fragments. These can be implemented in F#, in another .NET language, or in external engines.

The language-oriented programming techniques covered in this book (including some in this chapter) are the following:

- manipulating unstructured text and binary representations of languages, including writing parsers and lexers (Chapter 8)

- manipulating semi-structured language representations, such as XML (Chapter 8)

- using F# functions, types, and active patterns for abstract and symbolic representations of languages (Chapters 3, 9 and 12)

- using F# sequence expressions, asynchronous expressions, and, more generally, F# computation expressions for tightly language-integrated representations of some languages (Chapters 9, 11, and 13, and this chapter)

- using F# "dynamic" operators to give a slightly improved syntax for accessing information stored using dynamic (untyped) representation techniques (this chapter)

- using F# reflection and quotations to represent languages via meta-programming (this chapter)

- implementing F# type providers, a form of compile-time meta-programming (this chapter)

As you can see, language-oriented programming isn't a single technique; sometimes you work with fully concrete representations (for example, reading bits from disk) and sometimes with fully computational representations (for example, defining and using functions that compute the value of arithmetic expressions). Most often, you work somewhere in between (for example, manipulating abstract syntax trees). These tasks require different techniques, and there are trade-offs when choosing to work with different kinds of representations. For example, if you're generating human-readable formulae, then you may need to store more-concrete information, but if you're interested just in evaluating arithmetic expressions, then a purely computational encoding may be more effective. You can see some of those trade-offs in the different techniques just described.

■ **Note**   The term *language-oriented programming* was originally applied to F# by Robert Pickering in the Apress book *Beginning F#*, and it really captures a key facet of F# programming. Thanks, Robert!

Computation Expressions

Chapter 3 introduced a useful notation for generating sequences of data, called *sequence expressions*. For example:

```
> seq { for i in 0 .. 3 -> (i, i * i) };;

val it : seq<int * int> = seq [(0, 0); (1, 1); (2, 4); (3, 9)]
```

Sequence expressions are used extensively throughout this book. For example, Chapter 9 uses sequence expressions for a range of sequence-programming tasks. Likewise, Chapter 11 introduced a useful notation for generating individual results *asynchronously*, meaning that the result of a computation is eventually delivered to a continuation, and is called as *future*, *task*, or *promise*. Asynchronous computations can also represent actions that do not "block" .NET threads when waiting for I/O. For example, consider the body of an agent from Chapter 11, which asynchronously waits for a message and then recursively loops—this is a form of asynchronous state machine:

```
let rec loop n =
    async { printfn "n = %d, waiting..." n
            let! msg = inbox.Receive()
            return! loop (n + msg) }
```

It turns out that both sequence expressions and asynchronous expressions are just two instances of a more general construct called *computation expressions*. These are also sometimes called *workflows*, although they bear only a passing similarity to the workflows used to model business processes. The general form of a computation expression is builder { comp-expr }. Table 16-1 shows the primary constructs that can be used within the braces of a computation expression and how these constructs are converted by the F# compiler when given the computation-expression builder builder.

Table 16-1. Main Constructs in Computation Expressions and Their Conversion

Construct	De-sugared Form
let *pat* = *expr* in *cexpr*	let *pat* = *expr* in "*cexpr*"
let! *pat* = *expr* in *cexpr*	b.Bind (*expr*, (fun *pat* -> "*cexpr*"))
use *val* = *expr* in *cexpr*	b.Using(*expr*, (fun *val* -> "*cexpr*"))
use! *val* = *expr* in *cexpr*	b.Bind (*expr*, (fun *x* -> "use *val* = *expr* in *cexpr*"))
do *expr* in *cexpr*	*expr*; b.Delay (fun () -> "*cexpr*"))
do! *expr* in *cexpr*	b.Bind (*expr*, (fun () -> "*cexpr*"))
for *pat* in *expr* do *cexpr*	b.For (*expr*, (fun *pat* -> "*cexpr*"))
while *expr* do *cexpr*	b.While ((fun () -> *expr*), b.Delay (fun () -> "*cexpr*"))
try *cexpr1* with *val* -> *expr2*	b.TryWith(b.Delay(fun () -> "*cexpr1*"), (fun *val* -> "*cexpr2*"))
try *cexpr* finally *expr*	b.TryFinally(b.Delay(fun () -> "*cexpr*"),(fun () -> *expr*))
if *expr* then *cexpr1* else *cexpr2*	if *expr* then "*cexpr1*" else "*cexpr2*"
if *expr* then *cexpr*	if *expr* then "*cexpr*" else b.Zero()
cexpr1; *cexpr2*	v.Combine ("*cexpr1*", b.Delay(fun () -> "*cexpr2*"))
yield *expr*	b.Yield *expr*
yield! *Expr*	b.YieldFrom *expr*
return *expr*	b.Return *expr*
return! *Expr*	b.ReturnFrom *expr*

The three most important applications of computation expressions in F# programming are:

- general-purpose programming with sequences, lists, and arrays

- parallel, asynchronous, and concurrent programming using asynchronous workflows, discussed in detail in Chapter 11

- database queries, by quoting a workflow and translating it to SQL via the .NET LINQ libraries, a technique demonstrated in Chapter 13

This section will cover briefly how computation expressions work through some simple examples.

■ **Note** If you've never seen F# computation expressions before, you might find that computation expressions take a bit of getting used to. They give you a way to write computations that may behave and execute differently than normal programs do.

F# COMPUTATION EXPRESSIONS AND HASKELL MONADS

Computation expressions are the F# equivalent of monadic syntax, which is found in the programming language Haskell. Monads are a powerful and expressive design pattern; they are characterized by a generic type M<'T> combined with at least two operations:

```
bind : M<'T> -> ('T ->  M<'U>) -> M<'U>
return : 'T -> M<'T>
```

These correspond to the primitives `let!` and `return` in F# computation-expression syntax. Several other elements of the computation-expression syntax can be implemented in terms of these primitives, but the F# de-sugaring process leaves this up to the implementer of the workflow, because sometimes derived operations can have more efficient implementations. Well-behaved monads should satisfy three important rules, called the *monad laws*.

F# uses the terms *computation expression* and *workflow* for four reasons:

- When the designers of F# spoke with the designers of Haskell about this, they agreed that the word *monad* was obscure and sounded a little daunting and that using other names might be wise.

- There are some technical differences; for example, some F# computation expressions can be combined with imperative programming, taking advantage of the fact that computation expressions can have side effects that aren't tracked by the F# type system. In Haskell, all side-effecting operations must be lifted into the corresponding monad. The Haskell approach has some important advantages: you can know for sure what side effects a function can have by looking at its type. It also, however, makes it more difficult to use external libraries from within a computation expression.

- F# computation expressions can be reified using F# quotations, providing a way to execute the workflow by alternative means—for example, by translation to SQL. This gives them a different role in practice, because they can be used to model both concrete languages and computational languages.

- F# computation expressions can also be used to embed computations that generate multiple results (called *monoids*), such as sequence expressions (also known as *comprehension syntax*). These generally use `yield` and `yield!` instead of `return` and `return!` and often have no `let!`.

An Example: Success/Failure Computation Expressions

Perhaps the simplest kind of workflow is one in which failure of a computation is made explicit; for example, in which each step of the workflow may either *succeed*, by returning a result Some(v), or *fail*, by returning the value None. You can model such a workflow using functions of type unit -> 'T option—that is, functions that may or may not compute a result. In this section, assume that these functions are pure and terminating—they have no side effects, raise no exceptions, and always terminate.

Whenever you define a new kind of workflow, it's useful to give a name to the type of values or objects generated by that workflow. In this case, let's call them Attempt objects:

```
type Attempt<'T> = (unit -> 'T option)
```

Of course, you can use regular functional programming to start building Attempt<'T> objects:

```
let succeed x = (fun () -> Some(x)) : Attempt<'T>
let fail = (fun () -> None) : Attempt<'T>
let runAttempt (a : Attempt<'T>) = a()
```

These conform to the following types:

```
val succeed : x:'T -> Attempt<'T>
val fail : Attempt<'T>
val runAttempt : a:Attempt<'T> -> 'T option
```

Using only normal F# expressions to build Attempt values can be a little tedious and can lead to a proliferation of many different functions that stitch together Attempt values in straightforward ways. Luckily, as you've seen with sequence expressions, F# comes with predefined syntax for building objects such as Attempt values. You can use this syntax with a new type by defining a *builder* object that helps stitch together the fragments that make up the computation expression. Let's look at an example of the signature of an object that you have to define in order to use workflow syntax with a new type (note that this is a type signature for an object, not actual code; we show how to define the AttemptBuilder type and its members later in this section):

```
type AttemptBuilder =
    member Bind : p:Attempt<'T> * ('T -> Attempt<'U>) -> Attempt<'U>
    member Delay : f:(unit -> Attempt<'T>) -> Attempt<'T>
    member Return : x:'T -> Attempt<'T>
    member ReturnFrom : x:Attempt<'T> -> Attempt<'T>
```

Typically, there is one global instance of each such builder object. For example:

```
let attempt = new AttemptBuilder()
```

```
val attempt : AttemptBuilder
```

First, let's see how you can use F# syntax for computation expressions to build Attempt objects. You can build Attempt values that always succeed:

```
> let alwaysOne = attempt { return 1 };;
```

```
val alwaysOne : Attempt<int>
```

```
> let alwaysPair = attempt { return (1,"two") };;
```

```
val alwaysPair : Attempt<int * string>
```

```
> runAttempt alwaysOne;;
```

val it : int option = Some 1

```
> runAttempt alwaysPair;;
```

*val it : (int * string) option = Some (1, "two")*

Note that Attempt values such as alwaysOne are just functions; to run an Attempt value, just apply it by calling runAttempt. These correspond to uses of the succeed function, as you will see shortly.

You can also build more interesting Attempt values that check a condition and return different Attempt values on each branch, as shown in this example:

```
> let failIfBig n = attempt {if n > 1000 then return! fail else return n};;
```

val failIfBig : n:int -> Attempt<int>

```
> runAttempt (failIfBig 999);;
```

val it : int option = Some 999

```
> runAttempt (failIfBig 1001);;
```

val it : int option = None

Here, one branch uses return! to return the result of running another Attempt value, and the other branch uses return to give a single result. These correspond to yield! and yield in sequence expressions.

Next, you can build Attempt values that sequence together two Attempt values by running one, getting its result, binding it to a variable, and running the second. You do this by using the syntax form let! pat = expr, which is unique to computation expressions:

```
> let failIfEitherBig (inp1, inp2) = attempt {
        let! n1 = failIfBig inp1
        let! n2 = failIfBig inp2
        return (n1, n2)};;
```

*val failIfEitherBig : inp1:int * inp2:int -> Attempt<int * int>*

```
> runAttempt (failIfEitherBig (999, 998));;
```

*val it : (int * int) option = Some (999, 998)*

```
> runAttempt (failIfEitherBig (1003, 998));;
```

*val it : (int * int) option = None*

```
> runAttempt (failIfEitherBig (999, 1001));;
```

*val it : (int * int) option = None*

Let's look at this more closely. First, what does the first `let!` do? It runs the `Attempt` value `failIfBig inp1`, and if this returns None, the whole computation returns None. If the computation on the right delivers a value (that is, returns Some), then it binds the result to the variable `n1` and continues. Note the following for the expression `let! n1 = failIfBig inp1`:

- The expression on the right (`failIfBig inp1`) has type `Attempt<int>`.

- The variable on the left (`n1`) is of type `int`.

This is somewhat similar to a sequence of normal `let` binding, but `let!` also controls whether the rest of the computation is executed. In the case of the `Attempt` type, it executes the rest of the computation only when it receives a Some value. Otherwise, it returns None, and the rest of the code is never executed.

You can use normal `let` bindings in computation expressions. For example:

```
let sumIfBothSmall (inp1, inp2) =
    attempt { let! n1 = failIfBig inp1
              let! n2 = failIfBig inp2
              let sum = n1 + n2
              return sum}
```

In this case, the `let` binding executes exactly as you would expect; it takes the expression `n1 + n2` and binds its result to the value `sum`. To summarize, you've seen that computation expressions let you

- use an expression-like syntax to build `Attempt` computations;

- sequence these computations together using the `let!` construct;

- return results from these computations using `return` and `return!`; and

- compute intermediate results using `let`.

Computation expressions also let you do a good deal more than this, as you will see in the sections that follow.

Defining a Computation-Expression Builder

Listing 16-1 shows the implementation of the computation-expression builder for `Attempt` computation expressions; this is the simplest definition for `AttemptBuilder`.

Listing 16-1. Defining a computation-expression builder

```
let succeed x = (fun () -> Some(x))
let fail = (fun () -> None)
let runAttempt (a : Attempt<'T>) = a()
let bind p rest = match runAttempt p with None -> fail | Some r -> (rest r)
let delay f = (fun () -> runAttempt (f()))
let combine p1 p2 = (fun () -> match p1() with None -> p2() | res -> res)

type AttemptBuilder() =

    /// Used to de-sugar uses of 'let!' inside computation expressions.
    member b.Bind(p, rest) = bind p rest
```

```
    /// Delays the construction of an attempt until just before it is executed
    member b.Delay(f) = delay f

    /// Used to de-sugar uses of 'return' inside computation expressions.
    member b.Return(x) = succeed x

    /// Used to de-sugar uses of 'return!' inside computation expressions.
    member b.ReturnFrom(x : Attempt<'T>) = x

    /// Used to de-sugar uses of 'c1; c2' inside computation expressions.
    member b.Combine(p1 : Attempt<'T>, p2 : Attempt<'T>) = combine p1 p2

    /// Used to de-sugar uses of 'if .. then ..' inside computation expressions when
    /// the 'else' branch is empty
    member b.Zero() = fail
let attempt = new AttemptBuilder()
```

The inferred types here are:

```
type AttemptBuilder =
    new : unit -> AttemptBuilder
    member Bind : p:Attempt<'T> * rest:('T -> Attempt<'U>) -> Attempt<'U>
    member Combine : p1:Attempt<'T> * p2:Attempt<'T> -> Attempt<'T>
    member Delay : f:(unit -> Attempt<'T>) -> Attempt<'T>
    member Return : x:'T -> Attempt<'T>
    member ReturnFrom : x:Attempt<'T> -> Attempt<'T>
    member Zero : unit -> Attempt<'T>

val attempt : AttemptBuilder
```

F# implements computation expressions by de-sugaring them using a builder. For example, given the previous AttemptBuilder, then

```
attempt { let! n1 = failIfBig inp1
          let! n2 = failIfBig inp2
          let sum = n1 + n2
          return sum}
```

de-sugars to

```
attempt.Bind(failIfBig inp1, (fun n1 ->
    attempt.Bind(failIfBig inp2, (fun n2 ->
        let sum = n1 + n2
        attempt.Return sum))))
```

One purpose of the F# computation expression syntax is to make sure you don't have to write this sort of thing by hand. The de-sugaring of the workflow syntax is implemented by the F# compiler. Table 16-2 shows some of the typical signatures that a computation-expression builder needs to implement.

Table 16-2. *Some Typical Computation-Expression Builder Members, as Required by the F# Compiler*

Member	Description
`member Bind : M<'T>` `* ('T -> M<'U>) -> M<'U>`	Used to de-sugar `let!` and `do!` within computation expressions
`member Return : 'T -> M<'T>`	Used to de-sugar `return` within computation expressions
`member ReturnFrom : M<'T> -> M<'T>`	Used to de-sugar `return!` within computation expressions
`member Delay : (unit -> M<'T>) -> M<'T>`	Used to ensure that side effects within a computation expression are performed when expected
`member For : seq<'T> *` `('T -> M<'U>) -> M<'U>`	Used to de-sugar `for ... do ...` within computation expressions. M<'U> can optionally be M<unit>.
`member While : (unit -> bool) *` `M<'T> -> M<'T>`	Used to de-sugar `while ... do ...` within computation expressions. M<'T> may optionally be M<unit>.

`member Using : 'T *`
`('T -> M<'T>) -> M<'T>`
`when 'T :> IDisposable`
	Used to de-sugar `use` bindings within computation expressions

`member Combine : M<'T> * M<'T> -> M<'T>`	Used to de-sugar sequencing within computation expressions. The first M<'T> may optionally be M<unit>.
`member Zero : unit -> M<'T>`	Used to de-sugar empty `else` branches of `if`/`then` constructs within computation expressions

Most of the elements of a builder are usually implemented in terms of simpler primitives. For example, assume you're defining a builder for some type M<'T> and you already have implementations of functions bindM and returnM with the types:

```
val bindM : M<'T> -> ('T -> M<'U>) -> M<'U>
val returnM : 'T -> M<'T>
```

Then you can implement Delay using the functions:

```
let delayM f = bindM (returnM ()) f
```

You can also now define an overall builder in terms of all four functions:

```
type MBuilder() =
    member b.Return(x) = returnM x
    member b.Bind(v, f) = bindM v f
    member b.Delay(f) = delayM f
```

Bind and Delay may also have more efficient direct implementations, however, which is why F# doesn't insert the previous implementations automatically.

Computation Expressions and Untamed Side Effects

It's possible, and in some cases even common, to define computation expressions that cause side effects. For example, you can use printfn in the middle of an Attempt workflow:

```
let sumIfBothSmall (inp1, inp2) =
    attempt {
        let! n1 = failIfBig inp1
        printfn "Hey, n1 was small!"
        let! n2 = failIfBig inp2
        printfn "n2 was also small!"
        let sum = n1 + n2
        return sum
    }
```

Here's what happens when you call this function:

```
> runAttempt(sumIfBothSmall (999, 999));;

Hey, n1 was small!
n2 was also small!
val it : int option = Some 1998

> runAttempt(sumIfBothSmall (999, 1001));;

Hey, n1 was small!

val it : int option = None
```

Side effects in computation expressions must be used with care, particularly because computation expressions are typically used to construct delayed or on-demand computations. In the previous example, printing is a fairly benign side effect. More-significant side effects, such as mutable state, can also be sensibly combined with some kinds of computation expressions, but be sure you understand how the side effect will interact with the particular kind of workflow you're using. The following example allocates a piece of mutable state that is local to the Attempt workflow, and this is used to accumulate the sum:

```
let sumIfBothSmall (inp1, inp2) =
    attempt { let mutable sum = 0
              let! n1 = failIfBig inp1
              sum  <- sum + n1
              let! n2 = failIfBig inp2
              sum  <- sum + n2
              return sum }
```

We leave it as an exercise for you to examine the de-sugaring of this workflow to see that the mutable value is indeed local, in the sense that it doesn't escape the overall computation and that different executions of the same workflow will use different mutable values.

As mentioned, computation expressions are nearly always delayed computations. As you saw in Chapter 4, delayed computations and side effects can interact. For this reason, the de-sugaring of workflow syntax inserts a `Delay` operation around the entire workflow. This

```
let printThenSeven = attempt { printf "starting..."; return 3 + 4 }
```

de-sugars to

```
let printThenSeven =
    attempt.Delay(fun () ->
        printf "starting...";
        attempt.Return(3 + 4))
```

This means that "starting . . ." is printed each time the `printThenSeven` attempt object is executed.

Computation Expressions with Custom Query Operators

F# includes a set of extensions to computation expressions that allow builders to define additional "custom operators" associated with a computation-expression builder. This technique is used to define query-like languages that progressively add constraints, sorting, and other declarations to a query. For example, we can change the `Attempt` builder to custom query operator `condition` (to replace if/then):

```
type AttemptBuilder with

    [<CustomOperation("condition",MaintainsVariableSpaceUsingBind = true)>]
    member x.Condition(p, [<ProjectionParameter>] b) = condition p b

let attempt = new AttemptBuilder()
```

Note that custom operations are declared using the `CustomOperation` attribute. Loosely speaking, a custom operation gets to operate on the "whole" computation—any values already declared in the computation expression are packaged up into a tuple, the operation is applied, and the values are then unpackaged. The technique used to package and unpackage is either return/let! (`MaintainsVariableSpaceUsingBind` is true) or yield/for (`MaintainsVariableSpaceUsingBind` is false). Parameters to custom operations can access the variables defined in the computation expression via the `ProjectionParameter` attribute.

For example, a workflow to generate a pair of random numbers in the unit circle is as follows:

```
let randomNumberInCircle =
    attempt { let x, y = rand(), rand()
              condition (x * x + y * y < 1.0)
              return (x, y) }
```

Note that this is simply an alternative to an if/then expression. You must use either control-flow operators, such as if/then/else, or custom operators, such as `condition`, in your own computation expressions. Attempts to combine these are unlikely to be satisfying.

Custom operators are very rarely defined in F# programming and are primarily used with F# query expressions, seen in Chapter 13.

Example: Probabilistic Computations

Computation expressions provide a fascinating way to embed a range of nontrivial, nonstandard computations into F#. To give you a feel for this, this section will define a *probabilistic* workflow. That is, instead of writing expressions to compute, say, integers, you instead write expressions that compute *distributions* of integers. This case study is based on a paper by Ramsey and Pfeffer from 2002.

For the purposes of this section, you're interested in distributions over discrete domains characterized by three things:

- You want to be able to sample from a distribution (for example, sample an integer or a coin flip).

- You want to compute the support of a distribution; that is, a set of values in which all elements outside the set have zero chance of being sampled.

- You want to compute the expectation of a function over the distribution. For example, you can compute the probability of selecting element A by evaluating the expectation of the function (fun x -> if x = A then 1.0 else 0.0).

You can model this notion of a distribution with abstract objects. Listing 16-2 shows the definition of a type of distribution values and an implementation of the basic primitives always and coinFlip, which help build distributions.

Listing 16-2. Implementing probabilistic modeling using computation expressions

```
type Distribution<'T when 'T : comparison> =
    abstract Sample : 'T
    abstract Support : Set<'T>
    abstract Expectation: ('T -> float) -> float

let always x =
    { new Distribution<'T> with
        member d.Sample = x
        member d.Support = Set.singleton x
        member d.Expectation(H) = H(x) }

let rnd = System.Random()

let coinFlip (p : float) (d1 : Distribution<'T>) (d2 : Distribution<'T>) =
    if p < 0.0 || p > 1.0 then failwith "invalid probability in coinFlip"
    { new Distribution<'T> with
        member d.Sample =
            if rnd.NextDouble() < p then d1.Sample else d2.Sample
        member d.Support = Set.union d1.Support d2.Support
        member d.Expectation(H) =
            p * d1.Expectation(H) + (1.0 - p) * d2.Expectation(H) }
```

The types of these primitives are:

```
type Distribution<'T when 'T : comparison> =
  interface
    abstract member Expectation : ('T -> float) -> float
    abstract member Sample : 'T
    abstract member Support : Set<'T>
  end

val always : x:'T -> Distribution<'T> when 'T : comparison
val coinFlip :
  p:float -> d1:Distribution<'T> -> d2:Distribution<'T> -> Distribution<'T>
    when 'T : comparison
```

The simplest distribution is always x. This is a distribution that always samples to the same value. Its expectation and support are easy to calculate. The expectation of a function H is just H applied to the value, and the support is a set containing the single value x.

The next distribution defined is coinFlip, which is a distribution that models the ability to choose between two outcomes. Listing 16-3 shows how you can define a workflow builder for distribution objects.

Listing 16-3. Defining a builder for probabilistic modeling using computation expressions

```
let bind (dist : Distribution<'T>) (k : 'T -> Distribution<'U>) =
    { new Distribution<'U> with
          member d.Sample =
              (k dist.Sample).Sample
          member d.Support =
              Set.unionMany (dist.Support |> Set.map (fun d -> (k d).Support))
          member d.Expectation H =
              dist.Expectation(fun x -> (k x).Expectation H) }

type DistributionBuilder() =
    member x.Delay f = bind (always ()) f
    member x.Bind(d, f) = bind d f
    member x.Return v = always v
    member x.ReturnFrom vs = vs

let dist = new DistributionBuilder()
```

The types of these primitives are as follows:

```
val bind :
  dist:Distribution<'T> -> k:('T -> Distribution<'U>) -> Distribution<'U>
    when 'T : comparison and 'U : comparison
val dist: DistributionBuilder
```

Listing 16-4 shows the all-important bind primitive; it combines two distributions, using the sample from the first to guide the sample from the second. The support and expectation are calculated by taking the support from the first and splaying it over the support of the second. The expectation is computed by using the first distribution to compute the expectation of a function derived from the second. These are standard results in probability theory, and they are the basic machinery you need in order to get going with some interesting modeling.

Before you begin using workflow syntax, define two derived functions to compute distributions. Listing 16-4 shows the additional derived operations for distribution objects that you will use later in this example.

Listing 16-4. Defining the derived operations for probabilistic modeling using computation expressions

```
let weightedCases (inp : ('T * float) list) =
    let rec coinFlips w l =
        match l with
        | [] -> failwith "no coinFlips"
        | [(d, _)] -> always d
        | (d, p) :: rest -> coinFlip (p / (1.0 - w)) (always d) (coinFlips (w + p) rest)
    coinFlips 0.0 inp

let countedCases inp =
    let total = Seq.sumBy (fun (_, v) -> v) inp
    weightedCases (inp |> List.map (fun (x, v) -> (x, float v / float total)))
```

The two functions weightedCases and countedCases build distributions from the weighted selection of a finite number of cases. The types are:

```
val weightedCases :
  inp:('T * float) list -> Distribution<'T> when 'T : comparison
val countedCases :
  inp:('a * int) list -> Distribution<'a> when 'a : comparison
```

For example, here is the distribution of outcomes on a fair European roulette wheel:

```
type Outcome = Even | Odd | Zero
let roulette = countedCases [ Even,18; Odd,18; Zero,1]
```

You can now use sampling to draw from this distribution:

```
> roulette.Sample;;
val it : Outcome = Even

> roulette.Sample;;
val it : Outcome = Odd
```

You can compute the expected payout of a $5 bet on Even, where you would get a $10 return:

```
> roulette.Expectation (function Even -> 10.0 | Odd -> 0.0 | Zero -> 0.0);;
val it : float = 4.864864865
```

Now, let's model another scenario. Let's say you have a traffic light with the following probability distribution for showing red/yellow/green:

```
type Light = Red | Green | Yellow

let trafficLightD = weightedCases [Red, 0.50; Yellow, 0.10; Green, 0.40]
```

Drivers are defined by their behavior with respect to a traffic light. For example, a cautious driver is highly likely to brake on a yellow light and always stops on a red:

```
type Action = Stop | Drive

let cautiousDriver light =
    dist { match light with
           | Red -> return Stop
           | Yellow -> return! weightedCases [Stop, 0.9; Drive, 0.1]
           | Green -> return Drive}
```

An aggressive driver is unlikely to brake on yellow and may even go through a red light:

```
let aggressiveDriver light =
    dist { match light with
           | Red -> return! weightedCases [Stop, 0.9; Drive, 0.1]
           | Yellow -> return! weightedCases [Stop, 0.1; Drive, 0.9]
           | Green -> return Drive}
```

This gives the value of the light showing in the other direction:

```
let otherLight light =
    match light with
    | Red -> Green
    | Yellow -> Red
    | Green -> Red
```

You can now model the probability of a crash between two drivers given a traffic light. Assume there is a 10 percent chance that two drivers going through the intersection will avoid a crash:

```
type CrashResult = Crash | NoCrash

// Where the suffix D means distribution
let crash (driverOneD, driverTwoD, lightD) =
    dist { // Sample from the traffic light
           let! light = lightD

           // Sample the first driver's behavior given the traffic light
           let! driverOne = driverOneD light

           // Sample the second driver's behavior given the traffic light
           let! driverTwo = driverTwoD (otherLight light)
```

```
    // Work out the probability of a crash
    match driverOne, driverTwo with
    | Drive, Drive -> return! weightedCases [Crash, 0.9; NoCrash, 0.1]
    | _ -> return NoCrash}
```

You can now instantiate the model to a cautious/aggressive driver pair, sample the overall model, and compute the overall expectation of a crash as being approximately 3.7 percent:

```
> let model = crash (cautiousDriver, aggressiveDriver, trafficLightD);;
val model : Distribution<CrashResult>

> model.Sample;;

val it : CrashResult = NoCrash
...
> model.Sample;;

val it : CrashResult = Crash

> model.Expectation (function Crash -> 1.0 | NoCrash -> 0.0);;

val it : float = 0.0369
```

■ **Note**   This section showed how to define a simplistic embedded *computational probabilistic modeling language*. There are many more-efficient and more-sophisticated techniques to apply to the description, evaluation, and analysis of probabilistic models than those shown here, and you can make the implementation of the primitives shown here more efficient by being more careful about the underlying computational representations.

Combining Computation Expressions and Resources

In some situations, computation expressions can sensibly make use of transient resources, such as files. The tricky thing is that you still want to be careful about closing and disposing of resources when the workflow is complete or when it's no longer being used. For this reason, the workflow type must be carefully designed so as to correctly dispose of resources halfway through a computation, if necessary. This is useful, for example, in sequence expressions, such as this one that opens a file and reads lines on demand:

```
let linesOfFile fileName =
    seq { use textReader = System.IO.File.OpenText(fileName)
          while not textReader.EndOfStream do
              yield textReader.ReadLine()}
```

Chapter 4 discussed the construct use pat = expr. As shown in Table 16-2, you can also use this construct within computation expressions. In this case, the use pat = expr construct de-sugars into a call to seq.Using. In the case of sequence expressions, this function is carefully implemented to ensure that textReader is kept open for the duration of the process of reading from the file. Furthermore, the Dispose function on each generated IEnumerator object for a sequence calls the textReader.Dispose() method. This ensures that the file is closed even if you enumerate only half of the lines in the file. Computation expressions thus allow you to scope the lifetime of a resource over a delayed computation.

Recursive Workflow Expressions

Like functions, workflow expressions can be defined recursively using a standard recursive function. Many of the best examples are generative sequences. For example:

```
let rnd = System.Random()

let rec randomWalk k =
    seq { yield k
          yield! randomWalk (k + rnd.NextDouble() - 0.5) }
```

```
> randomWalk 10.0;;

val it : seq<float> = seq [10.0; 10.44456912; 10.52486359; 10.07400056; ...]

> randomWalk 10.0;;

val it : seq<float> = seq [10.0; 10.03566833; 10.12441613; 9.922847582; ...]
```

Using F# Reflection

The final topics in this chapter are *F# quotations*, which provide a way to access a representation of F# expressions as abstract syntax trees, and *reflection*, which lets you access representations of assemblies, type definitions, and member signatures. Let's look at reflection first.

Reflecting on Types

One of the simplest uses of reflection is to access the representation of types and generic type variables using the typeof operator. For example, typeof<int> and typeof<'T> are both expressions that generate values of type System.Type. Given a System.Type value, you can use the .NET APIs to access the System.Reflection. Assembly value that represents the .NET assembly that contains the definition of the type (.NET assemblies are described in Chapter 19). You can also access other types in the System.Reflection namespace, such as MethodInfo, PropertyInfo, MemberInfo, and ConstructorInfo. The following example examines the names associated with some common types:

```
> let intType = typeof<int>;;

val intType : System.Type = System.Int32

> intType.FullName;;

val it : string = "System.Int32"
```

```
> intType.AssemblyQualifiedName;;

val it : string =
  "System.Int32, mscorlib, Version=4.0.0.0, Culture=neutral, PublicKeyToken=b77a5c561934e089"

> let intListType = typeof<int list>;;

val intListType : System.Type =
  FSharp.Collections.FSharpList'1[System.Int32]

> intListType.FullName;;

val it : string =
  "FSharp.Collections.FSharpList'1[[System.Int32, mscorlib, Version=4.0.0.0,
Culture=neutral, PublicKeyToken=b77a5c561934e089]]"
```

Schema Compilation by Reflecting on Types

The F# library includes the namespace FSharp.Reflection, which contains types and functions that extend the functionality of the System.Reflection namespace. You can use the combination of .NET and F# reflection to provide generic implementations of language-related transformations. This section gives one example of this powerful technique. Listing 16-5 shows the definition of a *generic schema-reader compiler*, in which a data schema is described using F# types, and the schema compiler helps convert untyped data from comma-separated value text files into this data schema.

Listing 16-5. Using types and attributes to guide dynamic schema compilation

```
open System
open System.IO
open System.Globalization
open FSharp.Reflection

/// An attribute to be added to fields of a schema record type to indicate the
/// column used in the data format for the schema.
type ColumnAttribute(col : int) =
    inherit Attribute()
    member x.Column = col

/// SchemaReader builds an object that automatically transforms lines of text
/// files in comma-separated form into instances of the given type 'Schema.
/// 'Schema must be an F# record type where each field is attributed with a
/// ColumnAttribute attribute, thus indicating which column of the data the record
/// field is drawn from. This simple version of the reader understands
/// integer, string, and DateTime values in the CSV format.
type SchemaReader<'Schema>() =

    // Grab the object for the type that describes the schema
    let schemaType = typeof<'Schema>
```

```
// Grab the fields from that type
let fields = FSharpType.GetRecordFields(schemaType)

// For each field find the ColumnAttribute and compute a function
// to build a value for the field
let schema =
    fields |> Array.mapi (fun fldIdx fld ->
        let fieldInfo = schemaType.GetProperty(fld.Name)
        let fieldConverter =
            match fld.PropertyType with
            | ty when ty = typeof<string> -> (fun (s : string) -> box s)
            | ty when ty = typeof<int> -> (System.Int32.Parse >> box)
            | ty when ty = typeof<DateTime> ->
                (fun s -> box (DateTime.Parse(s, CultureInfo.InvariantCulture)))
            | ty -> failwithf "Unknown primitive type %A" ty

        let attrib =
            match fieldInfo.GetCustomAttributes(typeof<ColumnAttribute>, false) with
            | [|(:? ColumnAttribute as attrib)|] -> attrib
            | _ -> failwithf "No column attribute found on field %s" fld.Name
        (fldIdx, fld.Name, attrib.Column, fieldConverter))

// Compute the permutation defined by the ColumnAttribute indexes
let columnToFldIdxPermutation c =
    schema |> Array.pick (fun (fldIdx, _, colIdx, _) ->
        if colIdx = c then Some fldIdx else None)

// Drop the parts of the schema we don't need
let schema =
    schema |> Array.map (fun (_, fldName, _, fldConv) -> (fldName, fldConv))

// Compute a function to build instances of the schema type. This uses an
// F# library function.
let objectBuilder = FSharpValue.PreComputeRecordConstructor(schemaType)

// OK, now we're ready to implement a line reader
member reader.ReadLine(textReader : TextReader) =
    let line = textReader.ReadLine()
    let words = line.Split([|','|]) |> Array.map(fun s -> s.Trim())
    if words.Length <> schema.Length then
        failwith "unexpected number of columns in line %s" line
    let words = words |> Array.permute columnToFldIdxPermutation

    let convertColumn colText (fieldName, fieldConverter) =
        try fieldConverter colText
        with e ->
            failwithf "error converting '%s' to field '%s'" colText fieldName

    let obj = objectBuilder (Array.map2 convertColumn words schema)

    // OK, now we know we've dynamically built an object of the right type
    unbox<'Schema>(obj)
```

```
/// This reads an entire file
member reader.ReadFile(file) =
    seq { use textReader = File.OpenText(file)
          while not textReader.EndOfStream do
              yield reader.ReadLine(textReader)}
```

The type of SchemaReader is simple:

```
type SchemaReader<'Schema> =
    new : unit -> SchemaReader<'Schema>
    member ReadFile : file:string -> seq<'Schema>
    member ReadLine : textReader:System.IO.TextReader -> 'Schema
```

First, see how SchemaReader is used in practice. Let's say you have a text file containing lines such as:

```
Steve, 12 March 2010, Cheddar
Sally, 18 Feb 2010, Brie
...
```

It's reasonable to want to convert this data to a typed data representation. You can do this by defining an appropriate record type along with providing enough information to indicate how the data in the file maps into this type. This information is expressed using *custom attributes*, which are a way to add extra meta-information to assembly, type, member, property, and parameter definitions. Each custom attribute is specified as an instance of a typed object—here ColumnAttribute, defined in Listing 16-5. The suffix Attribute is required when defining custom attributes but can be dropped when using them:

```
type CheeseClub =
    { [<Column(0)>] Name : string
      [<Column(2)>] FavoriteCheese : string
      [<Column(1)>] LastAttendance : System.DateTime }
```

You can now instantiate the SchemaReader type and use it to read the data from the file into this typed format:

```
> let reader = new SchemaReader<CheeseClub>();;

val reader : SchemaReader<CheeseClub>

> fsi.AddPrinter(fun (c : System.DateTime) -> c.ToString());;
> System.IO.File.WriteAllLines("data.txt",
    [|"Steve, 12 March 2010, Cheddar"; "Sally, 18 Feb 2010, Brie"|]);;

> reader.ReadFile("data.txt");;

val it : seq<CheeseClub>
= seq
    [{Name = "Steve";
      FavoriteCheese = "Cheddar";
      LastAttendance = 12/03/2010 00:00:00;};
     {Name = "Sally";
      FavoriteCheese = "Brie";
      LastAttendance = 18/02/2010 00:00:00;}]
```

There is something somewhat magical about this; you've built a layer that automatically does the impedance matching between the untyped world of a text-file format into the typed world of F# programming. Amazingly, the SchemaReader type itself is only about 50 lines of code. The comments in Listing 16-5 show the basic steps being performed. The essential features of this technique are:

1. The schema information is passed to the SchemaReader as a type variable. The SchemaReader then uses the typeof operator to extract a System.Type representation of the schema type.

2. The information needed to drive the transformation process comes from custom attributes. Extra information can also be supplied to the constructor of the SchemaReader type if necessary.

3. The let bindings of the SchemaReader type are effectively a form of precomputation (they can also be seen as a form of compilation). They precompute as much information as possible given the schema. For example, the section analyzes the fields of the schema type and computes functions for creating objects of the field types. It also computes the permutation from the text-file columns to the record fields.

4. The data objects are ultimately constructed using reflection functions, in this case a function computed by FSharp.Reflection.Value.GetRecordConstructor or primitive values parsed using System.Int32.Parse and similar functions. This and other functions for creating F# objects dynamically are in the FSharp. Reflection library. Other functions for creating other .NET objects dynamically are in the System.Reflection library.

5. The member bindings of SchemaReader interpret the residue of the precomputation stage, in this case using the information and computed functions to process the results of splitting the text of a line.

This technique has many potential applications and has been used for CSV file reading, building F#-centric serializers/deserializers, implementing F# type providers, and building generic strongly typed database schema access.

Using the F# Dynamic Reflection Operators

F# lets you define two special operators, (?) and (?<-), to perform dynamic lookups of objects. These are conceptually very simple operators, but they add interesting new opportunities for interoperability between dynamic data and static data in F# programming.

These operators implicitly translate their second argument to a string if it's a simple identifier. That is, a use of these operators is translated as:

```
expr ? nm           ➤    (?) expr "nm"
expr1 ? nm <- expr2 ➤    (?<-) expr1 "nm" expr2
```

This means that the operators can be used to simulate a dynamic lookup of a property or a method on an object. This dynamic lookup can use any dynamic/reflective technique available to you. One such technique is to use .NET reflection to look up and/or set the properties of an object:

```
open System.Reflection

let (?) (obj : obj) (nm : string) : 'T =
    obj.GetType().InvokeMember(nm, BindingFlags.GetProperty, null, obj, [||])
    |> unbox<'T>
```

```
let (?<-) (obj : obj) (nm : string) (v : obj) : unit =
    obj.GetType().InvokeMember(nm, BindingFlags.SetProperty, null, obj, [|v|])
    |> ignore
```

Now, you can use the operators to dynamically query data:

```
type Record1 = {Length : int; mutable Values : int list}

let obj1 = box [1; 2; 3]
let obj2 = box {Length = 4; Values = [3; 4; 5; 7]}

let n1 : int = obj1?Length
let n2 : int = obj2?Length
let valuesOld : int list = obj2?Values
```

Here, both obj1 and obj2 have type obj, but you can do dynamic lookups of the properties Length and Values using the ? operator. Of course, these uses aren't strongly statically typed—this is why you need the type annotations : int and : int list to indicate the return type of the operation. Given the earlier definition of the (?<-) operator, you can also set a property dynamically::

```
obj2?Values <- [7; 8; 9]
let valuesNew : int list = obj2?Values
```

Using the (?) and (?<-) operators obviously comes with strong drawbacks: you lose considerable type safety, and performance may be affected by the use of dynamic techniques. Their use is recommended only when you're consistently interoperating with weakly typed objects, or when you continually find yourself doing string-based lookups of elements of an object.

Using F# Quotations

The other side to reflective meta-programming in F# is *quotations*. These allow you to reflect over expressions in much the same way that you've reflected over types in the previous section. It's simple to get going with F# quotations; you open the appropriate modules and surround an expression with <@ . . . @> symbols:

```
> open FSharp.Quotations;;

> let oneExpr = <@ 1 @>;;

val oneExpr : Expr<int> = Value (1)

> let plusExpr = <@ 1 + 1 @>;;

val plusExpr : Expr<int> = Call (None, op_Addition, [Value (1), Value (1)])
```

You can see here that the act of quoting an expression gives you back the expression as data. Those familiar with Lisp or Scheme know a sophisticated version of this in the form of Lisp quotations, and those familiar with C# 3.0 will find it familiar, as C# uses similar mechanisms for its lambda expressions. F# quotations are distinctive partly because they're *typed* (like C# lambda expressions) and because the functional, expression-based nature of F# means that so much of the language can be quoted and manipulated relatively easily.

Chapter 13 uses F# queries that implicitly convert F# quotations to SQL via the .NET LINQ library. Perhaps the most important application is in Chapter 14, where quotations are converted to JavaScript when using WebSharper. This may be implemented by a function with a type such as

```
val CompileToJavaScript : Expr<'T> -> string
```

WHAT ARE F# QUOTATIONS FOR?

The primary rationale for F# quotations is that they allow fragments of F# syntax to be executed by alternative means; for example, as an SQL query via LINQ or by being run on another device, such as a GPU or as JavaScript in a client-side web browser. F# aims to leverage heavy-hitting external components that map subsets of functional programs to other execution machinery. Another example usage involves executing a subset of F# array code by the dynamic generation of Fortran code and invoking a high-performance vectorizing Fortran compiler. The generated DLL is loaded and invoked dynamically.

This effectively means that you can convert from a computational representation of a language (for example, regular F# functions and F# workflow expressions) to an abstract syntax representation of the same language. This is a powerful technique, because it lets you design using a computational model of the language (for example, sampling from a distribution or running queries against local data) and then switch to a more concrete abstract-syntax representation of the same programs in order to analyze, execute, print, or compile those programs in other ways.

Example: Using F# Quotations for Error Estimation

Listing 16-6 shows a prototypical use of quotations, in this case to perform error estimation on F# arithmetic expressions.

Listing 16-6. Error analysis on F# expressions implemented with F# quotations

```
open FSharp.Quotations
open FSharp.Quotations.Patterns
open FSharp.Quotations.DerivedPatterns

type Error = Err of float

let rec errorEstimateAux (e : Expr) (env : Map<Var, _>) =
    match e with
    | SpecificCall <@@ (+) @@> (tyargs, _, [xt; yt]) ->
        let x, Err(xerr) = errorEstimateAux xt env
        let y, Err(yerr) = errorEstimateAux yt env
        (x + y, Err(xerr + yerr))
```

```
    | SpecificCall <@@ (-) @@> (tyargs, _, [xt; yt]) ->
        let x, Err(xerr) = errorEstimateAux xt env
        let y, Err(yerr) = errorEstimateAux yt env
        (x - y, Err(xerr + yerr))

    | SpecificCall <@@ ( * ) @@> (tyargs, _, [xt; yt]) ->
        let x, Err(xerr) = errorEstimateAux xt env
        let y, Err(yerr) = errorEstimateAux yt env
        (x * y, Err(xerr * abs(y) + yerr * abs(x) + xerr * yerr))

    | SpecificCall <@@ abs @@> (tyargs, _, [xt]) ->
        let x, Err(xerr) = errorEstimateAux xt env
        (abs(x), Err(xerr))

    | Let(var, vet, bodyt) ->
        let varv, verr = errorEstimateAux vet env
        errorEstimateAux bodyt (env.Add(var, (varv, verr)))

    | Call(None, MethodWithReflectedDefinition(Lambda(v, body)), [arg]) ->
        errorEstimateAux (Expr.Let(v, arg, body)) env

    | Var(x) -> env.[x]

    | Double(n) -> (n, Err(0.0))

    | _ -> failwithf "unrecognized term: %A" e

let rec errorEstimateRaw (t : Expr) =
    match t with
    | Lambda(x, t) ->
        (fun xv -> errorEstimateAux t (Map.ofSeq [(x, xv)]))
    | PropertyGet(None, PropertyGetterWithReflectedDefinition(body), []) ->
        errorEstimateRaw body
    | _ -> failwithf "unrecognized term: %A - expected a lambda" t

let errorEstimate (t : Expr<float -> float>) = errorEstimateRaw t
```

The inferred types of the functions are:

```
type Error = | Err of float
val errorEstimateAux : e:Expr -> env:Map<Var,(float * Error)> -> float * Error
val errorEstimateRaw : t:Expr -> (float * Error -> float * Error)
val errorEstimate :
  t:Expr<(float -> float)> -> (float * Error -> float * Error)
```

That is, errorEstimate is a function that takes an expression for a float -> float function and returns
a function value of type float * Error -> float * Error.

Let's see it in action. First, define the err function and a pretty-printer for float * Error pairs, using the Unicode symbol for error bounds on a value:

```
> let err x = Err x;;

val err : x:float -> Error

> fsi.AddPrinter (fun (x : float, Err v) -> sprintf "%g±%g" x v);;

> errorEstimate <@ fun x -> x + 2.0 * x + 3.0 * x * x @> (1.0, err 0.1);;

val it : float * Error = 6±0.93

> errorEstimate <@ fun x -> let y = x + x in y * y + 2.0 @> (1.0, err 0.1);;

val it : float * Error = 6±0.84
```

The key aspects of the implementation of errorEstimate are:

- The errorEstimate function converts the inputted expression to a raw expression, which is an untyped abstract-syntax representation of the expression designed for further processing. It then calls errorEstimateRaw. Traversals are generally much easier to perform using raw terms.

- The errorEstimateRaw function then checks that the expression given is a lambda expression, using the active pattern Lambda provided by the FSharp.Quotations. Patterns module.

- The errorEstimateRaw function then calls the auxiliary function errorEstimateAux. This function keeps track of a mapping from variables to value/error estimate pairs. It recursively analyzes the expression looking for +, -, * and abs operations. These are all overloaded operators and hence are called *generic functions* in F# terminology, so the function uses the active pattern SpecificCall to detect applications of these operators. At each point, it performs the appropriate error estimation.

- For variables, the environment map env is consulted. For constants, the error is zero.

- Two additional cases are covered in errorEstimateAux and errorEstimateRaw. The Let pattern allows you to include expressions of the form let x = e1 in e2 in the subset accepted by the quotation analyzer. The MethodWithReflectedDefinition case allows you to perform analyses on some function calls, as you will see next.

Resolving Reflected Definitions

One problem with meta-programming with explicit <@ ... @> quotation marks alone is that you can't analyze very large programs, as the entire expression to be analyzed must be delimited by these markers. This is solved in F# by allowing you to tag top-level member and let bindings as being reflected. This ensures that their definitions are persisted to a table attached to their compiled DLL or EXE. These functions can also be executed as normal F# code. For example, here is a function whose definition is persisted:

```
[<ReflectedDefinition>]
let poly x = x + 2.0 * x + 3.0 * (x * x)
```

You can retrieve definitions such as this using the `MethodWithReflectedDefinition` and `PropertyGetterWithReflectedDefinition` active patterns, as shown in Listing 16-6. You can now use this function in a regular `<@ ... @>` quotation and thus analyze it for errors:

```
> errorEstimate <@ poly @> (3.0, err 0.1);;

val it : float * Error = 36±2.13

> errorEstimate <@  poly @> (30271.3, err 0.0001);;

val it : float * Error = 2.74915e+09±18.1631
```

The `ReflectedDefinition` attribute can also be used on whole modules; for example:

```
[<ReflectedDefinition>]
module Polynomials =
    let poly1 x = x + 2.0 * x + 3.0 * (x * x)
    let poly2 x = x - 3.0 * x + 6.0 * (x * x)
```

From F# 4.0, the `ReflectedDefinition` attribute can also be used on parameters of members. This can be useful on an API where you want to arrange for the implicit quotation of code:

```
type Errors() =
    static member Estimate([<ReflectedDefinition>] expr) = errorEstimate expr
```

When this member is called, no explicit quotation delimiters are required:

```
let est1 = Errors.Estimate(fun x -> x - 3.0 * x + 6.0 * (x * x))
```

Writing an F# Type Provider

The last meta-programming topic we will consider in this chapter is a brief look at how you can write a type provider for F#. You have been using type providers to access and process data throughout this book, in Chapters 2, 8, and 13.

In this section, you will develop a very small type provider for F#. The type provider "generates" a type space where the number of types can be specified by the user. The user can also specify how many static properties each type contains. Once working, the type provider will allow a user of the provider to write the following code:

```
#r @"MyTypeProvider\bin\Debug\MyTypeProvider.dll"

type F = MyCode.ExampleProvider<60,100>

F.Type57.StaticProperty78
```

The two integers in the type provider invocation MyCode.ExampleProvider<60,100> are the number of types and the number of properties in each type respectively. When working in an editor, the provided types and properties are shown in auto-complete (see Figure 16-1):

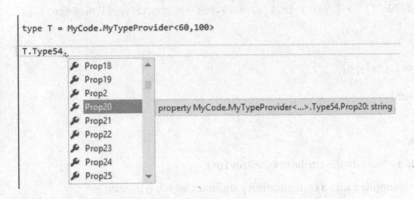

Figure 16-1. Using the Type Provider

The code for the type provider is shown in Listing 16-7.

Listing 16-7. Implementing a very simple type provider

```
module ExampleTypeProvider

open ProviderImplementation.ProvidedTypes
open FSharp.Core.CompilerServices
open System.Reflection

let createType (i, numProps) =
    let t = ProvidedTypeDefinition("Type"+string i, Some typeof<obj>)
    t.AddMembersDelayed(fun () ->
        [ for j in 1 .. numProps ->
            let propName = "StaticProp"+string j
            ProvidedProperty(propName, typeof<string>,
                IsStatic = true,
                GetterCode = (fun _ -> <@@ "Hello world: " + string j @@>)) ])
    t

[<TypeProvider>]
type ExampleProviderImpl (config : TypeProviderConfig) as this =
    inherit TypeProviderForNamespaces ()

    let ns = "MyCode"
    let asm = Assembly.GetExecutingAssembly()

    let myType = ProvidedTypeDefinition(asm, ns, "MyTypeProvider", Some typeof<obj>)
    let sparams =
        [ ProvidedStaticParameter("NumTypes", typeof<int>)
          ProvidedStaticParameter("NumProperties", typeof<int>) ]
```

```
    do myType.DefineStaticParameters(sparams, (fun typeName args ->
        let numTypes = unbox<int> args.[0]
        let numProps = unbox<int> args.[1]
        let t = ProvidedTypeDefinition(asm, ns, typeName, Some typeof<obj>)
        t.AddMembersDelayed(fun () -> [ for i in 1 .. numTypes -> createType(i,numProps) ])
        t))

    do
        this.AddNamespace(ns, [myType])

[<assembly:TypeProviderAssembly>]
do ()
```

In the code, note the following:

- The type provider is a class with the attribute TypeProvider.

- Each type provider is supplied with a configuration parameter, which is unused in this example.

- The provided types and members can be identified through the uses of ProvidedTypeDefinition and ProvidedPropertyDefinition. You may also use ProvidedMethodDefinition, ProvidedEventDefinition, and so on.

- Provided members (i.e., methods and nested types) are generated in an on-demand or "delayed" way.

- The outermost type is called MyTypeProvider, is in namespace MyCode, and takes two static parameters. These are called NumTypes and NumProperties, and both accept integer values.

- The static parameters are unboxed from objects using unbox<int>, and the second is passed to createType.

- The createType function is called for each provided type. Each type in turn includes numProps provided properties. In this short example, all the provided properties are static.

- Each of the provided properties has an implementation given by the quotation <@@ "Hello world: " + string j @@>, where j is the number of the property. This means that when the property is mentioned in user code, it is replaced by this code; the code is effectively the "macro expansion" of uses of the property.

■ **Note** The aim of this example is to show the form of the meta-programming code needed when writing a type provider. The sample code is intended to be used in conjunction with the Type Provider Starter Pack from https://github.com/fsprojects/FSharp.TypeProviders.StarterPack. Implementing type providers is a large topic. For more-complete information, see the F# Type Provider Starter Pack and other online guides.

Summary

This chapter covered key topics in a programming paradigm—*language-oriented programming*—that is central to F#. In previous chapters, you saw some techniques for traversing abstract syntax trees. These language-representation techniques give you powerful ways to manipulate concrete and abstract syntax fragments.

In this chapter, you saw two language-representation techniques that are tightly coupled to F#: F# computation expressions, which are useful for embedded computational languages involving sequencing, and F# quotations, which let you give an alternative meaning to existing F# program fragments. Along the way, the chapter touched on reflection and its use in mediating between typed and untyped representations. You also learned how to program a very simple F# type provider.

In the next chapter, you'll look at some of the interoperability mechanisms that come with the .NET implementation of F#.

CHAPTER 17

■ ■ ■

Libraries and Interoperability

> *Programming in different languages is like composing pieces in different keys, particularly if you work at the keyboard. If you have learned or written pieces in many keys, each key will have its own special emotional aura. Also, certain kinds of figurations "lie in the hand" in one key but are awkward in another. So you are channeled by your choice of key. In some ways, even enharmonic keys, such as C-sharp and D-flat, are quite distinct in feeling. This shows how a notational system can play a significant role in shaping the final product.*

> *Gödel, Escher, Bach: An Eternal Golden Braid*, Hofstadter, 1980, Chapter X

Software integration and reuse is becoming one of the most relevant activities in software development. This chapter will discuss how F# programs can interoperate with the outside world by accessing code available from both .NET and other languages.

Types, Memory, and Interoperability

F# programs need to call libraries, even for very basic tasks, such as printing or accessing files, and these libraries come in binary form as part of the Common Language Runtime (CLR), the piece of software responsible for running programs after compilation. Libraries can be, and have been, written using different programming languages, leveraging the fact that the output of the compilation has a common format that the CLR uses for executing the code. Even considering just the core libraries, such as mscorlib.dll (containing essential types such as System.String, the underlying type for the F# type string), most of the code has been written using C#.

You will need to understand language interoperability, at least to some extent, to be a proficient F# programmer. There are four levels of interoperability to consider:

- F# library
- Non-F# .NET library
- Native library
- Provided types

If a library has been compiled using the F# compiler and is meant to be used from F#, everything feels like F#—types, modules, and functions are available as in F# source form, except for scope restrictions introduced by visibility clauses, such as private. The F# compiler, unless told otherwise, generates additional information into the binary files that are meant to be used when compiling other F# source files that depend on them.

.NET libraries compiled with languages other than F# are easily accessible from F# programs in the form of a set of types and methods. F#-specific values, such function values, may need to be converted into .NET types. Apart from these small issues, using these libraries is seamless, because the runtime is shared and the .NET binary format contains meta-information, such as the type structure, that can be used by compilers to spare the programmer many details related to interoperability.

Native components are generally operating-system specific and have been a de facto standard for interoperability for many years. F# is capable of interoperating with C binary interfaces at the cost of manual annotations. Some marshalling may also be necessary: although simple in theory, sharing types and their values among different runtimes of programming languages results in many subtle issues in practice. Even a relatively simple type, such as the .NET string, has a memory representation very different from C.

F# type providers add an additional powerful form of interoperability to the languages. You learned about type providers in Chapters 3, 8, and 16. In addition to interoperating with data formats, type providers are also used for cross-language interoperability. This is not a topic explored extensively in this chapter, but see, for example, the "R Type Provider," which makes R packages available to F# code.

This chapter will explore the various levels of interoperability, giving an overview of the .NET libraries to begin. Finally, the platform-invoke API is introduced, showing how to link binary libraries and interact with C code; this interface is part of the .NET standard and is available on different CLR implementations running on Windows, MacOS X, and Linux.

■ **Note** For more information about designing F# libraries to be used from other .NET languages, see the F# component design guidelines, available at `http://tinyurl.com/fs-component-design-guidelines`

Libraries: A High-Level Overview

One way to get a quick overview of both the .NET Framework and F# libraries is to look at the primary DLLs and namespaces contained in them. Recall from Chapters 2 and 7 that DLLs correspond to the physical organization of libraries, and that namespaces and types give the logical organization of a naming hierarchy. Let's look at the physical organization first. The types and functions covered in this chapter are drawn from the DLLs in Table 17-1.

Table 17-1. *DLLs Containing the Library Constructs Referred to in This Chapter*

DLL Name	Notes
`mscorlib.dll`	Minimal system constructs, including the types in the `System` namespace
`System.dll`	Additional commonly used constructs in namespaces, such as `System` and `System.Text`
`System.Core.dll`	The foundation types for LINQ and some other useful types
`FSharp.Core.dll`	Minimal constructs for F# assemblies
`FSharp.Data.dll`	Modules, types, and type providers for XML, JSON, CSV, and HTML data-format manipulations, including web requests using these formats. See Chapter 8, "Programming with Text," and Chapter 13, "Integrating External Data and Services."
`System.Xml.dll`	See the corresponding namespace in Table 17-2.
`System.Data.dll`	See the corresponding namespace in Table 17-2.
`System.Net.dll`	See the corresponding namespace in Table 17-2.

To reference additional DLLs, you can embed a #r reference directly into your source code in F# scripting files that use the .fsx extension.

■ **Note** Hundreds of high-quality frameworks and libraries are available for .NET, and more are appearing all the time on http://nuget.org. For space reasons, this chapter covers only the .NET libraries and frameworks listed in Table 17-1.

Namespaces from the .NET Framework

Table 17-2 shows the primary namespaces found in the .NET Framework DLLs from Table 17-1. In some cases, parts of these libraries are covered elsewhere in this book; the table notes these cases. For example, Chapter 4 introduced portions of the .NET I/O library from the System.IO namespace.

Table 17-2. Namespaces in the DLLs from Table 17-1, with MSDN Descriptions

Namespace	Description
System	Types and methods that define commonly used value and reference data types, events and event handlers, interfaces, attributes, and processing exceptions, supporting data-type conversions, mathematics, application environment management, and runtime supervision of managed and unmanaged applications. See Chapter 3 for many of the basic types in this namespace.
System.Collections	Types that define various nongeneric collections of objects, such as lists, queues, and bit arrays. Partially covered in "Using Further F# and .NET Data Structures" later in this chapter.
System.Collections.Generic	Types that define generic collections. See Chapter 4 and "Using Further F# and .NET Data Structures" later in this chapter.
System.Configuration	Types that provide the programming model for handling configuration data
System.Data	Types that represent the ADO.NET database-access architecture. See Chapter 13.
System.Diagnostics	Types that allow you to interact with system processes, event logs, and performance counters. See Chapter 19.
System.Globalization	Types that define culture-related information, including the language, the country/region, the calendars in use, the format patterns for dates, the currency, the numbers, and the sort order for strings. Not covered in this book
System.IO	Types that allow the reading and writing of files and data streams, as well as types that provide basic file and directory support. See Chapter 4 for a basic overview.
System.Net	Types to programmatically access many of the protocols used on modern networks. See Chapters 2 and 14 for examples and a basic overview.

(continued)

Table 17-2. (*continued*)

Namespace	Description
System.Reflection	Types that retrieve information about assemblies, modules, members, parameters, and other entities in managed code. See Chapter 17 for a brief overview.
System.Reflection.Emit	Types for generating .NET code dynamically at runtime
System.Text	Types representing ASCII, Unicode, UTF-8, and other character encodings. Also abstract types for converting blocks of characters to and from blocks of bytes. See Chapter 3 and "Using Regular Expressions and Formatting" later in this chapter.
System.Threading	Types for creating and synchronizing threads and creating .NET tasks. Also, parallel operations and some functionality related to cancellation. See Chapter 11.
System.Xml	Types that implement standards-based support for processing XML. See Chapters 8 and 13.

Namespaces from FSharp.Core and FSharp.Data Libraries

Table 17-3 shows the primary namespaces found in the F# library DLLs from Table 17-1. The following are opened by default in F# code:

```
FSharp.Core
FSharp.Core.Operators
FSharp.Collections
FSharp.Control
FSharp.Text
```

Table 17-3. *Namespaces in the FSharp.Core DLL*

Namespace	Description
FSharp.Core	Provides primitive constructs related to the F# language, such as options. See Chapter 3.
FSharp.Collections	Provides functional programming collections, such as sets and maps implemented using binary trees. See Chapter 3 and "Using Further F# and .NET Data Structures" later in this chapter.
FSharp.Control	Provides functional programming control structures, including asynchronous and lazy programming. Chapter 11 covers programming with the IEvent<'T> type and the IEvent module, as well as the Async<'T> type.
FSharp.Data	Provides modules and types for data formats and unit-of-measure annotations, including type providers in the FSharp.Data library

(continued)

Table 17-3. (*continued*)

Namespace	Description
FSharp.Linq	Provides modules and types for language-integrated queries in F#
FSharp.Text	Provides modules and types for structured and printf-style textual formatting of data. See Chapter 4 for an introduction to printf formatting.
FSharp.Reflection	Provides extensions to the System.Reflection functionality that deal particularly with F# record and discriminated union values. See Chapter 17 for a brief introduction, and see "Further Libraries for Reflective Techniques" section later in this chapter for more details.
FSharp.Quotations	Provides access to F# expressions as abstract syntax trees. See Chapter 17.

Some F# Community Libraries

A very large range of .NET and F# Community libraries are available beyond those listed in this chapter. You can find .NET libraries for just about everything through simple searches on the web, and all these libraries are readily usable from F#. In addition, there are many F#-specific community libraries and tools available for use with F#. Table 17-4 shows some of these libraries.

Table 17-4. *Some .NET and F# Community Libraries, from* fsharp.org/community/projects

Library	Description
FSharp.Core.Fluent	Fluent-style extension members for core F# types. See Chapter 3.
FSharp.Charting	Provides charting suitable for use from F# scripting
Rx, FSharp.Control.Reactive	Supports asynchronous and event-based programming using observable sequences. FSharp.Control.Reactive is an F# wrapper over this library.
FSharp.Control.AsyncSeq	Asynchronous sequences, with some similarities to Rx
FSharp.Compiler.Service	Contains the logic of the F# compiler, for use in hosted editing, analysis, and execution tools.

Using the System Types

Table 17-5 shows some of the most useful core types from the System namespace. These types are particularly useful because of the care and attention taken in crafting them and the functionality they provide.

Table 17-5. *Useful Core Types from the System Namespace*

Function	Description
System.DateTime	A type representing a date and time
System.DayOfWeek	An enumeration type representing a day of the week
System.Decimal	A numeric type suitable for financial calculations requiring large numbers of significant integral and fractional digits and no round-off errors
System.Guid	A type representing a 128-bit globally unique ID
System.Nullable<'T>	A type with an underlying value type 'T but that can be assigned null like a reference type
System.TimeSpan	A type representing a time interval
System.Uri	A type representing a uniform resource identifier (URI), such as an Internet URL

Many .NET types are used to hold static functions, such as those for converting data from one format to another. Types such as System.Random play a similar role via objects with a small amount of state. Table 17-6 shows some of the most useful of these types.

Table 17-6. *Useful Services from the System Namespace*

Function	Description
System.BitConverter	Contains functions to convert numeric representations to and from bit representations
System.Convert	Contains functions to convert between various numeric representations
System.Math	Contains constants and static methods for trigonometric, logarithmic, and other common mathematical functions
System.Random	Provides objects to act as random-number generators
System.StringComparer	Provides objects to implement various types of comparisons on strings (case insensitive, and so on)

Using Further F# and .NET Data Structures

As you saw in Chapter 2, F# comes with a useful implementation of some functional programming data structures. Recall that functional data structures are persistent: you can't mutate them, and if you add an element or otherwise modify the collection, you generate a new collection value, perhaps sharing some internal nodes but from the outside appearing to be a new value.

Table 17-7 summarizes the most important persistent functional data structures that are included in FSharp.Core.dll. It's likely that additional functional data structures will be added in future F# releases.

Table 17-7. *The F# Functional Data Structures from* `FSharp.Collections`

Type	Description
`List<'T>`	Immutable lists implemented using linked lists
`Set<'T>`	Immutable sets implemented using trees
`Map<'Key,'Value>`	Immutable maps (dictionaries) implemented using trees
`LazyList<'T>`	Lists generated on demand, with each element computed only once

System.Collections.Generic and Other .NET Collections

Table 17-8 summarizes the imperative collections available in the `System.Collections.Generic` namespace.

Table 17-8. *The .NET and F# Imperative Data Structures from* `System.Collections.Generic`

Type	Description
`List<'T>`	Mutable, resizable integer-indexed arrays, usually called `ResizeArray<'T>` in F#
`SortedList<'T>`	Mutable, resizable lists implemented using sorted arrays
`Dictionary<'Key,'Value>`	Mutable, resizable dictionaries implemented using hash tables
`SortedDictionary<'Key,'Value>`	Mutable, resizable dictionaries implemented using sorted arrays
`Queue<'T>`	Mutable, first-in, first-out queues of unbounded size
`Stack<'T>`	Mutable, first-in, last-out stacks of unbounded size
`HashSet<'T>`	Mutable, resizable sets implemented using hash tables. New in .NET 3.5. The F# library also defines an `FSharp.Collections.HashSet` type usable in conjunction with earlier versions of .NET.

SOME OTHER COLLECTION LIBRARIES

Two additional libraries of .NET collections deserve particular attention. The first is `PowerCollections`. It provides additional generic types, such as `Bag<'T>`, `MultiDictionary<'Key,'Value>`, `OrderedDictionary<'Key,'Value>`, `OrderedMultiDictionary<'T>`, and `OrderedSet<'T>`.
The second is the `C5` collection library, provided by ITU in Denmark. It includes implementations of some persistent/functional data structures, such as persistent trees, that may be of particular interest for use from F#.

Supervising and Isolating Execution

The .NET System namespace includes a number of useful types that provide functionality related to the execution of running programs in the .NET Common Language Runtime. Table 17-9 summarizes them.

Table 17-9. *Types Related to Runtime Supervision of Applications*

Function	Description
System.Runtime	Contains advanced types that support compilation and native interoperability
System.Environment	Provides information about, and the means to manipulate, the current environment and platform
System.GC	Controls the system garbage collector. Garbage collection is discussed in more detail later in this chapter.
System.WeakReference	Represents a weak reference, which references an object while still allowing that object to be reclaimed by garbage collection
System.AppDomain	Represents an application domain, which is a software-isolated environment in which applications execute. Application domains can hold code generated at runtime and can be unloaded.

Further Libraries for Reflective Techniques

As discussed in Chapter 17, .NET and F# programming frequently use reflective techniques to analyze the types of objects, create objects at runtime, and use type information to drive generic functions in general ways. For example, in Chapter 17 you saw an example of a technique called schema compilation, which was based on .NET attributes and F# data types, and used a compiler to take these and use reflective techniques to generate an efficient text-file reader and translator. The combination of reflective techniques and .NET generics allows programs to operate at the boundary between statically typed code and dynamically typed data.

Using General Types

There are a number of facets to reflective programming with .NET. In one simple kind of reflective programming, a range of data structures are accessed in a general way. For example, .NET includes a type System.Array that is a parent type of all array types. The existence of this type allows you to write code that is generic over all array types, even one-dimensional and multidimensional arrays. This is occasionally useful, such as when you're writing a generic array printer.

Table 17-10 summarizes the primary general types defined in the .NET Framework.

Table 17-10. *General Types in the .NET Framework*

Function	Description
System.Array	General type of all array values
System.Delegate	General type of all delegates
System.Enum	General type of all enum values
System.Exception	General type of all exception values
System.Collections.IEnumerable	General type of all sequence values. This is the nongeneric version of the F# type seq<'T>, and all sequence and collection values are compatible with this type.
System.IComparable	General type of all comparable types
System.IDisposable	General type of all explicitly reclaimable resources
System.IFormattable	General type of all types supporting .NET formatting
System.Object	General type of all objects
System.Type	Runtime representation of .NET types
System.ValueType	General type of all value types

Using FSharp.Reflection

In Chapter 17, the schema compiler used functions from the FSharp.Reflection namespace. This namespace is a relatively thin extension of the System.Reflection namespace. It offers an interesting set of techniques for creating and analyzing F# values and types in ways that are somewhat simpler than those offered by the System.Reflection namespace. These operations are also designed to be used in precompilation phases to amortize costs associated with reflective programming.

Table 17-11 summarizes the two types in this namespace.

Table 17-11. *Some Operations in the FSharp.Reflection Namespace*

Class and Static Members	Description
FSharp.Reflection.FSharpType	Operations to analyze F# types
FSharp.Reflection.FSharpValue	Operations to analyze F# values

Some Other .NET Types You May Encounter

When .NET was first designed, the .NET type system didn't include generics or a general notion of a function type as used by F#. Instead of functions, .NET uses delegates, which you can think of as named function types (that is, each kind of function type is given a different name).

This means that you often encounter delegate types when using .NET libraries from F#. Since .NET 2.0, some of these are even generic, giving an approximation of the simple and unified view of function types used by F#. Every .NET delegate type has a corresponding F# function type. For example, the F# function type for the .NET delegate type System.Windows.Forms.PaintEventHandler is obj -> System.Windows.Forms.PaintEventArgs -> unit. You can figure out this type by looking at the signature for the Invoke method of the given delegate type.

.NET also comes with definitions for some generic delegate types. F# tends to use function types instead of these, so you don't see them often in your coding. However, Table 17-12 shows these delegate types just in case you meet them.

Table 17-12. *Delegate Types Encountered Occasionally in F# Coding*

Function	F# Function Type	Description
`System.Action<'T>`	`'T -> unit`	Used for imperative actions
`System.AsyncCallback`	`System.IAsyncResult -> unit`	Used for callbacks when asynchronous actions complete
`System.Converter<'T,'U>`	`'T -> 'U`	Used to convert between values
`System.Comparison<'T>`	`'T -> 'T -> int`	Used to compare values
`System.EventHandler<'T>`	`obj -> 'T -> unit`	Used as a generic event-handler type
`System.Func<'T,'U>`	`'T -> 'U`	A .NET 3.5 LINQ function delegate. Further arity-overloaded types exist that accept additional arguments: for example, `System.Func<'T,'U,'V>`, `System.Func<'T,'U,'V,'W>`.
`System.Predicate<'T>`	`'T -> bool`	Used to test a condition

Some F# Community Type Providers

There are F# type providers for a broad range of data formats available through the F# community. Table 17-13 shows a list of the most important of these at the time of writing. Check out `fsharp.org/community/projects` for more.

Table 17-13. *Some F# Community Type Providers*

Input Format	Library	Description
Xml	`FSharp.Data`	See Chapters 8, 13
CSV	`FSharp.Data`	See Chapters 8, 13
JSON	`FSharp.Data`	See Chapters 8, 13
HTML	`FSharp.Data`	See Chapters 3, 13
Regular Expressions	`FSharp.Text.RegexProvider`	See Chapter 8
SQL (codegen+queries)	`FSharp.Data.TypeProviders`	A SQL type provider using LINQ-to-SQL as the engine
SQL (Entity Framework)	`FSharp.Data.TypeProviders`	A SQL type provider using LINQ-to-Entities as the engine
WSDL	`FSharp.Data.TypeProviders`	Supports the WSDL web services protocol
T-SQL	`FSharp.Data.SqlClient`	See Chapter 13

(continued)

Table 17-13. *(continued)*

Input Format	Library	Description
Amazon S3	S3Provider	Access tables and data in Amazon Web Services cloud storage.
Azure	AzureStorageTypeProvider	Access tables and data in Azure Cloud storage
COM	FSharp.Interop.ComProvider	Access COM components
R	FSharpRProvider	Access R components
Configuration information	FSharp.Configuration	Access application settings, ResX resources, and YAML configuration
Files, WMI, Registry	FSharp.Management	Access files, PowerShell, WMI, and registry information

Under the Hood: Interoperating with C# and Other .NET Languages

Modern programs depend on a large number of libraries that are shipped in binary form, only some of which are written in the same language as the program. Libraries can be linked statically during compilation into the executable, or they can be loaded dynamically during program execution. Dynamic linking has become significantly more common to help share code (dynamic libraries can be linked by different programs and shared among them) and adapt program behavior while executing.

Interoperability among binaries compiled by different compilers, even of the same language, can be difficult. One of the goals of .NET was to ease this issue by introducing the Common Language Runtime (CLR), which is targeted by different compilers and different languages to aid in the interoperability between software developed in those languages. The CLR is a runtime designed to run programs compiled for the .NET platform. Because the F# compiler targets the CLR, its output is managed code, allowing compiled programs to interact directly with other programming languages targeting the .NET platform.

A DEEPER LOOK INSIDE .NET EXECUTABLES

Programs for the .NET platform are distributed in a form that is executed by the CLR. Binaries are expressed in an intermediate language that is compiled incrementally by the Just-In-Time (JIT) compiler during program execution. A .NET assembly, in the form of a .dll or an .exe file, contains the definition of a set of types and the definition of the method bodies, and the additional data describing the structure of the code in the intermediate language form are known as metadata. The intermediate language is used to define method bodies based on a stack-based machine, with operations performed by loading values on a stack of operands and then invoking methods or operators.

Consider the following simple F# program in the Program.fs source file:

```
open System
let i = 2
Console.WriteLine("Input a number:")
let v = Int32.Parse(Console.ReadLine())
Console.WriteLine(i * v)
```

The F# compiler generates an executable that can be disassembled using the `ildasm.exe` tool distributed with the .NET Framework. Because everything in the CLR is defined in terms of types, the F# compiler must introduce the class `$Program$Main` in the `<StartupCode$applicationname>` namespace. In this class, the definition of the `main@` static method is the entry point for the execution of the program. This method contains the intermediate language corresponding to the example F# program. The F# compiler generates several elements that aren't defined in the program whose goal is to preserve the semantics of the F# program in the intermediate language.

If you open the `main@` method, you will find the following code, which is annotated here with the corresponding F# statements:

```
.method public static void  main@() cil managed
{
  .entrypoint
  // Code size       38 (0x26)
  .maxstack  4

  // Console.WriteLine("Input a number:")
  IL_0000:  ldstr       "Input a number:"
  IL_0005:  call        void [mscorlib]System.Console::WriteLine(string)

  // let v = Int32.Parse(Console.ReadLine())
  IL_000a:  call        string [mscorlib]System.Console::ReadLine()
  IL_000f:  call        int32 [mscorlib]System.Int32::Parse(string)
  IL_0014:  stsfld      int32 '<StartupCode$ConsoleApplication1>'.$Program::v@4

  // Console.WriteLine(i * v) // Note that i is constant and its value has been inlined
  IL_0019:  ldc.i4.2
  IL_001a:  call        int32 Program::get_v()
  IL_001f:  mul
  IL_0020:  call        void [mscorlib]System.Console::WriteLine(int32)

// Exits
  IL_0025:  ret
} // end of method $Program$Main::main@
```

The `ldxxx` instructions are used to load values onto the operand stack of the abstract machine, and the `stxxx` instructions store values from that stack in locations (locals, arguments, or class fields). In this example, a static field is used for `v`, and the value of `i` is inlined using the `ldc` instruction. For method invocations, arguments are loaded on the stack, and a `call` operation is used to invoke the method.

The JIT compiler is responsible for generating the binary code that runs on the actual processor. The code generated by the JIT interacts with all the elements of the runtime, including external code loaded dynamically in the form of DLLs or COM components.

Memory Management at Runtime

Interoperability of F# programs with unmanaged code requires an understanding of the structure of the most important elements of a programming language's runtime. In particular, consider how program memory is organized at runtime. Memory used by a program is generally divided into three classes depending on the way it's handled:

- Static memory: Allocated for the entire lifetime of the program

- Automatic memory: Allocated and freed automatically when functions or methods are executed

- Dynamic memory: Explicitly allocated by the program, and freed explicitly or by an automatic program called the *garbage collector*

As a rule of thumb, top-level variables and static fields belong to the first class, function arguments and local variables belong to the second class, and memory explicitly allocated using the new operator belongs to the last class. The code generated by the JIT compiler uses different data structures to manage memory and automatically interacts with the operating system to request and release memory during program execution.

Each execution thread has a stack where local variables and arguments are allocated when a function or method is invoked. A stack is used because it naturally follows the execution flow of method and function calls. The topmost record contains data about the currently executing function; below that is the record of the caller of the function, which sits on top of another record of its caller, and so on. These activation records are memory blocks used to hold the memory required during the execution of the function and are naturally freed at the end of its execution by popping the record off the stack. The stack data structure is used to implement the automatic memory of the program, and because different threads execute different functions at the same time, a separate stack is assigned to each of them.

Dynamic memory is allocated in the heap, which is a data structure where data resides for an amount of time not directly related to the events of program execution. The memory is explicitly allocated by the program, and it's deallocated either explicitly or automatically, depending on the strategy adopted by the runtime to manage the heap. In the CLR, the heap is managed by a garbage collector, which is a program that tracks memory usage and reclaims memory that is no longer used by the program. Data in the heap is always referenced from the stack—or other known areas, such as static memory—either directly or indirectly. The garbage collector can deduce the memory potentially reachable by program execution in the future, and the remaining memory can be collected. During garbage collection, the running program may be suspended, because the collector may need to manipulate objects needed by its execution. In particular, a garbage collector may adopt a strategy called *copy collection* that can move objects in memory; during this process, the references may be inconsistent. To avoid dangling references, the memory model adopted by the CLR requires that methods access the heap through object references stored on the stack; objects in the heap are forbidden to reference data on the stack.

Data structures are the essential tool provided by programming languages to group values. A data structure is rendered as a contiguous area of memory in which the constituents are available at a given offset from the beginning of the memory. The actual layout of an object is determined by the compiler (or by the interpreter, for interpreted languages) and is usually irrelevant to the program, because the programming language provides operators to access fields without having to explicitly access the memory. System programming, however, often requires explicit manipulation of memory, and programming languages such as C let you control the in-memory layout of data structures. The C specification, for instance, defines that fields of a structure are laid out sequentially, although the compiler is allowed to insert extra space between them. Padding is used to align fields at word boundaries of the particular architecture in order to optimize the access to the fields of the structure. Thus, the same data structure in a program may lead to different memory layouts depending on the strategy of the compiler or the runtime, even in a language such as C, in which field ordering is well defined. By default, the CLR lays out structures in memory without any constraint, which gives you the freedom of optimizing memory usage on a particular architecture, although it may introduce interoperability issues if a portion of memory must be shared among the runtimes of different languages.[1]

Interoperability among different programming languages revolves mostly around memory layouts, because the execution of a compiled routine is a jump to a memory address. However, routines access memory explicitly, expecting that data are organized in a certain way. The rest of this chapter will discuss the mechanisms used by the CLR to interoperate with external code in the form of DLLs or native components.

Interoperating with C and C++ with PInvoke

F# implements a standard mechanism for interoperating with C and C++ code that is called "Platform Invoke," normally known as "PInvoke." This is a core feature of the standard available on all .NET implementations, including Mono.

The basic model underlying PInvoke is based on loading DLLs into the program, which allows managed code to invoke unmanaged functions exported from C and C++. DLLs don't provide information other than the entry-point location of a function; this isn't enough to perform the invocation unless additional information is made available to the runtime.

The invocation of a function requires

- the address of the code in memory;

- the calling convention, which is how parameters, return values, and other information are passed through the stack to the function; and

- the marshalling of values and pointers so that the different runtime supports can operate consistently on the same values.

You can obtain the address of the entry point using a system call that returns the pointer to the function given a string. You must provide the remaining information in order to instruct the CLR about how the function pointer should be used.

CALLING CONVENTIONS

Function and method calls (a method call is similar to a function call but with an additional pointer referring to the object passed to the method) are performed by using a shared stack between the caller and the callee. An activation record is pushed onto the stack when the function is called, and memory is allocated for arguments, the return value, and local variables. Additional information—such as information about exception handling and the return address when the execution of the function terminates—is also stored in the activation record.

The physical structure of the activation record is established by the compiler (or by the JIT, in the case of the CLR), and this knowledge must be shared between the caller and the called function. When the binary code is generated by a compiler, this isn't an issue, but when code generated by different compilers must interact, it may become a significant issue. Although each compiler may adopt a different convention, the need to perform system calls requires that the calling convention adopted by the operating system is implemented, and it's often used to interact with different runtimes.

---

[1]Languages targeting .NET aren't affected by these interoperability issues because they share the same CLR runtime.

Another popular approach is to support the calling convention adopted by C compilers, because it's widely used and has become a fairly universal language for interoperability. Note that although many operating systems are implemented in C, the libraries providing system calls may adopt different calling conventions. This is the case with Microsoft Windows: the operating system adopts the stdcall calling convention rather than cdecl, which is the C calling convention.

A significant dimension of the arena of possible calling conventions is the responsibility for removing the activation record from the thread stack. At first glance, it may seem obvious that before returning, the called function resets the stack pointer to the previous state. This isn't the case for programming languages such as C that allow functions with a variable number of arguments, such as printf. When variable arguments are allowed, the caller knows the exact size of the activation record; therefore, it's the caller's responsibility to free the stack at the end of the function call. Apart from being consistent with the chosen convention, there may seem to be little difference between the two choices, but if the caller is responsible for cleaning the stack, each function invocation requires more instructions, which leads to larger executables. For this reason, Windows uses the stdcall calling convention instead of the C calling convention. It's important to notice that the CLR uses an array of objects to pass a variable number of arguments, which is very different from the variable arguments of C, where the method receives a single pointer to the array that resides in the heap.

It's important to note that if the memory layout of the activation record is compatible, as it is in Windows, using the cdecl convention instead of the stdcall convention leads to a subtle memory leak. If the runtime assumes the stdcall convention (which is the default), and the callee assumes the cdecl convention, the arguments pushed on the stack aren't freed, and at each invocation, the height of the stack grows until a stack overflow happens.

The CLR supports a number of calling conventions. The two most important are stdcall and cdecl. Other implementations of the runtime may provide additional conventions to the user. In the PInvoke design, nothing restricts the supported conventions to these two.

The additional information required to perform the function call is provided by custom attributes that are used to decorate a function prototype and inform the runtime about the signature of the exported function.

Getting Started with PInvoke

This section starts with a simple example of a DLL developed using C++, to which you add code during your experiments using PInvoke. The CInteropDLL.h header file declares a macro defining the decorations associated with each exported function:

```
#define CINTEROPDLL_API __declspec(dllexport)
extern "C" {
void CINTEROPDLL_API HelloWorld();
}
```

The __declspec directive is specific to the Microsoft Visual C++ compiler. Other compilers may provide different ways to indicate the functions that must be exported when compiling a DLL.

The first function is HelloWorld; its definition is as expected:

```
void CINTEROPDLL_API HelloWorld()
{
    printf("Hello C world invoked by F#!\n");
}
```

Say you now want to invoke the HelloWorld function from an F# program. You have to define the prototype of the function and inform the runtime how to access the DLL and the other information needed to perform the invocation. The program performing the invocation is:

```
open System.Runtime.InteropServices

module CInterop =
    [<DllImport("CInteropDLL", CallingConvention = CallingConvention.Cdecl)>]
    extern void HelloWorld()

CInterop.HelloWorld()
```

The extern keyword informs the compiler that the function definition is external to the program and must be accessed through the PInvoke interface. A C-style prototype definition follows the keyword, and the whole declaration is annotated with a custom attribute defined in the System.Runtime.InteropServices namespace. The F# compiler adopts C-style syntax for extern prototypes, including argument types (as you will see later), because C headers and prototypes are widely used; this choice helps in the PInvoke definition. The DllImport custom attribute provides the information needed to perform the invocation. The first argument is the name of the DLL containing the function; the remaining option specifies the calling convention chosen to make the call. Because you don't specify otherwise, the runtime assumes that the name of the F# function is the same as the name of the entry point in the DLL. You can override this behavior using the EntryPoint parameter in the DllImport attribute.

It's important to note the declarative approach of the PInvoke interface. No code is involved in accessing external functions. The runtime interprets metadata in order to automatically interoperate with native code contained in a DLL. This is a different approach than the one adopted by different virtual machines, such as the Java virtual machine. The Java Native Interface (JNI) requires that you define a layer of code using types of the virtual machine and then invoke the native code.

PInvoke requires high privileges in order to execute native code, because the activation record of the native function is allocated on the same stack that contains the activation records of managed functions and methods. Moreover, as discussed shortly, it's also possible to have the native code invoking a delegate that is marshalled as a function pointer, allowing stacks with native and managed activation records to be interleaved.

The HelloWorld function is a simple case, because the function doesn't have input arguments and doesn't return any value. Consider this function with input arguments and a return value:

```
int CINTEROPDLL_API Sum(int i, int j)
{
    return i + j;
}
```

Invoking the Sum function requires integer values to be marshalled to the native code and the value returned to managed code. Simple types, such as integers, are easy to marshal, because they're usually passed by value and use types of the underlying architecture. The F# program using the Sum function is:

```
module CInterop =
    [<DllImport("CInteropDLL", CallingConvention = CallingConvention.Cdecl)>]
    extern int Sum(int i, int j)

printf "Sum(1, 1) = %d\n" (CInterop.Sum(1, 1));
```

Parameter passing assumes the same semantics of the CLR, and parameters are passed by value for value types and by the value of the reference for reference types. Again, you use the custom attribute to specify the calling convention for the invocation.

Mapping C Data Structures to F# Code

Let's first cover what happens when structured data are marshalled by the CLR in the case of nontrivial argument types. Here, you see the SumC function, which is responsible for adding two complex numbers defined by the Complex C data structure:

```
typedef struct _Complex {
    double re;
    double im;
} Complex;

Complex CINTEROPDLL_API SumC(Complex c1, Complex c2)
{
    Complex ret;
    ret.re = c1.re + c2.re;
    ret.im = c1.im + c2.im;
    return ret;
}
```

To invoke this function from F#, you must define a data structure in F# corresponding to the Complex C structure. If the memory layout of an instance of the F# structure is the same as that of the corresponding C structure, values can be shared between the two languages. How can you control the memory layout of a managed data structure? Fortunately, the PInvoke specification helps with custom attributes that let you specify the memory layout of data structures. The StructLayout custom attribute indicates the strategy adopted by the runtime to lay out fields of the data structure. By default, the runtime adopts its own strategy in an attempt to optimize the size of the structure, keeping fields aligned to the machine world in order to ensure fast access to the structure's fields. The C standard ensures that fields are laid out in memory sequentially in the order they appear in the structure definition; other languages may use different strategies. Using an appropriate argument, you can indicate that a C-like sequential layout strategy should be adopted. It's also possible to provide an explicit layout for the structure, indicating the offset in memory for each field of the structure. This example uses the sequential layout for the Complex value type:

```
module CInterop =
    [<Struct; StructLayout(LayoutKind.Sequential)>]
    type Complex =
        val mutable re : double
        val mutable im : double
```

```
    new(r, i) = {re = r; im = i}

[<DllImport("CInteropDLL", CallingConvention = CallingConvention.Cdecl)>]
extern Complex SumC(Complex c1, Complex c2)
```

Then uses, as follows:

```
let c1 = CInterop.Complex(1.0, 0.0)
let c2 = CInterop.Complex(0.0, 1.0)

let mutable c3 = CInterop.SumC(c1, c2)
printf "c3 = SumC(c1, c2) = %f + %fi\n" c3.re c3.im
```

The SumC prototype refers to the F# Complex value type. Yet because the layout of the structure in memory is the same as the layout in the corresponding C structure, the runtime passes the bits that are consistent with those expected by the C code.

Marshalling Parameters to and from C

A critical aspect of dealing with PInvoke is ensuring that values are marshalled correctly between managed and native code, and vice versa. A structure's memory layout doesn't depend only on the order of the fields. Compilers often introduce padding to align fields to memory addresses so that access to fields requires fewer memory operations, because CPUs load data into registers with the same strategy. Padding may speed up access to the data structure, but it introduces inefficiencies in memory usage; there may be gaps in the structures, leading to allocated but unused memory.

Consider, for instance, the C structure:

```
struct Foo {
    int i;
    char c;
    short s;
};
```

Depending on the compiler decision, it may occupy from 8 to 12 bytes. The most compact version of the structure uses the first 4 bytes for i, a single byte for c, and 2 more bytes for s. If the compiler aligns fields to addresses that are multiples of 4, then the integer i occupies the first slot, 4 more bytes are allocated for c (although only one is used), and the same happens for s.

Padding is a common practice in C programs; because it may affect performance and memory usage, directives instruct the compiler about padding. It's possible to have data structures with different padding strategies running within the same program.

The first step you face when using PInvoke to access native code is finding the definition of data structures, including information about padding. Then, you can annotate F# structures to have the same layout as the native ones, and the CLR can automate the marshalling of data. You can pass parameters by reference. Thus, the C code may access the memory managed by the runtime, and errors in memory layout may result in corrupted memory. For this reason, keep PInvoke code to a minimum and verify it accurately to ensure that the execution state of the virtual machine is preserved. The declarative nature of the interface is a great help in this respect, because you must check declarations and not interop code.

Not all the values are marshalled as-is to native code; some may require additional work from the runtime. Strings, for instance, have different memory representations between native and managed code. C strings are arrays of bytes that are null terminated, whereas runtime strings are .NET objects with a different layout. Also, function pointers are mediated by the runtime: the calling convention adopted by the CLR isn't compatible with external conventions, so code stubs are generated that can be called by native code from managed code, and vice versa.

In the SumC example, arguments are passed by value, but native code often requires data structures to be passed by reference so as to avoid the cost of copying the entire structure and passing only a pointer to the native data. The ZeroC function resets a complex number whose pointer is passed as an argument:

```
void CINTEROPDLL_API ZeroC(Complex* c)
{
    c->re = 0;
    c->im = 0;
}
```

The F# declaration for the function is the same as the C prototype:

```
[<DllImport("CInteropDLL", CallingConvention = CallingConvention.Cdecl)>]
extern void ZeroC(Complex* c)
```

Now, you need a way to obtain a pointer given a value of type Complex in F#. You can use the && operator to indicate a pass by reference; this results in passing the pointer to the structure expected by the C function:

```
let mutable c4 = CInterop.SumC(c1, c2)
printf "c4 = SumC(c1, c2) = %f + %fi\n" c4.re c4.im

CInterop.ZeroC(&&c4)
printf "c4 = %f + %fi\n" c4.re c4.im
```

In C and C++, the notion of objects (or struct instances) and the classes of memory are orthogonal: an object can be allocated either on the stack or on the heap and share the same declaration. In .NET, this isn't the case; objects are instances of classes and are allocated on the heap, and value types are stored in the stack or are wrapped into objects in the heap.

Can you pass objects to native functions through PInvoke? The main issue with objects is that the heap is managed by the garbage collector, and one possible strategy for garbage collection is copy collection (a technique that moves objects in the heap when a collection occurs). Thus, the base address in memory of an object may change over time, which can be a serious problem if the pointer to the object has been marshalled to a native function through a PInvoke invocation. The CLR provides an operation called *pinning* that prevents an object from moving during garbage collection. Pinned pointers are assigned to local variables, and pinning is released when the function performing the pinning exits. It's important to understand the scope of pinning: if the native code stores the pointer somewhere before returning, the pointer may become invalid but still be usable from native code.

Now, let's define an object type for Complex and marshal F# objects to a C function. The goal is to marshal the F# object to the ZeroC function. In this case, you can't use the pass-by-reference operator, and you must define everything so that the type checker is happy. You can define another function that refers to ZeroC but with a different signature involving ObjComplex, which is an object type similar to the Complex value type. The EntryPoint parameter maps the F# function onto the same ZeroC C function, although in this case, the argument is of type ObjComplex rather than Complex:

```
module CInterop =
    [<StructLayout(LayoutKind.Sequential)>]
    type ObjComplex =
        val mutable re : double
        val mutable im : double

        new() = {re = 0.0; im = 0.0}
        new(r : double, i : double) = {re = r; im = i}
```

```
    [<DllImport("CInteropDLL", EntryPoint = "ZeroC",
                CallingConvention = CallingConvention.Cdecl)>]
    extern void ObjZeroC(ObjComplex c)

let oc = CInterop.ObjComplex(2.0, 1.0)
printf "oc = %f + %fi\n" oc.re oc.im
CInterop.ObjZeroC(oc)
printf "oc = %f + %fi\n" oc.re oc.im
```

In this case, the object reference is marshalled as a pointer to the C code, and you don't need the && operator in order to call the function.

Marshalling Strings to and from C

PInvoke defines the default behavior for mapping common types used by the Win32 API. Table 17-14 shows the default conversions. Most of the mappings are natural, but note that there are several entries for strings. This is because strings are represented in different ways in different programming language runtimes.

Table 17-14. *Default Mapping for Types of the Win32 API Listed in* Wtypes.h

Unmanaged Type in Wtypes.h	Unmanaged C Type	Managed Class	Description
HANDLE	void*	System.IntPtr	32 bits on 32-bit Windows operating systems, 64 bits on 64-bit Windows operating systems
BYTE	unsigned char	System.Byte	8 bits
SHORT	Short	System.Int16	16 bits
WORD	unsigned short	System.UInt16	16 bits
INT	int	System.Int32	32 bits
UINT	unsigned int	System.UInt32	32 bits
LONG	long	System.Int32	32 bits
BOOL	long	System.Int32	32 bits
DWORD	unsigned long	System.UInt32	32 bits
ULONG	unsigned long	System.UInt32	32 bits
CHAR	char	System.Char	Decorate with ANSI
LPSTR	char*	System.String or System.Text.StringBuilder	Decorate with ANSI
LPCSTR	const char*	System.String or System.Text.StringBuilder	Decorate with ANSI
LPWSTR	wchar_t*	System.String or System.Text.StringBuilder	Decorate with Unicode
LPCWSTR	const wchar_t*	System.String or System.Text.StringBuilder	Decorate with Unicode
FLOAT	Float	System.Single	32 bits
DOUBLE	Double	System.Double	64 bits

To see how strings are marshalled, start with a simple C function that echoes a string on the console:

```
void CINTEROPDLL_API echo(char* str)
{
    puts(str);
}
```

The corresponding F# PInvoke prototype is:

```
[<DllImport("CInteropDLL", CallingConvention = CallingConvention.Cdecl)>]
extern void echo(string s)
```

What happens when the F# function echo is invoked? The managed string is represented by an array of Unicode characters that are described by an object in the heap; the C function expects a pointer to an array of single-byte ANSI characters that are null terminated. The runtime is responsible for performing the conversion between the two formats, which is performed by default when mapping a .NET string to an ANSI C string.

It's common to pass strings that are modified by C functions, yet .NET strings are immutable. For this reason, it's also possible to use a System.Text.StringBuilder object instead of a string. Instances of this class represent mutable strings and have an associated buffer containing the characters of the string. You can write a C function in the DLL that fills a string buffer given the size of the buffer:

```
void CINTEROPDLL_API sayhello(char* str, int sz)
{
    static char* data = "Hello from C code!";
    int len = min(sz, strlen(data));
    strncpy(str, data, len);
    str[len] = 0;
}
```

Because the function writes into the string buffer passed as an argument, use a StringBuilder rather than a string to ensure that the buffer has the appropriate room for the function to write. You can use the F# PInvoke prototype:

```
open System.Text
[<DllImport("CInteropDLL", CallingConvention = CallingConvention.Cdecl)>]
extern void sayhello(StringBuilder sb, int sz)
```

Because you have to indicate the size of the buffer, you can use a constructor of the StringBuilder class that allows you to do so:

```
let sb = new StringBuilder(50)
sayhello(sb, 50)
printf "%s\n" (sb.ToString())
```

You've used ANSI C strings so far, but this isn't the only type of string. Wide-character strings are becoming widely adopted and use 2 bytes to represent a single character. Following the C tradition, the string is terminated by a null character. Consider a wide-character version of the sayhello function:

```c
void CINTEROPDLL_API sayhellow(wchar_t* str, int sz)
{
    static wchar_t* data = L"Hello from C code Wide!";
    int len = min(sz, wcslen(data));
    wcsncpy(str, data, len);
    str[len] = 0;
}
```

How can you instruct the runtime that the StringBuilder should be marshalled as a wide-character string rather than as an ANSI string? The declarative nature of PInvoke helps by providing a custom attribute with which to annotate function parameters of the prototype and to inform the CLR about the marshalling strategy to be adopted. The sayhello function is declared in F# as:

```fsharp
open System.Text
[<DllImport("CInteropDLL", CallingConvention = CallingConvention.Cdecl)>]
extern void sayhellow([<MarshalAs(UnmanagedType.LPWStr)>]StringBuilder sb, int sz)
```

In this case, the MarshalAs attribute indicates that the string should be marshalled as LPWSTR rather than as LPSTR.

Passing Function Pointers to C

Another important data type that often should be passed to native code is a function pointer. Function pointers, which are widely used to implement callbacks, provide a simple form of functional programming; think, for instance, of a sort function that receives as input the pointer to the comparison function. Graphical toolkits have widely used this data type to implement event-driven programming, and they often have to pass a function that is invoked by another one.

PInvoke can marshal delegates as function pointers; again, the runtime is responsible for generating a suitable function pointer callable from native code. When the marshalled function pointer is invoked, a stub is called, and the activation record on the stack is rearranged to be compatible with the calling convention of the runtime. Then, the delegate function is invoked.

Although in principle the generated stub is responsible for implementing the calling convention adopted by the native code receiving the function pointer, the CLR supports only the stdcall calling convention for marshalling function pointers. Thus, the native code should adopt this calling convention when invoking the pointer. This restriction may cause problems, but in general, on the Windows platform, the stdcall calling convention is widely used.

The following C function uses a function pointer to apply a function to an array of integers:

```c
typedef int (_stdcall *TRANSFORM_CALLBACK)(int);

void CINTEROPDLL_API transformArray(int* data, int count, TRANSFORM_CALLBACK fn)
{
    int i;
    for (i = 0; i < count; i++)
        data[i] = fn(data[i]);
}
```

The TRANSFORM_CALLBACK type definition defines the prototype of the function pointer you're interested in here: a function takes an integer as the input argument and returns an integer as a result. The CALLBACK macro is specific to the Microsoft Visual C++ compiler and expands to __stdcall in order to indicate that the function pointer, when invoked, should adopt the stdcall calling convention instead of the cdecl calling convention.

The transformArray function takes as input an array of integers along with its length and the function to apply to its elements. You now have to define the F# prototype for this function by introducing a delegate type with the same signature as TRANSFORM_CALLBACK:

```
type Callback = delegate of int -> int

[<DllImport("CInteropDLL", CallingConvention = CallingConvention.Cdecl)>]
extern void transformArray(int[] data, int count, Callback transform)
```

Now you can increment all the elements of an array by using the C function:

```
let anyToString any = sprintf "%A" any
let data = [|1; 2; 3|]
printf "%s\n" (String.Join("; ", (Array.map anyToString data)))

transformArray(data, data.Length, new Callback(fun x -> x + 1))
printf "%s\n" (String.Join("; ", (Array.map anyToString data)))
```

PInvoke declarations are concise, but for data types such as function pointers, parameter passing can be expensive. In general, libraries assume that crossing the language boundary causes a loss of efficiency and that callbacks are less efficient than ordinary C functions. In this respect, the example represents a situation in which the overhead of PInvoke is significant: a single call to transformArray causes a number of callbacks without performing any real computation into the native code.

Wrapper Generation and the Limits of PInvoke

PInvoke is a flexible and customizable interface, and it's expressive enough to define prototypes for most libraries available. In some situations, however, it can be difficult to map directly the native interface into the corresponding signature. A significant example is function pointers embedded into structures, which are typical C programming patterns that approximate object-oriented programming. Here, the structure contains a number of pointers to functions that can be used as methods, but you must take care to pass the pointer to the structure as the first argument so as to simulate the this parameter. Oracle's Berkeley Database (BDB) is a popular database library that adopts this programming pattern. The core structure describing an open database is:

```
struct __db {
        /* ... */
        DB_ENV *dbenv;              /* Backing environment. */
        DBTYPE type;               /* DB access method type. */
        /* ... */
        int  (*close) __P((DB *, u_int32_t));
        int  (*cursor) __P((DB *, DB_TXN *, DBC **, u_int32_t));
        int  (*del) __P((DB *, DB_TXN *, DBT *, u_int32_t));
        // ...
}
```

The `System.Runtime.InteropServices.Marshal` class features the `GetFunctionPointerForDelegate` for obtaining a pointer to a function that invokes a given delegate. The caller of the function must guarantee that the delegate object will remain alive for the lifetime of the structure, because stubs generated by the runtime aren't moved by the garbage collector but can still be collected. Furthermore, callbacks must adopt the `stdcall` calling convention; if this isn't the case, the PInvoke interface can't interact with the library.

When PInvoke's expressivity isn't enough for wrapping a function call, you can still write an adapter library in a native language such as C. This is the approach followed by the BDB# library, in which an intermediate layer of code has been developed to make the interface to the library compatible with PInvoke. The trick has been, in this case, to define a function for each database function, taking as input the pointer to the structure and performing the appropriate call:

```
DB *db;
// BDB call
db->close(db, 0);
// Wrapper call
db_close(db, 0);
```

The problem with wrappers is that they must be maintained manually when the signatures of the original library change. The intermediate adapter makes it more difficult to maintain the code's overall interoperability.

Many libraries have a linear interface that can be easily wrapped using PInvoke, and, of course, wrapper generators have been developed. At the moment, there are no wrapper generators for F#, but the C-like syntax for PInvoke declarations makes it easy to translate C# wrappers into F# code. An example of such a tool is SWIG, which is a multi-language wrapper generator that reads C header files and generates interop code for a large number of programming languages, such as C#.

Summary

In this chapter, you saw a range of libraries and interoperability mechanisms associated with F#. You also learned how F# can interoperate with native code in the form of the standard Platform Invoke interface. Neither mechanism is dependent on F#, but the language exposes the appropriate abstractions built into the runtime.

CHAPTER 18

■ ■ ■

Developing and Testing F# Code

Successful programming must involve a healthy marriage of *good code* and *good software engineering*. Sometimes these overlap: functional programming is a good software-engineering technique. Among other benefits, anecdotal evidence indicates that functional programming frequently leads to a substantially reduced bug rate for good programmers. Programs built using functional techniques tend to be highly compositional, building correct programs out of correct building blocks. The functional programming style avoids or substantially reduces the use of side effects in the program, one property that makes programs more compositional and comprehensible.

Debugging and testing are still essential activities to ensure that a program is as close as possible to its specifications, however. Bugs and misbehaviors are facts of life, and F# programmers must learn techniques to find and remove them. Often, these techniques are not inherently "functional" or even particularly code related, but they are still critical to the process of writing robust, maintainable, and successful software components.

Developing Your Code

F# software engineering uses a range of tools. Table 18-1 shows some of the common tools you might use. One place to investigate these tools further is the "F# Project Scaffold" from https://github.com/fsprojects/ProjectScaffold.

Table 18-1. *Some Tools Used with F#*

Tool Category	Example Tools
Editors	Emacs, Spacemacs, Vim, Sublime Text, Atom, Xamarin Studio, Visual Studio
Build automation	XBuild, MSBuild, FAKE
Testing	NUnit, XUnit, FsCheck, NCrunch, FsUnit, Fuchu
Package formats	NuGet packages, Single github files with Paket
Package acquisition and dependency management	NuGet (nuget.exe), Paket (paket.exe)
Continuous integration	Travis, AppVeyor
Documentation generation	Markdown, FSharp.Formatting literate scripts, SourceLink
Code hosting and collaborative development	GitHub

Editing Your Code

F# support exists in most major editors. Table 18-2 shows some of the packages that give rich editing support (including auto-complete, type checking, and F# Interactive scripting integration) for F# in different editors:

Table 18-2. *Some Editor Packages for F#*

Editor	Description
Emacs	The `fsharp-mode` package provides full support for F# and is available from the popular MELPA package repository. See `github.com/fsharp/emacs-fsharp-mode`.
Vim	The `vim-fsharp` package provides support for F#. See `github.com/fsharp/vim-fsharp`. Vim-key bindings and modal editing can be added to most other editors.
Sublime	Support for `Sublime Text 3` can be found at `github.com/fsharp/sublime-fsharp-package`.
Atom	The `Ionide` package (`ionide.io`) provides F# support in the Atom editor.
MonoDevelop	`MonoDevelop` allows the use of the F# package, also used in the Xamarin Studio editor.
Xamarin Studio	`Xamarin` support F# in the Xamarin Studio editor.
Visual Studio	Microsoft makes the F# tools for Visual Studio. Be sure to also install the Visual F# Power Tools from `fsprojects.github.io/VisualFSharpPowerTools/`.

Mixing Scripting and Compiled Code

Small programs are often used both as interactive scripts and as small compiled applications. Here are some useful facts to know about scripting with F# and F# Interactive:

- F# scripts use the extension `.fsx`.

- A script file can contain `#r` directives. These reference a library or a type provider.

- A script file can contain `#load` directives. This is as if the files had been compiled using the command-line compiler and included in the same assembly as the referencing script.

- A script that is referenced via a `#load` can itself contain further `#load` and `#r` references. This means that a script can act like a "little library." If the same root file transitively references the same script more than once via `#load`, the file acts as if it is logically only referenced once.

- You can access command-line arguments from within scripts by using the expression `fsi.CommandLineArgs`. Within compiled code, use `System.Environment.GetCommandLineArgs`. Within code used in both modes, use conditional compilation to switch between these, as shown in the next coding example.

You can run a script on startup by using the `--exec` command-line option for `fsi.exe` or by giving a single file name on the command line. You can find other command-line options by using `fsi.exe --help`.

Conditional compilation is a particularly useful feature for scripts—especially the predefined conditional compilation symbols COMPILED and INTERACTIVE. The former is set whenever you compile code using the command-line compiler fsc.exe, and the latter is set whenever you load code interactively using F# Interactive. A common use for these flags is to start the GUI event loop for a Windows Forms or other graphical application, such as using System.Windows.Forms.Application.Run. F# Interactive starts an event loop automatically, so you require a call to this function in the compiled code only:

```
open System.Windows.Forms

let form = new Form(Width = 400, Height = 300,
                    Visible = true, Text = "F# Forms Sample")
#if COMPILED
// Run the main code
System.Windows.Forms.Application.Run(form)
#endif
```

■ **Note** You can specify additional conditional-compilation directives by using the --define command-line compiler option.

Choosing Optimization Settings

The F# compiler comes with a simple choice of optimization levels. You nearly always want to compile your final code using --optimize, which applies maximum optimizations to your code. This is also the default optimization setting when using fsc.exe or fsi.exe directly, but it is not the default for compiled code using project files. You learned about F# project files in Chapter 7, "Encapsulating and Organizing Your Code."

The F# compiler is a cross-module, cross-assembly optimizing compiler, and it attaches optimization information to each assembly you create when using optimization. This information may contain some code fragments of your assembly, which may be inlined into later assemblies by the optimizing compiler. In some situations, you may not want this information included in your assembly. For example, you may expect to independently version assemblies, and in this case, you may want to ensure that code is never duplicated from one assembly to another during compilation. In this case, you can use the --nooptimizationdata switch to prevent optimization data from being recorded with the assemblies that you create.

Generating Documentation

In Chapter 2, you saw that comments beginning with /// are XML documentation comments, which are also used by IDE tools. They can also be collected to generate either HTML or XML documentation. You generate HTML documentation using an auxiliary tool, such as FsHtmlDoc, which is available in the F# Power Pack.

You can also generate a simple XML documentation file using the --doc command-line option. You must name the output file. For example, using fsc -a --doc:whales.xml whales.fs for the code in Listing 7-11 in Chapter 7 generates the file whales.xml containing:

```
<?xml version="1.0" encoding="utf-8"?>

<doc>

    <assembly><name>whales</name></assembly>
```

```
<members>
  <member name="T:Whales.Fictional.WhaleKind">
    <summary> The three kinds of whales we cover in this release</summary>
  </member>
  <member name="P:Whales.Fictional.bluey">
  <summary> The backup whale</summary>
  </member>
  <member name="P:Whales.Fictional.moby">
   <summary>The main whale</summary>
  </member>

  <member name="P:Whales.Fictional.orca">
   <summary> This whale is for experimental use only</summary>
  </member>
  <member name="P:Whales.Fictional.whales">
    <summary> The collected whales</summary>
  </member>
  <member name="T:Whales.Fictional">
  </member>
</members>
</doc>
```

Building Libraries

You usually need to share libraries among multiple applications. You can do this by using any of these techniques:

- Including the same source file in multiple applications

- Creating a library binary, usually a DLL, and referencing it from multiple applications.

- Creating a library package, usually a NuGet package, published to nuget.org or another package feed, and referencing it from multiple applications

- Creating a strong name-shared library and installing it on the target machine. (Note that this is now rarely recommended, and it is better to package libraries with final applications.)

One of the easiest ways to create a NuGet package is to use FAKE, a build and packaging tool. You can also use FAKE to orchestrate your entire build-and-test pipeline. See fsharp.github.io/FAKE for full details.

■ **Note** If you're planning to write libraries for use by the rest of the world, we recommend that you take the time to read the .NET library-design guidelines, document them using XML and HTML docs, and learn how to version your libraries. Chapter 19 takes a deeper look at guidelines for library design.

Using Static Linking

Sometimes applications use a DLL as a library, but when it comes to deploying the application on a website or as installed software, it may be easier to bundle that DLL as part of the application. You can do this in two ways: by placing the DLL alongside the EXE for the application or by statically linking the DLL when you create the EXE. You select the DLL by using the --staticlink compiler option with the assembly name of the DLL.

You can also bundle the F# libraries into your application to result in a zero-dependency application. You statically link all DLLs by using the --standalone compiler option. Static linking can cause problems in some situations and should be used only for a final EXE or a DLL used as an application plug-in.

Packaging Different Kinds of Code

Table 18-3 lists some of the kinds of software implemented with F#. These tend to be organized in slightly different ways and tend to use encapsulation to varying degrees. For example, encapsulation is used heavily in frameworks, but not when you're writing 100-line scripts.

Table 18-3. *Some Kinds of Software Built Using F#*

Software Entity	Description
Script	A program or set of program fragments, usually in a single file and fewer than 1,000 lines long, usually with an .fsx extension, run through F# Interactive. Sometimes also compiled. Organized using functions and occasional type definitions. Freely uses static global state. Usually has no signature file or accessibility annotations.
Application	An EXE or a web application DLL, perhaps with some supporting DLLs. Organized using namespaces, modules, functions, and some abstract types. Often uses some static global state. Some internal files and data structures may have signatures, but often these aren't needed.
Application extension (plug-in or add-on)	A component that extends an application, often compiled as a DLL containing types along with an accompanying XML file that describes the plug-in to the application. The host application loads the DLLs using .NET reflection. Generally has no static state because this lets the application instantiate multiple instances of the plug-in. Example: the DLL plug-ins for Visual Studio, Xamarin Studio.
Type Provider	A specific application extension that extends the resolution logic of the F# compiler, F# Interactive, and the F# editing tools.
Framework	A collection of related type definitions, functions, and algorithms organized according to established .NET and F# library-design guidelines. Usually compiled as one or more DLLs and versioned as an independent entity. Generally has no static state except where it mediates essential state on the host computer or operating system.

Managing Dependencies

When your application references multiple packages and libraries, you will normally need a tool to help "manage" its dependencies. The two common tools to use are the following:

- Paket (paket.exe, fsprojects.github.io/Paket). A dependency manager for .NET and Mono projects, which is designed to work well with NuGet packages and also enables referencing files directly from GitHub repositories.

- NuGet client tooling (nuget.exe, nuget.org). A dependency manager for .NET that is the default tooling option for dependency management in Visual Studio and Xamarin Studio.

When using these tools, you must first specify your dependencies in files (or by using IDE tooling, which has the same effect as editing the files). For example, a paket.dependencies file looks like this:

```
source https://nuget.org/api/v2

nuget Castle.Windsor-log4net >= 3.2
nuget NUnit
```

You then ask the dependency manager to process this specification and work out what actual packages to depend on:

```
> .paket/paket.exe install
```

This generates a paket.lock file that records a resolution of the dependencies. You can commit this file as a "pinned-down" view of your dependencies that won't change until you run paket update. You can also ask Paket to manage which libraries are referenced by different project files. See the Paket documentation for more details.

Using Data and Configuration Settings

So far, this book has focused on code. In reality, almost every program comes with additional data resources that form an intrinsic part of the application. Common examples include the resource strings, sounds, fonts, and images for GUI applications. Applications typically select from among different data resources based on language or culture settings. Often, programs also access additional parameters, such as environment variables derived from the execution context or registry settings recording user-configuration options. It can be useful to understand the idioms used by .NET to make managing data and configuration settings more uniform.

You may need to access many different kinds of data resources and application settings. Table 18-4 summarizes the most common ones.

Table 18-4. Commonly Used Data and Configuration Settings

Data Resource	Notes
Source directory	The source directory containing the source file(s) at time of compilation. Often used to access further resources in F# Interactive scripts or for error reporting in compiled applications. Accessed using the `__SOURCE_DIRECTORY__` predefined identifier.
Command arguments	Arguments passed to the invocation of the program. Accessed using `System.Environment.GetCommandLineArgs` and `fsi.CommandLineArgs` when running in F# Interactive.
Installation location	Where a program EXE or DLL is installed. Accessed by reading the `Assembly.Location` of any of the types defined in your assembly. For F# Interactive scripts, the installation location is usually the same as the source directory.
User directories	Paths to common logical directories, such as `My Documents`. Accessed using `System.Environment.GetFolderPath`.
Environment variables	User- or machine-wide settings, such as `PATH` and `COMPUTERNAME`. Accessed using `System.Environment.GetEnvironmentVariable`.
Configuration settings	Database connection strings and other configuration settings, often used for web applications. If an application is called `MyApp.exe`, this is usually stored in a file such as `MyApp.exe.config` alongside the executable; web applications use a `Web.Config` file. Accessed using `System.Configuration.ConfigurationManager`.
Isolated storage	A special storage area accessible only to an installed application and that looks just like disk storage.

Many of these configuration settings are accessible in a strongly typed way through the `FSharp.Configuration` library of type providers, discussed in Chapter 17 You can embed resources in applications (or associate them with a DLL) by using the `--resource` compiler option.

Using F# Interactive Effectively

Functional programming languages have traditionally addressed many debugging and testing issues through their ability to interactively evaluate program statements and print the values of variables, thus inspecting the program state interactively. F# Interactive allows you to execute code fragments and quickly test them; you can also inspect the state of the `fsi` script by querying values from the top level.

Development and testing using F# Interactive can effectively reduce development time, because you can evaluate code fragments more than once without having to recompile the entire system. Code is edited in the development environment with type checking and auto-complete; you can send code to F# Interactive by selecting it and pressing the appropriate shortcut, such as `Alt+Enter` or `Ctrl+Enter`. You can develop code incrementally and test it by invoking it with test-input arguments. Once you find and fix issues, you can evaluate the function definition again and then test it for further bugs.

During software development, it's common practice to write simple programs to test specific features (the "Unit Testing" section discusses this topic more extensively). With F# Interactive, you can first define tests as functions stored in a file and then selectively evaluate them. This approach can be useful in developing and defining new tests, but you can use more-specific tools to run tests in a more systematic way.

Controlling F# Interactive

Programs run in F# Interactive have access to an object called fsi that lets you control some aspects of the interactive execution. It's contained in the assembly FSharp.Interactive.Settings.dll, which is automatically referenced in files ending with .fsx and in F# Interactive sessions.

Table 18-5 shows some of the methods supported by this object.

Table 18-5. *Members of the* fsi *Object*

Member	Type	Description
fsi.FloatingPointFormat	string	Gets or sets the format used for floating-point numbers, based on .NET formatting specifications
fsi.FormatProvider	System.IFormat Provider	Gets or sets the cultural format used for numbers, based on .NET formatting specifications
fsi.PrintWidth	int	Gets or sets the print width used for formatted text output
fsi.PrintDepth	int	Gets or sets the depth of output for tree-structured data
fsi.PrintLength	int	Gets or sets the length of output for lists and other linear data structures
fsi.ShowProperties	bool	Gets or sets a flag indicating whether properties should be printed for displayed values
fsi.ShowDeclarationValues	bool	Gets or sets a flag indicating whether declaration values should be printed
fsi.ShowIEnumerable	bool	Gets or sets a flag indicating whether sequences should be printed in the output of the interactive session
fsi.AddPrinter	('a -> string) -> unit	Adds a printer for values compatible with the specific type 'a
fsi.AddPrintTransformer	('a -> obj) -> unit	Adds a printer that shows any values compatible with the specific type 'a as if they were values returned by the given function
fsi.CommandLineArgs	string[]	Gets the command-line arguments after ignoring the arguments relevant to the interactive environment and replacing the first argument with the name of the last script file

Some Common F# Interactive Directives

Table 18-6 shows several common directives accepted by F# Interactive, some of which correspond to options for the F# command-line compiler.

Table 18-6. *Some Commonly Used F# Interactive Directives*

Directive	Description
#r path	References a DLL. The DLL is loaded dynamically when first required
#I path	Adds the given search path to that used to resolve referenced DLLs
#load file ... file	Loads the given file(s) as if it had been compiled by the F# command-line compiler
#time	Toggles timing information on/off
#quit	Exits F# Interactive

Understanding How F# Interactive Compiles Code

Although F# Interactive is reminiscent of the read-eval-print loops of interpreted languages, it's substantially different because it compiles code rather than interprets it. Whenever a code fragment is typed at the top level, it's compiled on the fly as part of a dynamic assembly and is evaluated for side effects. This is particularly important for types, because you can create new ones at the top level, and their dependencies may be tricky to understand fully.

Let's start with an example of a nontrivial use of F# Interactive that shows these intricacies. You define the class APoint, which represents points using an angle and a radius:

```
type APoint(angle, radius) =
    member x.Angle = angle
    member x.Radius = radius
    new() = APoint(angle = 0.0, radius = 0.0)
```

If you create an instance of the class using F# Interactive, you can inspect the actual type by using the GetType method. The output is:

```
> let p = APoint();;

val p : APoint

> p.GetType();;

val it : System.Type =
  FSI_0004+APoint
    {Assembly = FSI-ASSEMBLY, Version=0.0.0.0, Culture=neutral, PublicKeyToken=null;
     AssemblyQualifiedName = "FSI_0004+APoint, FSI-ASSEMBLY, Version=0.0.0.0, ...}
```

527

Now, suppose you want to extend the APoint class with an additional member that stretches the point radius a given amount; it's natural to type the new definition of the class into the top level and evaluate it. F# Interactive doesn't complain about the redefinition of the type:

```
type APoint(angle, radius) =
    member x.Angle = angle
    member x.Radius = radius
    member x.Stretch (k : double) = APoint(angle = x.Angle, radius = x.Radius + k)
    new() = APoint(angle = 0.0, radius = 0.0)
```

Because you've redefined the structure of APoint, you may be tempted to invoke the stretch method on it, but doing so results in an error:

```
> p.Stretch(22.0);;
```

```
error FS0039: The field, constructor or member 'Stretch' is not defined
```

To understand what's happening, create a new instance p2 of the class APoint and ask for the type:

```
> let p2 = APoint();;
```

```
val p2 : APoint
```

```
> p2.GetType();;
```

```
val it : System.Type =
  FSI_0007+APoint
    {Assembly = FSI-ASSEMBLY, Version=0.0.0.0, Culture=neutral, PublicKeyToken=null;
     AssemblyQualifiedName = "FSI_0007+APoint, FSI-ASSEMBLY, Version=0.0.0.0, ...}
```

As you can see, the name of p2's type is FSI_0007+APoint, whereas p's type is FSI_0004+APoint. Under the hood, F# Interactive compiles types into different modules to ensure that types can be redefined; it also ensures that the most recent definition of a type is used. The older definitions are still available, and their instances aren't affected by the type redefinition.

Understanding the inner mechanisms of F# Interactive is useful when you use it to test F# programs, because interactive evaluation isn't always equivalent to running code compiled using the command-line compiler. On the other hand, the compiled nature of the system guarantees that the code executed by F# Interactive performs as well as compiled code.

Using Tracing Diagnostics

A managed application can programmatically access the debugging services of .NET through the types contained in the System.Diagnostics namespace. Several types in the namespace encompass aspects of the runtime, including stack tracing, communicating with the debugger, accessing performance counters to read statistics about the computer state (memory and CPU usage are typically available using them), and handling operating-system processes.

This section will focus on the classes related to debugging and the debugger. You can interact with the debugging infrastructure in three primary ways:

- The Debug class programmatically asserts conditions in the program and outputs debugging and tracing information to debuggers and other listeners.

- The Trace class programmatically outputs diagnostics to trace listeners.

- The Debugger class interacts with the debugger, checks whether it's attached, and triggers breaks explicitly from the program.

The debugging attributes are a set of custom attributes that you can use to annotate the program to control its behavior (see Chapters 9 and 10 for more information about custom attributes).

The Debug class provides a way to output diagnostic messages without assuming that the program has been compiled as a console application; the debug output is collected by one or more *listeners* that receive the output notifications and do something with them. Each listener is an instance of a class inherited from the TraceListener class and typically sends the output to the console or to a file, or notifies the user with a dialog box (you can find more information about how to write a listener in the class library documentation). The following example demonstrates the isPalindrome function with tracing statements:

```
open System.Diagnostics

let isPalindrome (str : string) =
    let rec check(s : int, e : int) =
        Debug.WriteLine("check call")
        Debug.WriteLineIf((s = 0), "check: First call")
        Debug.Assert((s >= 0 || s < str.Length), sprintf "s is out of bounds: %d" s)
        Debug.Assert((e >= 0 || e < str.Length), sprintf "e is out of bounds: %d" e)
        if s = e || s = e + 1 then true
        else if str.[s] <> str.[e] then false
        else check(s + 1, e - 1)
    check(0, str.Length - 1)
```

The WriteXXX methods of the Debug class output data for a running program and are a sophisticated version of the printf debugging approach, where the program is enriched with print statements that output useful information about its current state. In this case, however, you can redirect all the messages to different media rather than just printing them to the console. You can also conditionally output messages to reduce the number of messages being sent to the debug output. The example outputs a message each time the check method is invoked and uses the conditional output to mark the first invocation.

■ **Note**   When a program is executed in debugging mode in an IDE, the diagnostic output is sent to the Output window. F# Interactive by default doesn't show diagnostic output.

Assertions are a well-known mechanism to assert conditions about the state of a running program, ensuring that at a given point in the program, certain preconditions must hold. For instance, assertions are often used to ensure that the content of an option-valued variable isn't None at some point in the program. During testing, if this precondition isn't satisfied, then program execution is suspended as soon as possible. This avoids your having to trace back from the point where the undefined value of the variable would lead to an exception. The Assert method lets you specify a Boolean condition that must hold; otherwise, the given message is displayed, prompting the user with the failed assertion.

When a release is made, debug output and assertions can introduce unnecessary overhead. The ConditionalAttribute custom attribute is used to label methods so the calls are only included in the program if a given compilation symbol is defined. The methods in the Debug type came pre-labelled to be conditional on the DEBUG symbol. The Debugger type lets you check whether the program is attached to a debugger and to trigger a break if required. You can also programmatically launch the debugger using this type and send log messages to it. This type is used less often than the Debug type, but it may be useful if a bug arises only when there is no attached debugger, such as when a web application starts up. In this case, you can programmatically start the debugging process when needed.

Another mechanism that lets you control the interaction between a program and the debugger is based on a set of custom attributes in the System.Diagnostics namespace. Table 18-7 shows the attributes that control in part the behavior of the debugger.

Table 18-7. *Attributes Controlling Program Behavior under Debug*

Attribute	Description
DebuggerBrowsableAttribute	Determines whether and how a member is displayed in the Debug window
DebuggerDisplayAttribute	Indicates how a type or field should be displayed in the Debug window
DebuggerHiddenAttribute	The debugger may interpret this attribute and forbid interaction with the member annotated by it
DebuggerNonUserCodeAttribute	Marks code that isn't user written (for instance, designer-generated code) and that can be skipped to avoid complicating the debugging experience
DebuggerStepperBoundaryAttribute	Locally overrides the use of DebuggerNonUserCodeAttribute
DebuggerStepThroughAttribute	The debugger may interpret this attribute and disallow stepping into the target method
DebuggerTypeProxyAttribute	Indicates a type that is responsible for defining how a type is displayed in the Debug window. It may affect debugging performance and should be used only when it's really necessary to radically change how a type is displayed.
DebuggerVisualizerAttribute	Indicates the type that defines how to render another type while debugging

These attributes allow you to control two aspects of debugging: how data are visualized by the debugger and how the debugger should behave with respect to the visibility of members.

The ability to control how types are displayed by the debugger can help you produce customized views of data that may significantly assist you in inspecting the program state in an aggregate view. The easiest way is to use DebuggerDisplayAttribute, which supports customizing the text associated with a value in the Debug window; an object of that type can still be inspected in every field. Consider the following simple example:

```
open System

[<DebuggerDisplay("{re}+{im}i")>]
type MyComplex = {re : double; im : double}

let c = {re = 0.0; im = 0.0}
Console.WriteLine("{0}+{1}i", c.re, c.im)
```

Here, you introduce a record named MyComplex with the classic definition of a complex number. The DebuggerDisplayAttribute attribute is used to annotate the type so that the debugger displays its instances using mathematical notation rather than just displaying the type name. The syntax allowed assumes that curly braces are used to indicate the name of a property whose value should be inserted in the format string. Figure 18-1 shows the result in the debugger: on the left is how the debugger window appears when MyComplex is without the DebuggerDisplay annotation; on the right, the custom string appears, with the properties in the string in curly braces. As you can see, the difference is in the value field, and the structure can still be inspected. You can use a custom visualizer to fully customize the appearance of the data in the debugger, but it may affect debugging performance.

Figure 18-1 is also interesting because it shows how the debugger displays information from the compiled program. In this case, the association between the name c and the runtime local variable has been lost, and the record appears because it has been compiled by the compiler as a pair of fields and public properties.

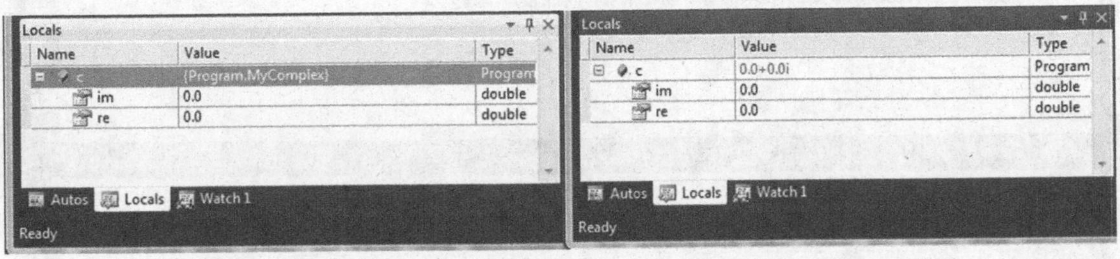

Figure 18-1. *The* MyComplex *type shown by the debugger without and with* DebuggerDisplay

The rest of the namespace contains classes to interact with the runtime: the event-logging infrastructure, process, and thread management, and the representation of a thread's stack. Stack manipulation can be useful if you need to know the call sequence that leads to executing a particular method. The StackTrace type exposes a list of StackFrame objects that provide information about each method call on the stack.

Debugging Your Code with an IDE

Programming systems such as .NET support debugging as a primary activity through tools that help you inspect programs for possible errors. The debugger is one of the most important of these tools, as it allows you to inspect the program state during execution. You can execute the program stepwise and analyze its state during execution.

Figure 18-2 shows the debugging session of the simple program. You set a breakpoint at the instruction that prints the result of the isPalindrome function for the "abba" string by clicking where the red circle is shown (the red circle will appear once the breakpoint is set). When you start the program in debug mode, its execution stops at the breakpoint, and you can step through the statements. The current instruction is indicated by the yellow arrow, and the current statement is highlighted.

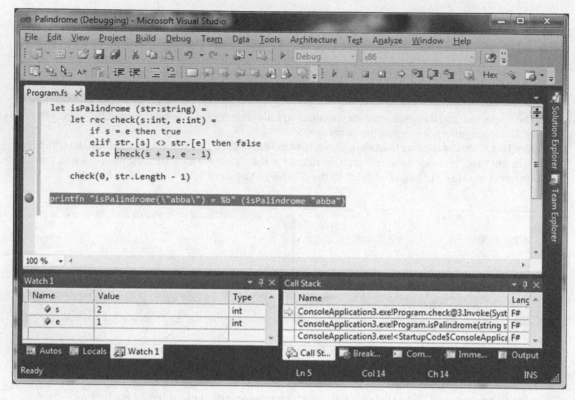

Figure 18-2. *Debugging F# code*

You can access the state of the program through a number of windows that show different aspects of the running program and that are usually docked at the bottom of the debugging window. For instance, you can inspect the state of the local variables of the current method (the Locals window shows the local variables and arguments; e and s in this example) or the state of the call stack to see the sequence of method calls (the Call Stack window). A watch view lets you write variable names and simple expressions and watch them change during execution. Be aware that the Watch window in most F# IDE tooling uses C# syntax; see the note below.

This simple example examines why isPalindrome misbehaves for an input string of even length. When the program breaks, the Watch window is used to monitor the s and e variables that are intended to define the bounds of the substring that has yet to be checked; in this case, the two indexes cross without ever becoming equal, which is the criterion used to successfully stop the recursion. This happens when s has value 2 and e has value 1 in the example. The symptom of the function misbehavior is that an exception is thrown; this is frequently where debugging starts. In this example, the exception is thrown a few steps forward, when e gets the value -1, which is an invalid index for accessing a character in a string. If you used str[e] as the watch expression or in the Immediate window, the problem would be evident. In more complicated situations, the ability to inspect the application state when the exception is raised makes it possible to determine what conditions to break on and where to set breakpoints before a bug occurs. Now that you've found the bug, you can fix it by extending the test from s = e to s >= e to ensure that even if the end index becomes smaller than the starting index, you can deal with the situation appropriately.

■ **Note**   In debugging tools, debugger expressions in Watch windows follow the C# syntax, and arrays don't require the dot before the square braces. The most noticeable difference between C# and F# expression syntax is that access to arrays uses [ ] rather than .[ ] and the equality operator is == rather than =. Also, the name of an enclosing object is always this.

Debugging Across Multiple Languages

Figure 18-3 shows a debugging session for a program combining F# and C code; you've stepped into the HelloWorld method, which is a C function accessed through the PInvoke interface as witnessed by the Call Stack window. To enable cross-language debugging, indicate in the project options' Debug section that the debugging scope is the whole program rather than just the current project.

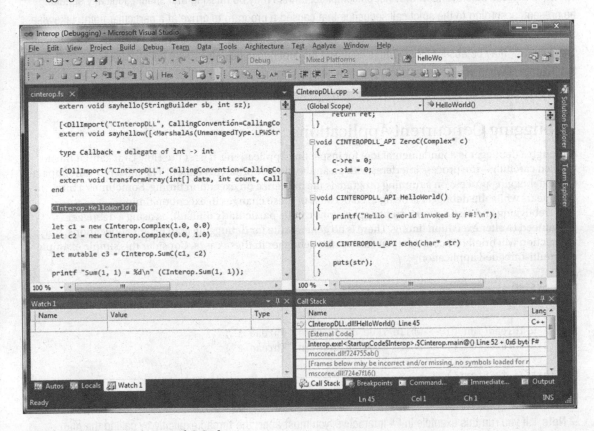

Figure 18-3.   *Debugging F# and C Code*

Sometimes you need to debug a running program that has been started without the debugger; a typical situation is one in which you're debugging a service or web application. In these situations, you can attach the debugger to a running process.

Debugging a program significantly slows down its execution speed, because the debugger infrastructure injects code to monitor program execution. Conditional breakpoints tend to worsen the situation, because every time the breakpoint is hit, the condition must be tested before standard execution can resume.

The .NET debugging infrastructure operates at the level of compiled assemblies. This has several implications. The objects and types that are visible to the debugger are those generated by the compiler and aren't always explicitly defined by you in the source code. The program database information tends to preserve the mapping between the source and the compiled program, but sometimes the underlying structure surfaces to the user. On the other hand, you can debug programs written in different programming languages, even when managed and unmanaged code must interoperate.

■ **Note** One problem with F# programs is debugging *tail calls*. (Chapter 9 described tail calls.) In particular, when a tail call is executed, the calling-stack frame is removed prior to the call. This means that the calls shown in the Call Stack window may not be complete. Entries may be missing that should, logically speaking, be present, according to the strict call sequence that caused a program to arrive at a particular point. Likewise, the debugger commands step-into and step-out can behave a little unusually when stepping into a tail call. This behavior may be absent for programs compiled for debugging, because many optimizations are disabled, but it appears when you're debugging a program compiled for release.

Debugging Concurrent Applications

Although a debugger is a fundamental tool for inspecting applications, it isn't the Holy Grail, and it must be used carefully—the process interferes with an application's normal execution. The most relevant impact of the debugging process on a running program is the influence on execution timing. Sometimes a bug disappears while the debugger is being used because of these changes in execution timing.

Debugging and testing concurrent applications can be particularly difficult, as using a debugger is guaranteed to alter execution timing. There is no general rule for debugging concurrent applications, but this section will briefly discuss how you can use the debugger in these cases. Consider this simple example of a multi-threaded application:

```
open System
open System.Threading

let t1 = Thread(fun () -> while true do printfn "Thread 1")
let t2 = Thread(fun () -> while true do printfn "Thread 2")

t1.Start(); t2.Start()
```

■ **Note** If you run this example in F# Interactive, you must abort the thread explicitly by calling the Abort method, right-clicking the F# Interactive window, and choosing Cancel Evaluation. If it doesn't resume, you may have to kill the fsi.exe process that is using the CPU most. This is a common solution when a computation gets out of control during interactive sessions.

Threads t1 and t2 access the console, which is a shared resource. When you run the program without a debugger attached, the string printed by the two threads appears interleaved on the console. If you set a breakpoint on the two printf statements and start a debugging session, stepping automatically moves from one thread to the other; the output of the program is completely different from that obtained without debugging. This is true also if you disable the breakpoints. The output is even more unbalanced if you set the breakpoint in only one of the two threads.

Chapter 11 discussed shared-memory, multi-threaded applications. In such applications, shared objects accessed by different threads are critical resources that may be viewed in the debugger. If the debug of a single thread fails, setting breakpoints in different threads may help you study the dynamic of the application, even if the full interaction of the threads can't be fully simulated. If this approach fails, it may be useful to introduce tests inside the application and use the Debugger type only when a given condition occurs. Channel-based message-passing applications are generally easier to debug than those that rely on shared memory, because you can monitor the communication endpoints using breakpoints or by logging messages. Although careful use of the debugger may help when you're debugging concurrent applications, sometimes external observation is enough to influence a running program. In these cases, tracing through debug output becomes a viable alternative; large systems have different levels of traces to monitor program execution.

Testing Your Code

This section discusses how you can develop unit tests in F# using the freely available NUnit tool (www.nunit.com). The tool was inspired by JUnit, a unit-testing suite for the Java programming language, but the programming interface has been redesigned to take advantage of the extensible metadata that the CLR provides by means of custom attributes. XUnit is a cross-platform-compatible unit-testing library that can also run NUnit tests.

Let's start with an example and develop a very simple test suite for the isPalindrome function. The first choice you face is whether tests should be embedded in the application. On the one hand, if you create tests as a separate application, you can invoke only the public interface of your software; features internal to the software can't be tested directly. On the other hand, if you embed unit tests in the program, you introduce a dependency from the nunit.framework.dll assembly, and the unit tests are available at runtime even where they aren't needed. Because the NUnit approach is based on custom attributes, performance isn't affected in either case. If you use tests during program development, it's more convenient to define them inside the program. In this case, conditional compilation may help you to include them only in checked builds.

Listing 18-1 shows tests for the isPalindrome function. Tests are functions annotated with the Test custom attribute. Inside a test case, you use methods of the Assert class to test conditions that must be satisfied during the test. If one of these fails, the entire test is considered a failure, and it's reported to the user by the tool that coordinates test execution.

Listing 18-1. A set of tests for the isPalindrome function

```
open System
open NUnit.Framework
open IsPalindrome

let posTests xs =
    for s in xs do
        Assert.That(isPalindrome s, Is.True,
                    sprintf "isPalindrome(\"%s\") must return true" s)
```

```
let negTests xs =
    for s in xs do
        Assert.That(isPalindrome s, Is.False,
                        sprintf "isPalindrome(\"%s\") must return false" s)

[<Test>]
let ``isPalindrome returns true on the empty string`` () =
    Assert.That(isPalindrome(""), Is.True,
                    "isPalindrome must return true on an empty string")

[<Test>]
let ``isPalindrome returns true for a single character``() =
    posTests ["a"]

[<Test>]
let ``isPalindrome returns true for even examples`` () =
    posTests ["aa"; "abba"; "abaaba"]

[<Test>]
let ``isPalindrome returns true for odd examples`` () =
    posTests ["aba"; "abbba"; "abababa"]

[<Test>]
let ``isPalindrome returns false for some examples`` () =
    negTests ["as"; "F# is wonderful"; "Nice"]
```

Unit tests are functions that invoke behaviors of the program and test return values to be sure their behavior conforms to the specification. Each is given a long, readable name using the `` ...`` form of specifying an identifier in F# code. When using this form, spaces and punctuation can be included in the identifier name. This example also introduces the posTests and negTests functions that are used in several tests.

Developing unit tests is a matter of defining types containing the tests. Although you can write a single test for a program, it's a good idea to have many small tests that check various features and different inputs. In this case, you introduce five tests: one for each significant input to the function. You could develop a single test containing all the code used for the individual tests, but, as you will see shortly, doing so would reduce the test suite's ability to spot problems in the program. In general, the choice of the test suite's granularity for a program is up to you. It's a matter of finding a reasonable tradeoff between having a large number of unit tests checking very specific conditions and having a small number of unit tests checking broader areas of the program.

To compile the project, you must reference the nunit.framework.dll assembly. After the program has been compiled, you can start NUnit and open the executable. As shown in Figure 18-4, the assembly containing the unit tests is inspected using the CLR's reflection capabilities; classes annotated with the TestFixture attribute are identified by NUnit; and searched-for methods are annotated with the Test attribute. Initially, all the fixtures and the tests are marked with gray dots. When you run tests, the dot is colored either green or red depending on the outcome of the particular test.

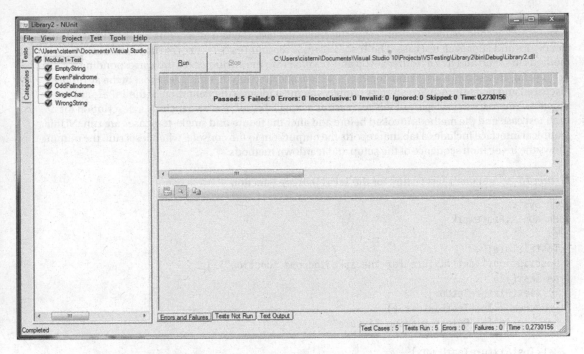

Figure 18-4. *Test unit of* `isPalindrome` *executed in NUnit*

If you reintroduce the original bug in the `isPalindrome` function and run NUnit again, two tests will fail. The corresponding dots are marked red, and the Errors and Failures tabs contain details about the test failures. This is the main benefit of having a large number of small unit tests: tools can run them automatically to identify problems in a program as well as the area potentially involved in the problem. Even in this simple example, a single test for the entire function would indicate the problem with the function, although it would fail to spot the kind of input responsible for the issue.

■ **Note**   This section shows how you can use NUnit to define test cases using F#. NUnit isn't the only tool for unit testing that's available for .NET, however. For example, XUnit is another tool you can use.

Using Test Fixtures in NUnit/XUnit

NUnit features a number of additional attributes to support the documentation and classification of test cases and test fixtures. The `Description` attribute lets you associate a description with annotated test fixtures and test cases. You can use the `Category` and `Culture` attributes to associate a category and a culture string with test fixtures and test cases. In addition, to provide more information about tests, NUnit lets you filter tests to be run by using the content of the attributes. The ability to select the tests that must be run is important, because running all tests for a system may require a significant amount of time. Other mechanisms to control the execution of tests are offered by the `Ignore` and `Explicit` attributes; you can use the former to disable a test fixture for a period without having to remove all the annotations, and the latter indicates that a test case or a fixture should only be run explicitly.

NUnit provides additional annotations to indicate the code that must be run to set up a fixture and the corresponding code to free the resources at the end of the test. You can also define a pair of methods that are run before and after each test case. The TestFixtureSetUp and TestFixtureTearDown attributes annotate methods to set up and free a fixture; SetUp and TearDown are the attributes for the corresponding test cases.

Listing 18-2 shows a test fixture for the isPalindrome function that includes most of the attributes discussed and one test case. To run the example, you must include the definition of the isPalindrome function. You mark the category of this test case as a "special case." You also include a description for each test case and the methods invoked before and after the fixture and single-test cases are run. NUnit's graphical interface includes a tab that reports the output sent to the console; when tests run, the output shows the invocation sequence of the setup and teardown methods.

Listing 18-2. *A Refined Test Fixture for the* isPalindrome *Function*

```
open System
open NUnit.Framework

[<TestFixture;
  Description("Test fixture for the isPalindrome function")>]
type Test() =
    [<TestFixtureSetUp>]
    member x.InitTestFixture () =
        printfn "Before running Fixture"

    [<TestFixtureTearDown>]
    member x.DoneTestFixture () =
        printfn "After running Fixture"

    [<SetUp>]
    member x.InitTest () =
        printfn "Before running test"

    [<TearDown>]
    member x.DoneTest () =
        Console.WriteLine("After running test")

    [<Test;
      Category("Special case");
      Description("An empty string is palindrome")>]
    member x.EmptyString () =
        Assert.That(isPalindrome(""), Is.True,
                    "isPalindrome must return true on an empty string")
```

The ability to set up resources for test cases may introduce problems during unit testing. In particular, you must treat the setup and teardown methods of test fixtures carefully, because the state shared by different test cases may affect the way they execute. Suppose, for instance, that a file is open during the setup of a fixture. This may save time, because the file is opened only once and not for each test case. If a test case fails and the file is closed, subsequent tests may fail, because they assume that the file has been opened during the fixture's setup. Nevertheless, in some situations, preloading resources only once for a fixture may save significant time.

Combining NUnit/XUnit and F# Interactive Debugging

It can be highly convenient to combine the unit testing and F# Interactive methodologies by allowing your unit tests to be easily run from F# Interactive. Listing 18-3 shows you one way to do this.

Listing 18-3. Making unit tests executable from F# Interactive

```
#if INTERACTIVE
#r "bin/Debug/IsPalindrome.dll "
#r "../packages/NUnit/lib/nunit.framework.dll"
#else
module IsPalindromeTests
#endif

open System
open NUnit.Framewbork
open IsPalindrome

[<Test>]
let ``isPalindrome returns true on the empty string`` () =
    Assert.That(isPalindrome(""), Is.True,
                "isPalindrome must return true on an empty string")
```

With the `#if INTERACTIVE` code at the top of your file of unit tests, you can now highlight your entire test file and send it to F# Interactive. You can then run through the contents of each test case by sending various fragments of tests (for example the body of the test shown) to F# Interactive and check the results:

```
> Assert.That(isPalindrome(""), Is.True,
             "isPalindrome must return true on an empty string")

val it: unit = ()    (the test has passed)
```

Property-based Testing Using FsCheck

Unit testing is not the only strategy for testing; other automatic testing approaches have been investigated and have led to tools implementing them. One of these is FsCheck (available at fscheck.github.io/FsCheck/). The approach focuses on *property verification*: a statement in the form of function is checked to find if potential inputs may falsify it.

To give an idea of uses of this tool, we introduce a very simple example taken from the quick start. The first property states the simple fact that a list twice reversed is the list itself:

```
let revTwice (xs: int list) = (List.rev(List.rev xs) = xs)
let revOnce (xs: int list) = (List.rev xs = xs)
```

Using the Check.Quick function, FsCheck generates 100 tests and verifies that the property holds for all of them.

```
> Check.Quick revTwice;;

//Ok, passed 100 tests.

> Check.Quick revOnce;;
//Falsifiable, after 2 tests (0 shrinks) (StdGen (1711668133,296077015)):
//Original:
//[0; 1]
```

An example showing a failing test case has been found and reported.

FsCheck generates inputs for verifying properties using strategies depending on involved types, and it features the ability to run multiple tests at once and control the number of cases to be generated and tested. With unit tests, the test cases are under control of the unit-test developer; with FsCheck, test cases are generated by the framework with pros and cons: tests may leave particular cases unchecked (this is also holds for programmer-developed unit tests), and the way properties are specified is more declarative, indicating that some property must hold rather testing for specific cases. Combining the two approaches may increase significantly the coverage and effectiveness of tests.

Summary

This chapter introduced techniques and tools you can use to package, debug, and test F# programs, and it also gave an overview of some of the libraries available for use with F# code. Many, many other libraries are available for .NET, and we couldn't possibly cover them in a single book. Many design patterns that you've seen here recur in those libraries; after you get to know the libraries discussed here, you'll find that other libraries are easy to use.

The final chapter covers another set of software engineering issues for F# code: library design in the context of F# and .NET.

CHAPTER 19

■ ■ ■

Designing F# Libraries

This book deals with F#, a functional-first language situated in a broader context of software construction and engineering. As an expert F# programmer, you need more than knowledge of the F# language; you also need to wisely use a range of software-engineering tools and methodologies to build software that is truly valuable for the situation in which it's deployed. The previous chapter touched on some important tools. This final chapter will look at some of the methodological issues related to F# library design, including the following:

- designing interoperable libraries that minimize the use of F#-specific constructs and doing so according to existing design conventions suitable for consuming the libraries from C# and other languages

- elements of *functional programming design methodology*, which offers important and deep insights into programming but doesn't address several important aspects of the library or component design problems

- specific suggestions for designing F# libraries, including naming conventions, how to design types and modules, and guidelines for using exceptions

F# is often seen as a functional language, but as this book emphasizes, it's really a multiparadigm language. The object, functional, imperative, and language-manipulation paradigms are all well supported. That is, F# is a *function-oriented* language, so many of the defaults are set up to encourage functional programming, but programming in the other paradigms is effective and efficient, and a combination is often the best course of all. Nonetheless, a multiparadigm language brings challenges for library designs and coding conventions.

It's a common misconception that the functional and OO programming methodologies compete; in fact, they're largely orthogonal. It's important to note, however, that functional programming doesn't directly solve many of the practical and prosaic issues associated with library design; for solutions to these problems, you must look elsewhere. In the context of .NET programming, this means turning first to the *.NET Library Design Guidelines*, published online by Microsoft and as a book by Addison-Wesley. In the official documents, the .NET library design is described in terms of conventions and guidelines for the use of the following constructs in public framework libraries:

- Assemblies, namespaces, and types (see Chapters 6 and 7 of this book)

- Classes and objects, containing properties, methods, and events (see Chapter 6)

- Interfaces (in other words, object-interface types; see Chapter 6)

- Delegate types (mentioned briefly in Chapters 5 and 6)

- Enumerations (that is, enums from languages such as C#, mentioned briefly in Chapter 6)

541

- Constants (that is, constant literals from languages such as C#)

- Type parameters (that is, generic parameters; see Chapter 5)

From the perspective of F# programming, you must also consider the following constructs:

- Discriminated union types and their tags (Chapters 3 and 9)

- Record types and their fields (Chapter 3)

- Type abbreviations (Chapter 3)

- Values and functions declared using `let` and `let rec` (Chapter 3)

- Modules (Chapter 6)

- Named arguments (Chapter 6)

- Optional arguments (Chapter 6)

- Asynchronous computations (Chapter 11)

- Provided types (Chapter 8, Chapter 13)

Framework library design is always nontrivial and often underestimated. This chapter will give opinions about how you can approach library design in the context of F# programming. These opinions are neither proscriptive nor official. More official recommendations are available from the Core Engineering Working Group of the F# Software Foundation at `http://fsharp.org`; these recommendations incorporate some of the material below. However, ultimately the final choices lie with F# programmers and software architects.

■ **Note**   Some F# programmers choose to use library and coding conventions much more closely associated with OCaml, Python, or a particular application domain, such as hardware verification. For example, OCaml coding uses underscores extensively in names, a practice generally avoided in F#. Some also choose to adjust coding conventions to their personal or team tastes.

Designing Vanilla .NET Libraries

One way to approach library design with F# is to design libraries according to the .NET Library Design Guidelines. This implicitly can mean avoiding or minimizing the use of F#-specific or F#-related constructs in the public API. We call these libraries *vanilla .NET libraries,* as opposed to libraries that use F# constructs without restriction and that are mostly intended for use by F# applications.

Designing vanilla .NET libraries means adopting the following rules:

- Apply the .NET Library Design Guidelines to the public API of your code. Your internal implementation can use any techniques you want.

- Restrict the constructs you use in your public APIs to those that are most easily used and recognized by .NET programmers. This means avoiding the use of some F# idioms in the public API.

Here are some specific recommendations from the authors of this book:

- Avoid using F# list types 'T list in vanilla .NET APIs. Use seq<'T> (i.e., IEnumerable<'T>) or arrays instead of lists.

- Avoid using F# function types in vanilla .NET APIs. F# function values tend to be a little difficult to create from other .NET languages. Instead, consider using .NET delegate types, such as the overloaded System.Func<...> types available from .NET 3.5 onward.

- Likewise, avoid using F# async or option types Async<'T> or 'T option in vanilla .NET APIs. Use Task<'T> or Nullable<'T> respectively instead.

- Avoid using F#-specific language constructs, such as discriminated unions and optional arguments, in vanilla .NET APIs.

For example, consider the code in Listing 19-1, which shows some F# code that you would adjust to be suitable for use as part of a .NET API.

Listing 19-1. An F# type prior to adjustment for use as part of a vanilla .NET API

```
namespace global

open System

type APoint(angle, radius) =
    member x.Angle = angle
    member x.Radius = radius
    member x.Stretch(l) = APoint(angle = x.Angle, radius = x.Radius * l)
    member x.Warp(f) = APoint(angle = f(x.Angle), radius = x.Radius)

    static member Circle(n) =
        [ for i in 1..n -> APoint(angle = 2.0 * Math.PI / float(n), radius = 1.0) ]

    new() = APoint(angle = 0.0, radius = 0.0)
```

The inferred F# type of this class is:

```
type APoint =
    class
        new : unit -> APoint
        new : angle:float * radius:float -> APoint
        member Stretch : l:float -> APoint
        member Warp : f:(float -> float) -> APoint
        member Angle : float
        member Radius : float
        static member Circle : n:int -> APoint list
    end
```

543

Let's look at how this F# type appears to a programmer using C# or another .NET library. The approximate C# signature is:

```
// C# signature for the unadjusted APoint class of Listing 19-1

[Serializable]
public class APoint
{
    public APoint();
    public APoint(double angle, double radius);

    public double Angle { get; }
    public double Radius { get; }

    public static FSharp.Collections.FSharpList<APoint> Circle(int n);
    public APoint Stretch(double l);
    public APoint Warp(FSharp.Core.FSharpFunc<double, double> f);
}
```

There are some important points to note about how F# has chosen to represent constructs here. For example:

- Metadata, such as argument names, has been preserved.

- F# methods that take tupled arguments become C# methods that take multiple arguments.

- Functions and lists become references to corresponding types in the F# library.

The full rules for how F# types, modules, and members are represented in the .NET Common Intermediary Language are explained in the F# language reference on the F# website.

To make a .NET component, place it in a file called component.fs and compile this code into a strong-name signed DLL:

```
C:\fsharp> sn -k component.snk
C:\fsharp> fsc --target:library --keyfile:component.snk  component.fs
```

The .NET Framework Design Guidelines require that

- types must be placed in namespaces;

- public identifiers must be spelled correctly; and

- additional attributes must be added to assemblies related to .NET Security and Common Language Specification (CLS) compliance.

Listing 19-2 shows how to adjust this code to take these things into account.

Listing 19-2. An F# type after adjustment for use as part of a vanilla .NET API

```
namespace ExpertFSharp.Types

open System

type RadialPoint(angle, radius) =
    member x.Angle = angle
    member x.Radius = radius
    member x.Stretch(factor) = RadialPoint(angle = x.Angle, radius = x.Radius * factor)
    member x.Warp(transform : Converter<_, _>) =
        RadialPoint(angle = transform.Invoke(x.Angle), radius = x.Radius)
    static member Circle(count) =
        seq { for i in 1..count ->
                    RadialPoint(angle = 2.0 * Math.PI / float(count), radius = 1.0)}
    new() = RadialPoint(angle = 0.0, radius = 0.0)
```

The inferred F# type of the code in Listing 19-2 is:

```
type RadialPoint =
  class
    new : unit -> RadialPoint
    new : angle:float * radius:float -> RadialPoint
    member Stretch : factor:float -> RadialPoint
    member Warp : transform:System.Converter<float,float> -> RadialPoint
    member Angle : float
    member Radius : float
    static member Circle : count:int -> seq<RadialPoint>
  end
```

The C# signature is now:

```
// C# signature for the unadjusted RadialPoint class of Listing 19-2
[Serializable]
public class RadialPoint
{
    public RadialPoint();
    public RadialPoint(double angle, double radius);

    public double Angle { get; }
    public double Radius { get; }

    public static IEnumerable<RadialPoint> Circle(int count);
    public RadialPoint Stretch(double factor);
    public RadialPoint Warp(Converter<double, double> transform);
}
```

The fixes you should make to prepare this type for use as part of a vanilla .NET library are as follows:

- Adjust several names: APoint, n, l, and f to become RadialPoint, count, factor, and transform, respectively.

- Use a return type of seq<RadialPoint> instead of RadialPoint list by changing a list construction using [...] to a sequence construction using seq { ... }. An alternative option would be to use an explicit upcast: ([...] :> seq<_>).

- Use the .NET delegate type System.Converter instead of an F# function type.

The last two points aren't essential, but, as mentioned, delegate types and sequence types tend to be easier for C# programmers to use than F# function and list types (F# function types aren't compiled to .NET delegate types, partly for performance reasons).

■ **Tip**   If you're designing libraries for use from any .NET language, there's no substitute for actually doing some experimental C# programming to ensure that any use of your libraries looks good from these languages. You can also use tools such as .NET Reflector to ensure that libraries and their documentation appear as expected to developers. If necessary, enlist the help of a C# programmer and ask what he or she thinks.

Understanding Functional-Design Methodology

So far, this chapter has looked at how to do vanilla .NET library design with F#. Frequently, however, F# programmers design libraries that are free to make more sophisticated use of F#, and they more or less assume that client users are using F# as well. To make the best use of F# in this situation, it's helpful to use functional programming design techniques as part of the library design process. For this reason, this section will cover what functional programming brings to the table with regard to design methodology.

Understanding Where Functional Programming Comes From

Let's recap the origins of the major programming paradigms from a design perspective:

- *Procedural programming* arises from the fundamentally imperative nature of processing devices: microprocessors are state machines that manipulate data using side effects.

- *Object-oriented programming* arises from the need to encapsulate and reuse large objects and associated behaviors, such as those used for GUI applications.

- *Functional programming* differs in that it arises from one view of the *mathematics* of computation. That is, functional programming, in its purest form, is a way of describing computations using constructs that have useful mathematical properties, independent of their implementations.

For example, the functional programming design methodology places great importance on constructs that are *compositional*. For instance, in F#, you can map a function over a list of lists as

```
let map2 f inp = List.map (List.map f) inp
```

This is a simple example of the inherent compositionality of generic functions: the expression `List.map f` produces a new function that can in turn be used as the argument to `List.map`. Understanding compositionality is the key to understanding much of what goes by the name of functional programming. For example, functional programmers aren't interested in a lack of side effects just for the sake of it—instead, they like programs that don't use side effects, because such programs tend to be more compositional than those that do.

Functional programming often goes further by emphasizing *transformations that preserve behavior*. For example, you expect to be able to make the following refactorings to your code regardless of the function `f` or of the values inp, x, or rest:

```
List.head (x :: rest)  ➤  x
```

```
List.concat (List.map (List.filter f) inp)  ➤  List.filter f (List.concat inp)
```

Equations such as these can be a source of useful documentation and test cases, and in some situations they can even be used to specify entire programs. Furthermore, good programmers routinely manipulate and optimize programs in ways that effectively assume these transformations are valid. If these transformations are *not* valid, it's easy to accidentally insert bugs when you're working with code. That said, many important transformation equations aren't guaranteed to *always* be valid—they typically hold only if additional assumptions are made. As in the first example, the expression rest shouldn't have side effects.

Transformational reasoning works well for some kinds of code and badly for others. Table 19-1 lists some of the F# and .NET constructs that are highly compositional and for which transformational reasoning tends to work well in practice.

Table 19-1. Some Compositional F# Library Constructs Amenable to Equational Reasoning

Constructs	Examples	Explanation
Basic types	int, float	Code using immutable basic types is often relatively easy to reason about. There are some exceptions to the rule: the presence of NaN values and approximations in floating-point operations can make it difficult to reason about floating-point code.
Collections	Set<'T>, Map<'Key, 'Value>	Immutable collection types are highly amenable to equational reasoning. For example, you expect equations such as Set.union Set.empty x = x to hold.
Control types	Lazy<'T>, Async<'T>	Control constructs are often highly compositional and have operators that allow you to combine them in interesting ways. For example, you expect equations such as (lazy x).Force() = x to hold.
Data abstractions	seq<'T>	F# sequences aren't pure values, as they may access data stores using major side effects, such as network I/O. In practice, uses of sequences tend to be very amenable to equational reasoning. This assumes that the side effects for each iteration of the sequence are isolated and independent.

Understanding Functional-Design Methodology

Functional-design methodology is rooted in compositionality and reasoning. In practice, it's largely about these steps:

1. Deciding what values you're interested in representing. These values may range from simple integers to more sophisticated objects, such as expression trees, seen in Chapter 9, or the asynchronous tasks from Chapter 13.

2. Deciding what operations are required to build these values, extract information from them, and combine and transform them.

3. Deciding what equations and other algebraic properties should hold between these values and assessing whether these properties hold for the implementation.

Steps 1 and 2 explain why functional programmers often prefer to define operations separately from types. As a result, functional programmers often find OO programming strange, because it emphasizes operations on *single* values, whereas functional programming emphasizes operations that *combine* values. This carries over to library implementation in functional programming, in which you often see types defined first and then modules containing operations on those types.

Because of this, one pattern that is common in the F# library is the following:

- The type is defined first.

- Then, a module defines the functions to work over the type.

- Finally, a with augmentation adds the most common functions as members. Chapter 6 describes augmentations.

One simple example of functional-programming methodology in this book appears in Chapter 12, where you saw how a representation for propositional logic is defined using a type:

```
type Var = string

type Prop =
    | And of Prop * Prop
    | Var of Var
    | Not of Prop
    | Exists of Var * Prop
    | False
```

Operations were then defined so as to combine and analyze values of type Prop. It wouldn't make sense to define all of these operations as being intrinsic to the Prop type, an approach often taken in OO design. In that same chapter, you saw another representation of propositional-logic formulae where two logically identical formulae were normalized to the same representations. This is an example of Step 3 of the functional-design methodology: the process of designing a type involves specifying the equations that should hold for values of that type.

You've seen many examples in this book of how OO programming and functional programming can work well together. For example, F# objects are often immutable, but use OO features to group together some functionality that is working on the same data. Also, F# object-interface types are often used as a convenient notation for collections of functions.

However, some tensions exist between functional programming and OO design methodology. For example, when you define operations independently of data (that is, the functional style), it's simple to add a new operation, but modifying the type is more difficult. In OO programming using abstract and virtual methods, it's easy to add a new inherited type, but adding new operations (that is, new virtual methods) is difficult.

Similarly, functional programming emphasizes *simple but compositional* types; for example, functions and tuples. OO programming tends to involve creating many (often large and complex) types with considerable amounts of additional metadata. These are often less compositional, but sometimes more self-documenting.

Finally, although functional programming doesn't provide a complete software design methodology, it's beautiful and powerful when it works, creating constructs that can be wielded with amazing expressivity and a low bug rate. However, not all constructs in software design are amenable to compositional descriptions and implementations, and an over-reliance on pure programming can leave you feeling bewildered and abandoned when the paradigm doesn't offer useful solutions that scale in practice. This is the primary reason why F# is a multiparadigm language: to ensure that functional techniques can be combined with other techniques where appropriate.

■ **Note**　Some functional languages such as Haskell place a strong emphasis on equational reasoning principles. In F#, equational reasoning is slightly less important; however, it still forms an essential part of understanding what functional programming brings to the arena of design methodology.

Applying the Good Library Design to F#

This section will present some additional recommendations for applying the .NET Library Design Guidelines to F# programming. We will make a series of recommendations that can be read as extensions to these guidelines.

Recommendation: Use Correct Naming and Capitalization Conventions Where Possible

Table 19-2 summarizes the F# guidelines for naming and capitalization in code. We've added our own recommendations for how these should be adjusted for some F# constructs. This table refers to the following categories of names:

- *PascalCase*: LeftButton and TopRight, for example
- *camelCase*: leftButton and topRight, for example
- *Verb*: A verb or verb phrase; performAction or SetValue, for example
- *Noun*: A noun or noun phrase; cost or ValueAfterDepreciation, for example
- *Adjective*: An adjective or adjectival phrase; Comparable or Disposable, for example

Table 19-2. *Conventions Associated with Public F# Constructs*

Construct	Case	Part	Examples	Notes
Concrete types	PascalCase	Noun/ adjective	`List`, `DoubleComplex`	Concrete types are structs, classes, enumerations, delegates, records, and unions. Type names are traditionally lowercase in OCaml, and F# code has generally followed this pattern. However, as F# has matured as a language, it has moved much more toward following standardized PascalCase idioms.
DLLs	PascalCase		`FSharp.Core.dll` `<Company>.<Component>.dll`	
Union tags	PascalCase	Noun	`Some`, `Add`, `Success`	Don't use a prefix in public APIs. Optionally use a prefix when internal, such as type `Teams = TAlpha | TBeta | TDelta`.
Event	PascalCase	Verb	`ValueChanged`	
Exceptions	PascalCase		`WebException`	
Field	PascalCase	Noun	`CurrentName`	
Interface types	IPascalCase	Noun/adjective	`IDisposable`	
Method	PascalCase	Verb	`ToString`	
Namespace	PascalCase		`FSharp.Core`	Generally use `<Organization>.<Technology>[.<Subnamespace>]`, but drop the organization if the technology is independent of organization.
Parameters	camelCase	Noun	`typeName`, `transform`, `range`	
let values (internal)	camelCase	Noun/verb	`getValue`, `myTable`	

(continued)

Table 19-2. (*continued*)

Construct	Case	Part	Examples	Notes
let values (external)	camelCase or PascalCase	Noun	`List.map`, `Dates.Today`	let-bound values are often public when following traditional functional-design patterns.
Property	PascalCase	Noun/adjective	`IsEndOfFile`, `BackColor`	Boolean properties generally use Is and Can and should be affirmative, as in IsEndOfFile, not IsNotEndOfFile.
Type parameters	TPascalCase	Noun/adjective	`'T`, `'Key`, `'Value`	Implicit type-inference variables are given lowercase names by the F# compiler.

In general, the F# component guidelines strongly discourage the use of abbreviations (for example, "use `OnButtonClick` rather than `OnBtnClick`"). Common abbreviations such as `Async` for `Asynchronous` are tolerated. This guideline has historically been broken by functional programming; for example, `List.iter` uses an abbreviation for `iterate`. For this reason, using abbreviations tends to be tolerated in F# programming, although we discourage using additional abbreviations beyond those found in existing F# libraries.

Acronyms such as XML aren't abbreviations and are widely used in F# libraries, although where necessary in Pascal Case form (Xml). Only well-known, widely recognized acronyms should be used.

We generally recommend using lowercase for value names, unless you're designing a library:

```
✓ let x = 1
✓ let now = System.DateTime.Now
```

We recommend using lowercase for all local value names bound in pattern matches, function definitions, and anonymous inner functions. Functions may also use uppercase:

```
✗ let add I J = I + J
✓ let add i j = i + j
```

Use uppercase when the natural convention is to do so, as in the case of matrices, proper nouns, and common abbreviations, such as I for the identity function:

```
✓ let f (A: matrix) (B: matrix) = A + B
✓ let Monday = 1
✓ let I x = x
```

We recommend using camelcase for other values, including:

- Ad hoc functions in scripts

- Values making up the internal implementation of a module

- Locally bound values in functions

```
✓ let emailMyBossTheLatestResults = ...
✓ let doSomething () =
        let firstResult = ...
        let secondResult = ...
```

Recommendation: Avoid Using Underscores in Names

In some older F# code, you will see the frequent use of underscores to qualify some names. For example:

- Suffixes such as _left and _right

- Prefix verbs such as add_, remove_, try_, and is_, do_

- Prefix connectives such as to_, of_, from_, and for_

We recommend avoiding this style because it clashes with recommended naming conventions. Using an underscore at the start of a name indicates that the value is unused and it turns off warnings associated with unused values.

■ **Note**　No rules are hard and fast. Some F# programmers ignore this advice and use underscores heavily, partly because functional programmers often dislike extensive capitalization. However this style is no longer seen as normal in F# coding.

Recommendation: Follow the Recommended Guidelines for Exceptions

The .NET Framework Design Guidelines give good advice about the use of exceptions relevant to F# programming. Some of these guidelines are as follows:

- Don't return error codes. Exceptions are the main way of reporting errors in frameworks.

- Don't use exceptions for normal flow of control. Instead, consider returning a None or Choice value to indicate failure.

- Document all exceptions thrown by your code when a function is used incorrectly.

- Where possible, throw existing exceptions in the System namespaces.

- Use invalidOp and invalidArg to throw exceptions where possible.

■ **Note**   Other exception-related topics covered by the .NET guidelines include advice on designing custom exceptions, wrapping exceptions, choosing exception messages, and special exceptions to avoid throwing (`OutOfMemoryException`, `ExecutionEngineException`, `COMException`, `SEHException`, `StackOverflowException`, `NullReferenceException`, `AccessViolationException`, and `InvalidCastException`).

Recommendation: Consider Using Option Values for Return Types Instead of Raising Exceptions

The F# approach to exceptions is that they should be exceptional. That is, they should occur relatively infrequently. However, some operations (for example, searching a table) may fail frequently. F# option values are an excellent way to represent the return types of these operations.

Recommendation: Follow the Recommended Guidelines for Value Types

The .NET guidelines give good guidance about when to use .NET value types (that is, structs, introduced in Chapter 6). In particular, they recommend using a struct in a public API only when the following are all true:

- A type logically represents a single value similar to a primitive type.
- It has a small instance size. (The original recommendation was to only use value types for objects of a size less than 16 bytes; with the rise of 64-bit architectures, this should now be regarded as conservative, and you should do your own testing).
- It's immutable.
- It won't have to be boxed frequently (that is, converted to/from the type `System.Object`).

Some programmers are much stricter and almost never use structs in public APIs.

Recommendation: Consider Using Explicit Signature Files for Your Framework

Chapter 7 describes explicit signature files. Using explicit signature files for framework code ensures that you know the full public surface of your API and can cleanly separate public documentation from internal implementation details.

Recommendation: Consider Avoiding the Use of Implementation Inheritance for Extensibility

Chapter 6 describes implementation inheritance. In general, in F#, implementation inheritance is used more rarely than in object-oriented languages. The main rationale for this is given in Chapter 6, which also presents many alternative techniques for designing and implementing OO types using F#. However, implementation inheritance is used heavily in GUI frameworks.

■ **Note**   Other OO extensibility topics discussed in the .NET guidelines include events and callbacks, virtual members, abstract types and inheritance, and limiting extensibility by sealing classes.

Recommendation: Use Properties and Methods for Attributes and Operations Essential to a Type

Here's an example:

```
✓ type HardwareDevice with
    ...
    member ID: string
    member SupportedProtocols: seq<Protocol>
```

Consider using methods for the intrinsic operations essential to a type:

```
✓ type HashTable<'Key,'Value> with
    ...
    member Add           : 'Key * 'Value -> unit
    member ContainsKey   : 'Key -> bool
    member ContainsValue : 'Value -> bool
```

Consider using static methods to hold a Create function instead of revealing object constructors:

```
✓ type HashTable<'Key,'Value> with
      static member Create : IHashProvider<'Key> -> HashTable<'Key,'Value>
```

Recommendation: Avoid Revealing Concrete Data Representations Such as Records

Where possible, avoid revealing concrete representations such as records, fields, and implementation-inheritance hierarchies in framework APIs.

The rationale is that one of the overriding aims of library design is to avoid revealing concrete representations of objects, for the obvious reason that you may want to change the implementation later. For example, the concrete representation of System.DateTime values isn't revealed by the external, public API of the core library design. At runtime, the Common Language Runtime knows the committed implementation that will be used throughout execution. However, compiled code doesn't pick up dependencies on the concrete representation.

Recommendation: Use Active Patterns to Hide the Implementations of Discriminated Unions

Where possible, avoid using large discriminated unions in framework APIs, especially if you suspect there is a chance that the representation of information in the discriminated union will undergo revision and change. For frameworks, you should typically either hide the type or use active patterns to reveal the ability to pattern match over language constructs. Chapter 9 describes active patterns.

This doesn't apply to the use of discriminated unions internal to an assembly or to an application. Likewise, it doesn't apply if the only likely future change is the addition of further cases, and you're willing to require that client code be revised for these cases. Finally, active patterns can incur a performance overhead, and this should be measured and tested, although the benefits of active patterns frequently outweigh this cost.

■ **Note**   Using large, volatile discriminated unions freely in APIs encourages people to use pattern matching against these discriminated union values. This is appropriate for unions that don't change. However, if you reveal discriminated unions indiscriminately, you may find it very hard to version your library without breaking user code.

Recommendation: Use Object-Interface Types Instead of Tuples or Records of Functions

In Chapter 5, you saw various ways to represent a dictionary of operations explicitly, such as using tuples of functions or records of functions. In general, we recommend that you use object-interface types for this purpose, because the syntax associated with implementing them is generally more convenient.

Recommendation: Understand When Currying Is Useful in Functional Programming APIs

Currying is the name used when functions take arguments in the iterated form—that is, when the functions can be partially applied. For example, the following function is curried:

```
let f x y z = x + y + z
```

This isn't curried:

```
let f (x, y, z) = x + y + z
```

Here are some of our guidelines for when to use currying and when not to use it:

- Use currying freely for rapid prototyping and scripting. Saving keystrokes can be very useful in these situations.

- Use currying when partial application of the function is highly likely to give a useful residual function (see Chapter 3).

- Use currying when partial application of the function is necessary to permit useful precomputation (see Chapter 8).

- Avoid using currying in vanilla .NET APIs or in APIs to be used from other .NET languages.

When using currying, place arguments in order from the least varying to the most varying. Doing so makes partial application of the function more useful and leads to more compact code. For example, List. map is curried with the function argument first because a typical program usually applies List.map not only to a handful of known function values but also to many different concrete list values. Likewise, you saw in Chapters 8 and 9 how recursive functions can be used to traverse tree structures. These traversals often carry an environment. The environment changes relatively rarely—only when you traverse the subtrees of structures that bind variables. For this reason, the environment is the first argument.

When you use currying, consider the importance of the pipelining operator; for example, place function arguments first and object arguments last.

F# also uses currying for let-bound binary operators and combinators, as follows:

✓ `let divmod n m = ...`
✓ `let map f x = ...`
✓ `let fold f z x = ...`

However, see Chapters 6 and 8 for how to define operators as static members in types, which aren't curried.

Recommendation: Use Tuples for Return Values, Arguments, and Intermediate Values

Here is an example of using a tuple in a return type:

✓ `val divmod : n:int -> m:int -> int * int`

Recommendation: Use Async for Asynchronous Computations

In F#-facing code, the type Async<_> should be used for the return type of asynchronous functions, as discussed in Chapter 11:

✓ `val GetResults : n:int -> Async<int * int>`

Recommendation: Use Choice or a Named Type for Alternative Results

In F#-facing code, it is often necessary to return one of multiple possibilities as a result. Consider using the Choice<_,_> type to represent these conditions:

✓ `val GetResultsOrFail : n:int -> Choice<int * int, Exception>`

Alternatively, define a new two-case union type to represent the possibilities:

✓ `type Result<'T> = Success of 'T | Failure of string`

✓ `val GetResultsOrFail : n:int -> Result<int * int>`

Some Recommended Coding Idioms

This section looks at a small number of recommendations for writing implementation code, as opposed to writing library designs. We don't give many recommendations on formatting, because formatting code is relatively simple for #light indentation-aware code. We do make a couple of formatting recommendations that early readers of this book asked about.

Recommendation: Use the Standard Operators

The following operators are defined in the F# standard library and should be used wherever possible instead of defining equivalents. Using these operators tends to make code much easier to read, so we strongly recommend it. This is spelled out explicitly, because other languages similar to F# don't support all of these operators, and thus some F# programmers aren't aware that these operators exist:

```
f >> g    -- forward composition
g << f    -- reverse composition
x |> f    -- forward pipeline
f <| x    -- reverse pipeline

x |> ignore   -- throwing away a value

x + y     -- overloaded addition (including string concatenation)
x - y     -- overloaded subtraction
x * y     -- overloaded multiplication
x / y     -- overloaded division
x % y     -- overloaded modulus

x <<< y   -- bitwise left shift
x >>> y   -- bitwise right shift
x ||| y   -- bitwise or, also for working with enumeration flags
x &&& y   -- bitwise and, also for working with enumeration flags
x ^^^ y   -- bitwise exclusive or, also for working with enumeration flags

x && y    -- lazy/short-circuit and
x || y    -- lazy/short-circuit or
```

Recommendation: Place the Pipeline Operator |> at the Start of a Line

People often ask how to format pipelines. We recommend this style:

```
let methods =
    System.AppDomain.CurrentDomain.GetAssemblies()
    |> List.ofArray
    |> List.map (fun assem -> assem.GetTypes())
    |> Array.concat
```

Recommendation: Format Object Expressions Using the member Syntax

People often ask how to format object expressions. We recommend this style:

```
open System

[<AbstractClass>]
type Organization() =
    abstract member Chief : string
    abstract member Underlings : string list
```

```
let thePlayers = {
    new Organization() with
        member x.Chief = "Peter Quince"
        member x.Underlings =
            ["Francis Flute"; "Robin Starveling"; "Tom Snout"; "Snug"; "Nick Bottom"]
    interface IDisposable with
        member x.Dispose() = ()}
```

■ **Note**   The discussion of F# design and engineering issues in Chapters 18 and 19 is necessarily limited. In particular, we haven't covered topics such as aspect-oriented programming, design and modeling methodologies, software quality assurance, or software metrics, all of which are outside the scope of this book.

Summary

This chapter covered some of the rules you may apply to library design in F#, particularly taking into account how F# code must interoperate with other languages and libraries. It also considered some of the elements of the functional programming design methodology, which offers many important and deep insights. Finally, we gave some specific suggestions to follow when you're designing F# libraries.

That concludes our tour of F#. We hope you enjoy a long and productive career working with the language.

F# Brief Language Guide

This appendix will describe the essential constructs of the F# language in a compact form. You can find a full guide to the F# language in the F# Language Specification on the F# website (http://fsharp.org/specs/).

Comments and Attributes

Comments (Chapter 2)

```// comment```
 	
```(* comment *)```
 	
```/// XML doc comment```
```let x = 1```

Attaching Attributes (Chapter 16)

```[<Obsolete("Deprecated at 1.2")>]```
```type Type =```
``` ...```
```[<Conditional("DEBUG")>]```
```let Function(x) =```
 	
```[<assembly: Note("argument")>]```
```do ()```

Basic Types and Literals

Basic Types and Literals (Chapter 3)

```
sbyte       = System.SByte    76y
byte        = System.Byte     76uy
int16       = System.Int16    76s
uint16      = System.UInt16   76us
int32       = System.Int32    76
uint32      = System.UInt32   76u
int64       = System.Int64    76L
uint64      = System.UInt64   76UL
string      = System.String   "abc", @"c:\etc"
single      = System.Single   3.14f
double      = System.Double   3.14, 3.2e5
char        = System.Char     '7'
nativeint   = System.IntPtr   76n
unativeint  = System.UIntPtr  76un
bool        = System.Boolean  true, false
unit        = FSharp.Core.Unit ()
```

Basic Type Abbreviations (Chapter 3)

```
int8    = sbyte
uint8   = byte
int     = int32
float32 = single
float   = double
```

Types

Types (Chapters 3 and 5)	
`ident`	Named type
`ident<type,...,type>`	Type instantiation
`type * ... * type`	Tuple type
`type[]`	Array type
`#type`	Flexible type (accepts any subtype)
`'ident`	Variable type
`type -> type`	Function type

Type instantiations can be postfix: `int list`

Patterns and Matching

Patterns (Chapters 3 and 9)	
`_`	Wildcard pattern
`literal`	Constant pattern
`ident`	Variable pattern
`(pat, ..., pat)`	Tuple pattern
`[ pat; ...; pat ]`	List pattern
`[| pat; ...; pat |]`	Array pattern
`{ id=pat; ...; id=pat }`	Record pattern
`id(pat, ..., pat)`	Union case pattern
`id expr ... expr (pat, ..., pat)`	Active pattern
`pat	pat`	"Or" pattern
`pat & pat`	"Both" pattern
`pat as id`	Named pattern
`:? type`	Type-test pattern
`:? type as id`	Type-cast pattern
`null`	Null pattern

Matching (Chapter 3)
`match expr with`
`| pat -> expr`
`...`
`| pat -> expr`
Note: Rules of a match may use
`| pat when expr -> expr`

Active Patterns (Chapter 9)
`let (|Tag1|Tag2|)  inp = ...`
`let (|Tag1|_|)  inp = ...`
`let (|Tag1|)  inp = ...`

Functions, Composition, and Pipelining

Function values (Chapter 3)	
`fun pat ... pat -> expr`	Function

`function`
`| pat -> expr`
`...`
`| pat -> expr`
	Match function

Application and Pipelining (Chapter 3)	
`f x`	Application
`x |> g`	Forward pipe
`f >> g`	Function composition

Binding and Control Flow

<table>
<tr><td colspan="2">Control Flow (Chapters 3 and 4)</td></tr>
<tr><td>expr
expr</td><td>Sequencing</td></tr>
<tr><td>do expr
expr</td><td>Sequencing</td></tr>
<tr><td>for id = expr to expr do
   expr</td><td>Simple loop</td></tr>
<tr><td>for pat in expr do
   expr</td><td>Sequence loop</td></tr>
<tr><td>while expr do
   expr</td><td>While loop</td></tr>
</table>

<table>
<tr><td colspan="2">Binding and Scoping (Chapter 3)</td></tr>
<tr><td>let pat = expr
expr</td><td>Value binding</td></tr>
<tr><td>let id args = expr
expr</td><td>Function binding</td></tr>
<tr><td>let rec id args = expr
expr</td><td>Recursive binding</td></tr>
<tr><td>use pat = expr
expr</td><td>Auto-dispose binding</td></tr>
</table>

<table>
<tr><td>Syntax Forms Without Indentation</td></tr>
<tr><td>let pat = expr in expr
while expr do expr done
for pat in expr do expr done
expr ; expr
do expr in expr</td></tr>
</table>

Exceptions

<table>
<tr><td colspan="2">Exception Handling</td></tr>
<tr><td>try
   expr
with
   | pat -> expr
   | pat -> expr</td><td>Handling</td></tr>
<tr><td>try
   expr
finally
   expr</td><td>Compensation</td></tr>
<tr><td>use id = expr</td><td>Automatic Dispose</td></tr>
</table>

<table>
<tr><td>Some Exceptions (Chapter 4)</td></tr>
<tr><td>Microsoft.FSharp.Core.FailureException
System.MatchFailureException
System.InvalidArgumentException
System.StackOverflowException</td></tr>
</table>

<table>
<tr><td colspan="2">Raising Exceptions (Common Forms)</td></tr>
<tr><td>raise expr</td><td>Throw exception</td></tr>
<tr><td>failwith expr</td><td>Throw FailureException</td></tr>
</table>

<table>
<tr><td>Catch and Rethrow</td></tr>
<tr><td>try expr
with
   | :? ThreadAbortException ->
   printfn "thrown!"
   reraise ()</td></tr>
</table>

Tuples, Arrays, Lists, and Collections

Tuples (Chapter 3)

(expr, ..., expr)	Tuple
fst expr	First of pair
snd expr	Second of pair

F# Lists (Chapter 3)

[expr; ...; expr]	List
[expr..expr]	Range list
[comp-expr]	Generated list
expr :: expr	List cons
expr @ expr	List append

Arrays (Chapter 4)

[| expr; ...; expr |]	Array literal
[| expr..expr |]	Range array
[| comp-expr |]	Generated array
Array.create size expr	Array creation
Array.init size expr	Array init
arr.[expr]	Lookup
arr.[expr] <- expr	Assignment
arr.[expr..expr]	Slice
arr.[expr..]	Right slice
arr.[..expr]	Left slice

See Chapter 4 for multi-dimensional operators.

F# Options (Chapter 3)

None	No value
Some(expr)	With value

Some Other Collection Types

```
System.Collections.Generic.Dictionary
System.Collections.Generic.List
System.Collections.Generic.SortedList
System.Collections.Generic.SortedDictionary
System.Collections.Generic.Stack
System.Collections.Generic.Queue
Microsoft.FSharp.Collections.Set
Microsoft.FSharp.Collections.Map
```

Operators

Overloaded Arithmetic (Chapter 3)

```
x + y    Addition
x - y    Subtraction
x * y    Multiplication
x / y    Division
x % y    Remainder/modulus
-x       Unary negation
```

Overloaded Math Operators

```
abs, acos, atan, atan2,
ceil, cos, cosh, exp,
floor, log, log10, pow,
pown, sqrt, sin, sinh,
tan, tanh
```

Overloaded Conversion Operators

```
byte, sbyte, int16, uint16,
int, int32, uint32, int64,
uint64, float32, float, single,
double, nativeint,
unativeint
```

Mutable Locals (Chapter 4)

```
let mutable var = expr   Declare
var                      Read
var <- expr              Update
```

Mutable Reference Cells (Chapter 4)

```
ref expr       Allocate
!expr          Read
expr.Value     Read
expr := expr   Assign
```

Booleans

```
not expr        Boolean negation
expr && expr    Boolean "and"
expr || expr    Boolean "or"
```

Overloaded Bitwise Operators (Chapter 3)

```
x >>> y    Shift right
x <<< y    Shift left
x &&& y    Bitwise logical and
x ||| y    Bitwise logical or
x ^^^ y    Bitwise exclusive or
~~~ x      Bitwise logical not
```

Generic Comparison and Hashing

```
hash x              Generic hashing
x = y               Generic equality
x <> y              Generic inequality
compare x y         Generic comparison
x >= y, x <= y,
x > y, x < y,
min x y, max x y
```

Note: Records, tuples, arrays, and unions automatically implement structural equality and hashing (see Chapters 5 and 8).

Indexed Lookup (Chapter 4)

```
expr.[idx]           Lookup
expr.[idx] <- expr   Assignment
expr.[idx..idx]      Slice
expr.[idx..]         Right slice
expr.[..idx]         Left slice
```

See Chapter 4 for multidimensional operators.

Object-Related Operators and Types

```
type obj = System.Object
box(x)             Convert to type obj
unbox<type>(x)     Extract from type obj
typeof<type>       Extract Sytem.Type
x :> type          Static cast to supertype
x :?> type         Dynamic cast to subtype
```

Type Definitions and Objects

Union Types (Chapters 3 and 6)

```
type UnionType =
  | TagA of type * ... * type
  | TagB of type * ... * type
```

Record Types (Chapters 3 and 6)

```
type Record =
  { Field1: type
    Field2: type }
```

Constructed Class Types (Chapter 6)

```
type ObjectType(args) =
  let internalValue = expr
  let internalFunction args = expr
  let mutable internalState = expr
  member x.Prop1 = expr
  member x.Meth2 args = expr
```

Object Expressions (Chapter 6)

```
{ new IObject with
    member x.Prop1 = expr
    member x.Meth1 args = expr }

{ new Object() with
    member x.Prop1 = expr
  interface IObject with
    member x.Meth1 args = expr
  interface IWidget with
    member x.Meth1 args = expr }
```

Object Interface Types (Chapter 6)

```
type IObject =
  interface ISimpleObject
  abstract Prop1 : type
  abstract Meth2 : type -> type
```

Some Special Members

```
member x.Prop                setter property
  with get() = expr
  and  set v = expr

member x.Item                indexer property
  with get idx = expr
  and  set idx v = expr

static member (+) (x,y) = expr operator
```

Implementation Inheritance

```
type ObjectType(args) as x =
  inherit BaseType(expr) as base
```

Named and Optional Arguments for Members

```
member obj.Method(?optArgA)        Declaring optional arg

new Object(x=expr, y=expr)         Call with named args
obj.Method(optArgA=expr, PropB=expr)  Call with optional args and properties
```

Namespaces and Modules

Namespaces (Chapter 7)

namespace Org.Product.Feature
 	
type TypeOne =
   ...
 	
module ModuleTwo =
   ...

Files As Modules (Chapter 7)

module Org.Product.Feature.Module
 	
type TypeOne =
   ...
 	
module ModuleTwo =
   ...

Sequence Expressions and Workflows

Sequence Expressions and Workflows (See Chapters 3 and 9)

`[ comp-expr ]`	Generated list
`[| comp-expr |]`	Generated array
`seq { comp-expr }`	Generated sequence
`async { comp-expr }`	Asynchronous workflow
`ident { comp-expr }`	Arbitrary workflow

Syntax for Workflows

`let! pat = expr` `comp-expr`	Execute and bind computation
`let pat = expr` `comp-expr`	Execute and bind expression
`do! expr` `comp-expr`	Execute computation
`do expr` `comp-expr`	Execute expression
`if expr then comp-expr else comp-expr`	Conditional workflow
`if expr then comp-expr`	Conditional workflow
`while expr do comp-expr`	Repeated workflow
`for pat in expr do comp-expr`	Enumeration loop
`try comp-expr with pat -> expr`	Workflow with catch
`try comp-expr finally expr`	Workflow with compensation
`use pat = expr in comp-expr`	Workflow with auto-dispose
`return expr`	Return expression
`return! expr`	Return computation
`yield expr`	Yield expression (for sequences only)
`yield! expr`	Yield sequence (for sequences only)

Queries and Quotations

F# Queries (Chapter 13)

`query { for x in expr do … }`	Query table
`query { … let v = expr in … }`	Query local
`query { … where expr … }`	Query filtering
`query { … select expr … }`	Query selection
`query { … averageBy/minBy/maxBy/sumBy expr }`	Query statistic
`query { … sortBy/sortByDescending expr }`	Query ordering
`query { … thenBy/thenByDescending expr }`	Query subsequent ordering
`query { … distinct }`	Query unique selection
`query { … count }`	Query count selection
`query { … first/last/exactlyOne }`	Query first/last/unique result
`query { … firstOrDefault/lastOrDefault/exactlyOneOrDefault }`	Query result or default
`query { … exists expr }`	Predicate satisfied at least once
`query { … all expr }`	Predicate always satisfied
`query { … skip expr }`	Query paging
`query { … take expr }`	Query paging
`query { … distinct }`	Query unique selection
`query { … groupBy expr }`	Query grouping
`query { … groupBy expr into id …}`	Query grouping
`query { … groupValBy expr expr }`	Query grouping value by key
`query { … groupValBy expr expr into id … }`	Query grouping value by key
`query { … join expr in expr on (expr = expr) }`	Query inner join
`query { … groupJoin expr in expr on (expr = expr) into id …}`	Query group join
`query { … leftOuterJoin expr in expr on (expr = expr) into id …}`	Query left outer join

+ nullable variations on statistics, sorting, and joining operators

---

Quotations (Chapter 16)

`<@ expr @>`	Quotation expression
`<@@ expr @@>`	Untyped quotation expression
`%expr`	Splice of typed quotation
`%%expr`	Splice of untyped quotation
`[<ReflectedDefinition>]`	Include quoted form of definition at runtime

Index

Get the eBook for only $5!

Why limit yourself?

Now you can take the weightless companion with you wherever you go and access your content on your PC, phone, tablet, or reader.

Since you've purchased this print book, we're happy to offer you the eBook in all 3 formats for just $5.

Convenient and fully searchable, the PDF version enables you to easily find and copy code—or perform examples by quickly toggling between instructions and applications. The MOBI format is ideal for your Kindle, while the ePUB can be utilized on a variety of mobile devices.

To learn more, go to www.apress.com/companion or contact support@apress.com.

Apress®
THE EXPERT'S VOICE™